GAL

MACROECONOMICS

MACROECONOMICS

James K. Galbraith
Lyndon B. Johnson School of Public Affairs
University of Texas at Austin

William Darity, Jr.
University of North Carolina at Chapel Hill

Houghton Mifflin Company Boston Toronto
Geneva, Illinois Palo Alto Princeton, New Jersey

For Aden, Douglas, Margaret, and William

Sponsoring Editor: Denise Clinton
Development Editor: Julie Hogenboom
Associate Project Editor: Susan Merrifield
Production/Design Coordinator: Sarah Ambrose
Senior Manufacturing Coordinator: Priscilla Bailey
Marketing Manager: Michael Ginley
Cover Design: Darci Mehall

Figure Illustrations: Tech-Graphics
Cover Image: Piero Dorazio (b. 1927)
 "Allaccio" (1966)
 Oil on Canvas, 78 3/4″ × 78 3/4″
 Collection F2, Terni
 Courtesy Achim Moeller Fine Art, New York
Photo Credit: Photo of William Darity, Jr., p. v, © 1993 by M. McQuown.

Library of Congress Catalog Card Number: 93-78636

ISBN: 0-395-52241-2

123456789-AM-98 97 96 95 94

ABOUT THE
AUTHORS

James K. Galbraith holds an A.B. *magna cum laude* from Harvard University and a Ph.D. in Economics from Yale. He has served as Executive Director of the Joint Economic Committee of the U.S. Congress, and is presently Professor at the Lyndon B. Johnson School of Public Affairs and in the Department of Government at The University of Texas at Austin, where he won a Texas Excellence in Teaching Award in 1990. He is the author of *Balancing Acts: Technology, Finance and the American Future* (Basic Books, 1989), and coauthor with Robert Heilbroner of *The Economic Problem* (9th edition, Prentice-Hall, 1990), a principles text. He lives in Austin with his wife Ying Tang, son Douglas, and daughter Margaret, who happens to share her birthday with John Maynard Keynes and Adam Smith.

William Darity, Jr., is the Cary C. Boshamer Professor of Economics at the University of North Carolina at Chapel Hill, where he has taught since 1983. He formerly has held faculty positions at the University of Texas at Austin as an assistant and associate professor, at the University of Maryland at College Park, and the University of Tulsa as a visitor. He is the author of over 90 published articles and reviews in numerous professional journals including the *American Economic Review*, the *Southern Economic Journal*, the *Journal of Economic History*, the *Review of Black Political Economy*, the *Journal of Money, Credit and Banking*, the *History of Political Economy*, and the *Journal of Macroeconomics*. His book publications also include *The Loan Pushers: The Role of Commercial Banks in the International Debt Crisis* (1988, coauthored with Bobbie Horn) and the edited volume *Labor Eco-*

nomics: Problems in Analyzing Labor Markets (1993). Professor Darity lives with his family in Durham, North Carolina, where he plays blues harmonica in local jam sessions, and coaches youth soccer and basketball.

Jamie Galbraith and William (Sandy) Dariety met as Marshall Scholars in England in the fall of 1974, and have been fast friends ever since.

Contents

PART III

MONETARISM AND NEW CLASSICAL ECONOMICS   177

PART IV

CONTEMPORARY DEPARTURES   **297**

Preface

As we write, in the summer of 1993, the American economy is recovering, very slowly, from a deep and lasting recession, the longest since World War II, with high unemployment, falling living standards, and a rising pessimism about our national economic future.

During the recession, there was a clamor in the land for the government to step in, to do something, to provide jobs, to cut taxes, to "get the economy moving." An election campaign was fought, in 1992, partly over this issue. And a new Administration took office in 1993, proposing a "stimulus package" to create jobs and speed economic expansion.

But what *should* have been done? *Should* the government have acted, or shouldn't it? At present, we can only note a deep division among our fellow economists over this issue. Some say yes, the hour was late, the needs urgent, the price small. Others say no, the proposed programs will not work, the budget deficit is already too large, and in any event recovery was just around the corner, whatever the government did or did not do.

None of this is new. Ever since the 1930s, the question of whether and how the government should take an active role to fight unemployment and promote economic expansion has been hotly debated. The lines of argument are broadly the same now, though with variations and innovations, as they were then. The divisions are the same. It is mainly the circumstances, the facts, and the personalities that have changed.

It is difficult to find much reassuring or encouraging about a stubborn recession, or a slow recovery, or about policy dissension and disagreement. But there is one thing that we can mention. This episode, or the memory of it, is an opportunity to alert students to the importance of understanding something about modern macroeconomics.

THE AIM OF THIS BOOK

This book aims to provide a broad exposure to issues in macroeconomic theory and in the conduct of monetary and fiscal policies. Our emphasis is, above all, on thinking clearly, and in presenting macroeconomics as it is, rather than as we, or anyone else, might like it to be.

For this reason, we do not plan to present a single body of doctrine (or "mainstream model"). In our view macroeconomics contains no such single coherent doctrine. Indeed, we believe that the attempt to patch together such a single view, so characteristic of the "textbook approach," leads to more confusion than it resolves.

We hope instead to teach students that the many current controversies in macroeconomics, including some of the most important policy issues of our time, are deeply rooted in disputes over points of theory. These disputes are between schools of economics that are opposed in very important and basic ways; they are longstanding. Macroeconomics originated in an intellectual revolution that was never definitively settled; and like the history of France for a century after 1789, the history of macroeconomics has been a history of conflict between revolutionary and counter-revolutionary traditions. It is not the case that macroeconomists agree on all of the major issues of theory and disagree only on secondary questions, such as of fact and of measurement. Instead, we believe, the disagreements extend through every root and branch of the theory and its practice, which is to say that disagreements over theory have profound consequences for the policy decisions that economists and those in authority must make in the real world.

THEORY AND POLICY

Many students seem to believe that there exists a kind of intellectual wall that separates questions of theory from decisions of policy. The theorists sit in their ivory towers, or so it seems, spinning abstract tales, while policymakers toil with the facts and figures, guided by the "common sense" of "practical men."

John Maynard Keynes, the man at the origin of our subject, provided the most famous refutation of this view:

> . . . the ideas of economists and political philosophers, both when they are right and when they are wrong, are more powerful than is commonly understood. Indeed the world is ruled by little else. Practical men, who believe themselves to be quite exempt from any intellectual influences, are usually the slaves of some defunct economist. Madmen in authority, who hear voices in the air, are distilling

their frenzy from some academic scribbler of a few years back. . . .
soon or late, it is ideas, not vested interests, which are dangerous
for good or evil.[1]

We, the authors, have experience both with the development of
economic theory and with its application to policy questions. On this
point, we believe that almost all economists (there are exceptions, even
to this!) would agree with Keynes. It is not true, as some suppose, that
policy issues are decided by an engineering process, in which economists
sharing a common perspective argue only about the interpretation of
new information. Quite to the contrary: the most critical policy choices
depend on the theoretical perspective one takes as a point of departure.
The critical policy changes occur, as with the arrival of the Reagan
Administration in 1981, when the controlling theoretical perspective
changes.

So how does theory get translated to policy? We believe that the
design of good policy in this complex and difficult field is a craft. It is a
skilled craft, one that requires the blunt and rigorous evaluation of evidence within a coherent framework of theory. There are rules, and it is
important to know and to use them. The macroeconomic artisan is ever
alert to assure consistency between assumptions and results, and always
looking at the facts, to seek out the guidance they offer and the problems
they pose.

Many who participate in policymaking, or attempt to, do not possess these skills, or perhaps have motives or special interests that would
in any event preclude their use. The policy arena is crowded with aspi-
rants to power and influence, from politicians to journalists to business
and union leaders, who lack training in economic theory and have a tin
ear for relevance in their use of economic fact. We expect students will
learn from this book how to distinguish the amateurish, the imprecise,
and the dogmatic, from those who have mastered the craft and who
abide by its rules.

The devilish thing is that mastering the craft is not the same thing as
arriving at a single "right" answer. For within the basic framework of
scientific macroeconomics, competing theoretical traditions flourish,
and these interpret the same facts through opposing theoretical lenses, to
arrive at opposing policy conclusions. To take the most fundamental
point of difference, which we have already mentioned, some economists
believe that the role of government in ending recessions and stabilizing
growth is necessarily large; others believe that it must be ideally small.

[1] John Maynard Keynes, *The General Theory of Employment Interest and Money*,
London: MacMillan, 1983, 384–5.
[2] Collected and exposed by Professor Donald McCloskey, *The Rhetoric of Economics*, Madison: University of Wisconsin Press, 1985, 31.

And this disagreement, unlike the views that we spoke of in the previous paragraph, does not stem from logical error nor from blatant disregard of the facts on either side.

Disagreements between well-trained and careful economists flow from the co-existence of competing theoretical traditions. Each of these competing traditions is honestly arrived at and carefully developed. Each has fervent partisans. Neither accounts for all the facts, but each has adherents who believe that the broad mass of facts fits better under their theory than under any other. We stress again, these are honest disagreements. And the job of this textbook is to provide a road map to the sources of the argument, so that students can decide for themselves.

Our approach to the "roadmap problem" is to present models in roughly chronological order and include some of the historical context in which they actually appeared. This too is a departure from much standard practice and from the many textbooks that emphasize the integration of strictly modern facts with modern theory. Our own primary interest is not, in fact, historical. But our teaching experience convinces us that presenting the context and development of theory helps students to grasp, order, and retain a complex presentation. On the other hand, we have built some flexibility into this text. Those instructors who do not share our view of the framesetting importance of the Great Depression and its dispute between Keynes and Classical economics are welcome to plunge in at Chapter Four, which is where the modern models make their appearance.

The roadmap is necessarily complex. For while the broad theoretical division in macroeconomics is between conservatives and liberals, classicals and Keynesians, each tradition has its own subdivisions. Each has a program of research and interpretation of the facts, which has over the years forced it to evolve and change as changing evidence and new situations present new puzzles for theory. And this has led to a diversity of schools and sub-schools, so that among "conservative" economists we have Classicals, Monetarists and New Classicals (not to mention Austrians and some other groups), while among the liberals we have Keynesians, New Keynesians and Post Keynesians (as well as institutionalists, new institutionalists and some self-described "eclectics").

We hope that this course will help students, to learn how to understand the basis for opposing points of view that exist between economists in the real world. It should also help them to recognize and expose inconsistent arguments that draw (often unwittingly) on opposing analytical frameworks. It cannot teach students how to make choices of their own between theories that are in conflict, but it can help them to recognize what the precise choices are. This process may not lead to simple and clear-cut solutions to the policy questions of the day. But it will, we hope, help them to understand the complex and fascinating world of macroeconomic policy debate. For there is nothing so alive, so vibrant, and so important, as a subject whose biggest questions remain unsettled.

HOW TO USE THIS BOOK

The most important thing about any book is readability. We have tried to make this an interesting book to read. To do that, we have tried very hard to tell a story *about* macroeconomics, to convey some of the history and context, at the same time that we teach the basic and the advanced concepts.

You will find the main elements of the story in the body of the text itself, along with all the essentials of the theory. At the beginning of each chapter, a box entitled *Looking Forward* gives a brief outline of where we are going, and structured learning objectives for this chapter. As you go along, boxes entitled *Taking a Closer Look* explore particular extensions of the theory, or provide a window onto illustrative data, including macroeconomic data from Europe and Japan as well as the United States. At the end of every chapter, an extended *Special Section* provides an opportunity to read about additional theoretical, historical or policy matters related to the main body of the chapter. Each chapter closes with four essentials: a *Summary, Review Questions* to think about and discuss, *Problems* to work on, and *Suggestions for Additional Reading.* For the professor, a combined *Instructor's Resource Manual / Test Bank* round out the package.

ACKNOWLEDGMENTS

This project originated in the summer of 1988, at the initiative of Nader Darehshori, then head of the College Division and now CEO of Houghton Mifflin. To him we owe our first thanks.

We thank our editor Denise Clinton and our development editor Julie Hogenboom for their inspiration, support, and criticism at every step of the way. Our production editor, Susan Merrifield, saw the manuscript through proofs with competence, efficiency, and good cheer. We thank our reviewers, anonymous to us but now listed below, especially those who picked at the manuscript page by page. At the LBJ School, Debbie Warden and Cynthia Bock-Goodner provided capable secretarial and also moral support.

In the fall of 1990 students at the LBJ School of Public Affairs read a draft manuscript and provided editorial and critical comments. Those who took this assignment most seriously were Christi Hawley, Shari Holland, Mary Ann Kaminksi, Brad Livingston, Mary Margaret Nicklas, John Puder, Margaret Shaw, and Andrew Wise. They have left their mark on this book.

Inevitably the style of textbooks we have used has influenced our own teaching, and traces of that influence are in these pages. We acknowledge the following: Geoffrey Woglom, *Modern Macroeconomics*; Rudiger Dornbusch and Stanley Fischer, *Macroeconomics*; and Richard Froyen, *Macroeconomics*. We hope that we have not crossed the line too often between influence and imitation.

Finally, we thank Kirsten Mullen and Ying Tang, *sine qua non*.

Reviewers

Christine Amsler
Michigan State University

Gary Barinshtein
University of Texas at Arlington

Scott Bloom
North Dakota State University

Robert D. Cruz
Florida International University

Steven Cunningham
University of Connecticut

Charles Engel
University of Washington

Rawle Farley
State University of New York, Brockport

Robert B. Fischer
California State University, Chico

James Gapinski
Florida State University

John Knudson
University of Idaho

Douglas Koritz
Buffalo State College

Rich MacDonald
Saint Cloud State University

David Martin
State University of New York, Geneseo

Christopher Waller
University of Illinois, Bloomington

J. K. G.
W. J. D., Jr.

TO THE STUDENT
A NOTE ON
NOTATION

In this text we have tried to develop a consistent and logical way of identifying our economic variables, so that you, the student, can tell at a glance what type of variable each symbol refers to.

The simplest kind of economic variable is the plain dollars-and-cents expression, which may be a wage rate, the price of a good or service, or the dollar value of all goods and services sold in the economy (gross national product and its components: consumption, investment, government spending, exports and imports). We call these *nominal* variables and use capital letters—W (wages), Y (national product or income), C (consumption), I (investment), G (government spending), X (exports), M (imports)—to express them in symbolic notation. We also use the block capital P to indicate the aggregate price level—an index number that tells you how much inflation there has been between any one time period and any other. And we use capital letters for the volume of employment (N) and the rate of unemployment (U), which are not dollars-and-cents expressions to begin with.

Often in macroeconomics our interest lies not so much in dollars-and-cents expressions, but in the underlying physical quantities, such as the volume of goods and services produced, or the amount of physical machinery purchased (investment). The measurement of these variables starts out in dollars-and-cents terms, but then an adjustment is applied to remove the effect of changing prices and so arrive at a measure of the underlying quantities. We call these derived expressions *real* variables, and say that they have been "deflated," which means that the effect of price inflation has been taken out. In this text, we will denote deflated variables with small letters. Thus, if nominal national income is "Y", real notation income is "y".

We calculate real national income by dividing the nominal value for a given year by the index value of the price level $(P/100)$[4] in that year.

[4] By convention, we divide the index number by 100. Thus, if 1982 is the base year, so that the price level in 1982 equals 100, the real or deflated value of any economic variable in that year is equal to the nominal value.

The price index is measured from an arbitrarily chosen base, a year whose value in that index is set to 100. (For most of the deflated series in this book, the index base year will be 1982, or 1987.) This gives us the value of real national income in terms of what the dollar was worth in the base year.

$$y_t = \frac{Y_t}{P_t/100}$$

Thus, if we are using a price index that uses 1982 for the base year, and the current value is 160, this would indicate $160/100 = 1.6$ or 60% inflation since 1982, which tells us that we must "deflate" nominal or "current" dollar national income by 1.6 in order to find real national income as expressed in "constant" 1982 dollars.

We use a dot on top to indicate the *rate of change* of economic variables, and we sometimes use a subscript to indicate the year in which a variable holds a certain value. Thus, if Y_t is nominal national income in year t, then

$$\dot{Y}_t = \left(\frac{Y_t - Y_{t-1}}{Y_{t-1}} * 100\% \right)$$

is the percentage change of Y since the last period, and $\dot{y}_t$ indicates the corresponding percentage change of real national income.

Next, we frequently will make reference to the *equilibrium* values of a variable, usually in the "Walrasian" sense of the values at which markets clear (quantities supplied equals quantities demanded), sometimes in the "Marshallian" sense of a stable value that does not normally change. We will use asterisks to denote equilibrium values in either sense. Thus N^* denotes the equilibrium value of employment. When we need to denote different values of a variable that are not necessarily equilibrium values, for example in a Figure, we will use a prime mark (N', not to be confused with the functional notation such as $N'(w)$, described below). If we need more than one such value, we will use numbered subscripts: y_1, y_2 and so on.

Finally, from time to time we need to express variables as *functions* of other variables—meaning simply that one variable depends on another. For example, we may wish to say that labor supply (N^s) is a function of the real wage (w), so that when real wages go up, more people seek employment. We do this with parentheses, as follows:

$$N^s = N^s(w)$$

When we wish to show how a function *changes* with respect to one of its variables (a variable in a function is known as an *argument* of that function), we will use a prime (') to indicate the direction of change. Thus

$$N^{s\prime}\ (w) > 0 \text{ is the same as}$$
$$d[\,N^s(w)]/dw > 0$$

in the routine notation of derivatives, meaning (in this case) that labor supply rises when the real wage rises.[5]

By arranging our notation in this way we hope to help clear the often critical distinction between nominal and real values, and to help keep them clear as you work your way through theoretical models that sometimes use one, sometimes the other. We also hope to provide a ready key that will help you distinguish equilibrium from dis-equilibrium values and rates of change from level measures. Finally, we hope that this system can clearly indicate the functional dependence of one variable on another.[6]

---

[5] If we need to show a second derivative (rate of change of the rate of change), we will use a double prime ($\prime\prime$). Thus:

$$y\prime(N) > 0 \text{ and}$$
$$y\prime\prime(N) < 0$$

would indicate that real production increases with employment but at a diminishing rate.

[6] In particular, we try to show functions without resort either to formal calculus notation or to restricting ourselves to linear equations. Linear equations are simpler, but they would not be consistent with the curves with which we frequently illustrate such relations.

THE MACROECONOMIC REVOLUTION

Chapter 1

REVOLUTION AND COUNTERREVOLUTION

Looking Forward

These first three chapters describe the Keynesian revolution. Read them with your eye on the big picture. What were the economic conditions of the Great Depression? How did prevailing economic theory attempt to account for mass unemployment? Why did Keynes rebel against this accounting, and what did he attempt to put in its place? Do not try to master every detail of macroeconomic theory at this stage. There is a lot of material in these chapters, and some of it may not become clear to you until you have had a chance to work through the formal models later on. But if you come away from these chapters with some appreciation of the climate of that time and an understanding of how Keynes attempted to "shift the goal posts" in economic thinking with respect to both labor and capital markets, then you will be well prepared for the task that lies ahead.

Macroeconomics began with a decisive event: the publication in 1936 of *The General Theory of Employment, Interest and Money*, by the British economist John Maynard Keynes (1883–1946). In large measure, all subsequent developments in macroeconomics have been reactions, either direct or indirect, to that book.

   The General Theory attempted in one blow to overturn most of economics as it then existed. Keynes considered the theoretical positions of his fellow economists to be both mistaken and dangerous. Indeed, he objected to positions that at one time he had himself held, although never uncritically.[1] In the Preface to *The General Theory*, he wrote: "The composition of this book has been for the author a long struggle of escape . . . a struggle of escape from habitual modes of thought and expression." He warned his readers that they, too, would have to wage such a struggle if the "assault upon them was to be successful."[2]

Escape from what? Assault on what?

THE CLASSICAL ECONOMICS

Keynes mounted his rebellion against a body of belief that he called "the classical economics." Classical economics had, by 1936, been dominant for precisely 160 years—since the publication of Adam Smith's *Inquiry into the Nature and Causes of the Wealth of Nations* in the American independence year of 1776. Classical theory's greatest nineteenth-century masters had included the Englishmen David Ricardo, W. S. Jevons, and John Stuart Mill and the Frenchman Jean-Baptiste Say. If there was, in Keynes's mind, a single leading modern master of the classical economics, it was probably his own teacher, Alfred Marshall (1842–1924), author of the first authoritative textbook in economics and inventor of the modern analysis of supply and demand.

Classical economics was a loose set of doctrines, rooted variously in moral philosophy, Newton's physics, and Darwin's biology; substantially nonmathematical; and lacking the systematic development and internal consistency that has come to characterize economics in our own time. We will present a synopsis, or more precisely a model, of the classical system when we get to Chapter 4. For now, we content ourselves with a mere description of three main points of doctrine.

First and foremost, classical economics held that the total volume of employment in society was determined in a labor market, by the supply of labor and other resources available and by the demand for them. Wages were the price that balanced the supply of labor with the demand. If, for some reason, the supply of workers increased relative to demand for them, wages would decline. In that event, it would become attractive for the additional workers to be hired. Wages would continue to fall, and additional workers would continue to be hired, until there were no more workers who were willing to work at the prevailing wage. At that point,

---

[1] Keynes was always less than orthodox in both his public and his private life. Robert Skidelsky's masterful biography of the young Keynes, *John Maynard Keynes: 1883–1920, Hopes Betrayed*, provides the essential details of Keynes's early life, personal history, and philosophical development.

[2] *The General Theory* (New York: Macmillan, 1986), p. viii.

in a phrase, *the labor market would clear*. There would be no unemployment, except for workers between jobs and those who were unwilling to work at the prevailing wage. In particular, there could not be a persistent excess supply of labor, of people willing to work at the prevailing wage but unable to find jobs, a condition otherwise known as mass unemployment.

Second, classical economics held that the interest rate, which is the rate of return on savings, investment, and capital formation, was also determined in a market. The classical capital market weighed the demand for investment funds against the willingness of savers to defer present consumption; to classical economists, the interest rate represented the balance of these two forces. If savings went up, interest rates would come down, and investment would go up to match the savings. Consequently, thrifty and virtuous peoples—for so the Victorian English viewed themselves—would be rewarded by the accumulation of wealth, while the supposedly feckless and spendthrift peoples of other countries would remain mired in poverty. Since there was no possibility of mass unemployment, investment and consumption were the only possible uses of current production, and an increase in consumption (at the expense of savings) could come only at the expense of future investment, capital formation, and wealth.

The notion of a balance between savings and investment was captured by a classical proposition known as *Say's Law*. Say's Law asserted, in effect, that all savings would necessarily be invested, that resources withdrawn from consumption by savers would automatically and necessarily return, in the form of demand for investment goods, to the general flow of demand for goods and services. Therefore, there was no possibility of what nineteenth-century economists called a "general glut" or an "underconsumption crisis," a persistent excess supply of goods that could not be sold. In a popular phrase that summarized Say's Law, "Supply creates its own demand."

The third main principle of the classical economic system concerned money. In an odd way, classical economics had almost no role for money. In an economy, according to the *quantity theory of money*, the total amount of circulating money in proportion to the total volume of circulating goods was responsible for the general level of prices. And the relationship between the two was thought to be quite steady over time. Since money earned no interest, whereas savings in other forms (such as bonds) did, it was not rational to hold money except as needed for transactions. And so, if the money supply increased more rapidly than the supply of goods, there would be price inflation; if it decreased, the general level of prices would fall.

Aside from that, classical economists believed, changing the quantity of money in an economy had no effects. It did not change the interest rate[3] and so would not change the balance between investment and consumption. It affected neither the supply of goods nor the demand for them; neither the supply of labor nor the demand for it. People had no reason to hoard money (over and above what they needed for transactions), so there was no possibility that savings could disappear into idle money holdings, disrupting the smooth operation of Say's Law. Inflation, deflation, or price stability would change nothing; the real volume of output, the level of employment, and the living standards of workers would remain exactly the same. Hence, in a phrase you will encounter again and again in this text, *money was neutral*.

KEYNES'S REVOLUTION

By 1936, Keynes had come to reject each and every one of these ideas. He had come to believe that there existed no labor market mechanism that would automatically keep the economy at full employment. Nor did he believe that the smooth functioning of the capital market would ensure that realized investment would always equal planned savings. Instead, he now believed that the supply of goods and the volume of employment depended on the demand for them, on the levels of consumption and planned investment—exactly the opposite of Say's Law. Keynes had also come to believe that the realized supply of savings, the amount that actually occurred as opposed to the amount that savers might plan for, depended not on the interest rate but instead on the level of income—on whether the economy was at full employment. And contradicting the quantity theory, he had come to see an intimate link between the money supply and the interest rate, and through them on the level of demand for output and on employment. In these links between topics that classical economics had kept separate, we find the very origin of macroeconomics as a distinct subject.

In consequence, where classical economics emphasized the virtues of thrift and savings, monetary stability, and *laissez-faire* (nonintervention) in labor markets, Keynes came to exactly opposite conclusions. In a comprehensive and dramatic break from the orthodoxies of his time, Keynes called for increased mass consumption, public spending, low interest rates, and easy credit. And he opposed the classical remedy of wage cutting for the then-inescapable problem of mass unemployment.

For Keynes this was no academic parlor game; the stakes were extremely high. The *Great Depression*, an unparalleled disaster, had by that time been going on in Britain for more than a decade. Double-digit unemployment had emerged in Britain as far back as 1921, when the rate

---

[3] At least not after taking out any (purely cosmetic) effects of inflation on the interest rate.

jumped from 3 to 19 percent. From 1930 to 1933, estimated British unemployment rates exceeded 20 percent.[4] Moreover, by September 1926 the index of economic production had declined to half of its September 1920 value; it was not to reach the 1920 level again until June 1936.[5]

The Great Depression in the United States of America was no less dramatic. Between 1929 and 1933, the unemployment rate rose from 3 percent to 25 percent, the U.S. economy's output fell by one-third, money wages and consumer prices both fell about 30 percent, and the prices of farm products fell by 50 percent.[6] The event that signaled the collapse was the crash of the New York Stock Exchange in late October 1929. By November 1929, the average price of fifty leading stocks was half of what it had been in September of the same year.[7] And the fall continued until July 1932, when the Dow Jones index of leading industrial companies' stocks dropped to 41, a 90 percent decline from its high in September 1929.[8]

The crisis in the securities market also hit hard at American commercial banking. After the crash, bank failures soared as panicked depositors withdrew their funds. Without deposit insurance, those who were unable to withdraw their money before their banks closed lost everything. Between 1929 and 1933, eleven thousand U.S. banks failed, over 40 percent of those in existence in 1929. About $2 billion in deposits were lost.

Keynes was convinced that these phenomena lay outside the comprehension of the economics and the economists of his day. Worse still, he had concluded, habitual economic modes of thought led to policies that would prolong, and perhaps perpetuate, the calamity. New policies, which were urgently required, could not be built on the old foundations. Rather, a new vision of how the economy functions, a new theoretical basis for policy, was required.

At first, and for quite a long time, Keynes's idea that the Depression broke with the past in a fundamental way was a minority view. There had been, particularly among Western countries, a long historical experience with financial panics and crashes, recoveries and collapses. The phrase "prosperity is just around the corner" was commonplace among political figures in 1930. Keynes, however, could be heard warning,

---

[4] Not until the British mobilization for World War II did the unemployment rate fall below 10 percent. See Forrest Capie and Michael Collins, *The Inter-War British Economy: A Statistical Abstract* (Manchester: Manchester University Press, 1983), pp. 62–69.

[5] *Ibid.,* p. 20.

[6] Gary Smith, *Money and Banking: Financial Markets and Institutions* (Reading, Mass.: Addison-Wesley Publishing, 1982), p. 292.

[7] "The Past," *Business Week*, September 3, 1979, pp. 9–10.

[8] Smith, *Money and Banking*, p. 292.

"The world has been slow to realize that we are living this year in the shadow of one of the greatest economic catastrophes of modern history."[9]

Yet Keynes argued—and here was another radical departure—that the Depression was all a nightmare that could, with the design and execution of proper policies, be put right by tomorrow morning:

> If our poverty were due to earthquake or famine or war—if we lacked material things and the resources to produce them, we could not expect to find the means to prosperity except in hard work, abstinence, and invention. In fact, our predicament is notoriously of another kind. It comes from some failure in the immaterial devices of the mind, in the working of the motives which should lead to the decisions and acts of will, necessary to put in movement the resources and technical means we already have. It is as though two motor-drivers, meeting in the middle of a highway, were unable to pass one another because neither knows the rules of the road. Their own muscles are no use; a motor engineer cannot help them; a better road will not serve. Nothing is required and nothing will avail, except a little clear thinking.[10]

AFTER KEYNES: COUNTERREVOLUTIONS

Unfortunately for Keynes, the "clear thinking" for which he called has never seemed quite so clear to other economists. Despite the fact that the policies he advocated were widely implemented, Keynes's theoretical perspective was never embraced in full by the economics profession. In that sense, Keynes's revolution remains incomplete. The long history of "Keynesian economics" has been one, in part, of repeated efforts to explain in simple, precise, and rigorous terms "what Keynes meant," followed by repeated attacks both on these explanations and on the theoretical perspective behind them.

In the beginning, which is to say from the 1940s through the early 1960s, Keynes's revolution certainly dominated the field. In this period, we see the elucidation of the simplest concepts of the Keynesian system, notably the relationship between the "multiplier" and the "marginal propensity to consume," from which Keynes had derived the first principles of his theory of the level of employment. These concepts provided a powerful way to explain why the mass unemployment of the 1930s did

[9] J. M. Keynes, "The Great Slump of 1930," in *Collected Writings,* Vol. IX, p. 126.
[10] "The Means to Prosperity" in *Collected Writings*, Vol. IX, p. 335.

not reappear, as many expected it would, after the end of World War II in 1945. We explore multiplier models and theories of consumption behavior in detail in Chapter 4.

Multiplier models and consumption functions were, however, only a part of the whole Keynesian system. They helped explain how government spending could prop up consumption and so keep an economy out of depression. But they ignored the roles of money, of the interest rate, and of demand for investment with which, as we have seen, Keynes was greatly concerned. And as the Keynesian era matured, many economists, especially in the United States, were drawn toward a much more complete effort to capture and represent the insights of *The General Theory*. This was the *IS-LM model*, generally attributed to Sir John Hicks of Oxford and Alvin Hansen of Harvard.

IS-LM, which we present in Chapter 5, has long formed the core of textbook Keynesianism and still does to this day. It represents an effort to integrate a model of the market for physical output (commodities), which incorporates the consumption function and the multiplier, with a model of the market for money, which incorporates Keynes's ideas about the determination of the rate of interest. IS-LM models are very broad, flexible, and useful. In more recent years, they have been modified to underpin models of international economic interrelationships (such as the exchange rate); we present an exposition of such a model in Chapter 11.

In the 1960s, another relationship was added to the Keynesian system, perhaps in an effort to make it even more relevant to the practical policy questions of the day. This was an empirical relationship between inflation and unemployment, known as the *Phillips curve*, after its originator, A. W. Phillips of the London School of Economics. The Phillips curve simply stated that the rate of inflation would be low so long as unemployment was high and that it would tend to rise when unemployment fell. There was, it was said, a trade-off between the desired objectives of full employment and price stability; policymakers could choose what sort of economy they desired by picking the particular combination of unemployment and inflation they might prefer from the Phillips curve's menu of possibilities. We discuss the Phillips curve in Chapter 5.

There were only two problems with the Phillips curve. First, try as one might, one could not derive, in any fully persuasive way, the relationship observed in the data from theoretical first principles. Second, the relationship observed in the data disappeared, catastrophically, with the high inflation and low growth rates that began to plague the American economy after 1968. By pulling on that string, critics of the whole Keynesian system were able to reemerge, to reassert themselves, and in the end very nearly to cause the entire system to unravel.

The first round of counterrevolution emerged under the banner of *monetarism*, led by Milton Friedman. Monetarists, whose ideas we treat in Chapter 7,[11] sought to reestablish the classical relationship between money growth and inflation and to refute the Phillips curve relationship between inflation and unemployment. In the long run, the monetarists argued, there was no trade-off between inflation and unemployment, and a slow rate of money growth would yield high employment with stable prices just as surely as a high rate of money growth would yield high employment with inflation.

The monetarist effort to overturn Keynesian theory and policy recommendations attracted wide support among economists but also generated a new round of theoretical criticism and innovation, largely among Friedman's own students and colleagues at the University of Chicago. This led, in the early 1970s, to a post-monetarist grouping that styled itself the *new classical economics*. We present new classical economics in Chapters 8 and 9.

The new classical economics combined monetarism with another idea drawn from the old classical repertory, namely the notion that markets for labor and capital are fully self-adjusting. To this, based on the notion that all individuals are able to make fully efficient use of all available information in making economic forecasts: proponents added a concept all their own: *rational expectations*. With the triple tools of monetarism, market clearing, and rational expectations, the new classical economists sought to demolish Keynesianism once and for all and to restore the basic noninterventionism policy conclusions that had prevailed among classical economists before the Great Depression.

They almost succeeded. For fifteen years or so, until the late 1980s, the new classical economists dominated the theoretical side of macroeconomics, and they remain highly influential to this day. But the initiative shifted with the emergence of yet another group in the late 1980s. This group, in conscious imitation of and opposition to the new classicals, has taken the designation of *new Keynesians*. The new Keynesians accept many of the theoretical arguments of the new classicals but reject the idea that markets self-adjust to ensure full employment. Thus, for new Keynesians, there remains an important role for the government to play in fighting unemployment, something that new classicals deny. We explore the new Keynesian position in Chapter 10.

In all of this complicated history, yet another group of macroeconomists has remained active. This group, usually known as *post-Keynesian*, is distinguished by its strong continuing interest in certain theoretical and policy issues that the other groups have tended to neglect. In particular, post-Keynesians predicate their analysis on a world of uncertainty, in which public policy plays a powerful function of coordinating and shaping the expectations of businesses, consumers, savers, and other economic actors. Post-Keynesians believe that their formula-

[11] After a chapter (6) devoted to ideas about money.

tions of macroeconomics are both closer to that of Keynes himself and more relevant to the politics of the modern world than are those of the other disputants. The post-Keynesian group is smaller and in many ways less influential than the Keynesians, monetarists, new classicals, and new Keynesians, but in our judgment their views are important. The post-Keynesians reject rational expectations and work with a model that stresses interest rates, the pricing of assets in capital markets, the level of effective demand, and the effects of technological change—all topics that are highly relevant to today's world. We round out our text with a presentation of post-Keynesian views in Chapters 12 and 13.

Thus, ever since Keynes invented macroeconomics in 1936, macroeconomists, whether self-consciously or incidentally, have supported either positions taken by Keynes in *The General Theory* or those from which he sought to escape. And even if the matter has not always been cast in these terms by its protagonists, the debate between those who have been with Keynes and those who have been against him has dominated macroeconomics for the past sixty years and still dominates it today. The flux continues, and the fact that the subject survives in part by a process of creative self-destruction provides another reason for learning about its evolution alongside its modern form. For one can be sure of only one thing about the subject on which you are about to embark: a few years from now, it will be different.

SPECIAL SECTION

Keynes, Einstein, and Scientific Revolution

One of the most intriguing and little-noted facts about Keynes's *The General Theory of Employment, Interest and Money* concerns the title itself. It evidently was cribbed, and quite consciously so, from Albert Einstein's historic 1915 paper, *The General Theory of Relativity*.[1]

The economists Hsieh and Ye have recently taken up this theme:[2]

Keynes was, probably, the first economist who recognized the importance of Einstein's theory of curved space-time. The following passage [from *The General Theory*] provides us with strong evidence that Keynes was well acquainted with Einstein's general theory.

The classical theorists resemble Euclidean geometers in a non-Euclidean world who, discovering that in experience straight lines apparently parallel often meet, rebuke the lines for not keeping straight—as the only remedy for the unfortunate collisions which are occurring. Yet, in truth, there is no remedy except to throw over the axiom of parallels and to work out a non-Euclidean geometry. Something similar is required in economics.

In our view, the parallelism that Keynes intended, between his revolution and Einstein's, runs very deep. It is therefore worthwhile to spend a few pages trying to explain how the two fields of physics and economics are related and what Keynes apparently had in mind.

Newton's Physics

Albert Einstein came of age in a world where the physics of Sir Isaac Newton still reigned largely supreme. Newton, the great seventeenth-century scientist and mathematician, had developed calculus to help explain the motion of matter in space and had set forth a system of laws that governed gravity, one of the most basic forces known.

Two features of Newton's world-view are especially important. First, it presupposes an absolute separation of *space* and *time*. Space is Euclidean: an empty, three-dimensional void stretching infinitely in all directions. The position of any particle in space can be defined, by means of a system of coordinates, with respect to any

observer or any fixed reference point.[3] Motion is simply the displacement of the particle from one position to another. Velocity is motion divided by the number of ticks on a clock required for the motion to occur. The clock that is used to measure velocity lies, in a strict sense, outside the universe itself. In other words, provided they were equipped with accurate timepieces, all observers of an event, no matter where they might be, would always agree on the exact time that the event occurred. Newton imagined time as an absolutely regular phenomenon that could not depend on the location of the clock or be affected by its movement or that of the observer or of any other physical force.

Second, Newton's system is *reductionist*. Gravity in Newton's system is the basic force exerted by one massive body on any other. Gravity produces the acceleration of a particle in space, according to the position and mass of all other particles in the universe that would be exerting gravitational force on the particle in question. And, in Newton's view, this interaction of each particle on every other *is all there is*. Once one knew the position, mass, direction, and velocity of every particle in the universe (admittedly a tall order), one would not need to know anything else. Every future event would be fully determined by the laws of motion. We can say that this complete dependence of the behavior of the whole universe on its individual parts reflects the reductionist character of Newton's physics: the whole is nothing more than the sum of its components.

Newton and Classical Economics

Newton's physics influenced the development of what Keynes called the classical economics as much as any single intellectual force. Indeed, as the economist Philip Mirowski has recently argued,[4] the imprint of Newton's mechanics is fundamental to economic thought even today. Without going into great detail, it is possible to trace the role of each of the above features in the classical economics of Keynes's time and in modern neoclassical economics.

The absolute separation of space and time was then and is now deeply embedded in the way economists reason. The analog of space is the *market*. Look at virtually any diagram in this text—for example, the simple labor market diagram in Figure 2.1, in the next chapter. The graph itself is a two-dimensional space.[5] Every point on the graph is a position defined unambiguously and uniquely with respect to the origin. The relationships between variables are presented as forces in this space: demand aligns wages and employment in a downward-sloping relation; supply aligns them along an upward slope. If two curves cross in that space, their point of intersection is an equilibrium position, where the forces balance. Where labor supply and labor demand intersect, there is the equilibrium of full employment.

The analog of Newtonian time, in classical economics, is money. Just as time is separated from space, money is separated from the market. Prices and wages may be measured in money terms, but this is only a convenience. The prices being measured are "relative prices," prices in relation to the prices of other goods. The wages being measured are "real wages," wages in terms of the commodities that wages purchase. Like time, money is only a unit of account. Just as it does not matter whether one measures time in seconds or in hours, it does not matter whether one measures prices in dollars or dimes or pesos or yen. The quantity of money has no effect on the equilibrium of the market; nothing "real" depends on money in any important way.

The reductionism of Newton's system was equally fundamental to classical economics—and remains so today. From the very beginning of their training, economists are taught that individual human action underlies all economic decisions. In this view, there is no economic "society" with independent laws of its own; societies are nothing more than the sum of their individual components. Macroeconomic expressions, which purport to describe the behavior of society as a whole, are in reality just a shorthand for the behaviors of large groups of individual people. In principle, therefore, it ought to be possible to develop a macroeconomics built strictly and rigidly from the theory of individual behavior, or *microfoundations*. If this has not yet been done, the problem must lie mainly in the difficulty of acquiring all the information that is necessary about all of the individuals whose preferences and behavior must be considered.[6]

Einstein and Newton's Mechanics

By the time Keynes came along, the Newtonian view of the physical universe had crumbled. Einstein's theories of relativity had done it in.

The absolute separation of time and space collapsed with Einstein's introduction of a new universal constant, the speed of light. If light traveled everywhere and always and irrespective of the direction and velocity of the observer (as Einstein argued and experiments have confirmed) at the same identical speed (300,000 kilometers per second), then the absolute simultaneity of two or more very distant events could no longer be defined. Clocks in different places will record these events at different times, and none is more "correct" than any other. Moreover, Einstein was able to show that space, time, and motion were interrelated—time moves more slowly near massive bodies than it does in empty space.[7]

Furthermore, this newly unified concept, space-time, also destroyed the Euclidean concept of emptiness extending forever in all directions. Space-time is *curved*. Near any massive body, the shortest distance between two points curves around it.[8] For this reason, parallel lines invariably meet if extended far enough. Keynes's reference to overthrowing the Greek geometer Euclid's "axiom of parallels" is an allusion to this feature of Einstein's theory.

But if space-time is curved by the presence of matter, then the shortest distance between two points is no longer defined independently of the distribution of matter in space. And then the system is no longer reductionist: you can no longer get to the whole merely by adding up the parts. The universe is, instead, more easily and more correctly understood by looking at the whole and placing the parts within it. The whole can impose rules on the parts: in a phrase, "space tells matter how to move; matter tells space how to curve."[9]

Keynes, the Classics, and Relativity Theory

There can be little doubt that Keynes had both of these troubled features of the Newtonian worldview, as reflected in classical economics, in his gun sights when he wrote *his General Theory*.

In the first place, Keynes sought to disestablish the "absolute space" of classical markets and to end the separation of these markets from the world of money. We shall see in the next chapters how he characterized his theory as a *monetary theory of production* and contrasted it with what he called the *real-exchange economics* of the classical view. In so doing, he broke down the traditional nonmonetary concepts of a "labor market" and a "capital market," suffusing both of these subjects with concepts—effective demand, liquidity preference—that cannot even be conceived except in monetary terms. *Monetary production* is Keynes's space-time: the marriage of two concepts previously held to be absolutely distinct.

Second, Keynes disavowed the reductionist, or bottom-to-top approach of the classical economists: the idea that the behavior of the system could always be explained by reference to the behavior of individuals within it. The pernicious influence of this view was especially apparent, in Keynes's opinion, in the theory of employment. Classical theory had focused the attention of those concerned with employment and unemployment on a labor market, an act of cognition that placed the actions of workers and the firms who hire them in a central perspective while relegating all other influences to the background. This led practitioners of classical economics to the unshakable conclusion that *involuntary* unemployment could not, in any strict sense, exist. The *apparently* unemployed person, in the classical view, should always be able to find work by cutting his wage requirements a sufficient amount. Supply

would intersect demand eventually, if this prescription only were followed.

Keynes sought to show that this was not, in fact, the case. The act of dropping wages would generate feedbacks through previously unrecognized—monetary—channels in the system. These would reduce the demand for workers and prevent total employment from rising. The system interacts with itself, and an equilibrium of the labor market cannot be achieved within the labor market. Economic space-time is curved. When Keynes speaks in the passage quoted above of overthrowing the axiom of parallels, he is referring specifically to the need to create a nonlinear economic world. The analog to the axiom of parallels, in his mind, was the classical theory of the supply of labor, the "second postulate of the classical doctrine"—precisely that part of the classical vision that reduced unemployment to a matter of individual decision:

> We need to throw over the second postulate of the classical doctrine and to work out the behavior of a system in which involuntary unemployment in the strict sense is possible.[10]

Macroeconomics, and Keynes's economics in particular, involve much more than the mere imitation or attempted imitation of modern developments in physics. Nevertheless, the parallels between what

Einstein did and what Keynes attempted to do provide insight, not only into the nature of the revolution that he was attempting, but also into the scale of his ambition.

---

[1] This point was first made to one of us in private conversation by Lord Robert Skidelsky, author of the definitive biography of Keynes.

[2] Ching-Yao Hsieh and Meng-Hua Ye, *Economics, Philosophy and Physics* (Armonk, N.Y.: M. E. Sharpe, 1991), pp. 80–81.

[3] This is done by placing the reference point at the origin of a (Cartesian) coordinate system and measuring the distance in each of the three dimensions of space from the origin to the projection of the particle on the coordinate axes—just as we locate points in graphs in this text by reference to x and y axes.

[4] See Philip Mirowski, *More Heat than Light: Economics as Social Physics, Physics as Nature's Economics* (Cambridge: Cambridge University Press, 1989).

[5] In more technical presentations of modern microeconomics, we frequently hear it said that different commodities define a "space," and that utility is a "field in commodity-space." In this simpler, two-dimensional representation, the y-axis represents price *in terms of all other commodities*; thus, the many dimensions of a commodity space are approximated by the two dimensions of a demand-supply diagram.

[6] This failure in no way invalidates economic laws, just as a failure to predict the future of the universe because of a lack of information about every particle in it would hardly invalidate the laws of motion.

[7] Experiments with atomic clocks in airplanes have since proved that increasing the altitude of a clock causes it to run faster (age more quickly).

[8] As does the path of a ray of light, as experiments confirming Einstein's hypothesis showed.

[9] John Archibald Wheeler, quoted in Hsieh and Ye, page 76.

[10] Hsieh and Ye, p. 81.

SUMMARY

The starting point for modern macroeconomic theory is *The General Theory of Employment, Interest and Money,* by John Maynard Keynes. All theoretic formulations since its publication have been either direct or indirect reactions to it.

The General Theory was itself seen by its author as a rebellion against what he called classical economic theory. Classical economic theory is popularly said to have begun with Adam Smith, but its actual formulation owes more to the economists that came between Smith and Keynes. In Keynes's view, classical economics has three basic tenets. The first, Say's Law, holds that supply creates its own demand. The second is that the interest rate is determined in a market for loanable funds. The third tenet is the quantity theory of money for the determination of the price level.

Keynes rejected all three of these tenets. He instead offered an explanation for the Great Depression that did not depend on the "real" explanations of, the classicals. In the chapters that follow, explanations of, reactions to, and extensions of the Keynesian system will be presented, including multiplier analysis, IS-LM analysis, the Phillips curve, monetarism, new classical economics, new Keynesian economics, and post-Keynesian economics. Also since it provides a convenient historical and theoretical counterpoint to Keynesian economics, the classical economic doctrine will be examined in some detail.

Review Questions

1. Where would you place the Keynesian and classical schools in the current political debate over macroeconomic issues? Which political parties line up with which schools? Since political parties are not homogeneous, distinguishing among personalities or "schools of thought" within the political parties may be important at times.

2. How did the most recent economic downturn (1989–1992) compare with the Great Depression? Make specific reference to economic statistics in your answer.

3. Policies suggested by a theoretical inquiry can sometimes be adopted by policymakers without their adopting the actual theory. Can this be a problem? Explain.

4. At the end of Chapter 1, a brief overview of the book is given, with specific reference to several schools and subschools of economics. Give your quick (and as yet uninformed) assessment of how each of these would formulate policy to fight unemployment.

5. How do the background and circumstances of Keynes and the Keynesian revolution compare with such other scientific revolutions as those associated with Newton, Darwin, and Einstein?

Suggested Readings

Robert Skidelsky, *John Maynard Keynes: 1883–1920, Hopes Betrayed* (New York: Viking, 1986).

Forrest Capie and Michael Collins, *The Inter-war British Economy: A Statistical Abstract* (Manchester: Manchester University Press, 1983).

Gary Smith, *Money and Banking: Financial Markets and Institutions* (Reading MA: Addison-Wesley, 1982).

Chapter 2

EMPLOYMENT AND
UNEMPLOYMENT

Can people be involuntarily unemployed? In the face of the Great
Depression, the then-prevailing economic theory maintained that
they could not. If mass unemployment existed, it must be because
workers were demanding wages that were too high in relation to
the value of what they produced. The problem would surely go
away if only workers would let wages fall and allow the markets
to work. Unemployment, therefore, was really the fault of those
unemployed workers who were making unreasonable demands; it
need not be a great concern of anyone else.

Keynes did not think the answer was so simple. Thinking afresh
about the labor market, he came to believe that lower *money*
wages might make unemployment worse rather than better and
that achieving lower *real* wages might be beyond the power of
workers alone to achieve, even if lower real wages would, in principle, erase unemployment. According to Keynes, if the cure for
unemployment lay beyond the powers of the unemployed, then
their unemployment was truly *involuntary*, and something more
than passive faith in the market would be required to correct it.

This chapter traces the intellectual steps that drove Keynes toward that conclusion. As you read, bear in mind that we are not
trying to present a formal macroeconomic model at this stage.
Rather, we are trying to think our way through a conceptual dispute. As you go along, you can test your understanding by asking
yourself the following questions:

- How was the classical labor market supposed to work? Why
  did that rule out involuntary unemployment?

- What criticisms did Keynes level at the classical labor market? How did these criticisms lead toward a coherent notion of involuntary unemployment?
- If a malfunctioning labor market was not the cause of mass unemployment, what was?

John Maynard Keynes opens *The General Theory* with a one-page chapter, in which he makes the claim that the classical theory from which he seeks escape is, at best, only a "special case." Of the many possible economic outcomes or positions of equilibrium, the classical theory acknowledges but one: the position of full employment. The *general* theory, Keynes's theory, asserts instead that many different equilibria are possible and that these are characterized, in general, by unemployment.

Keynes makes a further claim: that a world with unemployment is qualitatively different from the world of full employment. Propositions that hold under the special classical condition of full employment do not hold when there is persistent unemployment. Moreover, the classical theory rules out the very possibility of the particular type of unemployment that Keynes finds especially relevant to the Great Depression. This he calls *involuntary unemployment*. A new theory would be required to analyze such a world.

THE CLASSICAL THEORY OF EMPLOYMENT

Keynes provides a cogent description of the classical theory of employment against which he would rebel. We shall follow his description, both because it is reasonably fair and because in so doing we can most easily pinpoint the issues around which Keynes seeks to foment his revolution.

Two postulates sum it up. The first describes labor demand: *the wage equals the marginal product of labor*. Firms determine how many workers they wish to hire by adding employment until the last person hired is only just worth what he or she is paid. In Keynes's words: "The wage of an employed person is equal to the value which would be lost if employment were to be reduced by one unit (after deducting any other costs which this reduction of output would avoid)"[1]

As Keynes notes, the classicals admit to one qualification: the equality between wages and marginal products will not hold "if competition

---

[1] *The General Theory of Employment, Interest and Money* (London: Macmillan, 1936), p. 5. Unless otherwise noted, all quotations in this chapter are from this work; page numbers appear in parentheses following the quoted passage.

and markets are imperfect." In that case, firms are employing fewer workers than under perfect competition, and the marginal product of labor may be higher than the wage actually being paid.

The second classical postulate describes labor supply: *for any given amount of employment, the utility of the wage is equal to the marginal disutility of work*. People are willing to work up to the point at which the wage just ceases to compensate them for the inconvenience and effort of working. Again in Keynes's words: "The real wage of an employed person is that which is just sufficient (in the estimation of the employed persons themselves) to induce the volume of labor actually employed to be forthcoming" (p. 5). As used here, the phrase "real wage" means the commodity-content of the wage, or its purchasing power over the goods and services workers wish to consume.

The qualification the classicals admit here is that this equality will not hold if laborers combine (that is, if they form a union), producing circumstances "analogous to the imperfections of competition that qualify the first postulate" (pp. 5–6). In that case, the wage may be higher than strictly necessary to bring people into the labor market.

With the second postulate in place, a classical economist could acknowledge the possibility of unemployment, but only of very particular types. The types of unemployment consistent with the classical vision are frictional and voluntary.

Frictional unemployment involves temporary mismatches of jobs and skills or temporary bottlenecks in production, which might slow the movement of labor from one sector or from one region to another. Unemployment due to slow adjustment by workers to changes in patterns of supply and demand for goods, or to transitions from one job to another, also fall under this designation. Frictional unemployment is inherently temporary and wholly compatible with the view that "the existing economic system is in the long-run self-adjusting, though with creaks and groans and jerks."[2]

Voluntary unemployment arises when "a unit of labor" refuses or is unable "as a result of legislation or social practices or of combination or collective bargaining or of slow response to change or of mere human obstinacy, to accept a reward corresponding to the value of the product attributable to its marginal productivity" (p. 6). In short, voluntary unemployment occurs if there are laborers who refuse employment at a wage equivalent to the value of what they produce. Such workers *could* have found jobs, had they been willing to work for a "market" wage. They were not willing, and their consequent unemployment is entirely due to their own choice. Hence, it is voluntary.

These are the only types of unemployment that are permissible in

[2] J. M. Keynes, "A Self-adjusting Economic System?" *New Republic*, February 20, 1935, p. 35.

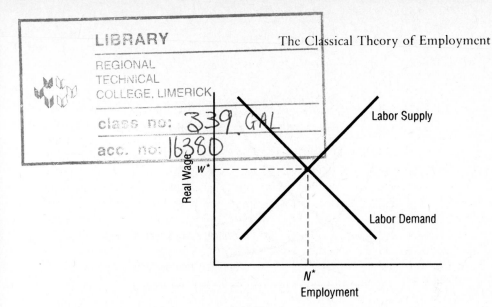

FIGURE 2.1   The Classical Labor Market

In the classical labor market, the market-clearing real wage and employment levels are
determined at the intersection of a downward-sloping demand curve and an upward-
sloping supply curve.

the classical analysis. From the standpoint of classical theory, they are
"comprehensive." They flow, directly and logically, from the two classical postulates.

In classical theory, the first postulate provides the basis for the
demand curve for labor. Labor demand depends on the productivity of
labor. The second postulate provides the basis for the *supply curve for
labor*. Labor supply depends on how willing workers are to put in additional hours in response to changing rates of pay.

Where these schedules intersect, the level of employment and the
real wage for the economy are determined. There is, in effect, an aggregate market for labor, and the position where that market clears establishes a *Walrasian general equilibrium*, in classical theory. Notice that there
is only one possible level at which the market can clear, since both
schedules depend exclusively on the real wage rate. That position is
given by N^* in Figure 2.1.

In the classical view, if a policymaker thought the existing level of
employment N^* was unsatisfactory for any reason, then he or she could
pursue only long-run strategies: strategies intended to change the mechanics of the labor market, or the tastes of workers for work, or the
techniques of production available to employers and hence the demand
for labor. For example, if technical change could raise the productivity of
labor in the sector producing consumption goods for workers, so that
workers become cheaper to hire, the demand schedule for employment
could shift to the right, raising employment to N^{**}, as shown in Figure
2.2. If there was a means of changing workers' tastes so that they had a

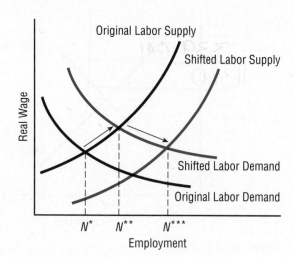

FIGURE 2.2   Shifts in Labor Demand and Supply

Shifts in the labor demand curve will cause a change in the equilibrium level of employment, as from N^* to N^{**}. A shift in the labor supply curve can cause a further shift, from
N^{**} to N^{***}. Note that the equilibrium real wage will rise when demand shifts outward
but will fall when supply shifts outward.

lower marginal disutility of labor, the supply curve for employment
could shift to the right, raising employment to the level N^{***}. But with
given tastes and technology and with real wages that can freely adjust to
clear the employment market, N^* would be the only possible (Walrasian) equilibrium level of employment.

Of course, if there were lags (and "creaks") in arriving at the market-clearing level of employment, then improved organization of the
employment market, improved information about job opportunities,
and other reforms could reduce the frictions. This would reduce the
incidence of unemployment of the *frictional* variety. Policymakers with
concerns about the slow adjustment of an employment market might
resort to the development of labor exchanges, public offices where the
unemployed could find out about available jobs. Such exchanges were
proposed by some economists in Britain in the 1920s, who were convinced that the new phenomenon of mass unemployment was nevertheless mainly frictional in character.

Still, in the classical view, if the economy were to settle at any level
of employment besides N^*, with given tastes and technology, it could
only be because the market for employment persistently failed to clear.
This would be the outcome of the failure of real wages—the "price" of
labor—to adjust. Figure 2.3 shows the excess supply of labor that would
result. If the real wage cannot fall below w_1 for some reason, then it can

Taking a Closer Look

TWO CONCEPTS OF EQUILIBRIUM

We have seen that Keynes's idea of unemployment equilibrium stresses that unemployment will not correct itself: it is an equilibrium. Yet, the instinctive response of most economists to this idea, then and now, has been to argue that a position of unemployment cannot by its nature be an equilibrium. And many expositions of Keynesian economics have tried to reconfigure his theory to explain unemployment as a persistent *disequilibrium* phenomenon (caused, for example, by "sticky wages"). Therefore, we may usefully ask: what did Keynes mean? And was his insistence on unemployment equilibrium based on confusion, as some asserted, or was it fundamental, as he believed?

Part of the puzzle comes clear as soon as we realize that the word *equilibrium* has at least two commonplace meanings in economics. One is attributable to Alfred Marshall, the great English economist and Keynes's own teacher. The other is owed to the French economist Leon Walras (1834–1910).[1]

Walrasian equilibrium, a mathematical construct, is the condition of equality between supply and demand in all markets, for all possible goods and services, at the same time. The economy is in "equilibrium" when *each* of the individual markets for goods and services is entirely free of excess demands and excess supplies; all markets clear. Walrasian equilibrium means universal market clearing. The absence of equality between supply and demand in any one market means, from the Walrasian standpoint, that the economy as a whole is in disequilibrium.

The *Marshallian* concept of equilibrium is more clearly related to the descriptive notion of equilibrium in the physical and biological sciences. It is simply a condition where there is no tendency for the system to change. An economy in Marshallian equilibrium is at a resting point; the forces that might ordinarily bring on a change are in abeyance or in mutual balance. Short of an externally induced shock, the economy will simply maintain its status quo. The parallel in the natural sciences can be seen, for example, in the concept of a chemical solution that is in equilibrium: the solution is at "rest," and no further changes in its composition will take place unless it is disturbed by the infusion of a new substance.

The Walrasian and Marshallian concepts of equilibrium are not the same. For example, all markets might clear, but rates of profit could differ among industries. This would create an incentive for capitalists to transfer resources from low-profit to high-profit activities. As long as profit rate differentials persist, the economy cannot be at a resting point; it still will be in a process of constant change. Therefore, an economy in Walrasian equilibrium need not be in Marshallian equilibrium.

Alternatively, all markets might not clear, but there might not be a tendency for further change to take place. The simplest case occurs when some price refuses to adjust. In this case, there is stability but with a persistent condition of non-market clearing. Therefore, an economy in Marshallian equilibrium need not be in Walrasian equilibrium.[2]

Keynes was a student of Marshall's and a Marshallian in much of his thinking. Consequently, he was not much concerned with whether markets were clearing—they might be, or they might not be—but he was deeply concerned with whether there were forces internal to the economic system that would

continue to alter its performance. When he argued that his general theory implied many possible positions of equilibrium—all, except the limiting classical case, being positions of unemployment equilibrium—he meant that there were ordinary circumstances under which an economy could get stuck producing at low output levels, and there would be no "natural" mechanism to restore full production and full employment.

---

[1] See Victoria Chick, *Macroeconomics After Keynes: A Reconsideration of the General Theory* (Cambridge, Mass.: MIT Press, 1983), pp. 21–24.
[2] An extreme example of Marshallian equilibrium and Walrasian disequilibrium occurs in socialist economies, where chronic shortages of goods of all kinds coexist with chronic excess supplies of money. In this case, rigid controls prevent the adjustment of prices and production, and the economy stagnates.

never reach the level $w^\star$ that will clear the market for employment. The classical economist would admit to this possibility but also would point out that the cure lies entirely in the workers' hands. If they would allow their wages to fall to $w^\star$, employment would rise to its market-clearing position at $N^\star$. So, in the classical view, the gap between N_1 and N_2 in Figure 2.3 represents voluntary unemployment. Note that the demand side of the market, not the supply side, sets the level of employment under conditions of excess supply. As the figure illustrates, there are more workers who want jobs at the real wage w_1 than there are jobs that employers are willing to offer at that wage. The classical economist concludes that if those hard-headed workers would accept wage cuts, then they would have jobs—at least, some of them would, while others who would have liked employment at the artificially high wages will no longer want it when wages fall.

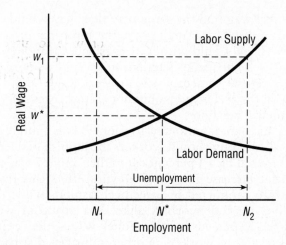

FIGURE 2.3   Classical Unemployment

If the real wage is above the level consistent with equilibrium employment, labor supply
will exceed labor demand, and unemployment is the result. Such unemployment is
voluntary because a fall in real wages will bring about a return to equilibrium employment.

A classical economist may sympathize with labour in refusing to
accept a cut in its money-wage, and he will admit that it may not
be wise to make it to meet conditions which are temporary; but
scientific integrity forces him to declare that this refusal is, nevertheless, at the bottom of the trouble. (p. 16)

KEYNES'S ATTACK ON THE CLASSICAL
LABOR MARKET

Keynes's aim, as we will see, is to shift economics away from the use of
labor supply and demand as the basis for determining real wages and the
level of employment. For Keynes, employment and wages will not be
determined in a "labor market"; rather, they will flow from the conditions of demand, *in product markets*, for the goods that workers produce.

Keynes begins his rejection by repudiating the *second* classical postulate—the utility of the wage equals the marginal disutility of employment—the postulate that provided the basis for the classical supply
schedule for labor. There are two reasons for this repudiation. The first,
which he describes as "not theoretically fundamental," is that the classical supply curve does not accurately describe the way workers behave.
Keynes points out (p. 8) that workers do not respond to reductions in
their real wage rate caused by cuts in their money wages (the numerator

of the real wage) in the same way that they would respond to real wage rate cuts caused by a small rise in the consumer price level (in the denominator). They would withdraw their labor if money wages fell but not if prices rose. Thus labor's refusal to accept cuts in money wages does not mean a refusal to accept a lower real wage, and a supply curve based solely on the real wage would not accurately predict or characterize such asymmetric behavior.

Is such an asymmetry irrational? Is it "money illusion," as it has been called? Why should workers distinguish between a reduction in real wages caused by a 1 percent cut in their money wage and one caused by a 1 percent increase in prices? Keynes offers this reason: cuts in money wages are conducted in piecemeal fashion, while the effects of a price inflation affect all workers alike. If a group of workers in the textile industry accept a cut in their money wages, they experience a fall in their wages *relative* to workers in other industries that have not yet accepted a cut. They would view such a cut as deliberate action of their own managements, and they would resist it. An inflation of the prices of the goods workers purchase, however, is of an all-around character, an anonymous event for which no one can be directly blamed; no group's relative position in the wage ladder will be affected.

Workers struggle over money wages, not because of an irrational attachment to *money illusion* but because, in Keynes's words, "the struggle about money-wages primarily affects the *distribution* of the aggregate real wage between different labour-groups" (p. 14, emphasis original). The struggle over money wages is a struggle to maintain the group's *relative wage*. If it were possible to reduce all labor groups' money wages by the same proportion at the same time, then laborers would indeed be indifferent between a reduction in the real wage achieved via wage cuts and a reduction achieved via inflation. But it is not, and so the asymmetry will exist:

> Since there is imperfect mobility of labour, and wages do not tend
> to an exact equality of net advantage in different occupations, any
> individual or group of individuals, who consent to a reduction of
> money-wages relatively to others, will suffer a *relative* reduction in
> real wages, which is a sufficient justification for them to resist it.
> On the other hand, it would be impracticable to resist every reduc-
> tion in real wages, due to a change in the purchasing-power of
> money which affects all workers alike; and in fact reductions of real
> wages arising in this way are not, as a rule, resisted unless they pro-
> ceed to an extreme degree. Every trade-union will put up some
> resistance to a cut in money-wages, however small. But since no
> trade union would dream of striking on every occasion of a rise in
> the cost of living, they do not raise the obstacle to any increase in
> aggregate employment which is attributed to them by the classical
> school. (p. 14)

In this argument, Keynes accepts the premise that to get more employment labor must accept a lower real wage. But, he argues, the superior practical method for achieving the required reduction is a price inflation, not a money wage cut. Yet if workers were willing to accept a price inflation with no change in behavior but not a money wage cut, as Keynes argues they would be, then the existing money wage could hardly be tied tightly to the real wage it supposedly represents, as classical economists believed. Thus, "the wage-goods equivalent of the existing money-wage is not an accurate indication of the marginal disutility of labour, and the second [classical] postulate does not hold" (p. 10). Instead, Keynes suggests, the marginal disutility of employment sets only an upper limit on employment at a given real wage. The actual level of employment might be lower, leading to a margin of workers who would like to work at the prevailing real wage but who cannot do so.

The idea that employment shifts along a demand curve for labor implies that as employment rises, the real wage must fall. In 1936, Keynes took the view that this was indeed necessarily the case. By 1939, the empirical investigations of John Dunlop and Lorie Tarshis[3] convinced him otherwise. If anything, it appeared that real wages and employment moved together rather than in opposite directions.[4] This finding unsettles the idea that one could get to full employment via price inflation and money wage stickiness and forces us to move on to Keynes's second, fundamental, objection to the second classical postulate.

His "more fundamental objection" stems from the observation that even if workers are willing to accept cuts in their *money wage*, they still can not ensure that a cut in their *real wage* will occur—if indeed such cuts are necessary to increase employment! The second classical postulate depends on the idea that real wages can be set by the money wage bargains that laborers make with business firms. Labor and capital bargain directly over the money wage; contracts are set in money terms. The classical theory presumes that labor can dictate its real wage by fixing its money wage, that labor can lower its real wage by accepting a lower money wage. Keynes argues that this is not necessarily true.

Why not? Because the decline in the money wage rate can spill over into a reduction in output prices, including the prices of wage goods. A

---

[3] J. T. Dunlop, "The Movement of Real and Money Wage Rates," *Economic Journal*, 1938, Vol. 48, pp. 413–34 and Lorie Tarshis, "Changes in Real and Money Wages," *Economic Journal*, 1939, Vol. 49, pp. 150–54.
[4] J. M. Keynes, "Relative Movements of Real Wages and Output," *Economic Journal*, Vol. 4 (March 1939), 35–51. More recently, Michael Dotsey and Robert G. King ("Business Cycles," in *The New Palgrave Dictionary: A Dictionary of Economics* [London: Macmillan, 1987], pp. 302–310) argue that "evidence concerning the cyclical behavior of the real wage is inconclusive; in part this reflects a variety of constructs used. In general, however, there does not appear to be a pronounced cyclical relation" (p. 303).

fall in money wages and in prices that is nearly equal in proportion would leave the real wage rate nearly unchanged. Keynes observes that this is exactly the argument one would have expected from a properly brought up classical economist:

> The classical theory [Marshall's in particular] . . . has taught us to believe that prices are governed by marginal prime cost in terms of money and that money-wages largely govern marginal prime costs. Thus if money-wages change one would have expected the classical school to argue that prices would change in almost the same proportion, leaving the real wage and the level of unemployment practically the same as before. (p. 12)

Keynes thinks that Marshall's argument is indeed valid, and he uses it in a detailed way in *The General Theory*'s Chapter 19, "Changes in Money-Wages." There he demonstrates that money wage flexibility would not ensure that the economy would self-adjust to full employment. Also, the British experience at the onset of their depression between 1920 and 1923 provides direct evidence to support Keynes's belief. As the government maintained its resolve to return to the gold standard at a high parity, money wages fell precipitously—more than 30 percent—under competitive pressure. But prices also fell by about the same amount. This left the real wage (for those lucky enough to be working) in 1923 unchanged from its 1920 level. For all the sound and fury, the real wage was unaffected by the joint price and wage deflation; meanwhile, unemployment soared.[5]

The classical economists, while asserting the neutrality of money in the economy (we will come back to this in the next chapter), do not perceive this argument, which establishes the neutrality of the money wage rate. Keynes believes the classicals have been "diverted from this line of thought" for two reasons. First, the classicals think it is a settled matter that labor can fix its own real wage through the money wage bargain. Second, they believe that the only determinant of the level of prices is the quantity of money. The classical economist simply ignores the interdependence between money wages and output prices.

This, then, is Keynes's "more fundamental objection" to the second classical postulate: there may be no avenue for "labour as a whole . . . [to] bring [the] wage-goods equivalent of the general level of money wages into conformity with the marginal disutility of the current volume of employment" (p. 13). There may be no way for labor to reduce its real wage by agreeing to a lower money wage.

---

[5] S. N. Broadberry, *The British Economy Between the Wars* (Oxford: Basil Blackwell, 1986), p. 86.

INVOLUNTARY UNEMPLOYMENT

Keynes now is prepared to introduce his third category of unemployment, *involuntary unemployment*, the category ruled out altogether by the classical mode of thought. He begins with a negative definition. Involuntary unemployment is not "the mere existence of an unexhausted capacity" nor "the withdrawal of their labour by a body of workers because they do not choose to work for less than a certain real reward"; nor is it frictional unemployment (p. 15).

His first definition of involuntary unemployment appears in *The General Theory* in italics:

> *Men are involuntarily unemployed, if in the event of a small rise in the price of wage-goods relatively to the money-wage, both the aggregate supply of labour willing to work for the current money-wage and the aggregate demand for it at that wage would be greater than the existing volume of employment. (p. 15)*

This definition remains bound up with the market for labor. It could be interpreted, from the perspective of a classical economist, as saying merely that the aggregate market for labor is in excess supply.

To move from this simple view toward Keynes's own view, we need to redefine the labor market in terms of money wages rather than real wages. Recall Keynes's claim that because of the piecemeal nature of money wage cuts workers resist money wage cuts more strongly than they resist inflation. This being so, the response of the supply of employment to a variation in the money wage will differ from its response to a variation in the price level. We should now write the labor supply function as $N_s = N_s(W, P)$ rather than as $N_s = N_s(w) = N_s(W/P)$, meaning that labor supply depends separately on the money wage rate and the price level, not just on the ratio between the two.

The employment market would now have to be drawn in terms of money wages and employment rather than real wages and employment. We present such a diagram in Figure 2.4. It becomes plausible to consider variations in the level of employment that correspond to different market-clearing positions in the labor market. Consider the initial market-clearing level of employment, N^*, in an economy with flexible money wages. Now suppose the economy experiences a small increase in the general price level. The *leftward* shift in the labor supply schedule will be small, because laborers are not inclined to reduce their supply significantly when their real wages fall due to a small increase in prices. But businesses will be encouraged to hire more workers nevertheless. As long as the *rightward* shift in the demand curve for labor is strong enough, the labor market can clear at a new and higher level of employment N^{**}. Although the money wage has risen, its proportionate in-

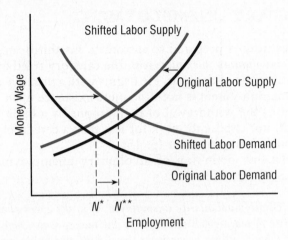

FIGURE 2.4   Keynes's Involuntary Unemployment

In Keynes's theory, inflation might cause a strong outward shift in labor demand but only a weak inward shift in labor supply. In that case, equilibrium employment will rise, and (by Keynes's definition) there was involuntary unemployment at the original equilibrium N^*.

crease is less than the increase in the price level, so the real wage rate has declined. Otherwise, employers would not be willing to put more people to work. Note that both the demand for and supply of labor are greater at N^{**} than at N^*. By Keynes's first definition, involuntary unemployment must have existed at employment level N^*, *despite* the fact that the labor market cleared.

A TWO-SECTOR ECONOMY

This is about as far as one can go with a simple supply-and-demand representation of a labor market. Keynes's own ideas required a further complication: that one distinguish between two sectors in the economy, a wage goods sector and a capital goods sector. The wage goods sector produces the products that workers consume, whereas the capital goods sector produces machinery and equipment for business investment.

With two sectors to work with, one can find another route toward involuntary unemployment. In this alternative, there is no reason to assume that labor's supply elasticity with respect to changes in the money wage rate differs from its supply elasticity with respect to changes in the price of wage goods. The aggregate price level is an index number that merges the respective prices of each sector's output. In

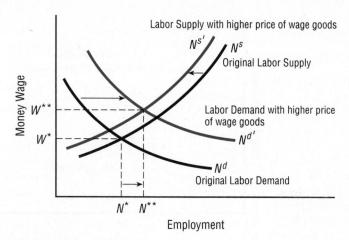

FIGURE 2.5   A Two-Sector Model

In a model with two sectors, wage goods and capital goods, changes in the price of wage goods shift both labor supply and labor demand. When there is inflation in wage goods, profits rise and labor demand shifts outward. Labor supply shifts inward but not by as much. Once again, equilibrium employment can rise.

mathematical notation, $P = P(P_w, P_k)$, where P is the general price level, P_w is the price of wage goods, and P_k is the price of capital goods. An increase in the price of wage goods will cause the general price level to increase, but the response of producers and workers to the increase in the general price level will not be precisely the same. Specifically, producers are concerned about movements in both components of the price index, while workers only are concerned about movements in the price of wage goods. We will assume, to make our point, that producers respond more strongly to (small) price inflations than do workers.

We display the implications in Figure 2.5, which also is drawn with money wages and employment on the axes rather than real wages and employment. We assume there is complete money wage flexibility. The economy is at an initial position with money wage rate $W^\star$ and employment level $N^\star$, both market-clearing values.

Now consider the effects of a small rise in the price of wage goods. At any nominal wage rate, workers will experience a lower real wage. If they are predisposed to reduce their supply of employment, the schedule N^s will shift to the left to $N^{s'}$. Employers, however, will perceive the price rise as beneficial to profitability, and their demand for labor schedule will shift to the right from N^d to $N^{d'}$.

At the new market-clearing combination of money wage rate $W^{\star\star}$ and employment level $N^{\star\star}$, both the demand for and the supply of labor exceed the level of employment $N^\star$ that prevailed before the inflation of wage goods prices. Involuntary unemployment, in a Keynesian sense,

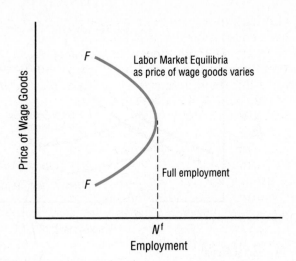

FIGURE 2.6   Full Employment

By varying the price of wage goods, we can trace out different equilibria in the labor
market. At low prices, profits are low and firms will increase their labor demand if prices
of wage goods rise. If such prices rise too far, eventually workers will refuse to supply
their labor. Thus there is a position of maximum employment at N^f.

existed at employment level $N^\star$ even though the labor market cleared.
Implicitly, although the money wage is higher at employment level $N^{\star\star}$
than at employment level $N^\star$, the real wage can be lower because the
price of wage goods could have risen more than the money wage rate.

Indeed, by making small changes in the price of wage goods, resulting in turn in small changes in the general price level, we can trace out a
set of market-clearing positions in the aggregate market for employment. Such a set appears as the curve *FF* in Figure 2.6. At the outermost
point of the curve, which corresponds to employment level N^f, any
further increase in the price of wage goods finally leads the labor supply
reduction to dominate the increase in labor demand. Although all levels
of employment along the curve are associated with supply-and-demand
equality in the aggregate labor market, only employment level N^f is *full*
employment. Thereafter, further increases in the price of wage goods
purchase less employment rather than more.

Again, keep in mind that this definition of involuntary unemployment is developed with reference to an aggregate labor market. In *The
General Theory*, Keynes writes that there is an alternative definition to
the first, which he says "amounts to the same thing" (pp. 15, 26). In this
alternative, Keynes defines full employment as simply "a situation in
which aggregate employment is inelastic in response to an increase in the
effective demand for its output" (p. 26). In terms of Figure 2.6, this

means nothing more nor less than that the economy is at N^f, the highest achievable equilibrium of employment. Full employment is the absence of involuntary unemployment. Involuntary unemployment prevails if more employment can be had by an expansion in aggregate demand.

But is this definition of full employment, as the maximum level of employment achievable by increases in effective demand, really equivalent to the definition of (the absence of) involuntary unemployment we have just discussed? As its criterion for the existence of involuntary unemployment, the first definition sets up the necessity of lowering real wages measured in terms of wage goods. The second definition makes no reference to the aggregate labor market nor any statement about what direction movements in the real wage must take.

The second definition of involuntary unemployment simply means that the following experiment determines whether or not involuntary unemployment exists. If an expansion of *aggregate demand*—an expansion of purchases of final products—leads to a higher level of employment, then involuntary unemployment prevailed prior to the expansion. If not, then the economy already was at full employment. It does not matter what may have happened to the real wage.

With the second definition, Keynes finally begins to shed his own classical skin. It is the second definition that Keynes uses in his discussion of involuntary unemployment in papers and correspondence after the publication of *The General Theory*.[6] Thus, while maintaining the formal equivalence of the two definitions, Keynes introduces the second in order to move the analysis of employment away from the market for labor.

[6] William Darity, Jr., and Bobbie Horn, "Involuntary Unemployment Reconsidered," *Southern Economic Journal*, 1983, Vol. 49, pp. 717–33 and Darity and Horn, "Involuntary Unemployment Independent of the Labor Market," *Journal of Post Keynesian Economics*, Winter 1987–88, Vol. 10, pp. 216–224.

SPECIAL SECTION

Keynes's Circus

"Keynes's Circus" refers to Keynes's circle of colleagues at the Cambridge University in England in the 1920s and 1930s, who played important roles in the development and immediate extension of the ideas put forth in *The General Theory of Employment, Interest and Money*. This remarkable group of individuals—a highly creative and tempestuous group—etched enduring marks on modern economics.

Central to the group was Richard Kahn, the originator of the formal version of the multiplier[1]—the idea that an increase in government spending can generate an even larger increase in national income and production—in English-speaking economics. Also at the core of the group was the aristocratic Roy Harrod, the conservative voice in the Circus, consistently pushing Keynes not to stray too far from orthodoxy. Harrod made the major conceptual breakthrough that was to spawn the development of mathematical growth theory, with his combination of the multiplier principle and an "accelerator principle" to build a dynamic version of Keynes's system.

Perhaps the most charismatic and contentious member of the Circus was Joan Robinson, whose contributions encompassed the theory of underemployment, the theory of economic growth, capital theory, the history of economic doctrine, and economic methodology. Robinson was unabashedly hostile to neoclassical economics. It was primarily she who sparked a famous series of debates (known as the "Cambridge Controversies") between economists in Cambridge, England, and their counterparts in Cambridge, Massachusetts, over the orthodox concept of capital and the conceptual validity of the neoclassical aggregate production function. This was one of the rare instances where the leading neoclassical economists (Paul Samuelson and Robert Solow of the Massachusetts Institute of Technology) were drawn into a substantive debate over the fundamentals of

their theory. Robinson was equally hostile to the American version of her own theory; the vast majority of what was called Keynesian economics in the United States she dubbed "bastard Keynesianism."

Kahn's version of the multiplier emphasized the relationship between investment in capital equipment and employment. Kahn's argument was very simple: a rise in capital expenditures would create jobs not only directly as workers were hired to build machines but also indirectly as workers were hired to feed and clothe the workers hired to build the machines. Most important, it did not matter what the machines were for. Nor did it matter who was doing the investment; if private businesses were depressed and unwilling, government could do just as well.

In his 1931 paper introducing the employment multiplier, Kahn used government expenditure on roads as his example of "home investment," while observing that "this simplification must not be taken to imply [that] . . . the building of more roads is a particularly desirable form of investment."[2] The circle of economists around Keynes drove this point home with élan. In the Depression, they were willing to countenance virtually any form of government expenditure as being superior to the extreme joblessness imposed by insufficient investment spending. Keynes wrote:

If the Treasury were to fill old bottles with banknotes, bury them at suitable depths in disused coal-mines which are then filled up to the surface with town rubbish, and leave it to private enterprise on well-tried principles of *laissez-faire* to dig the notes up again . . . there need be no more unemployment and, with the help of the repercussions, the real income of the community, and its capital wealth also, would probably become a good deal greater than it actually is. It would, indeed, be more sensible to build houses and the like; but if there are political and practical difficulties in the way of this, the above would be better than nothing.[3]

Keynes indeed argued that the great periods of prosperity in economic history, from the ancient Egyptians to the Middle Ages, could be viewed as having been caused by the multiplier effects of public investment:

Ancient Egypt was doubly fortunate, and doubtless owed to this its fabled wealth, in that it possessed *two* activities, namely pyramid-building as well as the search for the precious metals, the fruits of which, since they could not serve the needs of man by being consumed, did not stale with abundance. The Middle Ages built cathedrals and sang dirges. Two pyramids, two masses for the dead, are twice as good as one, but not so two railways from London to York.

What a tragedy then that in modern times political conservatism, doctrines of "sound finance" and "budget balancing," and the requirements of "profitability" prevent similar efforts:

Thus we are so sensible, have schooled ourselves to so close a semblance of prudent financiers, taking careful thought before we add to the "financial" burdens of posterity by building them houses to live in, that we have no such easy escape from the sufferings of unemployment.[4]

In a similar vein, Joan Robinson made the following trenchant remark about the policy position she and others in Keynes's Circus had taken in the 1930s:

We had to argue that any expenditure is better than none. Dig holes in the ground and fill them again, paint the Black Forest white; if men cannot be paid wages for doing something sensible, pay them to do something silly.[5]

Although their role was not as prominent nor as consistent as that of Kahn, Harrod, and Robinson, three other figures of note should be included in our description of the Circus. Among these was Dennis Robertson, who had been Keynes's student and one of his most intimate friends. Robertson and Keynes mutually built the Cambridge theory of money in the post-Marshall years. But as their friendship deteriorated, so did their intellectual compatibility. They split over *The General Theory*. Keynes was insistent on its revolutionary message; Robertson was insistent that its central tenets could be incorporated into the classical capital market. Thus Robertson moved from inside to outside the inner circle.

The Italian theorist Piero Sraffa also played an important role in the development of *The General Theory*, particularly with his seemingly jesting creation of the concept of the "own-rate of interest." Keynes took the concept seriously and made it the cornerstone of the value theory that he utilized in *The General Theory*. Sraffa published very little during his lifetime. (Rumor has it that there are many, many papers he left unpublished in drawers, simply content to have resolved a problem to his personal satisfaction.) However, what was published always took on striking significance—in particular, his brilliant insights about competition and equilibrium and his development of an alternative to the supply-and-demand theory of relative prices based upon classical political economy. The latter appeared in a deceptively slim volume, *Production of Commodities by Means of Commodities*, drafted in the late 1920s but not published until 1960. (See Suggested Readings.)

Also part of the Circus was Ralph Hawtrey. Although not a Cambridge academician, he developed, based upon his personal experiences as a speculator, an idiosyncratic macroeconomic theory rooted in the importance of the financial and credit markets. Keynes drew inspiration from Hawtrey's work and corresponded with him extensively in the development of *The General Theory*, although subsequently it seems that Hawtrey had difficulty understanding the book.

Finally, mention should be given to Nicholas Kaldor and James Meade. Feisty, rotund, Kaldor was an intellectual risk taker par excellence. Though he arrived in Cambridge (from the London School of Economics) only in the late 1940s, he had already in the 1930s seized upon various themes in *The General Theory*. From this starting point, Kaldor developed a profound analysis of speculation and an aggregative theory of income distribution. Seeing himself as a critic of neoclassical economics from a Cambridge (England) Keynesian vantage point, he went in a distinctly non-Keynesian but intriguing direction, that of exploring the consequences for economic theory of a world of increasing returns to scale. He was a regular adviser to Labour governments, commuting back to Cambridge on Saturdays to deliver lectures on growth and capital theory. His career continued into the 1980s, when he published scathing criticisms of the monetarist policies of Prime Minister Margaret Thatcher and eloquently denounced her government from his seat in the House of Lords.

James Meade, finally, was somewhat on the perimeter of the inner circle. Probably the most mathematically proficient of the group, Meade's technically dense papers often left his significant contributions undetected by more rhetorically minded readers. But he has placed his stamp on growth theory, the theory of international trade, and the theory of economic planning. Interestingly enough, it was Meade, the technician of the Circus, who did the most to carry the policy message of Keynes's economics into the British Labour party in the 1940s.

Keynes himself, a lifelong Liberal, never went that far to the left.

In a radical mood at the end of *The General Theory*, he did advocate what he termed a "socialization of investment."[6] By this, he meant that government would ensure that investment expenditure was consistently at its full employment level. But he realized that this also would mean a major transformation of the economic system, perhaps the eradication of capitalism itself. And these were revolutionary political positions of which Keynes was sometimes accused but that he never embraced. He carried to his grave in 1946 the unresolved tension in his blueprint for the future of a prosperous capitalism.

---

[1] We present the multiplier in detail in Chapter 4.
[2] Keynes, *The General Theory*, pp. 1–2.
[3] *Ibid.*, p. 129.
[4] *Ibid.*, p. 131.
[5] Joan Robinson, "What Has Become of the Keynesian Revolution?" *Challenge*, January–February 1974, p. 11.
[6] *The General Theory*, pp. 376–378.

SUMMARY

Keynes claimed that classical analysis applied only to the special case where full employment held. The classical theory of employment had two postulates. First, employers hire workers until the marginal product of workers in production is equal to the real wage. Second, workers offer their labor services until the marginal utility of the real wage is equal to the marginal disutility of work. Apart from imperfections, only frictional or voluntary unemployment can exist.

From a classical perspective, the equilibrium level of employment could be affected by long-run strategies that would enhance productivity or change the tastes of workers. Improvements in the efficiency of markets would reduce frictional unemployment.

Keynes's attack on the classical theory of wages and employment was twofold. First, workers are concerned not only with *absolute* wages but with their wage *relative* to that of other workers. It is therefore difficult to extract nominal wage concessions in a piecemeal fashion. Consequently, when real wages are too high, a significant part of the labor force may be unable to find work unless there is a general price inflation that brings real wages down. The second and more fundamental part of Keynes's attack was an argument that prices move with wages. Since wages constitute a large part of costs of production, a reduction in money wages will be followed by a fall in prices. It is impossible in this framework for workers to alter their real wage downward by making nominal wage agreements.

Keynes thus switched from an analysis that considered the real wage as the relevant measure of wages to an analysis that considered the nominal wage and the price level separately in the labor market. With this new conception and a more careful definition of involuntary unemployment, it is easy to show graphically the possibility of involuntary unemployment. Keynes differentiated between capital goods prices and wage goods prices, because in general the capital goods sector is more sensitive to price changes. A wage goods inflation could cause employment to rise until the full employment level is reached. After this point (when the labor supply becomes more elastic with respect to price changes), price increases can cause employment to fall.

The multiplier introduced by Keynes was originally due to Kahn. Kahn argued that since the wage goods industry is driven by activity in the capital goods industry, increases in investment result in a more than one-for-one increase in employment in the wage goods industry. A simple extension of multiplier analysis leads to government action to increase employment.

Review Questions

1. As a practical matter, what determines your success in the labor market? Compare your experiences, or prospects, with the views expressed by the classical and Keynesian schools of thought.

2. The word *neutral* was used to describe money in the classical theory. What exactly does the word mean in this context?

3. State carefully the definitions for involuntary unemployment as the concept would be understood by the classicals and by Keynes. Compare and contrast these definitions.

4. Although the classical school may be wrong theoretically, it can offer some insights into the phenomenon of persistent unemployment. Explain these insights. Are classical theory and Keynesian theory complementary?

5. Keynes described classical theory as a special case of his general theory. How is it a special case? In what ways is it not a special case but a theory independent of the general theory?

6. What exactly is meant by the "marginal disutility of labor"? Illustrate your answer with examples from everyday life if necessary, but do not limit your answer to these illustrations.

7. Empirically, how significant is the difference between the capital goods sector and the wage goods sector? A good answer will describe the small as well as the grand differences (e.g., what is the computer industry?).

8. In your view, which is more often the cause of rising prices: rising wages or an excess demand for goods? Or is there a third factor that is even more important?

9. Why is it that employment cannot increase indefinitely in the Keynesian system?

Review Problems

1. On a graph like the one in Figure 2.1, show the effects of an increase in productivity. Does the nature of the productivity increase make any difference in how you answer the question? For example, can you image a technological improvement that did not improve labor productivity?

2. Again on a graph like Figure 2.1's, show the effect of an increase in population. Will employment increase in the same proportion as the increase in population? Discuss what must happen for the entire increment of population to be absorbed into the economy? In what circumstances will the equilibrium wage increase through time?

3. It was mentioned in the text that a change in the tastes of the workers could increase employment. Show how this would happen with Figure 2.1. Explain how this simple analysis could turn into a cynical theory of unemployment, attributing unemployment to laziness.

4. An equilibrium condition in Keynes's system as described by Figure 2.4 might be the following equation: $N^s(W, P) = N^d(W, P)$. In this system, how might an increase in price inflation generate an increase in employment?

5. Draw, side by side, the classical and the Keynesian representations of involuntary unemployment. Discuss the difference between the two explanations, especially with respect to equilibrium and definitional issues.

6. Suppose that classical theory does in fact hold in reality. Show the effect of a government program to hire enough people to reach a total employment goal. What would the classical school say is the problem with this program? (Remember Say's Law.)

7. Using Figures 2.5 and 2.6, show the effect of a labor-enhancing productivity improvement. As discussed so far, would anything in these models lead you to believe that the economy can in fact generate these productivity increases? Explain.

8. Show graphically the difference between a Walrasian equilibrium and a Marshallian equilibrium. Describe what you have or have not done in light of the differences in the definitions.

Suggested Readings

Michael Dotsey and Robert G. King, "Business Cycles," *The New Palgrave Dictionary: A Dictionary of Economics* (London: Macmillan, 1987).

S. N. Broadberry, *The British Economy Between the Wars* (Oxford: Basil Blackwell, 1986).

Victoria Chick, *Macroeconomics After Keynes: A Reconsideration of the General Theory* (Cambridge: MIT Press, 1983).

Chapter 3

INTEREST, MONEY,

AND UNCERTAINTY

Looking Forward

In the classical economics, supply and demand in the labor market
determined employment, and employment determined output.
Meanwhile, supply and demand in a capital market determined the
rate of interest, producing the balance between consumption on
the one hand and savings and investment on the other.

Keynes broke down the barriers between the two markets by
calling on the total volume of consumption and investment spending to determine the level of employment and output. The volume
of savings then emerged in Keynes's system as a by-product of the
level of output, income, and consumption spending. Because this
undid the classical explanation of a mutual determination of savings, investment, and interest, Keynes needed some new theoretical device to explain the rate of interest. This he found by calling
on a market that classical economics had largely disregarded: the
market for money.

In this chapter, our concern once again is not with formal modeling but with the ideas that underlie the theory and with showing
how Keynes's ideas broke with the classical framework. As you
read, ask yourself:

- How did classical economics visualize the determination of
  savings, investment, and the interest rate?
- How did Keynes visualize the determination of the interest
  rate? What is liquidity preference? What is the market for
  money, and how does it differ from a market for capital?
- How did Keynes's theory break down the wall between monetary and "real" phenomena in economics?

41

Having broken free of the classical labor market, Keynes's conceptual imagination turned to the next item in his book's title, the theory of interest. Here he found another classical market model that, he determined, he would have to unravel.

THE CLASSICAL THEORY OF INTEREST

Classical theory viewed the rate of interest as a price, the price that would bring the "demand for investment" into equality with the "desire to save." The demand for investment would rise as the cost of borrowing in order to invest declined; this cost was represented by the interest rate on borrowed funds. The desire to save, and therefore the supply of savings, would rise as the return on saving rose, and this return was also represented by the interest rate.

Classical theory thus conceived of a *capital market*, in which the basic forces were, as in all markets, supply and demand. Figure 3.1 illustrates this market. There would be an *investment schedule*, or demand curve for saving (I), and a *saving schedule*, or supply curve of saving (S). The interest rate (r) would adjust to ensure that the quantity of investment demanded and the quantity of savings supplied just came into balance. In Walrasian fashion, there would be no excess supply or excess demand in this market for investable resources or "loanable funds."

The classical investment schedule (I) is a downward-sloping function of the rate of interest. Since the interest rate is the price at which

FIGURE 3.1   The Classical Capital Market

In the classical capital market, the supply of savings is brought into equality with the demand for investment by adjustments of the interest rate.

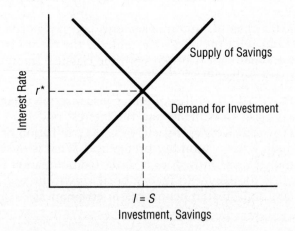

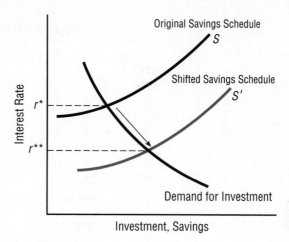

Original Savings Schedule

Shifted Savings Schedule

Demand for Investment

FIGURE 3.2   Shift of the Savings Function

An outward shift of the savings schedule lowers the interest rate and increases equilibrium investment.

potential investors can obtain a loan, they will be willing to borrow less as that price increases. Savers, on the other hand, will be willing to supply more investable resources to the capital market (by refraining from immediate consumption) as the price of saving becomes greater. Hence, the supply curve of savings (S) will be upward sloping.

The position of the supply curve of savings, its location on the diagram, will be determined by the underlying thriftiness (or extravagance) of the population. We might call this the *propensity to save*. If the propensity to save rises, the savings schedule would be displaced from S to S', as shown in Figure 3.2. This would lead to a lower market-clearing rate of interest (the interest rate falls from $r^\star$ to $r^{\star\star}$).

We can follow this process step by step. At first, as thriftiness rises, an *excess supply* of savings develops. Along the new savings schedule at the original interest rate, $r^\star$, there is more saving than businesses are willing to use at that interest rate. This puts downward pressure on the price of savings, the rate of interest. As the interest rate falls, businesses are willing to borrow more, whereas savers, though still on the new supply schedule, save less than they would have if the interest rate had not fallen. Eventually, the interest rate falls just enough so that savings supply and investment demand just match, and the capital market clears at the lower rate $r^{\star\star}$.

In similar fashion, the position of the investment demand curve is determined by an underlying inclination to invest, which may depend on the level of confidence (bullishness, bearishness) of business investors. If the inclination to invest rises, the investment schedule will be displaced

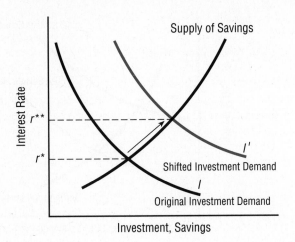

FIGURE 3.3   Shift of Investment Function

An outward shift of the demand for investment raises the interest rate and increases the
equilibrium volume of savings and investment.

from *I* to *I'*, as shown in Figure 3.3. This produces *excess demand* in the
capital market at the original interest rate *r*★; there will not be enough
savings at that interest rate to meet the demand for loans. As businesses
compete for loans, the interest rate will rise to *r*★★, reducing loan demand along the new investment demand schedule and raising savings
supply along the original savings supply schedule. At *r*★★, the capital
market clears, with a higher level of investment, savings, and interest.

KEYNES'S ATTACK ON THE CLASSICAL
CAPITAL MARKET

What did Keynes find unsatisfactory with this account of the determination of the interest rate? He objected to the idea that the positions of the
savings supply and investment demand curves, as well as shifts in those
curves that might occur, were attributed exclusively to the tastes of
savers and investors. Savings ultimately depended, in this theory, on
thriftiness, and investment on the spirit of enterprise, diligence, and
optimism among businesspeople. The interest rate merely served to
bring these forces into balance.

  This meant that classical theory had no place for an influence on
savings from another source, one Keynes considered to be of the highest
practical and theoretical importance. This was the effect of changes in the
level of national income. Keynes argued that the level of national income

had to be considered in two places from which the classical theory had excluded it by assumption. First, he believed, savings was a function of income (the more income one has, the more one is likely to save), and this force was much more important than the rate of interest. Second, the level of income itself was a function of the volume of investment. Thus, there was no capital market in which savings and investment were jointly determined; rather, there was a causal sequence that ran from the volume of investment to the level of income to the volume of savings. Keynes wrote: "The classical theory has not been alive to the relevance of changes in the level of income or to the possibility of the level of income being actually a function of the rate of investment."[1]

Along with mass unemployment, changes in the level of income, were, of course, the trademarks of the Great Depression. Keynes was arguing, in effect, that falling investment had killed incomes and falling incomes had killed savings. Changes in the rate of interest had had little to do with either of these calamities.

The intrusion of changes in the level of income onto the scene meant, in turn, that the classical capital market could not be used to explain the rate of interest. Both the level of national income and the rate of interest could now change. Within the framework of the classical capital market, each change in income would produce further shifts in S and I, the schedules governing the supply of savings and the demand for investment. Since the level of income was not pinned down, neither was the rate of interest. Once changes in the income level were allowed for, the savings and investment schedules could no longer provide, by themselves, a determinate explanation for the rate of interest.

The classical approach evaded this problem by treating the level of income as constant. Moreover, it treated the level of national income as constant *at the full employment level*. Keynes argued that it was possible for savings and investment to be equal—for savings-investment equilibrium to occur—at any number of different levels of income. Classical theory called the rate of interest consistent with savings-investment equality the *natural rate of interest*; it simply presumed that this rate would coincide with full employment. Keynes explicitly expressed his lack of interest in this concept because his view, a "natural [equilibrium] rate of interest" might be consistent with any amount of unemployment. He suggested that economics would do better to concern itself with the *neutral rate of interest*, that particular rate which is consistent with full employment (p. 243).

All this led to yet another question. If savings and investment alone did not determine the rate of interest, what did?

[1] *The General Theory of Employment, Interest and Money* (London: Macmillan, 1936), p. 180. Unless otherwise noted, all citations in this chapter refer to this work; page numbers appear in parentheses following the passage.

THE LIQUIDITY PREFERENCE THEORY
OF INTEREST

The classical school saw the rate of interest as a "reward for waiting," a reward savers would receive for forgoing consumption, building capital, or waiting until a later date to consume the interest they would earn by not consuming investable resources today. This explanation is rooted in the "real economy" of physical production and productivity. Interest itself, in this view, arises from the increased output that results from capital formation. Interest can be paid only because total production will be higher after a process of saving and capital accumulation than it would have been without that process.

This is a theory in which money and financial markets—markets for monetary instruments such as stocks and bonds—play no role at all. Loan contracts may be written in money terms and interest payments may be made in money units, but the underlying physical productivity is the real focus of the theory. Both savings and investment are perceived in physical rather than monetary terms: savings as consumption forgone, investment as the accumulation of resources into physical capital units. And it was at this point that Keynes made his attack.

Keynes, a speculator himself with a deep understanding of money and financial markets, decided to supplant the classical view with a *monetary* explanation for the rate of interest. Keynes's explanation would treat the rate of interest as the key to financial rather than to physical decisions: not to the decision to save rather than consume but instead to the decisions that must be made as to what financial form investment should take. In a word, interest was a reward for "not hoarding," for parting with liquidity—which is to say, for parting with money (p. 122).

Keynes developed his *liquidity preference* theory of the rate of interest as a substitute for the classical capital market apparatus of savings supply and investment demand. The rate of interest did not determine the margin between savings and consumption. That decision came before the interest rate entered into the picture, for, given the income level and the propensity to consume, the amount of savings was already fully determined. The question then was, in what form are savings to be held? The interest rate would influence the *portfolio decision*, the choice between holding savings as bonds or as money.

Typically, a saver has choices among a variety of assets. The most liquid among these is money. But money pays no interest,[2] whereas

[2] At the time Keynes wrote and for many decades thereafter, money was thought of as cash and checking deposits on which no interest was paid. Today, checking balances do pay interest. However, the interest rate they earn is typically the lowest available on the market, so that the basic principle of liquidity preference, that higher interest is the reward for holding less liquid assets, remains true today.

bonds, an alternative financial investment, do. To shift the composition of the portfolio away from money and toward less-liquid assets, assets that cannot be as readily or directly used to make purchases, the saver would have to be compensated. That compensation would take the form of the *money rate of interest*, the reward for giving up liquidity or, again, for "not hoarding" money. The interest rate, in this context, would bring the quantity of money into conformity with individuals' desires to hold money, as against alternative, less-liquid (and riskier) assets they might otherwise hold in their portfolios. Put another way, the lowest available interest rate on the safest available asset other than money measures the *liquidity premium* that makes the continued holding of money worthwhile in the opinion of the marginal holder of that money.

Thus, ultimate lenders and ultimate borrowers do not meet in a capital market in Keynes's world. Instead there is *intermediation*, carried out by the financial institutions that mobilize monetary deposits for productive use. The rate of interest plays its vital role, not by determining the volume of saving but by determining *the form in which savings are held*, on the one hand, and *the volume of investment and level of income*, on the other. (We return to the theory of investment in Chapter 5.)

KEYNES'S THEORY OF MONEY

Of the triad in his book's title—employment, interest, and money—money surely had the deepest roots in Keynes's thought and posed the greatest difficulties for him. Indeed, he had been brought up as a monetary theorist and was trained more thoroughly in the tenets of the classical view of money than in any other part of the classical canon.

In 1930, Keynes had published a two-volume *Treatise on Money*, which he had hoped would make his reputation. But his *Treatise* did not stir the hoped-for response,[3] and Keynes soon began to feel a sense of dissatisfaction with it. In particular, he perceived that the theory of money and the theory of output for the entire economy in *Treatise* were inadequate:

> When I began to write my *Treatise on Money* I was still moving along the traditional lines of regarding the influence of money as something so to speak separate from the general theory of supply

[3] More attention was drawn to an algebraic slip in some "fundamental equations," which occupied a small portion of *Treatise*, than to Keynes's overarching vision. See, for example, the exchange between Alvin Hansen and Keynes: Alvin H. Hansen, "A Fundamental Error in Keynes' 'Treatise on Money,'" *American Economic Review*, 22 (September 1932), 462; and J. M. Keynes, "Keynes' Fundamental Equations: A Note," *American Economic Review*, 22 (September 1932), 691-692.

and demand. When I finished it, I had made some progress towards pushing monetary theory back to becoming a theory of output as a whole. But my lack of emancipation from preconceived ideas showed itself in . . . that I failed to deal thoroughly with the effects of *changes* in the level of output. (pp. vi–vii)

To separate himself from classical monetary theory,[4] Keynes advanced a central distinction, between *real-exchange economics* and *monetary production economics*.[5] Real-exchange economics, according to Keynes, was Alfred Marshall's theoretical economics. First and foremost, it treated an economy that has a medium of exchange, money, as qualitatively the same as a barter economy. In real-exchange economics, money simply serves a convenience function. It facilitates transactions; it is not an "active agent" in the production process. Hence, money is neutral in that its presence or absence does not alter the way the economy works. *Relative* prices are the object of analysis. While the quantity of money in existence might affect the *absolute* level of prices, it will have no effect on their comparative values nor on interest, output, or employment.

The economics that should be taught, Keynes argued, is monetary production economics. Here money is not neutral. Rather, changes in monetary conditions affect interest rates and, through them, the output performance of the economy in both the short and long run. Instead of relative prices, instead of microeconomics, the main object of analysis must be *changes in output*—the missing piece of Keynes's *Treatise*. Crises, recessions, and depressions can occur and persist in a monetary production economy, and it may take active policies, exploiting devices like the multiplier, to bring them to an end.

Monetary production economics was theoretically relevant because

---

[4] When Keynes referred to "classical theory," he did not use the term as most economists now do, to refer to the economics of the classical school of political economy (Adam Smith, David Ricardo, James Mill). Rather, he used the term to refer to the economics of "the *followers* of Ricardo, those, that is to say, who adopted and perfected the theory of Ricardian economics, including (for example) J. S. Mill, Marshall, Edgeworth and Prof. Pigou" (p. 3). Keynes's colleague at Cambridge University, Piero Sraffa, would have called Keynes's "classical economists" the "marginalists," for strictly speaking they were the economists who immediately followed the classical school proper and who also could be labeled "neoclassicals." Out of this group, Keynes's real whipping boys were his own teacher Alfred Marshall and the person who took over Marshall's chair at his death, A. C. Pigou. Marshall and Pigou are the primary objects of Keynes's disdain in his essay "A Monetary Theory of Production"; they were the individuals whom he most wanted to place under the, in his opinion, invidious "classical" umbrella.

[5] J. M. Keynes, "A Monetary Theory of Production," *Collected Works*, XIV, ed. D. E. Moggridge (Cambridge: Cambridge University Press, 1933), pp. 408–411.

it described the type of economy in which "we actually live."[6] Keynes realized that his classical adversaries were aware of the unstable nature of the real economy and of the relationship between instability and money. Some of their practical advice to policymakers displayed a genuine sensitivity to real problems. Keynes made specific reference to Pigou's awareness of the stickiness of money wages and to Marshall's awareness "that the existence of debts gives a high degree of practical importance to changes in the value of money."[7] But Keynes's classicals lacked a theoretical framework that incorporated these factors.

The provision of such "a developed theory of monetary economics" was the task Keynes set for himself in *The General Theory*. Without such a theory, Keynes contended, the received doctrines would lead to the conclusion that an event such as the Great Depression could not happen:

> We are not told [by the proponents of real-exchange economics] what conditions have to be fulfilled if money is to be neutral. Nor is it easy to supply the gap. Now the conditions required for the "neutrality" of money . . . are, I suspect, precisely the same as those which will insure that crises *do not occur*. If this is true, the real-exchange economics, on which most of us have been brought up and with the conclusions of which our minds are deeply impregnated, though a valuable abstraction in itself and perfectly valid as an intellectual conception, is a singularly blunt weapon for dealing with the problem of booms and depressions. For it has assumed away the very matter under investigation.[8]

Such a "singularly blunt weapon" required replacement. For Keynes, after all, "Booms and depressions are phenomena peculiar to an economy in which . . . money is not neutral."[9]

Keynes's theory immediately established a relative price—the rate of interest—that depended on the quantity of money. In so doing, he dispensed with the neutrality of money. Any change in the quantity of money would disturb the rate of interest, which would then influence the volume of investment. And any change in the rate of investment would alter the level of income. As long as the economy had not yet reached Keynes's "true inflation" threshold, any change in money would lead to a change in real output and income. To that extent, money was not neutral.

[6] *Ibid.*, p. 410.
[7] *Ibid.*
[8] *Ibid.*, pp. 410–411.
[9] *Ibid.*, p. 411.

UNCERTAINTY AND THE
INVESTMENT DECISION

Keynes's theory of money introduced economists to the possibility that monetary instability might generate economic depression and mass unemployment. Indeed, attitudes toward money, and decisions to hold it or invest it, come to the front and center of his theory, forcing us to consider how individuals who dispose of money—the entrepreneurs and capitalists at the top of a free-market social structure—make decisions. In particular, Keynes focused attention on the investment decision, a decision about the future, precisely because that is a decision to forgo the holding of money in favor of a creative, and risky, economic activity.

In thinking about the prospects for a new investment, a classical economist tended to focus on the technical conditions of existing production. How great is the stock of capital in relation to the available labor? What does the production function tell us about the productivity of a new capital asset, which a Walrasian would call the *marginal product of capital*? This is a quantity that in principle can be known, and the choice of an optimal volume of new investment is essentially determinate once the marginal product of capital has been calculated.

How much new investment will there be? Keynes came at this problem in quite a different way. That decision, he believed, turned critically on the profit expectations of entrepreneurs: not how much the newly acquired capital stock would produce but rather how much newly produced output could be sold (and at what price). That is, the investment decision turned on the expected profitability, or prospective (monetary) yield, of a new investment, a quantity Keynes termed the *marginal efficiency of capital*. If profit expectations were poor, the marginal efficiency of capital might be too low to justify the volume of investment that would bring forth full employment; in that case, we would have a problem of entrepreneurs hoarding money rather than making investments that would put money to productive use.

Here it is useful to make another distinction between the Walrasian and the Marshallian habits of thought. This one concerns *expectations*.

To a Walrasian, expectations are essentially a matter of prediction. The economy follows definite laws, and the process of expectations formation is one of anticipating the results of the operation of those laws. For many things about the future, we may have a reasonable degree of confident knowledge. Perhaps we have seen similar situations before, possibly many times, and have a good feel for how such situations are likely to turn out. In these cases, we form our expectations based on the *probability* of an event occurring in certain circumstances. Indeed, in many situations, probabilities can be estimated with a fair degree of precision. (*Rational expectations*, as we see later, are Walrasian predictions made without systematic error.)

But to a Marshallian, expectations are not predictions of a (probabilistically) knowable future. Rather, they are the forces that motivate action, which itself shapes the future. Keynes was thus not concerned about whether forecasts were accurate; they might or might not be. He was concerned about whether expectations were optimistic or pessimistic, because the resulting actions determined investment, income, output, and employment.

Prospective yield—the expected return on any investment—is a concept necessarily bound up with expectations. Keynes said that forecasts of prospective yield depend upon two types of consideration: first, "existing facts which we can assume to be known more or less for certain"; second, "future events which can only be forecasted with more or less confidence" (p. 147). It is with the latter category that trouble arises.

Among existing facts, we can count such things as the existing stock of capital assets, both type and volume, as well as the "strength of existing consumers' demand for goods which require for their efficient production a relatively larger assistance from capital." Future events include changes in the type and volume of capital assets, alterations in consumer tastes, variations in the levels of effective demand, and changes in the money wage rate.

This second category, which may have a major effect on the actual returns realized from an investment, include some things about which probabilities are known. In these cases, we say that our predictions are subject to a calculable degree of risk. But there are also many future facts about which we are necessarily ignorant and of which we have no sense of the probabilities. In these cases, we say that the future is truly uncertain. *Pure uncertainty* describes situations about which not even degrees of probability are known.

Keynes offered pragmatic guidelines for action in the face of uncertainty. He wrote, "It would be foolish, in forming our expectations, to attach great weight to matters which are very uncertain." Accordingly, it would make more sense to form expectations primarily on the basis of "the facts about which we feel somewhat confident, even though they may be less decisively relevant to the issue than other facts about which our knowledge is vague and scanty." Thus, we tend to give greater weight to "the facts of the existing situation" in arriving at long-term expectations. Keynes even referred to "our usual practice being to take the existing situation and to project it into the future modified only to the extent that we have more or less definite reasons for expecting a change" (p. 148).

Thus, we seek to pierce the dark veil of the future by adopting rules of thumb, *or conventions*, one of which would be to project the present into the future indefinitely. Other rules of thumb are also possible. For example, one might assume "that the *existing* state of opinion as expressed in prices and the character of existing output is based on a *correct* summing up of future prospects, so that we can accept it as such unless and until something new and relevant comes into the picture." Or one might assume that our own "individual judgment is worthless, [so that] we endeavor to fall back on the judgment of the rest of the world which is perhaps better informed."[10] Keynes characterized such a community as "a society of individuals each of whom is endeavoring to copy the others," as possessing a psychology based upon "a *conventional* judgment."[11]

For Keynes, resorting to conventions to cope with uncertainty is the best we can do. He did not view the type of uncertainty that affects economic decisions as probabilistic in a quantifiable sense. It is not a mere lottery. It is not the type of uncertainty that is subject to calculable gambles. Writing in 1937, Keynes elaborated on the argument of *The General Theory* as follows:

> By "uncertain" knowledge . . . I do not mean merely to distinguish what is known for certain from what is only probable. The game of roulette is not subject, in this sense, to uncertainty; nor is the prospect of a Victory bond being drawn. Or, again, the expectation of life is only slightly uncertain. Even the weather is moderately uncertain. The sense in which I am using the term is that in which the prospect of a European war is uncertain, or the price of copper and the rate of interest twenty years hence, or the obsolescence of a new invention, or the position of private wealthowners in the social system of 1970. About these matters there is no scientific basis on which to form any calculable probability whatever. We simply do not know.[12]

Classical economics failed to acknowledge the nature of uncertainty in economic decision making. Instead, for the classicals,

> At any given time facts and expectations were assumed to be given in a definite and calculable form; and risks, of which, though admitted, not much notice was taken, were supposed to be calculable of an exact actuarial computation. The calculus of probability, though mention of it was kept in the background, was supposed to be capable of reducing uncertainty to the same calculable status as that of certainty.[13]

But for Keynes, in truth, "We simply do not know."

[10] J. M. Keynes, "The General Theory of Employment," *Quarterly Journal of Economics*, Vol. 52 February 1937, p. 214.
[11] *Ibid.*
[12] *Ibid.*, pp. 213–214.
[13] *Ibid.*, pp. 212–213.

Taking a Closer Look

WAS KEYNES A SOCIALIST?

Was Keynes a socialist? This is an intriguing question, particularly at a time when the formerly "socialist" countries of Eastern Europe are undergoing a tumultuous transformation toward the free market.

Certainly Keynes was not a Marxist in either a political or analytical sense. Politically, he was a liberal and not a member of the British Labour party, which was socialist in outlook and policy. It is not even apparent that Keynes ever read Marx closely, and he frequently teased his Italian Communist colleague, Piero Sraffa, about "that Karl Marx fellow."

But did Keynes favor central planning for the economic system in any form? To some extent, yes. His concerns about the cyclical instability of investment, and the corresponding swings between prosperity and depression under free-market capitalism, led Keynes to speculate about the potential advantages of driving the rate of interest to such a low level that full employment would be ensured. This would result, he wrote, in the "euthanasia of the rentier, of the functionless investor" who earns a return simply because of the unnecessary scarcity of capital.[1]

To the extent that the central bank's actions alone could not lower the rate of interest sufficiently to achieve these goals, then Keynes was prepared to countenance "a somewhat comprehensive socialization of investment." His idea was that guidance and control of investment might come from the public rather than the private sector.

This was socialism. But it was a cautious brand of socialism, for Keynes immediately added that such a socialization of investment "need not exclude all manner of compromises and of devices by which public authority will cooperate with private initiative." Moreover, only investment planning was involved: "Beyond this no obvious case is made out for a system of State Socialism which would embrace most of the economic life of the community." After all, argued Keynes, "It is not the ownership of the means of production which is important for the State to assume. If the State is able to determine the aggregate amount of resources devoted to augmenting the instruments and the basic rate of reward to those who own them, it will have accomplished all that is necessary."

Keynes was serious, then, when he expressed enthusiasm for the social philosophy of the idiosyncratic Argentinean émigré from Germany, Silvio Gesell, whom Keynes described as a "strange and unduly neglected prophet" albeit a "crank." Gesell had striven to construct, quite explicitly, what Keynes correctly described as an "anti-Marxian socialism."[2] And

Keynes himself, while contemplating "a somewhat comprehensive socialization of investment," was insistent that his own scheme would avoid authoritarianism while "preserving" the desirable aspects of "present-day capitalistic individualism," namely the twin goods of "efficiency and freedom." However, unless steps were taken to end the unemployment crisis, Keynes feared, few would continue to put up with the ills of "present-day capitalistic individualism."

There is no evidence to suggest that Keynes promoted his proposal for socializing investment, and it only surfaces briefly in the latter pages of *The General Theory*. After Keynes, Keynesian economics never took a strongly socialist turn. "Real socialists" in the British Labor party in the 1930s and 1940s (e.g., Evan Durbin and Hugh Gaitskell) sought a fundamental restructuring of the British economy. But the "liberal" Laborites such as Nobel laureate James Meade viewed Keynes's message as saying that unemployment could be cured through expansionary policy without disturbing the intrinsic character of private enterprise.[3] This view has prevailed among Keynesians to this day.

---

[1] Quoted material in this discussion is taken from J. M. Keynes, *The General Theory of Employment, Interest and Money* (London: Macmillan, 1936), pp. 353, 355, 376–378, 381.

[2] See Silvio Gesell, *The Natural Economic Order*, trans. by Philip Pye (London: Owen, 1958).

[3] Elizabeth Durbin, *New Jerusalem: The Labour Party and the Economics of Democratic Socialism* (London: Routledge and Kegan Paul, 1985), pp. 197–198.

INSTABILITY IN FINANCIAL MARKETS

With uncertainty counterbalanced by behavioral conventions, human affairs could proceed with stability and regularity as long as confidence held in the continuation of the prevailing convention. This would be especially true for the private investor:

> For if there exist organized investment markets and if we can rely on the maintenance of the convention, an investor can legitimately encourage himself with the idea that the only risk he runs is that of a genuine change in the news *over the near future*, as to the likelihood of which he can attempt to form his own judgment, and which is unlikely to be very large. For, assuming that the convention holds good, it is only these changes which can affect the value of his investment, and he need not lose his sleep merely because he has not any notion what his investment will be worth ten years hence. (pp. 152–153, emphasis in original)

The problem is that the convention of the moment will not hold indefinitely: "It is not surprising that a convention, in an absolute view of things so arbitrary, should have its weak points" (p. 153). Conventions are fragile things, and their fragility lends an inherent instability to the economy, particularly to the financial sector.

Keynes attributed the fragility of conventions in financial markets to five major factors. A presentation of these gives some of the flavor of the institutional features of modern financial relations that he considered important.

First, Keynes argued that the separation of ownership from control in major corporations, the devolution of power from stockholders to managers, meant that the owners/shareholders lacked "special knowledge of the circumstances, either actual or prospective, of the business in question [so that] the element of real knowledge in the valuation of investments by those who own them or contemplate purchasing them has seriously declined" (p. 153). With less real knowledge in the financial markets, behavior was likely to be less stable.

Second, Keynes argued that daily fluctuations in profits are given an excessive weight in equity markets. For example, he noted, "The shares of American companies which manufacture ice tend to sell at a higher price in the summer. . . . The recurrence of a bank-holiday may raise the market valuation of the British railway system by several million pounds" (pp. 153–154).[14]

Third, day-to-day news of all sorts, even those likely to have little relevance to the prospective yield of specific enterprise, generally tends to lead to sudden and drastic changes in a "conventional valuation which is established as the outcome of the mass psychology of a large number of ignorant individuals" (p. 154). The health of a president, the announcement of a summit meeting, the conclusion of a political convention—all are factors that might lead to sharp short-run changes in valuation on the equity markets.

The fourth factor[15] that renders financial markets precarious is the outlook of the captains of the lending institutions, the major bankers, whose decisions permit or inhibit the speculator from pursuing a series of ventures. This interaction between the "state of credit" and the prospective yield or marginal efficiency of capital is another contributor to prospects for financial crisis. For example, financial intermediaries may

[14] Note that this behavior, though "absurd," is not necessarily irrational for most investors. If there is one investor who will buy British railway stocks in anticipation of holiday traffic, others will rationally do the same, to take advantage of the price increases rationally expected as a result of the behavior of the first. Thus, this point ties in closely to later ones that have to do with instability arising from the interdependence of speculative behavior patterns.

[15] We have altered Keynes's ordering, switching his fourth and fifth factors for expositional clarity.

overlend, leading to a boom with questionable foundations. Or they may suddenly stop lending, go into "revulsion," and thereby starve the economy of resources on which it relies. And, as Keynes noted, "whereas the weakening of either [banks or speculators] is enough to cause a collapse, recovery requires the revival of *both*" (p. 158).

The fifth and final factor rendering conventions precarious is perhaps the most interesting and compelling. Keynes observed that one might expect professional investors to devote most of their time to careful calculation of the prospective yield of enterprises whose shares trade on the stock exchange. Competition should winnow out the most ignorant and least expert among them.

But, said Keynes, this is not the case. "The energies and skill of the professional investor and speculator are mainly occupied otherwise" (p. 154). They are not engaged in what Keynes termed *enterprise*, "the activity of forecasting the prospective yield of assets over their whole life"; rather, they devote their time to *speculation*, "the activity of forecasting the psychology of the market" (p. 158). Or, as Keynes also put it, the professional investor is primarily concerned "with foreseeing changes in the conventional basis of valuation a short time ahead of the general public" (p. 154).

The professional investor does not evaluate an investment in the same manner as a person who would seek to hold it for life. Instead, the primary objective is to evaluate "what the market will value it at, under the influence of mass psychology, three months or a year hence" (pp. 154–155). This is rational, given the nature of the uncertainty that envelops the calculation of prospective yield and given the existence of well-developed stock markets where ownership claims are rapidly transferable at low cost. The professional investor seeks "to anticipate the basis of conventional valuation a few months hence," " 'to beat the gun' . . . to outwit the crowd, and to pass the bad, or depreciating, half-crown to the other fellow" (p. 155). Keynes found analogies with children's games, such as "a game of Snap, of Old Maid, of Musical Chairs" (pp. 155–156). Ultimately, the game is played among the professionals themselves, each of whom seeks to anticipate the actions of the other. Keynes concluded: "We have reached the third degree where we devote our intelligences to anticipating what average opinion expects the average opinion to be. And there are some, I believe, who practice the fourth, fifth and higher degrees" (p. 156).[16]

Keynes also observed that professional investors who engage in speculation rather than enterprise tend to predominate in investment markets, which indicates that speculation is more profitable than enterprise, particularly in the short term. Speculation also is easier and garners

---

[16] Keynes himself may well have been among the latter group. He made large sums of money for King's College at Cambridge with his successful speculations in foreign exchange.

faster results. Also, "an investor who proposes to ignore near-term market fluctuations needs greater resources for safety and must not operate on so large a scale, if at all, with borrowed money." Finally, being "eccentric, unconventional and rash in the eyes of average opinion" (p. 157), the long-term investor is most likely to be subjected to derision.

The predominance of speculation rather than enterprise in investment markets accentuates the instability of the financial sector of the economy. This has, at least intermittently, disastrous implications for the performance of the economy:

> Speculators may do no harm as bubbles on a steady stream of enterprise. But the position is serious when enterprise becomes the bubble on a whirlpool of speculation. When the capital development of a country becomes a by-product of the activities of a casino, the job is likely to be ill-done.

> The measure of success attained by Wall Street, regarded as an institution of which the proper social purpose is to direct new investment into the most profitable channels in terms of future yield, cannot be claimed as one of the outstanding triumphs of *laissez faire* capitalism—which is not surprising, if I am right in thinking that the best brains of Wall Street have been in fact directed towards a different object (p. 159).

Classical theory could not incorporate the phenomenon of financial instability directly into its mode of thought. But Keynes's analysis could do so through his concepts of the marginal efficiency of capital and the corresponding uncertainty that overwhelms the direct calculation of the prospective yield of a capital asset.

A SYNOPSIS OF THE REVOLUTION

In Chapter 2, we showed how Keynes began his assault on the classical mode of thought by challenging the central idea of a labor market. In this chapter, you have seen that his critique went much farther than that, extending to the theories of interest and money and to a very basic departure from classical thinking about the underlying stability of markets. We can now summarize some of the stages of Keynes's revolution:

·   In Keynes's theory, the labor market does not establish an equilibrium at full employment. Many equilibria are possible, and most are characterized by involuntary unemployment.

·   Through changes in aggregate demand, the level of investment exercises a powerful effect on the level of national income or output. The magnitude of this effect is captured by the multiplier, a concept entirely absent from the classical mode of thought.

· Since aggregate demand may be altered by government action, there is a justification for such action (e.g., government spending on public works) to revive a depressed economy. No such justification can be found in classical economics.

· In classical theory, money is neutral, affecting neither interest nor investment nor employment and output. For Keynes, the money supply determines the interest rate and thus affects all parts of the real economy.

· The classical model is devoid of a financial sector whose behavior affects the real performance of the economy. Keynes's theory tried to incorporate the effects that he felt were present in real financial markets. As a result of the pervasive importance of uncertainty and speculative behaviors, he came to believe that capitalism itself was unstable. From this it is but a short step to a key role for stabilization policy—the lasting legacy of the Keynesian revolution.

In all of these matters, Keynes sought to replace a simple and powerful classical metaphor of a capital market with a more complex, more unified, more realistic theory relevant to the immediate crisis of the Great Depression. Did he succeed? That judgment you will have to make for yourself. But you will first have to master the technical representations of both theories in far greater detail, a task to which we turn in Chapter 4.

SPECIAL SECTION

The Great Depression in Britain and the United States

The Great Depression ended more than fifty years ago, its soup lines, railroad riders, and Hoovervilles swept away in the tumult of World War II. Yet the Depression still speaks to us as a time when our society, perhaps not unlike the societies of Eastern Europe and the former Soviet Union today, stopped working and no one seemed to know what to do.

Of course, then no more than now did the politicians, business leaders, and economists of the day admit to their helplessness in the face of the disaster. In the United States, President Herbert Hoover's response, as a generation of Americans remembered bitterly, was to repeat that nothing should be done, for "prosperity is just around the corner."

Robert Skidelsky has identified the main positions associated with the Conservative party, which was in power in Great Britain in the early 1920s.[1]

> Underlying the policy and interests of the "economic establishment" was a substratum of simplified economic theory which was known as the "treasury view." Briefly this view ignored the existence of unemployment, and maintained that existing resources of capital and labour were being fully utilized. . . . It followed that any attempt to increase the level of investment would be either inflationary or diversionary. If the Government created more money without a prior increase in demand to justify it, manufacturers would merely raise their prices. Employees would demand higher wages and a wage-price inflationary spiral would force Britain off the gold standard, disrupt the international currency structure, wipe out savings, and lead to the type of economic collapse that had overtaken European countries after the war.[2]

The official opposition to this view came from the British Labour (socialist) party, which achieved power for the first time in 1929. Skidelsky describes the socialist position on mass unemployment after 1920, which was caught up in the Labour party's prewar commitments to profits taxation, nationalization of industry, and something called the "counter-cycle policy":

> As the decade unfolded Labour's confidence was eroded by the harsh facts of postwar existence. The two "socialistic" policies it had inherited from before the war—the taxation of the "surplus" and the counter-cycle policy— became irrelevant: there was little surplus and no cycle. For its major solution, nationalization, there was no mandate and besides it was not clear that taking over one or two declining industries would have the slightest effect on unemployment. There is no evidence of any fresh research in the main body of the Party which was dominated by the visionless orthodoxy of Snowden and Graham, Labour's two financial "experts."[3]

> The Labour leaders thus accepted the "conservative" remedy for postwar unemployment in all its essentials. The traditional export industries were to be revived by deflation and rationalization; the return to the gold standard at the pre-war parity would assist the recovery of world trade. On the question of public works, whereas the Conservatives regarded them as no substitute for capitalism, the Labour Party regarded them as no substitute for socialism. . . .

Thus in the big unemployment debate at the end of the nineteen-twenties Labour Party leaders, insofar as they were aware that a debate was in progress at all, came down on the traditional side.[4]

Keynes's own Liberals were in political eclipse, having collapsed electorally in the early 1920s. Yet the Liberals fought the elections of 1929 with spirit and with the only program that might as a practical matter have attacked the problem of mass unemployment. The Liberal proposal was straightforward: the government would borrow 250 million pounds over two years and put six hundred thousand unemployed men directly to work, building trunk roads, ring roads, housing (especially low-rent housing), a telephone network, electrical distribution systems, and the London Transport. Taking into account the jobs that would be created directly and those that would result from increased activity stimulated by public works (through the multiplier, as we have seen), the Liberals calculated that they could put virtually all of Britain's one million unemployed back to work. Their program was expressed in a pamphlet entitled *We Can Conquer Unemployment* and supported by another coauthored by Keynes, *Can Lloyd George Do It?*
The Liberal manifesto provoked the Conservative government of Stanley Baldwin to rebut.

The Ministry of Transport did not agree. It was quite wrong to employ men, often with specialized skills, on what was essentially navvy [laborer's] work; besides, the Liberal expectations of an early start were hopelessly optimistic. . . . The Ministry of Health commented on the difficulty involved in the large-scale building of uneconomic houses. . . . The Post Office stated that there was no reason to suppose that in the following years people would want the telephones that Lloyd George proposed to build. . . .[5]

The treasury objections involved the familiar restatement of the "treasury view." There were no idle balances. Money on time deposit was not idle. It was regarded by industry as an essential liquid reserve which would not be available in any case for long term investment, and, in addition, it might be used for "commercial advances or credits and in taking up bills or acceptances for traders as well as in loans to the short-term money market." Insofar as the loan was raised by diverting money from foreign investment it would have unfavourable effects on foreign trade. . . . Even if the loan could be raised it would require a very high rate of interest to compete with foreign issues.[6]

Keynes was not impressed. "Abra would rise; cadabra would fall," he said. Mr. Baldwin's argument could be summarized: "You must not do anything because this will mean that you can't do something else."[7]

In America, too, when the Depression hit a few years later, the impulse to do nothing found formidable expression. Thurman Arnold, a lawyer who went on to found one of Washington's great law firms, published in 1937 an instructive volume entitled *The Folklore of Capitalism*.

In the spring of 1936 the writer heard a group of bankers, businessmen, lawyers, and professors . . . discussing a crisis in the affairs of the bankrupt New York, New Haven and Hartford Railroad. . . . They were expressing indignation that a bureaucratic Interstate Commerce Commission, operating from Washington, had decreed that passenger rates be cut almost in half. Every man there would directly benefit from the lower rate. None were stockholders. Yet all were convinced that the reduction in rate should be opposed by all conservative citizens and they were very unhappy about this new outrage committed by a government bent on destroying private business. . . .

The writer tried to get the picture of the impending catastrophe in clearer detail. Did the gentlemen think that, under the new rates, trains would stop running and maroon them in the City of Elms? It appeared that no one quite believed this. The collapse which they feared was more nebulous. Trains would keep on running, but with a sinister change in the character of the service. Under government influence, it would become as unpleasant as the income taxes were unpleasant. . . .

There was also the thought that investors would suffer. This was difficult to put into concrete terms because investors already had suffered. The railroad was bankrupt. . . . [But] one gentleman present had the statistical data on why the railroad would suffer. In order to take care of the increased traffic, new trains would have to be added, new brakemen and conductors hired, more money put into permanent equipment. All such expenditures would, of course, reflect advantageously on the economic life of New Haven, remove persons from relief rolls, stimulate the heavy goods industries, and so on. This, however, was argued to be unsound. Since it was done in violation of sound principle it would damage business confidence, and actually result in less capital goods expenditures, in spite of the fact that it appeared to the superficial observer to be creating more.[8]

A few pages later, Arnold winds up with an analogy between the accepted economics of his day and the practice of medicine in the Middle Ages:

Magic had the same importance in the art of healing physical ills in the Middle Ages that it has today in the determination of governmental policy. Practical remedies, like sanitation, were not sufficiently mysterious to be respected. . . . There was more magic in disagreeable drugs than in pleasant ones, because disease was personified as an evil element that had to be attacked and driven away through some sort of combat in which pleasant remedies were a sign of weakness in the face of the enemy. The tactics in the war against disease bore a striking resemblance to the tactics in the modern war

against social problems, in that the principles of medicine were much more sacred and important than the health of the patient.[9]

We are, of course, fortunate that such attitudes toward programs of action and experiment in the face of grave social problems were buried along with the Depression and do not afflict the era in which we live or the economics that we study today (though some might say they still do).

---

[1] Robert Skidelsky, *The Politicians and the Slump* (London: Macmillan, 1967), p. 23.

[2] *Ibid.*, pp. 24–25.

[3] *Ibid.*, pp. 37–38.

[4] *Ibid.*, pp. 44.

[5] *Ibid.*, pp. 56–57.

[6] *Ibid.*, p. 58.

[7] The quotes are from "Can Lloyd George Do It?" in *Collected Works*, IX, 124.

[8] Thurman Arnold, *The Folklore of Capitalism* (New Haven, Conn.: Yale University Press, 1937), pp. 48–50.

[9] *Ibid.*, pp. 56–57.

SUMMARY

The classicals viewed the capital market as they did any other market. This analysis included an upward-sloping savings schedule, a downward-sloping investment schedule, and an interest rate that responds to excess supplies and demands of loanable funds. Keynes, on the other hand, believed that savings also depend on the level of income. Any number of interest rates would be consistent with equilibrium in the capital market. The interest rate at which full employment would hold was called the neutral rate of interest.

The interest rate is determined by the composition of savings held. Savings can be held as cash or as an interest-bearing asset. The more interest-bearing assets are demanded relative to cash, the lower the interest rate will fall.

Closely related to this issue was Keynes's rejection of the classical view of the economy as a barter system. Keynes instead advocated a monetary theory of production. The interest rate acts in the allocation of resources much as any other relative price would act in the economy. The interest rate in this context is a relative price that depends on the quantity of money.

The investment decision, in Keynes's view, depends on prospective yields, which in turn depend partly on existing facts and expectations of the future. Expectations can be optimistic or pessimistic. They are not, however, objective. Instead, they are based on crude mass psychology or conventional judgment. In their arbitrariness, conventions are unstable. Fragility of expectations is due to five factors: (1) the separation of ownership from management; (2) the weight given in equity markets to daily fluctuations in profits is excessive; (3) day-to-day news is given too much importance; (4) is the weight given to the outlook of the captains of industry; (5) speculators don't actually calculate yields but attempt to guess the future psychology of the market. These speculators are particularly important to instability because they predominate numerically in equity markets.

Keynes had special theories of how investment is determined. Relative prices of existing assets are determined by portfolio theory. Producible assets are valued by their supply price. The investment decision rests on the difference between the prospective yield and the supply price. Investment increases until the marginal efficiency of capital falls to equal to the bank rate of interest. The bank rate of interest is determined by the liquidity preference theory.

Review Questions

1. "The classical theory has not been alive to the relevance of changes in the level of income or to the possibility of the level of income being actually a function of the rate of investment," said Keynes (*The General Theory*, p. 180). A classical economist might respond that, in the future, investments shift out the demand-for-labor curve and thus this problem described by Keynes is not a problem at all. What has the classical economist misunderstood about Keynes's argument?

2. Describe the difference between the classicals' natural rate of interest and Keynes's neutral theory of interest.

3. What is liquidity preference? Can you think of any actual examples of how this works in everyday life?

4. Explain in some detail how Keynes transformed the classicals' real theory of production into a monetary theory of production.

5. In Keynes's system, investment is unstable. In the text, several prices and costs were described that help to determine the level of investment; also, five reasons were given for the instability of investment. Explain specifically how these reasons relate to prices and costs.

Review Problems

1. Using Figure 3.1 as an expository device, show the effect of an increase in productivity. Does the nature of the productivity increase matter? Compare your answer to the answer for the similar question in Chapter 2.

2. On a diagram such as the ones in Figure 3.2, demonstrate the effects of uncertainty caused by failures in the banking system. Does this correspond to what actually happened in the late 1980s and early 1990s?

3. Answer question 2 again but use the theories developed by Keynes for your answer. Do you get more satisfying answers? Why do you think interest rates fell?

4. Using a diagram such as the one in Figure 3.4, show the effects of an increase in capital productivity. How does this analysis differ from the answer given for the classical system?

5. Can you think of any feedback mechanisms in the Keynesian system that would give you the same result as the classical result (referring to problem 4)? Redraw Figure 3.4 to reflect your amended analysis.

6. Draw arbitrary marginal efficiency schedules for three capital assets. Associate some numbers for several points on each schedule you have drawn. Show how to aggregate these three separate capital assets schedules into a marginal efficiency schedule for the entire capital market.

Suggested Readings

John Maynard Keynes, *Treatise on Money* (London: Macmillan, 1950).

Silvio Gesell, *The Natural Economic Order* (London: Owen, 1957).

Elizabeth Durbin, *New Jerusalem: The Labour Party and the Economics of Democratic Socialism* (London: Routledge and Kegan Paul, 1985).

Robert Skidelsky, *The Politicians and the Slump* (London: MacMillan, 1967).

Thurman Arnold, *The Folklore of Capitalism* (New Haven: Yale University Press, 1937).

THE RATE OF INTEREST AND
THE RATE OF INVESTMENT

One of Keynes's major complaints about classical economics was the breach he saw between monetary theory and the theory of value (theory of relative prices). The latter, which utilized the supply-and-demand, savings-investment apparatus in abstraction from monetary consider-ations, was the source of the image of the price-adjusting economy devoid of crises. Classical theory placed the determination of the rate of interest, a relative price, in the domain of the theory of value, separating it from the domain of the theory of money.

Keynes sought to construct a single, unified theory that would si-multaneously explain relative prices and provide a monetary theory that would account for economic fluctuations. Through his interest rate the-ory, in turn, he developed his own explanation for relative prices and for investment demand, one quite distinct from the ordinary theory of sup-ply and demand. (Keynes spelled out these ideas in Chapter 17 of *The General Theory*.)[1] We examine this approach to relative prices in detail in Chapter 12; here we merely provide a bare outline.

Keynes argued that the relative prices of existing assets depend on the economics of portfolio choice, whereas those of producible goods are determined largely by costs of production. Each capital asset possesses a *marginal efficiency*, which is defined as a relationship between what Keynes calls the prospective yield and the supply price of the capital asset. The *prospective yield* is the series of net (of expenses) monetary returns an investor expects to get from selling the output of the capital asset. This, of course, inherently takes on the character of a forecast of a stream of prospective net returns over the course of the lifetime of the capital asset.

The *supply price* of a capital asset is "*not* the market-price at which an asset of the type in question can actually be purchased in the market."[2] It is, instead, the price that would be just sufficient to induce a producer of that type of capital asset to make a new unit of it. Keynes also refers to the supply price of the capital asset as "replacement cost."

The prospective yield and the supply price of an additional unit of a capital asset give us the marginal efficiency of capital in the following

[1] J. M. Keynes, *The General Theory of Employment, Interest and Money* (London: Macmillan, 1936).
[2] Keynes, *The General Theory*, p. 135 (emphasis added).

way. The marginal efficiency of capital is defined as the *discount rate that will set the present value of the series of net returns* the investor anticipates receiving from the sale of the output of the capital asset over the course of its lifetime *exactly equal to its supply price* (or replacement cost). If (1) i_k is the marginal efficiency of capital, (2) P_k is the supply price, and (3) each Q_{tk} represents one year's net return on a capital asset of the kth type in the year t, then the following relationship defines the marginal efficiency of capital:[3]

$$P_k = \sum \frac{Q_{tk}}{1 + i_k}$$

(This same concept is recognized in microeconomics as the *internal rate of return*.)

The marginal efficiency of capital is defined in terms of expectations of the yield and estimates of the current replacement cost of the capital asset. Keynes argued that a rise in investment in a capital asset would reduce its marginal efficiency for two reasons. First, the prospective yield would fall as the supply increased; this happens because, with given supplies of other factors, additional units of a capital asset cannot be used as efficiently as earlier ones. Second, the production of an additional unit of a capital asset would make its supply price rise, due to increasing "pressure on the facilities for producing that type of capital." Both of these seem, indeed, to be straightforward applications of old-fashioned diminishing returns.[4]

Each capital asset has a schedule for its own marginal efficiency that is downward sloping in marginal efficiency, investment space (see the schedule for the kth asset in Figure 3.A1). Summing over all individual schedules yields the schedule of marginal efficiency of capital for the economy as a whole, with a similar slope (see Figure 3.A2). This can also be interpreted as an investment schedule.

What will be the equilibrium volume of investment? The volume of investment will be pushed to $I^\star$, "the point where there is no longer any class of capital-asset of which the marginal efficiency exceeds the current

---

[3] For example, if a capital asset is expected to offer an investor $100 per year in perpetuity, the expression on the right side of the equation simplifies to Q/i, where $Q = \$100$. Thus, if the supply price of the capital asset is $1,000, then the marginal efficiency of capital for this type of capital asset is 10 percent.

[4] Keynes, *The General Theory*, p.136.

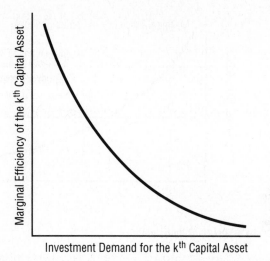

FIGURE 3.A1   The Marginal Efficiency of Capital

The marginal efficiency of each capital asset declines as the number of units purchased increases.

FIGURE 3.A2   The Aggregate MEC Schedule

The marginal efficiency of capital as a whole declines as investment increases, because increasing investment means purchasing capital assets of decreasing marginal efficiency.

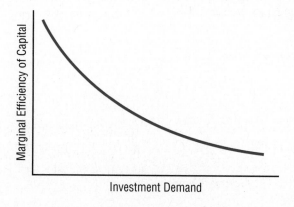

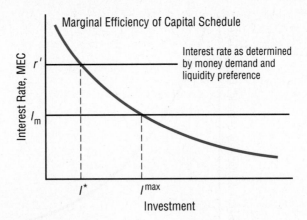

FIGURE 3.A3   Keynes's Theory of Investment

In Keynes's theory, the volume of investment is determined by the interest rate (r') and the marginal efficiency of capital schedule; investment projects with MEC greater than r' are chosen. The liquidity premium on money places a lower bound on the interest rate, making I^{max} the maximum volume of investment.

rate of interest" (see Figure 3.A3 above). Keep in mind that $I^{\star}$ need not be the full-employment level of investment and if it were possible to lower the rate of interest, it would be possible to get a higher volume of investment along this particular schedule of marginal efficiency of capital. The rate of interest cannot be lowered below the liquidity premium on money (since people would simply hold money rather than buy a bond at so low an interest rate), as depicted by the horizontal I_m schedule in Figure 3.A3. Therefore, getting a rate of investment above I^{max} would be impossible in this situation.

THE KEYNESIAN THEORY

Chapter 4

CLASSICAL AND KEYNESIAN MACROECONOMIC MODELS

Looking Forward

If you are accustomed to thinking of economics in terms of algebra and geometry, then the "real" textbook begins with this chapter.

First, we retrace our discussion of the classical theory, presenting it now in terms of a simple formal model. We then make a comparable presentation of a simple version of Keynes's theory, highlighting some of the most important departures of the latter from the former: the principle of effective demand, the consumption function, and the multiplier.

The chapter concludes with a special section on growth theory, which represented an effort to extend the basic Keynesian vision to the growing economy of the postwar world.

Read this chapter with pencil and paper in hand. Write down the equations as you come across them; sketch the graphs. Ask yourself how the equations and the graphs relate to each other. Can you see how both classicals and Keynesians sought to develop their theories of employment, interest, and money? Can you see how the theories differed?

By the end of this chapter, you should have a good understanding of:

> - The classical model, including the labor market, the production function, savings–investment equilibrium, and the classical dichotomy.
> - The Keynesian cross model and the multiplier.
> - The consumption function and alternative theories of the relationship between consumption and income.

In this chapter, we explore the development of macroeconomic models. A *macroeconomic model* is an attempt to capture the key features of an economy in a short set of formal propositions, which may be (and usually are) stated in mathematical form. We begin with an exposition of the classical system.

A CLASSICAL MACRO MODEL

The classical system had no single author, though its roots went back to Adam Smith. In the early twentieth century, its elements were scattered through the works of Marshall, Pigou, Robertson, and others on whom Keynes fastened the "classical" label.

It was Keynes himself who sought to synthesize the key features of the system against which he was rebelling, in order to understand clearly the reasons why he was rejecting it. In this chapter, we present first a compact exposition of the system that he saw and opposed and then one of the simplest (and earliest) representations of the system that he sought to erect in its stead.

Production Function

We start with an economy that has an *aggregate production function*—a relation that specifies how inputs produce outputs under a given state of technical know-how. Our inputs may be described in very simple terms, by an amount of employment of labor, N, and a variable that measures the machinery and equipment available, which we call the capital stock, K. The amount of real production, y, depends upon N and K. The capital stock is fixed in the short run, so we ignore it in this very simple model. Therefore, the aggregate production function can be expressed as

$$(4.1) \qquad\qquad y = y(N)$$

With a given capital stock, output will rise with increasing employment of labor. But as we add labor applied to an unchanging set of machines, the amount of additional output we can get out of each additional worker gradually declines. This is known as an assumption of *diminishing returns to the labor input.* The slope of the production function measures the amount of additional output that a small amount of additional labor can produce, or the *marginal product of labor*. Using our notation to express the rate of change of functions with respect to the variables they depend on, we can write that

$$(4.1')\qquad\qquad\qquad y'(N) > 0$$

which tells us that the marginal product of labor is a positive quantity, and

$$(4.1'')\qquad\qquad\qquad y''(N) < 0$$

which states the principle of diminishing returns.

The geometric representation of the relationship between labor and output will take the form given in Figure 4.1, where output rises with employment $[y'(N) > 0]$, but at a diminishing rate as employment grows $[y''(N) < 0]$. The production function slopes upward but becomes flatter and flatter as employment increases.

Demand Curve for Labor

From the shape of the production function, we can derive a demand curve for labor. This demand curve tells us how many workers firms will be willing to employ for any given rate of material compensation, or *real wage (w)*. Indeed, it turns out that the relationship between wages and labor demand is governed by the property of diminishing returns in the production function.

FIGURE 4.1   The Production Function

The production function relates employment to output/income. This function exhibits diminishing returns as employment increases.

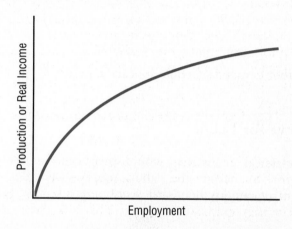

To see this, assume that the economy consists of competitive firms who try to maximize profits. Profit consists of all the revenue that remains to the owners of the firm after wages (and after any fixed payments for the fixed capital stock have been made). Since labor is the only variable factor of production, and so the only variable that firms actually control is the amount of employment they choose to provide, profit maximization actually consists of choosing a single best level of employment.

Now, if our firms are truly competitive, they must sell all of their output for a single price, and they must hire new labor at the prevailing wage. They may thus calculate the amount of employment to provide by comparing the selling price of an additional unit of output to the costs of producing that unit. If the price is greater, then it will pay to add employment. But if costs exceed price, then it will pay to reduce employment. At the employment level where price just equals the added cost of production, profits are maximized and no benefit is derived from either increasing or decreasing employment.

Thus, firms are willing to hire new workers so long as the resulting wage (which is the *marginal cost* of hiring additional labor) can be justified by the added value of production. In economic parlance, we say that the real wage cannot exceed the marginal product of labor, the extra product that would be made by employing one additional worker. Since, as we have seen, the addition of employment to a fixed stock of capital is subject to diminishing returns, the marginal product of labor falls as employment increases. When the marginal product falls below the real wage, then firms will cut back employment until the two are again equal. If the real wage falls below the marginal product, they will expand employment. Thus, the production-function relationship between labor and output implies that the demand for labor will fall as the real wage (w) rises.

Algebraically, the labor demand (N^d) relationship can be expressed as follows:

(4.2) $N^d = N^d(w)$

(4.2′) $N^{d\prime} < 0$

The labor demand schedule appears in Figure 4.2 as a downward-sloping curve.

Supply Curve for Labor

The classical economist would then call on a utilitarian theory of behavior to derive the labor supply schedule, which relates the amount of employment that workers are willing to supply to the real wage.

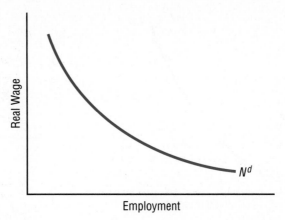

FIGURE 4.2   Demand for Labor

The demand for labor is derived from the production function. As employment increases, labor's marginal contribution to output declines, due to diminishing returns, and so does the real wage employers are willing to pay in order to hire additional workers.

In this view, the decision to work is essentially a choice between labor and leisure. Leisure is viewed as a direct source of pleasure, or utility. Work itself is correspondingly unpleasant; it has a *disutility*. But work is also a source of income that can be used to obtain satisfaction. Therefore, workers will choose to work as long as the utility that can be derived indirectly, through the real wage, is greater than the direct disutility of working. A higher real wage will offset the disutility of additional hours, so a higher wage will generate a greater work effort. In most cases, the supply curve (N_s) for labor will therefore be upward sloping (see Figure 4.3):

(4.3) $N^s = N^s(w)$

(4.3')[1] $N^{s\prime} > 0$

We can then combine supply and demand in the labor market, as we do in Figure 4.4. If the real wage is at $w^\star$, the level that clears the labor market, $N^\star$ workers will be put to work. Since in the classical labor

---

[1] At very high levels of work effort and of the wage, a rise in the wage rate can actually reduce the number of hours of work effort. This happens because an increase in the wage affects the amount earned on all hours, not just the additional one, while at high levels of income the marginal benefit or utility associated with additional income will start to decline. Thus, it is possible that the marginal utility of an additional hour's income will start to fall below the rising disutility of that additional hour's work. When this happens, we have a backward-bending *supply curve of labor*, which reflects the preference for leisure in an affluent population.

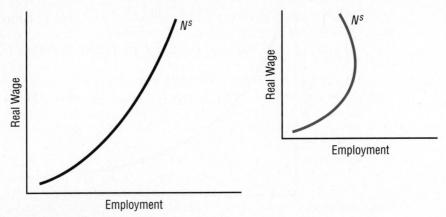

FIGURE 4.3   Supply of Labor

The supply of labor is determined by the rising marginal disutility of work. As people work more, a higher real wage is required to bring forth additional effort. (See curve on left.) At some point, the real wage gets so high that a further increase reduces the supply of labor. This is known as a backward-bending supply curve. (See curve on right.)

FIGURE 4.4   The Labor Market in Equilibrium

In the classical model, labor supply and demand determine the real wage and employment. Employment then determines the volume of real output, as shown on the right.

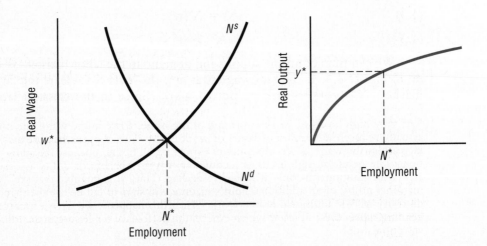

market the demand and supply of labor both depend solely upon the real wage, $N^\star$ is the maximum level of employment that can emerge from free and competitive markets. $N^\star$ is the classical employment equilibrium.

We can then insert the level of employment $N^\star$ into the production function to obtain the corresponding full employment level of output $y^\star$ (see Figure 4.4). We need no more information about this economy; once we know its aggregate labor market and its production function, we know all there is to know about its *real* performance.

Moreover, so long as the real wage is sufficiently flexible so that the classical labor market settles, or clears, at full employment, only long-run factors can alter the level of employment and output. Such factors include technical change, which could shift the production function upward and the labor demand schedule to the right. Capital accumulation over time could lead to a larger capital stock, which would also shift the production function upward and the labor demand schedule to the right. Also, changes in tastes and preferences in the labor versus leisure choice among workers could affect the position of the labor supply schedule.

Savings, Investment, and Interest

Once the level of employment and output was determined, classical economics turned to its theory of the interest rate to decide the allocation of that output between consumption and savings or investment. As we saw in the previous chapter, the classical interest rate comes from the *capital market*, the market that brings the supply of savings and demand for investment into equilibrium at a market-clearing rate of interest. Letting S and I represent supply of savings and demand for investment functions, each of them operating at the equilibrium volume of output $y^\star$, we have

$$(4.4) \qquad\qquad S(r, y^\star) = I(r, y^\star)$$

This relationship is graphed in Figure 4.5. Investment demand slopes downward and saving supply slopes upward, both with respect to the rate of interest, so we have

$$(4.4') \qquad\qquad S'(r) > 0; \; I'(r) < 0$$

The logic of the argument is again quite simple. Because of diminishing returns, investment demand falls with a rising rate of interest. In this case, the diminishing returns are to capital: as more capital is added to a given stock of available labor, the marginal productivity of capital falls. Therefore, additional investment will be demanded only if the interest rate on a loan to finance that much additional investment also declines.

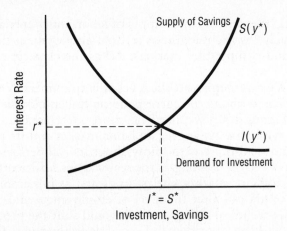

FIGURE 4.5   **Savings, Investment, and Interest**

In the classical capital market, the supply of savings and the demand for investment jointly determine savings, investment, and the rate of interest.

Savings, on the other hand, represent a choice between consumption today and consumption later. As the reward for deferring consumption rises, so must the supply of savings. This reward, of course, is the rate of interest paid on savings.

Thus, in Figure 4.5, the investment demand curve slopes downward, and the savings supply curve slopes upward. With the level of real income fixed at $y^\star$, real investment and real savings equalize at (real) interest rate $r^\star$.[2] Only long-run factors, such as those governing the tastes of savers and investors, can raise the equilibrium rate of capital formation.

Money and Prices

In the classical system, labor supply, labor demand, production, and the real interest rate are all determined without any reference to the price level.[3] The equilibrium level of employment determines the volume of output for any given capital stock, whereas the intersection of the sav-

---

[2] We deal with the distinction between real and nominal interest rates later on. For now, we note that a real interest rate measures the return on a loan or investment in terms of commodities rather than money and is not affected by changes in the price level.

[3] True, the price level, P, enters into the calculation of the real wage: given the money wage W, the real wage w is equal to W/P. But whatever happens to the price level (P), the money wage (W) will adjust, so that the real wage reaches the value that clears the labor market.

ings supply and investment demand schedules determine the partition of that output between consumption and savings/investment. Thus, there is only one possible level of output or income in equilibrium, $y^\star$, and only one real interest rate, $r^\star$.

Where then do the classicals get their price level? The simplest approach is to treat the aggregate price level as bearing a fixed, proportionate relationship to the quantity of money. A classical economist might start with the following relationship, known as the *equation of exchange*:[4] In this equation, M is the quantity of money, P is the price level, and y is the level of real income. V is the *velocity of circulation of money*, which may be thought of as the number of times each dollar changes hands in a given year.[5] This "income version" of the quantity equation states that in any given year the nominal level of income of the economy (Py), must be equal to the stock of money *times* the rate at which each dollar changes hands during the year (MV). The intuition behind this identity is quite simply that every transaction involving goods must coincide with a corresponding transaction involving money.

If the velocity of circulation V is approximately constant,[6] and if the level of real income in the economy y is determined by the relation between the labor market and the production function, so that $y = y^\star$, then the ratio $V/y^\star$ is an approximate constant. The following simple relationship emerges between the price level and the quantity of money:

$$(4.5) \qquad P = \alpha M \qquad \text{where } \alpha = \frac{V}{y^\star}$$

Equation (4.5) tells us that the money supply, perhaps controlled directly by the monetary authorities, governs the price level. Therefore, *changes* in the money supply will cause *changes* in the price level, or *inflation*. Inflation thus becomes a direct result of money growth: if M grows by 15 percent, so will P. And money growth is neutral in its effects on real activity, because the adjustment of money wages (a price, after all, like any other) will always ensure that the real wage is at $w^\star$ employment is at $N^\star$ and output is at $y^\star$. In fact, in this model, how much inflation, disinflation, or price instability there may be seems irrelevant. So long as the money wage can rise or fall proportionately with other prices to maintain real wage $w^\star$, the level of employment and output will not vary.

[4] Developed by the U.S. economist Irving Fisher (1867–1947).

$$MV = Py$$

[5] We provide full details on this concept in Chapter 6.
[6] By this we mean that velocity changes only slowly over time and mainly as a result of institutional forces, such as technical change in the banking system. The critical assumption is that velocity is independent of the other variables in the equation of exchange.

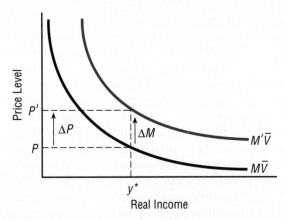

FIGURE 4.6   Money and Prices

The classical theory of the price level rests on the equation $MV = Py$. For any given money stock (M) and velocity (V), equilibrium output (y^*) is associated with a unique price level (P). Increase M, with V constant, and prices will rise proportionately to the rise in M.

Figure 4.6 plots the relationship between the price level P and the real output level y, which is mediated by the policy variable M, the money supply that is controlled by the central bank, and by the constant velocity of circulation V. For any given stock of money, the price level will vary inversely with the volume of output; however, once the volume of output is fixed (at the equilibrium employment level, as shown), then so is the price level. A change in the stock of money, from M to M', shifts the entire relationship between output and prices. But since such a shift cannot change the actual volume of output, which remains fixed by the operation of the labor market at $y^\star$ as determined by $N^\star$, the only possible effect is a proportionate increase in the price level, from P to P'.

The Classical Dichotomy

We then have the *classical dichotomy* between the real side of the economy where employment, output, and investment are determined and the monetary side of the economy where the general price level is determined (see Table 4.1).

Once the monetary side of the economy determines the price level and the real side determines the real wage rate, it becomes possible to calculate the money wage rate W—the earnings of workers unadjusted for the price level—since W, given P, must be set so that real wage w is consistent with classical full employment.

TABLE 4.1   The Classical Dichotomy

REAL	**MONETARY**
$N^d = N^d(w)$ (labor demand)	$P = \alpha M$ (prices)
$N^s = N^s(w)$ (labor supply)	
$N^d(w) = N^s(w)$ (employment)	
$y = y(N)$ (real output)	
$S(r) = I(r)$ (savings and investment)	

An important conclusion immediately followed from the classical view, as we have discussed in Chapter 2: there could be no such thing as *involuntary* unemployment. Any apparent unemployment could only come about for one of the following three reasons:

First, people could be unemployed temporarily, as they moved from one job to the next. This came to be known as *frictional unemployment*. We show this somewhat heuristically in Figure 4.7A; frictional unemployment is simply the measured unemployment that persists even though labor markets are clearing. Frictional unemployment is likely to be true for some number of people at all times, thus setting a floor under the minimum achievable rate of unemployment. But there is no good reason why frictional unemployment should vary greatly from year to year. It certainly could not explain the general and prolonged upturn in unemployment that engulfed the world economy in the early 1930s.

A second acceptable classical explanation for unemployment was that people could be out of work because their wage expectations were too high. They might be looking for work but at wages greater than the market value of their output. They would then be unwilling to accept work that might be offered at the prevailing wage. A glance at the supply curve shows that these people are located on it, above and to the right of the equilibrium point (Figure 4.7B). They therefore could work, if they chose to do so, simply by lowering their desired, or *reservation, wage* and so could not be described as involuntarily unemployed.

Finally, it might be possible for people to be unemployed even if they wanted to work at or for less than the equilibrium wage. This might happen, for example, if some combination of workers (e.g., a trade union) or a legislated policy (e.g., a minimum wage law) forced actual wages to levels above their equilibria (Figure 4.7C). But in that case, a social decision has been made to support wage levels above market-clearing values, and while individual workers might dissent from that decision and thus be "involuntarily" unemployed, society as a whole still could choose to employ them, if it wanted to, by breaking up the

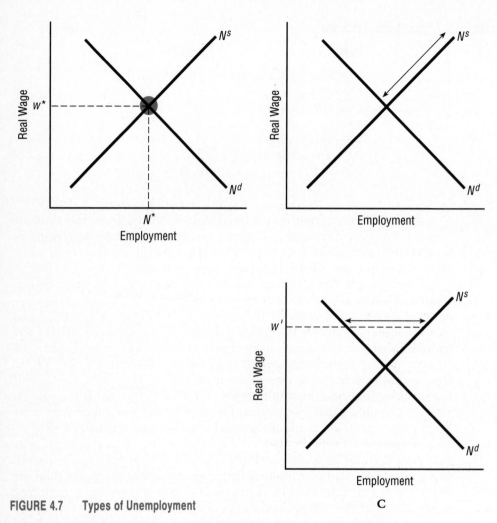

FIGURE 4.7   Types of Unemployment

All three classical varieties of unemployment are fundamentally voluntary.

wage-fixing institutions and allowing the wage to fall until it cleared the market.

Figure 4.7 illustrates these three possible cases. It is impossible, given the assumptions of the argument, to give meaning to the idea of involuntary unemployment within the framework of the three diagrams shown. And so it was quite impossible for the classical theory to explain the phenomenon of mass unemployment in any satisfactory way. In the Great Depression, a quarter of the work force could not find jobs, even at extraordinarily low wages. And yet unemployment theory could only opine that, for one reason or another, wages were just not low enough.

Taking a Closer Look

MONEY AND THE INTEREST RATE

A more complicated extension of the classical vision might admit to the possibility that the velocity of circulation of money is not constant. This approach is cast in terms of a supply and demand for money. The supply of money can be treated as dictated by the decisions of the monetary authorities, so that

$$M^s = M, \text{ a constant}$$

The demand for money relationship can be extrapolated from the quantity equation:

$$(4.\text{B}1) \qquad M^d = \frac{Py^\star}{V}$$

A classical economist might then specify that velocity is dependent upon the rate of interest and specifically that velocity increases in response to an increase in the rate of interest. This is tantamount to saying that people seek to get out of money and into other, less liquid and more rewarding assets when interest rates rise; thus, they use their remaining money balances more intensively:

$$(4.\text{B}2) \ V = V(r) \qquad V' > 0$$

Coupling (4.B1) with (4.B2), the demand for money function can be expressed as

$$M^d = \frac{Py^\star}{V(r)}$$

Setting $M^s = M^d$, as required for equilibrium in the money market, implies that the price level bears the following relationship to the quantity of money:

$$(4.\text{B}3) \qquad P = \frac{MV(r)}{y^\star}$$

A larger money supply implies a higher price level; a higher interest rate implies a higher price level. Note that an increase in real income, other things unchanged, has a deflationary effect on prices; this happens because an unchanged money stock must now accommodate a higher volume of transactions. With velocity fixed, it can only do so if prices fall.

The classical economist who inspects (4.B3) will discover a problem. The price level is now dependent, in part, on the interest rate! And so, unless the real interest rate is fixed so solidly by the savings and investment schedules that it never changes (not even when supply-siders alter tax rates), the classical dichotomy can no longer hold strictly true in this system.

Given mass unemployment, what could government do? The classical model implicitly replied: not very much. Everything important—employment, output, and the real rate of interest—is determined in a market, whether the market for labor or the market for capital. So long as these markets are competitive and working well, there can be no reason for government intervention to overcome a crisis of unemployment. The only conceivable justifications for intervention might be to shift the positions of the labor supply and demand schedules (raising total output) or to restore the requisite degree of money wage flexibility (by breaking up labor unions and other wage-fixing cartels) to ensure that the aggregate labor market clears.

Aside from helping markets work, what can government do? The classical theory left just one tool outside the purview of the markets: determination (through the central bank) of the stock of money. But this tool has only one consequence: determination of the general level of prices! So government (or its central bank) can control the price level (or, equivalently, the inflation rate) and just about nothing else.

The classical dichotomy thus separated the economic universe — into (1) a sphere of the market and (2) a sphere of money, prices, and government policy. By the very nature of the theory, then, *money was neutral*, and *monetary* causes could not have *real* consequences. Thus, the classical vision could not admit even the possibility that a failure of financial markets, such as occurred with the Great Crash of 1929, could be responsible for the Great Depression that immediately followed. It could not allow that a failure of purchasing power, of demand for goods, could precipitate a collapse of production. It could not even acknowledge the possibility that mass unemployment might result from any cause other than a malfunction of the labor market itself. The spheres of money and production were separate, and separate they would have to remain. We have seen and now attempt to explain in a more formal way how Keynes's revolution began as a rebellion against this separation.

A SIMPLE KEYNESIAN MODEL

As we have seen, Keynes reinterpreted a diverse and unconnected set of theories about labor markets, production, savings-investment, and money and the price level. In Keynes's general theory, all became linked: from money demand to interest, from interest to investment, from investment and effective demand to output and employment. Macroeconomics, as a unified science for the study of the behavior of the whole economy, was born.

Economists following Keynes began as he did, by emphasizing first the important but narrow range of issues directly related to the problem of mass unemployment. Later they broadened their approach to encompass the determination of interest rates, savings behavior, investment, and growth. We shall do the same.

The key element in the new intellectual structure was the displacement of the labor market from its central role in the determination of employment and unemployment. Let us explore this central transformation of perspective.

Aggregate Demand

Keynes reasoned that the volume of employment is determined by the volume of production. At any time, with a given capital stock and state of technology, employers hire enough workers at the prevailing wage to produce the goods they think they can sell at maximum profit.

What determines that volume of goods? Well, at the upper limit might be a maximum rate of production determined by the physical capacity of the capital stock. But below that, the amount of goods that employers think will yield maximum profits depends on their *totally subjective* estimate of the size of the market, of how much could be sold. If the estimate proves wrong, they might at any time choose to employ fewer workers than would be willing to work at the prevailing (real) wage.

And what determines the size of the market? Keynes argued that the crucial variable is *total spending*. In other words, the total volume of output is directly determined, and the level of employment is indirectly determined, by the total amounts that consumers, investors, and governments are able and prepared to bring to market to spend on the purchases of goods.

Once the determination of employment is viewed in this way, the possibility of strictly involuntary unemployment—that unemployed workers might be willing to work for the prevailing wage or less, perhaps even much less, and still not be able to find jobs—becomes frighteningly real. The size of the market, the total volume of spending (especially consumer spending), or *level of aggregate demand*, thus takes on a critical role.

At this point, formal statements of the Keynesian position begin to appear. We present a very basic one, known as the "Keynesian cross," in Figure 4.8.

The Keynesian cross diagram presents a relationship between two variables: income earned, on the horizontal axis, and income spent (the size of the market, or aggregate demand), on the vertical. The line that rises at 45 degrees from the origin reflects the truism that income earned and income spent must, in equilibrium, be equal. The plans of consumers, producers, and governments will govern what is spent, and

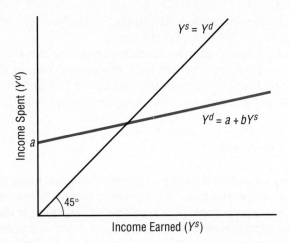

FIGURE 4.8   The Keynesian Cross

Income spent, or total expenditure, is often called aggregate demand. The simplest Keynesian model shows how spending, or aggregate demand, determines the equilibrium level of income.

what is spent by them will be earned by workers and firms. The other line, which intercepts the vertical axis at a and cuts the 45-degree line from above, shows, the resulting size of the market, or level of aggregate demand, for each level of income earned.

Aggregate demand (Y^d) is the sum of four components: spending by consumers, C, spending by businesses on investment in capital goods, I, spending by government on the purchases of goods and services, G, and *net exports*, or exports minus imports ($X - M$). All are measured here in money terms.[7] Expression (4.6) is a matter of definition and is therefore known as an *identity*; the two sides of the equation are always identically equal. We call this particular identity the *national income identity*.

(4.6) $$C + I + G + X - M = Y^d$$

We have much to say about how such spending is determined later on. For now, we need to note only that in order to simplify our problem, we assume here that investment and government spending are fixed and do not depend on the size of total earnings or national income. We also assume that trade is balanced, so that $X - M = 0$. This enables us to dispense with further treatment of the trade issue until Chapter 11.

---

[7] Investment spending by businesses is defined here as the purchase of physical capital goods, such as plant and machinery, *not* as the purchase by "investors" of financial assets such as stocks and bonds. Government spending is likewise restricted to purchases of goods and services; government transfer payments to individuals, such as Social Security payments, are counted only when spent by their recipients on consumption or investment goods.

Consumer Spending

Consumer spending is the principal variable that remains to be explained in our system. And consumer spending must depend on the earnings that consumers have received. This is true for an obvious reason: prosperous people can and do consume more than the impoverished and unemployed. We can represent this fact in the following simple, linear way, where C is consumption and Y^s is income earned (or supplied):

$$(4.7) \qquad\qquad C = a + bY^s$$

Equation (4.7) is a simple statement of the *consumption function*. It holds that consumption is a linear function of income, with a positive intercept at a. There will still be positive consumption if income is zero because people with no income continue to consume. As income rises, consumption rises but not as much. The coefficient b, which has a value between zero and one, gives the proportion that is consumed out of each additional dollar of income. It is known as the *marginal propensity to consume*, and it may be defined algebraically as $\Delta C/\Delta Y$, or the change in consumption per unit of change in income. The empirical statement that the marginal propensity to consume is a constant, Keynes termed a "fundamental psychological law."[8] We see below just how fundamental it is.

The Model

We are now into the building of a formal Keynesian model. At this point, you should review some general rules for the building of models, given in the box. You will need to understand very thoroughly the differences between *identities*, *structural equations*, and *equilibrium conditions*.

If we substitute the value for C given in (4.7), which is our structural equation (see the box) for consumption, $C = a + bY^s$, into the formal national income identity (4.6), we have equation (4.8) below. Then we note the *equilibrium condition* that aggregate demand (Y^d) and income (Y^s) must be equal. Stating this as equation (4.9) gives us the two-equation linear system in two variables, Y^s and Y^d, depicted as the intersection of the aggregate demand function and the 45-degree line in Figure 4.9:

$$(4.8) \qquad\qquad a + bY^s + I + G = Y^d$$

---

[8] J.M. Keynes, *The General Theory of Employment, Interest and Money* (London: Macmillan, 1936), p. 96.

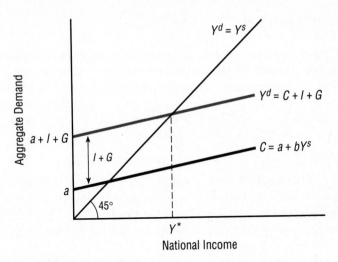

FIGURE 4.9   **Consumption, Demand, and Income**

In the Keynesian cross model, consumption is a simple linear function of income earned (Y^s). Investment and government spending are fixed outside the model. Total aggregate demand is the sum of consumption, investment, and government spending. Equilibrium income occurs where aggregate demand just absorbs total earned income.

(4.9) $Y^s = Y^d$

We then substitute Y^s into the right side of equation (4.8), subtract bY^s from both sides, and divide. We conclude with the *reduced form* result:

(4.10) $$Y\star = \frac{a + I + G}{1 - b}$$

where $Y\star$ signifies the equilibrium value of national income (nominal national income, measured in dollars).

Equation (4.10) presents the solution of the system in its simplest form. It states that the level of income at which income earned and income spent is equal is determined by the four fixed parameters of the system: $'a'$, the part of consumption that is unrelated to income; $'I'$ the amount of investment; $'G'$, the level of expenditure by government; and $'b'$, the marginal propensity to consume.

You can already see how the Keynesian vision overturned the classical world. In the classical world, as you recall, equilibrium and full employment were synonyms. When the labor market "cleared," so that labor supplied and demanded were equal, then full employment necessarily prevailed. Everyone wishing to work at the prevailing wage could find work; anyone not finding work had only their own excessive wage demands to blame.

Taking a Closer Look

SETTING UP A MODEL: SOME RULES AND DEFINITIONS

As we begin to work with models such as the simple Keynesian cross and the classical model presented in the text, we find it useful to set out some definitions and rules for setting up such models. In general, we can distinguish between two kinds of variables and four kinds of equations, all of them represented in the simple model presented. Variables can be either *exogenous* (i.e., given from outside the mathematical system of equations that make up the model) or *endogenous* (i.e., determined within it). In our system, investment (I) and government spending are exogenous; Y^s and Y^d are endogenous.

Equation (4.6) is an *identity*, which expresses a universal and uncontroversial truth: in this case, that total expenditure must equal the sum of its parts. Equation (4.7) is a *structural*, or *behavioral*, equation: it contains a statement about the way the economic system reacts to change. In this case, the equation states that consumption rises as income rises, but not by as much (because $b < 1$).[1]

Equation (4.8) is just a hybrid of the previous two, but equation (4.9) is quite different. We call it an *equilibrium condition*, a statement that is true if the economy as a whole is in equilibrium and false if the economy is out of equilibrium. Equilibrium conditions help us to discover "solutions," in the mathematical sense, to our systems of equations. It is by no means necessary that the economy be in equilibrium at any time. However, if it is not, then we have a situation that cannot be well modeled by the simple linear techniques we are, at the moment, attempting to employ. If we are in equilibrium, then equation (4.10) represents our final distinct equation type: a solution, or *reduced form*, equation, which tells us in terms of the known, fixed parameters of the system, what the equilibrium value of income will be.

---

[1] a and b are *parameters* of the system—fixed constants. One of the main purposes of econometrics is to estimate the value of parameters from real data.

In the Keynesian system this is not at all so. For Keynesians, the equilibrium of supply and demand in the market for output is represented by our Keynesian cross diagram. We have not discussed the relationship between this equilibrium and the classical idea of equilibrium in the labor market, for a simple reason: the two have no connection. More generally, there is *no necessary relationship* between this equilibrium and

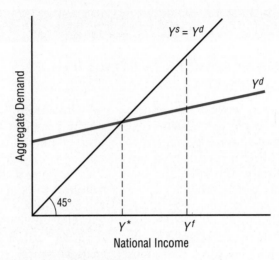

FIGURE 4.10   Equilibrium Output Below Full Employment

If aggregate demand is insufficient, there can be an equilibrium level of national income below that which corresponds to full employment (Y^f).

the level of employment that corresponds to some notion of full employment (Y^f, inserted arbitrarily in Figure 4.10). In fact, equilibrium is possible at low levels of output and with millions of involuntarily unemployed workers. Worse, at such an equilibrium, *no natural forces will intervene to put men and women back to work!*

Keynes advanced these ideas during the worst years of the Great Depression, when unemployment rates were near 25 percent in the United States and in Great Britain, money wages were spiraling downward, and prevailing economic theory held the problem to be that somehow wages were not falling fast enough. In those circumstances, for many people, Keynes's ideas had the force of a revelation.

The Multiplier

Returning to equation (4.10), what happens when we ask how the equilibrium level of national income, Y^*, changes if there is, for example, a small change in investment, I. Using ΔY to indicate the change in income and ΔI to indicate the change in investment, we can measure the effect of a change in investment with the following expression:

$$\Delta Y = \Delta\left(\frac{1}{1-b}\right) \quad \text{or}$$

$$Y'(I) = \frac{1}{(1-b)}$$

This equation states that a small rise in investment (say, one dollar) will produce a rise in equilibrium income of $1/(1-b)$ times as much. Note that $1/(1-b)$ is greater than 1 (since b is less than 1)! $1/(1-b)$ is another fundamental concept of this analysis: *the multiplier,* Q. For example, if the marginal propensity to consume, b, is 0.8, then $Q = (1/1 - 0.8) = (1/0.2) = 5$. In this case, each dollar's worth of investment must produce an increase of five dollars in the equilibrium level of income.

This multiplier will be the same for any change in any autonomous component of income, whether it is a change in 'a', in 'I', or in 'G'. Note too how the multiplier changes as the marginal propensity to consume (*MPC*) rises. As the marginal propensity to consume rises, the multiplier also rises, and the same increase in investment yields larger and larger increases in equilibrium income (and employment).

We can also define a *marginal propensity to save (MPS)*, which is equal to $1 - b$. This captures the proportion of each additional dollar of income that is *not* consumed. Of course, if the MPC is a constant, so will be the *MPS*. Moreover, as the *MPS* gets larger, the multiplier falls. For this reason, we say that savings are a *leakage* from the stream of spending—a higher propensity to save produces a lower equilibrium income. We shall encounter other leakages shortly.

The multiplier is a familiar part of every elementary economics course, and you have no doubt encountered it before. But consider its effect on economic thinking when it was first introduced, embedded in the new apparatus of effective demand, by Keynes's close collaborator Richard Kahn in 1931. Here was a theory that showed that the equilibrium level of output had nothing to do, in any necessary sense, with full employment. It also showed that the equilibrium level of income could be shifted, at any time, by any device that raised consumption, or investment, or government spending. It was, in one word, revolution.

The effects of the multiplier are illustrated graphically in Figure 4.11. Suppose, for example, that we start at an initial equilibrium given by the intersection of the lower aggregate demand function and the 45-degree line, so that equilibrium income is set at $Y^\star$. Now, the government raises its spending level from G to G'. The aggregate demand function shifts up by the amount of the increase in government spending, yielding a new equilibrium level of national income Y^f, (set in this case to the full employment level). As inspection of the diagram and perhaps a little geometry should persuade you, the increase in output

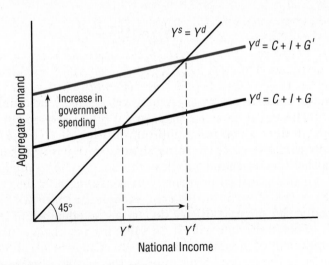

FIGURE 4.11   The Multiplier and Increases in Output

An increase in government spending from G to G' can raise equilibrium income from
Y* to Y^f, curing unemployment. The change in Y is greater than the change in G
because of the multiplier.

from $Y^\star$ to Y^f is greater than the increase in government spending. The
difference, which depends on the slope b of the consumption and aggregate demand functions, is attributable to the multiplier.

For example, suppose that national income is $5 trillion dollars, that
government spending is $1 trillion, and that the marginal propensity to
consume is 0.67. In this case, the multiplier is equal to three. If the
government raises its spending by, say, $50 billion, then total govern-
ment spending rises to $1,050 billion. But the total rise in equilibrium
income will be $150 billion, to a level of $5,150 billion.

A MULTIPLIER WITH TAXES

Our system of equations (4.6) through (4.10) rests on a single behavioral specification, the consumption function. From the facts that
consumption is a function of income ($C = a + bY^s$) and that the marginal
propensity to consume b is less than one, we derive the fact that the
multiplier is greater than one. And from this fact, the great Keynesian
prescription for unemployment, namely to increase government spending, flows naturally.

But how fundamental are these "facts"? What happens when the
model is made more complex, for example with taxes and foreign trade?

Are other specifications possible? And if so, what are the consequences for the multiplier and its policy implications?

Consider, for example, an extension of our first model that takes account of taxation and of transfer spending by the government. Taxes are of course a subtraction from income, while transfer payments (which include Social Security payments, welfare and other public assistance for the poor, and net interest paid on the government debt) are additions to the incomes individuals receive.[9] We may call the total volume of government tax revenue T and the total transfer expenditure TR. We then define disposable income, DY, as:

$$DY = Y^s + TR - T$$

which is to say that consumers actually spend out of the income that is left after paying taxes and receiving transfers.

We will allow transfer expenditures, investment, and government spending to be fixed constants in this simple model. But we need to allow for the fact that taxes vary with income. If we define t as the *average tax rate*, or proportion of income taken in taxes, we can specify that fiscal policy is set by varying t, which is applied to total income, Y^s. We also modify our consumption function, to allow that consumption is now a function not of total income Y^s but of disposable income DY.

We can write our model in three steps. Equation (4.11) is our familiar national income identity. Equation (4.12) is the consumption function, with disposable income rather than total income now the determining independent variable. Equation (4.13) expresses our simple system of taxation, that government revenue equals income earned times the tax rate:

(4.11) $$Y^d = C + I + G$$

(4.12) $$C = a + bDY$$

(4.13) $$T = tY^s$$

From (4.12) and (4.13), with a little rearrangement, it follows that the consumption function can be written in terms of Y^s and some constants, namely a, b, TR, and t:[10]

$$
\begin{aligned}
C &= a + b(Y^s + TR - T) \\
(4.12') \quad &= a + bY^s + bTR - btY^s \\
&= a + bTR + b(1 - t)Y^s
\end{aligned}
$$

---

[9] Recall that we excluded transfer payments from government spending when we presented the national income identity. They make their reappearance here.
[10] b is now the marginal propensity to consume out of disposable income, not total income as in our previous version of the model.

And now, by invoking the equilibrium condition we met in equation (4.9) above—that income earned equals income spent—we can derive a revised form of the multiplier that, unlike our earlier version, takes account of the effects of taxation. We do this first by substituting equilibrium income $Y\star$ for both Y^s and Y^d and by substituting the revised consumption function (4.12') into the national income identity:

(4.14) $Y\star = a + bTR + b(1 - t)Y\star + I + G$

If we now designate the sum of the four constant terms (a, bTR, I, and G) with the letter Z, so that

$$Z = a + bTR + I + G$$

we have, in equilibrium,

(4.14') $Y\star = Z + b(1 - t)Y\star$

From this it follows that equilibrium income is[11]

(4.15) $Y\star = Z\left[\dfrac{1}{1 - b(1 - t)}\right]$

And the multiplier, Q', for any small change in the fixed components of total spending, is the change of equilibrium income with respect to any change in Z:

(4.16) $Q' = Y\star'(Z) = \dfrac{1}{1 - b(1 - t)}$

Notice what happens to the value of Q' when taxation enters the picture. What, for example, happens to the multiplier if b is 0.7 and a tax rate of 0.3 (30 percent of income) is introduced into the system? We multiply $1 - t$, or 0.7, times b, also 0.7, and subtract the product, 0.49, from 1 to arrive at a figure of 0.51 in the denominator. The revised multiplier is now 1/0.51, or a little less than 2.

As the tax rate rises, the multiplier falls! The reason, of course, is that higher taxes depress the marginal propensity to consume. We say that the tax rate also is a leakage: it drains money out of the stream of spending. Try substituting some other values for b and t into equation (4.16) in order to get a feel for this effect. What happens, for example, if the marginal propensity to consume is 0.8 and the tax rate falls to 0.2?[12]

---

[11] To see this, subtract $b(1 - t)Y\star$ from both sides. Factor out $Y\star$ on the left side and divide through by $1 - b(1 - t)$.

[12] Tax rates are by no means the only leakage from the spending stream. Imports are another. We can model imports quite simply, starting from equation (4.6):

$$Y^d = C + I + G + X - M$$

Imports, like consumption, are a function of disposable income. We can define a

Taking a Closer Look

THE BALANCED BUDGET MULTIPLIER

What happens to national income when government policy changes so that spending and tax revenues rise by exactly the same amount? One might think, instinctively, that national income would not change. But the actual situation is quite different, as we shall now see.

Suppose that G is a constant and that the government decides to set the tax rate t so that the budget deficit D $(= G - T)$ is also held constant.

Ignoring transfers and foreign trade, we have the national income identity:

$$Y^d = C + I + G$$

the consumption function:

$$C = a + b(Y^s - T)$$

and a definition of the deficit:

$$D = G - T$$

Substituting our tax identity, we have

$$D = G - tY^s$$

which implies

(4.B1) $tY^s = G - D$

Substituting (4.B1) into the consumption function and the consumption function into the aggregate demand equation and invoking the equilibrium condition as before, we find:

$$Y^\star = a + b(Y^\star - G + D) + I + G$$

If we now subtract $bY^\star$ from both sides, group the two G terms, rearrange, and divide through by $(1 - b)$, we have:

$$Y^\star = \frac{a + bD + I + (1 - b)G}{1 - b}$$

Since a, b, D, and I are all constants, they do not change when government spending increases. It follows that the multiplier for a change in government spending for which the government deficit is held constant is merely:

$$\frac{\Delta Y^\star}{\Delta G} = \frac{1 - b}{1 - b} = 1$$

Thus, a dollar's worth of increased spending, if offset by a dollar in new tax revenues, must raise national income by exactly one dollar. This result is known as the *balanced budget multiplier theorem*.

---

parameter m, called the *propensity to import* out of disposable income DY. Disposable income, as before, is income earned plus government transfer payments minus taxes.

$$M = mDY = m(Y^s + TR - T)$$

As an exercise, you should now derive the multiplier for this system. Review equations (4.11) − (4.16) if you are unsure of how this is done.

THE CONSUMPTION FUNCTION

The Keynesian cross and its extensions capture an essential point put forward by Keynes, namely that national income is determined by the interaction of total spending and total income. Nevertheless, this is only one strand, and a comparatively simple one, in a much larger and richer tapestry. You will notice that it says nothing whatsoever about money or the interest rate or the price level, and indeed we cannot analyze these phenomena at all by looking at the system we have constructed. Shortly we will elaborate on these and other parts of the fabric. First, however, we need to spend some time on the one part of the model we have already constructed, namely the relationship between income and consumption.

As you will have noted, the consumption function of our simple model is specified in terms of a single period of time. We do not allow for spending and saving decisions to be made, as they surely are in real life, over the weeks and months that follow a change in the stream of income. When we do allow for this new element of complexity, we find that under some specifications the original Keynesian conclusions about the multiplier may no longer hold.

We have developed a simple Keynesian theory of consumption in deriving the multiplier. It takes the form of the *absolute income hypothesis (AIH)*, in which consumption C is a linear function of *the current level of disposable income* $(DY = Y + TR - T)$. Thus, as shown in equation (4.20),

$$C = a + b(Y + TR - T)$$

Here a is the autonomous component of consumption spending, b is again the propensity to consume, Y is national income, T is taxes, and TR is transfer payments. The difference $(T - TR)$ is net taxes, and the bracketed term $(Y - T + TR)$ is disposable income.

The consumption function in AIH form served as the underpinning for the forecast that the conclusion of World War II would be followed by a severe recession in the United States, perhaps by permanent stagnation. The assumption behind this prediction was the belief that as the economy went off a wartime footing, there would be a sharp drop in national income, leading to a sharp fall in aggregate demand. But such an economic collapse did not materialize, and the United States did not return to the Great Depression. In fact, real disposable income did fall between 1945 and 1947, but real consumption expenditure continued to rise steadily. Something was wrong with the AIH.

In addition, the research of 1971 Nobel prizewinner Simon Kuznets threw up another puzzle. Kuznets's long time-series of data for the period 1869–1938 led to an estimate of the propensity to consume of 85 percent, obtained by the statistical technique of regressing per capita real con-

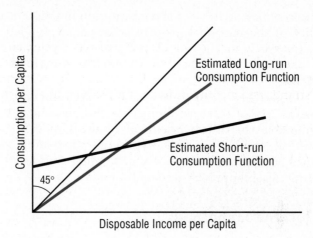

FIGURE 4.12   Different Estimates of the Consumption Function

Aggregate consumption functions over short periods of time seem much flatter, with a lower marginal propensity to consume, than do functions estimated over long periods.

sumption expenditures over time on per capita real income. Kuznets's fitted regression line for this seventy-year period passed through the origin, implying that the average propensity to consume and the marginal propensity to consume were identical and that there was no autonomous component of consumption spending independent of the variations attributable to changes in national income. Thus the parameter a in the AIH specification was estimated to be zero. (See Figure 4.12.)

When Kuznets examined shorter periods, however, (e.g., the years 1929–1944), the estimated consumption function was flatter and did not pass through the origin. This implied that in the short run the *average* propensity to consume, the simple ratio of consumption to income, generally was larger than the *marginal* propensity to consume. Thus, the consumption function intersected the y-axis above the origin, and there was an autonomous component to consumption. In addition, the marginal propensity to consume was lower than its value as estimated using a longer time period. A companion finding for shorter periods was that in periods of prosperity the marginal propensity to consume was comparatively low, whereas in periods of recession the marginal propensity to consume was comparatively high. This variability over the course of the business cycle was not evident in the estimates obtained for the long, seventy-year period. Thus, in several respects, the long-period data for the aggregate economy yielded an aggregate consumption function qualitatively different from the one estimated with shorter time series data.

These considerations—the failure of the expected postwar recession to occur, the inconsistency between the results of longer-run and shorter-run estimates of the consumption function, and the cyclical variability of the marginal propensity to consume—led to the conclusion that the Absolute Income Hypothesis was inadequate.[13] Three new approaches were developed which, for the most part, carry over to the present.

These three are the relative income hypothesis, attributable to James Duesenberry of Harvard University; the permanent income hypothesis, attributable to Milton Friedman of the University of Chicago (now Stanford); and the life cycle hypothesis attributable to Albert Ando and Franco Modigliani (of the Massachusetts Institute of Technology). We consider each approach in detail.

Relative Income Hypothesis

Duesenberry's work is especially interesting, because it involves a critique of orthodox notions of consumer behavior that bears the indirect stamp and influence of one of the most creative of all American economists, Thorstein Veblen (1857–1929).

Duesenberry's discussion began with an attack on two fundamental orthodox assumptions about consumers. First, he rejected the idea that every individual's consumption behavior is based on his or her own maximization decisions and is therefore independent of the behavior of every other individual or household. Second, he rejected the view that consumption relations are rapidly reversible over time.[14]

To replace the orthodox consumer theory, Duesenberry offered five primary reasons why people desire the articles that they purchase: (1) for sheer physical existence, for subsistence or basic comfort; (2) to facilitate participation in the activities of one's culture; (3) to facilitate the acquisition of other goods (e.g., the expense of traveling to work); (4) to attain or maintain social status; and (5) for pleasure.

That these desires lead to consumption decisions based upon learning, custom, and habit enabled Duesenberry to explain why consumption as a fraction of disposable income tends to be low in a boom and high in a bust. Past experience, the history of one's spending, becomes important, and adjustment to new circumstances is only a gradual process. Consumers are characterized as tending to follow their habitual patterns of spending, the patterns to which they have grown accus-

---

[13] Studies of family budget behavior, which compared consumption patterns for households at different levels of income, reinforced this conclusion.

[14] Or that consumption depends on current income independently of an individual or household's past pattern of consumption behavior. For the complete exegesis on Duesenberry's theory, see his book *Income, Saving and the Theory of Consumption Behavior* (Oxford: Oxford University Press, 1967; reprint of the 1952 ed.; orig. ed. 1949).

tomed. They can make mistakes and be surprised, but they will cling to their previous habits for longer than the original AIH hypothesis would suggest.

When real income rises abruptly, individuals will consume more—but not as much more as one might expect from long-run historical relationships. Recent spending habits hold them to comparatively low consumption expenditures. They adjust slowly to their newfound affluence. Similarly, when income falls, consumers adapt very slowly to a lower standard of living. Consumption, then, is not quickly altered in response to changes in income, and the marginal propensity to consume may rise when real income falls, and may fall when real income rises.

While consumers respond only gradually to changed income flows, their responses show a critical asymmetry. They are slower to reduce expenditures from a high level when income falls than to raise expenditures when income rises. There is more of a drag in their expenditure patterns to maintain a higher standard of living than to maintain a lower standard of living.

To capture this effect, Duesenberry argued, not only should real disposable income enter the consumption function but so should *previous peak real disposable income*. Over a short period of time, previous peak real disposable income will be given and can be treated as a constant. It is, in effect, the autonomous component of the shorter-run aggregate consumption function that caused the function not to pass through the origin in Kuznets's regressions. Over longer periods of time, the economy will pass through its cycle and achieve a new peak level of income. This will shift the short run consumption function up; the constant term *a* will then be permanently larger.

Duesenberry's theory thus introduces an irreversibility: once shifted up, the short-run consumption function cannot ever shift downward; the previous peak income will dictate its position. In shorter time periods, the economy will move along that consumption function until a new peak income is achieved; at that time the economy will bounce up to a new, higher short-run consumption function. This one-way series of shifts in the short-run consumption function is known as the *ratchet effect*. A series of short-run consumption functions appears in Figure 4.13.

To obtain a long-run consumption function that passes through the origin, assume the economy is growing at a steady trend rate. This abstraction washes out the short-run cyclical effects. Under steady growth, the previous year's real disposable income is the previous peak real disposable income. This year's real disposable income will be a stable multiple of last year's real disposable income. Algebraically, this means that previous peak income can be eliminated from the consumption function altogether. Under steady (long-run) growth, the aggregate consumption function takes the simple Keynesian form that Kuznets discerned. In Figure 4.14, the contrast between the short-run consumption

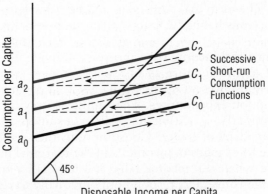

FIGURE 4.13   The Ratchet Effect

Duesenberry's ratchet effect held that the autonomous element (intercept) of the consumption function is determined by the previous peak level of income. In a slump, consumption does not fall with income. Dashes and arrows indicate the movements of C and Y over the cycle.

functions associated with the ratchet effect and the long-run consumption function associated with steady-state growth is displayed.

Duesenberry's ratchet effect could explain the apparent anomaly that immediately after World War II, real consumption expenditure continued to climb although real disposable income fell. From Duesenberry's perspective, the economy had simply "ratcheted" up to a new

FIGURE 4.14   The Ratchet Effect and Long-Run Consumption

If growth is steady over the long run, the ratchet effect is present but never visible.

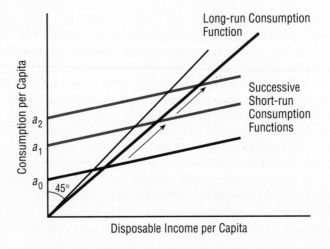

short-run consumption function. The relative income hypothesis offered a reconciliation of all the seemingly conflicting findings about aggregate consumption behavior, and it did so by emphasizing habit, custom, culture, and imitation.[15]

The theories of the consumption function that subsequently have gained the most respect and admiration in the economics profession are those of Friedman and of Ando and Modigliani. Relatively little attention is still drawn to the relative income hypothesis, probably because of its roots in an unorthodox theory of the consumer. But it should be recognized that Duesenberry's theory was successful in explaining the facts of his time and in all likelihood would be effective in explaining more recent phenomena as well.

Permanent Income Hypothesis

Another early and powerful attack on the Keynesian consumption function (or absolute income hypothesis) came from Milton Friedman in 1957. Friedman questioned the basis of the "fundamental psychological law"—Keynes's argument that the marginal propensity to consume was a constant. Why, Friedman asked, would rational men and women behave in so mechanical a way—always spending the same fraction of every additional dollar earned? Doesn't it make a difference how the income is earned? In particular, Friedman argued that people will spend money they expect to earn at a different rate from income that arrives without having been anticipated.

A discussion of Milton Friedman's *permanent income hypothesis* can begin with the observation that consumption and saving decisions are made simultaneously. Because income can be received over the course of a lifetime and because saving is possible, today's consumption need not depend solely upon present income flows. Indeed, since people can anticipate receiving income in the future, today's consumption need not depend exclusively upon today's income or presently available savings.

Friedman argued that current consumption depends on "normal" income, or average income over the course of an individual's anticipated lifetime. Friedman's consumer looks toward tomorrow and plans

---

[15] In the mid-1970s, Duesenberry gave a series of lectures in which he extended the relative income hypothesis to the structure of relative wages in an attempt to explain the puzzle of stagflation, the simultaneous occurrence of rising prices and unemployment. The relative wage hypothesis, of course, had been introduced by Keynes in Chapter 2 of *The General Theory*. In the 1970s, MIT economist Michael Piore toyed for a while with the development of a relative product price hypothesis, also seeking to explain stagflation. To the best of our knowledge no attempt has been made to construct a general macroeconomic model where all "agents" are concerned about how they fare relative to everyone else on all dimensions.

expenditure rationally, basing his or her decisions on beliefs about the course that income will take in the future. This is quite different from Duesenberry's backward-looking consumer, who seeks to maintain a habitual lifestyle. By pushing the analysis in exactly the opposite direction from Duesenberry, Friedman also was able to arrive at a theory of the aggregate consumption function consistent with then-known facts.[16]

Friedman called the individual's normal, or average, income, inclusive of expected future flows, the individual's *permanent income*—hence, the Permanent Income Hypothesis. He hypothesized that rational individuals form an idea of their expected, or permanent, income and base their consumption decisions on that amount. Even if the income rises in some particular year for unexpected reasons (a good year on the stock market, a hit on the state lottery), consumption remains unchanged. Instead of consuming, rational individuals would save the incremental income and add it to their wealth. Only changes in permanent income, Friedman suggested, would lead to changes in consumption.

Friedman's hypothesis can be modeled by dividing income into two components: a permanent part Y^P, which is expected to be present in the future, and a temporary part Y_t^T, which occurs only in time period t, (shown in the subscript). We may then distinguish between the marginal propensity to consume out of permanent income, b, and the marginal propensity to consume out of temporary income, c. The parameter b may well be of the same order as in the traditional Keynesian system, but Friedman's hypothesis holds that c is very small: transient windfalls are saved, not spent. Thus, we have

$$C_t = a + bY^P + cY_t^T$$

In this case, whether a change in some underlying component of income, such as government spending (fiscal policy), yields a large or a small multiplier depends on whether the rise in income is classed as Y^P or

---

[16] See Milton Friedman, *A Theory of the Consumption Function* (Princeton, N.J.: National Bureau of Economic Research, 1957).

[17] Formally, the size of the multiplier for a change in G (or any autonomous component of spending) will depend on what proportion of the change is perceived to be permanent and what proportion is perceived to be temporary. If we let w be the proportion that is permanent and $1 - w$ the proportion that is temporary, then we can derive a multiplier $\mathbf{Q}'''$ for this system.

$$Y_t = a + bY^P + cY_t^T + I + G$$

$$Y_t - bwY_t - c(1 - w)Y_t = a + I + G = Z$$

$$Y\star = \frac{Z}{1 - bw - c(1 - w)}$$

$$Q''' = \frac{\Delta Y\star}{\Delta Z} = \frac{1}{1 - bw - c(1 - w)}$$

which varies between $1/(1 - b)$ and $1/(1 - c)$ as w varies between zero and one.

as Y_t^T.[17] If the change is permanent, then it will induce an increase in consumption of b times the initial increase in income, with multiplier effects of $1/(1 - b)$, as before. But if the change is perceived to be temporary, then the multiplier will be $1/(1 - c)$, which is close to a value of 1, since c is close to a value of zero. Thus, a shock to transitory income raises total income, but there is no secondary, or multiplier, effect.

Friedman's permanent income hypothesis also is readily reconcilable with consumption functions estimated from shorter time series data. Recall the important finding that consumption as a fraction of disposable income was high during a recession and low during an expansion. Duesenberry's explanation was that people were slow to alter previous spending patterns. Friedman sought to explain the same finding by resorting to a distinction between *permanent* and *transitory* income.

In a recession, there will be a general decline in incomes, but it is a temporary fall—so that incomes are abnormally or transitorily low. The permanent income hypothesis says that expected normal incomes determine consumption behavior, so consumption as a percentage of current measured disposable income will tend to be comparatively high in a recession. A parallel argument applies to the marginal propensity to consume being comparatively low in a boom period, when incomes are abnormally or transitorily high.

Friedman's approach presents a difficult conceptual problem. How does an individual know where to peg his or her permanent income? Similarly, what is the permanent income level for the economy as a whole? Friedman's answer was clever insofar as it permitted him to construct a measure of permanent income from available data. He assumed that expected future incomes could be forecast from the history of past income, essentially by averaging past incomes to arrive at permanent income in the present.

The paradox of Friedman's theory lies in the fact that the forward-looking consumers have to look backward to determine their permanent income. Their expectations of normal income are formed adaptively, based upon actual incomes received.[18] Can the rationality of consumer choice between consumption and saving that underlies the permanent income hypothesis be sustained once we take into account the uncertainty that envelops our knowledge of our future income stream?

When Friedman won the Nobel Memorial Prize in economic science in 1976, the citation specifically included the permanent income hypothesis among his major contributions. In 1977, President Jimmy Carter proposed a one-time $50 tax rebate to stimulate economic growth. Opponents invoked Friedman's hypothesis to argue that such an explicitly transient boost to income would fail to stimulate additional

---

[18] Friedman later made use of adaptive expectations in his analysis of the formation of expectations of inflation, a key part of his attack on the Keynesian Phillips curve.

consumption. This argument helped fuel the controversy that forced the president to drop the proposal. It was heard again much more recently, as Congress and President Bush argued over whether to enact a temporary "middle-class tax cut" to help end the recession of 1990–92. Those in favor cited the multiplier effects; those opposed argued, with Friedman, that such a tax cut would not boost permanent income and so would not deliver the hoped-for results.

We encounter Professor Friedman again in Chapter 7, as the progenitor of the monetarist rebellion against Keynesian economics. The permanent income hypothesis represented a first skirmish in that rebellion. By casting doubt on the multiplier, it presaged the much more comprehensive assault on interventionist government policies that the monetarists and then their successors, the new classical economists, would launch over the 1960s and 1970s.

The Life-Cycle Consumption Model

For Keynes, consumption was a stable function of income. For Friedman, consumption was a stable function of expected or permanent income. Yet another view holds that people plan their consumption patterns over their whole lifetime and consume not just out of income but out of accumulated past income, or wealth. Thus, consumption is a variable fraction of income, depending on age and past accumulation.

In some respects, Ando and Modigliani push the rational choice argument even further than Friedman. They characterize consumers as planning an optimal lifetime pattern of consumption based upon their expectations of earnings or receipt of income of all types over an expected lifetime horizon. People seek to smooth their consumption stream relative to what usually would be a less even flow of income.[19]

Consider a representative individual over the course of the life cycle. During the schooling years, consumption is out of expected future earnings, financed by borrowing. During the work years, consumption is out of current labor income and expected future earnings. Simultaneously, debts are being paid and saving is likely to be occurring for retirement, leading to the accumulation of wealth. During retirement, consumption is out of wealth in the form of dissaving. In the aggregate, the relative importance of expenditure out of current earnings, expected

[19] See especially Albert Ando and Franco Modigliani, "The Life Cycle Hypothesis of Saving," *American Economic Review*, Vol. 53, March 1963, pp. 55–84; Franco Modigliani and R. E. Brumberg, "Utility Analysis and the Consumption Function: An Interpretation of the Cross-section Data," in *Post Keynesian Economics*, ed. K. K. Kurihara (New Brunswick, N.J.: Princeton University Press, 1954).

future earnings, and wealth would depend upon the age composition of the population as well as the nature of the income distribution.

To formalize these ideas, suppose that: L is the expected lifetime of a consumer, N is her total working life, and T is her age. $AY = CL/N$ is her income averaged over her entire life, which is equal to her average annual consumption. W is her stock of accumulated wealth, saved out of past income. We then have, Modigliani hypothesized, a consumption function of the following form:

$$C_t = aW + cAY$$

where

- $a = 1/(L - T)$ is the reciprocal of the number of years left to live. Thus, if expected lifetime is seventy-five years and an individual is fifty years old, a takes on the value of $1/25$, or 0.04.
- $c = (N - T)/(L - T)$ is the ratio of our worker's remaining working years to her years left to live, so long as she has not yet retired. Thus, if our worker expects to retire at sixty-five, c takes on the value of $15/25$, or 0.6. For a worker who has retired, c is set equal to zero.

According to the first part of this specification, a worker consumes an increasing fraction of her wealth each year as she ages, exhausting all of it before death (there are no bequests). According to the second part, she consumes out of her expected lifetime income, each year, a fraction that decreases as she ages and approaches retirement. This scheme is illustrated in Figure 4.15, which shows the relationship between income and consumption at different stages of life. (Wealth, of course, appears on this graph as the area of accumulated savings.)[20]

[20] There is no straightforward route from this approach to Kuznets's long-run consumption function. Even if steady growth is assumed, the presence of the wealth effect means that there is a component of consumption expenditure that is not dependent upon variations in income. Ando and Modigliani would have to assume that the wealth effect washes out over long periods to derive the Kuznets long time series consumption function, and there is no clear reason why one should make such an assumption.

Like Friedman's hypothesis, the forward-looking life-cycle hypothesis requires a measure of expected future income. Initially, the Ando-Modigliani strategy was somewhat similar to Friedman's; they assumed that expected labor income bore a direct and fixed proportional relationship to current labor income. But this strategy missed business cycle effects altogether. As Ando and Modigliani pointed out, in recessions expected future incomes ought to be high relative to the current level, so that expected future labor income would *not* stand in fixed proportion to current income. To overcome this problem, they weighted current labor income by the ratio of the total labor force to total employment and so raised their measure of expected future labor income. The theoretical motivation for such an adjustment is not altogether clear, but *ad hoc* or not it had the desired effect of reconciling their theory with the facts.

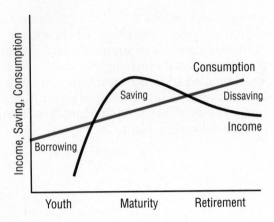

FIGURE 4.15   The Life-Cycle Model

The life-cycle model of consumption behavior assumes that people save in their middle years for their old age. Thus, wealth and age enter as independent forces in the consumption function.

The life-cycle model has interesting practical implications. For example, a windfall increase in income adds to wealth but not much to annual average income. This increase is consumed at an annual rate given by $1/(L - T)$ per year, which for the population as a whole is a small fraction. For example, if the average age of the population is thirty-five and the average life expectancy is seventy-five, then a is on the order of 1/40, or 2.5 percent. Thus, the multiplier for any given year of a windfall will be slight, on the order of $1/(1 - .025)$, or just a little more than one.

In the immediate wake of the stock market crash of October 19, 1987, the life-cycle model was used to make a rough estimate of the effect of the vast losses of paper wealth on gross national product (GNP) in 1988. The crash caused an estimated one to two trillion dollars in losses. Applying the $1/(L - T)$ formula above (for the "average" person) suggested that the lost GNP as a result would be much smaller—on the order of twenty-five to fifty billion dollars. This was only about 0.6 to 1.2 percent of then-existing GNP. So, using the model, analysts predicted correctly that the stock market crash of late 1987 would not lead to a recession in 1988.[21]

Philosophically, the relative income hypothesis is far removed from the permanent income and life-cycle hypotheses. The former grew out of a critique of the conventional theory of choice, whereas the latter two

[21] At a public meeting within a few days after the stock market crash, one of the authors heard such a prediction based exactly on the logic outlined above. Aggressive actions by the authorities to lower interest rates also helped prevent the crash from producing a recession. Such actions were not taken in the wake of the Great Crash of 1929.

approaches were intended to pursue the implications of the conventional theory of choice to its limits. All three approaches can be mobilized to explain the "facts" as they were known at the time the three theories were introduced in the 1950s.

However, in the case of the latter two approaches, all household saving is for future consumption, even if it is for the future consumption of one's offspring via bequests. But this does not explain why people seek to amass enormous fortunes. Some people who succeed clearly have accumulated more wealth than can reasonably or even unreasonably be consumed as goods and services by themselves or their children. Lester Thurow has suggested that the desire for power and status is predominant in such activities, particularly among paper entrepreneurs on Wall Street.[22] Such motivations fit more comfortably in the relative income hypothesis than in either of the other two approaches and leave us with a conclusion that we will encounter again: the relative success of competing hypotheses in economics may depend as much on how well they can be reconciled with prevailing theory as on how well they explain the prevailing facts.

[22] Lester Thurow, "Popular Mechanics: The Redistribution of Wealth," *Working Papers for a New Society,* 3 (Winter 1976) pp. 23–27, 69–77.

SPECIAL SECTION

Growth Theory and the Management of Growth

The multiplier framework lets us look at the interplay of aggregate supply and aggregate demand in the determination of the level of output. But it has the severe limitation of *static analysis*. In the multiplier model, we are concerned with the equilibrium relationship of the level of national income and production. To isolate that relationship, we first assume that almost everything else is fixed. Specifi-cally, we assume a fixed stock of capital and state of technique, fixed conditions for the supply of labor, and a fixed state of expectation about profits (or marginal efficiency of capital).

Having made these assumptions, we can experiment (as we have done in the preceding pages) with two basic analytical techniques. First, we can explore the consequence of particular underlying assumptions, which affect the slope or position of our aggregate demand functions. For example, we can ask what will happen if the marginal propensity to consume is zero, or one, or some value in between. Second, we can compare the equilibria that will be achieved under different assumptions. For example, we can ask how reducing the fiscal deficit will affect the equilibrium values of the interest rate and national income. This exercise of comparing two different static equilibria is known as the method of *comparative statics*.

What the multiplier apparatus cannot do, as it stands, is help to predict the evolution of the economy over time. It does not tell us whether, left to itself, our economy is likely to grow or to stagnate or perhaps to fluctuate in a regular or irregular cycle. It thus leaves unanswered one of the most important sets of questions that necessarily concern macroeconomists.

It is easy to understand why the multiplier analysis ignores the growth process. In the Depression, when Keynes and his followers made their assault on the citadel of classical economics, the great problem was unemployment. Millions were out of work despite their demonstrated willingness to cut wages—a situation that classical economics could not explain. The theory of effective demand, which is captured in great part by this alternative model, provided an explanation. But it was an explanation of the low level of output and employment and of how to correct that low level—not an explanation of the development of a healthy economy over time.

World War II ended the Depression and brought to the fore a new set of economic questions. As economists came to feel that economies were moving toward the limits of their production possibilities, the behavior of production possibility frontiers themselves—of the way in which the maximum capabilities of an economy develop—became a critical question.

Growth theory is an effort to move beyond static general equilibrium to a formal theory of the laws of motion of the system. The approach taken—initially by Sir Roy Harrod at Oxford in 1939 and by Evsey Domar at MIT in 1946—was to move toward a macroeconomics based on the mathematics of systems of differential equations. We shall set out below the simplest of these systems, a combination of Harrod's and Domar's ideas offered by Robert Solow.[1] We can call their method *pseudo-dynamics* because, although the model traces out a path over time, the entire evolution of the path is determined at the outset by the structural equations and the starting values, or *initial conditions*.

To develop a growth model, we start by specifying the production possibility frontier, as it may appear at any single moment of time. A very simple way to do this (ignoring many problems) is to stipulate that total output (in physical units) is a function of the quantities of two inputs, or *factors of production*, which we will call labor or employment, N, and capital, K:

$$y = y\,(K,\,N)$$

$$y'\,(N) > 0$$

$$y'\,(K) > 0$$

We will allow that adding more of either factor, holding the other constant, adds to output but at a diminishing rate. There may be *substitutability* between factors, but a law of diminishing marginal productivity holds. Thus, the production function, which expresses the possible combinations of K and N that can yield a given level of output y, has the characteristic shape shown in Figure 4.1. This should be familiar to all students from an introductory course in microeconomics, and we will not deal with it in greater depth here. Instead, we turn to the question, how does this system grow?

Let us start with some definitions. The proportionate rate of growth of the labor supply, we will call $\dot{N}$ (pronounced "N-dot"). We will call the rate of savings, defined as a proportion of income, σ. $\sigma y = I$ is the volume of physical investment and therefore the increase in a given time period of the capital stock, so that $I/K = \dot{K}$. The ratio of the capital stock to output, we will call $K/y = \phi$.

To understand the growth of our system, we need to know how an increase in population, yielding more workers, interacts with the propensity to save, yielding more capital, so as to produce a larger amount of output. Growth theorists have been particularly interested in *steady-state,* or *balanced, growth*, the theoretical condition that is analogous to the comparative-static concept of equilibrium. Balanced growth is said to occur when, and only when, all three of our basic variables—capital, labor, and output—are growing at the same proportional rates: $\dot{y} = \dot{K} = \dot{N}$. Balanced growth is interesting for a simple reason: it is the only kind of growth that, by its nature, can last for a long time. If growth is unbalanced, the underlying structure of the economy must be changing, and so the conditions for growth itself will change as time passes. This situation is interesting and much more realistic as a description of how the economy actually behaves, but it is also much more difficult to analyze than balanced growth.

The basic approach to the problem of balanced growth, known loosely as the *Harrod-Domar model*, approaches this issue with the following basic assumptions:

1. Population and labor force growth are exogenous and proceed at a constant proportional rate; $\dot{N}$ is therefore a fixed constant.
2. Net saving σy is a fixed fraction of income; σ is also a fixed constant.
3. Technology is described by two parameters, both constant:

    a. Labor per unit of output: N/y
    b. Capital per unit of output (as above): $K/y = \phi$

In this simple version, there is no technical change; for the moment, we rule out substitution between K and N (coefficients of production are, for purposes of simplicity only, assumed to be fixed).

What then is the condition of steady growth? We can derive it by making the following substitutions into the equation above.

$$\dot{K} = \sigma \frac{y}{K} = \frac{\sigma}{\phi}$$

$$\dot{N} = \dot{K}$$

The answer is that steady growth can only occur when the following holds true: $\sigma/\phi = \dot{N}$ and $\sigma = \phi\dot{N}$.

We have seen that σ is the rate of saving out of income. ϕN is the product of the ratio of capital to output ϕ and the rate of growth of the labor force $\dot{N}$. ϕN is therefore the proportion of investment in output "just necessary to keep the stock of capital growing at the same rate as the supply of labor."[2] To put it another way, the ratio of savings to capital, $\sigma y/K = \sigma/\phi$, gives us the actual rate of growth of the capital stock. The expression $\dot{N}$ is known as the *natural rate of growth* of the economy. Only if these are equal, if $\sigma/\phi = \dot{N}$, will steady growth of output prevail.

If savings σ are greater than $\phi\dot{N}$, then the economy will experience too much investment. Capital will accumulate more rapidly than the labor force can use it, and there will be increasing overcapacity and labor shortage. As workers are used more intensively than they would ideally like, output will rise more rapidly, at least for a time, than it would on the steady path. But the excess output will be fun-

neled into excess capital investment, and the living standards of the workers will be lower than on the steady path, both because the workers are working too hard and because the excess investment deprives them of the consumption goods that might otherwise become the fruits of their labor. (One might think of the model of forced industrialization of the Soviet Union under Stalin as a case of chronically excessive capital investment.)

If, on the other hand, savings σ are less than $\phi\dot{N}$, investment will not be adequate to keep up with the increasing number of workers. This must lead to unemployment and, again, a failure to produce the consumer goods that might otherwise be made available. Worse still, unemployment and deficient demand will lead to failure of the incentive to save and invest, and the unemployment will be chronic. Here again the economy cannot remain on a stable path and cannot sustain the long-term rise in consumption and well-being that would characterize that path.

Remarkably, σ, ϕ, and $\dot{N}$ are all independently determined quantities: σ is a behavioral parameter; ϕ is a fact of technology, and $\dot{N}$ is largely determined by births fifteen to twenty years earlier. We have no reason so far to expect that they will bear any particular relationship to each other. Moreover, we have given no reason at all why the economy would adjust to make the balance equation $\dot{y} = \dot{K} = \dot{N}$ true if it happens, at some given time, to be false.

This is the Harrod-Domar knife-edge problem: the fundamental conditions for balanced growth to occur will only be met by the sheerest accident, if they are met at all! (See Figure 4.S1.)

Thus, as stated by Harrod and Domar (in quite separate ways at the outset), theory provided no essential reason why an economy moving through time in accordance with certain laws of motion should remain on a stable growth path. Harrod, and to a lesser extent Domar, felt that knife-edge phenomena were characteristic of Keynesian economies viewed dynamically. They were, in fact, the dynamic equivalent of static underemployment equilibrium. Harrod was thus a "gloomy Keynesian," who argued that in the postwar period, the advanced economies would likely return to chronic instability unless ways could be found to overcome the knife-edge problem.

As did the representation of Keynesian economics in general, growth theory changed when it crossed the Atlantic. Most U.S. economists did not share Harrod's stagnationist view. And, as time passed, the "stylized facts" of successful postwar development seemed to confirm that steady state was not only possible but actually the normal condition of advanced industrial economies. For these economists, the question became how to account for the historical experience of steady state.

There are three possible ways to address this issue. First, one can dispute that steady-state, balanced growth actually occurred in the period from about 1946 to 1970.

FIGURE 4.S1   Instability of the Growth Path

If savings, technology, and labor force growth are not exactly in balance, the Harrod-Domar model produces cumulative instability in income over time. The graph is drawn on a log scale, so the straight line represents growth at a steady rate.

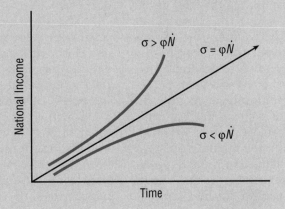

Although that point can be argued both ways, it does seem clear that, steady or not, growth was steadier than it had been before.

Second, one can argue that growth was steady but that Keynesian policies made it so by adjusting either σ or ϕ to bring a rough equality of σ and ϕN into being. Since Keynesian policy influences income and income determines saving, the savings rate σ is the variable under policy control. So the argument might be that government policies raised the rate of savings/investment over what would otherwise have occurred, perhaps by stabilizing the climate of profit expectations with monetary and fiscal policies. This then could account for the more stable growth performance of the postwar years.

The actual course taken by growth theory was something else again. It tried to explain the satisfaction of $\sigma = \phi N$ in terms of market mechanisms, which might automatically bring about an adjustment of one of the three variables so that the equation would be satisfied. There were three possibilities, corresponding to the three terms σ, ϕ, and N.

First, there could be adjustment of population growth N. Classical economics had long previously considered this grim possibility; unemployment could be taken care of by famine and mass migration. Still, it did not seem entirely sensible (or humane!) to rely on this mechanism in modern economies where the welfare state tended to guarantee at least a minimal living standard for most people.

Adjustment of the savings rate was the second possibility. If one allows for different groups in the economy with different propensities to save, then this could occur with large shifts in the distribution of income between the groups. Suppose, for instance, that there were two large social groupings, capitalists (who earn profits) and workers (who earn wages). Suppose that savings out of profits were higher than savings out of wages (because capitalists are richer than workers). Then, if the savings ratio were too high, the accumulation of excess capital would lead to a shortage of labor, a redistribution of income in favor of workers, and a fall of total savings toward the balanced level. Conversely, a shortfall of savings would lead to capital shortage, rising profits, and rising savings. The Cambridge economist Nicholas Kaldor suggested this mechanism as a possible solution to the steady-state growth problem. But it too did not meet broad acceptance on the U.S. side of the Atlantic.

The third possibility was adjustment of the capital-output ratio ϕ. This could happen, it was argued, in response to a change in the relative prices of capital and labor. An excess of savings would lead to a fall in the price of capital equipment (rate of interest), which would induce employers to use more capital per worker. ϕ would rise, bring ϕN into line with σ, at which point the excess of savings would disappear. Once again, the system would tend toward equilibrium around the Harrod-Domar stability condition.

This third possibility, the favored view of neoclassical economists and American Keynesians (including Robert Solow), engendered massive controversies in the 1950s and 1960s. Known as the "capital controversies" or the "Cambridge controversies," these arguments stemmed from the observation, mainly by Joan Robinson at Cambridge, England that it was not true in principle that a fall in the rate of interest would lead in general to a smoothly increasing capital intensity of production. (And, if it did not, then ϕ would not rise to bring ϕN into balance with σ, to ensure steady growth.) Indeed, the debate over the plausibility of such an adjustment mechanism became a key issue in an argument over whether capitalist economies were self-regulating over the long run.

For a time, growth theory seemed to be one of the most promising fields of economic research. But, in the early 1970s, it was overtaken by events. In an economic climate of extreme instability characterized by episodic inflation, oil price shocks, and periodic recessions and high unemployment, pursuing the development of theories that sought to explain the persistence of steady growth began to seem beside the point. Growth theory lost its reason for being— and has yet to fully recover it.[3]

---

[1] This entire presentation draws heavily on Robert Solow, *Growth Theory: An Exposition* (Oxford: Oxford University Press, 1969).
[2] Solow, *Growth Theory*, p. 9.
[3] But stay tuned. Recent promising developments in the theory of *nonlinear dynamics* may have application to the problem of economic growth. The essence of this theory is that economies tend to cycle in a fully determined but irregular way around the steady-state paths.

SUMMARY

A mathematical model of the Classical macromodel comprises three parts. Each determines macroeconomic variables independently of the other two. Output, real wages, and employment are determined in the first part by the labor market and an aggregate production function. The interest rate is determined in a separate market. Finally, the price level is determined by the level of real national output, the level of the money supply, and the income velocity of circulation. The "classical dichotomy" is present here. The real performance of the economy with respect to output and employment is determined separately from monetary influences.

Involuntary unemployment is impossible in the classical system. Unemployment or joblessness is mainly for these whose wage expectations are too high. Otherwise, unemployment could be attributed to labor market imperfections, but this must be a comparatively minor and transient problem.

The simple Keynesian model, called the "Keynesian cross," explains the determination of a subset of the macroeconomic variables of the classical system. The analysis in this model revolves around an equilibrium condition: that aggregate supply must come to equal aggregate demand. Aggregate demand in the more sophisticated version of the Keynesian cross consists of consumption, investment, government spending, and net exports. Aggregate supply is simply national income.

Special emphasis is placed on the consumption function. In the simplest case, consumption consisted of an autonomous part and a part that depended on disposable income. The variable portion of consumption was a constant proportion of disposable income, a relationship based upon an observation made by Keynes, which he termed a *fundamental psychological law*. More sophisticated versions of the consumption function were presented in particular detail. These were the relative income hypothesis of James Duesenberry, the permanent income hypothesis of Milton Friedman, and the "life-cycle consumption model" of Albert Ando and Franco Modigliani.

A major difference between the classical model and the Keynesian cross model is that involuntary unemployment is possible in the simple Keynesian model. A second difference is that the simple Keynesian model offers the possibility for government intervention to remedy the problem of unemployment. The multiplier is an indicator of the power of the government's hand in this regard.

Review Questions

1. The general observation of students over summer vacation is that the third month of vacation does not seem to be as enjoyable as the first month of vacation. Explain why this observation is or is not consistent with a downward-sloping labor supply curve.

2. Derive a multiplier for the Keynesian cross model when a constant proportion of income is spent on imports.

3. Discuss the effects Duesenberry's relative income hypothesis, Friedman's permanent income hypothesis, and Ando and Modigliani's life-cycle consumption model have on the multiplier of the Keynesian cross model.

4. What will be the effect on current consumption of a rise in the rate of interest that can be earned on savings under Duesenbery's relative income hypothesis, Friedman's permanent income hypothesis, and Ando and Modigliani's life-cycle hypothesis?

5. The consumption function is argued to have an autonomous part because even a person who has no income will still spend some money. Explain why this makes sense in the aggregate economy, especially with respect to an aggregate autonomous component to consumption.

6. Savings and investment and government spending and taxes are in no way guaranteed to be equal in the Keynesian cross model. Describe how the difference between savings and investment is related to the difference between government spending and investment and between government spending and taxes. What will be the balancing effects if the imbalances are not permanent?

7. Is market clearing in the capital market and labor market in the classical model completely consistent with the full employment equilibrium in the Keynesian cross model?

8. Is neutral money relevant to the classical model, the simple Keynesian model, neither, or both? Explain.

Review Problems

1. Put together your own set of equations within a Keynesian cross framework, using the following information. Autonomous domestic consumption spending is $2,000. The marginal propensity to consume domestic goods is 70 percent. The marginal propensity to consume foreign goods is 10 percent. There is no autonomous component to expenditures on foreign goods. Foreign consumers spend $500 on the goods domestically produced. The government spends $2,000, of which $1,000 is spent directly and $1,000 is given to consumers to do with as they please. Investment is a constant $3,000. What is the equilibrium income in this economy? What effect does increased spending on foreign goods have on national income? What is the savings rate? Is this equal to one minus the marginal propensity to consume? Now, double foreign consumption of domestic goods to $1,000, calculate the new equilibrium income, and determine a multiplier for this economy.

2. The following equations describe the important features of an economy according to an economist who adheres to the Keynesian cross model:

Consumption: $C = 1,000 + .8y^s$
Investment: $I = 200$
Government: $G = 400$
Equilibrium: $Y^s = Y^d$

What is the equilibrium income in this economy? Does investment spending equal savings? Comment on why this is possible. Suppose the full employment level of output is $9,000. By how much should government spending increase to reach this level of output?

Now, suppose that a 5 percent tax on all income is levied to cover the amount of government spending. Will this be successful in covering the deficit? (Use the original level of government spending.) Explain why the deficit was *not* covered. With the 5 percent tax, calculate a new multiplier and determine the level of government expenditures for full employment.

3. The classical labor demand function is based on rational hiring decisions by employers. Use the following data to construct a labor demand curve.

Number of Workers	Output	Marginal Output	Marginal Output per Worker
5	1,000		
10	1,500		
15	1,900		
20	2,200		
25	2,400		
30	2,500		

You also know the labor supply in this fictitious economy:

Number of Workers	Wage
5	10
10	20
15	35
20	60
25	100
30	150

Now plot the labor supply and the labor demand on a single graph to determine the equilibrium employment in the economy. There are a total of thirty people in this macroeconomy. What is the rate of involuntary unemployment? Defend your answer, remembering that you are in a classical economy.

4. Put together a graph similar to Figure 4–14 with the following short-term consumption functions:

At income of 5,000 $c = 3,000 + .1y$
At income of 6,000 $c = 3,500 + .1y$
At income of 7,000 $c = 4,100 + .1y$
At income of 8,000 $c = 4,800 + .1y$

What shape does the long-run consumption curve have? How well does this set of short-run consumption curves and the associated long-run consumption curve correlate with Keynes's observation about consumption? With Kuznets's empirical study? Duesenberry's consumption function? Friedman's consumption function? Ando and Modigliani's consumption function?

5. By drawing figures like Figures 4.4, 4.5, and 4.6 and shifting curves as necessary, demonstrate the effects of the following on income, employment, prices, and the interest rate:

a. an improvement in productivity
b. an increase in the money supply
c. a minimum wage below the equilibrium wage
d. a minimum wage above the equilibrium wage
e. price controls that impose a ceiling on the price level in general
f. an interest rate ceiling set below the equilibrium interest rate

In all cases, think carefully about whether repercussions will occur in other markets, especially when a disequilibrium situation is being imposed.

6. In each of the cases below, compare the simple Keynesian cross model (constant marginal propensity to consume, no imports, no exports, exogeneous government spending, exogenous investment spending, and no taxes) with a model where a small adjustment has been made by drawing two aggregate demand curves on a single Keynesian cross diagram. In each case, comment on how equilibrium income is affected. In particular, comment on how the intensity of the effect affects equilibrium income.

a. Imports are included as an autonomous quantity.
b. Imports are included as a constant proportion of income.
c. Investment, instead of being exogenous, is made to be a constant proportion of income.
d. A lump-sum tax is imposed.
e. A fixed proportion tax is imposed.

Suggested Readings

James, Duesenberry, *Income Saving and the Theory of Consumption Behavior* (Oxford: Oxford University Press, 1967).

Milton Friedman, *A Theory of the Consumption Function* (Princeton: NBER, 1957).

Robert Solow, *Growth Theory: An Exposition* (Oxford University Press, 1969).

Appendix

NATIONAL ACCOUNTS

National income and product accounts[1] provide us with measures of performance for the economy as a whole. As the name suggests, there is duality in these measures. On the one hand, they capture the types of *income*—wages, profits, and rent—that are received by the different participants in economic activity. On the other hand, they measure the value of *production* that is generated in the pursuit of those incomes. That the two measures, of national income and of the value of national product, must be equal is a fundamental accounting truism on which the whole system of measurement is based.

Gross national income = gross national product

[1] Pioneering work on national accounts was undertaken in the 1930s by two economists, Sir Richard Stone at Cambridge in England and Simon Kuznets at Harvard in the United States. Both Stone and Kuznets later received the Nobel prize in economics for their work.

Gross National Product

Consider first the most well-known national account, the *gross national product (GNP)*. The GNP is a measure of the *value* of the *flow* of *final* goods and services produced during a given period of time. Each of the qualifying words—*value*, flow, and final—bears emphasizing.

The fact that GNP is a measure of *value* tells us that it is measured in monetary units. To measure value, we use market price. Activities that are not valued in the market (e.g., cooking, cleaning, and other labor in the household) may have value in the ordinary sense of the term but are not part of GNP. Activities that hurt human welfare, such as pollution or cigarette smoking, may have a net negative value but, because they have no market price, are not subtracted from GNP.[2]

The fact that GNP is a measure of *flow* tells us that only *currently produced* goods and services can be counted. The sale and resale of old automobiles adds nothing to GNP, except for the value of services rendered by the used car dealers. The appreciation in value of a house built fifty years ago does not add to GNP, even if that house is sold this year. GNP this year is concerned only with production, and with services rendered, this year.

Finally, the fact that GNP measures a flow of *final* goods and services tells us that inventories and other *intermediate* goods do not count. Any good produced for the sole purpose of contributing to the production of some other good will disappear from the stream of production when that other good is produced. To count it in GNP and then to count again the final good into which it disappears would mean counting double. Thus, in the final analysis, the production of crude oil does not count in GNP: only the production of gasoline and other refined petroleum products is counted. The significant exception to this rule consists of goods that make a sustained contribution to the production of other goods. These *investment goods*, or *capital goods*, are counted in GNP; indeed, they form one of the major categories of current production.

GNP has both a product and an expenditure interpretation. The *product* interpretation defines GNP as the sum of the value of all types of goods and services produced in the economy. Broadly speaking, goods can be produced for four purposes: for consumption, for investment, for the government, and for export. To make sure we are measuring domestic production, we subtract the value of domestic consumption that is actually produced elsewhere, which is to say the value of imports. In symbols, GNP can be written:

---

[2] One significant exception bears noting. Owner-occupied housing does not generate regular market transactions, but national income accountants do estimate an "imputed rent," which represents an estimate of the value of housing services "purchased" (from themselves) by people who own their own houses. This measure is included in GNP.

(4.A1) $GNP = C + I + G + (X - M)$

C represents the value of current consumption, I the value of current investment, G the value of government-produced goods and services, X exports, and M imports. The difference between exports and imports, $X - M$, is *net exports*.

If this definition is used to measure GNP for the United States, all the goods would be valued in U.S. dollars; if it is used to measure GNP for Chile, all the goods would be valued in pesos. To compare GNP measures across countries in a given year, we would have to convert all to a measure in a common currency. Typically this is accomplished by converting one currency into another, using the *exchange rate* between the two. So, to know how the U.S.'s and Chile's respective GNPs compare, the dollar-peso exchange rate would be used to change U.S. GNP into a peso measure or to change Chilean GNP into a dollar measure.

Analysts commonly want to determine how GNP has changed for a single country over time. In particular, they may be interested in estimating the country's rate of growth from one period to another. In this case, the unit of measure, the currency unit, is unchanged. But the value of the currency may be different in the two periods, and for this reason a different kind of adjustment may be required.

Recall that GNP calculations for a particular year are made on the basis of the current market prices of goods and services—that is, the prices that pertain in the year being measured. If, however, there is a general inflation between one period and another, a general rise in most or all prices in the economy, then the measure of money GNP will increase, even though there may have been no change in the actual volume of goods and services. Since we are often interested in the actual physical volume of production, and not so much in its money measure, we need to take the effects of inflationary (or deflationary) price changes out of our measure of GNP.

To meet this need, a distinction is made between *nominal* and *real* GNP. Nominal GNP is measured in *current dollars*—in the market prices of each year's output, whatever those prices may be. No adjustment is made for inflation. Real GNP is measured in *constant dollars*—in dollars adjusted so that they have the same purchasing power in both years being compared. A measure of real GNP is *deflated*, or divided by a measure of the price level, to adjust for the effects of a general rise in prices. The price index that the U.S. Department of Commerce uses to convert nominal GNP measures into real GNP measures is known as the *GNP deflator*.

The difference between the two measures of nominal and real GNP has palpable consequences for conclusions about the performance of an economy. For example, the Department of Commerce's estimate for nominal GNP (GNP in current dollars) for the U.S. economy in 1950 was $288.3 billion and for 1991 was $5,694.9 billion. These figures imply an astronomical thirty-year growth of 1,877 percent, or nearly twentyfold! In contrast, the Department of Commerce's estimate of real GNP (GNP in constant dollars) for 1950 was $1,416.2 billion (dollars of 1987 purchasing power); for 1991, their estimate was $4,842.8 billion. Thirty-year growth would have been 241 percent, a considerably more modest figure than that implied by the GNP numbers unadjusted for the effects of inflation.

The alternative interpretation of GNP is by categories of *expenditure*. That is, instead of a breakdown of the economy by types of goods, a breakdown can be undertaken by types of buyers. Instead of directing attention to production decisions, the expenditure interpretation of GNP focuses on the purchasing decisions of major types of buyers: consumers, corporations engaged in investment activity, the government, foreign buyers of domestic products, and domestic importers of foreign-made goods. So, once again, the identity

$$(4.A1')\qquad GNP = C + I + G + (X - M)$$

covers this interpretation.

The expenditure approach is helpful in understanding subcomponents of GNP that underlie the categories in accounting identity (4.A1'). Consumption spending can be directed to durables (e.g., furniture), nondurables (e.g., as food), and consumer services. Investment expenditure can be directed to purchases of capital goods and to residential and nonresidential construction. Government spending can cover the gamut of currently produced goods and services, from military equipment to the services of social workers and even tax collectors. Spending by the government in the national income accounts does not, however, include transfer payments, such as Social Security or welfare or payments of interest on the national debt. To include these would be double counting, since they turn up again behind the purchases of those who receive the transfer.

Spending on net exports must be added to the three categories of domestic expenditure, because GNP must reflect all types of spending associated with the nation in question. It is not just spending on goods produced domestically or sold domestically; it is all spending on production by the nation, whether that spending originates domestically or not.

GNP and GDP

GNP has been the primary measure of national economic performance for over forty years. Recently, however, interest has shifted to a slightly different measure, called *gross domestic product (GDP)*. GDP includes the value of output produced in the United States but transferred abroad to the foreign owners of U.S.-based operations, while excluding the value of incomes earned abroad by U.S. citizens. GNP excludes the former but includes the latter: it is a measure equivalent to gross national income, whereas GDP measures the value of *domestic* production.[3] Most of the empirical examples in this book will involve GDP measures.

Definitions possess a certain intrinsic arbitrariness, as do accounting conventions. Certain conventions in the measurement of GNP are practiced to ensure consistency in measurement over time and across countries. For example, the entire value of capital goods produced or sold during a period is included in the measure of GNP for that period. Subsequently, however, when capital goods are valued in the market, an estimate of their depreciation is included as a component of their price. Such depreciation is called the *capital consumption allowance*.

The measure referred to as *net national product (NNP)* (see next section) deducts depreciation of the capital stock from the gross national product. Contrary to the general rule that the conventions used for calculating GNP seek to avoid double counting—counting the same goods or the same purchases twice—including depreciation on the capital stock used to produce the capital goods as an element of their price is a form of double counting.

To avoid double counting, GNP is supposed to be calculated on the basis of final goods and services evaluated at market prices. But the actual conventions of measuring GNP lead to some exceptions. For example, additions to inventories are included in GNP although these are not final sales. On the other hand, the convention is not to include reductions of inventories in GNP calculations.

To get a flavor of the relative magnitudes of the components of GNP and GDP in 1991, the breakdown given in Table 4.A1 should be helpful. Obviously, consumption spending, at over 68 percent, constituted the largest single component of GNP for the United States. Among the three subcomponents of consumption, expenditure on services have been the largest since 1965. While gross investment spending amounted to under 13 percent of the total, it is the most volatile component of GNP. For this reason, Keynesian economists in particular highlight the role of investment swings in driving fluctuations in the economy as a whole. Note also that out of the $447.3 billion in government spending on goods and services in 1991, $323.8 billion was for national defense. The data also reveal that in 1991 the United States ran a trade deficit (or a deficit on current account): the money value of imports exceeded the money value of exports.

---

[3] There were two reasons for the change: (1) GDP is the measure most widely used elsewhere in the world; (2) with foreign ownership of U.S. assets growing and U.S. ownership of foreign assets in decline, the performance of GDP began to look better to the government than did the performance of GNP. But the difference is not very large.

TABLE 4.A1   1991 Gross National and Gross Domestic Product

(in billions of current dollars)

Gross domestic product	$5,677.5
Gross domestic product	5,694.9
Personal consumption expenditures (C)	3,887.7
Durable goods	446.1
Nondurable goods	1,251.5
Services	2,190.1
Gross private domestic investment (I)	721.1
Residential structures	190.3
Nonresidential structures	541.1
Producers' durable equipment	360.9
Change in business inventories	−10.2
Government purchases (G)	1,090.5
Federal	447.3
State and local	643.2
Net export of goods and services (X − M)	−21.8

Source: Economic Report of the President; January 1993.

Net National Income

Another type of aggregate performance measure, mentioned above, is *net national income* (NNI). NNI is the sum of all *factor earnings*—wages, profits, and rent—from current production of goods and services. To be precise, net national income consists of employees' compensation, corporate profits, proprietors' incomes, rental income, and net interest income. Therefore, net national income can be written as the following identity:

$$NNI = W + C + P + R + N$$

Here NNI is national income, the sum of the aggregate wage bill (W), aggregate corporate profits (C), proprietors' income, (P), rents (R), and net interest payments, (N).

Table 4.A2 shows net national income by type for 1991. National income as a measure of the aggregate performance of the economy directs our attention to the distribution of income in a given year. The fundamental split is between wage and nonwage income—or, to echo themes from the classical political economy of the nineteenth century, between income going to labor and income going to capital. Classical growth theory comprised three great social classes: labor, capitalists, and landlords. The capitalists were viewed as the only class that would save a high proportion of their income to be mobilized for capital

Taking a Closer Look

THE GROSS DOMESTIC PRODUCT

The gross domestic product (GDP) is the sum of private consumption spending, private investment spending on plant and equipment and other physical capital assets, and spending by government on goods and services. To this add export sales, which are the demand by foreigners for domestic output, and subtract import purchases, which are demand by home country residents for foreign output. Exclude spending by the government on transfer payments from some individuals to others, because the effect of transfers is picked up in the spending decisions individuals make out of posttransfer income. GDP differs from GNP only in excluding payments of wages and profits on foreign assets owned by Americans, while including profits and wages paid to foreigners in the United States. Since it measures domestic production, it is slightly more appropriate for comparing output in different countries.

The charts in Figures 4.A1–4.A3 show the major components of gross domestic product—consumption, investment, and government—over thirty years for the

FIGURE 4.A1 Real Gross Domestic Product

Gross domestic product is the sum of private consumption spending, private investment, and government spending (plus exports, minus imports, which we don't show here). When GDP falls for two consecutive quarters, as in 1970, 1974, 1981–82, and 1990–91, there is a recession.

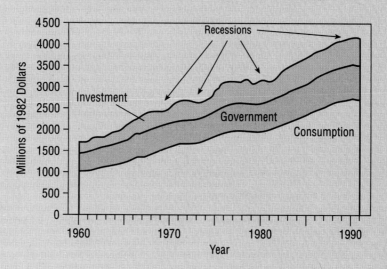

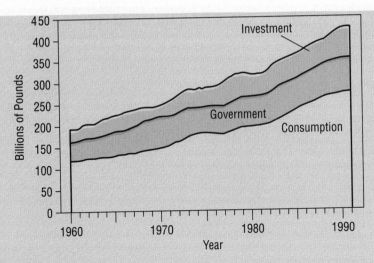

FIGURE 4.A2   British Components of GDP

United States, Great Britain, and Japan. Note that consumption is by far the largest component, averaging about two-thirds of GDP in all three countries; government spending and investment divide the remaining one-third. In Japan, the government sector is slightly

FIGURE 4.A3   Japanese Components of GDP

Investment has become much larger as a share of GDP in Japan, compared with Britain or the United States.

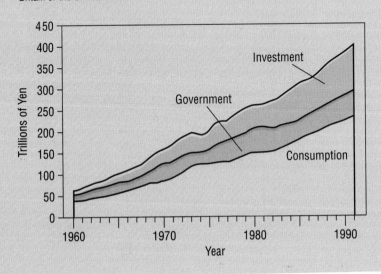

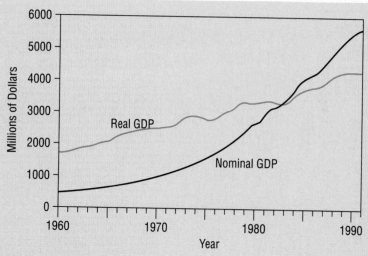

FIGURE 4.A4   Nominal and Real GDP

Real GDP is calculated by dividing current dollar or nominal GDP by an index of prices. The index is arbitrarily based so that nominal and real GDP are equal in a given year. In this case, the base year is 1982, and we say that real GDP is expressed in "1982 dollars." Note that recessions that are clear in the real GDP series are barely visible in the nominal series.

FIGURE 4.A5   Comparing Growth Rates: United States and Great Britain Real GDP

American and British growth rates have been very closely aligned over the years, and both are highly cyclical.

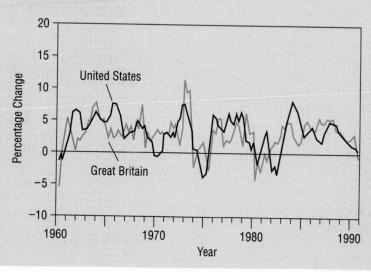

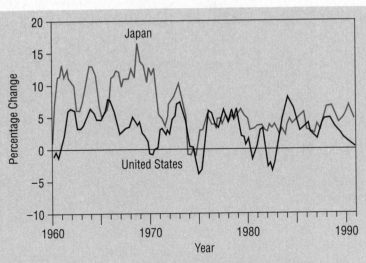

FIGURE 4.A6   Comparing Growth Rates: United States and Japan Real GDP

Japanese growth rates greatly exceeded those in the United States until the oil crisis of 1974. Since then, average growth in the two countries has been more similar. However, Japanese growth has been much more stable than the United States growth.

smaller than the private investment sector, whereas in the United States and United Kingdom, it is slightly larger.

Of all the sectors, investment is the most variable, and changes in investment are principally responsible for periods of decline in the overall volume of output. Such periods, known as *recessions*, show up quite clearly on the U.S. and British charts. But Japanese growth has been higher than Anglo-Saxon growth for almost this whole period, and Japan has rarely known a recession.

Nominal and Real GDP

Figures 4.A1–4.A3 show GDP for the United States, Great Britain, and Japan in *real* terms, or constant dollars, constant pounds, and con-

stant yen. The value of GDP and its components in each year has been divided by a *price index*, so that the effects of price changes have been removed and the index measures the change in the physical quantity of production. We say that the measure of real GDP has been deflated, or inflation-adjusted.

Figure 4.A4 shows the relationship between money GDP and real GDP for the United States. Note that money GDP is almost always rising, and it is hard to detect the fluctuations that seem so apparent in the series for inflation-adjusted GDP.

Comparing Growth Rates

The charts titled "Comparing Growth Rates" (Figures 4.A5 and 4.A6) compare the rates of change of real GDP in the United States and Britain, and in the United States and Japan. These numbers are measured for each quarter from 1960 through 1991, and a moving average formula is applied to each series, which smoothes out some of the bigger bumps in the data. The results show clearly how closely U.S. and British growth has been aligned over the years. They also show that the Japanese growth advantage, which was once phenomenal, is no longer so. Today, Japan's main advantage over the United States seems to be an ability to maintain a much more stable growth path, not necessarily a higher one.

accumulation. Thus, the rapid economic growth in a capitalist economy would be advanced by a rising proportion of income going to the capitalists.

In Table 4.A2, the largest share goes to the aggregate wage bill. In 1991, W constituted 74 percent of NNI. In the post–World War II era, the wage share has tended to be in the vicinity of 70 percent in the United States, although fluctuations have been sufficiently wide to preclude the assertion that the proportion is stable. For example, in 1950 the aggregate wage bill was 64 percent of net national income, whereas in 1975 it reached 76 percent.

Corporate profits have tended to decline as a share of nonwage income, from close to 50 percent of all nonwage income in 1970 to 34 percent by 1980 and a mere 29 percent in 1991. Net interest, in contrast, has undergone a dramatic increase as a proportion of nonwage income, suggestive of the great rise in the importance of financial activity in the

TABLE 4.A2   1991 Net National Income

(in billions of current dollars)

National income	$4,544.2
Compensation for employees (W)	3,390.8
Wages and salaries	2,812.2
Supplements to wages and salaries	578.7
Corporate profits (C)*	346.3
Proprietors' income (P)*	368.0
Non-farm	332.0
Farm	35.8
Rental income (R)*	−10.4
Net interest (N)	449.5

Source: Economic Report of the President, January 1993
* These figures include an adjustment for depreciation called the "capital consumption adjustment."

U.S. economy relative to productive activity. Net interest was a little more than 18 percent of nonwage income in 1970; by 1991 it was nearly 40 percent of nonwage income.

Conceptually, as noted at the outset, gross national product and gross national income are equal. From the expenditure perspective, GNP is the total sum spent in a given period of time on goods and services. The amounts received by participants in the economy in exchange for the goods and services must be equal to the former total via the circular flow between income and expenditure. The principles of double-entry bookkeeping for individual businesses lead to the conclusion that aggregate costs and aggregate product value are equal. There is also a companion sense in which national income accounts of these types apply to economies where monetary exchanges are prominent activities.

However, the data in Table 4.A2 are for net national income rather than for gross national income. GNP exceeded NNI by $1,155 billion in 1991. To arrive at the gross concept of national income (GNI) we would have to add in depreciation on the capital stock (or the capital consumption allowance) and indirect business taxes for that year.

After the transformation from net to gross national income is made, measured GNP and measured GNI still may not balance exactly. Therefore, the U.S. Department of Commerce adds the remaining difference, labeled the *statistical discrepancy*, to gross national income. This ensures that GNP and GNI match. Thereby, the gross national product (GNP) will be equal to the charges against gross national income (GNI). The statistical discrepancy typically amounts to less than 1/10 of 1 percent in the estimates issued by the U.S. Department of Commerce.

Personal Income

The definition of aggregate *personal income* (*PI*) used in the national accounts takes net national income and deducts corporate profits taxes (*CPRT*), undistributed profits or the retained earnings of corporations (*U*), and business contributions to social security (*SSB*). Then government and business transfer payments (*TR*) and government interest payments (*GN*) are added to the remaining amount to arrive at the personal income measure:

$$PI = NNI - CPRT - U - SSB + TR + GN$$

Personal income is a measure that seeks to capture the amount of income that actually is received by the household sector. Households cannot spend the full amount, because they still incur personal taxes (*PT*), which come out of their incomes. Once personal taxes are removed from personal income, one arrives at the definition of disposable personal income (*DPI*), the total amount of income available for households to spend:

$$DPI = PI - PT$$

As already seen in this chapter, the concept of disposable personal income plays a role of special importance in the development of the theory of aggregate consumption behavior.

Disposable personal income can be partitioned into different categories of use of personal income: personal consumption expenditures, net personal transfer payments to foreigners, and personal savings.

Price Indices

As noted earlier, the best overall measure of the aggregate price level, and the one most used for calculating the economywide rate of inflation, is the GNP deflator. Constant dollar measures of both *PI* and *DPI* can be calculated, for purposes of making comparisons over time, by using the *consumer price index (CPI)* as the deflator. The CPI is the appropriate price index for this purpose because it gauges the overall change in retail prices for a fixed market basket of consumer goods. It omits measures of the change of prices of investment goods, which are not relevant to the consumption decisions of households.

The *producer price index (PPI)* provides a parallel index for wholesale prices. Analysts often use the PPI to forecast changes in the consumer price index because the PPI consists largely of intermediate goods.

You can derive an additional variant of a national accounting identity by making some simplifying assumptions. First, treat the economy as "closed" (i.e., there is no foreign sector). Second, ignore any discrepancies between gross national product and national income. Third, ignore depreciation on the capital stock. And fourth, assume away retained corporate earnings and business transfers, so that all taxes are imposed directly on households. Disposable income becomes simply national income less net taxes.

Now label the indistinguishable concepts of gross national product and national income as Y. In this closed-economy context, the GNP accounts reduce to:

(4.A2) $Y = C + I + G$

Based upon the disposition of income by *all* households, including both wage and nonwage income recipients, we can construct an alternative account:

(4.A3) $Y = C + S + T$

where C is aggregate consumption spending, S is aggregate saving, and T is net taxes imposed on households. Equation 4.A3, then, is a different version of a national income identity that emphasizes the disposition of income rather than its distribution. (Of course, the distribution of income will affect its disposition between the three categories, C, S, and T.)

Combining (4.A2) and (4.A3), rearranging terms, and eliminating C by substitution yield a different view of aggregate economic relations:

(4.A4) $I + G = S + T$

Here investment plus government expenditure equals national saving plus net taxes. In short, equation (4.A4) gives an expression where the left side represents two categories of spending and the right side represents the sources of funds to support the expenditures.

In effect, (4.A4) says that, taken together, *investment plus government expenditure must be financed by the sum of national saving and tax revenues.* This sort of national account indicates that if the government runs a deficit ($G < T$), then saving must exceed investment by the corresponding amount, and vice versa, by definition. Aggregate expenditure cannot exceed the funds that are withdrawn from the stream of expenditures either through acts of personal saving or through governmental tax collections.

The conclusion displayed in equation (4.A4) does not depend upon ignoring the foreign sector. So long as the foreign sector only takes the form of net exports, as in the definition of gross national product given in (4.A1), you can add it back in and show that it has no effect. If the net export sector is incorporated into equations (4.A2) and (4.A3), it simply will cancel out when the identities are combined. This will result in equation (4.A4) once again, in precisely the same form.

What would alter the identity in (4.A4) is the capacity of an economy to borrow or lend abroad. To take this into account, expand the right side of (4.A4) with respect to the sources of funds for investment and government spending. Equation (4.A4) would become

(4.A5) $I + G = S + T + F + FN$

where F represents net inflows of foreign capital (a positive value indicates that the country is a net borrower in the current period) and FN represents net interest payments from abroad (a positive value indicates that the country is a net recipient of interest payments on preexisting debt). Equation (4.A5) shows clearly that the expenditure/sources-of-funds type of national income identity changes substantially when financial activities in the foreign sector are brought into the picture. In particular, it becomes possible to finance an investment boom or a budget deficit without matching them with domestic savings or tax revenues. This, of course, is precisely what the United States did during most of the 1980s.

Chapter 5

THE *IS-LM* MODEL AND THE *PHILLIPS* CURVE

Looking Forward

This chapter presents the Keynesian theory in its most familiar form, the IS-LM model. IS-LM grew from the efforts of Keynes's followers to interpret his *General Theory* in a rigorous way and is surely the most successful textbook model in the history of macroeconomics. In the United States especially, IS-LM *was* Keynesianism, as generally understood, from the arrival of Kennedy-era New Economics in 1961 until the crisis of U.S. Keynesianism in the 1970s. This flexible and resilient framework is still used by Keynesians today.

Just as the classical model had two main markets (labor and capital), there are two main elements to IS-LM: the market for goods and services and the market for money. The interaction of these markets jointly determines real production (gross domestic product) and the rate of interest. Real production, of course, determines employment and unemployment.

To establish a connection between the real economy and the rate of inflation, Keynesians brought in a purely empirical relationship between unemployment and inflation, known as the Phillips curve. Yet, at a moment when reliance on this concept was at its zenith, in the late 1960s, the Phillips curve failed. The history of the Phillips curve explains, in large measure, why this brand of Keynesian economics faced a crisis and lost both political and academic influence nearly two decades ago.

The chapter also includes a special section on varieties of the investment function.

As you read this chapter and work through the mechanics of the equations and the graphs. Ask yourself the following questions:

- How is equilibrium determined in the market for goods and services? How does this lead to a downward-sloping IS curve?
- How is equilibrium determined in the market for money? How does this lead to an upward-sloping LM curve?
- How do IS and LM jointly determine the equilibrium rates of output and interest?
- How does policy shift the IS and LM curves? What happens to equilibrium output and interest when policies change?
- What are the implications of special cases when IS and LM are either horizontal or vertical?
- What did the Phillips curve bring to the IS-LM analysis?

Leaving the theory of the consumption function, we now expand our Keynesian theory of production and employment to encompass the vital issue of investment.

The theory of consumption has given us, automatically and without further ado, a corresponding theory of saving: any income earned (Y^s) that is not consumed must be saved:

$$(5.1) \qquad\qquad Y^s = C + S$$

Therefore, if we take the simplest form of the Keynesian theory, the idea that consumption is a (simple, linear) function of income also tells us that saving is a (simple, linear) function of income. In general,

$$(5.2) \qquad\qquad S = Y^s - C(Y^s) = S(Y^s)$$
$$S' > 0$$

In the linear case,

$$(5.2') \qquad\qquad S = Y^s - (a + bY^s) = -a + (1 - b)Y^s$$

As noted in Chapter 3, this is a dramatic departure from classical thinking. In that theory, savings and investment were linked directly in a capital market, where savings were supplied in increasing volumes in response to a rising rate of interest. In the Keynesian theory, savings are more or less insensitive to interest rates. They are passive, a mere residual of the consumption decision, and total savings rise and fall strictly in accordance with the rise and fall of incomes.

But must not savings also equal investment? Certainly, in equilibrium this must be true (whether one is Keynesian or not!), for we know that[1]

(5.3) $$Y^d = C + I$$

and since Y^s must equal aggregate demand Y^d in equilibrium incomes, equations (5.1) and (5.3) together show that, in equilibrium, savings S must equal investment I. But doesn't investment (for a Keynesian or a classical) depend on the rate of interest? Assuredly it must. So we will now show how to integrate this theory of investment and this theory of saving.

THE THEORY OF INVESTMENT

Keynes rooted his theory of investment firmly in the microeconomics of the circumstances facing entrepreneurs who make the investment decision. Entrepreneurs dispose of capital, of access to resources, and must decide whether or not to use it to create new plant and equipment. On what do they base this decision? Keynes saw that the crucial consideration must be *opportunity cost*, or the highest reward that might be earned if the same resources were used in some other way.

Specifically, business managers must form an idea of the *expected rate of return*, the percentage profit to be carried on capital, associated with each investment project that they may be contemplating. The expected rate of return is not directly observed. It is, rather, a subjective judgment, inferred from the mass of present economic conditions, large and small. It differs for different projects and may vary with the state of confidence that is felt toward future economic conditions in general. Nevertheless, expected rate of return is a notion that is virtually instinctive in free enterprise, as simple and straightforward as the question, "Can I make money on this or not?"

The opportunity cost of capital investment, on the other hand, is directly observable. It is simply the interest rate available, from the bank or other financial markets, in return for allowing someone else to carry out their investment plans, rather than one's own. For any given project, businesspeople compare the expected rate of return on that project with the interest rate that the same capital might earn if left in the bank (or that would have to be paid on funds borrowed from the bank in the first place). Projects expected to yield more than the opportunity cost, as measured by the interest rate, will be undertaken. Projects that fail the test will be deferred.

---

[1] For convenience, ignore government and taxes at this stage.

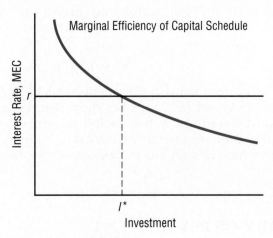

FIGURE 5.1   The Theory of Investment Revisited

Businesses invest up to the point where the marginal efficiency of capital, or expected rate of return on new investment, falls to the prevailing rate of interest.

Of course, businesses will take on the most profitable projects first and the less profitable ones later. Thus, as investment increases, the expected rate of return declines. One may therefore imagine a schedule of the expected rate of return on investment, for different rates of investment as a whole. Such a schedule appears in Figure 5.1. Keynes called this function the *marginal efficiency of capital schedule.*

Investment takes place until the most profitable investment contemplated (but not yet undertaken) by any business is expected to yield no more than the prevailing rate of interest. At that point, new investments are no longer profitable. And so, the separate decisions of all business enterprises taken together at any moment in time determine the rate of investment in the whole economy. Should the interest rate fall, investment again will increase; if the interest rate rises, investment will decline. In a given state of expectation about future economic conditions, therefore, the rate of investment is a decreasing function of the rate of interest, r.

$$(5.4) \qquad\qquad I = I(r)$$
$$I' < 0$$

We now have one theory of saving, related to income, and another of investment, related to the interest rate. To tie them together, we need only an equilibrium condition. And this is readily provided. As we have already shown, it follows directly from the macroeconomic equilibrium $Y^s = Y^d$ that, in equilibrium, savings must equal investment:

$$Y^s = C + S \text{ and}$$

(5.5)
$$Y^d = C + I \text{ therefore}$$

$$I = S$$

It is therefore possible to create a model subsystem that tells us the relationship between investment, savings, income, and interest. The subsystem consists of equations (5.2), (5.4), and (5.5), which may be mapped together (a process we show in Figure 5.2).

Equation (5.2) provides the general form of the determination of savings. Savings is a passive function of income: it rises when income

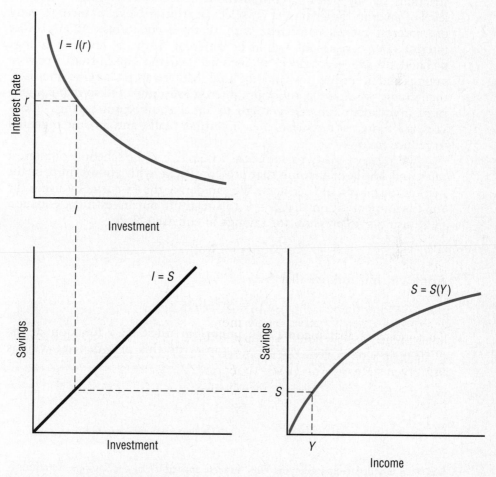

FIGURE 5.2   Savings and Investment

Investment is a function of the interest rate, whereas savings depends on income. The two are linked through the equilibrium condition that savings equals investment.

rises. We graph this in the lower right of Figure 5.2, where savings is shown as a smooth, upward-sloping curve.

Equation (5.4) supplies the general form of the determination of investment. Investment is a function of the interest rate: it rises as the interest rate falls. We graph this in Figure 5.2 (upper left), where investment is shown as a smooth, downward-sloping curve.

Equation (5.5), finally, gives the equilibrium condition that savings must equal investment. We show this in the lower left of Figure 5.2, which takes savings and investment together and shows that in equilibrium they must be equal.

When Equations (5.2), (5.4), and (5.5) all hold, they establish restrictions on the possible combinations of the interest rate, r, and the level of income, Y. That is, if we select an arbitrary level of income, only one interest rate is consistent with all three equations. At any other interest rate, investment would be different from the level of savings dictated by the given level of income, and the equilibrium between savings and investment would not hold. Moreover, if (say) income rises, then savings rise, and equilibrium interest rates must fall so that equilibrium investment can rise enough to equal equilibrium savings. Conversely, if interest rates rise, then investment falls, and income must fall to reduce savings.

We are now ready to define the *IS curve*. It is the schedule of interest rates and levels of income that are consistent with equilibrium in the market for goods and services. We can derive the *IS* curve by using the equilibrium condition that $S = I$ to substitute our investment equation (5.4) into our expression for savings in equation (5.2):

$$I(r) = S(Y)$$

from which it follows that

$$Y = S^{-1}[I(r)]$$

This indicates that income in equilibrium must be a function of the interest rate, and vice versa.[2] We can write this in a general way as follows:

(5.6)
$$Y = IS(r)$$
$$IS' < 0$$

---

[2] $S^{-1}(\ )$ is a notation signifying the "inverse function" of the savings function. For any function $S(Y)$, S^{-1} is defined as that function for which it is true that $S^{-1}[S(Y)] = Y$. Applying S^{-1} to both sides of the equation above yields an easy general form of the *IS* function.

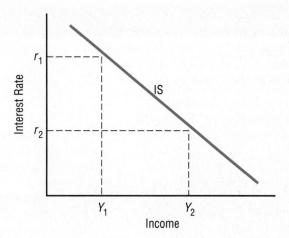

FIGURE 5.3   IS Curve

The IS curve shows the combinations of the interest rate and the income level that are
compatible with savings-investment equilibrium.

Equation (5.6) is illustrated by the relationship in Figure 5.3, which
shows the interest rate/income level combinations that are consistent
with the savings = investment equilibrium. Since investment and interest rates are inversely related and the links from savings to income and
investment to savings are both positive, we can deduce that interest rates
and income must be inversely related so long as equilibrium prevails.
Thus, the equilibrium relationship between income and interest lies
along a downward-sloping curve.

The curve so formed is known as the IS curve,[3] and it supplies half
of the necessary conditions for a full and unique equilibrium of the
macroeconomy. Each point along it is an equilibrium point; indeed,
there are an infinite number of such points. But this information
is insufficient to tell which among the infinitely numerous equilibria
that lie along the IS curve will actually be the one at which the
economy settles. To narrow the range, we need more information; for
that, we turn to the financial side of the economy, to the market for
money.

---

[3] Note that "IS" here is the name for the curve and does not signify multiplica-
tion of investment (I) and savings (S). Rather, the equation simply says that
when equilibrium prevails in the markets for goods and services (and therefore
savings equals investment), income (Y) is a downward-sloping function of the
interest rate (r).

Taking a Closer Look

A LINEAR VERSION OF THE IS CURVE

Although in the text and drawings the IS curve and its associated relationships appear for the most part as a series of smooth curves, many students find it helpful to work through the case where all of these relationships are straight lines as in Figure 5.3.

Start with a linear savings function, based on the linear consumption function $C = a + bY$. Note that this function is upward sloping $[(1 - b) > 1]$, with a negative intercept:

$$S = Y - C = Y - (a + bY)$$

$$= (1 - b)Y - a$$

(5.B1)[1]

Add to this a downward-sloping investment function:

(5.B2)[2] $I = g - kr$

And you have, as before, the equilibrium condition

(5.B3)[3] $I = S$

Substituting (5.B1) into the right side of (5.B3) and (5.B2) into the left side yields

$$g - kr = (1 - b)Y - a$$

Solving for Y, add a to both sides and divide through by $(1 - b)$:

$$\frac{a + g}{1 - b} - \left(\frac{k}{1 - b}\right) r = Y$$

This equation for the IS curve in a linear form—a linear version of equation 5.6—has a positive intercept because a, g, and $(1 - b)$ are all positive constants. And it has a negative slope because k is also a positive constant. Note that the greater the marginal propensity to consume b, the steeper the slope of the IS curve (a familiar result from the multiplier theory of Chapter 4). Note too that larger autonomous components of spending shift the position of the IS curve (and raise equilibrium income for any given interest rate) by a factor of $1/(1 - b)$. This result is again very familiar from the multiplier model, since $1/(1 - b)$ is simply equal to Q, the multiplier. A bigger coefficient k, indicating a greater response of investment to changes in the interest rate, will also produce a steeper IS curve.

---

[1] Compare text equation (5.2)', page 132.
[2] Compare text equation (5.4), page 134.
[3] Compare text equation (5.5), page 135.

THE MARKET FOR MONEY

As we have seen, most economists before Keynes believed that money itself was not subject to the laws of supply and demand. A certain amount would be created, and that amount would be used, with prices of goods adjusting to ensure that all the money in circulation was in fact also in use. Thus the quantity theory of money held that money determined the general level of prices but was neutral in its effects on output and employment. In the classical expression, money was "a veil"; it might conceal but would not change the functioning of the real economy underneath.

Keynes was a monetary theorist, and his *General Theory*[4] (as we have discussed) was above all a revolutionary work of monetary theory. In it, Keynes advanced the idea that money might serve as an asset, rather than simply as a medium for exchange. In that case, there would exist a *demand curve for money:* people would seek to hold more or less of it according to the cost and the expected returns. With this basic idea, Keynes set out to overturn the classical neutrality of money.

Keynes's first departure was to note that at a given price level, the volume of money needed for the circulation of goods would rise and fall with the volume of that circulation, or transactions. Thus, if prices are not perfectly flexible, one element of changing demand for money will stem from a changing level of production, commerce, and spending (Y^d). This element, termed the *transactions demand* for money, can be simplified to the following, where L_1' signifies the transactions demand for money.

(5.7)
$$L_1 = L_1(Y^d)$$
$$L_1' > 0$$

Keynes further noted that money—a medium that bears no interest—was an alternative to holding interest-bearing financial instruments, such as bonds. Bonds do bear interest, but they also are subject to capital risk. That is, their price in terms of money fluctuates from day to day on the market. For this reason, investors may at times prefer to forgo the interest that might be earned on a bond and to hold money instead. The holding of money thus provides a way for investors (or speculators) in the financial markets to reduce the risk in their portfolios.

The price of a bond moves inversely with the rate of interest, rising when interest rates fall and falling when interest rates rise.[5] Because smart investors seek to anticipate these movements, their willingness to hold bonds depends not only on the interest rate today but also on what the interest rate is expected to be in the future. Suppose, for example, that an investor expects the interest rate available on the market next week to be higher than it is today. If, despite that expectation, he or she buys a bond today to hold for a week, there will be an expected capital

---

[4] *The General Theory of Employment, Interest and Money* (London: Macmillan, 1936).
[5] To see this, suppose that in April, company X issues to investor Y a $10,000 bond bearing 10 percent interest, or $1,000 per year. In May, the market interest rate on bonds falls to 8 percent. If investor Z wishes to buy the bond held by

loss, which may greatly offset the interest earned during the week. Better to hold money for a week, giving up the interest, and buy bonds at that later time. If the speculation about the movement of interest rates proves correct, then bond yields will be up and their prices will be down, and the interest forgone will be a pittance compared to the capital loss avoided.

The degree to which speculators engage in this behavior, holding money now in order to be able to make financial transactions at a later date, is known as their *liquidity preference*, or *speculative demand for money*. And Keynes's theory of liquidity preference is perhaps his fundamental contribution to our understanding of money.

Extending this reasoning, we can argue that interest rates generally will be expected to rise when they are low (by standards of past history) and to fall when they are high. Therefore, the speculative demand for money will be related inversely to the rate of interest:

(5.8)
$$L_2 = L_2(r)$$
$$L_2' < 0$$

Further, we know that the total demand for money must equal the sum of the transactions and the speculative demands:

(5.9)
$$M^d = M^d(Y, r) = L_1 + L_2$$

In need of an equilibrium condition, we can find one in the simple assertion that the amount of money demanded must equal, in equilibrium, the quantity supplied. We can make an assertion that the amount of money supplied is at any one time strictly determined by the central bank (this is a bit too simple, as we shall see, but it must do for now):

(5.10)
$$M^d = M^s$$

The three diagrams of Figure 5.4 present equations (5.7) through (5.10).

In Figure 5.4 (top left), we see the inverse relationship between interest rates and the demand to hold money for speculative reasons. This is the graph of equation (5.8). As we have explained, speculative demand for money rises when the interest rate falls.

In Figure 5.4 (bottom right), we see the positive relationship between income and the transactions demand for money, or the graph of equation (5.7). As income rises, more goods are bought and sold, and more money is demanded to facilitate these transactions.

---

investor Y, she must pay just enough so that investor Y could, if he chose, use the proceeds to buy a bundle of new bonds yielding only 8 percent that would be exactly equivalent to the bond she is selling. How much would investor Z have to pay? The answer is $12,500, since $12,500 × .08 = $1,000, the same return as investor Y presently enjoys. Thus, the price of investor Y's bond has risen 25 percent.

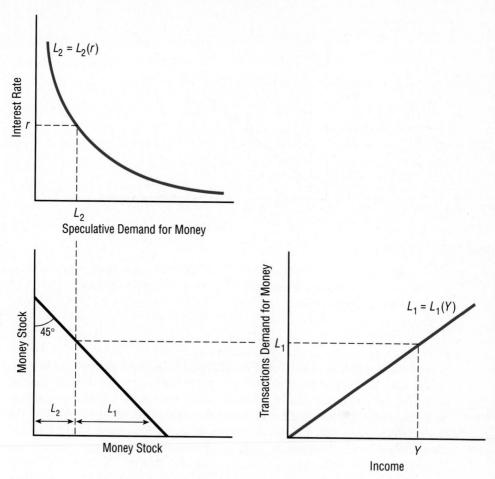

FIGURE 5.4   Speculative and Transactions Demand for Money

Speculative demands for money depend on the interest rate, whereas transactions demand depends on income. The two are linked by the equilibrium requirement that their sum, total money demand, must equal the quantity of money supplied.

Figure 5.4 (bottom left) shows our equilibrium condition, a combination of equations (5.9) and (5.10). Here the speculative demand for money and the transactions demand, which together sum to the total demand for money, must in equilibrium also sum to a fixed money supply. The size of the money supply is given by the intercept of the diagonal line along either axis. By taking any point on the diagonal line and measuring its position on each axis, we can divide the money supply into its two constituent parts.

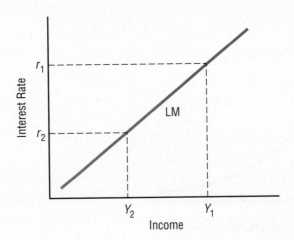

FIGURE 5.5   LM Curve

The LM curve shows the combinations of the interest rate and the income level that are compatible with total money demand equal to total money supplied (the equilibrium condition in the money market).

Once again we notice that when equations (5.7) through (5.10) all hold, they establish restrictions on the possible combinations of the interest rate, r, and the level of income, Y. If we select an arbitrary rate of interest, only one level of income is consistent with all four equations and therefore with equilibrium in the market for money. And if the interest rate rises, then the speculative demand for money will fall and the income level must rise in order to bring forth the extra transactions demand for money that equilibrium in the money market will now require.

And so we turn to Figure 5.5. Equations (5.7) through (5.10) map out a set of combinations of r and Y that are consistent with equilibrium in the market for money; as with the IS analysis, these combinations define a curve. It is clearly an upward-sloping relation: if interest rates rise, less money is demanded for speculative purposes, and income must also rise if the available money is to be absorbed by transactions demand. The points that define the possible equilibria in the financial markets are known as the *LM curve*.

The LM curve's equation can be derived directly from our expressions for the demand for money. Simply substitute equations (5.7) and (5.8) into (5.9), obtaining

$$M^d = L_1(Y) + L_2(r)$$

and then exploit equilibrium condition (5.10) that $M^s = M^d$, so that

Taking a Closer Look

A LINEAR VERSION OF THE LM CURVE

As we did for the IS curve, we can easily present our derivation of the LM curve in a linear form.

We start with a linear transactions demand for money, assumed to have an intercept of zero because if there were no output there would be no transactions:

(5.B1)[1] $L_1 = \beta Y$

Add to this a downward-sloping speculative demand for money function:

(5.B2)[2] $L_2 = \Gamma - \rho r$

We have, once again, our equilibrium condition, combined with the definition that total demand for money equals the sum of transactions and speculative demands:

(5.B3)[3] $M^s = M^d = L_1 + L_2$

Substitute (5.B1) and (5.B2) into the right side of (5.B3) yields

$$M^s = \beta Y + \Gamma - \rho r$$

from which the value of Y in terms of r (or vice versa) is easily derived:

(5.B4)[4] $Y = \dfrac{\rho r + M^s - \Gamma}{\beta}$

This LM curve is an upward-sloping line, with slope ρ/β, indicating that the more sensitive the speculative demand for money is to the interest rate, the flatter the LM curve. Likewise, the more sensitive the transactions demand for money is to income, the flatter is the LM curve. Finally, the presence of the money supply in the intercept term shows that when the money supply increases, other things equal, income must grow.

---

[1] Compare text equation (5.7), page 139.
[2] Compare text equation (5.8), page 140.
[3] Compare text equation (5.10), page 140.
[4] Compare text equation (5.11), page 143.

$$M^s = L_1(Y) + L_2(r)$$

Solving for Y in terms of r gives us

$$Y = L_1^{-1}[M^s - L_2(r)]$$

This is the general equation of the LM curve, which we can write in simple form as:

(5.11) $Y = LM(r)$
                          $LM' > 0$

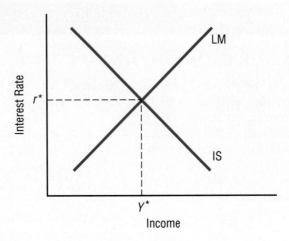

FIGURE 5.6   IS and LM

The IS and LM curves separately show the possible equilibrium positions of the goods and money markets. They jointly show the general equilibrium of interest and income in the economy.

THE GENERAL EQUILIBRIUM
OF INTEREST AND OUTPUT

We now have a downward-sloping IS curve and an upward-sloping LM curve, both defined in terms of the rate of interest and total income. Each curve shows the possible equilibria in its respective market: IS for goods, LM for money. Each establishes a sliding scale of Y in terms of r, and vice versa. But neither, taken alone, pins down the exact requirements for both variables to arrive at a single equilibrium value.

Together, on the other hand, the two can define a complete model. In mathematical terms, equations (5.6) (IS) and (5.11) (LM) present a system of two variables and two simultaneous equations. Solving them together yields a unique solution for both r and Y. That is, only one level of income and only one rate of interest are consistent with equilibrium in both the real and the money markets. Figure 5.6 shows this *general equilibrium* of the macroeconomy.

The IS-LM framework shows how a certain part of the Keynesian insight can be expressed in a setting of mathematical equilibrium. The elements included are the marginal efficiency of capital from the theory of investment, the income theory of saving, and the transactions and speculative demands for money. From these elements, we can derive an equilibrium that is an equilibrium in every mathematical sense and yet defies the classical notion that equilibrium only occurs at full employ-

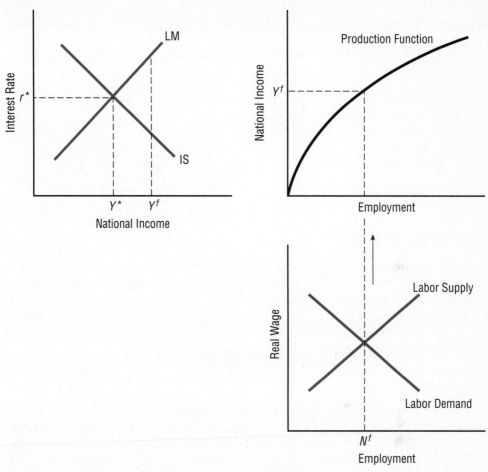

FIGURE 5.7   IS-LM, Labor Market, and Production Function

In this Keynesian model, IS-LM determines the equilibrium level of national income. The labor market determines what the "full employment" level of national income would be. But there is no reason why full employment in the labor market must prevail. If Y^* is at less than full employment, there will be an underemployment equilibrium.

ment. As a quick check of each component will verify, neither IS nor LM depends in any way on the achievement of full employment in the labor market.

In fact, we can now sketch in some remaining elements of the macroeconomy, including a labor market (relating labor supplied and demanded) and a production function (relating the volume of employment to the volume of output). These elements appear, along with IS-LM, in Figure 5.7. Note that the volume of output corresponding to equilibrium or full employment in the labor market, denoted by Y^f,

Taking a Closer Look

IS-LM IN LINEAR FORM: ALGEBRAIC SOLUTIONS FOR Y AND r

Taking our linearized equations for IS and for LM, we can readily solve them together for the equilibrium values of r and Y.

Recall that IS is given by

(5.B1) $\quad \dfrac{a + g - kr}{1 - b} = Y$

and that LM is given by

(5.B2) $\quad Y = \dfrac{\rho r + M^s - \Gamma}{\beta}$

Rearranging these expressions, we can derive the corresponding expressions for the interest rate, r:

$$r = \frac{a + g - Y(1 - b)}{k}$$

and

$$r = \frac{\beta Y - M^s + \Gamma}{\rho}$$

By setting these expressions to equal each other, we can establish a unique equilibrium value for national income while eliminating the interest rate variable from the calculation:

$$\frac{a + g - Y(1 - b)}{k}$$
$$= \frac{\beta Y - M^s + \Gamma}{\rho}$$

Rearranging terms and multiplying through by ρ/ρ and k/k yields

$$\rho(a + g) + k(M^s - \Gamma)$$
$$= Y\rho(1 - b) + k\beta Y$$

and, finally,

(5.B3)

$$Y = \frac{\rho(a + g) + k(M^s - \Gamma)}{\rho(1 - b) + k\beta}$$

This complicated-looking expression tells us that we can bypass the determination of the interest rate, if we choose, and compute the equilibrium level of national income directly from knowledge of eight basic facts about the economic world. Four of these come from the IS analysis: the autonomous components of consumption and investment spending (a and g), the response of investment demand to the interest rate (k), and the marginal propensity to consume (b). Three other facts are parameters from the LM analysis (denoted here with Greek letters): the response of money demand to the interest rate (ρ), the autonomous component of speculative demand for money (Γ), and the response of transactions demand for money to income (β). Last, one is a policy variable, the money supply (M^s).

This expression shows that equilibrium income rises in response to increases in autonomous spending (a, g) and in the money stock (M^s). The size of the increase grows with the marginal propensity to consume (b), whose familiar presence in the denominator indicates the continuing presence of the multiplier relationship, in modified form, in the IS-LM model. Income falls in response to increases in the autonomous component of speculative demand for money (Γ) and in the need for money to finance transactions (β).[1]

We solve for r by substituting (5.B2) into the right side of (5.B1):

$$\frac{a + g}{1 - b} - \frac{kr}{1 - b} = \frac{\rho r + M^s - \Gamma}{\beta}$$

so that

$$\frac{\beta(a + g)}{1 - b} - M^s + \Gamma$$

$$= \left(\frac{\beta k}{1 - b} + \rho\right) r$$

and

$$r = \frac{\dfrac{\beta(a + g)}{1 - b} - M^s + \Gamma}{\dfrac{\rho + \beta k}{1 - b}}$$

This tells us, among other things, that the equilibrium value of the interest rate falls when the money stock rises—money is not neutral with respect to the interest rate. It also tells us, not surprisingly, that a higher speculative component of the demand for money will raise the equilibrium interest rate. And so will increases in autonomous spending for consumption or investment. An increase in the interest sensitivity of the speculative demand for money (ρ) will, however, lower the equilibrium rate of interest.

---

[1] The direction of change of Y in response to changes in ρ and k is uncertain and will depend on the relative size of the other quantities in the expression.

bears no necessary relationship to the joint equilibrium of the goods and financial markets (denoted $Y^\star$). The labor market in this Keynesian model only provides a benchmark, telling us whether or not we are at full employment. So long as we allow the IS-LM model to determine the real level of output, the labor market has no operational role.[6]

FISCAL AND MONETARY POLICY

An immediate use of the IS-LM framework is to show how the position of the joint equilibrium of interest rates and income levels might change, if certain underlying conditions change.

[6] We shall see later that the new classical economists restore the role of the labor market in determining employment and real output, and they correspondingly change the role of the IS-LM framework to determination of the interest rate and price level.

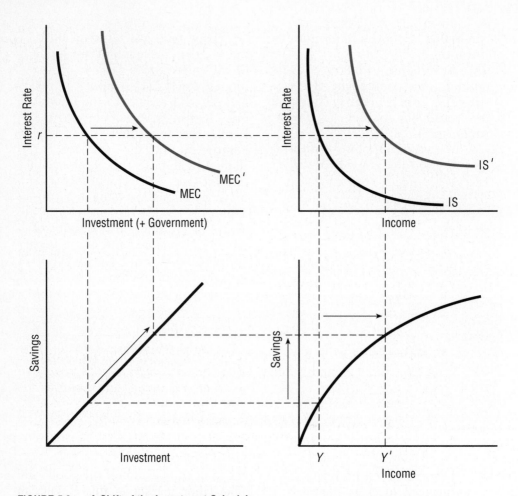

FIGURE 5.8   A Shift of the Investment Schedule

An outward shift of the MEC schedule generates an outward shift of the IS curve. For any given interest rate, equilibrium income will rise. The effect of an increase in government spending is the same as the effect of any increase in investment.

Suppose there is a change in the climate of confidence, so that, at every interest rate, businesspeople are prepared to undertake a larger amount of investment. This can be depicted as an outward shift (to the right) of the schedule of the marginal efficiency of capital, as in Figure 5.8. Because for any given interest rate there is now a higher level of investment, there must be a higher equilibrium level of savings. Since savings depends on income, this can only happen if the rise in investment raises income.

Thus, the consequence: the IS curve must also shift outward (to the right), and each interest rate must now be consistent with a higher level of income. The new IS curve, IS', must intercept the LM curve at a higher interest rate than before. The basic result is that an autonomous expansion of investment will, other things equal, raise both income (through the multiplier process) and interest rates.

Increases in government spending (fiscal policy), so far left entirely out of the model, can be analyzed in essentially the same way. Instead of I alone, we put $I + G$ on the horizontal axis; algebraically, we include government spending as part of the autonomous component of investment demand (g) in box equation (5.B2) on page 146. Increases in G will now shift the whole MEC schedule, as augmented by government spending, to the right and thus shift the IS schedule to the right in the same way as an autonomous increase in investment would do. Equilibrium income and interest rates both rise. As we can tell from examining equation (5.B3) on page 146, equilibrium income will rise by a modified multiplier, equal (in the linear case) to:[7]

$$\frac{\Delta Y}{\Delta g} = \frac{\rho}{\rho(1 - b) + k\beta}$$

Now consider a decrease in the supply of money, shown as a move from M to M' in Figure 5.9. This means that there is less money to divide between L_1 and L_2, the transactions and speculative demands for money. Thus, interest rates are forced up, and income will be forced down, until a new equilibrium in the money market has been reached. In graphical terms, the LM curve must now shift in and to the left, to LM'.

How can you satisfy yourself of the consequences for equilibrium income and the interest rate of (1) a simultaneous expansion of the money supply *and* increase of government spending and (2) an increase in government spending accompanied by a decrease in the supply of money? You can approach these problems by sketching your own IS and LM curves and shifting each in response to the various policy changes.

How would you model the imposition of an income tax? To see this, consider what happens to the slope of the savings function if consumption is out of aftertax rather than pretax income, so that $C = a + b(1 - t)Y$. The higher the tax rate t, the less is disposable income $(1 - t)Y$ and the less is savings for any given level of pretax income. Thus, the savings function pivots inward and so must the IS curve.

---

[7] Note that if either k or β approaches zero, so that investment demand is unaffected by rising interest rates or new money is not required to finance increased transactions, then this expression will tend toward our familiar Keynesian multiplier, $1/(1 - b)$.

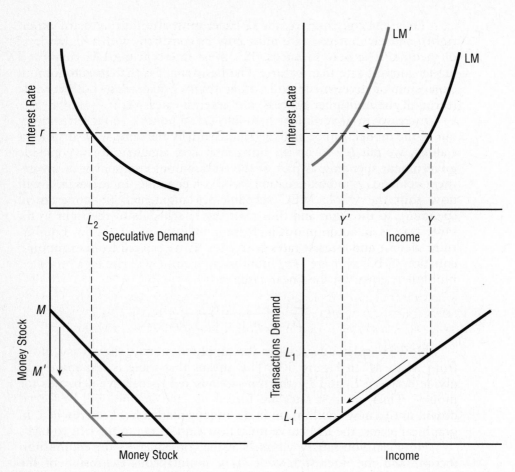

FIGURE 5.9   A Monetary Contraction

A reduction of the money supply (lower left) leads to an inward shift of the LM curve.
Now, any given interest rate is associated with a lower level of income.

LIQUIDITY TRAPS AND CROWDING OUT

So far, we have provided equations of only the most general and abstract kind for IS and LM. About the actual shape of these curves, we have avoided saying anything definite beyond the fact that IS slopes downward and LM upward. But you may now easily investigate the consequences if one or the other is either flat or vertical.

If interest rates are extraordinarily low, the speculative demand for money may become indefinitely large. That is, everyone expects that interest rates will soon rise and therefore bond prices will fall, inflicting huge capital losses on anyone foolish enough to hold bonds or other interest-bearing financial assets. Market participants are seized with an inordinate fear of these capital losses—and equally inordinate hopes of taking advantage of the imminent fall in bond prices. Under these circumstances, new money that may be created is snapped up and hoarded by speculators in the anticipation of increases in interest rates and declines in bond prices.

The LM curve will then assume a horizontal slope, as shown in Figure 5.10. When this happens, it becomes impossible, simply by creating money, either to reduce interest rates and stimulate investment or to stimulate transactions. Such policy shifts, which ordinarily produce an outward movement of the LM curve, now simply map the new curve directly over the old one. Monetary policy is impotent. On the other hand, fiscal policy is extremely effective, since an outward shift in the IS curve along a horizontal LM curve can raise income without affecting interest rates.

This hypothetical situation, which became known as the *liquidity trap,* has sometimes been thought to convey the essence of the Keynesian policy message. Keynes himself, however, discounted its importance, saying that he knew of no historical instance when this extreme case in fact prevailed.

> There is the possibility . . . that, after the rate of interest has fallen to a certain level, liquidity preference may become virtually absolute

FIGURE 5.10   The Liquidity Trap

In a liquidity trap, monetary policy has no effect. But shifts in the IS schedule, caused for example by expansionary fiscal policy, can easily raise output without raising interest rates.

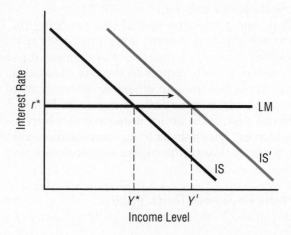

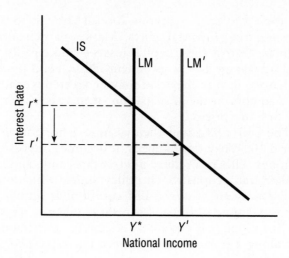

FIGURE 5.11   Vertical LM Curve

If the LM curve is vertical, fiscal policy is helpless. A shift in the IS curve will raise or
lower interest but can have no effect on output. But monetary policy can easily increase the level of output and lower the interest rate.

in the sense that almost everyone prefers cash to holding a debt
which yields so low a rate of interest. In this event the monetary
authority would have lost effective control over the rate of interest.
But whilst this limiting case might become practically important in
future, I know of no example of it hitherto.[8]

Moreover, Keynes was not particularly worried by this problem, for "if
such a situation were to arise, it would mean that the public authority
itself could borrow through the banking system on an unlimited scale at
a nominal rate of interest."

A second interesting special case can bring the IS-LM model nearly
back to the classical theory. This case arises if there is no speculative
demand for money, so that the total demand for money becomes completely inelastic with respect to the rate of interest. In this scenario, the
money supply becomes an inflexible determinant of the level of income,
and the LM curve is vertical, as shown in Figure 5.11.

In this case, fiscal policy is ineffective. Shifts in the IS curve raise and
lower interest rates but have no consequences for the level of employment because, due to the higher interest costs, any increase in govern-

[8]   Keynes, *The General Theory*, p. 207.

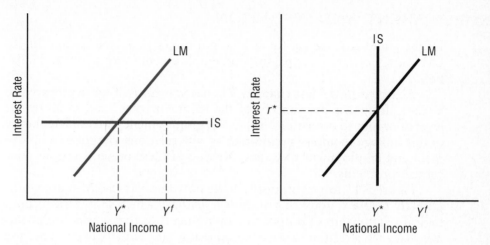

FIGURE 5.12   Horizontal and Vertical IS Curves

When the IS schedule is perfectly flat, as in the graph on the left, fiscal policy is again helpless. There is complete crowding out of private investment by public spending. But monetary policy can move the economy toward full employment. What can policy do and not do in the case depicted in the graph on the right?

ment spending is completely offset by reductions in private investment spending. This is an extreme case of *complete crowding out* (of private investment by public spending). There is a single equilibrium level of real income, governed at fixed prices by the money supply. Only by changing the quantity of circulating money can the level of output be raised or lowered (and then only if, in fact, changes in money can affect real output rather than merely affecting prices).

Horizontal or vertical IS curves, which also can be imagined, are shown in Figure 5.12, although they have been much less important to the history of disputes over Keynesian economics. A horizontal IS curve (on the left of Figure 5.12) will arise if the interest–elasticity of demand for investment rises to an indefinitely high level. In this case, a rise in government spending does not affect income, because the slight rise of interest rates it causes forces private investment down by an exactly equal amount. Likewise, there is dollar-for-dollar "crowding in" when spending and interest rates fall. Monetary policy can therefore easily be set to generate full employment.

The vertical IS curve (on the right of Figure 5.12) arises if investment is, for practical purposes, fixed and insensitive to changes in the interest rate. In this case, crowding out does not occur, and increases in government spending can readily produce full employment. Shifts in monetary policy, on the other hand, are useless.

EMPLOYMENT AND INFLATION

Of the issues that are *not* (or at least not directly) treated within the IS-LM framework, two are paramount: employment (once again) and inflation.

As noted in the last chapter, Keynes was himself quite prepared to discard altogether the concept of the labor "market" and to allow the level of output to determine the level of employment. A complete theory of this linkage requires specification of two relations: output to employment and employment to wages. Neither of these presents serious conceptual problems.

Figure 5.13(top right) displays the now familiar IS-LM framework. Directly below is graphed a *production function*, which shows the technological relationship of output to employment. In this world, we postulate that such a relationship exists and that it is essentially one to one: any given level of output implies a specific, unique volume of employment. To put it another way, technology is fixed in the short run. The production function graphed here has a conventional (indeed classical) shape, denoting diminishing returns to labor: as employment increases, output increases but at an ever diminishing rate.

The curve at the bottom left in Figure 5.13 represents the demand for labor. This curve shows the relationship between levels of employment and the wages that firms are willing to pay. It is derived from the production function itself, on the principle that wages reflect the marginal productivity of labor. Since the production function has diminishing returns, as employment increases, marginal productivity declines and wages fall. Given a level of employment, the wage is therefore fully determined.

There is no need, or role, in this argument for a supply curve for labor. Unemployment is defined in the usual empirical way actually used by the Bureau of Labor Statistics, through surveys that measure and compare the number actually working with the number actively seeking work but unable to find "acceptable" employment.[9] No theoretical presumption exists that such workers could find work if they were prepared to lower their asking wage. To the contrary, the only way unemployed resources can be absorbed within this framework is to increase the level of *effective demand*—of total spending in the economy. In that case, there will be higher employment and lower real wages.[10]

[9] The Bureau of Labor Statistics publishes numerous measures of unemployment, of which this one is the most prominent. It excludes all those who are not seeking work, either because they do not wish to work or because they may believe that finding work is impossible under prevailing conditions ("discouraged workers").

[10] This, as noted briefly in Chapter 2, was what Keynes believed would happen if stimulative policies were adopted to end the Great Depression. He later came to believe that real wages need not fall with rising employment, thus casting doubt on the validity of diminishing returns.

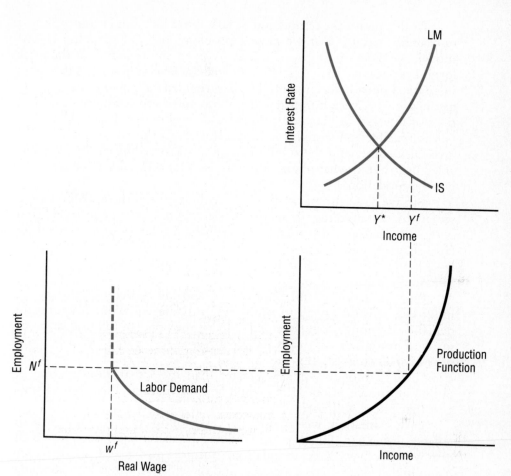

FIGURE 5.13   IS-LM and Labor Demand

As monetary and fiscal policies push employment toward the full employment level, the marginal product of labor falls, and so does the real wage that firms are willing to pay. At employment levels lower than N^f, real wages fall below w^f, which is the minimum that society is prepared to permit.

Within this framework, it is clearly not possible for demand and output to increase in real terms indefinitely. Indeed, in the vicinity of the point denoted by Y^f, because of diminishing returns, increases in expenditures cease to yield corresponding increases in real output. At that point, the real wage that firms are willing to offer to hire additional workers to meet that demand falls below the minimum—if there is one—at which society is willing to permit people to work. Real output is therefore constrained to an upper limit by the fact of full employment.

At this point, the temptation to talk about inflation becomes almost unbearably strong. But we have a problem. In presenting the IS-LM model, we have up to now carefully avoided all discussion of the price level. In effect, we have treated P, the general level of prices, as though it were fixed outside the system. This has enabled us to avoid making any distinctions between nominal and real income, between money and real rates of interest, or between nominal and "real money balances" and to talk in sensible and straightforward terms about the rate of interest, the level of income, and the stock of money.[11] Proceeding in this way enabled us to avoid what might otherwise be a lot of head-scratching as we got the model out.

But we have also paid a price: an inability, with the tools presented so far, to say anything about the determinants of the price level. And without a theory of the price level, we have no theory of how the price level changes, which is to say no theory of the rate of inflation. The price level has simply been left out of the IS-LM model up to now. It is the "missing equation" of our Keynesian system.

Our discussion of full employment and full capacity output points intuitively toward a way to supply the missing equation. If aggregate demands in money terms are pressed past the point of full utilization of physical resources, the capacity to increase real output at prevailing prices ceases to exist. But the demand is there. Expenditures are being attempted at money volumes greater than the actual money value of output at present prices. What could be more natural, then, but to suggest that prices will rise?

In this situation, we say with the early followers of Keynes[12] that an *inflation gap* exists. This gap can be closed by increasing prices, in which case we effectively have an inflation. Business profits rise, workers demand higher wages, costs increase, and the inflation gap is recreated in a continuing pattern known as a *wage-price spiral*.

These notions of full employment and the inflation gap never achieved the status of a fully accepted theory. Their failure to do so occurred partly for theoretical and partly for empirical reasons. On the theoretical side, American economists proved unwilling to throw over the fundamental concept of a market—governed by demand *and* supply—for labor. And the concept of the inflation gap seemed to imply a threshold, or *full employment barrier*, below which inflation would not be a problem. This seemed to contradict the empirical observation that inflation tended to rise smoothly as the unemployment rate fell; there was an inflation problem before the economy reached full employment.

---

[11] This has also enabled us to use our capital letter variable names, $C, I, G, Y,$ M, and so on, as though they measured real as well as nominal quantities.
[12] For example, Arthur Smithies of Harvard.

THE PHILLIPS CURVE

In the mid-1950s, A. W. Phillips, an engineer from New Zealand who was then working at the London School of Economics, measured changes in unemployment and wages for the United Kingdom from 1862 through 1957. From this data, he offered a remarkable generalization: there seemed to be a stable association between changes in employment and the rate of wage inflation. As employment increased, in other words, money wage rates seemed also to increase.

This may not seem surprising, but remember that it was not at all what the classical theory either of labor markets or of inflation predicted. That theory, after all, held that labor supply and labor demand depend only on movements of *real* wages. Nominal wages are, of course, just one special kind of price, and nominal wage inflation, if accompanied by corresponding changes in other prices, need not affect real wages or have any particular relationship to changes in employment. Phillips found that one hundred years of British history suggested that such an empirical relationship did, in fact, exist.

It was a short step from Phillips's finding to a parallel assertion about the *price level* and unemployment. This step was taken by Paul Samuelson and Robert Solow in 1960.[13] They converted wage change to price change by applying a simple formula: prices are a markup over wages, so price changes (P in the formulas below) must be a function of wage changes and therefore, if Phillips was correct, also of the rate of unemployment (U). For example,

$$(5.12) \qquad \dot{P} = \alpha + \beta \dot{W}(U)$$

This relationship between inflation and unemployment came to be known as the *Phillips curve*. For the specific case where $\dot{W}(U) = 1/U$ and so $P = \alpha + \beta(1/U)$, a convenient functional form that makes the rate of inflation a linear function of the reciprocal of the rate of unemployment, we have the relationship shown in Figure 5.14.

The coefficient α has a simple interpretation: it is the negative of the rate of labor productivity growth, π. As average output per worker rises, the total output level in the economy is rising. If wages for each worker are unchanged, prices must necessarily decline or this extra output could not be purchased. If wage changes are just equal to the rate of productivity growth, then all the output can be purchased at unchanged prices, and prices will be stable. In general, the rate of price inflation must equal the rate of wage inflation minus the rate of labor productivity growth. So we can rewrite (5.12) as

$$\dot{P} = \beta \dot{W}(U) - \pi$$

[13] Paul Samuelson and Robert Solow, "Analytical Aspects of Anti-Inflation Policy," *American Economic Review*, Vol. 50, May 1960, pp. 177–194.

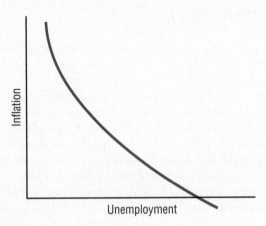

FIGURE 5.14   Phillips Curve

> The Phillips curve shows an empirical relationship between inflation and unemployment. This relationship held for a very long time (1860–1913) in the United Kingdom and for most of the postwar period up to 1969 in the United States. It became an important part of Keynesian models of the macroeconomy because it provided a way of incorporating inflation into the model.

Samuelson and Solow replicated Phillips's empirical work for the twenty-five years of post-Depression data then available for the United States, using their revised association between inflation and unemployment. They came up with a stable, negatively sloped relation similar to that which Phillips had found. They then suggested that this relation represented the menu of U.S. policy choices.

As Solow has related, the result was a boon to estimators of macro models.[14] Armed with the Phillips curve and a computer, anyone could simulate the consequences of differing paths of monetary and fiscal policy and come up with results of immediately evident significance for social well-being. Unemployment and inflation were (as they remain) the principal variables at play in macroeconomic policy discussion. This was a big improvement over the unadorned IS-LM model, since what, after all, is the precise welfare significance of the level of GDP or the interest rate?

From 1960 through 1966, as Figure 5.15 shows, the Phillips curve estimates for the United States held up remarkably well, leading to a dramatic reinforcement of the Samuelson-Solow conjecture. As the Vietnam War gathered steam, there seemed to be a clear choice: if unemployment declined, inflation would rise; for inflation to fall, unemployment would have to rise. Phillips curve arguments had direct significance both for economists involved in policymaking and for the

[14] R. M. Solow, "What We Know and Don't Know About Inflation," *Technology Review*, 81 (January 1979), pp. 31–46.

politicians they associated with, seeming to force a clear choice between price stability and full employment.

But what was the theoretical basis for the Phillips curve? Essentially, there was none.

Some economists felt that Phillips's observations, and those of Samuelson and Solow, could be explained by telling a story about *disequilibrium* in labor markets. Assume that changes in the level of money wages respond to changes in the difference between the quantity of labor demanded (N^d) and the quantity supplied (N^s) and that the unemployment rate itself reflects this difference. If, for any reason, the quantity of labor that firms wish to hire at a given wage goes up, there will be competitive pressure in labor markets, unemployment will fall, and money wages will rise as employment rises. Conversely, if the demand for labor falls relative to the supply at the going wage, then employment will fall and wages will fall with it. The argument is summarized in the following mathematical relation:

$$\dot{W} = \dot{W}\,(N^s - N^d) = \dot{W}\,(U) \qquad \dot{W} < 0$$

where W represents the proportionate change in money wages and U is the measured rate of unemployment, equal to the difference between labor supplied and labor demanded.

But that little scenario does not withstand close scrutiny very well. For instance, one could argue that unions become more aggressive when unemployment rates are low, so that wage *demands* go up. But why would employers give in to union demands for higher rates of increase in money wages? And even if higher wages are paid, shouldn't that lead to

FIGURE 5.15   Phillips Curve 1948–1969

The Phillips Curve once fit the data pretty well.

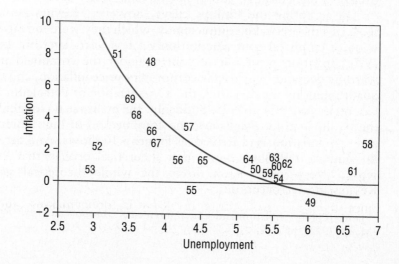

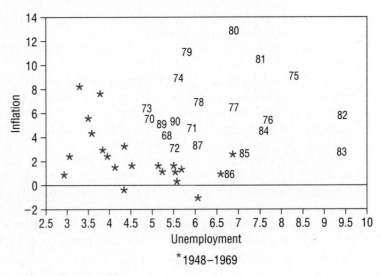

FIGURE 5.16   Phillips Curve 1948–1990

The data no longer supports the Phillips curve.

more unemployment rather than to higher prices? In the words of James Tobin, the Phillips curve was "an empirical finding in search of a theory, like Pirandello characters in search of an author."[15]

In the end, the Phillips curve amounted to the proposition that, as a matter of empirical fact, shifts in demand dominated labor markets and produced rises or declines in wages and prices. As such, the Phillips curve plugged the inflation gap in Keynesian theory, providing an operational and seemingly reliable equation that related unemployment to inflation. Macroeconomic model–building in the Keynesian tradition became a big business, and policy-advising thrived.

In accepting the Phillips curve, however, Keynesians sowed the seeds of a theoretical incompleteness, which they were to reap in a whirlwind of empirical contradiction only a few years later on. In the early 1970s, inflation went out of control under the combined pressure of wartime demand, worldwide commodity price inflation, and then price-quadrupling by the oil cartel, the Organization of Petroleum Exporting Countries (OPEC) in 1973. Suddenly, the evidence no longer supported the Phillips curve. *Stagflation*, the combination of high unemployment and high inflation, had arrived, as Figure 5.16 shows. And the collapse of the empirical Phillips curve, that theoretical orphan that "seemed to work," very nearly took down the whole theoretical structure of Keynesian macroeconomics.

[15] James Tobin, "Inflation and Unemployment," *American Economic Review*, 62 (March 1972), pp. 1,9.

Taking a Closer Look

SOME COMPARATIVE PHILLIPS CURVES

Figures 5.15 and 5.16 tell the standard story of the Phillips curve, with annual data for the United States from the early postwar years to the present. This story is of a relationship that failed, of a Phillips curve that holds up through 1969 and then collapses.

    Is this really what happened? In the three charts that accompany this box, we look again at the U.S. data, as well as at data for Great Britain and Japan. But instead of looking at yearly average data, we will use a *moving average* of *monthly data* over thirty years. Monthly data give us many more datapoints, and taking a moving average helps to smooth the series and reduce purely random disturbances (statistical

"noise") that monthly numbers often reflect.

    Looking first at the U.S. numbers (Figure 5.B1), we see clearly the original Phillips curve, smooth and shallow, from 1962 to 1970. During all of these years, there was steady decline in unemployment and rise in inflation. The Phillips curve in those years was always moving in one direction. When recession hit in 1970, with sharply rising unemployment, the relationship did not exactly fail; events merely established that it did not work both ways. Unemployment could not fall without raising inflation, but unemployment could rise, it turned out, without forcing inflation back down.

FIGURE 5.B1   **Inflation and Unemployment: United States**

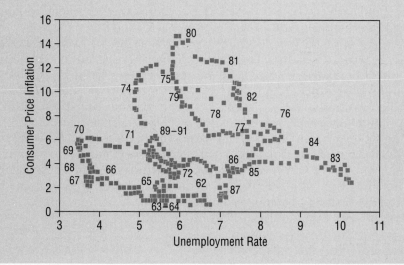

The expansion from 1971 to 1974 seemed to repeat the pattern of the 1960s, although from a higher base rate of unemployment. The recession of 1974–75 made the non-reversibility point again: higher unemployment does not cure inflation as quickly as falling unemployment produces inflation. Finally, the lesson has to be learned a third time, in the expansion of 1977 to 1980 and the double recessions of 1980 and 1981–1983.

The Phillips curve did not exactly collapse into chaos after 1970. Rather, as Keynesians at the time tended to argue, it seems to have shifted to the left with each recession—making for higher and higher unemployment at each rate of inflation. Why did this happen? For one reason, as one of us has argued,[1] the experience of recessions forced many more people, especially women and young people, into the work force. This created a huge strain on relatively unskilled labor markets, while at the same time not affecting by very much the wages and other costs that determine most prices in the economy. As a result, inflation accelerated with each expansion, but high unemployment persisted for less skilled workers.

Not until the years of the Reagan expansion from 1983 to 1989 do we see a real change in this pattern. As the chart shows, the United States saw six years of steadily falling unemployment with no increase in inflation. Good news? Unfortunately, it would appear not. For the achievement in

this period seems to have been accomplished by creating a huge number of low-skilled and poorly paid jobs—eighteen million jobs in all and not very many in high-wage sectors. Meanwhile, a high-dollar policy held prices in check by creating a flood of cheap imported goods. The price of flattening out the Phillips curve was a huge and persistent trade deficit (which rose to $150 billion or more per year) and a corresponding accumulation of foreign debt. This price eventually proved unsustainable, and the economy slipped back into recession after 1989.

The next two charts show similar data for Great Britain and Japan. Britain (Figure 5.B2) seems to have virtually no Phillips curve in the pre-1973 years, a time of full employment and nearly stable prices. Then came the oil shock of 1974, which in Great Britain took the form of a sharp increase in inflation. This was followed by more than a decade of austerity under the Labour government of James Callaghan and then the long Conservative rule of Margaret Thatcher. During this time, a Phillips curve, by then seemingly extinct in the United States, seems to have arisen in Britain; but it is one of slowly falling inflation in the face of rising unemployment. After 1987 or so, recovery finally began, and the British economy appears to move back along a fairly flat Phillips curve. Will this stability last? Only time will tell.

The Japanese case (Figure 5.B3) appears similar to the British,

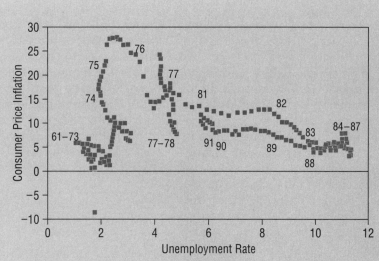

FIGURE 5.B2   Inflation and Unemployment: Great Britain

although we present data only for the years from 1970 to the present. Once again, the oil shock disrupted a phase of stability and set the stage for a long period of slowly falling inflation and slowly rising unemployment. (Note however, the difference in scale: unemployment in Japan rises only to 2.9 percent by official measures.) Once again,

FIGURE 5.B3   Inflation and Unemployment: Japan

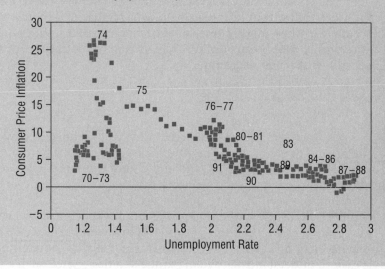

there is a recent recovery that seems to track back along the Phillips curve reasonably well.

In both the British and Japanese cases since 1974, as in the U.S. case after 1983, the Phillips relationship appears to be comparatively flat. This indicates that it is costly to reduce inflation by raising unemployment and relatively painless, in terms of inflation, to cut unemployment. This is a far cry from the arguments you will encounter in the next few chapters, which

present reasons why the Phillips curve should, in principle, be vertical!

Will these new facts lead to a new theoretical view on this subject? They have not done so yet, and many economists would like to have a lot more evidence about this tricky relationship before jumping, once again, to conclusions.

---

[1] James K. Galbraith, *Balancing Acts: Technology, Finance and the American Future* (Basic Books, 1989).

IS-LM IN MODERN MACROECONOMICS

The debacle of the Phillips curve led to a reformulation of the IS-LM analysis, which was then incorporated into modern non-Keynesian theories of macroeconomics. We develop these theories in greater detail later, but here it is already possible to sketch several key points of this reformulation.

The essential step is to reintroduce the supply curve for labor into Figure 5.13 (bottom left)—as is done in Figure 5.17 (bottom left). Now we have a labor market once again, characterized in the purely classical way with a supply curve and a demand curve, both functions solely and strictly of the real wage:

$$N^d = N^d(w) \qquad N^{d\prime} < 0$$
$$N^s = N^s(w) \qquad N^{s\prime} > 0$$

As in any market characterized by well-defined and well-behaved supply and demand, two magnitudes are determined jointly: the equilibrium level of employment and the equilibrium real wage. For unemployment to exist in such a model, real wages must for some reason be "too high"—so that more people want to work than would be true at equilibrium, while at the same time employers choose to provide fewer jobs than they would if the labor market were in balance. We are back, in other words, all the way to the classical explanation of unemployment! It is easy to understand why Paul Samuelson designated such a marriage of

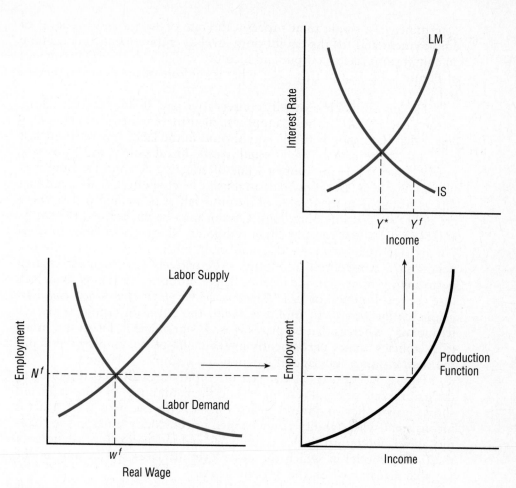

FIGURE 5.17   IS-LM and the Labor Market

If the labor market determines the levels of employment and production, then IS-LM's only role is to set a level of effective demand (Y^*) consistent with full employment without inflation. In this case, we show how a deflationary inconsistency might arise.

Keynesian demand analysis with pre-Keynesian labor market theory as the *neoclassical synthesis.*

The neoclassical synthesis changes entirely the interpretation of the role of policy. It is possible for IS and LM jointly to determine income and output, for output to determine employment, and for employment to determine wages, which is the sequence depicted in Figure 5.13. Fiscal and monetary policies then play the essential role in setting real output leveis and in controlling the rate of unemployment, just as Keynes and his followers believed they did. Or, it is possible for the labor market to determine, in a single joint process, the rate of wages and the level of employment and for the equilibrium level of employment to determine an equilibrium rate of output and income, which is the revised sequence of Figure 5.17. But in that case, what is the role of fiscal and monetary policy?

The answer is a profoundly conservative one. If labor markets clear, as the neoclassical synthesis supposes, then there exists a *natural rate of output* that corresponds to the equilibrium in the labor market (which is itself called the *natural rate of employment*). Fiscal policy and monetary policy codetermine the money value of effective demand for output at prevailing prices. But if policies establish a level of effective demand that differs from the money value of output itself at prevailing prices, there are only two possible outcomes. Output may be pushed away from its equilibrium values, causing either temporary shortages of labor or temporary unemployment—a disequilibrium phenomenon that will not persist in a competitive economy. Alternatively, prices must change permanently to accommodate the change in money demands, in which case the real function of IS-LM is *to model the effects of monetary and fiscal policies on the price level*. In either event, the effect on output is always temporary, whereas that on prices is always permanent. Fiscal and monetary policies cannot permanently increase output and employment, and the central policy message of Keynesian economics is refuted.

Figure 5.17 illustrates the rate of employment that corresponds to the natural rate of employment N^f and the natural rate of output Y^f and shows how policy might establish a value of effective demand $Y^\star$ that is inconsistent with stability at unchanged prices. Many times in the chapters ahead, we return to this framework and indeed explore versions of the IS-LM model in which the price level displaces real income as the variable determined on the horizontal axis.

APPRAISAL OF IS-LM MODELS

A few final comments are in order on this important, still pivotal phase in the evolution of macroeconomic model–building.

The IS-LM framework goes a long way toward elucidating the insights of *The General Theory*. The theory of investment, for example, shows the dependence of investment on the interest rate that Keynes suggested. The theory of interest is rooted, as Keynes maintained it should be, in liquidity preference rather than in the supply and demand for loanable funds (the classical capital market). The level of employment in the model depends, as Keynes argued, on effective demand. And the framework provides a clear, intuitive, and in many ways compelling framework for evaluating the effects of changes in monetary and fiscal policies in widely varying combinations and under a wide range of differing external conditions. In all of this, the IS-LM framework helps to clarify for us many critical points of departure of Keynesian macroeconomics from the classical tradition that came before it.

Yet the framework also simplifies and even omits much that is critical to a full understanding of Keynesian theory. While the developers and users of IS-LM generally think of the model as Keynesian, many Keynesians are profoundly uncomfortable with it. We try in this appraisal to convey some of the flavor of their discomfort, to bring into focus some theoretical considerations that the IS-LM model tends to obscure.

Part of the difficulty can be traced to the fact that most representations of IS-LM present their argument exclusively in "real" terms. Thus, the LM curve is said to represent the equilibrium between supply and demand for "real balances," defined as the stock of money adjusted by the price level ($M/P = m$). Correspondingly, the IS curve measures the equilibrium of savings and investment in real terms: savings is a set-aside of commodities out of the consumption of commodities; investment is the physical conversion of these saved commodities to productive use. The interest rate against which investment decisions are taken (or not taken) must therefore be a "real" rate, the money rate of interest (i) reduced by expected future changes in the price level ($\dot{P}^e$):

$$r = i - \dot{P}^e$$

An IS-LM model conceived exclusively in real terms is logically coherent, for it permits one to stipulate a separate theory, perhaps a monetary theory, of the price level and so to fill in the missing inflation equation without disrupting the IS-LM analysis. But to do so is, in effect, to reestablish the classical dichotomy between monetary and real phenomena in economics. And this does great violence to *The General Theory*. The IS-LM model was developed by students and contemporaries of Keynes to help interpret and formalize his ideas. But as we saw in Chapter 3, Keynes was very clear on the need to have a monetary theory — not only of prices, but of production. The money rate of interest, not the real rate of interest, is determined by the interaction of liquidity preference and the actions of the central bank. It is the money wage, not the real wage, in terms of which workers rent their services to companies in the labor market. And effective demand is money demand, not demand for real commodities except as mediated by money.

A monetary theory of production requires that money be treated seriously as a part of every economic process. And, in contrast to IS-LM's emphasis on the determination of a general equilibrium for output and interest, a monetary production model aims inherently at explaining fluctuations and instability.

For Keynes, the essential role of money was to help economic actors cope with modern economic life's vast instabilities. In particular, Keynes stressed the importance of expectations, and of changing expectations, to the development of economic events. Expectations determine the hopes or fears of businessmen about their future profits and therefore guide the pricing of capital assets and the all-important rate of investment. Expectations relate the past to the future—and money holdings provide the evidence of what expectations are. Shifting demands for money reflect shifting expectations.

By their nature, expectations were and are immensely volatile. Partly, this is because the future cannot be known. Beyond this, the climate of expectations is determined in large part by the estimates of individuals about what other individuals are thinking—by a game of second-guessing and one-upmanship. Keynes felt that the fact that much objective economic activity (especially business investment) depends on the subjective state of expectations rendered much of the economic future inherently unpredictable. And therefore (contrary to the lifework of many subsequent Keynesian economists), the proper purpose of economics was less to predict the future than to understand the mechanisms whereby capitalist economies sometimes became radically unstable.

As the IS-LM model developed (especially in the hands of American economists), the problems of time and uncertainty, and the treatment of economic problems as involving decisions about an uncertain and unknowable future, gradually faded into the background. One could so easily forget that the marginal efficiency of capital and the speculative demand for money are purely subjective, susceptible to changing on a whim! Instead, the development of IS-LM promoted an impression of general equilibrium stability that, while it largely preserved the structural relationships Keynes argued for, neglected and de-emphasized the inherent instability of their movement through time.

Armed with its new-found specificity, macroeconomists turned to the task of forecasting, generally with large-scale linear models set up on computers. In this effort, they were forced to attempt to find deterministic relationships between the past and the future, relationships of the sort Keynes would have denied were present. For example, the theory of interest and liquidity preference came to depend exclusively on current and past, rather than current and expected future, interest rates. The theory of investment came to view the marginal efficiency of capital as a known and stable, rather than as an expected and unstable, quantity. To arrive at numerical predictions of the future, Keynesian economists revised their theories so that the future could be modeled as a systematic outgrowth of the past. In doing so, they parted company with Keynes.

The consequence of these attempts to build deterministic forecasting models on Keynesian premises was large-scale, periodic, and embarrassing forecasting failures. It became apparent that a theory of investment based only on past behavior could not reliably forecast downturns of investment. Nor could a theory of demand for money that was based only on past behavior forecast times when the speculative demand for money might be especially great or especially small. Models that could not anticipate either of these might have been useful and reasonably accurate when the economy was stable (precisely when such models were least needed), but they did not reliably get the economic boats of their subscribers into port in advance of a storm. As a result, the great econometric forecasting enterprises have, after about two decades of commercial success, largely lost the esteem and respect that they once commanded.

As it happened, these weaknesses also gave weight to theoretical objections raised by economists who either had never accepted the Keynesian perspective or who felt that the failures of Keynesian modeling techniques proved the failure of Keynesian theory as a whole. New models were written, some of which incorporated time and risk in explicit ways. Their idea was to give an intertemporal dimension to the solution of the model, incorporating the element of riskiness in predicting the future without departing from the general equilibrium framework. Thus, the crisis of IS-LM gave rise to the framework of *rational expectations*, to which we devote considerable time and space in the chapters ahead.

SPECIAL SECTION

Varieties of the Investment Function

The theory of aggregative investment has taken many forms, but these do not stem from empirical findings, as was the case with the aggregate consumption function. Instead, the investment function really emerges out of competing visions of how capitalists—those making investments—behave.

Underlying Keynes's investment function—the marginal effi-ciency of capital schedule—is the belief that the decision to produce a new capital asset must occur in a climate of impenetrable uncertainty about the profitability of such an asset. To gauge the capital asset's prospective yield, which we have seen is an indispensable element in the calculation of its marginal efficiency, is virtually impossible. In the effort to do so, Keynes would argue, there are more grounds for expecting things to go wrong than right. Therefore, "Individual initiative will only be adequate when reasonable calculation is supplemented and supported by animal spirits, so that the thought of ultimate loss which often overtakes pioneers, as experience undoubtedly tells us and them, is put aside as a healthy man puts aside the expectation of death."[1]

Faced with intractable uncertainty, individuals may resort to the adoption of rules of thumb or *conventions*. Based upon beliefs about the future size of the market, they might seek to identify a target level of the capital stock. They may use the current rate of growth of output as a guide to next year's demand. This would mean that if the economy is growing more rapidly, investment will be expanding, reinforcing the expansion, and the capital stock will be increasing. In contrast, if national income declines, investment will drop, reinforcing the contraction, and the capital stock will erode.

Keynes was not specific about the conventions that individuals may follow in the face of an uncertain future. But this particular convention for the investment decision underlies an investment function of the *accelerator* variety,[2] so named because of the reinforcing effects of an increase in income on investment, and subsequently on income again, via the multiplier. As long as producers of capital goods forecast future demand from the current growth of national income and project their desired stocks of fixed capital on that basis, the economy's growth rate increases progressively as it moves into a positive growth path. In parallel fashion, if there is a downward shock to the level of income, the economy's growth will decelerate.

The accelerator could be modified to introduce adjustment lags. In one well-known version, firms only make plans to reduce a part of the discrepancy between desired and actual capital stock in each production period. However, the larger the gap, the greater the volume of investment. This adaptation is known as the *flexible accelerator*.

The mechanical structure of the accelerator did not satisfy classically-minded modern economists, who also were uncomfortable with the open-endedness of Keynes's marginal efficiency of capital schedule. They argued that the decision to invest should be placed on the same footing as rational optimizing decisions in any aspect of economic activity. Consequently, they downplayed or ignored the radical nature of Keynes's claims about uncertainty. Instead, the neoclassicals argued that a far more complex story should be told about the determinants of the desired capital stock, a story that includes costs of production of new capital goods—real wages, the real rate of interest at which the producer can borrow funds, the depreciation rate of the existing stock of capital, investment taxes or subsidies—as well as expectations of future demand. The accelerator model could be adapted to take these additional considerations into account. But then, of course, the model no longer offers the same income-driven theory of investment.

The *cost of capital* model has taken pride of place as the neoclassical theory of investment. Harvard University economist Dale W. Jorgenson has been especially prominent in the development of this approach to the investment function.[3] In his model, the representative producer of capital goods assesses the returns and expenses associated with the production of the marginal unit of each capital asset. This does not happen in an environment of uncertainty; instead, decisions are made with complete certainty or at least rational expectations of the net income stream.

James Tobin's *q-theory* approach to the investment function, a third alternative, finds its origins in Thorstein Veblen's *Theory of Business Enterprise*.[4] Tobin incorporates themes from Keynes's analysis of the stock exchange and from Veblen's still earlier analysis of the valuation of firms.[5]

Tobin's q is the ratio of the valuation of the existing capital stock to its replacement cost. The existing capital stock is found in ongoing business enterprises. Claims to these enterprises, equities, are traded on a stock exchange. Their valuation is based upon the number of shares of stock issued times the price of each share. If this valuation exceeds the cost of constructing an entirely new enterprise of the same type, then it would pay a producer to start up such a new business. On the other hand, if the valuation is less than the cost of constructing an entirely new enterprise type, then it would instead pay a producer to buy up shares in an enterprise that already exists.

Tobin therefore reasons that if $q > 1$, there is a positive stimulus to net investment; if $q < 1$, net investment will be retarded. In the intermediate case where the valuation of existing enterprises is exactly equivalent to their replacement cost, then the volume of net investment will remain stable.

The Tobin q theory can drift toward the neoclassical formulation of cost of capital if the stock exchange is dominated by individuals who price corporate shares on the basis of the "fundamentals"—the genuine underlying profit performance of the enterprises in question. However, the Tobin q-theory takes on a Keynesian flavor if the stock exchange is dominated by individuals engaged in sheer speculation—merely trying to outguess the buy-and-sell strategies of other traders.[6] Because individuals can only follow the fundamentals if they have solid knowledge about the future, whether the q-theory is Keynesian or neoclassical depends on whether one accepts or rejects Keynes's views about uncertainty.

A final approach of note is the investment theory of Michal Kalecki, a Polish economist who ventured into Cambridge, England, in the 1930s. It is now acknowledged that Kalecki conceived of the modern theory of effective aggregate demand independently of Keynes at virtually the same time.[7] But three of his papers that advanced his theory of the capitalist economy were published (in 1933, 1934, and

1935) in Polish and remained largely inaccessible to English-reading audiences until the late 1960s.

In Kalecki's investment function, net additions to fixed capital occur in response to increases in the general rate of profit. Gross profitability in an economy is the ratio of gross profits to the existing capital stock. As that ratio rises, the rate of investment goes up; as it falls, the rate of investment declines. At any moment, the greater the level of capitalists' spending, which mainly takes the form of investment, the greater the level of capitalists' profits. If capitalists spend less, they receive less profits. Hence, the famous Kaleckian aphorism: "Workers spend what they get; capitalists get what they spend." Kalecki wrote that "capitalists, as a whole, determine their own profits by the extent of their investment and personal consumption. In a way they are 'masters of their fate.'"[8]

Profitability swings up and down with investment, and investment swings up and down with profitability. In this way, Kalecki derived a capitalist business cycle linked directly to swings in investment activity, much as Keynes tied the business cycles to fluctuations in the more elusive marginal efficiency of capital.[9]

[1] J. M. Keynes, *The General Theory of Employment, Interest and Money* (London: Macmillan, 1936), p. 162.

[2] Paul Samuelson, "Interactions Between the Multiplier Analysis and the Principle of Acceleration," *Review of Economics and Statistics,* 21 (May 1939), 75–78.

[3] See, for example, Dale W. Jorgenson, "Econometric Studies of Investment Behavior: A Survey," *Journal of Economic Literature,* Vol. 9, December 1971, pp. 1111–1147.

[4] Thorstein Veblen, *The Theory of Business Enterprise* (New York: Charles Scribner's Sons, 1904; reprinted by Augustus M. Kelley, 1975).

[5] See, for example, James Tobin, "A General Equilibrium Approach to Monetary Theory," *Journal of Money, Credit and Banking,* Vol. 1, February 1969, pp. 421–431; and James Tobin, "Monetary Policies and the Economy: The Transmission Mechanism," *Southern Economic Journal,* Vol. 44, January 1978.

[6] See Keynes, *The General Theory,* chap. 12.

[7] See especially the first three essays in Michal Kalecki, *Selected Essays in the Dynamics of the Capitalist Economy* (Cambridge: Cambridge University Press, 1971), pp. 1–34.

[8] Ibid., p. 13. Note that increases in capitalists' consumption, even on luxury items such as yachts and furs, also raise the total volume of capitalists' profits. The intuition behind this is that spending on such items creates wage income for the artisans and others who produce such commodities, increasing the demand for wage goods relative to the supply and driving down the real wage.

[9] Kalecki omitted the rate of interest from his theory on the grounds that it follows swings in profitability and changes only slowly relative to changes in the profit rate. He also abstracted from the financial sector because, he argued, capitalists really only borrow from other capitalists in that sector.

SUMMARY

The more complete, more sophisticated Keynesian model, known as the IS-LM model, includes monetary considerations and an explanation of investment behavior.

The IS curve is the set of interest rate and income pairs that equilibrate savings and investment. Savings is the residual of income minus consumption. With consumption remaining a function of disposable income, saving is by extension also a function of disposable income.

Investment is dependent on the marginal efficiency of capital (*MEC*) in this model. As new investment is made, less profitable ventures are taken up, and the *MEC* decreases. Because the marginal efficiency of capital is identified with profitability, investment is carried to the point where the *MEC* just equals the rate of interest. The higher the interest rate, the earlier that new investment comes to a halt; the lower the rate of interest, the more new investment there will be. Therefore, investment is a decreasing function of the interest rate. Combining the savings function with the investment function produces a downward-sloping IS curve.

The LM curve provides the set of interest rate and income pairs that clear the money market. There are two types of demand for money. The first is the transactions demand for money: as income increases, more money is demanded to make transactions. The second type is the speculative demand: when bond interest rates are low, speculators hold on to money in expectation of higher interest rates in the future. Thus, the speculative demand for money is a decreasing function of the interest rate. In conjunction with a fixed money supply, the speculative and transactions demands for money trace out a positively sloped LM curve.

The intersection of the LM and IS curves determines a macroeconomic equilibrium that is independent of the labor market. Indeed, nothing guarantees that the IS-LM equilibrium is the same as the equilibrium of the classical labor market. If the IS-LM national income equilibrium occurs at less than that of full employment, policy intervention can bring the economy to full employment. For example, government deficit spending could cause the marginal efficiency of capital schedule to shift out. The new marginal efficiency of capital schedule then produces a new IS curve and a higher equilibrium income level.

Monetary expansion offers a second means of raising income. Increasing the money supply shifts the LM curve down and to the right, also producing a higher level of income. The relative elasticities of the IS and the LM curves determine which policy is most effective.

The IS-LM analysis has at least two serious flaws: price level and employment are not addressed. An intuitive explanation for inflation is that when money demand exceeds the full capacity point, inflation will ensue. Followers of Keynes called this the inflation gap. An explanation of the connection between inflation and employment that gained more acceptance for a time is the Phillips curve. The Phillips curve started out as the empirical observation that for the period 1862 through 1957 in Great Britain, changes in employment and wage inflation had a stable relation. Samuelson and Solow extended this empirical observation to a statement about changes in employment and the price level in general. The Phillips curve led policymakers, at the urging of economists, to form policy in the 1960s and early 1970s based on the presumption of a tradeoff between unemployment and inflation. In the late 1970s, the empirical relation broke down, and high inflation occurred simultaneously with high unemployment; the lack of theoretical underpinnings for the Phillips curve became glaringly apparent. Unfortunately for the reputation of Keynesian economics, many saw the failure of the Phillips curve also as a failure of Keynesian economics itself.

The Phillips curve, however, was never an integral part of the Keynesian analysis, and it actually plays no part in a faithful interpretation of Keynes's work. In fact, the IS-LM analysis also does some violence to Keynes's own economics. Keynes had a monetary theory of production, in which the money rate of interest and effective monetary demand were what was important. These features contrast with the real rate of interest and the price-deflated or real output demand that play a central role in the standard IS-LM framework. Where the IS-LM model strives to determine a general equilibrium, a monetary theory of production strives to explain fluctuations and instability.

Keynes also believed that expectations were an essential source of instability. By ignoring the volatility of expectations, IS-LM contributed to the perceived failure of Keynesian economics. The framework set up in the name of Keynes was essentially static, whereas Keynes imagined a system that was decidedly unstable.

Review Questions

1. Describe how a foreign sector with autonomous exports and autonomous imports could be added to the IS-LM analysis. Emphasize the effect on the goods market equilibrium. How would your answer change if imports were dependent on domestic income?

2. Suppose a government wanted to design a fiscal and monetary policy that would increase national income but not change the interest rate. What should it do?

3. Suppose an economywide increase in productivity occurred. How would the IS-LM analysis be affected? How would your answer fit into a wider critique of the IS-LM analysis? Is the classical framework more useful in analyzing changes in productivity?

4. Suppose the goods market was in equilibrium (on the IS curve) but income was too low for equilibrium in the money market. Describe how total macroeconomic equilibrium could be restored. Then suppose the money market was in equilibrium but income was too high for equilibrium in the goods market. Describe how total macroeconomic equilibrium could be restored.

5. Would any of the different economic classes of society (e.g., workers, business interests) have a vested interest in the existence or nonexistence of a Phillips curve? Explain.

6. Suppose a period of great political turmoil is under way. How might the IS-LM analysis be affected? Pay particular attention to how the uncertainty would affect absolute levels of the various demands—money demand, consumption demand, and investment demand.

Review Problems

1. The following equations describe a macroeconomy that follows the IS-LM framework:

Consumption:	$C = 120 + .8Y$
Savings:	$S = Y - C$
Investment:	$I = 80 - 10r$
Transactions demand for money:	$L_1 = .5Y$
Speculative demand for money:	$L_2 = 500 - 10r$
Money supply:	$1,000$

Explain why each equation does or does not make sense. Determine an equation for the IS curve and for the LM curve. Calculate an equilibrium level of income. Graph the solution.

2. To the model above, add a government sector that spends 140. Determine the equation of the new IS curve? Why is the LM curve unaffected? What is the new equilibrium? Using the results above and the just-calculated equilibrium, determine a fiscal multiplier for this economy. Draw a graph that shows the new equilibrium and its relation to the equilibrium in problem 1.

3. Suppose the money supply in problem 1 is increased to 1,700. Determine the equation of the new LM curve? What is the new equilibrium? Using the results above and the just-calculated equilibrium, determine a fiscal multiplier for this economy. Draw a graph that shows the new equilibrium and its relation to the equilibrium of problem 1.

4. Referring to equation 5.B3 as needed, explain in economic terms the effects of the following on the fiscal multiplier defined as $\Delta Y/\Delta G$:
a. An increase in the interest sensitivity of investment
b. An increase in the marginal propensity to consume
c. An increase in the transactions demand for money
d. An increase in the interest rate sensitivity of the LM curve

5. Explain in economic terms the effects of the following on the money multiplier, defined as $\Delta Y/\Delta M$:
a. An increase in the interest sensitivity of investment
b. An increase in the marginal propensity to consume
c. An increase in the transactions demand for money
d. An increase in the interest rate sensitivity of the LM curve

6. Draw the graphs in Figure 5.7. Draw in a shift to the IS curve that would cause employment greater than full employment. Explain why this situation is not permanently stable. Emphasize in particular the effects vis-à-vis the labor market.

SUGGESTED READINGS

James K. Galbraith, *Balancing Acts: Technology, Finance and the American Future* (Basic Books, 1989).

Thorstein Veblen, *The Theory of Business Enterprise* (New York: Charles Scribners Sons, 1904). Reprinted by Augustus M. Kelley in 1975

Michael Kalecki, *Selected Essays in the Dynamics of the Capitalist Economy* (Cambridge: Cambridge University Press, 1971).

MONETARISM AND NEW CLASSICAL ECONOMICS

Chapter 6

AN INTRODUCTION
TO MONEY

Looking Forward

The four chapters in Part 3 explore the anti-Keynesian counterrevolution, which began with the rise of monetarism in the late 1960s and developed into the full-blown new classical economics of the 1970s and early 1980s.

We have already introduced the role of money in developing the IS-LM model. But we have not spent much time exploring monetary theory or trying to understand some of the larger issues in the treatment of money in economics. To understand monetarism, you need first to acquire some of this background knowledge.

As you read this chapter, consider the following questions:

• What is money, and how is it measured?
• What are the different kinds of monetary systems?
• How is money created? What are the functions of a central bank, and how does central bank monetary policy work?
• What is the relationship between money and credit?

You have now explored in a general way three different theories of the nature and economic role of money.

First, the classical vision, embodied in the classical dichotomy between real and monetary phenomena, relegated money to a role on the sidelines of economic life. In this theory, the quantity of money controls the general level of prices but has no effect on employment, production, or the real standard of living. Money is neutral; money is "a veil."

Keynes, as we saw in Chapter 3, tried to overturn the classical theory and replace it with a monetary theory of production. In Keynes's vision, money is no veil; rather, it is the essence of economic activity itself. Shifting demands for money are governed by the psychologies of businesspeople and by the actions of financial investors and speculators. These demands play a central role in setting the interest rate, the prices of capital assets, and through these two phenomena the level of output in a capitalist economy. Keynes emphasized subjectivity, uncertainty, and volatility in financial markets, with a resulting risk of instability in output and employment. His theory is one of why the "equilibrium" level of output may change and why it may have no tendency to coincide with full employment.

The IS-LM model, finally, recast Keynes's monetary vision in a model of mathematical equilibrium. In IS-LM, there is a speculative demand for money; for this reason, money is not neutral. Changes in monetary policy under most conditions will change the interest rate and so will have real effects on production and employment. On the other hand, the focus of attention in IS-LM is not on subjective and volatile phenomena. Concepts that for Keynes were abstract and difficult to pin down, such as the marginal efficiency of capital schedule and the schedule of speculative demands for money, become well-defined, stable functions in IS-LM. Whether they are so stable and well defined in real life is an important question, one that has often bedeviled economic forecasters trying to build empirical models on Keynesian foundations.

Money obviously plays a critical role, one way or another, in our understanding of macroeconomics. We see much more on this in the chapters ahead. But what do we understand, up to this point, about money? Not very much, beyond some bare-bones concepts of the quantity theory and of transactions and speculative demand. In this chapter, we will explore what money really is, how it is created, and how monetary policy actually works.

WHAT IS MONEY?

Money is vexatious. For economists, particularly those who charge themselves with interpreting its nature and function, money is also often a subject for vague, even occasionally mystical, reflection. The quotations that follow illustrate:[1]

> Sir John Hicks: "Money is defined by its functions. . . . Money is as money does."

[1] These quotations were collected by Paul Davidson in *Money and the Real World*, 2nd ed. London: Macmillan, 1978, p. 140.

As Hicks observes, the physical character of money varies according to circumstances. During biblical times, cattle and oxen served as money; certain island cultures used seashells; in classical Greece and Rome, it was coins of gold, silver, and copper; banknotes first saw use in Medieval Europe; and now we have a vast array of paper instruments and proliferation of purely electronic ones. How do we know these things are money? Not by what they *are* but by what they *do*: money is whatever people use to perform the functions of money.

> Sir Roy Harrod: "Money is a social phenomenon, and many of its current features depend on what people think it is or ought to be."

Thus, "moneyness" rests on social convention. Whatever is routinely accepted as a means of payment *is* money. Anything that becomes accepted (e.g., cigarettes in occupied Germany in 1945; the U.S. dollar in Peru and Bolivia in the past few years) becomes money. Anything that ceases to be accepted (such as the German reichsmark at the time of the great inflation of 1923) ceases to be money.

But what are those social conventions?

> Tibor Scitovsky: "Money is a difficult concept to define, partly because it fulfills not one, but three functions, each of them providing a criterion of moneyness . . . a unit of account, a medium of exchange, and a store of value."

Scitovsky's categorization of the three roles of money—unit of account, medium of exchange, and store of value—is the standard one in modern economics. Let us consider each in turn.

As a *unit of account*, money is the measuring rod by which the value of goods, services, and capital assets can be compared. This function is indispensable for exchange; it enables us to decide how much of any one commodity (bushels of wheat, hours of labor) are required for the acquisition of any other (rocket ships, microcomputers).

The measuring function is also useful even if no exchange is to occur. If, for example, we want to know which of two people is richer, we need not actually put all their assets up for immediate auction. Instead, we can merely make a mental conversion of physical asset holdings, such as houses, stocks, bonds, and artwork (which are not themselves directly comparable), into their equivalent sums of money. By adding up the money-equivalents, we are able to measure the asset wealth of each person and make the comparison. Comparison of values requires that money exist *as a measure* but not that any particular person hold any particular amount of it (nor indeed any amount at all).

Money as a physical entity is only required when *exchange*—Scitovsky's second function—is contemplated. Then the existence of money becomes a powerful convenience, which makes easy and efficient what might otherwise prove cumbersome and impractical. Suppose someone wishes to sell a car and buy a boat. In the absence of money, she would need first to locate the precise boat she wanted and then to persuade the owner of that particular boat to accept her particular car in exchange. Needless to say, if he did not like her car, indeed if he did not like it at least as much as he liked his own boat, no exchange could occur. The requirement for a *double coincidence of wants,* as economists have called it, defeats all efforts to organize society along principles of barter and makes life miserable in some societies (such as the Soviet Union a few years ago) where free markets do not exist.

With money, the problem vanishes. All our car seller has to do now is to take her car to anyone, anyone at all, who values it as highly as the boat owner values his boat. She needs only one such person from which she can get money to then offer to the boat owner, and the deal will be done. There may, indeed, be a car dealer willing, for a fee, to speculate on the existence of such a person and to undertake the search. In that case, the dealer buys the car, advancing to its owner the money to buy the boat even though an ultimate buyer for the car has not yet been found. The car owner can buy the boat, and the boat owner need no longer want her car. He may buy another boat, a horse, an Adriatic or Antarctic cruise, or anything else that strikes his fancy and that he can afford with the money he has received.

If it happens that the now former boat owner has no immediate wish for anything in particular, then Scitovsky's third function of money, as a *store of value,* comes into play. He can simply leave the money in a bank (or in a pillowcase, for that matter) where, undisturbed, it serves as an asset that might at any moment be converted into something useful. Of course, there are many other ways to store value, most of them superior to holding money. They may be either immediately useful (a house one can live in) or increase in value over time (a stock or a painting), or they may pay interest, yielding a return to the holder, as a bond does but as money characteristically does not.

Money, however, has a special virtue; it is *liquid.* Money can be converted immediately and without cost into other goods, services, or assets. A house, a painting, or a stock cannot be so easily converted, for it must first be sold (converted into money). Thus, even though money is *barren* as an asset, most people will choose to hold some of it as a store of value. We say that their willingness to do so reflects their *liquidity preference*—a concept we have seen before and to which we shall return.

IS MONEY RATIONAL?

These three roles for money—unit of account, means of exchange, and store of value—have led to what may be called a *rationalist* explanation for the development and existence of money. Essentially, this explanation holds that trade caused money. In other words, the rationalist idea is that a need for money came to exist, at some long distant date in the past, as trade developed between individuals and communities and as societies wrestled with the difficulties of systems of barter (nonmonetary exchange). Money was invented, in this view, specifically to overcome these difficulties and to cope with related problems, such as the need for a consistent means of accounting.

Whether the rationalist interpretation is valid as history is doubtful. Anthropological evidence on primitive societies suggests that where money is absent, so too is exchange itself, at least in the form the modern mind conceives it. That is, without money no alternative mechanisms, such as barter, exist for establishing the equivalence of value of one good for another. Of course, goods still pass from hand to hand. But these transfers are not trade; rather, they resemble the modern exchange of holiday gifts (a familiar example in which strict equivalence of value is in general neither expected nor delivered). If the anthropological evidence is a guide to history, it would be more accurate to say that the invention of money coincides with the innovation of trade rather than that money merely provides a convenient and efficient way to conduct a human activity conceived and initiated without it.

The use of money in trade is ages old; indeed, some of the earliest known written records are of monetary transactions. But the extension of the use of money to the domain of production is much more recent. The medieval serf, the peasant, the soldier, and the slave were not paid cash for services. Instead, they provided labor directly for the necessities of life or for a share of the product. These institutions of bonded labor were dominant in Europe and the United States, in agriculture especially, until the eighteenth century. Slavery formed a major element in the U.S. economy until the middle of the nineteenth. And sharecropping, a modern nonmonetary production relationship, remained important in some areas through the first half of the twentieth century.

Initially and in limited circumstances, the monetized economy emerged alongside the development of towns and of artisans' guilds in medieval Europe. An artisan could sell handiwork for cash; a mason or an artist could exchange a specified product or service for a specified sum. In systems of piecework, production on a larger scale could be organized. An employer would offer cash for cloth without worrying whether the cloth itself was produced in a day or a week. In this way, the principles of trade and the exchange economy could be, and gradually were, extended into the domain of production.

With the arrival of the *division of labor*, and particularly as the industrial revolution took hold in Europe in the late eighteenth century, the system of handicraft production and piecework reached its limits. Single workers could no longer claim undivided and clear-cut responsibility for any particular phase of production, making piecework impractical as a generalized basis for payment. It then became necessary to assess labor input directly, to measure and compensate for hours worked (and also to control what was being done during those hours). The incorporation of free labor into the money economy thus seemed to wait on the development of a metric for measuring work. And this, of course, required the use of the clock, a mechanical invention. Thus, only with the mechanical age does the path open for the universal spread of the wage system. Or, one might say that the conjunction of time-measure and value-measure, of clocks and money, actually made possible the creation of a production economy based on the division of labor.

The historical relationship of money and production suggests something about the nature of instability in the production process. So long as the use of money is restricted to trade—that is, to the exchange of previously produced goods—it is quite impossible for monetary disorders to disrupt the stream of production of real goods. Inflations and deflations surely can occur if the stock of money grows out of proportion to the stock of traded goods. But even in the face of such disorders, production goes on quite independently and quite smoothly, since production is organized not on the basis of exchange of money for labor time but rather, for the most part, on nonpecuniary principles. Medieval European agriculture was not disturbed, and indeed could not be disturbed, by the arrival of gold from the Americas in the sixteenth century.

With the advent of the division of labor and the wage system, everything changes. Changes in the value of money now interact with the value of the reimbursement of labor. It therefore becomes possible, in principle, for monetary disorders to disrupt production. In particular, disorders in the markets for financial instruments, such as bonds, can raise interest rates and cause unemployment. Whether this happens in practice, and whether we therefore need a monetary theory of production as Keynes argued that we did, remains the single greatest issue in macroeconomics.

It is a hotly disputed issue. If one holds with the rationalist vision of money (and many economists do), then it is hard to see how monetary disorders of any importance can arise. Indeed, in the theories that correspond to rationalist thinking, they do not arise, and the disorders that one does see are not essentially monetary in nature. In the next chapters, we present such theories according to which (in the long run, at least) monetary disruptions of real production cannot and do not occur.

THE OFFICIAL MONEY STOCK

Yes, but what is it?

We have talked of what money does, of its social character, and of its rational purposes and historical development. We have still not said what it is. Kenneth Boulding speaks elegantly to that point:[2]

> We must have a good definition of Money,
> For if we do not, then what have we got,
> But a Quantity Theory of no-one-knows-what?

The indefinite character of money is reflected in official statistics, which do not give us a single measure of money. Rather, they provide for a hierarchy of measures of money, from narrow to broad, that encompass different kinds of financial assets.

The narrowest of the measures, known as M1, consists of currency in circulation and demand deposits (checking accounts in banks). These are the basic constituents of what most of us would in day-to-day conversation describe as money. M1 also includes traveler's checks, which are very much like money, and "other checkable deposits," such as money market accounts on which large checks may be written. However, while M1 covers most of the types of money that most of us use every day, it is not considered by most economists to correspond to all of the money stock. Rather, M1 tries to measure that part of the money stock most closely associated with transactions demand, with money's function as a means of exchange.

M2 is a broader measure intended to capture some of the function of store of value as well as the transactions demand. M2 includes all of the items in M1 plus various short-term financial instruments that serve as repositories of savings. These include individuals' holdings, such as savings and small time deposits, (uncheckable) money market mutual funds and deposit accounts, and also some holdings of banks and other institutions, such as overnight repurchase agreements and Eurodollar deposits. In general, the financial instruments included in M2 have some store-of-value characteristics but are also reasonably liquid and can be converted to transactions use within a comparatively short time.

M3 expands the definition to include large time deposits and other term deposits, such as large certificates of deposit. These carry penalties if cashed before maturity and generally do not circulate in exchange for goods. Beyond M3, the government maintains a measure known as "L," for total liquid assets (which may include, for example, short-term debts of corporations), and an additional measure of the total debt of the domestic nonfinancial sector. Again, each of these measures, which move progressively away from the concept we would recognize as *money* and toward a concept we might recognize as *credit*, includes all of the elements of the narrower versions. The measures of money are thus

[2] The full quotation may be found in John Hotson, "*Stagflation and the Bastard Keynesians*" (Waterloo, Ont.: University of Waterloo Press, 1976), p. 53.

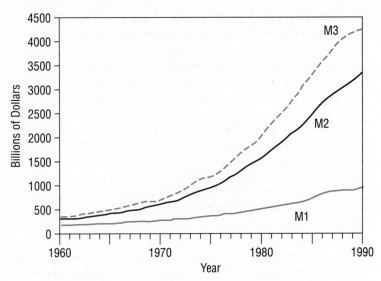

FIGURE 6.1   **Measures of Money**

This chart shows the growth of three measures of the money stock, M1, M2, and M3, over thirty years from 1960 to the present. The increasing gap between the measures reflects in part the growing diversity of money market assets.

nested within each other. (Figure 6.1 gives recent data for these variables for the United States.)

Economists agree that these empirical definitions do not correspond exactly to the concept of money. As noted above, M1 is more closely akin to the idea of transactions balances, of assets held and used mainly for their convenience in buying and selling. M2, with its short-term savings, is more of a mixture of both the store-of-value and means-of-exchange functions; it includes deposits held mainly as assets and not regularly liquidated in order to finance the purchase of goods. Changes in M2 are also more closely correlated with changes in national income than are changes in M1, a feature that some economists exploit for forecasting purposes. M3 and higher measures progressively incorporate more stores of value but also move away from the property of liquidity that is associated with money.

The M's are affected by financial innovation. As new liquid instruments (in recent years: overnight repurchase agreements, NOW accounts, money market mutual funds) are invented, they must be assigned to one of the empirical M's.[3] Because this is done according to the

---

[3] Matters get especially complicated because new financial entities must be *assigned* to one of the preexisting M's, and the criteria for assignment may include

degree of liquidity of the new instruments, the historical data measuring the M's do not reflect continuous, consistently defined series, and it is sometimes difficult to know exactly what is being measured. The money measures are among the most interesting data series that the government collects, and they are widely used by economists doing empirical research; but like all numbers from the real world, they must be interpreted with caution!

MONETARY SYSTEMS AND MONEY SUPPLY

Our definitions of money have told us that money does not exist in a vacuum. Rather, it is a *social* construct, a feature of the society, the culture, and the technology in which we live. Indeed, it might be said that one of the defining characteristics of any society is the nature of its monetary system.

We turn now from the questions of what money is and how it evolved to an examination of how monetary systems can differ and how various monetary systems can work. For while monies can take on many forms, few broad lines of classification will tell us much about the nature and role of money in differing social contexts.

The *monetary standard* is a set of rules, or *conventions*, that govern the creation of money and its relationship to other commodities.

There are two basic types of monetary standard and thus two basic monetary systems. One we call a *commodity* standard; the other is a *paper* standard. We will say that a commodity standard is *convertible*: at fixed rates of exchange guaranteed by the government, money can be exchanged for the commodities in terms of which the money is defined. We say that a paper standard is *inconvertible*, because there is no commodity backing the issue of paper money. Paper money is also called *fiat money* because it is simply declared to be money by arbitrary injunction, or "fiat." Paper money remains money only so long as people accept it as such.

---

the results of statistical analysis after the new entity has been in existence for some time. For example, money market mutual funds, are assigned to an M, say M2, on the basis of an observed relation to income over time that is similar to that of previously defined components of M2. In such cases, the statistical relationship of M2 to national income will acquire a spurious stability, because the measure of money has actually been constructed to conform with a preconceived notion of how money behaves.

A Commodity Standard

Under a commodity standard, the government sets the commodity content of the currency unit. In other words, the government specifies exactly what a unit of the money is worth, in terms of the commodity that defines the standard. The most famous commodity standard is *a gold standard*, in which the commodity content of a dollar will be specified as grains of fine gold. Under the "old gold parity" in the United States from 1900 to World War I, the dollar was fixed at $20.67 per fine ounce. After World War II, under the very different rules established at the Bretton Woods conference in 1944, a "gold-exchange standard" parity was set at $35 per fine ounce.[4]

Under a gold standard, in principle at least, price stability comes about directly. The price of the monetized commodity—gold—is fixed, and other prices remain stable insofar as they continue to bear a stable relation to that commodity. So long as the price of gold in relation to prices of other commodities does not change, the gold standard fixes the price level of the economy as a whole. Thus, the gold standard is supposed to provide stability of prices and confidence in the stability of money.

On the other hand, the gold standard removes government's control over the creation of currency itself. The coinage of gold coins and the printing of bank notes backed by gold are unrestricted within the limits established by the quantity of gold. People can take gold to the mint and there have it assayed and coined, thus converting jewelry, keepsakes, or freshly mined gold bullion into money. Moreover, banks can issue whatever scrip (or bank notes) they like, subject to the proviso that it be convertible into gold held by the bank. Bank notes circulate as money, sometimes at a discount related to the reliability of the bank. Thus, in principle, a gold standard in principle supplies money to the economy in accordance with the demand for it, so long as gold is available to serve as backing for that money.

The actual operation of the gold standard in the nineteenth century was not so simple, and the stability it promised is often hard to find in the historical record. Relative prices of commodities and gold varied from year to year despite the discipline of a fixed money price for gold. Some of the disruption was due to changes in gold supply. Gold rushes

[4] The gold-exchange standard was a means of fixing exchange rates between currencies while allowing individual nations some independent control of their domestic money supplies. Under this standard, most nations pegged their currencies to the dollar at fixed rates, and the dollar itself was pegged to gold. Where trade payment imbalances arose, settlement between central banks could be made either in dollars or in gold at the fixed rate. However, gold no longer circulated as currency. In the United States, private ownership of monetary gold was actually prohibited from 1934 until 1974.

in Australia and South Africa brought inflation. Long periods with little new discovery produced a falling price level as a fixed money stock was forced to accommodate an increasing volume of transactions. Other disruptions were due to changes in the business climate—booms and panics—that were perhaps more sudden, if not so durable, than those we experience today.

The United States abandoned the gold standard on the eve of World War I, with the passage of the Federal Reserve Act of 1913. There was a return to gold after the war, but the gold standard foundered with the economy in the Great Depression, and Franklin Roosevelt ended it for good in 1934. From 1944 through 1971, gold played a role in determining the value of the dollar in international transactions but had no part in the domestic economy (where, indeed, private holdings of gold coins and bullion were illegal). Since 1971, gold's role in monetary systems has all but disappeared.

Gold is a relic, and like many relics, it retains a hold on the imagination. To this day, advocates of a return to gold can be found, and they cite the anti-inflationary properties of the gold standard as their major reason. In 1981, the Reagan administration convened a commission to study the international and domestic monetary roles of gold. Beyond the minting of a gold medallion, however, the commission was unable to make any recommendations that would have restored any real role to the yellow metal. Modern economies seem destined to remain with the alternative system that we call a paper standard.

A Paper Standard

Actually, the term *paper standard* is misleading, for (as we have seen) only a small fraction of money in a modern economy is made of paper. We use the term as shorthand to denote all the modern forms of money, most of which are electronic. The distinguishing characteristic of a paper standard is not what the money is made of but how the quantity is controlled. We use the term for any monetary system in which the government sets the quantity of money through direct or indirect control over monetary issue.

Government may, of course, issue paper notes that are the direct liability of the Treasury Department, as were the famous greenbacks of the U.S. Civil War.[5] However, such notes are rare in modern economies, and U.S. paper money—Federal Reserve notes—is a liability of the central bank, not of the treasury itself. And even Federal Reserve

---

[5] Greenbacks bore the memorable image of Salmon P. Chase, then secretary of the treasury, a man who aspired to be president and who apparently thought this a good way to become well known!

paper is only a small fraction of the total money stock. Most money is created through the commercial banking system, and the government regulates the money stock outstanding by buying and selling (for money) government bonds and other nonmonetary debt instruments. This form of monetary control, is known as *open market operations*, is discussed at greater length below.

Money Creation

How is money created, and how is the process of money creation controlled?

In the United States today, the basic requirements are simple enough: private, commercial banks; a central bank, operated by the government, to oversee the private banks; and borrowers, who have some need for the money that is to be created. Key to money creation is that it is done by private banks for the benefit of their customers and to earn a profit. The central bank does not print money. The role of the central bank is merely to *regulate* money creation that occurs in the course of private banking.

A bank loan creates money. How? By creating a deposit in the account of the borrower. This deposit is, by definition, money that did not previously exist. The borrower is then free to spend this money, withdrawing it as needed from the account. At that point, the money becomes income to the recipient and a deposit in the income-earner's own bank account. Thus the money that did not exist until the bank created it by making a loan remains in existence as the loan is withdrawn and spent. It becomes part of the money stock in circulation through the economy.

The central bank regulates the amount of new lending that any private commercial bank can undertake. It does so by imposing *reserve requirements*, according to which a specified fraction of all deposits (say, 15 percent) must be held either as cash or as a deposit at the appropriate regional branch of the central bank. These *required reserves* are idle; they may not be lent to other borrowers or otherwise put at risk. Their function is not, as one might at first suspect, to ensure that the bank has enough cash in its vault to pay off all depositors who wish to make withdrawals. Rather, reserve requirements exist to permit the government to exercise influence over the total volume of lending that banks undertake.

Reserve requirements determine the amount of reserves banks must hold to satisfy the requirements of the central bank. Open market operations influence the aggregate volume of reserves available to the banking system as a whole. In this way, the government can alter banks' lending behavior, by making more readily available, or more scarce, the reserves that must be available to back up new lending.

For example, suppose that the Federal Reserve, our central bank, places an order with a dealer in government bonds (debts of the government held by private citizens) to purchase $1 billion of such bonds. The dealer supplies the bonds from her inventory and receives payment by check from the Federal Reserve. She deposits that check at her bank. This new deposit is, of course, money, and it is also a new reserve from the standpoint of the bank. No loans have yet been made against this reserve. Total bank reserves have now risen by $1 billion.

With a 15 percent reserve requirement, the specific bank in question now has $850 million in *excess reserves*. With this excess, it may now make a new loan of $850 million, effectively lending the dealer's money, while retaining only $150 million in reserves. It makes that loan by creating a new deposit in the account of the borrower. The money stock rises immediately by *another* $850 million. The remaining $150 million remains idle. The *total* increase in the money stock, from the initial injection *and* the new loan, is now $1,850 million.

The process does not end here. The newly created $850 million is drawn down by the borrower, who spends the money, creating incomes of $850 million elsewhere and new bank deposits of the same amount. This raises reserves at other banks, which may now make loans in the amount of $850 million less the 15 percent, or $127.5 million, reserve requirement imposed on them. Thus, in the second round, as the process continues, $722.5 million of new loans, new deposits, and new money are created. After the second round, the total increase in the money stock is $2,572.5 million.

As you can see, the process can go on for a long time. It is, in fact, the start of a potentially infinite series of transactions. If we define the initial injection of new reserves as ΔH (for high-powered money) and the required reserve ratio (.15 in our example) as ρ, then we can see that in each round of new lending, the total money supply rises by a factor of $1 - \rho$ times the increase in the previous round:

(6.1)
$$\Delta M = \Delta H + \Delta H(1 - \rho) + \Delta H(1 - \rho)^2 \\ + \Delta H(1 - \rho)^3 + \ldots$$

However, in a short time, the amount of new money created in each subsequent round diminishes to a very small number. Ultimately, the total new money created from a single injection of reserves is a finite and determinate sum; the series in equation (6.1) converges to a final value. This value can be calculated by multiplying both sides of equation (6.1) by $1 - \rho$ and then subtracting both sides of the second equation from the first:

(6.2)
$$(1 - \rho) \Delta M = \Delta H(1 - \rho) + \Delta H (1 - \rho)^2 \\ + \Delta H(1 - \rho)^3 + \Delta H(1 - \rho)^4 + \ldots$$

Since the terms on the right side in both equations go on forever, all the terms after ΔH on the right side of equation (6.1) are canceled by equivalent terms in equation (6.2), and we are left with $\Delta M - (1 - \rho)$ $\Delta M = \Delta H$, or $\rho \Delta M = \Delta H$, from which it follows that the total increase in the money supply will in the limit converge to:

$$\Delta M = \frac{\Delta H}{\rho}$$

In our example, the initial injection of $1 billion with a 15 percent reserve requirement generates an ultimate, total increase in the money stock of $6.667 billion. The initial increase in total bank reserves increases total lending by a multiplied amount, determined by the inverse of the required reserve ratio. This fraction is known as the *required reserve multiplier*; in our case it takes a value of 1/0.15, or 6.67.

From this example, we can easily understand two of the most important instruments that, in principle, make control over the size of the money stock possible. The first, open market operations, works through the purchase and sale by the central bank of debt instruments (mostly government bonds), which raises or lowers the total volume of reserves available to the banking system and, thus, the freedom that banks enjoy to make new loans and create new money.

The second instrument is change of the reserve requirement itself. This has the effect of forcing a sweeping adjustment on private commercial banks. An increase in reserve requirements may force banks to liquidate, or call in, old loans for repayment in order to increase cash reserves. Liquidating loans reduces the corresponding deposits and, consequently, the stock of money.

Because of their sweeping nature, across-the-board changes in reserve requirements happen rarely, usually as part of a major attack on inflation, when reserve requirements may be raised, or on unemployment, when they will be lowered. The Federal Reserve System has at times altered reserve requirements selectively, creating and manipulating different ratios for different types of deposits, in order to make some flexible use of this instrument.

A third principal instrument of monetary control is the use of the *discount window*. The discount window is merely a facility at the Federal Reserve for making a short-term loan to a bank. It is used when the Federal Reserve wishes to increase the deposits of, and therefore reserves available to, a particular institution. For example, a bank that is in trouble and is having difficulty raising funds on the private financial market may request a *discount loan*, which the Federal Reserve may or may not make, at its discretion. Discount operations affect the money supply just as open market operations do, through changing the total volume of reserves and the volume of lending via the required reserve multiplier.

The *discount rate*, the interest rate charged on such loans, is a uniform rate for all discount loans, set administratively by the Federal Reserve Board in Washington. In principle, it is set a little bit higher than the market rate at which banks can borrow reserves (also called federal funds) from each other, which is the *federal funds rate*. The intent behind this practice is to establish a slight penalty for use of the discount window, so that banks do not make a practice of borrowing to cover reserve shortfalls. Since heavy use of the discount window may also attract regulatory attention to a bank, economists say that, in addition to the penalty rate on discount loans, there is also a regulatory "frown cost" to excessive discounting.

Because the discount rate is set administratively and not in an open market, it has another use as well: as a signal of the direction in which the Federal Reserve Board wishes interest rates to move. Thus, when the Federal Reserve acted in late 1991 to cut interest rates in the hope of generating an economic recovery, the action took the form of a full one-point cut in the discount rate, announced by the Federal Reserve Board chairman, Alan Greenspan.

THE QUANTITY EQUATION

Whether we are under a commodity standard, a paper standard, or any other imaginable monetary system, the following equation holds:

(6.3) $$MV = PT$$

Equation (6.3) is sometimes known as the *Fisher equation* (or *Fisher identity*), after U.S. economist Irving Fisher (1867–1947), and more often as the *equation of exchange* or as the *quantity equation*. It holds that the quantity of money, M, times its *velocity of circulation, V*, must equal the product of the price level, P, times the volume of transactions of goods, T.[6] The Fisher equation is an identity and, like all identities, is true by definition, everywhere and under all circumstances. It is true simply because there is no independent statistical measure of the *velocity* of money. Velocity is, rather, defined internally by the ratio

$$V = PT/M.$$

When we say that V represents the number of times the average dollar changes hands in a year, we are simply restating this arithmetic truism in an intuitive way. (We show measures of velocity in Figure 6.2.) The Fisher equation by itself tells us nothing about the structural relationship between money, prices, and output nor indeed about any

[6] This equation is often written $MV = Py$, where y represents the volume of new production, or real gross national product, rather than transactions. In the short run, Y and T are roughly proportional, so this substitution has little effect.

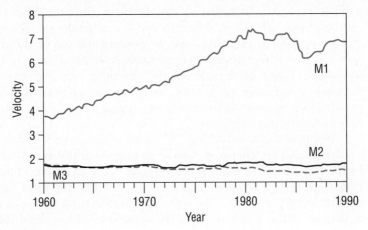

FIGURE 6.2   Velocities of Money

The velocity of M1 rose steadily until 1979 but then fell, evidently because lower rates of inflation reduced the opportunity cost of holding demand deposits and cash. The velocity of M2 has held constant, while that of M3 has fallen slowly since the early 1980s.

other structural relationship in the economy—unless and until we invoke some specific rules that govern the adjustments of M, V, P, and T. In these rules, we can find the essence of a monetary standard.

Under a classical gold standard, such as the one the United States lived under from the turn of the century until 1913, the government in effect controls P, the price level. M, the money stock, must in this case be left to market forces, because convertibility requires that gold holders be able to freely convert their gold into money. In a more general case, commodities other than gold (such as silver) may also be convertible.

Conversely, if the government controls M, then we have fiat money, or a paper standard. Under a paper standard, commodities cannot be sold freely at a fixed price. Rather, given the quantity of money and the level of output, the price level depends on velocity, which is a feature of the social system and especially of the technology we use for financial transactions.

THE MARKET FOR MONEY

The monetary system tells something about the terms and conditions under which money can be created and made available for public use. Combining this information with an understanding of why people might choose to hold (or demand) money, one can begin to form a view of the workings of the market for money as a whole.

Money Demand

When we derived the LM curve, we already saw two reasons why people have liquidity preference, or a demand to hold money. They do so for *transactions*, which rise and fall with the volume of economic activity and with the general price level. And they do so for *speculation*, shifting their portfolios between non–interest-bearing money and interest-bearing assets such as bonds, depending on current and expected future rates of interest.

The overall demand for money thus depends on several distinct variables: the level of real output, the price level, the current rate of interest, and the expected future rate of interest. We can write

$$M^d = M^d(P, y, r, r^e)$$

where M_d stands for the demand for money, P is the price level, y is real output, r is the interest rate, and r^e is the expected interest rate at some time in the future.

Demand for money rises when prices, real output, and expected future interest rates rise.[7] The demand for money generally falls when the interest rate rises; in that case, there is a tendency to believe that bonds are becoming cheap, and investors move to purchase bonds instead of holding money. We show these effects by writing the direction of change of the demand function with respect to each of its arguments, in the usual way:

$$M^{d'}(P, y, r^e) > 0 \qquad M^{d'}(r) < 0$$

A Pure Commodity Standard Model

Some simple diagrams showing the demand for and supply of money can clarify further how different monetary systems work. Since we only have two dimensions on a piece of paper, we need to freeze three of the four variables and portray our demand curve for money by putting the remaining dimension on the vertical axis. Changes in any of the three not shown will then shift the curve to the left or to the right, depending on the direction of change of the variable and its direction of influence on the demand for money. For example, a rise in prices shifts the demand function to the right, a rise in interest rates shifts it to the left.

---

[7] The effect of rising expected future interest rates is to discourage current purchases of bonds, which will fall in price when the interest rate increase occurs. Thus, speculators shift their portfolios toward more liquid positions.

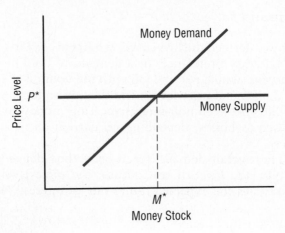

FIGURE 6.3   Commodity Standard

Under a pure commodity standard, the price level is fixed and the quantity of money
varies with shifts in demand for money. Money demand can vary because people bring
the monetary commodity (gold, for example) to the mint and convert it from bullion into
money.

In Figure 6.3, we see a simple representation of a commodity standard. The supply curve for money is a horizontal line; any quantity of
money that may be demanded will be supplied, so long as there is no
physical limit to the amount of the underlying commodity that is available. We can draw the diagram with P on the vertical axis because the
purpose of the commodity standard is to fix the price level.[8]

In this diagram, the demand curve slopes upward. Were the authorities to raise the price level, shifting the supply curve upward (e.g., by
raising the money price of gold), then more money would be demanded
(and supplied). A rise in the interest rate shifts the demand curve inward,
lowering the quantity demanded and supplied but having no consequences for the price level. Correspondingly, an increase in output may
shift the demand curve outward, increasing the money stock (again
without changing the price level).

Under the purest (hypothetical) commodity standard, therefore, we
can say that the supply of money is *perfectly*, or *infinitely*, *elastic*. Prices in
essence are fixed, and the actual quantity of money in circulation is free
to vary in line with variations in demand, there being no limit on the
conversion of commodities into money. It is also fair to say that this is a
model of a "system that never was." No actual commodity standard,

---

[8] If we are speaking specifically of a gold standard, then the price level, or vertical axis, is merely the money price of gold. Money will be supplied in return for
gold in unlimited quantities at the given price.

particularly not the gold standard, has come close to resembling a perfectly elastic money supply.

A More Realistic Gold Standard Model

Why does gold not provide an elastic money supply? Simply, gold, a special commodity quite unlike commodities in general, is scarce. Indeed, it is very scarce. Countries that operated on a gold standard, such as the United States from 1900 to 1913 and Great Britain from 1880 to 1913, did so precisely because the limited stocks of gold placed (in principle) strict quantity limits on the issue of money. Banks and governments could issue notes only to the extent that they were able to, or that it was widely believed they were able to, cover their note issue with gold.

If word or rumor got about that a bank note was not "backed," the note would quickly depreciate. And ordinary people could not expand the money stock (shift the demand curve of money to the right), because they lacked gold, the one commodity legally convertible into money. For this reason, we may say that economies under the gold standard were typically *liquidity constrained*, in that they had a greater demand for money than was supplied. Even though the government was formally obligated to convert gold into money on demand, liquidity constraints arose because the people lacked the gold.

This situation is depicted in Figure 6.4. Because the money stock in circulation was insufficient to satisfy transactions demand, such economies often experienced interest rates that were too high and downward pressures on the commodity prices and output levels. Only in the brief moments of a gold rush did free convertibility come close to satisfying money demands.

In this context, it is easy to understand the populist revolt against the "cross of gold" that threatened to burden commerce, industry, labor, and (above all) agriculture in the late nineteenth century United States. One of the main populist demands of that time was for *free silver*, or *bimetallism*, meaning that silver should be made as freely convertible into money as gold was, and at a fixed rate. Silver convertibility had a straightforward purpose: it would remove the liquidity constraint. There was a lot more silver around than gold; specifically, there was more of it in the hands of people in the South and West. Silver convertibility would give these people a chance to form their own banks and thus to participate in the monetary system, independent of the hated Eastern financial powers who controlled most of the stocks of gold.

The rhetoric of William Jennings Bryan, "boy orator of the Platte" and Democratic candidate for president in 1896, speaks with the passion that this issue once aroused. While the economic model just discussed is

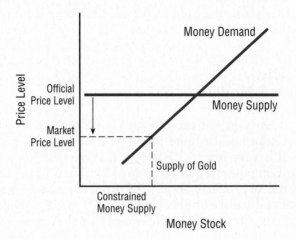

FIGURE 6.4   Gold Standard with Gold Shortage

If a gold standard economy is short of gold, the price level will tend to fall to reconcile demand for money with the limited available supply. This is a formula for depression in farming and among other primary producers, and it explains their hostility to the gold standard.

fresh in your mind, read from his speech to the Democratic convention in that year:

> If they ask us why it is that we say more on the money question than we say upon the tariff question, I reply that, if protection has slain its thousands, the gold standard has slain its tens of thousands. . . . You [turning to the gold men] tell us that the great cities are in favor of the gold standard; we reply that the great cities rest upon our broad and fertile prairies. Burn down your cities and leave your farms, and your cities will spring up again as if by magic; but destroy our farms and the grass will grow in the streets of every city in the country.
>   . . . It is the issue of 1776 over again. . . . We care not upon what lines the battle is fought. . . . If they dare to come out in the open field and defend the gold standard as a good thing, we will fight them to the uttermost. Having behind us the producing masses of this nation, . . . we will answer their demands for a gold standard by saying to them: "You shall not press down upon the brow of labor this crown of thorns, you shall not crucify mankind on a cross of gold."[9]

[9] Quoted in Paolo E. Coletta, *William Jennings Bryan* (Lincoln: University of Nebraska Press, 1964), 1, pp. 140–141.

The gold standard, in principle, combined free convertibility and unlimited money creation, with the severe practical limitation that in order to take advantage of free convertibility you had to have gold. Why not dispense with this complication and control the money stock directly? In so doing, a government would have a monetary system working on a quantity principle.

A Model of a Paper Standard

In Figure 6.5, we represent the supply of and demand for money under a strict quantity principle. The supply curve for money is vertical, indicating that a fixed quantity has been issued. This is true whether we examine different possible price levels (6.5a), output levels (6.5b), or interest rates (6.5c).

Shifts in the demand for money cannot now affect the quantity of money in existence, M. They can only change the variates on the vertical axes (P, y, or r). An increase in money demand, for example, must lower either or both P and y, the price level and output, since fewer transactions can be financed from a given stock of money if more of it is being held. Equally, a rise in money demand will raise the interest rate. In the attempt to satisfy the rising demand for money, people will sell bonds for money. This will depress the price of bonds and raise their yield (the

FIGURE 6.5   Paper Standard

If the monetary system operates on the quantity principle, shifts in money demand will change the price level, real national income, and the interest rate. Note that the money demand curve slopes upward with respect to P and y but down with respect to r. Thus, a shift in the money supply curve to the right will raise prices and income but lower the rate of interest.

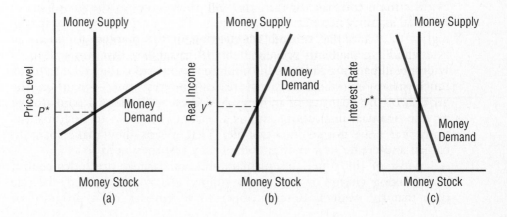

rate of interest). Once again, the money supply is fixed and does not change. It can change, of course, but only if the monetary authorities shift the supply curve bodily to the left or right.

THE MONETARY SYSTEM IN REAL LIFE

Our institutions, which issue inconvertible paper currency, and our theories, which speak in terms of a money supply set by policymakers, seem to presume that the real-life economy of the United States operates under a paper standard. For many purposes this is not a bad assumption. Still, in practice, real life once again is more complicated.

The actual monetary system of the United States has a paper core. This core includes the Federal Reserve System, an unbacked paper currency, a network of commercial banks operating on fractional required reserves, and a set of instruments and policies designed to control the issue of new money. By means of open market operations, discount loans, and occasional changes in reserve requirements, the Federal Reserve retains a technical capacity to influence the volume of money in circulation directly, both through the banking system and outside it, at any time.

But does the Federal Reserve actually use these means to control the stock of money in the sense of setting a target for the money stock and trying to hit it? Many influential economists (the monetarists, to whom we come again shortly) maintain that it should work in this way. But monetarists are the first to admit that central banks, our Federal Reserve especially, rarely follow this advice.

Lender of Last Resort

Central bankers generally do not regard fixing the quantity of money as their main mission. Rather, they see themselves as the guardians of financial stability in a more general sense. Their purpose, broadly speaking, is to ensure the smooth functioning of the markets for financial assets and especially to prevent financial instability that might lead to widespread banking failures. In fulfilling this mission, they tend to focus much more on stable financial prices—interest rates—than on the growth of the quantity of money. And they act both as a regulator of private financial institutions and as a *lender of last resort* to such institutions that have gotten into trouble. That means they make loans to banks, and create new money, when they feel they need to.

Most of the time, this primary mission largely precludes central banks taking charge of the money supply as a whole. Indeed, the one time that the Federal Reserve appeared to embark on a program of monetary targeting and control, the experiment lasted only from the end of 1979 until the middle of 1982. It was abandoned because of the costs of the recession, which the very restrictive monetary policy apparently had provoked. Given a test between monetary control and economic and financial stability, the desire for stability won out.

Interest Rate Targeting

This evidence leads to a diagram that may be the most accurate representation of the money creation process as it actually exists. In Figure 6.6, the supply curve for money is now horizontal. However, it is the interest rate, not the price of gold or the price level, that is the policy-determined variable on the vertical axis. The quantity of money issued is then determined by the borrowers, whose demand for loans fixes the position of the demand curve for money.

If the Federal Reserve wishes to alter the equilibrium of the money market as shown in Figure 6.6, it acts to shift the money supply curve up or down by buying or selling government bonds to the public (open market operations). This changes the interest rate. A new interest rate then indirectly affects the equilibrium quantity of money in existence, through movement along the demand curve. Nevertheless, an increase in demand for money will result in an increased supply, so long as the Federal Reserve does not react again by shifting the interest rate another time.

FIGURE 6.6   Interest Rate Targeting

When the Federal Reserve targets interest rates, it effectively manipulates an elastic money supply function by shifting that function up and down.

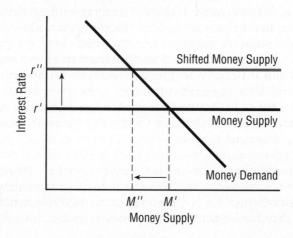

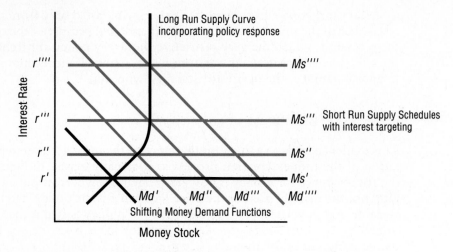

FIGURE 6.7   The Supply of Money in the Long Run

When nominal money demand shifts outward, for example with rising inflation, the
Federal Reserve reacts by raising interest rates, tracing out the long-run relationship
between money growth and interest rates that is shown. Eventually, high interest rates
choke off the inflation and money growth.

Interest Rate Changes over Time

The horizontal money supply curve in Figure 6.6 is a short-run curve. It
captures the day-to-day method of operation of the Federal Reserve and
does not imply that interest rates are held constant by monetary policy
for long periods of time. Indeed, interest rates change all the time—
because policy changes. And policies change because the Federal Reserve
detects shifts in the demand curve for money.

A shift outward in the demand for money indicates a strong economy, inflation pressures, or perhaps only a widespread expectation that
interest rates are going to rise (and that bond prices will therefore fall,
making it profitable to sell bonds today and buy them back tomorrow).
The Federal Reserve will react to such a shift by raising the interest rate.
Looking at a sequence of such actions, we can trace out a long-run
supply curve for money, or *policy response function* (see Figure 6.7).

Ultimately, if demand for money shifts "too far" to the right, the
policy response is to raise interest rates so much that the quantity demanded along the new curve is no greater than it was under the interest
rate and demand curves that prevailed earlier. At this point, the policy
response function resembles the vertical money supply curve of Figure
6.5. But Figure 6.5 is a representation of hypothetical short-run operating procedures, whereas the policy response function traces the conse-

quences over time of certain actions that occur under a completely opposite set of operating procedures.[10]

THE CREDIT SYSTEM

In the IS-LM model, as you will recall, we explicitly assume that there is perfect control over the quantity of money. The supply of M, which can be allocated between transactions and speculative demand, is fixed. This assumption is clearly a major simplification, and some argue that it is seriously mistaken. We have already examined part of the reason. It may be that the central bank's policy is to fix interest rates rather than the money stock. In this case, the LM curve is horizontal and changes in fiscal policy alone affect GNP, at least in the short run when monetary policy is holding the interest rate constant.

Indeed it may be that the way our banking institutions are set up makes strict monetary control quite impractical, ensuring that, in the short run at least, the money supply curve has to be effectively horizontal.

The basic institutional evidence for this is the fact that about 70 percent of all new loans made by banks are made under previously negotiated standing lines of credit to individuals and companies. These arrangements effectively give the debtor a right to borrow.[11] The interest rate on such loans may change, but their extension, and the creation of money that results, does not depend on central bank actions. Rather, once the loans have been made, the central bank is effectively obliged to supply the reserves that the new loans and deposits require; to fail to do so would risk provoking a crisis. Thus, the central bank has little direct, short-run control over money creation and at most can influence events indirectly by changing the interest rate at which new loans are offered.

Some of those who argue that the money supply curve is flat also attach great importance to the ability of corporations, especially the largest, to create their own liquidity, effectively in unregulated competition with the policy of the state. Corporations do this by issuing highly liquid short-term debts, called *commercial paper*. In essence, commercial paper effectively allows them to write their own loans.

If the money supply curve truly is flat, then in reality we live in a world that behaves rather more like a pure convertible commodity world, in that demand rather than supply determines the quantity of

[10] As an exercise, try to trace out a policy response function for monetary policy that exercises strict control over the quantity of money but seeks to stabilize the interest rate.
[11] Basil J. Moore, *Horizontalists and Verticalists: The Macroeconomics of Credit Money* (Cambridge: Cambridge University Press, 1988).

money in the system as a whole.[12] This is a curious phenomenon, in which the model we characterized earlier in this chapter as being the most fanciful may turn out to be one of the better representations of the world in which we actually live!

Thus, there is merit to the convertible commodity view of the monetary world and to its implication that the money stock is determined within the system, "endogenously," rather than by policy. Still, it is a minority view. In normal times, most economists assume that within broad limits the instruments of monetary policy are used effectively to control the size of the money stock. They assume, in effect, that interest rates normally adjust by enough to keep in existence whatever quantity of money the Federal Reserve chooses to create. Indeed, explaining the development of macroeconomics from this point forward is quite difficult unless one sticks with a paper standard operating on the principle of monetary control. For the sake of moving forward with a simple and clear exposition, we will therefore assume a paper money standard for the time being, ignoring central bank passivity, interest rate targeting, and institutional endogeneity of money and credit creation. If we did not do so, we could hardly bring you the story of monetarism and rational expectations in Chapter 7.

[12] Both the late Nicholas Kaldor of Cambridge and Axel Leijonhufvud of the University of California at Los Angeles seem to have shared this view.

SPECIAL SECTION

Bank Stability and Financial Reform[1]

In the modern economy, the creation of money is entrusted to private financial institutions. As we have seen, banks create money by the act of making a loan. If banks make a great many new loans at one time, the money supply will expand rapidly, and there is a risk of inflation. If banks are unable or unwilling to make new loans at all, the money supply and the economy will stagnate together.

Governments and central banks therefore have a strong interest in ensuring that the banking system functions smoothly, that it makes just enough new loans to keep the economy moving forward but not so many as to cause a speculative and inflationary "bubble." The government can encourage new lending by making additional reserves available to banks through open market operations, specifically by purchasing outstanding government bonds from the private sector. It restrains lending by imposing reserve requirements, which ensure that a portion of each increment to reserves remains in the form of a secure asset (government bonds or cash). In this way, a well-regulated banking system ought to make new loans at just the rate intended by the central bankers.

But the government has an additional concern. Loans made by banks are *assets* on the balance sheet of the banks. The deposits created in extending those loans represent the *liabilities* of the banks. For a bank to remain solvent and to function in a normal way, the value of its assets must exceed the value of its liabilities: the bank must have a positive *equity,* or *net worth*. Therefore, the loans made must be, by and large, good loans. They must have a reasonable prospect of full repayment on their original terms. Alternatively, they must have strong collateral to ensure that in the event they are not repaid, the bank can recover its principal by selling off the collateralized asset.

You might think that the profit motive would guarantee that banks themselves would attend to the quality of their loans. Alas, history shows that this is not always the case. Just in the past twenty-five years, we have seen a series of waves of overlending by banks and savings and loans, followed by heavy losses: in the real estate investment trusts (REITs) of the early 1970s, in Third World loans in the late 1970s, and in commercial office buildings (especially on the East Coast) in the 1980s. In each case, an area of economic development strongly supported by the banks turned into a bust.

Hedge, Speculative, and Ponzi Finance

Some argue that this instability is a feature of the system, that banks are prone to march together, like lemmings, into disaster. The economist Hyman Minsky has given this financial instability hypothesis its most careful and complete development. Minsky distinguishes three basic financial positions, or strategies, available to borrowing firms. *Hedge firms* construct a financial profile that enables them to cover their financial obligations out of current receipts. Theirs is the most conservative and secure financial position but also the least flexible and least able to take advantage of distant and risky opportunities for large future profits. *Speculative firms* anticipate occasional cash shortfalls in the near term but are able to cover their obligations out of revenues in the long run. These firms issue debt and refinance it as needed. *Ponzi firms,* finally, are those that can meet neither current nor medium-term obligations except by adding continuously to their debts. These firms are headed for bankruptcy while gambling on a big strike to save them.

In an economic expansion, Minsky argues, the proportion of business firms assuming speculative or Ponzi finance postures rises as businesses seek ever more lucrative but ever more distant and uncertain prospects for profit. Banks, for their part, come to share the enthusiasm of business for risky ventures. As banks lend to these businesses, they themselves take on the speculative and Ponzi characteristics of their borrowers. Debt-to-income ratios rise in the productive sectors, as well as for individual households and families; the stock and real estate markets experience a price run-up that has no apparent limit; and the economy slowly becomes unhinged.

Now the economy is poised for a downturn. Any event that interrupts the flow of credit—a run-up in interest rates, a jump in the price of oil—will precipitate a chain of bankruptcies and business failures. And these failures will quickly reverse the rising tides of spending, investment, and profitability that fed the boom.

Bank Runs and Deposit Insurance

In extreme circumstances, even worse can happen: bank depositors may lose confidence in the banking system. Fearing that banks rendered insolvent by loans gone bad will be forced to close their doors, worried depositors may seek to withdraw their money in cash from the banks.

Because banks maintain only a fraction of their deposits on hand as reserves, they cannot possibly pay out cash to more than a fraction of depositors at any one time. And if a bank runs out of cash, it must close. In that case, panic may cascade through the system, causing runs and forcing the closure even of banks whose assets are relatively sound. Panics and crashes were a periodic feature of the U.S. financial system in the 19th century.

The desire to put an end to such financial instability was a major reason behind the creation of the Federal Reserve System in 1913. The Federal Reserve brought several new tools to this task, including an ability to regulate the "safety and soundness" of loans made by banks and the power to make emergency loans, through the discount window, to banks that were threatened by panics or runs.

Unfortunately, the plan didn't work. The banking crisis of the early 1930s overwhelmed the Federal Reserve System; over 9,000 banks failed during that time. In response, the Roosevelt administration introduced a new concept: federal *insurance* of bank deposits. The Federal Deposit Insurance Corporation (FDIC) provided depositors with a guarantee: they would *always* be able to get their money back (up to the insurance limit), no matter what happened to a bank's loans. To finance this system, depositors pay a small premium on the accounts they hold.

The FDIC restored confidence in the banking system. And for the next half-century, very few banks failed. But in the late 1970s and through the 1980s, the number of bank failures began creeping up. By the early 1990s, it had reached several hundred a year. In some parts of the country (notably

Texas), virtually every major commercial bank failed during the real estate and oil slump of the late 1980s. The savings and loan industry, which had been regulated and insured by separate mechanisms (the Federal Home Loan Bank Board [FHLBB] and Federal Savings and Loan Insurance Corporation [FSLIC], respectively), collapsed altogether. Many observers began to wonder whether deposit insurance was still working as its designers intended.

Moral Hazard and Narrow Banking

One concern raised by critics of the deposit insurance system involves the concept of *moral hazard*. *Moral hazard*, a term from the economics of insurance, tells us that depositors will respond to the existence of insurance by seeking out banks that run unusually high levels of risk. Such banks are generally willing to pay slightly higher interest rates on deposits in order to attract funds. But, since the deposits are insured, depositors are indifferent to the higher level of risk that accompanies the higher return. If such behavior is pervasive in the system, critics argue, deposit insurance aggravates the tendency of the banking system to take too many risks.

What to do? Some advocate the abolition of deposit insurance, and urge that the market be allowed to discipline banks that take excessive risks—as well as the depositors who entrust them with their money. But it is unlikely that the U.S. public would now accept a return to an uninsured banking system.

Another possible solution, advanced by leading economists such as James Tobin of Yale University and Robert Litan of the Brookings Institution, is to restrict deposit insurance to what are called "narrow banks": banking institutions that lend only to a restricted set of safe and liquid borrowers (such as the government itself). Such a bank would pay a relatively low rate of interest on its deposits, but the money would be safe. If a customer sought a higher return, he or she would have to invest in a "broad bank," losing the benefit of deposit insurance and accepting the possibility of loss.

There are difficulties with the "narrow bank" proposal. Perhaps the most important problem involves the nature of the risk against which deposit insurance is offered. Whereas narrow bank proposals would protect depositors against involuntary exposure to the reckless lending practices of an individual bank, it would not necessarily serve the function of the FDIC, which was and is to ensure confidence in the banking system as a whole.

If narrow banking were enacted, the overwhelming majority of depositors likely would forgo deposit insurance, in favor of the promise of a market rate of return—just as millions of households today invest in uninsured mutual funds rather than leave their money in the bank. In that case, uninsured "broad banks" would quickly come to dominate the banking industry. And then, in the event of a bank run, all of the systemic problems that plagued the banking system until the 1930s would be present. The government would face a crisis and would probably feel constrained to attempt to save the banking system, irrespective of whether or not deposits were insured.

More Regulation?

Of course, there is another route to bank stability, which is to regulate bank lending practices to avoid excessive concentrations of risky lending in the first place. Bank regulators have been arguing in recent years for more decisive early intervention of this kind against "high-flying banks." And in the aftermath of every banking crisis, notably of the savings and loan disaster of the 1980s, it is always possible to identify instances of foolish, reckless, even fraudulent lending behavior.

The problem here, however, is how to know *in advance* that a particular type of loan is economically risky. How can a regulator distinguish, before the facts are in, between a speculation and a brilliant investment? And how can one expect regulators to do this for banks, when bankers themselves have been unable to come up with any routinely successful way of making this same distinction? (As for fraud, that also poses a regulatory problem. Crooked bank operators generally make a point of concealing their illegalities if they can!)

Because market mechanisms do not eliminate system risk, they are unlikely to be relied upon to the exclusion of regulatory measures in any new round of banking reform. And because regulators cannot wholly eliminate the risk in individual bank lending decisions, it is also unlikely that new regulatory initiatives will entirely restore confidence in the banking system either. Indeed, the more one looks at the endemic problems of instability in the financial system, the harder it is to foresee any substantial solution for this problem at any near date.

---

[1] Parts of this section are adapted from William Darity, Jr., "Financial Instability Hypothesis," in *The New Palgrave Dictionary of Money and Finance,* ed. Peter Newman, Murray Milgate, and John Eatwell. Vol. 2, (London: Macmillan, 1992), pp. 75–76.

SUMMARY

Money is central to macroeconomic analysis, especially when expectations and uncertainty are important. The definition of money is elusive. At times, it has been given a functional definition. At other times, it has been given a definition deriving from social convention. Tibor Scitovsky said money had three uses: as a unit of account, as a medium of exchange, and as a store of value. Liquidity preference derives from money's easy convertibility.

The innovation of money coincides with the introduction of trade. But only in the past 250 years or so has money played an integral role in the process of production. It is this role that becomes a key source of instability. In rationalist theories of money, such instability is impossible.

Money is not a homogeneous entity. The Federal Reserve has established a set of operational definitions of money to reflect this. M1 is currency and demand deposits; in large measure, it is the money that corresponds to transactions demand. M2 is M1 plus savings and small time deposits; it has some store-of-value properties and some transactions demand properties. M3 is M2 plus longer time deposits such as CDs. M2 and M3 add in money that could be used for speculative purposes.

Money is a social construct that can take many forms. The simplest conceptually are fiat money and commodity-backed money. With commodity money, inflation is (in principle) controlled because the monetary authority sets the value of money in terms of a fixed quantity of gold. The supply of money is fixed, except in the case of gold discoveries or similar events. Fiat money is any money of which the government controls the supply. In the modern economy, the money supply is controlled within a banking system consisting of a central bank and commercial banks. Money is created within this banking system by the placement of a deposit in the account of a borrower.

The creation of money can be controlled by policy in at least three ways. First, the central bank can vary the level of required reserves. Second, the central bank can affect the amount of money available for reserves through open market operations. Third, the central bank can vary the discount rate on its own short-term loans.

The market for money can be viewed as the site of interaction between the supply of and demand for money. The demand for money depends on the price level, real output, the interest rate, and the expected rate of interest.

In principle, the supply of money is infinitely elastic in a commodity money system. In fact, the demand for money in such systems often has been greater than the supply, causing a deflation of commodity prices.

In principle, the fiat money system has a perfectly inelastic money supply that is controlled by the monetary authority. In fact, the existence of economic and financial stability indicates that monetary control is incomplete. Often, the interest rate, rather than the money supply, is the policy variable. A further argument against the complete inelasticity of the money supply is the "endogenous money" argument. This argument is based in part on the existence of standing lines of credit and commercial paper, so that the central bank in practice has little choice but to validate private demands for credit with increased supply.

Review Questions

1. What is the reserve multiplier when the required reserve ratio is zero? Describe what actually happens in this case.

2. Which is more important to target: the money supply or the interest level? Be specific about any value judgments in your answer.

3. Describe why in practice it is impossible to fix the value of commodity money.

4. Explain why it is or is not possible to have an exogenously determined supply of money.

5. On the basis of history and anthropological evidence, the text questioned the validity of rationalist theories of the existence of money. Present counterexamples, or evidence that might rebut the criticisms raised in the text.

6. The quantity equation of money was presented in both Chapter 4 and this chapter. Discuss the differences in emphasis in each of the discussions.

Review Problems

1. Suppose the current money supply is $2 billion and the reserve requirement is 15 percent. If an open market sale of $100 million is carried out by the government, by how much will the money supply increase?

2. Suppose the current money supply is $10 billion and the reserve requirement is 15 percent. If the reserve requirement is increased to 20 percent, by how much will the money supply decrease?

3. On graphs like those of Figure 6.6, show the effect of an increase in the reserve requirement. On a separate set of graphs, show the effect of an open market operation.

4. On a graph such as the one in Figure 6.4, where equilibrium in the money market holds under a commodity standard, show the effect of the discovery of a new source of gold. Describe the disequilibrium situation.

5. Prepare graphs like those of Figure 6.6 for the case of commodity money. What determines the level of national income and the interest rate?

6. What is the effect of the discovery of gold on the graphs drawn in problem 5?

SUGGESTED READINGS

Paul Davidson, *Money and the Real World,* 2nd edition

John Hotson, *Stagflation and the Bastard Keynesians* (University of Waterloo Press, 1976).

Basil J. Moore, *Horizontalists and Verticalists: The macroeconomics of credit money* (Cambridge (UK): Cambridge University Press, 1988).

Chapter 7

MONETARISM

Looking Forward

Monetarism embodied and brought back the basic classical idea that, in the long run, the money stock and nothing else determines the price level, and therefore, that the growth of the money stock determines the rate of inflation.

To arrive at this conclusion, Milton Friedman and Edmund S. Phelps developed models that incorporated *adaptive expectations* of the rate of inflation into a Phillips curve framework. They then showed that when inflation expectations were proved correct, the Phillips curve would be vertical, establishing a single rate of unemployment, the *natural rate of unemployment*, compatible with any stable rate of inflation. From this it followed that steady money growth, leading to stable inflation at the natural rate of unemployment, was the best course for monetary policy. In particular, government should never pursue stimulative policies designed to drive unemployment below the natural rate.

The chapter includes a special section on the practical administration of monetary policies.

As you study this chapter, make sure you understand each stage of the monetarist argument:

- What is the monetarist view of inflation, and how does it differ from the Keynesian view?
- How did Milton Friedman reconcile an asset demand for money (an idea introduced by Keynes, as we have seen) with the classical conclusion that money is neutral in the long run?
- In the monetarist model, how do changes in the rate of growth of the money stock lead to changes in output and employment in the short run but not in the long run?

• How do the monetarists arrive at the concept of a natural rate of unemployment? In particular, what are adaptive expectations, and what role do they play?

The macroeconomic role of money can be viewed from a perspective quite different from, and indeed opposed to, the LM curve framework of Chapter 5. In that framework, the shifts in the quantity of money influenced the interest rate and real production. Meanwhile, the price level remained a "missing equation." This missing equation was eventually filled in by the Phillips curve relationship between inflation and unemployment. Yet, while the Phillips curve plugged a hole in the IS-LM framework, its weak theoretical foundation left many economists uneasy. And when the stable empirical relationship between inflation and unemployment collapsed after 1969, the way was open to a reformulation, and revival, of a more theoretically coherent and rigorous classical view.

The first step in that reformulation sought to reestablish the classical direct linkage between money and the price level while returning the interest rate and real production to the real, or nonmonetary, sector. This part of the revival of classical theory, Milton Friedman's answer to Keynes, is called *monetarism*.

THE OLD QUANTITY THEORY

As you have seen, classical theory before Keynes had two very distinct and separate elements. The first of these was a *barter economy*, in which, for theoretical purposes, money makes no appearance at all. In the classical system, commodities are exchanged for other commodities, and production is the transformation of physical inputs into physical outputs. The systems of demand and supply relations that express these conditions are written in physical terms, without reference to money.

The second distinct element in the classical system is a monetary theory. In the long run equilibrium of a classical model, money affects the price level and nothing else. Double the quantity of money and you will double the price level. Nothing else will be affected. And the price level *per se* is of no importance nor even of any intrinsic interest. It merely measures, in effect, the scale of the monetary unit. Whether you measure all the transactions of the real economy in terms of dollars or of dimes is unimportant.

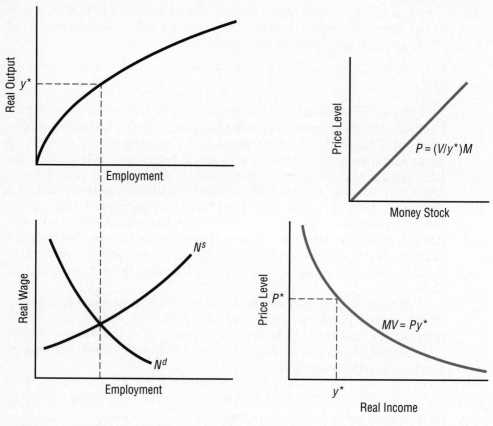

FIGURE 7.1   The Classical Dichotomy Revisited

Real Economy   Monetary Economy

Classical economists before Keynes knew that money had other qualities and other purposes, that it did not exist solely and exclusively as a unit of account. But they did not incorporate these properties into their theory. And so, they did not integrate the existence of money into the real world of exchange and, especially, of production. For them, in a phrase, money was a veil; it lay lightly and irrelevantly over the face of the real economy. Thus money, in the classical tradition, is *neutral*.

In terms of the income version of the quantity equation, $MV = Py$, money neutrality means that y, the volume of output, is unaffected by M or by changes in M. In terms of Figure 7.1, it means that the labor market alone determines the level of employment and, through that, the volume of output. Variables affecting total spending in monetary terms can affect only the price level. These propositions are known as the *quantity theory of money*.

MONETARISM

We now reintroduce Milton Friedman, professor and Nobel laureate in economics, the preeminent player in the restoration of classical thinking about monetary problems that has occurred over the half-century since Keynes. In Chapter 4, we encountered Friedman's early challenge to the Keynesian consumption function. Now we pass to his major thrust, his theory of money, the doctrine known as *monetarism*.[1]

Milton Friedman was from Chicago.[2] His outlook and economics are linked to the university there, to its blend of Middle European theory and Middle American empiricism, in much the same way that Keynes was linked to Cambridge and its embodiment of the British intellectual elite. Both, oddly, might describe themselves as liberals. But where Keynes was steeped in a progressive liberalism characteristic of Britain's emergence from the Victorian age, Friedman's liberalism was and is classical in character, rooted in individualism and distrust of the state.[3]

Friedman was convinced that the IS-LM model and the Phillips curve, core Keynesian propositions that established the roles of monetary and fiscal policy in stabilizing the level of output and employment, were wrong. In essence, they were wrong because they filtered the price level through the labor market. According to the Phillips curve, inflation would rise when unemployment was low and would fall when unemployment was high. And according to IS-LM, labor market conditions themselves depended on fiscal and monetary policies, so that both of these policies could indirectly determine the rate of inflation.

Friedman thought this was confused. In his often expressed and strongly held view, inflation was always and everywhere a monetary

---

[1] "Monetarism Mark I" is a designation originated by James Tobin to describe the version of monetarism initially advanced by Friedman. It incorporated "adaptive expectations" (see below) and explained unemployment as a short-run phenomenon mainly caused by sticky wages. "Monetarism Mark II" is the version compatible with "rational expectations" and the "new classical economics." We take it up in the next chapter.

[2] In recent years, he has moved to the Hoover Institution at Stanford University in California.

[3] This has made Friedman into a conservative on most questions of U.S. politics. But there are notable exceptions, such as his strong stand in favor of the decriminalization of drugs on the ground that this area is properly one of individual rather than governmental responsibility.

phenomenon.[4] Fiscal policy could not cause inflation unless the expansion of government spending were financed by the creation of new money. And an expansionary (or loose) monetary policy could not fail to cause inflation, for if the money stock grew more rapidly than the real volume of transactions required, then with stable velocity the quantity equation dictated that a rising price level would necessarily result.

Friedman backed this basic belief with a weighty statistical and historical argument,[5] designed to show that changes in the growth rate of the money stock over long periods of U.S. history were closely associated with changes in the rate of inflation and not so closely, if at all, with changes in the level of output. Thus, Friedman started from the empirical position that money had been, as he perceived it, more or less neutral in the long run of U.S. history.

Friedman's theoretical task became the designing of a model consistent with this observation. And the theoretical problem in so doing can be stated simply. Keynes and *The General Theory* had destroyed the foundations of the classical position on money.[6] Keynes had shown the indispensable role of money as an asset, or store of value. Anyone reconsidering monetary theory after Keynes was bound to acknowledge this function and to incorporate demand for money as an asset into their theory. But did that necessarily mean, as Keynes claimed, that the long-run neutrality of money also had to be abandoned? Milton Friedman did not think so. So he set out to construct an economic model that introduced a productive function for money holdings but under which function money would still be neutral in the long run.

Basic Model

Friedman's method, put forth in a famous essay,[7] was to invent a highly simplified model world, as a kind of metaphor for essential features of the real world. This model world has a constant population of immortal people with fixed and unchanging tastes. They have at their disposal a

---

[4] Milton Friedman and Anna S. Schwartz, *Monetary Trends in the United States and the United Kingdom* (Chicago, University of Chicago Press, 1982), p. 19. In this work Friedman and Schwartz write "substantial changes in prices and nominal income are almost invariably the result of changes in the nominal supply of money."

[5] Milton Friedman and Anna S. Schwartz, *A Monetary History of the United States* (Chicago: University of Chicago Press, 1963).

[6] J. M. Keynes, *The General Theory of Employment, Interest and Money* (London: Macmillan, 1936).

[7] Milton Friedman, "The Optimum Quantity of Money," in *The Optimum Quantity of Money and Other Essays* (Chicago: Aldine, 1971), pp. 1–50.

fixed and unchanging technology and a fixed and unchanging stock of resources, which they exploit by organizing perfectly competitive firms and free markets. Capital goods exist, and last forever, but they cannot be exchanged, and there is no lending or borrowing and hence no rate of interest. Thus, the only exchanges that actually occur are of goods and services for money, or vice versa. The money consists of pieces of paper, marked as dollars, of which (let us say) 1,000 are in circulation.

Friedman argued that life in this world would go beyond the classical quantity theory, but in only one respect. Individuals may live forever, but they do not necessarily also have the same incomes in every period of time. That is, they have a notion of permanent income (harking back to Friedman's own earlier theoretical work) and suffer occasional fluctuations of transient income around that permanent level. Friedman argued that to guard against the possibility of an unusually low income, they would seek to hold a reserve as a *precaution*. Since money is the only asset, he allowed money to serve the role of a store of value.

In this world of Friedman's, there are just two reasons to hold money. One may need money to purchase a service, or one may wish to have a small store of money in reserve to purchase services in the future in the event of a fluctuation in future demand for the services one sells. These are the transactions motive and the precautionary motive giving money an asset property. There is no speculative motive (see Chapter 5), for there is no capital market, no rate of interest, and so nothing to speculate on. Friedman's model thus does not take on the whole of Keynes's monetary theory; its purpose is only to ask whether the role of money *as an asset* is necessarily inconsistent with money neutrality in the long run.

To understand the logic of Friedman's argument, fix in mind two essential concepts: nominal balances and real balances. *Nominal balances* (B) are the money holdings of individuals in actual dollar terms. We are accustomed to thinking of money as a circulating medium, which exists in order to change hands in return for services and goods. At any moment, however, all money is necessarily held by some individual, as a result of the preceding transaction and pending the next one. This distribution of holdings is known as the distribution of nominal balances.

Real balances ($b = B/P$) are nominal balances deflated by a price level. They thus represent the purchasing power of individuals' money holdings, after adjustment for inflation.

We now state the *stock identity*, which is that the money stock must equal the sum of all nominal balances (where the subscript i denotes the holdings of each individual). This is straightforward. The community as a whole can hold neither more nor less than the total stock of money.

$$M = \sum_i B_i$$

Friedman argued that individuals would not care much about the nominal balances they held. They would, however, care about the purchasing power of those balances—about real balances—because the purchasing power of money holdings would determine just how much a given reserve would be worth. Therefore, Friedman constructed a theory of money *supply* in terms of nominal balances but a theory of money *demand* based on the desire for real balances.

Real balances in terms of what? Friedman argued that the value of money holdings to an individual consisted of the length of time that such a balance could support a normal level of consumption. Therefore, he measured the real balances held by a community as days or weeks of "normal" income—a concept once again not unlike the notion of permanent income, which you have already met. Real balances thus measured the reserve set aside for financing consumption in the absence of new income.

In other words, real balances are the financial wealth of the community. Any independent change in either the prices of goods or the money income levels of the community affects real balances. Inflation, in particular, drives down the real value of a given nominal income and reduces the purchasing power of a given store of wealth. An increase in the money stock without inflation will increase real balances and so financial wealth. But if an increase in money could be shown always to lead to a parallel increase in inflation, then real balances would be unaffected, money neutrality would hold, and there would never be any good reason for increasing the stock of money. The question therefore was: would money creation in this model world always lead to inflation?

Suppose, Friedman argued, that people choose to hold one-tenth of their annual income, or 5.2 weeks of pay, as a reserve for emergencies. Then, since we have a money stock (M) of \$1,000, we know that nominal national income (Py) must equal \$10,000. Why do we know this? Because the reserve is, in fact, equal to the whole of the money stock, the only asset that can be held in reserve. Since we know that reserve balances are \$1,000 and that individuals on average adjust their balances until they equal one-tenth of income, turnover must adjust to give us an income of ten times the balances, or \$10,000. This merely reflects the quantity equation rule that total money balances (M), multiplied by the number of times each dollar is used in each year (V, or velocity) must equal this total of income generated by the same transactions (Py): $MV = Py$.

Friedman then constructed a thought experiment: Suppose that a one-time increase in nominal money stock occurs. For example, a helicopter may fly overhead and drop, at random, an additional \$1,000 in fresh one dollar bills. What happens?

There are two basic possibilities. The public may simply add the extra cash to its idle balances. In that case, prices do not change, and turnover must fall in half. However, the people are twice as rich in wealth as before. They are holding, on average, 10.4 rather than 5.2 weeks of money reserves as assets. Friedman rejected this possibility. Since people had previously chosen to reserve 5.2 weeks of income, why would they be interested in doubling that reserve to 10.4 weeks?

This leaves the second possibility: that people will choose to recreate the old situation by reducing their money-swollen balances to the one-tenth of income that they had previously decided was desirable. And this, Friedman argued, is indeed what rational people will want to do.

But there is a problem. It is impossible, with a fixed stock of money, for all individuals to reduce their nominal balances at the same time. Indeed, the average level of nominal balances cannot fall at all! The money stock has doubled; the population is unchanged. It must therefore be true that average nominal balances are twice what they were.

The supply of money has doubled. To get cash balances back to one-tenth of national income, national income must necessarily double. And since the supply of services is fixed, there is only one way for this to happen. Prices will double. And money neutrality holds in the long run, despite the asset role of money. Friedman had nearly proved his case.

The Case for
Stable Money Growth

Next Friedman examined the case where an increase in money is not simply a once-for-all event but rather a continuing phenomenon. Assume a continuing increase in M at a rate of 10 percent per annum; our helicopter is returning on regular missions, dropping off additional cash in a gradual but ever increasing crescendo.

In this case, the community must add to its nominal balances at 10 percent per year. Once again, logic requires that individuals attempt to adjust their nominal balances to achieve the same ratio to income, the same 10 percent reserve, as before. And then prices must rise at 10 percent per year. Once more, no real magnitudes will be affected, and the neutrality of money is again observed.[8]

Why do prices rise? Here a critical assumption slips in, expressed by Friedman this way: "Because everyone confidently anticipates that prices will rise."[9] That is, we assume that the community is aware of the flights of the helicopter—it knows, or believes it knows, that the money supply is rising at 10 percent per annum. Further, individual sellers of services are aware that, on average, a 10 percent increase in the money demand for their services can be expected simply because there is 10 percent more money to spend. They therefore raise prices by 10 percent. This spares

---

[8] This effect, the neutrality of the rate of growth of the money stock, is sometimes known as *superneutrality*.
[9] Friedman, "The Optimum Quantity," p. 10.

them from misregistering the purely monetary part of the increase in demand as a rise in the real demand for their services and in any way altering, on that account, their real supply of services. Thus, *confident expectations* play the critical role of guaranteeing that the neutrality of money holds true.

There is one crucial qualification. In the dynamic case, Friedman pointed out, inflation is reducing, by 10 percent yearly, the real purchasing power of the monetary reserves that were previously being held. This is the same as imposing a 10 percent annual tax on the real value of previously existing cash balances. It thus makes holding those balances more expensive relative to the purchase of services with the same money. If one makes cash-holding decisions rationally, as Friedman assumed, then one will decide rationally in response to this price change to reduce balances and increase purchases.

This action pushes prices up by an additional step change. That is, inflation will rise by more than 10 percent for a brief time, as people adjust their real money balances downward in response to the inflation tax. This case therefore violates the neutrality of money in the short run: there is a real behavioral consequence to a change in the rate of growth of the money stock. Only in the long run does this effect disappear and inflation converge to a 10 percent annual rate, as Figure 7.2 illustrates.

FIGURE 7.2   A Change in the Money Growth Rate

A rise in the money stock generates a parallel rise in the price level. An acceleration of money growth increases inflation and also causes a one-time step change in the price level as individuals cut their real balances.

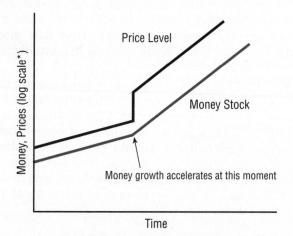

*Use of a log scale means that a constant rate of change will appear as a straight line on this graph.

Taking a Closer Look

MONEY, INFLATION, AND GDP

How well does the monetarist view of money and prices hold up? To form a rough idea, to compare the movements of various measures of the money stock with the inflation rate in recent years.

The charts in Figure 7.B1 compare the growth rates of M1, the narrow money stock, and M3, a broad measure, with the rate of price inflation in the United States from 1960 to the present. As 7.B1(a) shows, M1 growth tracked price inflation reasonably well for the first twenty years of this period, lending empirical support to the monetarist view that control of the money stock would effectively help to control inflation. But in the mid-1980s, this relationship broke down completely. M1 growth surged in the aftermath of the 1982 recession and then again in 1985–1987, yet there was no inflation effect; indeed, inflation continued to fall.

As figure 7.B1(b) shows, the growth rate of M3 was never a particularly close correlate of the inflation rate. But as you can see from Figure 7.B2, this broad aggregate has tracked the rate of change of nominal gross domestic product,

FIGURE 7.B1a   Inflation and Money (MI)

The simplest versions of monetarism held that increases in transactions money, measured by M1, would lead to rising inflation. This idea seemed to draw support from the data up to 1980 (except for the oil shock in 1974–1975), but it has not done very well in the past decade.

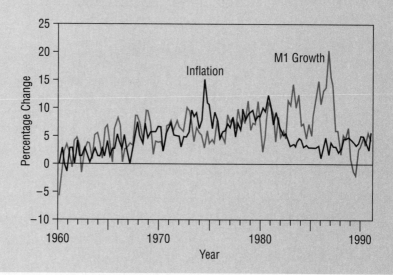

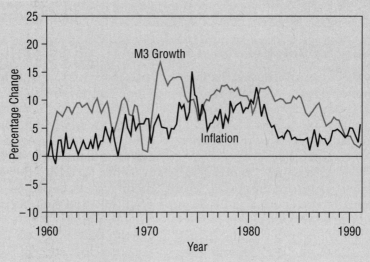

FIGURE 7.B1b   Inflation and Money (M3)

M3 growth has a poor fit to the rate of inflation.

FIGURE 7.B2   Money and Nominal GDP

Broad monetary aggregates such as M3 track the growth of nominal gross product fairly well. But some economists argue that the causality in this case runs from economic activity to money creation, so that M3 should not be considered a policy instrument.

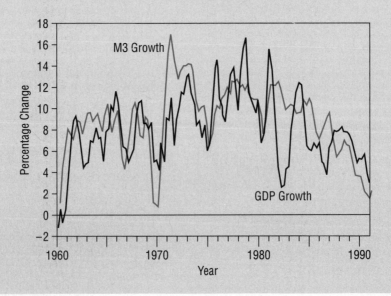

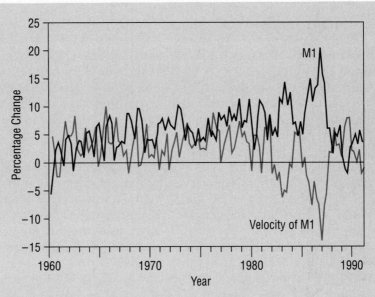

FIGURE 7.B3   **How Stable Is Velocity?**

Strict application of the quantity theory's principle that inflation must follow high money growth would require that velocity be reasonably constant. In fact, velocity has fallen in the past decade when money growth rose. One reason for this may be that, because of lower inflation, there was increasing demand for currency and low-interest demand deposits.

including the effects of both inflation and output changes, reasonably well over the years.

Does this mean that M3 can be
used to control nominal GDP?
While some economists have made
that argument, many believe that
the causality runs the other way:
changes in either the volume or the
price of output lead to changes in
demands for credit, and these are
supplied by the banking and financial systems and ratified, after the
fact, by the Federal Reserve. Thus,
the M3-GDP relationship does not
reflect the use of M3 as a policy instrument, and this broadly defined

aggregate would probably not
prove useful as a policy instrument.

As we have seen, a useful way
to summarize the stability of the
relationship between money and
nominal GDP growth is to look at
the stability of the ratio between the
two. This ratio is, of course, the
velocity of circulation of money.
Figure 7.B3 shows the rate of
change of the velocity of M1, compared to the rate of growth of M1
itself. As the chart demonstrates,
M1 velocity fluctuation has long
tended to be opposite to the movements of M1 itself, rising when M1
falls and falling when it rises. This

reflects the fact that it would take time for any change in M1 to have an effect on GDP, whether on real output or on prices.

Until 1980, the fluctuations of M1 velocity growth remained within a fairly narrow range and tended to reverse themselves within a year or two. But after 1980, things became much more unstable. M1 growth rose, and velocity growth fell, indicating that the growth of M1 had little impact on either money or prices.

Why did the stability of M1 velocity fall apart so abruptly in the 1980s? A basic explanation has been suggested: with the falling rate of inflation after 1980 (itself due, perhaps, to a very high exchange rate and intense competitive pressures from low-wage manufactured imports), people became more willing to hold additional quantities of cash and demand deposits—despite very high real interest rates that tended to induce them to put their cash into interest-bearing assets. As people demanded cash to hold, M1 rose but without major effect on either output or prices, and so velocity fell.

This qualification to Friedman's model has an important consequence for thinking about policy. It shows that changes (specifically increases) in the rate of inflation impose a real welfare loss on the community. Why? Because real wealth, in the form of real money balances, is a smaller fraction of current income than it was before. Conversely, cuts in inflation (or increases in deflation) must raise real wealth. They provide an increased return on real balances and cause the community to add to its financial wealth.

Thus, we have Friedman's basic theoretical conclusion. In a world of full employment, stable velocity, and confident expectations, the growth rate of M will determine the growth rate of P, once initial effects of changes in the rate of growth of the money stock subside. Money is therefore, despite its asset character, neutral in the long run. It will only be nonneutral if policy behaves erratically, causing changes in the rate of inflation. And this led Friedman to his famous, fundamental monetary policy recommendation: that the Federal Reserve should set (and publish) an unchanging rule stipulating a constant rate of growth of the money stock, year in and year out.

MONETARISM AND UNEMPLOYMENT

In the real world, of course, full employment is not a guaranteed condition. On the other hand, a stable money growth rule is not commonly seen in the real world either. Is there a connection between monetary instability and unemployment? In examining this question, Friedman and his followers saw the outlines of a theory of unemployment consistent with their theories of money and prices.

According to the classical supply-and-demand model of labor markets, unemployment may occur if wages fail to adjust so that quantities demanded and supplied become equal. Unemployment results if nominal wages are, in a word, "sticky." In that case, the labor market does not clear. People will exist who are willing to work at the prevailing wage or lower but who nevertheless cannot find work. The actual level of employment is determined by the number of workers that firms are willing to hire at the given wage (in other words, on the demand curve), while the level of unemployment is given by the difference between this quantity and the amount of labor that workers wish to supply (on the supply curve).

Why should nominal wages be sticky? One argument is the now familiar relative wage hypothesis attributed to Keynes (first presented in Chapter 2). By this line of argument, the wage bargain of any worker affects not only his real wage but also his relative standing among fellow workers. This gives each worker a reason to resist cuts in nominal wages, even though more employment would result and even though reductions in the real wage that might result from a price inflation would not be resisted.

The monetarists accept this argument but question how well it holds up in the real world. They note that the unemployed's desire for work will undermine the capacity of existing workers to resist nominal wage cuts. Therefore, nominal wage stickiness, and the unemployment it produces, only can persist as long as labor markets fail to respond to the applications for work (at lower wages) submitted by the unemployed. And while such a situation could continue for some time (particularly if governments intervene, for example with minimum wage laws), monetarists believe that competitive forces will sooner or later cause wages to fall to levels that clear the labor market.[10]

How then can persistent unemployment occur? It must be the case that other obstacles prevent the adjustment of real wages to market-clearing levels. Under what circumstances, if at all, can such a thing happen? Why do labor markets not clear continuously at full employment?

---

[10] A second and much more important argument in Keynes's reasoning was that even if nominal wages do fall, markup pricing rules ensure that prices will fall by similar amounts and so cause real wages to remain stable. Since it is real rather than nominal wages that matter to the classical labor market, nominal wage bargains will not bring about the requisite fall in real wages. Monetarists answer this argument by rejecting markup pricing in favor of a strict reliance on the quantity theory of money to explain price inflation and deflation.

The Accelerationist Hypothesis

Monetarists, beginning with Friedman himself in 1968, have offered several answers to this question. Friedman's argument has an institutional flavor. It emphasizes ways in which policy can exploit forces, such as labor contracts fixed for a definite period of time, that slow down the speed of adjustment of money wages (relative to that of prices). At the same time, another argument arose from Edmund S. Phelps, who emphasized the difficulties that individuals face in evaluating the information presented to them by the market. Phelps's argument is noninstitutional and is, as we shall see, a precursor of the modern postmonetarist view, known as new classical economics.[11]

Both Phelps and Friedman came to the same conclusion. Persistent unemployment is possible but only if policy produces falling prices at an accelerating rate. Employment at levels above equilibrium is also possible but only if policy produces inflation at an accelerating rate. When the rate of inflation is itself changing, and only then, the effects of policies on market conditions can outrun the reactions of individuals that would otherwise neutralize those effects. We call this result the *accelerationist hypothesis*.

Adaptive Expectations

Why can policies run ahead of reactions to them? Because it takes time for workers to realize that the price increases they see are connected to the wage increases they have just received. Why does it take time? Because price expectations (or more precisely, inflation expectations) in this model are *adaptive*. They depend, in a predictable way, on a stream of past prices (rates of inflation).

So long as the rate of inflation is constant, workers and other economic agents have no problem appreciating it for what it is. But when the rate of inflation changes, for example when it accelerates, then problems surface. Workers see the most recent price increases, but in forming their view of future price increases, they average the most recent data with earlier data that were based on a lower rate of inflation. Expected future prices do rise but not as much as prices are in fact going to rise. And this discrepancy—unexpectedly rapid rates of inflation—leads, in the Phelps-Friedman argument, to changes in behavior that would not otherwise occur.

[11] See Edmund S. Phelps, *Inflation Policy and Unemployment Theory* (New York: W. W. Norton, 1972), for a complete account of this thinking. The original Phelps article is "Phillips Curves, Expectations of Inflation and Optimal Unemployment," *Economica*, vol. 34, August 1967. Friedman's answer is in his presidential address to the American Economics Association: "The Role of Monetary Policy," *American Economic Review*, vol. 58, March 1968.

Adaptive expectations are easy to model, since all the needed information is contained in the past history of the variable. One form of adaptive expectations is the *distributed lag specification*, popularized by Philip Cagan in a famous study of hyperinflations:[12]

$$(7.1) \qquad E\dot{P}_{t+1} = \alpha_t \dot{P}_t + \alpha_{t-1}\dot{P}_{t-1} + \alpha_{t-2}\dot{P}_{t-2} + \ldots + \alpha_{t-n}\dot{P}_{t-n}$$

$$0 < \alpha_i < 1$$

$$\sum_i \alpha_i = 1$$

$$\alpha_t \geq \alpha_{t-1} \geq \ldots \geq \alpha_{t-n}$$

In this model, the inflation rate expected in the next period is treated as a weighted average of the past history of actual inflation rates, with the weights given by each α_i. The largest weight is given to the most recently experienced rate of inflation. Therefore, the coefficients decline as the years recede into the past. The coefficients also sum to one. In this specification, individuals calculate their expectations on the basis of the present and past n periods' inflation rates (where n could be twelve months ago or ten years ago).

If the inflation rate has been increasing in recent months or years, the forecast for next month or next year will be a further increase in prices. This approach provides a rule of thumb for the formation of expectations, one that may be workable under conditions of a fairly consistent, even if explosive, pattern of change.

Another form of the adaptive expectations approach is the *error-learning specification*.[13] Here the expected rate of inflation is adjusted upward or downward in response to the error in expectation in the most recent period observed. The expected rate of inflation in the next period would then be the current rate plus an error adjustment term:

$$(7.2) \qquad E_t\dot{P}_{t+1} = \dot{P}_t + \beta \, [\dot{P}_t - E_{t-1}\dot{P}_t]$$

If the actual rate of inflation in the current period exceeds the expectation formed in the previous period, the expectation of the next period's inflation rate will be revised upward. If the current-period inflation rate is less than the expectation formed previously, the expectation will be revised downward. The positive number β is a *reaction-response coefficient*, indicating the magnitude and speed of adjustment of the new expectation to the expectational error.

For example, if β is equal to one, there is a one-for-one adjustment in the expected rate of inflation in response to the error made in the

[12] Philip Cagan, "The Monetary Dynamics of Hyperinflation," in *Studies in the Quantity Theory of Money* (Chicago: University of Chicago Press, 1956).
[13] David Meiselman, *The Term Structure of Interest Rates* (Englewood Cliffs, N.J.: Prentice-Hall, 1962).

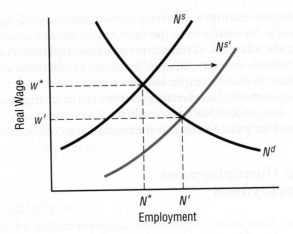

FIGURE 7.3   Inflation Misperceptions and Labor Supply

If workers underpredict the inflation rate, they will accept more employment at a lower real wage than they would have chosen with correct information.

accelerating inflation, why do workers supply the additional labor that employers are demanding? Why don't workers realize that their real wages have fallen and react in time by reducing their labor supply? Second, why are money wage contracts, alone among all prices, set in this particularly inflexible way? Why not provide workers with full *indexation* to protect their wages automatically from inflation, thus stabilizing the labor supply curve with respect to the inflation rate and neutralizing the consequences of expectational error? Friedman's story appears to rest on the same sort of arbitrary institutional assumptions that characterized the prevailing U.S. version of the Keynesian theory.

Information Asymmetry

Phelps offered a different version of the accelerationist story, one intended to be more consistent with freely functioning markets and rational individuals making well-informed decisions about how much labor to supply. The linchpin of this story is not sticky wages but rather the difficulty that rational people have in making correct inferences about the situation in the world economy when their only direct information comes from the events (in this case, price changes) they observe locally. We call this difficulty a problem of *information asymmetry*. In particular, important asymmetries can arise between business firms, who have good access to new information, and their workers, who may not.

To help make the problem clear, Phelps proposed a metaphor. Imagine, he said, that workers live on an archipelago and that they know just about everything that happens on their own island but less and less about what is happening on islands that are further and further away. Suppose, too, that the monetary authorities, whose emissions of new paper currency determine the general movement of prices, all reside on a separate, particularly distant island.

Now suppose, that, unannounced and unpredicted, the monetary authorities decide to try to stimulate economic activity by raising the growth rate of the money supply. Eventually, the inevitable effects will be felt, and price rises will accelerate on the workers' home island. That bare fact, of course, will be no secret to the worker. But is it a sign of a general increase in inflation, which would call for a compensating rise in the rate of change of money wages? Or is it a sign of changing relative prices, perhaps due to some unanticipated change in purely local conditions (e.g., a drought affecting local farming but not the farming on other islands)?

Phelps argued that workers would at first be unsure, so they would hesitate to raise their money wages. Firms, on the other hand, being organizations with the capacity to gather information for their own use, would be quicker to realize the true situation and to act. Seeing the rising price level and the sluggish money wage, they will seize the opportunity to hire more workers while the uncertainty lasts. The final effect is the same as in Friedman's version of the story: real wages fall at each level of labor supplied, and the quantity of labor demanded rises.

Phelps's story, however, offers an explanation for the two ends left loose in Friedman's version. Workers do not restore original conditions by demanding higher money wages in immediate response to higher prices because they are not certain that they are in fact experiencing a general inflation and a concomitant decline in the general level of the real wage. It takes time to arrive at a confident understanding of what part of the price change is global and what part is merely local.

MONETARISM AND THE PHILLIPS CURVE

In the short run, the Phelps–Friedman model produces a downward-sloping Phillips curve relationship. If the inflation rate rises, unemployment falls, and vice versa; both Phillips's and Samuelson-Solow's observations are accounted for. The ability of the Phelps–Friedman model, which appeared in the late 1960s, to account for what then seemed an established empirical regularity was an important point in its favor.

Two things set Phelps and Friedman apart from the empirical Phillips curve. First, their argument placed a seemingly rigorous foundation in individual behavior under the Phillips curve—Tobin's "Pirandello characters" now had their authors. Second, the model yielded a set of implications for the economy in the long run. We turn next to these implications.

The Natural Rate of Unemployment

Sooner or later, if the new rate of inflation remains constant, expectations catch up to reality. Workers observe that price inflation is permanently higher and that real wages have fallen. Naturally, they demand a wage adjustment that will establish the unique real wage that will clear the labor market. But the inflation rate, which is determined by the new, permanently higher rate of money growth, remains at its own new, permanently higher rate!

Hence, the short-run Phillips curve has shifted to the right. The same equilibrium unemployment rate now corresponds to a higher rate of expected inflation. To reduce unemployment again, it will be necessary once again to increase the rate of inflation and to mispersuade workers that real wages in the production period just ahead are higher than, in fact, they are.

The *Phelps-Friedman long run* can now be defined as those times when inflation (and therefore real-wage) expectations are shown to be correct. We can say that, in the long run, workers are not misled by rate-of-return misperceptions into offering either more or less work than they would, in retrospect and with complete information, have agreed to do. This happens any time workers correctly forecast the rate of inflation—which, with adaptive expectations, they will do when, and only when, the rate of inflation has been constant over a sustained period of time.

The rate of inflation can be at any value at all, so long as it is *constant*. And at any constant rate of inflation, the amount of labor offered and employed will be the equilibrium rate—the same rate as at any other constant rate of inflation. At that rate of unemployment, with a constant rate of inflation, the classical condition that money is neutral—the chief concern of Friedman's earlier monetary model—is satisfied. Friedman gave this special rate of unemployment a name: the *natural rate of unemployment*.[15]

---

[15] Subsequent Keynesian scholars have tried to rename the same concept as the nonaccelerating inflation rate of unemployment, or NAIRU. The more cumbersome term has not spread very far.

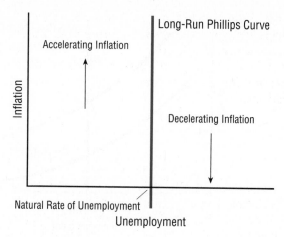

FIGURE 7.4   The Natural Rate of Unemployment

In the Phelps-Friedman model, the Phillips curve is vertical in the long run and determines a natural rate of unemployment. Inflation can be any constant value at the natural
rate of unemployment.

The Vertical Long–Run Phillips Curve

As Figure 7.4 shows, there is a clear conclusion. In the Phelps-Friedman
long run, *the Phillips curve must be vertical*, intercepting the horizontal axis
at the natural rate of unemployment. So long as inflation rates are correctly anticipated, the labor market will clear at the natural rate. It will
fail to clear, or clear at a rate different from the natural rate, only if
inflation is forecast incorrectly, which under adaptive expectations will
occur only when the inflation rate is varying.

To see how the vertical Phillips curve emerges analytically, return
to a proposition derived in Chapter 5, where we showed that the rate of
inflation must equal the rate of wage increase, minus the rate of productivity growth, π:

$$(7.3) \qquad\qquad \dot{P} = \dot{W} - \pi$$

The Friedman argument, in its simplest form, holds that the rate of
wage increase will be determined in part by the expected rate of inflation
and in part by the actual rate of unemployment. The effect of unemployment on wage increases is negative, so the effect of rising unemployment
is to depress wage increases, and vice versa. And in the equation following, λ is a parameter whose value lies between zero and one, indicating
how rapidly a change in price expectations is incorporated into rising
wages.

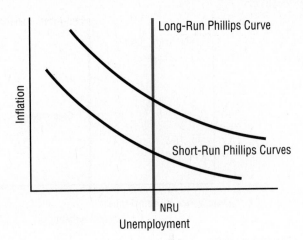

FIGURE 7.5   Short- and Long-Run Phillips Curves

Each short-run Phillips curve corresponds to a different expected rate of inflation. When expected inflation coincides with actual inflation, the Phillips curve is vertical.

$$\dot{W} = \dot{W}(U) + \lambda E \dot{P} \tag{7.4}$$

$$\dot{W}' < 0$$

$$0 \le \lambda \le 1$$

Combining (7.3) and (7.4), we see that the rate of price inflation depends on the rate of productivity growth, the rate of unemployment, and the expected rate of inflation. This relationship is known as the *expectations-augmented Phillips curve*:

$$\dot{P} = \dot{W}(U) - \pi + \lambda E \dot{P} \tag{7.5}$$

Since the first two terms of the right side of (7.5) are the equation of a short-run Phillips curve, one may think of this equation as representing a family of ordinary short-run Phillips curves. Any change in expected inflation merely shifts the short-run curve up or down by an amount corresponding to the size of the change in the final term. Figure 7.5 illustrates such a family of curves.

We can now solve for the special case—the Phelps-Friedman long run—where actual and expected rates of inflation are equal. In that case, we have

$$\dot{P} = \frac{\dot{W}(U)}{1 - \lambda} - \frac{\pi}{1 - \lambda} \tag{7.6}$$

Equation (7.6) is the equation of the *long-run Phillips curve*. It too is very similar to that of the regular, or short-run, Phillips curve—except

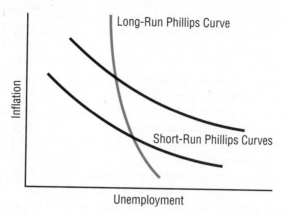

FIGURE 7.6   The Expectations-Augmented Phillips Curve

If adjustment of inflation expectations to reality is not complete in one period, then the long-run Phillips curve may not be vertical. It will still be steeper than the short-run Phillips curve.

that the intercept is different and, importantly, the slope is steeper by a factor of $1/(1 - \lambda)$. As equation (7.4) demonstrates, when λ is equal to one, a change in inflation expectations is reflected one-for-one in wages, and we have the case that interested Friedman and Phelps: the long-run Phillips curve is vertical, and the rate of inflation does not depend on the rate of unemployment. Figure 7.5 illustrates this case, and Figure 7.6 shows the case where $\lambda < 1$ and the long-run Phillips curve is not vertical.[16]

We can also solve for the rate of unemployment in the long run from equation (7.6):[17]

$$U = \dot{W}^{-1} \left[(1 - \lambda) \, \dot{P} + \pi \right]$$

When $\lambda = 1$, once again the rate of inflation does not influence the rate of unemployment. Unemployment then reduces to

$$U\star = \dot{W}^{-1} (\pi)$$

This is the natural rate of unemployment. It depends only on π, the growth rate of labor productivity, and on the function that determines

---

[16] This case was once a major part of the response of Keynesians to Friedman's argument because it continued to permit policies aimed at expanding output to have a permanent effect on unemployment. However, it has been hard to justify an incomplete incorporation of price expectations into wages, so even self-described Keynesians have come increasingly to accept a vertical Phillips curve in the long run.

[17] Recall that $\dot{W}^{-1}$ is mathematical notation ("W-dot inverse") indicating that the effect of the function W-dot is reversed. It is analogous to taking the reciprocal of a fraction: $\dot{W}^{-1}[\dot{W}(\pi)] = \pi$.

how a change in the actual unemployment rate is reflected in the rate of change of money wages. Since that original function has a negative slope, its inverse must also have a negative slope. Thus, the faster labor productivity grows, the lower the natural rate of unemployment, and vice versa. (This formulation underpins the idea that the rising unemployment rates of the 1970s and 1980s were due to slower rates of productivity growth, with a policy implication that only high rates of productivity growth can reduce the natural rate of unemployment.)

In this way, Friedman and Phelps provided a theoretical basis for a downward-sloping short-run Phillips relation, consistent with the facts up to that time, that simultaneously denied its usefulness as a tool for permanently affecting the rate of unemployment. At any moment, government policy could force the unemployment rate down by persuading workers to offer more labor supply than they would if they had full and accurate information. But the inevitable consequence would be a rising rate of inflation, and a new equilibrium could only be established by returning to the natural rate of unemployment at the new, higher rate of inflation. Thus, short of hyperinflation, there could be no permanent gains from Keynesian policies to stimulate aggregate demand; and under hyperinflation, of course, the whole economy would collapse.

The Collapse of the Phillips Curve

Friedman and Phelps had thrown down the gauntlet at the U.S. Keynesians, who were then (in 1968) at the height of their power and prestige. Unemployment had been falling continuously since the beginning of the Kennedy administration eight years before. The price, so far, in terms of increased inflation, had been small. Friedman was warning, in effect, that there would be a larger price to pay later on.

The Phelps-Friedman position enjoyed an enormous vindication after 1969, when the vaunted stability of the measured short-run Phillips curve collapsed. We showed in Figure 5.16 how the inflation-unemployment tradeoff broke down after 1969; this figure is reproduced as Figure 7.7. With the fall of the Phillips curve, the self-confidence of U.S. Keynesians that they could manage the economy to produce full employment without inflation also broke down, and the political position of politicians associated with Keynesian ideas sharply eroded.

Robert Lucas, writing in 1981, described the triumph of the anti-Keynesian view:

> Now, Friedman and Phelps had no way of foreseeing the inflation of the 1970s, any more than did the rest of us, but the central forecast to which their reasoning led was a conditional one, to the effect that a high inflation decade should not have less unemployment on

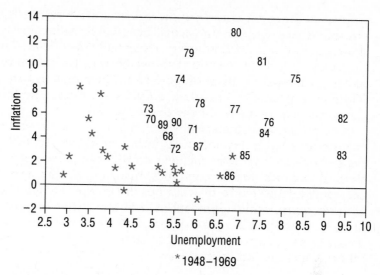

FIGURE 7.7   The Collapse of the Phillips Curve

The Phillips curve fell apart after 1970, seeming to confirm the argument of Milton Friedman and the monetarists.

average than a low-inflation decade. We got the high inflation decade, and with it as clear-cut an experimental discrimination as macroeconomics is ever likely to see, and Friedman and Phelps were right.[18]

Axel Leijonhufvud, in 1983, echoed this judgment:

> It was a debacle. A bad enough debacle that the profession proclaimed the long controversy a Monetarist victory and, by and large, turned its interest elsewhere.[19]

What actually went wrong? The explanation favored by Lucas and Leijonhufvud is very clear. Samuelson and Solow, they argued, failed to incorporate the effect of price expectations on wage formation when they developed their original formulation of the Phillips curve as a simple relationship between unemployment and wage demands. Therefore, when inflation expectations grew to a noticeable size after 1968, the

---

[18] "Tobin and Monetarism: A Review Article," *Journal of Economic Literature*, 29 (June 1981), 558–585.
[19] "What would Keynes Have Thought of Rational Expectations?" in *Keynes and the Modern World*, ed. James Worswick and David Trevithick, (Cambridge, Cambridge University Press, 1983).

collapse of the stable short-run curve was inevitable. The only argument remaining was whether the actual events reflected a family of shifting short-run Phillips curves (the Keynesian fallback—Figure 7.6) or a vertical curve with temporary deviations about it due to forecasting errors (the monetarist alternative—Figure 7.4). The monetarist alternative won out in this argument, because it provided a simpler and more coherent argument that accounts for the observed facts.

As the next chapters will show, this was not the end of the story. Further theoretical developments in line of descent from Friedman and Phelps were to lead, over the next decade, to the emergence of the new classical school of macroeconomics, based on the idea of rational expectations and dedicated to the rigorous integration of aggregative analysis with microeconomic "foundations" of competitive market theory. And then, in the 1980s, the propositions of the rational expectationists were themselves to confront reality, with results that led to still more theoretical development and controversy.

SPECIAL SECTION

The Federal Reserve and the Control of Money

The powers of monetary policy in the United States are vested in the Federal Reserve, our central bank. In this Special Section, we provide an overview of the Federal Reserve System and of its relationship to the rest of the government and to the banking system.

The Federal Reserve, the "bankers' bank," was created by an act of Congress in 1913 to help furnish an "elastic currency" to the nation and to serve as a "lender of last resort" to the banking system. The act was, in large measure, a response to the monetary crises of the late nineteenth and early twentieth centuries, in particular the financial panic of 1907. These events had led many U.S. observers to conclude that the gold standard, a strict version of which was then in force, was not a sufficiently flexible basis for a system of money and credit. Yet many also feared the powers that would accrue to a central bank, especially if that bank came too much under the thrall of the "hard money" men at the New York banks or if it became a political tool in the hands of the president. The structure, governance, and purposes of the Federal Reserve thus reflected a long national history of struggle over monetary matters, of popular distrust of central banking dating back to the time of Andrew Jackson, and of efforts to achieve financial stability without compromising the independence of private banking institutions.

To arrive at a workable compromise between these interests, Congress established a decentralized Federal Reserve System, dividing the country into twelve financial districts. Each district Federal Reserve Bank would be a semiprivate institution, "owned" by shareholding "member" banks and governed by a president and by a board of directors nominated by the local community, including especially local bankers. District banks thus would feel a special commitment to stabilize the banks in their own regions and would act as a voice for regional concerns with the Federal Reserve in Washington, D.C. Each district bank would manage its own discount window and thus have the power to lend to banks within the district. Presiding over all would be, in Washington, a board of governors, appointed by the president and confirmed by the U.S. Senate. The seven governors would be appointed for fourteen-year terms and thus be largely independent of the president of the moment. On the other hand, the agency would remain a "creature of Congress," subject to congressional mandate because Congress was, of course, the body that enacted and that retains the power to change the Federal Reserve Act.

Over the course of this century, actual power at the Federal Reserve has become concentrated in Washington. Perhaps the major turn in this direction occurred in the 1920s, when open market oper-

ations were devised as a means of exerting central control over a national market for bank reserves—and so over a nationwide rate of interest (the overnight rate on deposits that banks lend to and borrow from each other in order to meet their reserve requirements, known as the *federal funds rate*). Open market operations—the buying and selling of government bonds—are carried out by a desk at the New York Federal Reserve Bank, but open market policy has been set in Washington by the Federal Open Market Committee since 1934. This policymaking body comprises the seven presidentially appointed Federal Reserve governors and, on a rotating basis, five of the twelve district bank presidents. The powers to set reserve requirements and discount rates and also to take many regulatory decisions are now also vested in the board of governors in Washington. The district banks no longer exercise (if they ever did) much practical autonomy in major policy matters.

The Great Crash of 1929 provided the first big test of the grand design of the nation's central bank. As thousands of bank failures and the Great Depression proved, the design was not especially effective. Although the Federal Reserve was quite able to provide interim discount loans to help individual banks that might be in trouble, it was either unable or unwilling to provide the massive infusions of cash that became necessary when the entire banking system as a whole was thrown into crisis. As a result, bank runs and bank failures were epidemic from 1929 to 1933, and both the money supply and the economy itself collapsed. Only deposit insurance, a New Deal measure enacted in 1934 and embodied in the Federal Deposit Insurance Corporation (FDIC), proved able to restore confidence in the banking system as a whole.

These developments spawned an interesting and persistent controversy in the history of economics. Monetarists, led by Milton Friedman and Anna Schwartz,[1] have maintained that had the Federal Reserve been attempting to control the level of the money supply rather than interest rates, it would have been able to print enough money to forestall the banking collapse and the Depression itself. All the Federal Reserve needed to do, in this interpretation, was to buy up outstanding debts from the private sector, thereby flooding the economy with cash.

Keynesians, not surprisingly, resist this conclusion. They argue that the Depression saw a large-scale collapse in effective demand. Since people without jobs had no way of getting money, either as income or as loans, to finance their transactions, they would not have been helped by the creation of money per se. Therefore, any amount of money printing would have been largely futile unless accompanied by measures to distribute the printed money, as incomes, to the population. Such measures—whether jobs programs or welfare—of course are described as fiscal policy.

To support their position, Keynesians point to the experience of 1937–38. At that time, the Federal Reserve, by then itself under the influence of Keynesian ideas, attempted to fight a deepening of the Depression by aggressively creating money and reducing interest rates. In the face of a sharply more restrictive fiscal policy, brought about by the Roosevelt administration's attempt that year to balance the federal budget, the effort failed. Indeed, even though the interest rate fell almost to zero, the economy did not recover. U.S. Keynesians drew from this the lesson that an expansionary fiscal policy was essential; they coined the phrase "pushing on a string" to describe the ineffectiveness of expansionary Federal Reserve policy during a depression.[2]

In 1942, the Federal Reserve was, in effect, "drafted" into the war effort and given the mission of ensuring that the price of U.S. government bonds be maintained at par—100 cents on the dollar—for the duration. In practice, this meant that the Federal Reserve would have to buy government bonds from the public and so create money, enough to ensure that the long-term interest rate on government bonds did not rise above the then-prevailing rate of about 2 percent.

Interestingly, this step was considered necessary in order to encourage saving at low interest rates. Policymakers believed that people would not put their money into government bonds if they felt that the price of those bonds might fall if interest rates were to rise in the future. If that happened, there would be a flight from bonds to money and from money to goods, which would bid up prices and generate runaway inflation. Thus, an ironclad commitment to low and stable interest rates alongside an expansionary monetary policy and price controls, became part and parcel of the successful effort to hold down inflation in wartime.

After the war and with the dismantling of price controls in 1946, the governors of the Federal Reserve wished to return open market operations to the conventional role of monetary control and macroeconomic stabilization. They did not achieve the power to do so until 1951, when the "Federal Reserve–Treasury Accord" permitted renewed movement of the government bond rate. From that point forward, monetary policy took the form it largely retains to the present day.

As a legal matter, the Federal Reserve's mandate is to support the goals of the Employment Act of 1946, as amended by the Humphrey-Hawkins Full Employment Act of 1978, which sets a national goal of full employment with reasonably stable prices. However, in enacting both of these measures, Congress refrained from specifying exactly how they were to be achieved. The result has been that the Federal Reserve retains very substantial discretion over its conduct of monetary policy; in practice, the oversight powers of Congress are limited.

With some significant exceptions, the basic macroeconomic operating rule of the Federal Reserve since the 1950s has been to "lean against the prevailing wind" of the business cycle. That is, when the Board of Governors judges the prevailing threat to be inflation, interest rates are driven up and the growth rate of the economy is slowed down. When, as happened on five occasions since 1970, these actions resulted in an actual fall in gross domestic product (GDP)—a recession—then the Federal Reserve responded by easing policy, allowing interest rates to fall and therefore facilitating renewed economic expansion.

In the middle and late 1970s, an academic debate swirled around the question of whether the operating procedures of the Federal Open Market Committee, which emphasized the control of short-term interest rates, were compatible with the basic philosophy of leaning against the wind. In particular, monetarists argued that interest rate stabilization amounted to leaning *into* the wind. If the economy and the demand for money were growing rapidly, a policy of providing enough bank reserves to keep the federal funds rate stable would entail meeting all of the rising demand for money. In a recession, conversely, a policy of stabilizing the federal funds rate would mean that the Federal Reserve would "follow the economy down." While in principle the FOMC could change its interest rate targets up or down rapidly enough so that policy would be countercyclical in effect, monetarists argued that in practice it would fail to do so.

Moreover, even if officials did move quickly and presciently, the lags between the implementation of an expansionary or contractionary policy and its eventual effects were so long and variable that, as often as not, the effects would come too late. A policy intended to reverse a downturn by cutting interest rates would end up accelerating an inflationary expansion, and policies aimed at curbing inflation would end up making a recession worse. For all of these reasons, the monetarists said, a policy of stabilizing money growth would be much more effective, because it would tend, in their view, to prevent fluctuations of demand growth from occurring in the first place.

Federal Reserve officials, along with most theoretical Keynesians, doubted the monetarist argument for at least three practical reasons. First, they knew that the federal funds rate could be controlled precisely, day to day, by the means of open market operations; they also knew that the linkage from open market operations to money creation was not as precise. For one thing, whereas minute-to-minute information was available about what the federal funds rate was, money supply data were (and are) collected only on a weekly basis and were subject to revision in the following weeks. Thus, although interest rate control was an established art, money supply control might amount to chasing a moving target.

Second, the empirical definition of the money supply was (and remains) quite imprecise, and the monetarists themselves were divided as to whether M1 or M2 should be the object of control. If effective control of one aggregate were sought and achieved, critics could always object that the target should have been the other. Finally, Federal Reserve officials doubted that the relationship between money growth and GDP growth, or between money and prices, was as tight as monetarists believed. There arose among central bankers an aphorism known as Goodhart's law (named after a Bank of England economist), which holds that when you convert an econometric relationship into an instrument of policy, the relationship always changes.

Against these doubts, there emerged an unlikely coalition of theoretical monetarists, whose reasons for favoring monetary control have been described, and of liberals in Congress. This latter group had practical reasons of its own for favoring monetary targets.[3] Leaders of the two banking committees, Henry Reuss in the House and William Proxmire in the Senate, were frustrated by the secrecy that surrounded the operations of the Federal Reserve. Congress could not get even routine information about what policy was. Congressional hearings with the Federal Reserve chairman (at that time, Arthur F. Burns) were notorious occasions for evasion and stonewalling, stoutly defended on the ground that giving out public information about future movements of the interest rate would lead to rampant speculation and financial disorder. Without information, Congress could not exercise even minimal oversight over monetary policy. And by 1975, in congressional eyes, monetary policy bore responsibility for two recent deep and painful recessions, with no effective cure for inflation and no end in sight.

The result was legislation known as House Concurrent Resolution 133, passed in early 1975. It required the chairman of the Federal Reserve Board to appear at regular intervals before Congress to present and explain the Federal Reserve's annual targets for the growth of the money supply. Within a short time, Congress also got the Federal Reserve to present its forecasts for the behavior of the economy itself: real growth, inflation, and unemployment. With this information, Congress could effectively discuss and, if need be, criticize the direction that monetary policy was planning to take.

The creation, announcement, and public discussion of annual monetary targets did not, of course, give Congress power to change those targets or to force the Federal Reserve to meet them. And the Federal Reserve, having met the letter of the congressional mandate,

routinely defied the spirit. High officials of the Federal Reserve were no more monetarist after H. Con. Res. 133 (or its incorporation into law in the Full Employment Act of 1978) than they had been before. Actual money growth rose above or fell below the announced targets, depending on the decisions of policymakers taken after the targets were announced, or on changes in underlying economic conditions.

In late 1979, however, the Federal Reserve found it convenient to adopt the monetarist label for purposes of its own. With the second oil shock, the inflation rate was running above 10 percent, and strong calls came from the financial community and elsewhere for decisive action to bring inflation down. In spring 1979, President Jimmy Carter had named Paul A. Volcker, a professional central banker of conservative credentials, as Chairman of the Federal Reserve Board. Volcker, though not himself a theoretical monetarist, determined to act.

On October 6, 1979, Volcker announced that monetary policy would no longer attempt to stabilize interest rates even in the short term; monetary control would be the order of the day. The results were dramatic: short-term interest rates rose to above 20 percent.

The recession of 1980 was caused by a combination of two factors: the tight monetary policies inaugurated in October 1979 and quantitative credit controls imposed briefly in March 1980. Of the two measures, credit controls probably had the greater effect. Abruptly, that spring, people simply stopped using their consumer credit cards, and the economy plunged into recession. When credit controls were lifted in the early summer, there was a rapid recovery.

In 1981, monetary policy put an end to the recovery, and with a vengeance. In March, under pressure from the newly installed Reagan administration, Chairman Volcker determined to tighten again. Money growth rates fell to zero and stayed there for six months, while the economy went into its steepest downturn since World War II. In vain a few congressional liberals protested that, under this purported monetarism, actual money growth was far *below* the announced monetary targets! In truth, the Federal Reserve was no more monetarist in the early 1980s than it had ever been; it merely found for a time that monetarist arguments could be used to justify a severe credit crunch, and resulting recession, when these were felt necessary to bring about a rapid end to inflation.

The crisis of the Federal Reserve's commitment to monetarism came in late summer 1982, when the recession reached bottom amid growing signs of a financial crisis. In August, Mexico announced that it could not pay its debts, and the country's largest banks, deeply embroiled in shaky loans to Latin America and elsewhere, seemed to teeter on the brink of collapse. The Federal Reserve's response was in keeping with its larger mandate to preserve the stability of the financial system. Monetarism was abandoned, the growth rate of the money supply exploded, and the economy and the financial system were brought back from the brink.

In the years after the 1982 debacle, the Federal Reserve moved away from paying even lip service to monetarism. It never, however, returned entirely to its former preoccupation with short-term interest rates. Rather, one gets the impression that the Federal Reserve moved in three different policy directions more or less at once. First, it became more directly concerned with the movements of the macroeconomy and tried to stabilize the aggregate growth rate at a low level—moving the interest rate down when the growth rate was too low or falling, raising it when real growth exceeded an annual rate of 3 or 4 percent. As the recession of 1991–1992 wore on, falling interest rates became the main weapon in the government's efforts to restore positive economic growth; by the end of 1992, short-term interest rates were at their lowest levels in twenty-seven years.

Second, the Federal Reserve became ever more conscious of the role of monetary policy in setting the exchange value of the dollar. At times when the concern with growth was not overriding, U.S. interest rate policy alternated between driving the dollar down (in the late 80s) and holding it up. Third, as savings and loan and

banking instabilities grew more severe, the Federal Reserve increasingly conducted monetary policy
with an eye to reinforcing the stability and profitability of its primary institutional clients, the large
commercial banks. Where this tendency will lead us, in an era when
bank instability is likely to get
more serious rather than less, is
anybody's guess.

---

[1] See M. Friedman and A. Schwartz, *A Monetary History of the United States*

(Chicago: University of Chicago Press, 1963).

[2] This experience led Paul Samuelson to argue that the simple, one-variable 45-degree Keynesian cross diagram wasn't such a bad depression model after all. Investment *was* insensitive to falling interest rates at this time—although another possible interpretation is that since prices were falling at the same time, real interest rates may not have fallen very much.

[3] These observations are based on James Galbraith's personal experience as staff economist for the House Banking Committee between 1975 and 1980.

SUMMARY

As an economic point of view, monetarism shares much common ground with classical theory. The leading proponent of monetarism, Milton Friedman, has written that inflation "is always and everywhere a monetary phenomenon." This view was shared by the classicals, but in the monetarist theory it is complicated by a more sophisticated theory of the demand for money. In addition to the transactions demand for money, monetarists also posit an asset demand for money. This asset demand serves to smooth out consumption in the face of fluctuations in income; in other words, people hold some money as a contingency or *precaution* against random adverse events.

The money set aside as assets is measured in real balances. Concep-tually, this is the length of time that the assets could be used to maintain a person's normal spending habits. With inflation, real balances will fall for any given value of the money supply. Friedman argued that people hold a constant percentage of their income as real balances. With this assumption, he was able to show that an asset demand for money was consistent with the classical theory of money. To be exact, he showed that if the nominal money supply doubled, then prices also would dou-ble. When this argument is made with a steadily growing money supply, monetary policy is shown to be ineffective, and money is neutral in its impact on the economy.

Monetarism is a theory of money neutrality in the long run. In the short run, an expansionary monetary policy can have some effect on real output and employment because people will spend a bit more money before the value of their nominal balances falls. This will cause inflation to be somewhat lower than would be expected, but in the longer run the rate of inflation will converge with the growth rate of money.

The monetarists have a theory of unemployment based on the idea that nominal wages are sticky. Wage bargains between workers and employers are struck in real terms, based on an expected rate of price inflation. Expectations of inflation are assumed to be formed adaptively, based on the past history of the rate of inflation itself. If inflation accelerates, then employment may increase because, under adaptive expectations, the acceleration cannot be anticipated and real wages will fall. With the adaptive expectations framework, stabilization policy is effective in raising employment as long as the actual rate of inflation outruns the adaptively formed expected rate of inflation. This is, of course, a recipe for indefinitely accelerating inflation.

In the long run, the monetarists argue, the Phillips curve is vertical at the natural rate of unemployment. Two arguments are advanced to allow for possible deviations from the vertical Phillips curve in the short run. The first is that the long-run Phillips curve is actually a series of several short-run Phillips curves. Because the adjustment to a new short-run curve is not instantaneous, deviations from the natural rate are possible. The second argument rests on forecasting errors within the adaptive expectations framework.

Review Questions

1. Is it possible to create an adaptive expectations framework that would perfectly predict an accelerating inflation rate? How?

2. Describe two justifications for the long-run vertical Phillips curve. In particular, discuss how each justification changes the content of policy discussions.

3. Discuss how to implement a way of forming expectations that is superior to adaptive expectations.

4. Friedman came to conclusions very similar to those of the classical economists. How is Friedman's argument better than the simple quantity equation of the classical economists?

5. Does Friedman restrict his analysis of real balances to any one kind of money (M1, M2, etc.)? Explain.

6. Discuss how monetarists explain the persistence of unemployment. In particular, highlight the similarities and differences between the monetarist view and that of the Keynesians.

Review Problems

1. Consider equation (7.1), which describes an adaptive expectations framework for predicting future inflation. Assume only three periods are used for predicting. The present period is weighted 0.5, one period back is weighted 0.25, and two periods back is also weighted 0.25. The inflation in the present period is 10 percent, one period back it was 15 percent, and two periods back it was 8 percent. What is the prediction of inflation for the next period?

2. Repeat the same exercise with the following information. The weightings are exactly the same. The inflation in the present period is 100 percent, one period back it was 50 percent, and two periods back it was 25 percent. Does the inflation predicted by equation (7.1) make what you would consider a good guess? What is a better guess?

3. Create an adaptive expectations equation that would better predict the series of inflation rates given in problem 2.

4. Now turn to equation (7.3). Suppose workers expect an inflation rate of 10 percent and they expect this to be fully incorporated into wages. If productivity growth is 2.5 percent per year, what will be the inflation rate? Does your result pose any problems for consistency?

5. Taking up equation (7.5), continue to use the numbers in problem 4. Suppose further that workers cut back their wage demands by 0.5 percent for every 1 percent of inflation. What would be an equilibrium level of unemployment? Is there a rate of inflation that would generate no unemployment? (Assume that eventually the workers' expectations of inflation would converge to the actual level of inflation.)

6. Suppose that the productivity growth rate doubled. What would happen to the results in problem 5? Explain why this makes sense intuitively.

SUGGESTED READINGS

Milton Friedman and Anna S. Schwartz, *A Monetary History of the United States* (Chicago: University of Chicago Press, 1963).

Milton Friedman, *The Optimum Quantity of Money and Other Essays* (Chicago: Aldine, 1971).

Edmund S. Phelps, *Inflation Policy and Unemployment Theory* (New York: Norton, 1972).

Philip Cagan, *Studies in the Quantity Theory of Money* (Chicago: University of Chicago Press, 1956).

David Meiselman, *The Term Structure of Interest Rates* (Englewood Cliffs, New Jersey: Prentice-Hall, 1962).

Michael Hadjimichalakis, *Macroeconomics: an Intermediate Text* (Englewood Cliffs: Prentice-Hall, 1982).

Chapter 8

RATIONAL

EXPECTATIONS

The task of new classical economics was to build a complete macroeconomic theory on the foundation laid down by the monetarists. This new macroeconomics would seek to explain the actual behavior of the economy from the first principles of rational maximizing individual behavior and perfectly competitive markets. It thus sought to reconcile macro- and microeconomics in a way that neither the Keynesianism of IS-LM and the Phillips curve nor monetarism alone could do.

This chapter presents the core assertions of new classical economics as a combination of monetarism, market clearing, and rational expectations. It concludes with a special section on alternative ways of modeling and measuring expectations.

As you study the core assertions, keep these questions in mind:

- How does an economy achieve universal clearing of markets? In particular, what practical obstacles to this achievement would have to be overcome?
- What are rational expectations, and how do they differ from adaptive expectations?
- What implications do rational expectations have for the Phillips curve relationship between inflation and unemployment?

New classical economics surged to the forefront of economic theory in the 1970s. The early new classicals were monetarists, anti-Keynesian students and allies of Milton Friedman.[1] Yet they were not entirely happy with the logical underpinnings of the monetarist theory. They felt that monetarism shared too much the Keynesian habit of analyzing the behavior of economic aggregates, such as inflation and unemployment, from the top down—of looking for empirical regularities[2] first and seeking to explain them later. Further, both monetarists and Keynesians explained economic behavior too much in terms of "adjustment lags," "sticky wages," and other *market imperfections*. These, the new classicals felt, were *obiter dicta*, assertions not rigorously justified by theory. Adaptive expectations, a case of sticky adjustment of forecasts, fell under the same cloud of suspicion.

The new classicals set out to reconstruct macroeconomics from the ground up. Their model, unlike Keynesian and even monetarist models, would be based rigorously on the rational behavior of self-interested individuals operating in competitive markets. Where Friedman's monetarism was at least implicitly Marshallian in its concern with the movement of economic conditions through time, the new classicals would take a rigorously Walrasian analytical approach (see the discussion of Marshallian and Walrasian equilibria in Chapter Two). In this way, they would create a model world where money is neutral and a continuous equilibrium prevails in the labor market. The resulting macroeconomics would be based, for the first time, on *microfoundations*.

The new classical model combines three fundamental elements, or assumptions. Monetarism, the basic belief that the money stock is an exogenous policy variable and that money is neutral, is retained as the first of these. The other two are market clearing and rational expectations.

MARKET CLEARING

The *market clearing* assumption asserts a basic faith in the price mechanism. The new classicals reject sticky wages, sticky prices, and lags in adjustment. If such rigidities exist for even a short time, they argue, opportunities for profit must arise. Rational individuals will move either to meet the excess demands that rigidities cause or to remove the excess supplies. In so doing, they correct the rigidities and earn the profits. Therefore, new classicals have come to believe that price rigidities are *per se* irrational, except in the very short run. And they do not believe that a

---

[1] The principal new classicals included Robert Lucas, Jr., at the University of Chicago, Thomas Sargent and Neil Wallace, both then at the University of Minnesota, and Robert Barro, then at the University of Rochester.

[2] Such as the aggregate consumption function, or the relationship of money growth to price changes.

coherent macroeconomic theory can be built on phenomena that would not endure in a rational world.

Instead, new classicals hold that relative prices will adjust with sufficient speed to ensure that quantities supplied will come into balance with quantities demanded, leaving no persistent shortages or surpluses anywhere in the economic system. The new classicals apply this assumption particularly to the labor market. In so doing, they retrieve the "old" classical view that the level of employment is determined by supply-and-demand curves for labor, which themselves depend solely on the real wage. The labor market will clear at full employment unless the government or some other external force interferes with the setting of wages.

When the real wage rises, the quantity of labor demanded falls, but the supply of labor rises. There is one, and only one, real wage at which quantities of labor demanded and supplied will be equal; this is the only real wage that will clear the labor market. This combination of real wage and employment level is represented by the point $(w\star, N\star)$ in Figure 8.1. Unemployment can exist at the $N\star$ level of employment, but it must be strictly frictional or voluntary. New classicals reject altogether the conceptual validity of involuntary unemployment.[3] For them, the only possible equilibrium unemployment rate is the natural rate of unemployment, at which any remaining unemployment must be voluntary.

A *natural rate of output* is associated with the natural rate of unemployment. Given the labor market–clearing level of employment $N\star$, we need the full employment level of output, $y\star$, from the now familiar aggregate production function, also shown in Figure 8.1. As long as no excess demand or excess supply exists in the labor market, an economy with this production structure must produce the natural rate of output.

A key point here is that market clearing must be universal: it is not sufficient, for full employment, that the labor market alone have flexible adjustment of real wages. All markets have to clear, or the excess demand in some product market may spill over and cause excess supply (unemployment) in the market for labor.

To ensure that excess demand and excess supply do not arise in the labor market or anywhere else, relative prices of all commodities (including wages of labor) must move in the appropriate direction and quickly enough to eliminate excess demands and excess supplies in all markets at once. The pricing mechanism must ensure that markets clear throughout a multimarket economy. When this condition is met, the economic system inherently tends toward *Walrasian* equilibrium, that hypothetical state in which all exchanges occur at just the right prices, ensuring that all markets are in balance.

---

[3] Robert E. Lucas, Jr., "Unemployment Policy," *American Economic Review*, 68: No. 2 (May 1978), pp. 353–357.

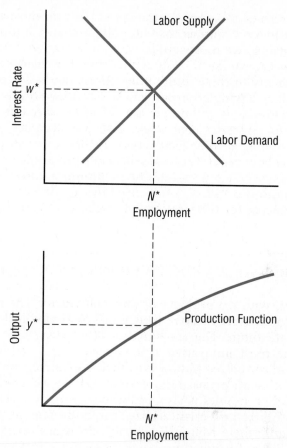

FIGURE 8.1   Natural Rates of Employment and Output

The natural rate of output is determined by supply and demand in the labor market.

Even without rigidities, there remains a big problem in principle with universal market clearing. This is the existence of a large class of transactions for which actual markets simply do not exist. Especially prominent among these are the transactions that will occur entirely in the future. Future markets may clear or they may not: how would we know? It is not possible, after all, to make all of one's purchases for all future time all at once. And yet, complete market clearing now and in the future must at least require that decisions taken today not be a source of a failure of market clearing down the road.

Modern economies provide a limited set of *futures markets* and *forward markets*, in which traders can make future purchases at predetermined prices. For example, one may buy wheat in March for delivery in

September at a fixed and certain price. But for most transactions, buyers cannot make a contract today for all purchases in future time. As a rule, for instance, we must simply wait until next week to buy groceries for next week, paying in cash at that time the then-prevailing prices. Because many of these future transactions can be foreseen (we know that we will be buying groceries next week), they do affect decisions taken in markets today (I will decide how much to save out of this week's paycheck for groceries next week, based on my guess as to what grocery prices are likely to be next week). Errors, or even strong differences of opinion between buyers and sellers in anticipating the condition of markets next week, can lead to disequilibrium in those markets. In decision making, this is called a problem of *time consistency*, and it poses a potential problem for the idea that all markets are clearing all of the time.

THE RATIONAL EXPECTATIONS HYPOTHESIS

To deal with the problem of time consistency, the new classical school introduced a provocative theory of how individuals form expectations about the future. Known as the *rational expectations hypothesis*, it is probably the most innovative aspect of new classical thinking. It was put forward to replace Milton Friedman's adaptive expectations.

Although primarily a reaction against Keynesian economics, new classical economics is also a mutiny against monetarism in its original form. All the new classicals have had important ties to the University of Chicago, where Milton Friedman's doctrines reigned in the 1960s and early 1970s. Friedman proposed to model expectations *adaptively*, with equations that predicted the future of each economic variable from its own past behavior. This hypothesis was instrumental to Friedman's accelerationist argument and to his justification for a constant money growth rule.

Friedman's proposal of adaptive expectations was meant to underpin a theoretical attack on the IS-LM model, which contains no model of expectations. It was also partly an operational alternative to the use of survey expectations, which were deemed costly and unreliable (see the Special Section at the end of the chapter). Adaptive expectations are readily calculated; one needs to know only the past history of the variable involved and the form of the expectations equation. They also provide an inflation prediction that appears, at first glance, to be reasonably close.

The problem with adaptive expectations is illustrated in Figure 8.2. In this simple adaptive model, expected inflation depends on actual inflation one, two, and three periods in the past, with declining weights. When inflation is rising, our adaptive model always underpredicts infla-

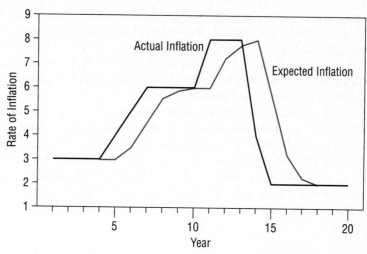

FIGURE 8.2   Adaptive Expectations

Expectation formed adaptively will track the rate of inflation with a lag. In this case, expectations catch up after three periods. In the meantime, the authorities can "fool" the public if they wish to do so. The formula for adaptive expectations in this example gives a 0.6 weight to the immediate past period, a 0.3 weight to the period before that, and a 0.1 weight to the third period back.

tion. And when inflation is falling, our adaptive model always over-predicts inflation. These are *systematic errors*, and adaptive expectations makes them whenever the authorities are pursuing a systematic policy of accelerating or decelerating inflation. Leading critics of this approach are moved to ask:

> Is it sensible to assume that people will continue to form expectations in a way which leads them to underpredict the inflation rate every period? Won't they realize that their current method of forming expectations is leading to an obvious, systematic pattern in their forecasting errors and won't they therefore change the method they are using to forecast the inflation rate?[4]

Of course, in the face of systematic error, people do change the method they are using to forecast the inflation rate. For example, they would certainly take into account the behavior of the monetary authorities if the latter were pursuing policies with a detectable, regular impact on the inflation rate. If the monetary authorities were actively accelerating inflation, we would surely expect the general public eventually to

[4] C. L. F. Attfield, D. Demery, & N. W. Duck, *Rational Expectations: An Introduction to Theory and Evidence* (Oxford: Basil Blackwell, 2nd ed., 1991), p. 10.

catch on. In fact, if any information (beyond the observed history of past inflation rates) relevant to the determination of the future inflation rate were available, we would expect individuals to take that into account. Indeed, we might expect that over time people would learn how the economy actually works and that their inflation forecasts would come to incorporate and reflect this learning.

So, although adaptive expectations provides economists with the luxury of a procedure for deriving measures of expectations directly from available data, it appears "irrational" for individuals to stick with this convention for forecasting. The *rational expectations hypothesis* provides an alternative method for expectations formation. It overcomes the problems associated with adaptive expectations and yet is still amenable to measurement from available data, although in a more complex manner.

The Origins of Rational Expectations

The formal concept of rational expectations originated in 1961 with an article by John Muth.[5] Ironically, Muth developed his perspective at Carnegie-Mellon University during the late 1950s and early 1960s, at the same time that his colleague Herbert Simon, another later Nobel prize-winner in economics, was emphasizing the limits to human rationality in decision making.

Simon's project was to reduce economics' reliance on the assumption that rational individuals seek to maximize their well-being and that business firms maximize profits. Simon felt that these assumptions placed an untenable burden on real people and real organizations and that the resulting theory was therefore doomed to be unrealistic. He sought to replace the maximizing assumptions with an alternative construct he called *satisficing*: the idea that individuals and firms develop a notion of what is acceptable and search among the feasible courses of action until they come across one that meets, at a minimum, their expectations.

Muth, instead, made a plea for the use of an assumption of a *greater* degree of rationality in the theory of human decisions, as observed by Daniel Colander and Robert Guthrie:

> Rational expectations evolved from a management science inquiry
> of Charles Holt, Franco Modigliani, John Muth, and Herbert
> Simon. . . . This study was to serve as representative of "satisfic-

---

[5] "Rational Expectations and the Theory of Price Movements," *Econometrica* 29 (1961), pp. 299–306.

ing" behavior under uncertainty. . . . Muth turned that work on its head.[6]

As his springboard for the development of a thoroughly rational approach, Muth took the venerable *cobweb theorem* sometimes associated with farmers' planting decisions. The cobweb theorem demonstrates how cycles in the price and quantity of agricultural goods can arise simply because farmers based current production on current prices, rather than on the prices that will prevail when crops are harvested. Thus, if corn prices are high this year, farmers have an incentive to raise production, which will cause a market glut and falling prices next year, which will be followed by reduced production and rising prices the year after that. Muth noted that although "few students of agricultural problems or business cycles seem to take the cobweb theorem very seriously . . . its implications do occasionally appear. . . . A major cause of price fluctuations in cattle and hog markets is sometimes believed to be the expectations of farmers themselves."[7]

Muth observed that the erratic price fluctuations associated with the cobweb theorem arose because of the assumption that price expectations were of the adaptive variety (that they were formed by looking solely at the past and present behavior of prices). It would be more reasonable, according to Muth, to suppose that farm price expectations were formed from knowledge of the full range of supply-and-demand conditions in agriculture—to suppose that farmers actually understand something about the economic conditions in which they operate. If so, Muth was able to demonstrate, the cobweb would not arise; instead, prices would converge toward an equilibrium value. Muth generalized this conclusion to argue that "expectations, since they are informed predictions of future events, are essentially the same as the predictions of the relevant economic theory."[8] This is the type of expectation that Muth labeled a *rational expectation*.

Thus, the *expected value* of a variable should be derived from knowledge of the theoretical structure—the supply-and-demand conditions—that explains how that variable is determined. Such expectations will be *model-consistent*; they will be consistent with the model that is used to explain the variable being forecast. The rational expectation of a variable, therefore, equals the objective *mathematical expectation*, or average expected value, conditioned on the theory of the variable and on the data available at the time the expectation is formed.

---

[6] David C. Colander and Robert S. Guthrie, "Great Expectations: What in the Dickens Do 'Rational Expectations' Mean?" *Journal of Post-Keynesian Economics*, 3 (Winter 1980–1981), pp. 219–234.

[7] Muth, "Rational Expectations," p. 330.

[8] Ibid., p. 316.

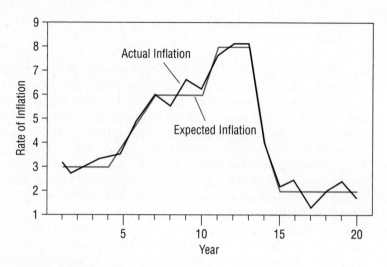

FIGURE 8.3   Rational Expectations

In this rational expectations model, inflation expectations are formed by observation of
the money growth rate in the previous period. Actual inflation differs from expected only
by a random error.

Figure 8.3 illustrates a simple rational expectations process. In this case, the expected rate of inflation in this period is determined by the rate of money growth one period before. The actual rate of inflation is also determined by that rate of money growth, plus or minus a random error. As the figure shows, the expectation of inflation in this case will predict actual inflation without systematic error.

It took a decade for the rational expectations hypothesis to be incorporated into macroeconomic theory and macroeconomic model-building. Robert Lucas took the major steps in three papers written in the early 1970s, followed closely by contributions by Thomas Sargent and Neil Wallace.[9] With these papers, new classical economics supplanted monetarism as the preeminent voice of economic conservatism and inheritor of the classical tradition.

[9] R. E. Lucas, Jr., "Expectations and the Neutrality of Money," *Journal of Economic Theory*, 4 (April 1972), pp. 103–124; Thomas Sargent and Neil Wallace, "Rational Expectations, the Optimal Money Instrument, and the Optimal Money Supply Rule," *Journal of Political Economy*, 83 (April 1975), pp. 241–254; Thomas Sargent, "A Classical Macroeconometric Model for the United States," *Journal of Political Economy*, 84 (April 1976), pp. 207–237. The title of this paper makes a conscious link to classical economics in the sense that Keynes used the term. Also, Thomas Sargent and Neil Wallace, "Rational Expectations and the Theory of Economic Policy," Research Department, Federal Reserve Bank of Minneapolis, June 1978; "Rational Expectations and the Theory of Economic Policy: Arguments and Evidence," Research Department, Federal Reserve Bank of Minneapolis, December 1977.

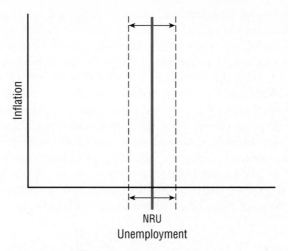

FIGURE 8.4   The New Classical Phillips Curve

In the new classical model, the rate of unemployment can vary randomly about the natural rate, but it is not possible to drive down the unemployment rate systematically, even at the price of hyperinflation.

RATIONAL EXPECTATIONS AND THE PHILLIPS CURVE

In this somewhat technical section, we work through the precise implications of rational expectations for a model of the economy. When we remove Milton Friedman's assumption of adaptive expectations from our model and replace it with rational expectations, the world shifts. In particular, Phillips curves become vertical in both the short and the long run, as Figure 8.4 illustrates, and policymakers lose their grip on the unemployment rate altogether. Under adaptive expectations, policymakers can lower the unemployment rate by continuously accelerating inflation. If expectations are rational, even this option is denied to them.

Friedman's expectations-augmented Phillips curve, explored in Chapter 7, holds that the actual rate of inflation bears a systematic relationship to the unemployment rate and to the expected rate of inflation. In linearized form, the relationship appears thus:

(8.1) $$\dot{P}_t = \alpha - \beta U_t + \gamma E_{t-1}(\dot{P}_t)$$

In equation (8.1), $\dot{P}_t$ is the actual inflation rate at time t, U_t is the unemployment rate in the same period, and $E_{t-1}(\dot{P}_t)$ is the expected rate of inflation, an expectation formed in the previous period. The coefficients α, β, and γ all represent positive constants. The equation indicates that the inflation rate rises when it is expected to rise and falls when the unemployment rate rises.

Friedman claimed that once expectations become accurate, that is, when the actual inflation rate equals the expected inflation rate, $\dot{P}_t = E_{t-1}(\dot{P}_t)$, then there will be no tradeoff between inflation and unemployment. You can see this by solving for the natural rate of unemployment; if the coefficient γ on the expected rate of inflation, $E_{t-1}(\dot{P}_t)$, has a value very close to unity, then the expressions for inflation drop out of the equation. Friedman would argue on grounds of principle that γ should be close to unity, because rational individuals' price expectations should not differ systematically from actual prices. When γ is equal to one and $\dot{P}_t = E_{t-1}(\dot{P}_t)$, there is one and only one possible unemployment rate regardless of how large or small the inflation rate is:

$$(8.2) \qquad\qquad U_t = \frac{\alpha}{\beta}$$

This is the natural rate of unemployment. It is the value the unemployment rate takes when the Phillips curve, which depicts the relation between inflation and unemployment, becomes vertical. It depends only on two structural parameters of the economy, α and β. α is the underlying rate of inflation, the rate that would occur if there were no unemployment and no expected inflation; β is the rate at which inflation adjusts to a change in unemployment in the short run. If, for example, the coefficient α was estimated to be .04, or 4 percent (per year), and the coefficient β was estimated to be 1 (so that a change in the percentage rate of unemployment yields a one-for-one percentage change in inflation), the natural rate of unemployment would be .04, or 4 percent.

Friedman thus argued that the monetary authorities could succeed in driving the unemployment rate below, say, 4 percent only if they could engineer a policy of accelerating inflation and thus a systematic misforecasting by the public of the actual inflation rate. The cost of reducing unemployment below its natural rate would be a policy-induced momentum toward *hyperinflation*. Nevertheless, the accelerationist strategy would be available to the monetary authorities as long as the public formed its inflation expectations adaptively. Therefore, while Friedman acknowledged that a tradeoff between inflation and unemployment could exist (so long as the actual rate and the expected rate of inflation continued to diverge) and that such a divergence might be due to the active efforts of the central bank, he was driven to the conclusion that the consequence would be disaster.

This led directly to Friedman's policy conclusion. It would be best, he reasoned, for the monetary authorities to maintain a constant rate of growth of the money supply. In that case, the public's adaptively formed expectations eventually will converge with the actual inflation rate. And in that long run, any constant inflation rate is possible, but unemployment can only be at the natural rate. Hence, Friedman made a distinction between the *expectational short run*, where an exploitable tradeoff between inflation and unemployment exists, and the *expectational long run*, where the Phillips curve is vertical and no such tradeoff exists.

Rational expectations obliterates Friedman's distinction between the short and long run. To see why, suppose there is a known process that generates the actual rate of inflation, in which the rate of inflation depends on the rate of money growth $\dot{M}$ and, perhaps, a list of other short-run variables X (changes in the unemployment rate, the oil price, and so on):

$$(8.3) \qquad \dot{P}_t = q\dot{M}_{t-1} + z\dot{X}_{t-1} + \varepsilon_t$$

Again $\dot{P}_t$ is the inflation rate at time t, $\dot{M}_{t-1}$ is the rate of growth of the money supply in the current period, and X_{t-1} is an index of all other presently known variables that affect the forthcoming inflation rate in the next period. The equation tells us that the actual rate of inflation is a function of monetary policy on the one hand and some possible outside shocks on the other.

ε_t is a purely random disturbance, an error term, that affects the inflation rate at time t. Being random, it is unpredictable. A spontaneous panic in the stock market, a volcanic eruption or earthquake, a presidential assassination, or any other purely unpredictable event will show up as part of ε_t. The average, or expected, value of ε_t is zero however— since we do not know whether our random error is likely to raise the inflation rate above its predicted value or to reduce it.

An expectation of the next period's inflation rate, formed rationally, will be the mathematical expectation of equation (8.3), which is just the equation itself with the error term set to its expected value, which is zero:

$$(8.4) \qquad E\dot{P}_t = q\dot{M}_{t-1} + z\dot{X}_{t-1}$$

Since $\dot{M}_{t-1}$ and $\dot{X}_{t-1}$ are known to the public at the start of period t, whereas the random disturbance is not, the mathematical expectation of a random disturbance is zero, so the term ε_t vanishes from equation (8.4). As we can see from comparing equations (8.3) and (8.4), the rational expectations forecast of the inflation rate utilizes all of the relevant information available at the start of period t. It is the rational *short-run* forecast; nothing in it requires that the economy be in some long-term expectational equilibrium.

Still assuming that $\gamma = 1$, we can substitute (8.3) (our inflation equation) into the left side of (8.1) (our original expectations-augmented Phillips curve equation) and (8.4) (our equation for inflation expectations) into the right side:

$$q\dot{M}_{t-1} + z\dot{X}_{t-1} + \varepsilon_t = \alpha - \beta U_t + q\dot{M}_{t-1} + z\dot{X}_{t-1}$$

This equation tells us how actual inflation, expected inflation, and unemployment are related. Solving for the unemployment rate yields the following:

$$(8.5) \qquad\qquad U_t = \frac{\alpha - \varepsilon_t}{\beta}$$

This equation shows that under rational expectations the unemployment rate must always be at its natural rate (α/β), aside from the random disturbance ε_t. Entirely unforeseeable and unpredictable random shocks will be the sole cause of any departures from the natural rate of unemployment. There is no exploitable tradeoff between inflation and unemployment in either the short or the long run.

Indeed, if there was no random change, then the economy would maintain the natural (or permanent) rate of unemployment continuously. A lower rate of unemployment would be possible only if the natural rate itself fell, for example as the result of policy measures that raise labor productivity and thereby reduce the inertial rate of inflation α in equation (8.2). In the absence of random effects on the unemployment rate, rational expectations would amount to *perfect foresight* if in fact the Phillips curve (8.1) and the inflation equation (8.3) captured the actual structural relationships that prevail in the economy.

Even if it were true that *contemporaneous* (as opposed to lagged) changes in the supply of money drive the actual inflation rate, this would not matter as long as the public knew or could discern the process that governs policy decisions about money growth. For example, suppose that equation (8.3) is rewritten as follows:

$$(8.6) \qquad\qquad \dot{P}_t = q\dot{M}_t + z\dot{X}_{t-1} + \varepsilon_t$$

Here the current period's change in the money supply partially determines the inflation rate, rather than the lagged change from the previous period. $\dot{M}_t$, the money stock in period t, is not known at the start of period t, when the public's forecast is made. But suppose the monetary authorities follow an accelerationist strategy, where each period's rate of monetary growth is a multiple, g, of the previous period's rate of increase:

$$(8.7) \qquad\qquad \dot{M}_t = g\dot{M}_{t-1} + u_t$$

The term u_t now captures *random variations in the growth rate* of the money supply beyond the control of the authorities.

Under rational expectations, the public would take this monetary growth rule into immediate account when forming its expectation of the inflation rate. Therefore, the structural relationship (8.7) that captures the behavior of the central bank (the Federal Reserve) will be substituted into equation (8.6) to yield the following expression for the inflation rate:

(8.8) $$\dot{P}_t = qg\dot{M}_{t-1} + z\dot{X}_{t-1} + qu_t + \varepsilon_t$$

Now the rationally formed expectation of $\dot{P}$ will take the following form, because the expected value (or average, over time) of both random disturbances is zero:

(8.9) $$E\dot{P}_t = qg\dot{M}_{t-1} + z\dot{X}_{t-1}$$

We can now substitute (8.8), our price equation, into the left side of (8.1), our Phillips curve and (8.9), our expected price equation, into the right side of (8.1). If we then solve for U_t, the unemployment rate, we can find the following rational expectations solution for the unemployment rate:

(8.10) $$U_t = \frac{\alpha - qu_t - \varepsilon_t}{\beta}$$

Qualitatively, this is the same result that we obtained under equation (8.5). The economy again will always be at the natural rate of unemployment, aside from the effects of random disturbances. However, now the random disturbance has two components: an *indirect component* associated with the imprecision of the ability of the monetary authorities to fine-tune the rate of increase of the money supply, qu_t, and a *direct component* associated with immediate shocks to the inflation rate ε_t. Again, if the shocks were not present, the public under rational expectations would possess perfect foresight, and U_t would equal the ratio α/β at all times; unemployment would always be at the natural rate. Note, finally, that the money growth acceleration parameter, g, is entirely absent from equation (8.10). The rate of increase of money growth has no effect on unemployment. Policymakers cannot exploit a tradeoff between inflation and unemployment in any period, because there is no such tradeoff in new classical economics.

THE INEFFECTIVENESS OF POLICY

The new classical school thus combines monetarism, market clearing, and rational expectations. Together, these assumptions lead to four often startling propositions about economic behavior and the role of policy:

First, in the new classical world, the distinction between the short-run and the long-run Phillips curve has no basis. The economy will always be at the natural rate of unemployment unless disturbed by a "random shock," affecting either labor supply or labor demand.[10] Such

---

[10] A random shock might be a war, a change in the price of oil, or a shift in the social climate affecting the willingness of some part of the labor force to supply their labor for a given real wage.

disturbances are always temporary: left to itself, the economy will always return to the natural rate of unemployment if displaced from it.

Second, so long as they are anticipated by the public, increases or decreases in the stock of money have no effect on the real performance of the economy, on employment or output. Therefore, *neither* countercyclical policies nor even a constant money growth rule (of the sort advocated by Milton Friedman and the monetarists) has any real effect of any kind. Indeed, the monetary authorities can follow any rule they like. So long as the rule is understood by the public, the result will be the same.

Third, and more generally, all fiscal and monetary measures that seek to alter the level of aggregate demand are *neutral* in their effects. They can affect only the general price level, not real quantities nor relative prices.

Fourth, business cycles, or persistent deviations of the economy from the natural rates of output and employment, can only be the persistent effects of forecasting errors by economic agents. The forecasting errors themselves are random and unsystematic; they persist only because of certain adjustment lags (such as the time it takes for the level of inventories to change), which even the new classicals do not completely purge from their analysis. Hence, the twists and turns of the business cycle are inherently unpredictable.

Taken together, these propositions rule out virtually any justification for government intervention to stabilize the economy. Attempts to improve output and employment are not necessary, because the economy automatically gravitates toward the natural rate of unemployment. And if the government does pursue predictable monetary or fiscal policies, its actions will have no effect on output and employment.

Departures from full employment, when they occur, can be attributed to two sources only. Government actions may be taken that are not predictable and hence are not predicted. Or there may be other random shocks. For the monetary authorities to succeed over time in pushing the level of employment and output away from their "natural" levels, they must deceive the public continuously. And this, from the new classical perspective, requires entirely random or nonsystematic policies. But why would central bankers want to pursue activist policies if these policies must be conducted on a random basis?

Of course, they wouldn't. The theoretical thrust of new classical thinking is to refurbish the ideas of the old classical economists. Similarly, the policy thrust of new classical thinking is to restore the *laissez-faire* position taken by the old school.

Can Economic Expectations Be Measured?

Almost all human decisions are made under uncertainty. This is particularly true of important economic decisions, such as those that involve long-term contracts for the purchase or sale of goods and services, the arrangement of portfolios between more and less liquid assets, and the commitment to invest in the production of new capital assets. Therefore, any serious macroeconomic theory must address the formation of anticipations about the future and the effect of those anticipations on human decisions. Rational expectations provide one particular framework within which such behavior can be modeled.

Just how expectations should be brought into a macroeconomic model has been a vital issue for theory. One position, associated with Keynes and one of his disciples, G. L. S. Shackle, maintains that relevant information about the future is so sparse and so inadequate that, for most economic purposes, the formation of precise expectations is impossible. The response of economic actors is therefore to adopt a convention, to follow rules of thumb, when "our existing knowledge does not provide a sufficient basis for a calculated mathematical expectation."[1] A macroeconomist taking this position should then ex-

plore the content of actual conventions and behavior patterns, examine why certain conventions are adopted instead of alternatives, and study the conditions that result in changes in the conventions of the moment.

In fact, modern macroeconomists have devoted little time to the study of conventions. Exceptions include the work of Herbert Simon and others at Carnegie-Mellon in the late 1950s and early 1960s on *bounded rationality*.[2] Macroeconomic models frequently seem to require the measurement or estimation of expectations, particularly expectations of the inflation rate. Yet the analysis of actual conventions, as suggested by the Keynes-Shackle view of expectations, does not suggest a straightforward procedure for constructing or obtaining such measures.

One tactic for obtaining measures of expectations in empirical work is simply to ask people what they believe. Public opinion pollsters' surveys of expectations can be used to derive the average expectation of a macroeconomic variable from a sample of the general population or from a sample of experts.[3] But public opinion surveys necessarily reflect only short-term forecasts. In general, people are not able to offer meaningful responses about what they expect the inflation rate or unemployment rate or the level of interest rates to be five or ten years from now. Yet people frequently must make decisions that can be affected by events five or ten years or more from today. Such decisions may be governed by implicit long-term forecasts, even though those forecasts cannot be detected by survey methods.

Moreover, survey expectations cannot capture the beliefs people hold, even about the near future, at the moment when economic commitments are actually made on the basis of those beliefs:

> Since we generally want to incorporate expectations variables in an economic model that describes human behaviour, we are likely to want any variable measuring economic expectations to represent the actual thoughts of individuals *before* they were forced to sit down at a questionnaire and carefully think about how to forecast an economic variable.

When we try to characterize a person's frame of mind at these times, we should recognize that the expectations are likely to differ through time qualitatively as well as quantitatively. For example, an expectation of a future rise in income may become more vividly impressed on individuals' consciousness by some public event that reminds that person of the reasons to expect income to rise. At the same time, the expectation as measured on a survey may be unchanged.[4]

There is another reason why economists have generally preferred to adopt a mathematical approach to modeling expectations rather than a survey approach or the empirical study of conventions. Adaptive and even rational expectations are much easier to model. For adaptive expectations, all one needs is the past history of the variable itself; to get rational expectations, you need a full structural model of the macroeconomy, but even that can be constructed from the aggregative data and does not require the kind of expensive field research that investigation into the actual state of expectations would demand.

---

[1] J. M. Keynes, *The General Theory of Employment, Interest and Money* (London: Macmillan, 1936), p. 152.
[2] Herbert A. Simon, "Rational Decision-Making in Business Organizations." *American Economic Review*, Vol. 69, No. 4, September 1979, pp. 500–501.
[3] George Katona, *Psychological Economics* (New York: Elsevier, 1975).
[4] Robert J. Schiller, "Expectations," *The New Palgrave: A Dictionary of Economics* (London: Macmillan, 1987), 2, p. 255.

SUMMARY

New classical economics attempts to provide microfoundations for macroeconomics, to build a theory from the bottom up rather than from the top down. The three main tenets of new classical economics are monetarism, market clearing, and rational expectations. Market clearing in the labor market implies that any observed unemployment is either frictional or voluntary.

A major problem with the new classical assumption of universal market clearing is that future as well as current markets must clear. To deal with the disequilibrium that might arise from such a time inconsistency problem, rational expectations are brought into the analysis. They are also offered as an improvement on the adaptive expectations of Milton Friedman.

Rational expectations rest on the assumption that individuals will use all available information in the best available way to form their expectations. The rational expectation of the value of a variable is the objective mathematical expectation based on the best theory and data available. Rational expectations will render both the short-run and the long-run Phillips curves vertical. Now, even a policy of money growth leading to accelerating inflation is rendered ineffectual. In a carefully derived expectational framework, the unemployment rate differs from its natural rate only because of random disturbances.

The policy ineffectiveness doctrine of the new classical economics has at least four tenets: (1) There is no essential distinction between the long run and the short run. (2) Changes in the supply of money have no effect so long as the monetary policy rule is known. (3) Predictable, or anticipated, monetary and fiscal policies are both neutral. (4) The only reasons for departures of the unemployment rate from the natural rate are persistent forecast errors due to ignorance about the structure of the economy, consistently unpredictable policy, or sheer randomness.

Review Questions

1. Describe the relationship between the assumptions of rational expectations and market clearing in the new classical theoretical framework.

2. How would the rational expectations result be affected if not all information needed for a perfect prediction were available at the time when expectations were formed? How is this related to policymaking?

3. If the random term ε_t turned out to be greater than 3^{zero} over several periods, how would the rational expectations of future periods be affected?

4. Explain how random policy by central bankers can have an effect under a new classical regime. Explain why the central bankers probably would not want to pursue such policies.

5. The rational expectations hypothesis claims that people learn from their mistakes. Explain how rational expectations differs from the error adjustment model in Chapter 7.

6. Examine Figures 8.2 and 8.3. Is it possible that any amount of shifting will make the curves of Figure 8.2

more closely fit together than do the curves of Figure 8.3? (Caution: in any expectational framework, information that does not yet exist cannot be used.)

Review Problems

1. Redraw Figure 8.2 by putting all weight on the immediately preceding period. Compare the new graph with Figure 8.3. Describe how the graphs differ.

2. Suppose economic agents consistently underpredicted the inflation level by 10 percent for a period of time. Rework the solution to equation (8.1) to relate this fact. Graph and compare this equation with equation (8.2).

3. Suppose that expectations were perfect but that the coefficient of adjustment γ in equation (8.1) were 0.8 instead of unity. Graph and discuss this result.

4. Suppose that the expected value of ε_t in equation (8.3) were ten instead of zero. Taking this into account, reproduce the steps leading to equation (8.5). How are the results affected?

5. Repeat problem 4, but this time assume that the economic agents continue to think the expected value of ε_t is zero. How are the results affected?

6. By making the small change in problem 5, have you now created a downward-sloping Phillips curve? Draw a graph with the result of problem 5. How does this compare with rational expectations results?

Suggested Readings

C. L. F. Attfield, D. Demery, & N. W. Duck, *Rational Expectations: An Introduction to Theory and Evidence* (Oxford: Basil Blackwell, 1985).

R. E. Lucas, "Expectations and the Neutrality of Money," *Journal of Economic Theory,* Vol. 4, No. 2 (April 1972).

Thomas Sargent, "A Classical Macroeconometric Model for the United States," *Journal of Political Economy,* Vol. 84, No. 2 (April 1976).

George Katona, *Psychological Economics* (New York: Elsevier, 1975).

Chapter 9

NEW CLASSICAL
ECONOMICS

Looking Forward

This chapter shows how new classical economics attempts to
come to grips with the great disorders of the macroeconomy: unemployment and the business cycle.

   To begin, we present the new classical position in terms of a
formal equilibrium model of aggregate supply and aggregate demand. We discuss the various ways in which this model can be
reconciled with the observed existence of unemployment. We
show how new classical assumptions lead to the policy conclusions
that activist fiscal and monetary policies can only affect real output
if they come as a surprise to the population. And we explore the
new classical theory that the business cycle is a product of random
shocks to the macroeconomy.

   The chapter concludes with a special section on natural laws of
interest and money. It shows some other ways that the concept of
"naturalness" has been handed down in economics over the years.

   Warning! This is not an easy chapter. As you proceed, it may
help to ask yourself these questions:

- What determines aggregate demand in the new classical model?
  What determines aggregate supply?
- How do aggregate supply and aggregate demand interact to
  determine the price level in an economy characterized by a
  natural rate of unemployment?
- How does the AS-AD model establish the neutrality of
  money?

- How do new classical economists treat the neutrality of fiscal policy?
- How does new classical economics explain the business cycle?

The new classical economics eliminates the Phillips curve. The economy is always at the natural rate of unemployment except for the influences of random events. This, as we have seen, makes government policy almost irrelevant. Predictable changes in the quantity of money can have no effect on the unemployment rate; only random and genuinely unforeseen shocks to the quantity of money, shocks that are surprises to the general public, can push workers off their supply curve and the unemployment rate away from its natural level. Whereas under monetarism we have neutral money in the long run, new classical doctrine gives us neutral money in both the short and long run, but with a twist. *Anticipated* changes in the money stock are purely neutral; *unanticipated* changes may not be.

Though cast originally in terms of unemployment, these new classical propositions can be formulated to provide a theory of the level of output. To spell it out, we specify the price level–real output equilibrium of the macroeconomy. We do this in much the same way that microeconomists specify the simple price-quantity equilibrium of an individual market, by presenting a model of supply and demand. However, instead of supply and demand, we will now have aggregate supply and aggregate demand. And our aggregate demand and supply functions will distinguish between the effects of anticipated and unanticipated changes in policy.

AGGREGATE DEMAND

Aggregate demand represents the total amount of expenditures individuals and companies are willing to make in a given period of time. It is a function of three forces. The first of these is habit: individuals maintain certain routine patterns of spending in order to maintain their accustomed standard of life. But while habit (or permanent income) sets a base level of consumption demand, unexpected variations in prices or incomes (the second force) will cause demand to fluctuate around that base level. Thus, individuals will tend to spend more when their incomes rise in comparison with the prices of goods that they would like to buy or when prices offered seem unusually favorable in relation to the incomes they have. Conversely, individuals will spend less when their incomes appear to fall in relation to prices or when prices seem unusually high. And finally, in addition to these forces, aggregate spending may contain a purely random element, which is the consequence of "shocks" that cannot be predicted.

Taking these three forces into account, an aggregate demand curve at time t can be specified as

$$(9.1) \qquad y^d_t = A + \alpha[M_t - \mathrm{E}_{t-1}(P_t)] + \lambda_t$$

In this equation, y^d_t represents the real level of demand. A represents a stable level of autonomous real expenditures, of expenditures that will occur irrespective of circumstance or policy; we might think of it as the level of expenditures that will occur when actual income is equal to permanent income. The term α is a positive coefficient, which governs the size of the effect on spending of a change in the term following, namely $M_t - \mathrm{E}_{t-1}(P_t)$. M_t is the quantity of money at time t, and $\mathrm{E}_{t-1}(P_t)$ is the price level expected (at time $t - 1$) to prevail at time t.

Assuming that changes in the money stock are normally reflected one-for-one in the price level,[1] $M_t - \mathrm{E}_{t-1}(P_t)$ represents the *unanticipated movement of the money stock*. Recall from Chapter 7 the condition that changes in nominal money balances have to accrue to individuals as income. Therefore, an unanticipated change in the money stock is nothing more nor less than an unanticipated change in incomes. The term $M_t - \mathrm{E}_{t-1}(P_t)$, the difference between the money stock at time t and the price level that was expected to hold at time t, therefore measures (1) the amount by which individuals have received, at time t, money incomes higher than their expectation of inflation would have led them to expect and, as a result, (2) the amount by which they now think that their real incomes are higher or lower than they previously expected them to be.

What is the import of all of this? If the money stock has risen by more than the expected rate of inflation, then people believe that their real incomes have risen, and their total real spending will therefore rise. If the money stock rises by less than expected inflation, aggregate demand will fall. Thus, in this model, the monetary authorities can influence real spending but only by manipulating money growth in ways that are not immediately offset by changing inflation expectations.

λ_t, finally, is a random real demand shock (such as a change of weather or a war), an unpredictable event that may or may not occur at any time.

Having explained the forces that will govern how much individuals will choose to spend in a given period of time, we next take up the

---

[1] We are also assuming that the money stock and the price level are measured here in comparable units. This could be done, for instance, by using an index number to represent the money stock, just as index numbers are used to represent the price level.

symmetrical question: how much will sellers of goods choose to offer on the markets at any given time?

AGGREGATE SUPPLY

This brings us to the *aggregate supply* function. The aggregate supply function in new classical economics has some very special features, leading it to be labeled the *Lucas supply function* (again after Robert Lucas, who introduced the curve in this form).

Aggregate supply is the amount of output sellers are willing to bring to market at any given moment of time. Lucas postulated that this (like aggregate demand) depends on three forces. First, just as aggregate demand is based on permanent income, aggregate supply is rooted in the natural rate of output. But it may vary from that rate if suppliers perceive that conditions are unusually favorable, in which case they will increase supply, or if conditions are unusually bleak, in which case suppliers will cut back on what they are prepared to offer. To be precise, if actual market prices appear high relative to expectations, then suppliers will dip into inventories or expand production to make additional product available. If actual market prices seem low, then suppliers will hold back until the disequilibrium is removed. Finally, as with aggregate demand, there is the possibility of purely random shocks to supply.

Taking these three forces together, the aggregate supply curve is specified in Lucas fashion as

(9.2) $$y^s_t = y^\star + \beta[P_t - E_{t-1}(P_t)] + \mu_t$$

In this equation, y^s_t is the aggregate supply of real output, and $y^\star$ is the natural rate of output, or that level of output associated the natural rate of unemployment. μ_t is a supply shock, again a random disturbance, such as the oil "shock" of 1973 or 1979. It is a *real* supply shock. Again, β is a positive constant.

The expression $P_t - E_{t-1}(P_t)$ is the expectational error, the difference between what people expected prices to be in time t and what they actually are. If the public underestimates the true inflation rate (or price level at time t), then the supply of output will rise above the natural level. If the public overestimates the actual inflation rate (or price level), then the supply of output will fall below the natural level.

Why is that so? The concept that mispredictions of inflation have real consequences on the supply side requires some justification. One argument, which we have seen before, is our old friend sticky wages, specifically a variant associated with Friedman and his short-run Phillips curve. According to this argument, money wage rates are set by contract before the actual price level is known. Real wages will therefore fall when the public underestimates the true price level (inflation rate) in setting nominal wages. In that case, workers will accept lower real wages than they otherwise would do. So long as the nominal wage level lags behind inflation, workers are unusually cheap, and employers have an incentive to hire more workers than they would at the natural rate. The output level will then rise above the natural rate.

By the same reasoning, real wages will rise above the level consistent with the natural rate of unemployment when the public overestimates the true price level (inflation rate). In that case, employers have an incentive to hire fewer workers, and the output level will fall.

Friedman's argument isn't entirely satisfactory from a new classical standpoint, for the same reason that his adaptive expectations argument (on the demand side) wasn't entirely satisfactory. The wage lag thesis relies, in the end, on an institutional rigidity—in this case, wage contracting—that itself has no basis in economic rationality. If price uncertainty is a problem, why would workers not insist on complete indexing of all wage contracts, so that real wages paid *ex post* are always exactly consistent with employment at the natural rate? Even though we do not observe perfect indexation in practice, there is no completely satisfactory answer to this question in principle.

The new classicals were determined to purge such arbitrary elements from their system. So they tend to prefer an alternative justification for (9.2), originated at about the same time by the economist Edmund S. Phelps.

This is the global-local argument[2] first encountered in Chapter 7. As you recall, this argument rests on a metaphor. Suppose we think of workers as independent contractors living on semi-isolated "islands." They have first-hand knowledge of the price they can receive for their own products but no immediate knowledge of what is happening to the general, or average, level of prices.

In this state of semi-isolation, workers and other economic agents simply cannot tell, at first sight, whether an observed increase in the price of their product (beyond the level they anticipated) is due to a *relative price change* in their favor, which would justify expanded production, or to a change in the *absolute price level*, which would justify standing pat.

Phelps argues that, in the face of this uncertainty and until they are able to learn at the end of the production period exactly what has happened to the general price level, producers are likely to respond to an increase in the prices of their own products (beyond the level they anticipated) by expanding production. They will do this because it is prudent

[2] E. S. Phelps et al., "The New Microeconomics in Employment and Inflation Theory," in *Microeconomic Foundations of Employment and Inflation Theory* (New York: W. W. Norton, 1970), pp. 1–27.

to allow for the possibility that their real/relative position truly has improved. That might well be the case. Certainly, in any event, the real/relative position cannot have declined. Thus, workers will compute the subjective probability that they are truly better off and will respond at least in part to this possibility by raising their effective supply.

They will respond in the opposite manner when the prices they actually receive for their products fall below the prices they expected. Again they do not actually know that the relative price they can command for their output has fallen. But it is prudent to allow for the possibility that a decline in real/relative position has occurred; certainly if local product prices are falling, it is unlikely that their real purchasing power (local prices divided by general prices) is getting better. So our independent contractors will withdraw at least some supply from the market, pending clarification of what may be happening to the general level of prices.

THE AS-AD MODEL

The new classical determination of the level of output may be presented geometrically through an *aggregate demand and supply* diagram (Figure 9.1). For convenience, we work with the levels of the money stock and of prices, not with their rate of change. This shift has no practical importance, because (for example), a lower than expected rate of inflation necessarily implies a lower than expected price level in the forecast period, and vice versa.

When we draw the aggregate demand curve (AD) with the price level on the vertical axis, we are depicting the value of the aggregate demand, or total expenditure on goods and services, at time t, given a forecast of the general price level at that time. The curve is downward sloping because the lower the realized price level at time t in relation to the forecast, the cheaper goods and services appear to be in relation to what was expected, and the more consumers will be willing to purchase. Conversely, if actual prices are higher than expected, consumers will purchase less and save more, and real aggregate expenditure will be reduced.

For the same reason, the aggregate supply curve (AS) is upward sloping in the space defined by the price level and real output. Aggregate supply is an increasing function of the actual price level, given once again (along a particular aggregate supply curve) a forecast of the expected price level. If market prices are high relative to forecast, more will be supplied. If they are low, less will be supplied. Whether the underlying story is of wage contracting or of producers on islands, only expectational errors lead to shifts in the aggregate supply curve and therefore, as we shall see below, to departures from the natural level of output.

NEW CLASSICAL UNEMPLOYMENT

To see why rising prices received by workers might lead to both rising labor supply and falling unemployment (and vice versa), it is useful to review the kinds of unemployment with which Phelps was concerned. Phelps identified three types: speculative, wait, and search unemployment. All share one essential, common characteristic: they are caused by asymmetries in information due to costs of acquiring information. Because of these asymmetries, he argued, rising (locally perceived) normal prices (wages) might lead to a belief that real wages are rising, causing an increase in work accepted and a fall in measured unemployment. Only when the production period was already under way would workers realize—too late—that their prices paid had also risen and that real wages had not changed.

Speculative Unemployment

Speculative unemployment can arise, Phelps reasoned, when workers attempt to base a decision to work or not work on their perception of the present (as against the future) real value of the wage. Thus, given a fall in the money wage, relative to expectation, that is perceived to be temporary, a worker may quit the job in the expectation of returning to it or to a comparable job when conditions improve. At the moment, it so happens that the command of the wage over commodities is not favorable. But there is the hope and expectation that money wages will rise again, relative to the price level, perhaps in a month or a year. Thus, it's a good time to vacation, a bad time to be employed. Unemployment rises; conversely, when the money wage rises (as perceived, temporarily), unemployment falls.

Wait, or Precautionary, Unemployment

Many jobs have a discrete character; taking one precludes taking another while the first is in progress. For such jobs, a crucial question is whether to accept an offer today knowing that to do so precludes accepting a better offer tomorrow. Conditions that increase the likelihood that a worker will decline a job offer today raise the total number of unemployed people.

To make this decision, Phelps argued, workers set a *reservation wage*. If the contract offered is above that wage, they work; if it's below it, they wait for the next contract. Thus, if a housepainter is between jobs and, while he is waiting, average money wages fall, he will generally not find a new job at or above his reservation wage quite as quickly as he would have expected. In the meantime, he rejects jobs at "below normal" offers so that he will not be tied up when the right offer comes through. Thus, he remains unemployed, waiting for an acceptable offer, and the aggregate level of unemployment will rise.

In this case, once again, a decline in money wages caused by a far-off decision to reduce money growth is associated with a rise in unemployment. The information asymmetry occurs because workers are unable to read the government's actions in time to adjust their reservation wages and are unable to distinguish the global fall in the money wage level from a purely local run of ordinary bad luck.

Search Unemployment

A third type of unemployment affects people who are dissatisfied in their present employment and quit in order to find something better. Such people will tend to find new jobs that are acceptable (at or above the reservation wage) more quickly if money wage increases are accelerating and more slowly if money wages are falling as they look. The logic is essentially the same as for wait unemployment.

In contrast with Friedman, Phelps's reasoning about the behavior of the nominal wage and unemployment does not necessarily require that any change in the real wage actually occur. If a carpenter commits to work because she thinks that wages have risen relative to the prices she must pay, she will discover in the course of the construction project that this is not so. But it is too late; by the nature of her commitments, she is obliged to finish the work or not get paid at all. Likewise, the misperception

that real wages are rising will shorten search periods, even though workers will realize once they are reemployed that they are not better off and that they might ideally have preferred to continue searching.

Moreover, as noted above, Phelps's argument does not even strictly require that workers be short of locally available information about either wages or prices as they make decisions to work or vacation. If, for example, money wages rise and prices also rise immediately by the same proportion, so that there is no actual current increase in the real wage, labor supply may still rise and unemployment may still fall. This happens because workers cannot be sure what will happen to wages and prices in the next period. If they think that the price and wage rises are temporary (though with full information they would know them to be permanent) they may perceive a change in the real wage and so alter their behavior. Their temporary misperception of the real rate of return to present employment (manifested in this case as an overestimate of the value of saving out of present wages) is responsible for temporary changes in the level of employment and unemployment. Given the misperception, there is no disequilibrium in the labor market. Labor supply comes into balance with labor demand. However, the equilibrium so achieved is a short-run equilibrium: it will decay over time, as workers realize that their underlying real wage has not changed after all.

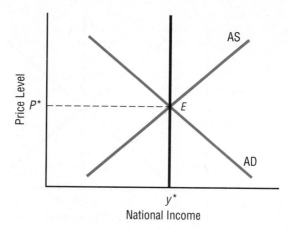

FIGURE 9.1   Aggregate Supply and Demand

In the full new classical equilibrium, both sellers and buyers correctly foresee the rate of inflation, and they set their money demands at rates consistent with the natural rate of real output and an unchanged rate of inflation. This means that they correctly foresee the next period's price level, as shown.

Finally, we incorporate into Figure 9.1 the vertical line $y\star$, which shows the relationship between the price level and real output when there are no forecast errors and no random shocks. In effect, under such circumstances, there is no relationship, because in the absence of forecast errors the economy will always be at its natural level of output, whereas the price level will be whatever level is determined by the quantity and velocity of money. This line is exactly analogous to the vertical Phillips curve.

Imagine that a new classical economy is in full equilibrium at point E in Figure 9.1. The schedules AD and AS intersect at point E in the diagram, which lies along the vertical line $y\star$. The price level is at $P\star$.

Now consider what happens if there is an unannounced increase in the quantity of money. The first effect, given the expected rate of inflation, will be to increase the real quantity of money. This will lead to a rightward shift in the position of the AD curve from AD to AD', as shown in Figure 9.2. If the expected price level stays the same, then the economy will move along the aggregate supply curve by the full amount of the shift in the aggregate demand curve. The result will be a temporary position at output level y' and an increase in the actual price level to P' from $P\star$.

With static expectations of the price level, an expansionary monetary policy obviously is effective in changing the real performance of the economy; output shifts from $y\star$ to y'. But the actual price level becomes P', whereas the public, unaware of the policy change, maintains the belief that the price level will stay at $P\star$. There is both a disturbance of

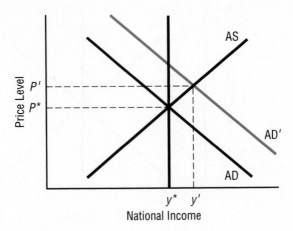

FIGURE 9.2   A "Surprise" Demand Shock

If the money supply is increased unexpectedly, actual demands will be higher than is consistent with stable prices. Production will be displaced temporarily above the natural rate.

real output and employment and a discrepancy between the expected and the actual rates of inflation.

Quite a different result arises when the public becomes aware of the policy change. In this case, the rational public will run the known policy change through their model of the macroeconomy and come up with an expected rate of inflation that is an unbiased predictor of the actual rate. Suppose, therefore, that the public anticipates that the price level will change from $P\star$ to $P\star\star$ in response to the growth of money. Not only does the AD curve shift from AD to AD', but now the AS curve shifts from AS to AS'. Suppliers know that the real value of prices received will be eroded by inflation; they therefore insist on higher nominal prices for each and every possible level of supply. The result appears in Figure 9.3: prices rise, but there is no change in real output.

So long as policy is known, the rational expectations hypothesis effectively dictates that the public will expect the aggregate demand curve to shift to AD' and the aggregate supply curve to shift to AS' in response to the increase of money supply. Given the underlying theory of the natural rate, the expectation of the price level formed rationally must be $P\star\star$. This is the only expected price level that will be consistent with the actual price level, given the shift in aggregate demand. There could, of course, be other expected price levels between $P\star$ and $P\star\star$; these would involve increases in output that were smaller than the extreme of static expectations (where output rises to y' in Figure 9.2). There could even be expectations of deflation, which would raise output, or expectations of price level increases above $P\star\star$, that would be accom-

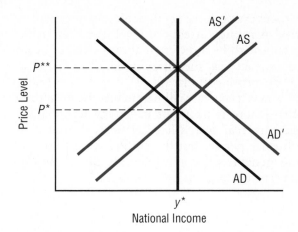

FIGURE 9.3   Effect of Expected Money Growth

If the change in money growth is fully anticipated, then both *AS* and *AD* will shift upward, raising prices but leaving real income unchanged.

panied by a decline in production. But only an expected price level $P^{\star\star}$ will be compatible with unchanged output at the actual price level $P^{\star\star}$; thus, only that expected price level is rational, given knowledge of what policy is.

Because nominal wages now rise, in advance of any transactions, by enough to offset the rise in commodity prices, the real wage stays at its original level. This preserves the level of employment that clears the labor market and the corresponding level of output, $y^{\star}$. Under the islands metaphor, producers have recognized that the increase in the price of their own output is the same as the increase in the general level of prices. So there is no change in relative prices and no reason to raise output beyond the natural level.[3] The fully anticipated price level change that accompanied the increase in the quantity of money has rendered monetary policy ineffective.

This result is known in the literature as an *invariance proposition.*[4] The real performance of the economy is entirely invariant to, or independent of, the particular policy pursued by the Federal Reserve, whether that policy is countercyclical or a constant money growth rule, so long as the policy leads to predictable changes in the money supply. Only unpredictable variations in the quantity of money can affect y_t.

[3] See C. L. F. Attfield, D. Demery, and N. W. Duck, *Rational Expectations: An Introduction to Theory and Evidence* (Oxford: Basil Blackwell, 1985), pp. 40–41, for this argument.
[4] A fuller demonstration of the neutrality of money is presented in the appendix to this chapter. For discussion of invariance propositions, see S. M. Sheffrin, *Rational Expectations* (Cambridge: Cambridge University Press, 1983), p. 40.

However, both the predictable and unpredictable components of the quantity of money affect the level of prices. Although a new classicist might appear to be indifferent about whether or not the Federal Reserve pursues an activist monetary policy, all increases in the quantity of money do produce inflation. To the extent that inflation is viewed as "bad," a new classical will be inclined to urge the Federal Reserve to be cautious—there is no point in having an inflation if it can be avoided without any real cost. New classicals do not care for constant money growth rules per se, but the emphasis on a strong link between money and the general price level reveals the somewhat forlorn imprint of monetarism on new classical thought.[5]

NEW CLASSICAL ECONOMICS AND FISCAL POLICY

We have just shown how anticipated monetary policy can have no effect on the rate of output. What about anticipated *fiscal* policy?

Consider, for example, the potential effects of a credible, preannounced cut in the income tax. The main effect of such a change is to raise disposable income in the short run. In a Keynesian world, one would expect to set off a multiplier process leading to an increase in real output. And one instinctively realizes that in a new classical world, where the Phillips curve is vertical and where anticipated upward shifts in the aggregate demand curve are fully offset by upward shifts in aggregate supply, this will not be the case.

An argument made famous by Robert Barro,[6] the *Ricardian equivalence theorem,* explains why. It suggests that the way in which a government chooses to finance its expenditure, whether by tax or deficit, does not matter. Indeed, Barro argued, all fiscal procedures are equivalent.

Barro traced the consequences of a tax reduction initiated to raise aggregate demand, when aggregate demand is (perceived as being) low. The current shortfall in revenue will be remedied by government borrowing, which requires future interest and principal payments on the debt so incurred. These must eventually be paid for, out of new taxes.

---

[5] For a related discussion see Rudiger Dornbusch and Stanley Fischer, *Macroeconomics,* 3rd ed. (New York: McGraw Hill, 1984), p. 572.

[6] Robert Barro, "Are Government Bonds Net Wealth?" *Journal of Political Economy,* 82 (November/December 1974). Also see Andrew Abel, "Ricardian Equivalence Theorem," in *The New Palgrave: A Dictionary of Economics,* 4 (London: Macmillan Press, 1987). The association with David Ricardo was taken from an argument in Chapter 17 of Ricardo's *Principles of Political Economy* (Volume One of Piero Snaffa, ed., *The Works and Correspondence of David Ricardo,* Cambridge [UK]: Cambridge University Press, 1975).

Barro therefore argued that the current tax reduction must imply a future tax increase, given the prevailing level of government spending. And rational expectations tells us that the voters will come to know this.

The life-cycle microeconomic analysis of consumption decisions tells us that people are attempting to make lifetime consumption decisions. Faced with a reorganization over time of their income stream, they will make offsetting adjustments in their savings. Therefore, people will take the additional revenue they earn from tax reduction, save it, and earn interest on it, in order to be able to offset exactly their increased future tax liability. The term A—autonomous real expenditure in our aggregate demand equation—will remain absolutely unchanged. Thus, the "stimulative" fiscal policy of tax cuts has no effect on aggregate demand or on real output.

Parallel reasoning could be applied to the case of a tax increase designed to restrain aggregate demand when the economy appears to be overheating. If the government originally runs a balanced budget, a common hypothetical analytical starting point, the tax increase would put it in a surplus position. The public therefore anticipates a compensatory tax reduction in the future. The value of tomorrow's disposable income would rise, and the public would maintain its current level of expenditure, just as in the earlier case, despite the reduction in disposable income. It may do so by reducing its present savings on the confident assumption that the shortfall will be made up by future tax reduction. Or it may actually borrow to keep up living standards, again confident that future tax cuts will permit repayment of the loans. Again A stays fixed, and the aggregate demand schedule does not shift.

The recognition that increased government spending must be financed and public debt incurred, to be paid by future taxes, leads inexorably to the same conclusion. People reduce their private expenditures in anticipation of a greater future tax burden, offsetting the increased government expenditure and leaving aggregate demand unaltered. Thus, the Barro argument augments the new classical claims about the neutrality of money with a parallel claim about the neutrality of fiscal policy. In general in the new classical analysis, any anticipated stabilization measure is found to be neutral.

The situation is a little more complicated if the anticipated tax measure changes a real price, such as the relative price of leisure. It will do so, for example, if it reduces the marginal tax rate—for example, lowering the tax paid on the earnings of the last hour worked. In principle, this affects the willingness of the population to work and to produce real output. One might expect that this would shift the natural rate of unemployment to the left and increase the natural rate of output.[7] Since

---

[7] Attfield, Demery, and Duck, *Rational Expectations,* p. 61.

taxation is a relative price affecting the choice between income and leisure, the invariance proposition does not appear to hold.

This argument, which is associated with "supply-siders," is not one with which most new classical economists would be comfortable. Their response would be "yes, but." To be sure, if marginal tax rates are reduced, the price of leisure increases, and people will choose to work more and to play less. There will be more output. Yet they must, as the Ricardian equivalence theorem tells us, recognize that the change in relative prices that has occurred will be temporary and will be followed in due course by an offsetting change in the opposite direction: leisure is expensive today; it will be cheap tomorrow. Thus, they will anticipate a future in which today's hard work and low taxes will be succeeded by tomorrow's high taxes and strong incentives to vacation. The result, for those with a rational desire to smooth their consumption over time, must be a strong incentive to save the excess incomes that low taxes induce them to earn today. Thus, although real production rises, real consumption will not—and once again the Keynesian multiplier process will be defeated.

NEW CLASSICAL BUSINESS CYCLE THEORY

A major challenge that faces new classical economics in the real world is how to account for the business cycle. Why are there recessions and booms in the economy of the United States?

To see the problem, remember that in the new classical model, output only deviates from the natural rate if there are random shocks to aggregate demand or to the money supply. These shocks are the only possible sources of prediction error. And since these shocks are entirely random, they do not assist the public in predicting future shocks.

In short, each period's deviation of output from the full employment level $y\star$ does not correlate with another period's deviation; the errors from period to period are uncorrelated. One cannot predict the mistakes people will make from the mistakes they made in the past.

Correspondingly, we would expect output from period to period to be uncorrelated. As Steven Sheffrin has written:

> Practically, this means that if output is greater than full employment this period, there is no reason whatsoever to predict that the next period's output will be anything but full employment.[8]

The problem is that this implication of the new classical approach is not at all supported by actual data on the movements of real output. Again

[8] Sheffrin, *Rational Expectations*, p. 55.

Taking a Closer Look

INFLATION AND OIL PRICES

While new classical economists agree with the monetarists that inflation is always and everywhere a monetary phenomenon, nonmonetarist economists tend to see other causes at work. One of these, in the past several decades, has been fluctuations in the price of oil. In this box we examine the effect of "oil shocks" on the price level.

There have been two major oil shocks in recent years. The first came in 1974, with a quadrupling of prices following the Yom Kippur war between Israel and its Arab neighbors in October 1973. The second came in 1979, with a further doubling of prices (from the already much higher base) following the revolution in Iran.

Figures 9.B1 and 9.B2 show the effect of these shocks on inflation rates in the United States, Japan, and Great Britain. The charts show that the oil shocks affected all three countries. However, there are also revealing differences.

As Figure 9.B1 shows, Japan (which imports nearly all its oil from members of the Organization of Petroleum Exporting Countries, or OPEC), suffered very high inflation in the wake of the first oil shock. However, Japan reduced its inflation quickly after that episode and was much less affected by the

FIGURE 9.B1   Comparing Rates of Inflation: Japan and the United States 1960 to 1991

Japan had very high inflation in the oil shock of 1974 but much less inflation than the United States in the late 1970s and even during the 1980s.

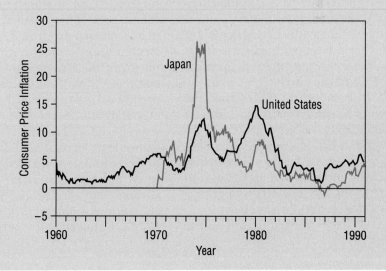

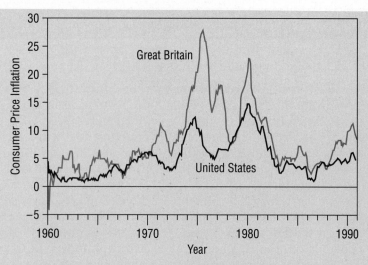

FIGURE 9.B2   **Comparing Rates of Inflation: Great Britain and the United States 1960 to 1991**

British inflation is usually higher than in the United States, especially during periods of external shock.

second shock than was the United States. Specialists in labor relations have suggested that a main reason for Japan's superior performance in the second episode lies in the coordination of wage settlements in Japan, which enabled the country to weather the oil price increase without incorporating the rise in prices into domestic costs.

In comparison with Japan, the United States suffered less inflation immediately from the first oil shock but had more difficulty keeping inflation under control thereafter. And indeed, U.S. inflation rose sharply in the late 1970s, peaking with the second oil shock.

U.S. performance, in turn, looks good compared to that of Great Britain (see Figure 9.B2), which experienced inflation higher than the United States did in both oil shocks and in almost every year thereafter. This dismal performance occurred despite the fact that Britain became a major producer of oil (from the North Sea) in this period and that British unemployment was also higher than U.S. unemployment for most of this time. Again, the fractionated and conflict-ridden character of British labor relations is sometimes deemed to be a major reason for Britain's chronic high-inflation experience and serious vulnerability to external price shocks.

Sheffrin's observation is informative:

> This implication of the theory is strongly rejected by the data. If the
> economy is in a boom this period, most likely it will continue next
> period and, conversely, for recessions. In other words, movements
> of output, employment, and unemployment all tend to *persist*. If
> they exceed their trend or normal levels in a given period, these
> variables tend to remain above trend.[9]

The persistence of cyclical changes in the real performance of the
economy undermines the new classical concept that output fluctuations
are attributable to random shocks, whether real or monetary. And
movements of real variables, such as employment, output, and real
wages, do appear to be strongly correlated across time and with one
another.

> All of the quantity series—including real balances—exhibit signifi-
> cant positive serial correlation at the annual or quarterly interval.
> They all display positive covariation, both with output and with
> each other. They differ somewhat in relative volatilities, notably
> investment is more volatile than output, which in turn is more vola-
> tile than consumption.[10]

In other words, it appears that deviations from the natural rate of output
are correlated. Indeed, we call this correlation the *business cycle*.[11]
Given these facts, the challenge for new classicals was to reconcile
their theoretical belief, that only random disturbances affect real output
and employment, with the evidence that real output movements display
strong serial correlation. The challenge was to develop a new classical
theory of the business cycle, to explain the persistence of movements in
real variables away from the values ostensibly dictated by their natural
rates.

New classical economists have advanced several possible answers.[12]
One argument relies on informational time lags. For example, the public

---

[9] Ibid., p. 55.

[10] Michael Dotsey and Robert G. King, "Rational Expectations Business Cycle
Models: A Survey," *Federal Reserve Bank of Richmond Economic Review*, 74 (April
1988), 4. According to Dotsey and King, "Evidence concerning the cyclical behavior of the real wage is inconclusive. . . . In general . . . there does not appear
to be a pronounced cyclical relation." But the cyclical movement of real output
and employment is undeniable.

[11] The observed persistence in movements of output, employment, and unemployment is often referred to as *hysteresis*.

[12] G. K. Shaw, *Keynesian Economics: The Permanent Revolution* (Brookfield, VT:
Gower Publishing Company, 1988), p. 98.

may not become aware of the error in its forecast at time *t* until several periods in the future. In that case, it is possible for a sequence of forecast errors to occur, leading to serial correlation in real variables. In a word, people cannot correct their systematic mistakes because they do not become aware of them in a sufficiently timely way.[13]

A second answer is based upon the dynamics of inventory adjustment.[14] Businesses hold precautionary stocks of inventories of their goods. Suppose an unexpected fall in aggregate demand occurs at time *t* due to the random shock to the *AD* schedule (λ_t). Businesses will experience an unexpected accumulation in their inventories. To get inventories back to the preferred levels, they must decrease future production. That decrease in production will account for the serial correlation evident in time series data on real output and employment, even though the causative random shocks are entirely uncorrelated. A shock leading to a surprise rise in aggregate demand will lead, by parallel reasoning, to an undesired drawing down of inventories. This will be compensated for in subsequent periods by a (cyclical) upturn in production.

A third answer extends the logic of the global-local argument. It takes longer to acquire "global" information than to find out what is going on in the home neighborhood. Due to these lags, misperceptions by businesses attempting to distinguish between absolute and relative price changes may persist. And this too may lead to output and employment variations that move in the same direction over several periods.[15]

The global-local argument can be combined with an argument about adjustments over time in the desired size of the capital stock. Suppose, for example, that an unforeseen aggregate price increase leads to an overestimate of the real rate of return on new investment. Home prices seem high relative to global prices, and worker-contractors decide that the real rate of return on new capital investment has gone up. They place orders for new machinery, and this leads directly to a rise in the stock of fixed capital. In short order, the economy has a capital stock that is higher than the level that would have been desired if the global-local problem did not exist. So once the error is realized, the rate of capital accumulation will decline below normal.

From this argument, we get a full cyclical swing. The boom raises the economy's capital stock above its normal level and will be followed by a downturn in new investment to restore the capital stock to its

[13] Robert E. Lucas, Jr., "An Equilibrium Model of the Business Cycle," *Journal of Political Economy*, 83: No. 6 (December 1975), pp. 1113–44.

[14] Alan Blinder and Stanley Fischer, "Inventories, Rational Expectations, and the Business Cycle," *Journal of Monetary Economics*, 8: No. 3 (November 1981), pp. 277–304.

[15] Shaw, *Keynesian Economics*, p. 99.

normal level. The driving mechanism here is incomplete information. However, this is a problem, for arguments based on incomplete information are precisely the sort of argument that the rational expectations hypothesis was intended to escape.

A fourth answer, attributable to Thomas Sargent,[16] points to costs of changing the number of workers a business employs. If businesses are confronted with adjustment costs in altering their stock of labor, then the labor demand for each business will be a function, in part, of the last period's employment. Once again, the past will exert a hold over the present, and we can expect persistence and cyclicity in the data.

Incomplete information about forecast errors, adjustment costs, inventory adjustments— lags and frictions—become the basis for the new classical theory of the business cycle. There are interesting parallels between these ideas and those of Keynes. While mainly interested in demonstrating on theoretical grounds that the economy could settle into positions of *underemployment equilibrium*, a possibility that new classical economics hotly denies, Keynes also did discuss a theory of the trade cycle toward the end of *The General Theory*:

> The explanation of the *time-element* in the trade cycle, of the fact that
> an interval of time of a particular order of magnitude must usually
> elapse before recovery begins, is to be sought in the influences
> which govern the recovery of the marginal efficiency of capital.
> There are reasons, given firstly by the length of life of durable assets
> in relation to the normal rate of growth in a given epoch, and sec-
> ondly by the carrying-costs of surplus stocks, why the duration of
> the downward movement should have an order of magnitude which
> is not fortuitous, which does not fluctuate between, say, one year
> this time and ten years next time, but which shows some regularity
> of habit between, let us say, three and five years.[17]

Thus, Keynes argued, the physical conditions of the real world would likely impose a regularity on the business cycle, accounting in part for its persistence. New classical economists draw on some of these elements as well (in particular, inventory and capital stock adjustments) to reconcile their theoretical view of a world in which deviations from full employment are purely random, with the data that show that they are not.

---

[16] Thomas Sargent, *Macroeconomic Theory*, 2nd ed. (Boston: Academic Press, 1987).
[17] Keynes, *The General Theory*, p. 317.

SPECIAL SECTION

More Natural Laws: Interest and Money

You have now seen a careful theoretical development of the natural rate of unemployment and again of the natural rate of output. In this section, we present yet another natural rate, that of interest. This concept is especially interesting because the existence of a natural rate of interest is not inconsistent, as Keynes discovered, with the persistence of unemployment.

This special section concludes with a historical excursion, tracing the idea of the neutrality of money and showing how the development of the theory of interest led Keynes eventually to reject the notion that money was neutral.

The Natural Rate of Interest

The concept of a natural rate of interest is owed originally to the Swedish economist Knut Wicksell, who introduced the idea in his famous work, *Interest and Prices*.[1] The concept made its way into English-speaking economics by way of the research concerns of the Cambridge University economists in the early part of the twentieth century.

The natural rate of interest has several alternative definitions; we will mention the two most prominent here. The first holds that the natural rate of interest is the rate that is consistent with a zero rate of inflation. The second definition holds that the natural rate is the rate consistent with equality between saving and investment in a market for loanable funds.

If inflation is treated as a *demand-pull* phenomenon, where prices rise when there is excess demand and desired investment is greater than available savings, then the two definitions could converge. The rate of interest associated with the loanable funds market's failure to clear will then be a disequilibrium, or "unnatural" rate. Only that rate which eliminates excess demand and supply in the loanable funds market, and hence in the economy overall, will maintain price stability. That will be the natural rate of interest. On the other hand, if inflation has *cost-push* or supply-side elements, the natural rate of interest that generates savings and investment equality may not guarantee stable prices and, conversely, the rate of interest that gives price stability may be too high to clear the market for loanable funds.[2]

In Keynes's *General Theory*, the natural rate appears mainly in its second guise—as the price that equalizes saving and investment. Indeed, it was Keynes and his associates who discovered—in the early 1930s—that there was no reason to believe that equality between saving and investment meant that the economy was at full employment. For this reason, they also came to question whether reaching the natural rate was a desirable policy objective in the first place. Keynes and his colleagues saw nothing particularly attractive about market clearing between savings and investment, or even about price stability, if they were accompanied by large-scale unemployment. Why not have, instead, a disequilibrium rate of interest at full employment?

Keynes professed a much stronger interest in what he termed the *neutral rate of interest*, which he described in the following passage:

> I am now no longer of the opinion that the concept of a "natural" rate of interest, which previously seemed to me a most promising idea, has anything very useful or significant to contribute to our analysis. It is merely the rate of interest which will preserve the *status quo*; and, in general, we have no predominant interest in the *status quo* as such.

> If there is any such rate of interest, which is unique and significant, it must be the rate which we might term the *neutral* rate of interest, namely, the natural rate in the above sense, which is consistent with *full* employment, given the other parameters of the system; though this rate might be better described, perhaps, as the *optimum* rate.[3]

There could be many natural rates of interest but only one neutral rate among these: the equilibrium rate

of interest consistent with full employment.

The Neutrality of Money

The idea that money is neutral has an even longer history in economics than the natural rate of interest does. It stems from the intuition that a change in the quantity of the circulating medium of exchange should not have effects on the real performance of the economy. Such changes, in equilibrium, are essentially equivalent to changes in the way that prices are measured. So why should it matter, as one economist has expressed it, whether the money stock circulates as so many dollars or so many dimes?

The notion that money is neutral means that an increase in the quantity of money should lead to an increase in the absolute level of prices, affecting all prices uniformly and in the same proportion, leaving relative exchange values unchanged. That being the case, there would be no ultimate effects on output and employment from a doubling or a halving or any other change in the quantity of money.

Even in such a neutral-money economy, most economists would concede, a change in the quantity of money might have some short-term effects on production. Indeed, they would have to, unless somehow an instantaneous proportionate rise in all prices occurred with every change in the money stock. The most orthodox-minded economist would admit that, if, for example, output prices initially rose at a faster rate than wages, creating a profit-making price-cost wedge for private businesses, then there would be an incentive for those businesses to increase their output; conversely, if wages rose more rapidly than prices, profits and output would fall. The neutral-money orthodoxy merely held that in the long run, which is to say after allowing for a reasonable period of adjustment, the relation of prices to costs would have to return to its original position, along with the level of output.

In a 1752 version of the neutral-money hypothesis, the Scottish schoolmaster David Hume placed the burden of adjustment in a single-currency world on what came to be known as the *price-specie-flow mechanism:*

> Suppose four-fifths of all the money in Great Britain to be annihilated in one night, and the nation reduced to the same condition, with regard to specie, as in the reigns of the Harrys and Edwards, what would be the consequence? Must not the price of all labour and commodities sink in proportion, and everything be sold as cheap as they were in those ages? What nation could then dispute with us in any foreign market, or pretend to navigate or sell manufactures at the same price, which to us would afford sufficient profit? In how little time, therefore, must this bring back the money which we had lost, raise us to the level of all the neighbouring nations? Where, after we have arrived, we immediately lose the advantage of the cheapness of labour and commodities; and the farther flowing in of money is stopped by our fullness and repletion.
>
> Again, suppose that all the money of Great Britain were multiplied fivefold in a night, must not the contrary effect follow? Must not all labour and commodities rise to such an exorbitant height, that no neighbouring nations could afford to buy from us; while their commodities, on the other hand, became so comparatively cheap, that, in spite of all the laws which could be formed, they would run in upon us, and our money flow out; till we fall to a level with foreigners, and lose that great superiority of riches, which had laid us under such disadvantage?[4]

But Hume admitted that in the process of adjustment to a smaller or larger quantity of money, there could be employment- and productive capacity–enhancing effects. Even in Hume's hypothetical case, where a domestic deflation stimulates an external demand for the comparatively cheaper British products, the renewed inflow of specie that restores the original level of prices only can be forthcoming after an expansion of production takes place to meet the new foreign demand. And in his essay "Of Interest," Hume wrote, "In the progress towards these changes, the augmentation may have some influence, by exciting industry; but after prices are settled, suitably to the new abundance of gold and silver, it has no manner of influence."[5] Although the influence is only temporary, the new output and productive capacity has been brought into existence and presumably will not disappear when the influence is gone.

Eugene Rotwein has observed that acknowledging that output can change with a monetary change led Hume into a stance that was far from bedrock on the neutrality of money, "for, as [Hume] here assumes a condition of less than full employment, there is no obvious reason why the resulting increase in output should be wholly ephemeral."[6] Indeed, it should not.

Keynes's analysis contributes something entirely new and different to this familiar story. Keynes argued that the nonneutrality of money arises because the primary effect of changes in the money stock is on money's own rate of interest. Such a change affects all asset prices relative to their production costs, and therefore the volume of investment expenditure, and thereby the general level of production of the economy.[7] Keynes dismissed the idea that money changes would, in general, leave output and employment undisturbed; he

viewed it as a somewhat silly vestige of what he called "the Classical economics" or "real exchange economics."

James Tobin has provided an interesting extension of Keynes's perspective. Tobin treats money as one of several capital assets that individuals could choose to hold in their wealth portfolio. If these assets are treated as *gross substitutes*, then holding money is simply an alternative to holding claims to real physical assets or to the fixed capital of the economy. An increase in the quantity of money affects the relative prices of assets (driving down that of money and raising that of all other assets) and so alters the composition of portfolios and, hence, the pace of investment, which in turn determines the rate of growth of the capital stock. As the capital stock varies, the potential and actual output of the economy varies as well.[8]

---

[1] Wicksell, Knut, translated by Carl G. Uhr, *Interest and Prices: A study of the causes regulating the value of money* (New York: AM Kelley, 1962).

[2] For example, when Federal Reserve chairman Paul Volcker acted to drive interest rates up to 20 percent in early 1981, his objective was to restore price stability, a goal he largely achieved. But because much of the inflation at that time was in fact driven by supply factors, 20 percent interest rates produced an enormous excess of planned saving over desired investment, a deep recession, and double-digit rates of unemployment. Thus, at that time, 20 percent may have corresponded to the

natural rate of interest in terms of the first definition but not of the second.

[3] J. M. Keynes, *The General Theory of Employment, Interest and Money* (London: Macmillan, 1936), p. 243. Emphases in original.

[4] David Hume, "Of the Balance of Trade," in *David Hume: Writings on Economics*, ed. Eugene Rotwein (Madison: University of Wisconsin Press, 1955), pp. 62–63.

[5] David Hume, "Of Interest," ibid., p. 48.

[6] Eugene Rotwein, "Introduction," ibid., p. lxiv.

[7] For example, a rise in the money stock drives down the rate of interest, raising the price of capital assets, making production of new capital assets profitable and thereby increasing both investment and output in the economy as a whole. For a more detailed discussion of this process, see Chapter 13.

[8] James Tobin, "A Dynamic Aggregative Model," *Journal of Political Economy*, 68 (April 1955), pp. 103–115.

SUMMARY

New classical economists use the aggregate supply and aggregate demand analysis in the same way that microeconomists analyze the behavior of individual markets. The aggregate demand curve is based on habit, relative prices, and a random element. In operationalizing the model, relative prices are modeled by how much people are fooled in their estimates of the growth of the money stock. Aggregate supply depends on permanent income, the ratio of market prices to expectations of prices, and a random element.

New classical economists have both an unsophisticated and a sophisticated explanation for the difference between prices and their expected values. The unsophisticated explanation is, once again, sticky wages. But this argument is unsatisfactory to new classical purists, because a rational scheme of wage indexation would eliminate stickiness. The more sophisticated explanation is the islands paradigm first proposed by Phelps. In this explanation, people know local conditions (prices/relative prices) well, but they do not know global conditions (the absolute price level).

Equilibrium is displayed in a diagram with a positively sloped aggregate supply curve and a negatively sloped aggregate demand curve. The intersection of these curves constitutes the equilibrium. In the absence of forecast errors and randomness, only one value of national income is possible. With an unexpected change in the money stock, national income may be displaced. But once the changed money supply is reflected in the supply and demand curves, the net effect is an inflation and an unchanged level of real income. In this model, real income characteristically is stable only when the expected price level equals the actual price level.

The ineffectiveness of monetary policy also can be shown algebraically. The rational expectation of the price level is substituted for the expected price level. The expected price level and income are the same as the actual price and actual income, with the only difference being due to random error. The reborn neutrality result that is then derived is also known as an invariance proposition.

An extension of the new classical argument by Robert Barro holds that fiscal policy is also ineffectual. A tax cut is not acted on by consumers, because they know that future taxes will be levied to cover the present shortfall in the government budget. So rational consumers will save their present-day tax cut in order to pay future taxes. This is an argument derived in large measure from the lifetime consumption hypothesis. Parallel arguments may be made to show the ineffectiveness of government spending and of marginal tax decreases.

Business cycles have posed particular problems for the new classical economists. Random fluctuations about the natural rate of income are to be expected, but empirically it has been shown that if income strays above the natural level, it is likely to stay above that level for some time. This is called serial correlation, or persistence, and it is not readily explained by the core new classical propositions.

At least four responses have been made. First, due to information lags, it may be that the economy cannot respond in timely fashion to shocks. Second, inventory stocks may respond, over time, in a manner to accentuate the cycle. Third, global-local information asymmetries (of the Phelps variety) may persist. Finally, it is hypothesized that the costs of hiring and firing may prevent the complete and rapid adjustment of real income back to its equilibrium value that the new classical paradigm would otherwise predict.

Review Questions

1. True equilibrium in the new classical framework occurs when the expected price level is equal to the actual price level. Explain why this causes the aggregate supply curve, but not the aggregate demand curve, to be vertical.

2. Given the mass of information on all economic variables, one might argue that the local-versus-global explanation for expectational errors is not very satisfactory. Reply to this argument the way a new classical economist would.

3. The Ricardian equivalence theorem was presented without a lot of the mathematical trappings of the monetary theory of the new classical economists. Explain how this theorem is still very much in the spirit of new classical economics.

4. The Ricardian equivalence theorem is based in large measure on the lifetime consumption hypothesis. Assuming this is all true, what group of people should be most boisterous in support of tax increases? Explain.

5. It seems at times that nothing will increase income in the new classical framework. Explain why this is not true.

6. The new classical economists have several explanations for business cycles. Discuss whether or not these explanations are consistent with the general spirit of their theories.

Review Problems

1. Solve equations (9.1) and (9.2) to find the equilibrium real income. In what instances is this income level greater than, less than, or equal to the natural level of income?

2. Into the equation found in problem 1, substitute for the case where the price level is correctly predicted. What is the level of income in this case? What is the price level? How does this compare to the strict classical quantity equation?

3. Run through the calculations of problem 2 once again, but this time assume there are no shocks or random disturbances. How do the results compare to the results of models in previous chapters?

4. On a graph like the one in Figure 9.1, show the effects of an unexpected restriction in the money supply. Compare the long run in the model with the short run.

5. What might cause the aggregate supply curve to shift in Figure 9.1? With the help of a graph, show both the short-run and long-run adjustment.

6. Draw and explain, with the help of Figure 9.1 and equations (9.1) and (9.2), how income could rise without a decrease in the price level.

Suggested Readings

E. S. Phelps et al., *Microeconomic Foundations of Employment and Inflation Theory* (New York: W. W. Norton, 1970).

Steven Sheffrin, *Rational Expectations* (Cambridge: Cambridge University Press, 1983).

Robert Barro, "Are Government Bonds Net Wealth?" *Journal of Political Economy,* Vol. 82, Nov/Dec 1974.

G. K. Shaw, *Keynesian Economics: The Permanent Revolution* (Brookfield, VT: Gower Publishing Co., 1988).

Robert E. Lucas Jr., "An Equilibrium Model of the Business Cycle," *Journal of Political Economy,* Vol. 83, 1975.

Thomas Sargent, *Macroeconomic Theory,* 2nd edition (Boston: Academic Press, 1987).

Eugene Rotwein, ed., *David Hume: Writings on Economics* (Madison: University of Wisconsin Press, 1955).

THE NEUTRALITY OF MONEY REVISITED

We now will present the new classical proof of the neutrality of money in algebraic fashion, retaining the structure associated with the aggregate demand/aggregate supply apparatus of equation (9.2). The actual price level is determined when aggregate demand is equal to aggregate supply. Setting the right sides of (9.1) and (9.2) (demand and supply, respectively) equal and rearranging terms, we can solve for the actual price level at time t:

$$(9.\text{A}1) \quad P_t = \frac{-y^\star + A + \alpha M_t + (\beta - \alpha)\text{E}_{t-1}P_t + (\lambda_t - \mu_t)}{\beta}$$

As this equation shows, the actual price level depends on the natural rate of output $y^\star$, the level of autonomous expenditure A, the money stock M_t, the expected price level $\text{E}_{t-1}P_t$, and disturbances λ and μ. If any one of these variables changes, so will the actual price level. Note, in particular, that the actual price level at time t depends upon the expected price level for time t, held at time $t - 1$. A crucial question, again, is how to treat the formation of the expected price level.

The new classical answer, of course, is to constrain the anticipated price level to be formed according to the rational expectations hypothesis. This means, as we have seen, that in forming its expectation of the price level at time t, the public takes into account all available information that is relevant to the determination of the actual price level at time t. The public can be presumed to know the correct values of $y^\star$, A, α, and β, as these are structural features of the economic system. Since the price level at time t also depends on the quantity of money at time t, the public will also use its knowledge of the process determining M_t in forming its expectation of P_t.

Suppose now that the monetary authorities do indeed follow a simple money growth rule, increasing the size of the money stock by a factor n each period. Then M_t merely will be a multiple of M_{t-1}:

$$(9.\text{A}2) \quad M_t = (1 + \eta)M_{t-1} + \nu_t$$

ν_t is a random disturbance that captures the inability of the monetary authorities to fix the size of the money stock in an exact fashion.

The money growth rule presumably will be known to the public. That permits us to substitute the right side of (9.A2) for M_t in (9.A1), so that we can express the price level at time t entirely in terms of variables known with certainty at $t - 1$, plus random errors. If we do so and rearrange the random terms so that all are grouped together at the end of the expression, we obtain

$$P_t = \frac{-y\star + A + \alpha(1 + \eta)M_{t-1} + (\beta - \alpha)E_{t-1}P_t + \lambda_t - \mu_t + \alpha\nu_t}{\beta}$$

(9.A3)

All that remains to complete this exercise is to solve for $E_{t-1}P_t$, the expected price level for time t that is held at time $t - 1$. To come up with such a solution, we need to purge from the equation the actual price level at time t, which is now the only variable (other than the random errors) that cannot be known with certainty at time $t - 1$. How are we going to do this?

The answer once again invokes the spirit of rational expectations. The expected price level for time t must be equal to what the actual price level at time t would be, except for purely random errors. So on the assumption that expectations will be rational, we can write down, and substitute for the expected price level, a general solution for the price level at time t, or P_t, that is written strictly in terms of known variables and random errors. In this case, the known variables are of two types: the structural values and coefficients ($y\star$, A, α, β, η) and the policy variable M. We can assign a new coefficient, w^0, to represent the appropriate combination of the first four structural values and a second, w^1, to the money growth rule.

A general solution for P_t will take the following form:

(9.A4) $$P_t = w^0 + w^1(1 + \eta)M_{t-1} + \frac{1}{\beta}(\lambda_t - \mu_t + \alpha\nu_t)$$

Since the disturbances have an expected value of zero, we can forget about them. In technical terms, we take the mathematical expectation of the price level at time t, which gives us

$$EP_t = w^0 + w^1(1 + \eta)M_{t-1}$$

This is a perfectly good expression for the expected value of the price level at time t, that will prevail under rational expectations at time $t - 1$. We can substitute it into our general expression (9.A4) for P_t, and then put that into the left side of (9.A3). This gives us an expression that can be simplified quite radically in just a few steps. The complicated expression is:

$$E_{t-1}P_t + \frac{1}{\beta}(\lambda_t - \mu_t + \alpha\nu_t) = \frac{A - y\star}{\beta} + \frac{\alpha}{\beta}(1 + \eta)M_{t-1}$$

(9.A5)

$$+ \left(\frac{\beta - \alpha}{\beta}\right)E_{t-1}P_t + \frac{1}{\beta}(\lambda_t - \mu_t + \alpha\nu_t)$$

Since the random terms on both sides of equation (9.A5) must be identically equal, we can eliminate them. Next we can take both terms in $E_{t-1}P_t$ to the left side and solve, in which case we obtain

$$E_{t-1}P_t = \frac{\dfrac{A - y^\star}{\beta} + \dfrac{\alpha}{\beta}(1 + \eta)M_{t-1}}{1 - \dfrac{\beta - \alpha}{\beta}}$$

From this equation, we can isolate all the terms that play a role in the coefficient w^0; and we solve for that coefficient:

$$w^0 = \frac{\dfrac{A - y^\star}{\beta}}{1 - \dfrac{\beta - \alpha}{\beta}}$$

After a little simplification, this reduces to

$$w^0 = \frac{A - y^\star}{\alpha}$$

Meanwhile, all the terms that play a role in the coefficient w^1 can be brought together, giving the solution for that coefficient, as well:

$$w^1 = \frac{\left(\dfrac{\alpha}{\beta}\right)}{1 - \dfrac{\beta - \alpha}{\beta}} = \frac{\alpha}{\alpha} = 1$$

Substituting the solutions for the parameters w^0 and w^1 back into equation (9.A4) yields the following solutions for the actual price level at time t:

$$(9.A6) \qquad P_t = A - y^\star + M_{t-1} + \frac{\lambda_t - \mu_t + \alpha v_t}{\beta}$$

and, because expectations are rational,

$$(9.A7) \qquad E_{t-1}P_t = A - y^\star + M_{t-1}$$

$E_{t-1}(P_t)$ in equation (9.A7) is the rational expectation of the price level. It only differs from the actual price level by the term $(l_t - v_t + Ad_t)/\beta$, the term that contains all the random disturbances that impinge upon the actual price level.

In principle, the price expectation can be measured on the basis of data currently available at time $t - 1$. All one needs to know are the level of autonomous real expenditures A, the natural rate of output $y^\star$, and the money stock M_{t-1} in period $t - 1$, the most recent for which data are available. The assumption of rational expectations provides empirical macroeconometricians with a procedure for calculating expected values of variables that is a viable alternative to adaptive expectations.

Finally, we can derive the rational expectations solution for the *level of output* of the economy at time t by substituting (9.A6) and (9.A7) into the aggregate supply function (9.2). The rational expectations equilibrium level of output, y_t, will be

$$(9.A8) \qquad\qquad y_t = y^\star + \lambda_t + \alpha v_t$$

This is the striking new classical result that exactly parallels new classical conclusions with respect to the Phillips curve. The *equilibrium* level of output under rational expectations is equal to the *natural* level of output, apart from random shocks. In this case, the supply shock, μ_t, has no effect, but the aggregate demand shock, λ_t, and the *unanticipated* innovation in the money supply, v_t, both influence y_t.

Notice, too, that the anticipated increase in the quantity of money, ηM_{t-1}, is entirely absent from equation (9.A8). Anticipated variations in the quantity of money are entirely neutral in their consequences for the real performance of the economy. The classical dichotomy between the real and monetary sides of the economy is reborn. The neutrality of predicted changes in money is reasserted. And monetary policy, to the extent that it is predictable, is rendered impotent.

CONTEMPORARY DEPARTURES

Chapter 10

NEW KEYNESIAN
MACROECONOMICS

Looking Forward

Just as new classical economics attempts to obliterate all theoretical justification for activist government policy, new Keynesian macroeconomics sets out to revive it.

New Keynesians accept two-thirds of the new classical worldview: monetarism (at least in the long run) and rational expectations. But they argue that universal market clearing is not necessarily a feature of rational economic conduct in the real world. Also, where markets do not clear, persistent unemployment is possible, and expansionary government policies will have an effect on real output and employment. Why don't markets clear? New Keynesians have offered a range of answers to this question, without (so far) coming to definitive agreement on any one.

The chapter concludes with a special section on a topic of interest to macroeconomists, policymakers, and the public: the budget deficit and the public debt.

As you read this chapter, make sure you understand the answers to these questions:

- If workers care about their relative wages, how can this lead to sticky wages in general and therefore to unemployment?
- What are efficiency wages, and why might it be rational for firms to pay them?
- Under what circumstances can "insiders" use their economic power to extract higher wages for themselves than would be paid to "outsiders" performing the same jobs?

- Under what circumstances might workers be willing to trade job security for a higher wage rate? Under what circumstances would employers be interested in offering such a bargain?
- What are the menu costs of changing wages and prices, and how might a large number of individually small menu costs lead to persistent unemployment?
- What are the dynamics of a general disequilibrium system, and how might they lead to a theory of the business cycle?

In 1946, the United States Congress enacted the Employment Act, which created a President's Council of Economic Advisers and a Joint Economic Committee of Congress and declared that the economic goals of the nation were to achieve "maximum employment, production and purchasing power."[1] Since that time, Keynesian economic principles and the macroeconomic activism they require have been the law of the land. In practice, U.S. governments have taken responsibility for ending recessions and reducing unemployment, and voters have come to expect that they will do so. As recent presidential elections demonstrate, voters also get angry when they think that politicians are not doing enough to fight unemployment.

New classical economics threatens to obliterate the theoretical justification for macroeconomic policy and indeed for the very notion that the rate of unemployment should be a matter of policy concern. If the three new classical assumptions of rational expectations, monetarism, and market clearing all hold, then the economy will have an inherent predisposition to reach and maintain production at full employment. Any anticipated macropolicy intervention will be offset in full by the reactions of private individuals and can have no effect on macroeconomic performance. The only way to push the economy above full employment is to conduct policies that consistently surprise the public. Yet how can such "consistent inconsistency" be contrived? And (since the economy is already at full employment) what useful purpose would it serve? In the final analysis, new classical assumptions provide no practical reason for a full employment policy of any kind.

Not surprisingly, many economists are not comfortable with this conclusion. Many, perhaps most, still believe that the mass unemployment of the Great Depression was a failure of classical economics and of the economic policies of that time. Many, perhaps most, believe that the

---

[1] In 1978, Congress passed the Humphrey-Hawkins Full Employment Act, which changed the wording of the employment objective from "maximum employment" to "full employment."

period of high employment from about 1948 through 1973 represented the crowning achievement of Keynesian economics and of activist government. And, while most accept that Keynesian policies failed after 1969, leading to a decade of *stagflation*[2] in the 1970s, many believe that it was Keynesian demand stimulus (in the form of the Reagan tax cuts of 1981, 1982, and 1983) that produced the recovery of the 1980s. And many still believe that when there is a recession and unemployment, as at the beginning of the 1990s, government has a responsibility to do something about it.

How can these lingering beliefs be reconciled with the rigorous, implacable, and contrary logic of new classical economics? By themselves, the raw facts cannot help. For (as generations of professors never tire of trying to explain to skeptical students) facts can only be viewed through the prism of a theory. Theoretical concepts, definitions, and logical links in the argument are what help define and interpret observed facts.

For example, suppose analysts want to decide whether the unemployment of the Great Depression was voluntary or involuntary. The facts can tell us how much unemployment there was—up to 25 percent at the worst times—but they cannot tell what kind it was. The analysts cannot know whether the unemployment was voluntary or involuntary, except through the intermediation of a theory—new classical or Keynesian—that tells whether or not real wages might have fallen enough to clear labor markets and eliminate that unemployment. If they accept the new classical theory, they immediately "know" that the unemployment of the Great Depression was not involuntary, because involuntary unemployment does not exist under the terms of that theory.

If they still want to believe that the unemployment of the Great Depression was involuntary (or that government policies helped produce full employment after World War II, or that Reagan's tax cuts stimulated a demand-side recovery after 1982), the analysts must have a logical, rigorous, theoretical reason for not accepting some part of the new classical argument. And they must show that when they take the step of rejecting some part of the new classical argument, the possibility of involuntary unemployment (or effective government policy to fight unemployment) emerges.

As it turns out, there are responses to the new classical challenge. And we shall concern ourselves with theoretical responses, which repudiate one or more of the three central assumptions of new classical economics. Since NCE rests on three distinct assumptions (monetarism, market clearing, and rational expectations), alternatives to it take several forms.

---

[2] *Stagflation* is an informal term meaning a time when high unemployment and inflation occur together.

In fact, there is a complex pattern of possible positions. The particular approach that we ourselves prefer is to return to the spirit of Keynes's *General Theory*[3] and to reject both monetarism (the quantity theory of money) and the rational expectations hypothesis. In this, we join some of the older generation of U.S. Keynesians, such as Nobel laureate James Tobin.[4]

This has not been the approach taken by the most prominent group of younger North American economists who have attempted to find a new underpinning for the activist policies of the Keynesian tradition.[5] (We call this group by the name they have chosen for themselves: the new Keynesians.) Largely sympathetic to rational expectations and to the radical reconstruction of the core propositions of the older theories to which rational expectations leads, the new Keynesians have also been willing to accept the broad outlines of monetarism, at least as a description of the theoretical long run. So they have devoted most of their ammunition to an attack on the third new classical assumption, perfect price flexibility, which is required if markets for commodities and especially markets for labor are to clear.[6]

What causes unemployment? The new classicals answer that transitory mistakes and misperceptions due to transitory shocks cause unemployment. Because they are transitory, these mistakes and their consequences must and will disappear in a short time if left alone. The new Keynesians counter that unemployment occurs because relative prices, especially wage rates in the labor market, do not adjust quickly enough. When conditions of excess demand or excess supply arise, to be quite specific, prices do not adjust before transactions are made. Transactions therefore occur at "wrong" prices, and this has the effect of freezing an excess demand or excess supply condition into place. In a nutshell, new Keynesian economics is the economics of *disequilibrium* caused by transactions at prices that do not clear markets.

[3] J. M. Keynes, *The General Theory of Employment, Interest and Money* (London: Macmillan, 1936).

[4] Tobin rejects rational expectations and also emphasizes non–market clearing as the basis for the theory of unemployment. See, for example, James Tobin's Yrjo Jahnsson Lectures for 1978, published as *Asset Accumulation and Economic Activity* (Chicago: University of Chicago Press, 1980), especially pp. 20–48. Meanwhile the new Keynesians accept rational expectations and base their theory of unemployment solely on a rejection of market clearing. For our part, we reject rational expectations and rest our critique of the new classical theory principally on that ground; we do not believe that a rejection of market clearing is essential.

[5] Among the most prominent new Keynesians, we would mention Lawrence Summers and N. Gregory Mankiw of Harvard University, Janet Yellen of the University of California, Berkeley, and Joseph Stiglitz of Stanford University, a member of President Clinton's Council of Economic Advisors.

[6] Lately, as we shall see, a line of new Keynesian reasoning based on imperfect competition in commodity markets has made an appearance, but this is not a major part of the story.

But why do such non-market-clearing transactions occur? If an economic process is inefficient (and what could be more inefficient than mass unemployment?), then most economists would argue that there must be something wrong with it. In the particular case of the labor market, we are told that unemployment results from real wages that are too high and from a failure of real wages to fall sharply and quickly enough. There are obvious personal and social gains to be had if only wages could be made to adjust faster, for then the unemployed could find jobs (though at a lower wage) and both they and those who would hire them would be better off. To paraphrase a favorite new classical parable, it would seem that $500 bills are being left in the street and no one is picking them up. We need a theory to explain why not.

The old Keynesian approach, at least in the American tradition, contented itself with the institutional assertion that wages were sticky. It did not explain why. The new Keynesian research agenda has been devoted to providing a rational basis for sticky wages and prices.

New Keynesian economics seeks to construct a theory that generates Keynesian results and policy implications consistent with individual optimizing behavior over time. As part of this, new Keynesians seek particularly to offer reasons why slow price adjustment in some markets may be consistent with individuals acting in an optimal, self-interested fashion. As Olivier Blanchard and Stanley Fischer observe in an advanced macroeconomics textbook written very much in the spirit of new Keynesian economics,

> By the end of the 1970s . . . it had become clear to many that the [traditional Keynesian] approach had reached a dead end: the assumption of given prices, which had appeared initially to be a useful shortcut, turned out to be a misleading one. Further, in the absence of microfoundations that accounted for the price stickiness, it was difficult to make progress on several ambiguities that emerged from the framework.
>
> These problems led in the 1980s, to a change in research strategy. *Recent research has started from explicitly specified market imperfections and attempted to derive price or wage stickiness and other macroeconomic implications by examining optimal behavior under such imperfections.*[7]

New Keynesians describe their models as *disequilibrium systems*, meaning that universal equality between supply and demand does not hold in all markets at the same time. You may recall the discussion in Chapter 2 of concepts of equilibrium and the distinction drawn between Marshallian equilibrium (a situation in which nothing is expected to

[7] Olivier Blanchard and Stanley Fischer, *Lectures on Macroeconomics* (Cambridge: MIT Press, 1989), p. 373. (Emphasis added.)

change over time) and Walrasian equilibrium (a situation in which the prices in all markets equalize supply and demand). The new Keynesian concept of equilibrium is Walrasian; it has to do with a balance of supply and demand in each micromarket, one by one. The economy could be in *Walrasian disequilibrium* if one or more markets fail to clear and in persistent Walrasian disequilibrium if this failure is persistent. In some new Keynesian analyses, all markets fail to achieve equality of supply and demand initially, but the emphasis typically is placed on the failure of one particular market to clear—the labor market, of course.[8]

SIX REASONS FOR STICKY WAGES

The labor market is as central to the new Keynesians as it is to the new classicals. In both theories, supply and demand in the labor market directly determine both the level of real output and the level of employment. To the new Keynesians, however, the labor market exhibits *market failure*. The price in that market, which is the real wage, fails to adjust to ensure continuous full employment. Therefore, the new Keynesians must devote special attention to explaining why, in their theory, the real wage rate is slow to change.

Robert Solow's December 1979 presidential address before the American Economic Association crystallized the new Keynesian position.[9] Solow provided a list of six major reasons for the existence of wage rigidity. These six reasons were presumed to be consistent with rational, optimizing behavior on the part of individual participants in the economy and hence to be entirely compatible with the other core premises of new classical economics.

Solow gave the following six reasons for the stickiness of wages:

(1) Workers may resist changes in nominal wage because these disturb the relative position of different groups of workers in the wage structure.

(2) Firms may wish to pay non-market-clearing wage rates in order to elicit higher levels of work effort; this is the doctrine of *efficiency wages*.

---

[8] Representative of the latter sort of disequilibrium macroeconomics are Robert M. Solow, "Alternative Approaches to Macroeconomic Theory: A Partial View," *Canadian Journal of Economics*, 12: No. 3 (August 1979), pp 339–354; Robert M. Solow, "On Theories of Unemployment," *American Economic Review*, 70: No. 1 (March 1980), 1–11; and Joseph Stiglitz, "Theories of Wage Rigidity," in *Keynes' Economic Legacy: Contemporary Economic Theories*, ed. James L. Butkiewicz et al. (New York: Praeger Publishers, 1986), pp. 153–206.
[9] "On Theories of Unemployment," *American Economic Review*, 70: No. 1, pp. 8–9.

(3)   Social forces outside of economics proper may play a role in creating a solidarity against wage changes, even when this may not be in the short-run economic interest of individual workers.
(4)   Workers may implicitly extract an agreement from employers, in which sticky wage rates compensate them for an increased probability of unemployment; this is the doctrine of *implicit contracts.*
(5)   It is a simple institutional fact that wage contracts are imperfectly indexed and often fail to keep up with changing inflation conditions.
(6)   Wages remain sticky because it is costly to change them; this is the doctrine of *transactions cost.*

We explore the six reasons in detail below. Note that some of them provide direct reasons why *real* wages may be sticky; others, especially the first, provide reasons why *money* wages may not move in a fully flexible way. In a model of supply and demand in the labor market, the distinction is very important for the following reason. If real wages alone are sticky, then unemployment is, in effect, *structural* in character, which means that it cannot be remedied by the normal processes of increased government spending or tax cuts. Increased nominal spending will simply raise prices along with wages, leaving real wages and unemployment unchanged. We may have an explanation for unemployment, but stabilization policies provide no cure. However, if sticky money wages are the fundamental source of a real-wage disequilibrium, there is a ready solution. Raise the level of nominal spending, and therefore the price level, and the real wage can be brought down toward the full employment level. With sticky money wages and a downward-sloping labor demand curve, inflationary policies can remedy unemployment, at least in the short run.

1. Relative Wages

The relative wage argument—that workers care about relative wages as well as absolute wage levels—originated with Keynes, is about money wage inflexibility, and leads straightforwardly to an inflationary cure for unemployment.

Many economists in Keynes's time had noted that workers resisted piecemeal reductions in their money wage rates, even though prices might also be falling. The alternative to a money wage cut under the circumstances was likely to be rising real wages and unemployment. Yet workers seemed to prefer the risk of unemployment, even their own unemployment, to accepting money wage cuts.

Many saw this as evidence that workers were beset by a form of irrationality known as *money illusion*: workers seemed to pay heed to the monetary value of their wages, and not to the real value. Economists who took this view believed that workers were incapable of piercing the "veil of money" to understand where a worker's true economic interests lay. They therefore saw irrational behavior as the explanation for unemployment—something that of course would not be consistent with the principles of new classical economics.

For his part, Keynes denied that workers suffer money illusion or from any other distinctive irrationalities. He offered an alternative, quite rational explanation of their behavior. Workers, he said, have a concern not only for the absolute level of their wages but also for the level of their wage in comparison with other groups of workers. Because reductions in money wages are "seldom or never of an all-around character," they will inevitably alter the relative position of those who accept them. Keynes argued that labor's resistance to money wage cuts did not mean that labor was unalterably opposed to real wage reductions. If such reductions could be achieved by raising the price of workers' consumption goods (*wage goods*) relative to money wages, then they would not affect relativities, and the problem of *real-wage resistance* would not arise.[10] The virtue of an inflationary policy was that it reduces all real wages by the same amount, thus avoiding destructive competition for relative position between different groups of workers.[11]

This argument depends critically on the existence of a downward-sloping demand curve for labor. It must be true that a fall in real wages leads to a higher volume of employment. When Keynes made the argument, he still believed this a useful approximation to reality: that the falling volume of employment in the Great Depression had led to higher real wages for those workers who had been able to keep their jobs. But this belief was not borne out by the evidence, a fact that Keynes later acknowledged.[12] In the Great Depression and later, real wages did not necessarily rise when employment declined; they may actually have fallen. In that case, there is no reason to think that a policy of reducing real wages by inflation (or otherwise) would lead in any direct way to a

[10] Keynes, *The General Theory*, pp. 7–15.

[11] In presenting this argument, Solow omits discussion of what Keynes felt was an even more important point. Even if workers agreed to reductions in money wages, Keynes argued, they could not guarantee that this would in fact reduce real wages and so raise employment. In Keynes's thinking, money wage levels affect the price level, since prices are determined by costs and wages are the largest element in costs. Money wage cuts, therefore, would go hand in hand with price deflation—potentially leaving the real wage virtually unchanged. To repeat, this argument, though central to Keynes, is not part of the new Keynesian canon, and for a straightforward reason. It is inconsistent with the idea, which new Keynesians generally accept, that the quantity of money as set by the central bank ultimately determines the price level.

[12] J. M. Keynes, "Relative Movements of Real Wages and Output," *Economic Journal*, 69 (March 1939), pp. 34–51.

rise in employment. Nevertheless, the new Keynesians retain the relative wage argument and the standard labor market model as part of their arsenal of objections to new classical market clearing.

2. Efficiency Wages

Solow's second argument was pioneered by Berkeley economists George Akerlof and Janet Yellen.[13] It provides a reason why real wages may be structurally too high for full employment but does not lead to a solution as easily as the relative wage argument.

The efficiency wage hypothesis posits a possible connection between labor productivity in business firms and the level of real wages. The connection is quite simple: workers may be motivated to give more effort by higher wages. If so, it becomes profitable for employers to raise wage payments above the level that will clear the labor market, to employ fewer workers, and to get more out of them. The wage rate–productivity connection gives rise, in microeconomic terms, to an *externality*—an effect the higher wage payment has on a worker that conveys a benefit back to the employer. This, in turn, raises the real wage actually paid above the level that would be consistent with full employment. These higher real-wage rates are known as *efficiency wages*.

Unlike the first argument on Solow's list, this one is a strict argument for *real-wage rigidity*. There is no reason why workers who are paid efficiency wages would not be willing to let their nominal wages float to reflect changes in the price level, thereby maintaining whatever level of real wages and employment is optimal for them.[14] In that case, efficiency wages will lead to a permanent problem of unemployment for a class of workers who, for whatever reason, cannot persuade employers that their *inferior* productivity can be offset by a sufficiently *lower* wage.

The hypothesis of efficiency wages arises in part as an effort to square the classical labor market theory with empirical observations about wage patterns that might otherwise seem inconsistent with it. In industries where workers have high measured productivity levels, they

[13] For a recent discussion, George Akerlof and Janet Yellen, "The Fair Wage-effort Hypothesis and Unemployment," *Quarterly Journal of Economics*, 105: No. 2 (May 1990), pp. 255–284.

[14] In a relative wage version of the efficiency wage hypothesis, workers produce more effort in response to a wage that raises their comparative standing among all workers. See Jeremy Bulow and Lawrence H. Summers, "A Theory of Dual Labor Markets with Application to Industrial Policy, Discrimination, and Keynesian Unemployment," *Journal of Labor Economics*, Vol. 4, No. 3 (1986), pp. 376–414; Lawrence H. Summers, "Relative Wages, Efficiency Wages, and Keynesian Unemployment," *American Economic Review*, 78: No. 2 (May 1988), pp. 383–388.

in fact also enjoy high rates of pay. This is true even when one controls for measurable differences in the characteristics of the workers. Given two groups of otherwise identical workers, those with the higher average productivity will, in general, be more highly paid.

Classical labor market theory predicts quite the opposite. In classical equilibrium, since members of the two groups of workers are indistinguishable, they can in principle be substituted freely one for another. Therefore, their pay should be equal. But it is not. The efficiency wage hypothesis reconciles theoretical prediction with observed reality by arguing that the apparent similarity of workers' characteristics masks an essential difference. Those with higher pay are working harder because they have been induced (by higher pay) to do so.[15]

In the background of this argument is a series of market imperfections. The first is known as an *information asymmetry*, not unlike the information asymmetries invoked by new classical economists to explain unemployment. But where new classical asymmetries concern the state of workers' information about the real value of their pay packet, new Keynesian asymmetries have to do with the state of employers' information about the productivity of their workers.

Individual workers are said to know their own propensity to shirk (or goof off) on the job and their own propensity to put forth a hard effort in the workplace. But their employers do not. As a result, the employers confront what economists now call a *signal extraction problem:* they cannot tell which workers are the shirkers and which ones are the grinds. Further, employers ostensibly have no test they can administer to distinguish one group from the other. On the other hand, workers face an information asymmetry of their own: they cannot always be sure whether their shirking will or will not be detected.

The sensible alternative is to raise the cost, to the worker, of being discovered goofing off on the job. This can be done by paying an efficiency wage: a worker fired from such a job will carry the stigma of having been fired into the next job, will not be able to earn the same efficiency wage, and will therefore suffer a significant *cost of job loss.* For this reason, the higher pay serves as an inducement not to shirk. And since the employers do know that all workers' efforts respond favorably to higher wages, their optimal strategy is to set the wage rate at a level

---

[15] Whether this explanation is persuasive remains unsettled. Could wage differentials perhaps be due to a sharing of the technological or market advantages of an industry with its workers? This would account for the high wages paid in capital-intensive, high-technology industries, but only if there is a general failure of even closely similar groups of workers to serve as substitutes for each other. This would indeed be our preferred interpretation, but it is unavailable to the new Keynesians because it entails a systematic move away from reliance on a supply-and-demand model of the labor market.

that reduces the average worker's propensity to shirk by just enough to ensure maximum profits for the business.[16]

The efficiency wage hypothesis starts by *assuming* that monitoring is costly and that it is cheaper to rely on the general payment of high wages to prompt greater individual effort. The hypothesis does not quite explain why the signal extraction problem should be so difficult, nor indeed does it establish that it is so in practice. Not surprisingly, this is an area of continuing controversy.

For example, if shirking is a problem, some economists have asked, why aren't cheaper and more effective monitoring schemes devised? For example, why not link compensation to output through piecework (payment per unit of measured output) and bonuses, so that individual workers are rewarded after the fact for good performance?[17] Shirkers would not get the Christmas bonuses; grinders would. In this case, total reward need not be higher than actual measured effort, and the incentives to deliver a high-productivity work effort would be even greater than if all workers were receiving an equal efficiency wage.

Alternatively, if monitoring the performance of individuals is too difficult, why not try teamwork? After organizing workers into teams, management might reward groups of workers for successfully performing tasks and so induce group members to police the efforts of one another. Setting the average wage above market-clearing levels in such a system would be unnecessary, since rewards would be tailored to the efforts made and the employer's funds would not be dissipated on those who might shirk despite being paid an efficiency wage.

The new Keynesian response to such questions must be that all feasible innovations affecting monitoring and compensation (at any given time) have already been made. We observe, in the real world, some cases of piecework, bonuses, and teamwork, but there must not be a lot more scope for gains from such practices. It must not be possible with existing technologies to distinguish good from poor workforce performers even after the fact, and this must be no more feasible for groups of workers than for managers. Efficiency wages therefore operate at the margin; they are paid to discourage shirking that could not otherwise be deterred with existing technologies.

[16] Or, more precisely, they raise the wage until the declining marginal losses from shirking are just offset by the marginal increases in the wage bill.

[17] Piecework is useful where output can clearly be attributed to the effort of individual workers, as for example in harvesting strawberries or in the "putting out" system of garment manufacture in the home. Bonuses are useful where piecework is infeasible, as in assembly lines where all workers contribute to a stream of products but it is possible to evaluate worker performance after the fact. As a historical matter, piecework, sliding scales, and other effort-related forms of compensation tended to disappear in favor of fixed wages with the rise of the factory system, precisely because shirking could be monitored directly and efficiently in the factory.

The presence of a wage differential between those who have jobs and those would like to work but cannot find employment at even a significantly lower real wage suggests the presence of a second type of asymmetry, or imperfection—one in the structure of the product market. If firms are going to pay above-market wages, they must have the ability to set wages. They cannot be the purely competitive price-takers (wage-takers) that the assumption of perfect competition in all markets would seem to require.

Where does this ability to pay above-market wages come from? One possible answer might be monopoly and monopoly profits. But for firms to be able to set wages, holding a monopolistic position is not strictly necessary. It is, for example, possible to imagine a very large number of competitive firms, all of whom realize that by paying a slightly higher wage and employing slightly fewer workers, they can achieve the same or higher profits than if wages were allowed to fall to the point where labor markets cleared. Since all firms are identical, all behave in exactly the same way, and the wage rises above the market-clearing level.

An obvious question arises. Since all workers are also identical (including the unemployed), why are new firms not formed that will hire the unemployed at the prevailing efficiency wages? Something, somewhere in this argument, must be blocking the operation of free competition and particularly the formation of new firms. In other words, the efficiency wage argument appears to rest on the bedrock of imperfect competition; there must be a *barrier to entry* that underlies the linkage between efficiency wages and unemployment.[18] So far, however, the efficiency wage literature does not clearly specify what those barriers are or why they exist.

One final puzzle needs to be addressed. Assuming that firms can, for whatever reason, change the wages they offer, why should they want to? Why do higher wages lead to increased effort and productivity in the first place? We know that along the classical labor supply curve more labor hours will be supplied as real wages rise. But does this say anything about the quality of work performed in those hours? Hours are a measured quantity, punched in on the clock in the morning and punched out in the afternoon. Efficiency wages are paid, by construction of the hypothesis, to call forth increases in effort that cannot be measured profitably; if they could be, firms would do so and would reward workers individually for their work effort. And since the difference between

---

[18] Alternatively, it might be the case that the unemployed are stigmatized in some direct or indirect way, perhaps by external characteristics (gender or race) or by the very fact of their unemployment. In this case, firms looking at the unemployed become convinced that they are not suitable candidates for the payment of efficiency wages.

shirkers and grinds cannot be detected, won't the workers become aware of this fact and conscious that the cost of job loss created by the efficiency wage cannot be related in a systematic way to the *risk of job loss* engendered by management's efforts to find and deter shirkers?

In the final analysis, are there strong reasons to believe that workers whose skills, training, and job effort are in every measurable way identical do in fact perform better when they are more highly paid? To believe that firms paying efficiency wages will do better than those who hire the unemployed (who presumably will be highly grateful for any opportunity to work) at market-clearing wages? So far, these questions remain open for continued economic research. Efficiency wages are an immensely interesting and theoretically flexible idea, but many economists, including ourselves, remain skeptical about how much of real-world real-wage rigidity they can actually explain.

3. Fair Wages and Insider–Outsider Models

As a third reason, Solow suggests that there may exist in society a *fair wage standard*, which is recognized as customary by employed and unemployed workers alike and which will not be undercut by those who are unemployed even though it may be in their short-term, purely economic interest to do so.[19]

How can such a standard survive? Perhaps because if the unemployed (or their prospective employers) do seek to underbid the "fair" wage, they will face harsh social sanctions. Such sanctions might come from existing workers whose long-range earnings prospects are undermined by the competition. Just as would-be strikebreakers are inhibited by the brutal treatment they may face from the strikers and their allies, Solow argues, those who underbid the fair wage will be treated as scab workers.

The extension of this argument from strikes to ordinary labor markets requires careful examination. What are the content and force of these hypothesized social sanctions? Strikers and strikebreakers face a clear-cut conflict over well-defined jobs. But in the case of, say, cut-rate barbershops, the situation is quite different. Can an old-style barber enforce a social sanction on a college student who has been offered a competing job in a lower-wage Supercuts salon down the road? More broadly, can garment workers in North Carolina enforce social sanctions on garment workers in Hong Kong? Obviously not.

[19] This suggestion of Solow's has been developed into a formal model of the "insider-outsider" type by Assar Lindbeck and Dennis J. Snower, "Cooperation, Harassment, and Involuntary Unemployment," *American Economic Review*, 78 (March 1988), pp. 167–188.

The fair standards argument would seem to require that the new jobs being offered be recognizably the same, and in the same places, as the high-wage jobs that are being underbid; they must be jobs over which the existing workers (the *insiders*) have some leverage. The argument also must presume that those out of work (the *outsiders*) are not so desperate as to have lost fear of repercussions when they weigh that against the fear of remaining out of work. The labor market cannot be perfect in this situation; there must be some power of the employed to discipline the unemployed who seek to become competitors for their jobs.[20] Since in any large (indeed, global) economy this power cannot be unlimited, the fair wage argument may explain some real-wage rigidity but cannot plausibly explain very much. In practice, the *insider-outsider model*, as it is called, is usually thought to be more applicable to the tightly organized labor markets of Western Europe than to the loosely organized case of the United States.

4. Implicit Contracts

The next argument on Solow's list, the *implicit contracts* hypothesis, holds that real wages become sticky because of an informal, or implicit, agreement that employers will provide higher wages as a form of insurance against spells of unemployment. Workers obtain higher than market-clearing wages when they have work; in exchange, employers are free to vary the total volume of employment without complaint from their employees. Workers may be laid off and rehired whenever the employers find it convenient.

This argument implies that workers have a predominant preference for high wages over employment security. Further, workers with this predominant preference must have the means to ensure that they are not undercut by those who do not share that preference. And finally, workers seemingly must save at least part of their high wages in order to be prepared for the spells of unemployment they expect to come along with the job.

Under this model, in contrast with insider-outsider models, the employed and the unemployed do not necessarily come into conflict. The preference for high wages over employment stability may be shared by both groups. The employed prefer higher wages with some risk of unemployment to lower wages and steady work. The unemployed, for

[20] This is tantamount to the unionized portion of the work force being able to protect its occupational turf from potential rivals. The argument would be more compelling in the 1990s if there was not so much evidence of the deterioration of the commanding position of organized labor, particularly in the U.S. labor market, where union membership has declined to about 15 percent of the work force.

their part, prefer to wait for a spell of high-wage employment, rather than attempt to underbid wage standards in order to secure immediate jobs. Thus, the implicit contracts hypothesis largely escapes from the difficulty faced by insider-outsider models, namely the necessity of assuming that employed workers can impose stiff sanctions on those who would take away their jobs.

Do we know whether, in fact, the preference for high wages with unstable employment is widely shared? No. As with the previous two arguments, this one is offered as a *plausible basis* for real-wage inflexibility. Little or no direct or indirect evidence exists on workers' actual preferences with respect to the choice between high wages and job security.[21] If the argument happens to be correct, then it implies the logical result: sticky real wages and persistent unemployment. But is it true in practice? Again, we don't know.

5. Long-term Labor Contracts and Imperfect Indexation

Fifth on Solow's list is the tendency of collective bargaining procedures to establish long-term contracts that do not adapt nominal wages to rapidly changing output prices.

When a wage contract is adjusted regularly and automatically to compensate for inflation, we say it is *indexed*. Indexation clauses in U.S. labor contracts are known as automatic *cost-of-living adjustments* (*COLAs*). Ever since the late 1940s there have been such adjustments, either automatic or regular enough to be virtually automatic, in the pay rates of the best-organized industrial workers, such as those in automobiles and steel. Automatic COLAs have also been built into the Social Security system since 1972, and tax rates have been adjusted automatically to offset the effects of inflation since 1981.

But many long-term labor contracts are not indexed to inflation or are, at best, only weakly indexed. For example, a cost-of-living Adjustment clause will generally provide for an inflation adjustment only once a year. In such cases, when inflation accelerates, real wages fall and employment rises.[22] Conversely, disinflation leads to rising real wages and unemployment.

---

[21] We do observe many female workers in the U.S. in recent years accepting low-wage work, evidently in order to increase the stability of employment and incomes in their families. This suggests that if the implicit contracts argument was once true, it may not be any longer.

[22] In hyperinflationary Brazil, even a once-a-month 100 percent adjustment of wages to past inflation may still mean a substantial erosion of real wages over the course of each month, from one adjustment to the next.

Economists who advance this argument must, of course, explain the rationality of nonindexation or weak indexation. They argue that there are costs, inherent in the collective bargaining process, to procedures that would permit a rapid adjustment of nominal wages to nominal prices. For example, unions may prefer a regular schedule, neither continuous nor overly infrequent, of negotiations with employers. This schedule ensures that they have the periodic opportunity to revisit a range of employment-related issues; yearly negotiations serve this purpose. It would be much harder to justify having such negotiations if full indexation to inflation were ensured automatically without them.

A preference by different groups of workers for regular, periodic negotiations does not imply that different groups will hold their negotiations at the same times. Rather, accidents of history will ensure that labor contracts are staggered and overlapping. At any given moment, some workers will have just completed their negotiations, and others will be on the verge of going to the bargaining table. Each negotiating team thus faces an environment set by the wage contracts concluded by other workers a short while before.

This, in turn, leads back to the relative wages argument. In any particular negotiation, a failure to conform precisely to the historic pattern of wage indexation must imply a rise or a fall in relative wages, which in turn will destabilize the pattern of settlements in negotiations to follow. In this spirit, a literature on staggered, overlapping labor contracts has developed; it attributes a rigidity of nominal wage settlement patterns to the inevitable distributive conflicts that any departure from settled patterns would necessarily cause.

In a sense, such arguments are not much different from the attribution of rigid wages to trade union power. Such arguments indicate an "imperfect" or quasi-monopolistic labor market, in which workers set the terms of their employment partly by organized, collective action. Criticism of trade union power was, of course, commonplace in pre-Keynesian economics. Indeed, much of the new Keynesian argument, in a high irony, circles back to the sort of position from which Keynes sought a theoretical escape:[23] once again, the stubborn behavior of workers (or their organizations) is, in the final analysis, responsible for unemployment.

---

[23] The long-term contracts view prompted a debate over whether an aggregate labor market is best conceived of as a contract market, in which wages are set for long periods of time, or as an auction market, in which wages are changed quickly in response to changing general economic conditions. Empirical evidence, to say the least, has left the matter unresolved. See, for example, Thomas J. Kniesner and Arthur H. Goldsmith, "A Survey of Alternative Models of the Aggregate U.S. Labor Market," *Journal of Economic Literature*, 25 (September 1987), pp. 1241–80.

6. Transactions Costs and Countervailing Power

Finally, Solow suggests an argument for money wage rigidity that emphasizes that costs are associated with making changes in wages. He posits that both employers and employees may be fearful that wage revisions made today, in response to the conditions of the moment, could prove too hard to reverse at a later date. Faced with the alternatives of making changes at some cost that might have to be reversed later at more cost and of doing nothing for free, this argument suggests that there will be a bias toward doing nothing.

For example, employers might be tempted to agree to higher wages on an upswing of the economy. But they could fear that labor will not agree to reductions when the economy turns down. Conversely, employees might be tempted to accept wage cuts in a depressed economy but be nervous about whether high wages will return when the economy recovers. Faced with such doubts on both sides, all may agree that the rational course lies in fixing wages and not changing them until overwhelming evidence suggests that permanent, once-for-all changes are essential.

The transactions cost argument thus provides a basis for both upward and downward nominal wage rigidity. Under this argument, parties on both sides would seek to preserve the prevailing wage rate unless driven to change it by overwhelming circumstance.

This argument also presumes an imperfection in the labor market. Both labor and capital must be sufficiently organized and disciplined so that no employers will offer higher wages on the upturn and no workers will underbid on the downturn. The workers' side of this argument really is another variant of trade union power; the employers' side amounts to the power of a collectively organized business community. The argument is reminiscent of John Kenneth Galbraith's *American Capitalism: The Concept of Countervailing Power*,[24] which argued that the mixed U.S. economy was characterized by the mutually offsetting power of large organizations. Given Galbraith's position as a leading economic dissident, his book is surely an odd place to look for an argument that is supposed to be consistent with the canons of rationality and perfect competition underpinning new classical economics.

STICKY PRICES

Most of the new Keynesian arguments have focused on reasons for sticky wages and labor market failure. However, one very recent strand

[24] (Boston: Houghton Mifflin, 1952.)

of the literature emphasizes general reasons for *price inflexibility* instead.[25] This type of inflexibility goes by the name of *menu costs,* and in principle it affects all kinds of nominal prices (including but not limited to nominal wages).

Menu Costs

The basic intuition behind menu costs is very simple. It takes some resources to make changes in prices and to inform customers, clients, and workers that changes have been made. Changes will therefore not be made until the marginal benefit to the *price changer* from doing so exceeds the marginal cost. So long as some changes are not made, transactions may occur at disequilibrium prices, leading to the possibility of excess supply of goods and services, or unemployment.[26]

Of course, the menu costs of physically changing prices in the modern grocery store or pharmacy are not very large. In most cases, the inventory turns over every few days, and the adjustment lags to changing wholesale prices cannot be very long. Even restaurants and catalog stores, which print menus and price lists, can in principle devise ways to change those prices on short notice (for example, by writing the menu on a blackboard or on a list of "daily specials").

But this is not the main line of the argument. Rather, the menu cost argument is essentially similar to the imperfect information arguments of the new classicals, with a twist. The twist comes from *game theory.* Firms, proponents argue, cannot predict the reaction of their competitive rivals to a change in their own prices, so they calculate the possible consequences of each different course of action. A price cut, for example, might lead to a great expansion of market share and profit. Or it might lead to a general round of price cuts from other firms—a price war with no relative gains but with lost profits for everybody. Game theory tells us that the second outcome is more likely. Since all firms reason alike, all will realize that they will be individually better off if they follow a price cut than if they resist it. And since all realize this, all may (wisely) refrain from precipitating just such a price war by cutting their own prices.

By parallel reasoning, firms will avoid attempting to raise prices, even in the face of moderately rising costs, if they do not know how their competition will react. If price increases are not followed, firms will lose

---

[25] See, for example, Joseph Stiglitz, "Toward a Theory of Rigidities," *American Economic Review,* 79: No. 2 (May 1989), p. 364.

[26] An alternative argument, important for some cases, holds that prices, because they are an important indicator to consumers of the quality of the goods being sold, will not be changed. Thus, a firm that cuts price in response to a decline in costs risks losing sales, because customers regard the price cut as a sign of declining quality and difficulty in clearing the goods off the shelf.

market share. And since all realize this, none will follow (and none will lead).

The menu cost argument thus puts a foundation of game-theoretic microrationality under two ideas that were first developed in U.S. economics before World War II. One of these is the idea of *administered pricing*, developed by Adolph Berle and Gardiner C. Means, who argued that stable pricing policies would be observed for bureaucratic reasons in large corporations.[27] The other, the *kinked oligopoly demand curve* developed by Paul M. Sweezy in 1939, is still well known as an explanation of price inflexibility in oligopolistic markets.[28]

The menu cost argument gives plausible reasons why many prices may not adjust spontaneously, giving rise to disequilibrium transactions. But how important can small deviations from equilibrium prices be? One might think that if the deviations are small, then the consequences in terms of unemployed resources cannot be very large.

Menu cost theorists meet this argument in the following way. Certainly, they point out, firms will change prices when the private benefit from doing so exceeds the private cost. But the private benefit to the firm only includes the higher profit that can be earned; it does not include the reduction of unemployment that a more rapid price adjustment would produce. This external effect, they suggest, is cumulative. If each small, uncorrected price disequilibrium leads to a little unemployment, the sum of all such disequilibria may produce large-scale unemployment. And there will be no tendency for this unemployment to be eliminated by the normal functioning of private markets.

Increasing Returns to Scale

We have not been able to treat all of the possible permutations of wage and price stickiness. One of the most interesting is to focus on the presence of increasing returns to scale in the production process or, alternatively, on the existence of monopolistic competition among firms. Martin Weitzman of MIT has sought to argue that the only logical theory of unemployment is one based upon an environment of increasing returns.[29] The work of Oliver Hart and Olivier Blanchard has em-

[27] See A. A. Berle and Gardiner C. Means, *The Modern Corporation and Private Property* (New York: Harcourt Brace & World, 1968).

[28] Paul M. Sweezy, "Demand Under Conditions of Oligopoly," *Journal of Political Economy*, 47: No. 4, August (1939), pp. 568–573; George J. Stigler, "The Kinked Oligopoly Demand Curve and Rigid Prices," *Journal of Political Economy*, 55: No. 5, October (1947), pp. 432–447.

[29] See Martin Weitzman, "Increasing Returns and the Foundations of Unemployment Theory," *Economic Journal*, 92: No. 368 (December 1982), pp. 787–804. For a critical reply, see William Darity, Jr., "On Involuntary Unemployment and Increasing Returns," *Journal of Post-Keynesian Economics*, 7 (Spring 1985), pp. 363–372.

phasized, as the cornerstone of unemployment theory, the role of a world of rivalrous firms engaged in product differentiation. The theoretical developments here are highly interesting, though it somewhat stretches the nomenclature to describe them as Keynesian. Increasing returns and monopolistic competition may play a major role in new Keynesian economics, but like the emphasis on wage and price stickiness as the sources of unemployment, this work has very little to do with the theoretical content of Keynes's economics.

Policy Implications of Rational Stickiness

The new Keynesian vision is, in general, one of an economy beset by imperfections in the workings of its market system. These arise because of information asymmetries, monopoly positions, or externalities. Information asymmetries feature the unknowable linkages between wages and productivity; monopoly positions flow from trade union power, and externalities flow from game-theoretic pricing decisions by firms. The persistent or innate nature of these imperfections is sometimes left unexplained, but once their existence is accepted, they provide the backdrop to the rational, optimizing behavior that results in price or wage rigidity.

What of it? Whether one accepts one version of new Keynesian non–market clearing or another, the conclusions for policy point in the same way. If the markets are failing, then the government has a role.

The new Keynesian arguments for wage and price rigidity avoid attributing the inflexibilities to government policy. For example, it would be easy to claim that a floor on wages exists due to the presence of minimum wage laws. But then the solution to the resulting unemployment or production shortfalls would be to eliminate these types of government intervention. Of course, this would vitiate the new Keynesian policy agenda. For that agenda to survive, inflexibilities must be due to the consequences of actions taken by individuals, or by groups of individuals, functioning independently of the state.

If, on the other hand, wage rigidities do arise in the course of rational, optimizing behavior by individuals and do lead to unemployment, then government action will be needed either to alleviate the wage rigidity or to uplift the economy despite the persistence of the wage rigidity.[30] If the rigidities are nominal, then policies that raise the level of

---

[30] It is not always obvious that new Keynesians believe wage rigidities must be eliminated by government action. Martin Weitzman has made a case for the adoption of profit-sharing arrangements by businesses with the obvious goal of making wages flexible through outcome-based compensation schemes. However, the fact that such arrangements have not been adopted on a sufficiently wide scale may suggest a need for government to prompt businesses to adopt these payment schemes that Weitzman believes will push the economy to full employment.

aggregate demand can be justified. If the rigidities are real, then structural change to permit real wages to adjust is the appropriate solution.

GENERAL DISEQUILIBRIUM

So far, our discussion of new Keynesian economics has focused on the reasons why a rational world may nevertheless be characterized by sticky wages and prices. We now turn to a more formal exposition of the consequences. In particular, how can the effects of disequilibrium transactions, and the spillovers from disequilibrium in one market to disequilibrium in another, be conceptualized?

A good starting point for such an investigation is the old-fashioned IS-LM diagram, which gives a model of equilibrium conditions in several distinct markets. However, accepting the new classical view that employment and real output are determined in the labor market requires adjustment of IS-LM accordingly. Once employment and real output are set, only the price level is to be determined in the long run by IS and LM. Thus, Figure 10.1 is drawn in interest rate/price level space rather than in interest rate/real output space as in the earlier version.

The IS schedule is now interpreted as a set of all combinations of interest rates, r, and the price level, P, compatible with supply-and-demand equality in the market for commodities. We presume that in this market the price level rises to eliminate an excess demand for goods and services and falls to eliminate an excess supply. Similarly, the LM

FIGURE 10.1   **IS-LM and the Price Level**

In the new Keynesian model, the IS and LM schedules determine the interest rate and the price level, but not the level of real output.

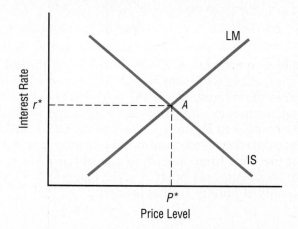

Taking a Closer Look

IS-LM AND THE PRICE LEVEL

Instructors in basic economics courses frequently remind their students to label the axes of their diagrams. That lesson is doubly important for use of the IS-LM apparatus, as differing versions of the same model have different variables on the horizontal axis.

In the text up to now, the IS and LM schedules appear on diagrams where the vertical axis represents the rate of interest (r) and the horizontal axis represents the level of real national output or income (y). In this case, we say that the two schedules are drawn in (r,y) *space*. The general price level, P, is treated as a constant, given by some process (such as the Phillips curve) external to the aggregate market processes analyzed by IS-LM. The IS curve indicates the combination of interest rates and real income that clear the commodity markets at a specific price level, and the LM curve indicates the combination of interest rates and real incomes that clear the financial markets at the same price level. If the general price

level changes, both curves will shift; variations in interest rates and real income lead to movements along the schedules. This is the more familiar version of IS-LM.

A less familiar version of IS-LM can be made compatible with the new classical economics. In this version, the horizontal axis represents the general price level, P, and we can say that the two schedules are drawn in (r,P) *space*. This means that the IS curve is now the combination of interest rates and price levels that clear the commodity markets, and the LM curve is the combination of interest rates and price levels that clear the financial markets, *for a given level of real output or income*. In other words, the output level of the economy is given outside the model, by the equilibration of supply and demand in the labor market. Any change in the level of real national income will now result in a shift in the schedules, and changes in interest rates or in the price level lead to movements along the schedules.

schedule is interpreted as all combinations of the interest rate and price level compatible with supply-and-demand equality in the money market. Here the interest rate is the price that rises to eliminate an excess demand for money and that falls to eliminate an excess supply.

At point A in Figure 10.1, where the two schedules intersect, both aggregate markets—the commodity market and the money market—clear at the same time. Indeed, in a world of perfect price flexibility and full employment, only point A in the diagram is relevant. Point A is the only center of gravity for the economy.

A new Keynesian economist would argue that point *A* is not sufficiently general to describe the full range of positions attainable by a real-world economy. Although relative prices might move in the appropriate direction (up to choke off excess demand, down to offset excess supply), a new Keynesian would protest that there is no reason to believe that they change with enough speed to clear the markets continuously, as equilibrium requires. Therefore, we cannot be assured that no transactions occur at non–market-clearing prices. And if transactions actually do occur at disequilibrium prices, point *A* will not be attained.

For example, suppose that the rate of interest adjusts instantaneously to eliminate any condition of excess demand or supply in the money market. On the other hand, suppose that the commodity price level is friction bound, changing only gradually in response to changing market conditions. Then, given the dynamics we have just imputed to each relative price, the money market always will clear. The economy of necessity will be always somewhere along the LM schedule. However, the slower adjustment of the price level means that the economy customarily will be off of the IS curve.

The IS-LM diagram can be divided into two regions by the IS curve, as shown in Figure 10.2. In the region to the left of the curve, the price level is too low relative to the values of *P* that will clear the commodity market; the economy experiences an excess demand for goods and services and upward, inflationary pressure on the commodity price level. Yet, that pressure is not quite strong enough to close immediately the gap between demand and supply. Therefore, transactions do

FIGURE 10.2   Disequilibrium in the Goods Market

The IS schedule represents equilibrium in the market for commodities. Above it, there is excess supply and prices are falling; below it, there is excess demand and prices are rising.

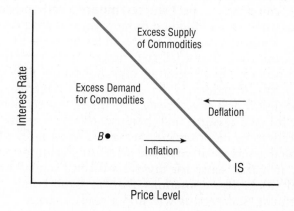

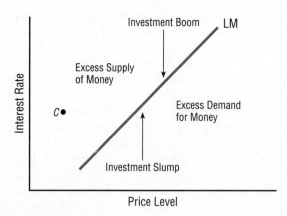

FIGURE 10.3   Disequilibrium in the Money Market

The LM schedule represents equilibrium in the market for money. Above it, there is excess supply and interest rates are falling, which stimulates investment. Below it, there is excess demand for money, interest rates are rising, bond prices are falling, and investment is in a slump.

occur at those disequilibrium prices. Economies are, at point *B*, experiencing inflation. By similar reasoning, to the right of the IS curve, the price level will be too high relative to the market-clearing values of *P*. Here we have a region of excess supply for goods and services—in effect, a region of *price deflation*.

A parallel argument can be made about the LM curve (see Figure 10.3). Suppose the interest rate, instead of the price level, is sluggish. If the price level adjusts instantaneously to clear the commodity market, as we may assume, then the economy always would be somewhere along the IS curve but off of the LM curve. The LM curve divides the space in Figure 10.3 into two regions. To the left of the curve, all interest rates are too high to clear the money market. People are holding on to their bonds, since they expect interest rates to fall and bond prices to rise. Because they are not holding money, there is an excess supply of money. Interest rates in this situation are under pressure to fall (bond prices are rising), but they do not fall fast enough to clear the financial market. We are, at point *C*, in a region of high but falling interest rates.

In this situation, if the interest rate governs the choice between consumption and investment, we might expect a bias toward investment, for two reasons: first, because interest rates are high, savings rates are likely to be high; second, because interest rates are falling, the prices of capital assets (relative to the prices of consumption goods) are rising. Thus, it makes sense for investors to buy capital assets, increasing the capital stock. If corporations wish to issue bonds in order to finance investment, such bonds will find a ready market.

To the right of the LM curve, interest rates are too low to clear the money market, and the region is one of excess demand for money. People are dumping bonds in favor of money, because they expect interest rates to rise and bond prices to fall. Savings are low, and there is a corresponding bias against investment. Corporations will have trouble issuing bonds to finance investment, because investors are afraid of a capital loss when interest rates rise and bond prices fall.

If the world is one of new Keynesian *general disequilibrium*, both markets could fail to clear because of rigidities in both the price level and the interest rate. The IS and LM schedules jointly divide the space in Figure 10.4 into four regions. Region I features an excess supply of money and commodities. Both prices (including wages) and interest rates are high, and both are tending to fall. Bond prices are correspondingly low and expected to rise, which makes this deflationary environment a good one for investment. Think of the period just at the end of a recession, when inflation has been arrested, inflationary expectations are down, and interest rates are adjusting to the new climate. An investment-led recovery can happen in this situation.

Moving counterclockwise, region II couples an excess supply of money with an excess demand for goods and services. Commodity prices are rising, but interest rates continue to fall and bond prices to rise. This might be an inflationary investment boom, such as may follow the investment-led recovery of region I.

In region III, both commodities and money are in excess demand. The good times clearly are coming to an end. The economy experiences both price inflation and, potentially, an investment slump—the exact

FIGURE 10.4   General Disequilibrium

In a general model of sluggish price and interest rate adjustment, the analyst can generate a plausible theory of the business cycle.

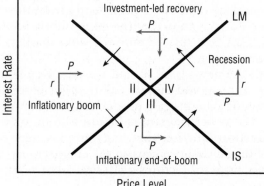

opposite of the deflationary recovery of region I. Think of the situation just before a recession, when incomes are strong but investors nevertheless fear that prosperity cannot last.

In region IV, finally, the downturn comes. This region is one of excess demand for money but of excess supply of commodities. Prices are still falling, but interest rates are now pushing upward. Correspondingly high bond prices are expected to fall along with commodity prices. This is not a good environment for investment and might be characterized as a new Keynesian recession.

These four major permutations of the IS-LM world, when prices and interest rates both adjust slowly, come close to a fairly plausible new Keynesian theory of the business cycle. To complete the theory, explaining why the cycle moves counterclockwise is necessary. You can get a feel for this by observing the directions in which r and P adjust in each region. If both variables adjust sluggishly, then the disequilibrium of the economy will tend to follow the crossover arrows, from recovery to boom to stagnation to slump.

PERSISTENT UNEMPLOYMENT

Along each schedule in Figure 10.4, the level of real national income, y, must, for the moment, be taken as given. If the horizontal axis of the IS-LM analysis is shifted from real income to the price level, IS-LM no longer seems to have anything useful to say about unemployment. But, of course, this is not the point of new Keynesian economics in general, for we have seen that a good part of the new Keynesian argument is aimed at an understanding of unemployment.

The new classicals would presume that unemployment must be at the full employment level, aside from the temporary effects of random shocks. Of course, the new Keynesians disagree. In their view, real national income can deviate persistently from the full employment level. However, for this to occur, the disequilibria in the goods and financial markets must be displaced onto the labor market. We now explore how this might happen.

Both the new classicals and the new Keynesians embrace the view that employment and output will be determined in an economy by the interaction of an aggregate production function with an aggregate labor market. The upper diagram in Figure 10.5 shows an aggregate neoclassical production function that links employment to real output, where there are diminishing returns to the employment of additional workers. The lower diagram pictures a classical labor market, where the demand

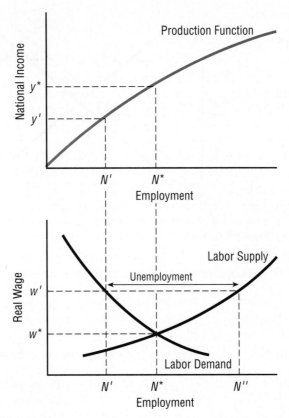

FIGURE 10.5   A Nonclearing Labor Market

If real wages are stuck at w', employment at N' will be below the equilibrium N^*, output y' will be below y^*, and there will be unemployment N'' minus N'.

and supply curves for labor take the traditional slopes and depend exclusively on the real wage rate.

The new classical position is straightforward. The nominal wage rate is perfectly flexible and will adapt to any level of commodity prices to ensure that the real wage will take the value $w^\star$ that will clear the labor market. In a classical labor market, the position where supply and demand balance is full employment, $N^\star$. When employment is at the $N^\star$ level, we can read off the corresponding level of real output or real national income from the aggregate production function. That level is $y^\star$. With $y^\star$ as the level of real national income and complete price flexibility, the IS and LM schedules will intersect at point A in Figure 10.6.

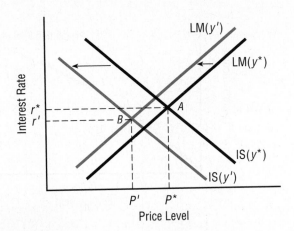

FIGURE 10.6   Displacement of IS-LM

When the rate of output is displaced from y^* to y', the price level and interest rate consistent with all other markets clearing are displaced from A to B.

Displaced Equilibria

The simplest new Keynesian counterargument is based, as we saw earlier in the chapter, on rigidities in the labor market. The labor market can be treated as the single market where prices (wages) are slow to adjust, a *fixprice* market.[31] If the nominal wage is sufficiently sticky, then the real wage itself may be stuck at the level w', which is too high to bring about supply-and-demand equality in the labor market. At such a real wage rate, workers want to offer N'' level of employment, but businesses only want to hire N' workers. The short side of the market prevails because, in an environment of free contracting, employers cannot be forced to take on more workers than they perceive as being profitable to hire. As a result, the economy's level of real national income will be y', lower than if the labor market also was a flexprice market. This is fixwage unemployment, exactly of the type (actually) that Keynes's classical antagonists had in mind.

Consequently, and here is the crux of the matter, the demand for goods and services and the demand for money will also be constrained to be lower than in the new classical case. This result arises because the lower level of real national income limits the incomes that can be earned (in real terms) by households and, therefore, their need for cash balances

---

[31] Both the commodity and money markets can be treated as markets where prices adjust rapidly, as *flexprice* markets. The fixprice/flexprice distinction was given detailed elaboration in John Hicks's Yrjo Jahnsson Lectures, subsequently published as *The Crisis in Keynesian Economics* (Oxford: Basil Blackwell, 1974).

to finance their transactions. As a result, both the IS and LM schedules will be displaced toward the left. The economy will settle at a different equilibrium configuration of interest rate and price level (point *B* in Figure 10.6). The price level will be unambiguously lower, whereas the interest rate could be higher, lower, or unchanged in comparison with point *A*.

Point *B* is a pseudoequilibrium. It is an equilibrium of the goods and money markets, given the disequilibrium in the labor market. We can call it a *constrained equilibrium*—constrained, in this case, by the insufficient stream of incomes generated at less than full employment.

To restate the argument: because the labor market does not clear, consumers of goods and services and purchasers of assets find themselves confronted with *quantity constraints* when making their optimal choices about how much to save (as opposed to consume) and about how much money to keep on hand for transactions. A spillover effect from the disequilibrium condition in the labor market to the commodity and money markets alters the decisions and outcomes there. Specifically, unemployment reduces the constrained equilibrium value of real output and the price level. It thereby creates the conditions under which even a temporary disruption of the labor market can become a persistent recession or depression.

Notional and Actual Demands

The consumption function underlying the IS curve and the money demand function underlying the LM curve that intersect at point *A* can be called the *notional demands*. These are the demand relationships that would prevail if participants in this economy did not face any quantity constraints, were able to purchase unlimited supplies of a good, and could do so solely on the basis of relative prices.

The consumption and investment demand function underlying the IS curve and the money demand function underlying the LM curve that intersect at point *B* may be described as the *actual demands*. Because firms are not hiring, economic agents will find themselves quantity-constrained in the labor market, unable to supply as much labor as they would prefer to do at the prevailing (non-market-clearing) real price for labor, w'. Less employment equals less income, so agents demand fewer goods and services at initial prices than they would if the labor market cleared. Thus, there is an initial excess supply of goods, which forces the price level to fall.

Spillovers in All Directions

Must the fixprice market be the labor market? Of course not. From the market that fails to clear, spillover effects onto markets where prices are

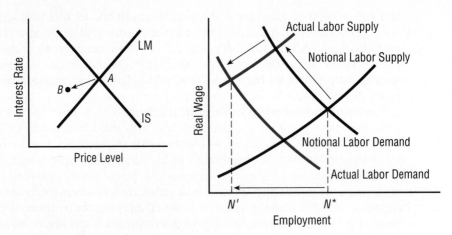

FIGURE 10.7   Displacement of the Labor Market

If prices rather than wages fail to adjust, then disequilibrium in commodity markets
may cause labor supply and/or labor demand to shift, displacing market-clearing
employment from its true equilibrium value.

flexible can occur in all directions. And from this fact we can finally
arrive at a general new Keynesian theory of unemployment.

For instance, a sluggish rise in the general price level will generate
transactions at prices that are too low. This will deplete the stock of
goods and leave consumers unable to buy all the goods and services they
desire at the prevailing price level. That shortfall will then spill over onto
consumers' decisions to supply employment in the labor market. Con-
sumer-workers who anticipate being unable to purchase all the goods
and services they might desire at the prevailing price level will supply
less labor at all real-wage rates. They will then enjoy the leisure that is
always available to them as an alternative to the goods that are the fruit of
labor. This, in turn, will shift the labor supply schedule from its notional
(not quantity-constrained) position to an actual (quantity-constrained)
position, with lower employment. Figure 10.7 illustrates this spillover
from a fixprice commodity market to persistent unemployment.

Alternatively, businesses may find excess supply in the commodity
market, because prices are slow to fall and transactions have used up all
the available money before depleting the available stocks of goods. Firms
will then reduce their demand for labor at every real wage rate in the
labor market, and the demand curve for labor will shift to the left.
Again, this will cause both employment and real output to fall. This
situation is equally well illustrated by Figure 10.7.

In an environment with general price sluggishness across markets,
careful treatment of all the spillover effects will lead to the construction

of a model that combines the displaced equilibria of shifted IS-LM and labor supply and demand curves with the general disequilibrium already discussed. This yields the fullest new Keynesian vision of how the economy works.[32] In such a world, individuals are quantity-constrained in each market in which they participate, and this affects their decisions in every other market in which they also participate. They will be on actual rather than notional schedules in all markets.

Policy Implications

The new Keynesians follow the new classicals in accepting rational expectations and monetarism. They reject only market clearing, on the ground that perfect market clearing would not be rational in the real world even if it could be attained. They show that persistent disequilibrium in any market can result in *persistent displaced equilibrium* in any other. In particular, they show that non–market clearing can lead to persistent unemployment.

What difference does that make for policy? A great deal. Take the case, described briefly above, where the trouble starts with excess supply in the commodity markets. As we saw, there could be an induced shift of labor demand to the left and persistent unemployment. But now there is also a simple cure, at least in the short run: let the government absorb the excess supply of commodities. It can do this, of course, by an expansionary policy, either monetary or fiscal. If both are expansionary to just the right extent, then point B (the disequilibrium in the left graph) in Figure 10.7 can essentially be dragged over to coincide with point A (the notional equilibrium). When this happens, the reason for an underemployment displacement of labor demand will disappear. Once again, policy is nonneutral, at least in the short run.

---

[32] This vision is influenced by Donald Patinkin's recognition, in *Money, Interest and Prices*, 2nd ed., Cambridge: MIT Press, 1989, of the spillover effects the failure of the labor market to clear have on consumption and asset demands, and by similar arguments in Robert W. Clower, "The Keynesian Counterrevolution: A Theoretical Appraisal," in *The Theory of Interest Rates*, ed. F. Hahn and F. Brechling (London: Macmillan, 1965). Robert Barro and Herschel Grossman were first to formalize a model of general macroeconomic disequilibrium; see Barro and Grossman, *Money, Employment and Inflation* (Cambridge: Cambridge University Press, 1976). For an additional useful explication, see John Muellbauer and Richard Portes, "Macroeconomic Models with Quantity Rationing," *Economic Journal* 88 (December 1978), pp. 788–821. Significant contributions to this literature also have come from French economists; see especially Edmond Malinvaud, *The Theory of Unemployment Reconsidered* (Oxford: Basil Blackwell, 1977), and Antoine d'Autume, "Non-Walrasian Equilibria and Macroeconomics," in *The Foundations of Keynesian Analysis*, ed. Alain Barrere (New York: St. Martin's Press, 1988), pp. 66–92.

Taking a Closer Look

DEFICITS, SAVINGS, PROFITS, AND INVESTMENT

Perhaps the biggest issue in popular and policy discussion of the deficit controversy concerns the effect of government borrowing on private savings and investment.

From a theoretical perspective, as we know, the effect of a budget deficit on private investment spending can cut in either direction, depending particularly on the shape of the LM curves. If the LM is relatively flat, then an increase in government deficits may stimulate private investment spending through the multiplier and accelerator process. But if the LM curve is vertical or nearly so, then an increase in government deficit spending must draw on a fixed pool of lendable resources, and interest rates will rise to "crowd out" an equivalent amount of private investment spending.

With a near-vertical LM curve at least implicitly in mind, some economists have argued that federal budget deficits should be subtracted from private savings (the sum of business and personal savings) to measure the pool of *national savings* actually available to finance private investment spending. When the level of national savings falls, they argue, either private investment

FIGURE 10.B1   Deficits and Savings

All components of national savings—the sum of business and personal savings, minus the budget deficit—drifted downward in the 1980s.

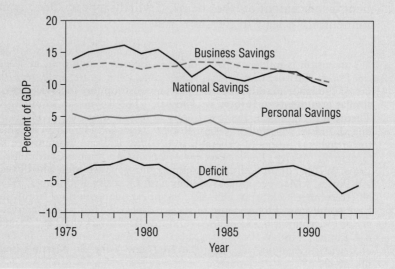

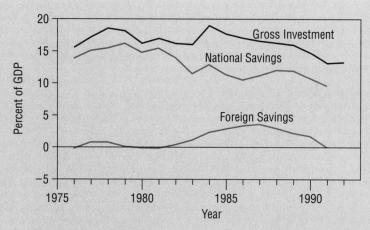

FIGURE 10.B2   National and Foreign Savings

The rise in the current account deficit in the mid-1980s meant a capital inflow that helped sustain gross investment in the United States, despite falling national savings. When growth slowed at the end of the decade, trade came into balance, in part because investment fell. "Foreign savings" is the negative of the current account balance.

must fall or foreign investment in the U.S. economy must rise (which implies, as we see in the next chapter, a deficit in the current account or balance of trade in goods and services).

Figure 10.B1 shows how this measure of national savings fell as a share of gross domestic product (GDP) in the middle 1980s in the United States. By this measure, the budget deficit was absorbing all of personal savings and some of business savings as well.

Some of the consequences are shown in Figure 10.B2, which shows the path of national savings alongside that of the share of investment in GDP. Investment fell in the late 1970s and early 1980s as national savings fell. But it revived in 1983–1984 while national sav-

ings continued to fall. The reason for this is shown in the bottom line on the graph: a rising current account deficit, which corresponded to a capital inflow that financed domestic investment with foreign savings.

The correspondence of a foreign savings inflow to a rising government budget deficit in the 1980s meant that large increases in the budget and trade deficits occurred at the same time. This led some prominent observers, and in particular Chairman Paul Volcker of the Federal Reserve Board, to argue that the two deficits were "twin" deficits, that the budget deficit had caused the trade deficit. Figure 10.B3 shows this relationship in the mid-1980s; it also shows that the trade deficit shrank in the late 1980s

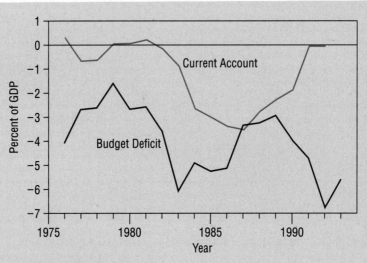

FIGURE 10.B3   The Twin Deficits?

The budget and trade deficits moved together in the early 1980s but in opposite directions at the end of the decade.

as the budget deficit exploded. This tells us that the budget and trade deficits are twins only in an economic expansion characterized by tight money (a vertical LM curve); in a recession with a low interest rate monetary policy, they can go in opposite directions.

FIGURE 10.B4   Deficits and Profits

Some economists believe the rise in inflation-adjusted deficits after 1980 helped to restore profits and so end the recession.

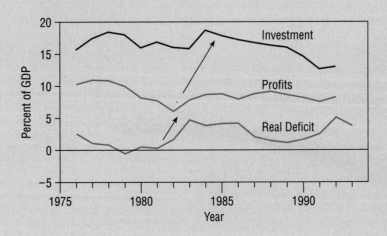

What do economists who do not accept a near-vertical LM curve think? Some of the flavor of the competing argument is shown in Figure 10.B4. The argument rests on the fact that deficit spending by the government *raises* private incomes—particularly corporate profits—since the extra spending or reduced taxes represent additional disposable income to consumers and business. Thus, the rise in the deficit (shown here in inflation-adjusted terms) in 1982–1983 gets direct credit for raising corporate profits and indirect credit for raising the share of investment in GDP—particularly since most business investment is not financed by borrowing out of personal savings but rather directly out of retained corporate profits.

We will not pursue the new Keynesian vision any further at this time, for two reasons. First, you are now pretty much at the frontier: the new Keynesians are only just now articulating their view, and we must all wait to see how they proceed from here. Second, it may be more important at this stage for you, the student, to understand one more alternative theoretical vision. In Chapter 12, we turn to that vision, which is Keynesian but does not rely on general disequilibrium to explain unemployment.

SPECIAL SECTION

A Guide to the Deficit

The federal government of the United States has been in deficit continuously since 1970 (see Figure 10.S1). The annual budget deficit rose above $100 billion dollars in 1982 and has been above $150 billion every year but one since 1983. For the recession year of 1991, the budget deficit exceeded $300 billion dollars for the first time in history, and it remained above $300 billion in 1992.

For most of the past decade, and even in the late 1970s when the actual deficit was only a fraction of what it is today, the budget deficit has held a role of great, even mythic importance in our public discussions. Many observers have feared the worst. The most eloquent among them, Benjamin Friedman of Harvard University, has written an elegant and austere treatise, *Day of Reckoning*, which begins with these words:

> What can you say to a man on a binge who asks why it matters? Flush with cash from

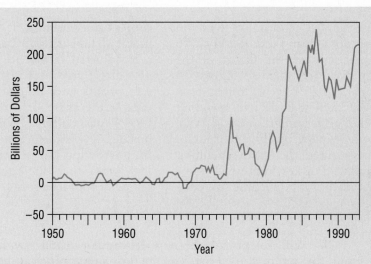

FIGURE 10.S1   U.S. Budget Deficit

liquidating his modest investment portfolio and from taking out a second mortgage on
the inflated value of his house,
he can seemingly spend without limit. The vacation cruise
his family has dreamed about
for years, the foreign sports
car he has always wanted, new
designer clothes for his wife
and even his children, meals in
all the most expensive restaurants—life is wonderful. What
difference does it make if he
has to pay some interest? If
necessary, next year he can sell
his house for enough to pay
off both mortgages and have
enough left over to buy an
even faster car. What difference does it make whether he
owns a house at all? For the
price of the extra sports car, he
can afford the first year's rent

in the fanciest apartment
building in town. Why
worry?[1]

Friedman goes on to level the following indictment of the budget
deficits incurred under the presi-
dency of Ronald Reagan:

The thesis of this book is that
the radical course upon which
the United States economic
policy was launched in the
1980s violated the basic moral
principle that had bound each
generation of Americans to the
next since the founding of the
republic: that men and women
should work and eat, earn and
spend, both privately and collectively, so that their children
and their children's children
would inherit a better world.
Since 1980 we have broken

with that tradition by pursuing a policy that amounts to living not just in, but for, the present. We are living by running up our debts and selling off our assets. America has thrown itself a party and billed the tab to the future. The costs, which are only beginning to come due, will include a lower standard of living for individual Americans and reduced American influence and importance in world affairs.[2]

But is it really as bad as all that? If the sky were going to fall, why hasn't it done so by now? Robert Eisner of Northwestern University, a recent president of the American Economics Association, offers a sharp and critical dissent from the gloom-and-doom view of deficits. In a book entitled *How Real Is the Federal Deficit?* Eisner writes:

> For most of the American public, debt and deficits are like sin: morally wrong, difficult to avoid, but not easy to keep track of. Our federal deficits have each year been adding huge, $200 billion chunks to the "national debt." The sheer magnitude of that debt, currently [in 1986] approaching $2 trillion, suggests to some the danger of national bankruptcy. . . .
>
> The real story is that federal deficits *can* have great consequences for the economy.

Startling as this may seem, these may be good as well as bad. And deficits can be too small as well as too large. We cannot begin to know the consequences of deficits until we measure them correctly.[3]

In Eisner's view, the fact that government expenditures exceed tax revenues by $200 or $300 billion may be very important—or it may not be. It may have a large effect on interest rates, savings, and investment—or it may not. Everything depends on a bewildering array of other variables, including the rate of inflation, the size of the previously existing public debt, the rate of unemployment and capacity utilization in the economy, and (last but not least) the purposes to which public spending is being put.

In this section, we present the main issues that surround and confound the discussion of the budget deficit and its economic importance (or lack thereof). We provide a guided tour of deficit concepts, discuss the issue of deficit sustainability, and explore how goals for the deficit might reasonably be set. Our discussion relies heavily on Eisner, particularly in the next two subsections.

Nominal and Real Deficits

The budget deficit is, of course, nothing more than the difference between the expenditures of government and the tax revenues that government receives. In the conventional notation where G_t is government spending this year, T_t is taxes this year, and D_t is the deficit this year:

$$D_t = G_t - T_t$$

Since all three of these variables are measured in current, or nominal, dollars, we will call this the *nominal deficit*.

As the subscripts tell us, the deficit itself is a time-limited concept. This year's deficit may be a record, and next year's budget could be balanced. But does that mean that this year's record deficit has no effects next year? Evidently not—many commentators speak of the effects of the deficit not only this year and next but on our children and grandchildren.

The link between deficits today and their consequences in the future lies in the fact that today's government borrowings, which finance the deficit, generally take the form of interest-bearing bonds that add to the national debt. Thus, if R_t represents the debt at the end of this year,

$$R_t - R_{t-1} = D_t$$

When we consider the effects of the deficit and the debt on the economy, perhaps the most important conceptual question concerns the role played by inflation. To see this role, consider the following proposition, on which all economists are certain to agree irrespective of theoretical persuasion:

If spending and taxes both rise by 10 percent this year and if the rate of inflation in the same year is also 10 percent, all economists of all persuasions would agree that no real changes have occurred, either in fiscal policy itself or in the effects one would expect for the economy as a whole.

And since no real effects have occurred, the increase in real debt imposed by the deficit on the economy should be no greater than it would have been if the inflation had not occurred.

To confirm that, suppose government spending last year was $1 trillion, and tax revenues came to $900 billion, leaving a deficit and increase in the debt of $100 billion, which is added to a previously existing national debt of $2 trillion. If there was no inflation, and we use last year's price level as the base year, then these nominal numbers are also the real numbers and accurately measure the increase in the real value of the debt. The real debt has therefore risen by $100 billion/$2,000 billion, or 5 percent.

Now introduce a yearly inflation rate of 10 percent. In nominal terms, this year's government spending is $1.1 trillion, taxes are $990 billion, and the nominal deficit is $110 billion. Deflating by the rise in the price level since last year's base ($1 + \pi$, where π is the rate of inflation, or 1.1), we have real values of

$$\frac{1{,}100}{1.1} - \frac{990}{1.1} = \frac{110}{1.1} = 100$$

or, in other words, a real situation no different from that in the previous year.

Extending this argument to the relationship between the deficit and the debt, we can see that the *real change* in the debt (the difference between the value of the debt now, expressed in last year's prices, and the value of the debt last year) is equal to the real value of the deficit:

$$\frac{2,110}{1.1} - \frac{2,000}{1} = ?$$

Whoops. The difference in the real value of the debt on the left side is −$81.8 billion, not the same as the +$100 billion in the previous equation. In fact, the real value of the debt seems actually to have fallen, in spite of the rise in the nominal deficit!

How can this be? An answer quickly emerges in the algebraic relationship between changes in the real debt and the value of the real deficit. Let R_t stand for the nominal debt as before, P_t for the value of the price index (with base set arbitrarily in year $t-1$, so that we only have to deflate nominal values in the current year), π for rate of inflation between $t-1$ and t. Thus, R_t/P_t represents the real value of this year's debt, correctly deflated to the prices of year $t-1$. We then have an expression for the stock change in the real debt, or real deficit:

$$\frac{R_t}{P_t} - R_{t-1} = \frac{R_t - P_t R_{t-1}}{P_t}$$

Since $P_t = 1 + \pi$, we can substitute that into our expression on the right side and expand as follows:

$$(\text{Real deficit})_t = \frac{R_t}{P_t} - \frac{R_{t-1}}{P_t} - \frac{\pi R_{t-1}}{P_t}$$

The first two terms are the same, or nearly so, as the mistaken definition of the real deficit we first offered. The key to the mystery lies in the third term, πR_{t-1}. This term represents the *depreciation* of the previously existing national debt. Debt depreciation occurs because inflation makes repayment of that debt less onerous to the government than it otherwise would be. This depreciation, which does not show up at all in official measures of either government spending or taxation, is in effect an inflation tax levied on holders of government bonds, who lose some of their wealth as a result of inflation. It must be subtracted from the measure of the deficit in order to arrive at a correct evaluation of the change in the *real burden* of an increasing nominal national debt.

In our example, the depreciation on the previously existing $2,000 billion debt was $200 billion this year, or $181.81 billion in last year's prices. This was enough to turn our nominal deficit of $100 billion into a *real surplus* of over $81 billion.

We dwell on this example because we believe that the mismeasurement of deficits in countries with high rates of inflation and large national debts is a pervasive real-world problem. In Latin America, where inflation rates are often above 100 percent per year and the internally held national debt may be as large as the annual gross

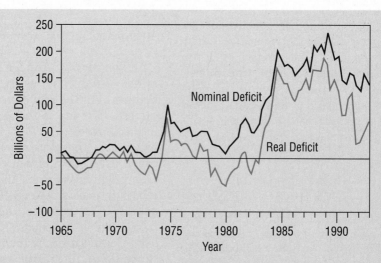

FIGURE 10.S2   Nominal and Real Deficits

Inflation adjustments converted nominal deficits into real surpluses in the late 1970s and greatly reduced the deficit in the late 1980s.

national product, the effects are simply enormous—a Brazil or a Mexico may finance most government expenditure by depreciating old national debt. Even in the United States, where inflation rates are comparatively low, the inflation of the late 1970s was enough to convert an apparent deficit into a real surplus, slowing the economy in a way that almost no one at the time understood. The modest 5 percent inflation of the late 1980s nearly wiped out the $150 billion deficits of that time, before the recession of 1990–1991 sent inflation down and the deficit soaring (see Figure 10.S2).

Does this mean that governments can rely on inflation, and the inflation tax, to keep the deficit from getting out of hand? No, unfortunately not. While bondholders may well be willing (or have no alternative than) to accept a certain depreciation of their holdings, so that the device works at low and moderate rates of inflation, it can quite easily get out of hand. At high rates of inflation, the credit markets are likely to demand extremely high nominal interest rates from the government, with the result that government spending and nominal deficits rise with inflation, offsetting the depreciation on the old debt. High nominal deficits, which reimburse bondholders for the losses that they are incurring on their capital accounts, should not be interpreted as providing a net new stimulus to the real economy.

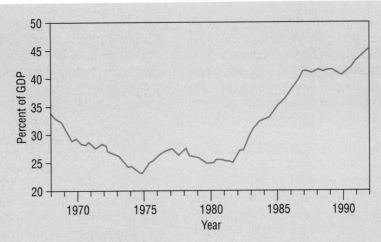

FIGURE 10.S3   **Ratio of Debt to GNP**

The ratio of debt to GNP fell steadily until the recession of 1974. It rose in that recession but then leveled off and fell again until 1982. With the 1982 recession, tax cuts, and military buildup, it rose sharply until it leveled off again in 1987. It has risen again in the latest recession.

Deficits, Debt, and GDP

There is an appropriate and simple way to measure the real burden that high deficits and a rising national debt may impose on future taxpayers (who will have to pay interest to future bondholders) and also to capture the real stimulus of the deficit to the economy: the ratio of the nominal national debt to nominal gross domestic product (GDP) (see Figure 10.S3). This ratio automatically accounts for inflation and the inflation tax, because the price level appears (implicitly) in both numerator and denominator.

Thus, if inflation pushes up nominal dollar GDP more rapidly than the national debt rises, the inflation tax is eating away at the real value of debt. On the other hand, if interest rates and payments keep pace with inflation, the ratio of the debt to GDP will be unaltered in spite of a rising nominal dollar deficit. And if, in a recession or period of Keynesian stimulus, the "burden" of the national debt is actually rising, we can be sure that there is a real increase taking place in the wealth of private bondholders, which may well translate into higher consumption, expenditure, output, and income.

Structural and Cyclical Deficits

So far, we have been concerned with measuring deficits and changes in the debt in ways that avoid distortions imposed by inflation. Planners of fiscal policy make another type of distinction, based not on inflation but on employment and capacity utilization. This distinction concerns causes rather than consequences of the deficit. It particularly tries to separate the part of the deficit caused by deliberate actions of goverment policy, a *structural* component, from a part solely due to the position of the economy in the business cycle, a *cyclical* component.

The easiest way to see the structural/cyclical decomposition is to define the structural deficit as what the actual deficit would be were the economy operating at a full employment level of income (Y_f). Ignoring the effect of economic expenditure on government spending and taking advantage of the fact that tax revenues, T, are the product of the tax rate, t, and the income level, Y, we have

$$SD = G - tY_f$$

and, for the cyclical deficit,

$$CD = D - SD$$

Applying these formulas in a rough way[4] to the nominal deficit for the years 1960 through 1990 shows that the vast bulk of the deficits in that time have been cyclical rather than structural in nature. In fact, we have had very few instances, other than in actual recession years, when fiscal policy sought actively to speed the growth of the economy.

Once again, a word of caution is in order. People—in our experience, both students and professionals who ought to know better—often speak as though the ability to distinguish structural and cyclical components of the deficits can lead directly to policy conclusions. Here are arguments dealing with three common fallacies:

1. Fallacy: Periods of high structural deficits are times when fiscal policy is too stimulative. Not true. The late 1970s were such a period, as unemployment was low. But because of the rising inflation tax, the real deficit was actually in surplus in those years, and the net effect of fiscal policy was contractionary.

2. Fallacy: The structural budget should always be balanced, allowing for changes in the actual deficit to reflect the cyclical position of the economy. Not true. In a time of high unemployment, such as 1981–1982, it may be entirely appropriate to lower tax rates or raise discretionary spending and so raise the structural deficit, even though the cyclical deficit is already very large. These actions will have the effect of ending the recession more rapidly, which may be desirable policy.

3. Fallacy: Changes in discretionary policies, such as in G or t, affect only the structural, not the cyclical, element of the deficit. Not true. To see this, define Y_g as the difference (or gap) between the actual level of income Y and the full employment level Y_f. Note that

$$CD = D - SD$$
$$= (G - tY) - (G - tY_f)$$
$$= tY_g$$

The cyclical deficit is thus nothing more than a simple function of the income gap. Cutting tax rates in a recession raises the structural deficit but actually reduces the cyclical deficit.

Because of these common misperceptions and pitfalls, we do not share the enthusiasm of many who work on budget issues for the structural/cyclical dichotomy. Understanding it, however, is important, for it remains in very widespread use.

Sustainable Deficits

When we turn next from definitions and measurement to the question of what deficits do to the economy, we move onto very murky and hotly contested terrain. Rather than providing a comprehensive survey of results, we will suggest three broad generalizations consistent with most of the reputable empirical work we know of.

First, in principle, deficits can cause inflation, but it is not generally true that they actually do so. Since most deficits are cyclical—incurred when the economy is in recession and inflationary pressures are low and falling—this can hardly be a surprise. Even large, measured structural deficits may not be inflationary if they occur when unemployment is high or result from a prior inflationary process that pushes up interest payments on the national debt while not counting the depreciation of the national debt that offsets it.

Second, deficits do tend to stimulate economic growth. A weak form of this stimulus occurs when tax collections fall. In a progressive tax system, effective tax rates fall as a result of falling output and rising unemployment in a recession. A stronger form of stimulus occurs when government policies deliberately raise spending and cut tax rates. We credit the recoveries from the deep recessions of 1974–1975 and 1981–1982 to the strongly expansionary fiscal policies adopted at those times. And it appears that deficits do not displace private investment; rather (as we would expect on theoretical grounds), they tend to raise profitability and, therefore, to stimulate rather than restrict private investment.

Third, properly measured deficits do appear to have some effect on interest rates when all other variables are controlled for and the deficit measures are properly adjusted for inflation. But this effect is quite small. In the mid-1980s, for example, careful estimates indicated that even the very large deficits of those years could not be charged with more than two points of the then exorbitantly high interest rates; most of the high interest rates were due to the deliberate actions of the Federal Reserve.

Of course, a deeper anxiety

underlies many objections to high deficits. If the government is borrowing too much today, people worry about whether it will continue to be able to borrow in the future. "Is the country going bankrupt?" appears to be the unstated question and deep concern of many. It is certainly the clear message of Benjamin Friedman's broadside quoted at the beginning of this special section.

In the early 1980s, Olivier Blanchard (then of Harvard, now at MIT) devised a simple framework for the analysis of this question. Suppose that G_0 is the minimum value that government spending (not including interest payments on the debt) can take; any value of G lower than G_0 would entail so much social upheaval that it is excluded for political reasons. Suppose again, for similar reasons that T^0 is the maximum feasible level of taxes T. Then we have the following expression for the *largest feasible primary surplus* (surplus excluding interest payments):

$$LFPS = -(G_0 - T^0) = T^0 - G_0$$

Now suppose that the total existing national debt is given by D and the real rate of interest on that debt is given by r. rD is therefore the real burden of interest due on the existing debt. In that case, Blanchard argued, the debt may be considered unsustainably large when

$$rD > LFPS$$

For, if the interest due on the existing debt exceeds the largest possible amount by which the noninterest deficit can be reduced, then the debt itself necessarily must grow. And since this condition holds for all future periods, the debt will grow indefinitely, without ever being reduced or repaid. In that case, the burden of interest due on the debt eventually must exceed the capacity of the debtor, and default is inevitable. Creditors, knowing this, will therefore refuse to lend, and the debt becomes unsustainable because it cannot be financed.

As Blanchard was first to acknowledge, this little piece of analysis is too simple in many ways. Nevertheless, it can provide a revealing benchmark by which to make an initial rough judgment as to the maximum sustainable national debt (MSD) of any country, which is readily derived from the preceding equation:

$$MSD = \frac{LFPS}{r}$$

To put some rough (and admittedly arbitrary) numerical bones on this proposition, consider that in 1988 (the last year before the onset of economic stagnation, which raised the budget deficit) the nominal federal budget deficit of the United States was on the order of $155 billion. Net interest payments were about $159 billion, accounting for all of the actual deficit, so that the actual primary surplus was about $4 billion. If one allows that there could have been, at most, a combination of higher taxes and smaller government spending in that year totaling $150 billion and that the real long-term interest rate was on the order of 3 percent, then the maximum sustainable debt of the United States in 1988 was

$$\frac{\$150 \text{ billion}}{0.03} = \$5 \text{ trillion}$$

This is comfortably above the actual debt of $2 trillion, which may explain why the United States was not insolvent in 1988.

Objectives for the Deficit

A range of possible policy rules have been advanced, or in some cases might have been advanced, to govern the federal budget deficit. The brief comments here will show that we are not particularly enamored of hard-and-fast rules in this arena.

1. *Balance the budget.* Surely the oldest and most widely believed of all economic prescriptions, this was the embodiment of the "Treasury View" in Keynes's day and is the subject of daily preaching of the financially righteous in our own time. In our view, there is nothing wrong with government borrowing, within limits and with reason, for the purposes of capital improvement and economic stabilization. We accept the evidence of several generations that federal budget deficits help renew growth in times of recession. Therefore, we reject the general rule that the federal budget should be balanced under all circumstances, and we oppose all constitutional amendments and budget statutes (such as the Gramm-Rudman-Hollings law) that attempt to force the government toward budget balance on a fixed timetable, disrupting needed government services or imposing burdensome new taxes in order to get there.

2. *Balance the budget over the business cycle.* For many years, the Committee for Economic Development (CED), a group of progressive U.S. businesses, has advocated setting fiscal policy so that deficits in recessions were offset by surpluses in times of full employment. By educating the business community, the CED has done much over the years to legitimize budget deficits that occur in times of economic weakness. It has, of course, been far less successful in bringing about surpluses in times of full employment.

While a rule that the budget should be balanced over the cycle would be better than a naive policy of "budget balance at all times," such a rule is still fundamentally unrealistic. The notion that the budget should be balanced "on average" implies that the total public debt should not grow over time. We disagree. We see no reason why the infrastructure and service obligations of the government should not grow as the economy grows and, therefore, no reason why the national debt cannot properly grow as well. This implies larger deficits on average than surpluses, even over the business cycle.

3. *Balance the high-employment budget*, or *balance the high employment budget over the cycle*. This amounts to arguing that the structural deficit should be held at zero, at all times (in the first alternative) or on average over the business cycle (in the second), allowing only deficits that reflect the gap between actual and full employment. Thus, a rising national debt overall (the sum of the structural and cyclical deficits) would be permitted during periods when the economy persisted at less than full employment.

Once again, these positions represent improvement. However, we have already rejected the idea that the structural deficit should ideally be held at zero. As argued in an earlier section, it is entirely proper to expand the structural deficit when the economy needs a stimulus toward full employment.

A rule that the structural budget should be balanced over the cycle would allow for countercyclical increases in structural deficits, which is nice. But this proposal merely collapses into the previous one, that the whole budget should be balanced over the cycle, once one allows the definition of whether one is in the top or the bottom part of the cycle to be the same definition that governs whether one is at, above, or below high employment. By this rule, when the economy is above the high-employment norms both the structural and cyclical budgets must be in surplus, the former by policy mandate and the latter by the simple fact that the income gap will be negative. If the two parts are in surplus, then so must be the whole.

4. *Balance the price-adjusted high-employment budget over the cycle*. None of the preceding formulas take account of the rising real tax collections caused by inflation. All may therefore be criticized for failing to provide fiscal stability in inflationary times. When inflation rises, fiscal policy under any of the above rules would turn sharply contractionary in real terms, whether or not such a turn were justified by a condition of excess demand.

A way around this problem is to mandate that the price-adjusted (or real) high-employment budget be balanced over the business cycle. This would permit nominal deficits to rise and fall with inflation. Such movements may have little effect on the real posture of fiscal policy, because the inflation that causes them also engenders uncounted depreciation of the debt. At the same time, this policy would permit strong stimulus in recessions and require fiscal stringency in booms (whether they were inflationary or not).

Although this would be an improvement, it does not answer our basic objection to the previous formula. If balancing the structural budget over the cycle does not necessarily make sense, neither does balancing an inflation-adjusted structural deficit.

In the end, we urge the rejection of all hard-and-fast fiscal policy rules. In their stead, we would offer some basic principles. First, in normal times, the government properly should borrow to finance capital improvements and should tax to cover operating expenses. Second, borrowing to stabilize and stimulate the economy is appropriate when there is less than full employment. There is no necessity that debt so incurred be retired during years of high employment.

Can deficits be too large? Absolutely. A government can fail to operate an effective tax system. It can borrow for operating expenses at high employment and allow the share of interest payments in its expenditures to rise promiscuously without taking steps to generate a corresponding growth in its ability to pay. Worse still, it can deliberately cause a recession and use the rise in the deficit, plus deficit-increasing discretionary actions such as tax cuts, merely to restore production to where it was before the recession. When governments do these things, they risk financial ruin.

Of course, as Benjamin Friedman has argued, these were the things done by the Reagan administration. Though many economists agree that they were bad, we do not believe, on the evidence we have seen, that they were bad enough to bring the United States to the verge of financial ruin.

---

[1] Benjamin Friedman, *Day of Reckoning* (New York: Random House, 1988), pp. 3–4.
[2] Ibid.
[3] Robert Eisner, *How Real Is the Federal Deficit?* (New York: Free Press of Macmillan, 1986), pp. 1, 2.
[4] For example, we make no effort here to disentangle possible shifts in the *full employment* rate of unemployment.

SUMMARY

New Keynesian economics is a response to new classical economics. In general, new Keynesians accept the monetarist and rational expectations propositions of the new classical school, but they reject the market clearing doctrine. They take special issue with the assumption of perfect price flexibility, holding that unemployment can persist because prices do not adjust quickly enough. They also posit that disequilibrium is the usual state of economic affairs, because transactions are made before prices adjust. Persistent disequilibrium in the labor market leads to a general disequilibrium in the Walrasian sense.

A large part of the new Keynesians' energy has been devoted to giving rational explanations for sticky wages. They include: (1) worker resistance to reductions in nominal wages that would change their relative wage; (2) the efficiency wage hypothesis, under which employers pay a premium to prevent shirking; (3) social forces outside the sphere of economics that prevent quick adjustment; (4) the implicit contracts argument that employers pay higher-than-equilibrium wages in return for offering jobs with a higher risk of unemployment; (5) the imperfect indexation of wages in the face of inflation; (6) costliness of changing wages, due to transactions costs.

Recently, new Keynesians have focused attention on price stickiness in general, using the theory of menu costs advanced by Stiglitz. This theory is supported in its weak form by the high cost of changing prices; its stronger form relies on game theory, when the repercussions of an individual price change cannot be predicted with any certainty. This uncertainty promotes maintaining current prices rather than risking a ruinous outbreak of price warfare. The menu cost theories do not predict large-scale price stickiness. Rather, the sum effect of many markets slightly out of equilibrium is a large disequilibrium in the labor market.

The policy agenda of the new Keynesians is twofold. For disequilibrium due to rigidities in real wages and prices, they advocate the elimination of structural rigidities. If the disequilibrium is due to nominal rigidities (traditional wage stickiness, however caused), then they advocate an activist aggregate demand policy.

The IS-LM analysis may be modified to sketch the results of disequilibrium in the macroeconomy. Since, in the new Keynesian analysis, real output and employment are determined in the labor market, the aggregate price level is substituted for the real income level on the horizontal axis of the IS and LM curves. The IS curve is the schedule of all interest rate and price pairs that clear the goods market. The LM curve is the schedule of interest rates and prices consistent with equilibrium in the money market. The intersection of these curves is still the center of gravity of the system if perfect information and price flexibility hold. But if any disequilibrium trades are made, then general equilibrium is impossible to reach. By positing sluggish interest rate and price adjustments, various disequilibrium situations may be described. In fact, a new Keynesian theory of business cycles can be mapped out as the economy moves counterclockwise around the IS-LM axes.

New Keynesians explain unemployment with our old friend, sticky nominal wages that cannot be lowered to the classical equilibrium. The disequilibrium position in the labor market then acts on the money and goods markets, to create a pseudoequilibrium where prices are lower than in the true equilibrium. A distinction between notional and effective schedules is particularly useful for the general model of the new Keynesians, in which price rigidity in any market leads to quantity rationing. The restrictions on quantity are then carried over to other markets, leading to lower economic activity elsewhere. These sorts of disequilibrium may be remedied, in the new Keynesian view, with aggregate demand policies that take up the slack caused by the quantity restrictions.

Review Questions

1. New Keynesians generally accept rational expectations. But are their six major explanations for sticky wages consistent with rational expectations?

2. Explain how disequilibrium in a goods market can cause disequilibrium in the labor market.

3. Describe how the difference between real and nominal wage stickiness has an effect on the policy prescription offered by the new Keynesians.

4. A general observation is that prices are more flexible upward than they are downward. Do the new Keynesians explain this phenomenon satisfactorily? Explain your answer.

5. Why is the IS-LM analysis sometimes presented in terms of interest rates and prices instead of interest rates and real income? Does this imply a disinterest in issues of employment and unemployment? Explain.

6. Explain how the pseudoequilibrium arrived at in the new Keynesian model differs from a true equilibrium.

Review Problems

1. Using a diagram like the one in Figure 10.1 and a diagram showing the labor market, chart the effects of an increase in labor productivity. Describe these effects.

2. Using the same sort of diagrams as in problem 1, show the effect of an increase in the money supply. Explain all effects (and noneffects). How is this similar to the new classical argument?

3. For each of the four partitions in Figure 10.4, find a period in economic history that corresponds. For each of these periods, cite some economic aggregates that support your assessment.

4. Describe a pseudoequilibrium analogous to that in Figure 10.6, where the price level would be too high. Draw a graph showing the situation.

5. Analyze the labor market in terms of notional and effective demand for a situation where there is excess demand in the commodity market. How is the IS-LM analysis affected?

6. Analyze diagrammatically the effect of an aggregate demand policy that acts on the disequilibrium cited in problem 5.

Suggested Readings

James Tobin, *Asset Accumulation and Economic Activity* (Chicago: The University of Chicago Press, 1980).

Olivier Blanchard and Stanley Fischer, *Lectures on Macroeconomics* (Cambridge: MIT Press, 1989).

Robert M. Solow, "On Theories of Unemployment," *American Economic Review,* March 1980.

James L. Butkiewicz et. al. (eds.), *Keynes' Economic Legacy: Contemporary Economic Theories* (New York: Praeger Publishers, 1986).

John Kenneth Galbraith, *American Capitalism: The Concept of Countervailing Power* (Boston: Houghton Mifflin, 1952).

A. A. Berle and Gardiner C. Means, *The Modern Corporation and Private Property* (New York: Harcourt Brace & World, 1968).

John Hicks, *The Crisis in Keynesian Economics* (Oxford: Basil Blackwell, 1974).

Donald Patinkin, *Money, Interest and Prices* (New York: Harper & Row, 1965).

Robert Barro and Herschel Grossman, *Money, Employment and Inflation* (Cambridge: Cambridge University Press, 1976).

Edmond Malinvaud, *The Theory of Unemployment Reconsidered* (Oxford: Basil Blackwell, 1977).

Benjamin Friedman, *Day of Reckoning* (New York: Random House, 1988).

Robert Eisner, *How Real is the Federal Deficit?* (New York: Free Press of MacMillan, 1986).

Chapter 11

THE MACROECONOMICS

OF OPEN ECONOMIES

Looking Forward

In this chapter, we turn our attention to world trade. For convenience and continuity, we restrict ourselves to a model built upon
the Keynesian IS-LM analysis. Exchange rates and the balance of
trade can be introduced into this framework by means of an upward-sloping BP schedule. With this framework we can analyze
the simple effects of expansionary or contractionary monetary and
fiscal policies, as well as the problems of capital flow and foreign
reserve flows under fixed exchange rates.

The chapter includes an important special section on North-
South models, a growing and increasingly vital field. These
models briefly introduce the problems of modeling multiple economies simultaneously, and they provide some elementary explanations for the persistence of inequality across countries in the
world.

The chapter is structured with these questions in mind:

- How can foreign trade be incorporated into a simple multiplier
  model of equilibrium income?
- How can a variable exchange rate be used to reconcile internal
  equilibrium and external balance?
- How are flows of capital, as well as flows of goods, accounted
  for in our model?
- What effects does a floating exchange rate system have, and
  how do they compare with a system of fixed exchange rates?

So far, this text has dealt exclusively with the macroeconomics of economies *closed* to foreign trade and to flows of payments across frontiers. In this chapter, the discussion broadens to the macroeconomics of *open* economies, which are economies of countries whose citizens participate with citizens of other countries in trade and in the buying and selling of assets.[1] In a series of steps, we modify the models presented earlier to show how they can incorporate the *external sector*.

We begin with a simple modification of the consumption multiplier model. The closed-economy version of this model starts with the familiar national income identity:

$$(11.1) \qquad\qquad Y = C + I + G$$

where Y is national expenditure, C is consumption expenditure, I is investment expenditure, and G is government expenditure. Deflating each term by a price index yields an equivalent expression in constant dollar, inflation-adjusted values:

$$(11.1') \qquad\qquad y = c + i + g$$

Equations (11.1) and (11.1') are applicable to any closed economy.

OPEN ECONOMIES

For the open economy, in its most spare form, real aggregate demand can be expressed as

$$(11.2) \qquad\qquad y = (c + i + g) + (x - m)$$

The variable x represents export demand, or foreigners' expenditures to buy goods produced in the home economy; m represents import demand, or the expenditures of domestic residents on goods produced abroad. The bracketed difference between x and m also is referred to as *net exports* or the *trade balance* or the *current account balance*. If x exceeds m, or exports exceed imports, then the home economy is running a *trade surplus* or a *surplus on current account*. When the imports exceed exports, then the home economy is running a *trade deficit* or a *deficit on current account*.

There is a clear dichotomy in equation (11.2) between internal, or domestic, expenditure flows $(c + i + g)$ and *external*, or *foreign sector*,

[1] General references for material in this chapter include Graham Bird, *International Macroeconomics: Theory, Policy and Applications* (Basingstoke: Macmillan, 1987); William Scarth, *Macroeconomics: An Introduction to Advanced Methods* (Toronto: Harcourt Brace Jovanovich, 1988); Richard T. Froyen, *Macroeconomics: Theories and Policies* (New York: Macmillan, 1983), pp. 507–519; Rudiger Dornbusch, *Open Economy Macroeconomics* (New York: Basic Books, 1984).

expenditure flows $(x - m)$. If the economy experiences a surplus on current account (if $x > m$), then it also experiences a net addition to the demand for home goods. On the other hand, if $x < m$, an economy incurring a current account deficit will experience a net reduction in aggregate demand, as compared with conditions when the economy is closed to foreign trade.

A third possibility is for trade balance, so that exports and imports exactly offset one another. In this case, when $x = m$, both internal and external balance can hold simultaneously. Before exploring this possibility in greater detail, let us first consider cases where exports and imports do not equalize—so that the economy in question has either a surplus or deficit on current account.

To fix the contrast between the closed and open economy, we use very simple, uncluttered specifications for each of the components of aggregate demand:

$$c = \bar{c} + \gamma y$$

$$i = \bar{i}$$

(11.3) $$g = \bar{g}$$

$$x = \bar{x}$$

$$m = \bar{m} + \mu y$$

Investment demand (i), government spending (g), and export demand (x) all are treated here as autonomous expenditures, fixed for the purposes of the model and not explained by it. This is, of course, a simplification. Export demand is likely to depend on the level of real income in the rest of the world, but it cannot depend, at least not in any straightforward way, on the domestic level of income or output; hence, $x = \bar{x}$.

The Propensity to Import

However, while both consumption and import demand have an autonomous or exogenous component ($\bar{c}$ and $\bar{m}$, respectively), each also possesses an induced or endogenous component (γy and μy). This reflects the fact that a part of both consumption and import demand is sensitive to changes in the level of home income. The more people produce and spend, the more they will consume of both home and foreign goods. The proportions depend upon the *propensity to consume*, γ, and the *propensity to import*, μ.

Two potential explanations can account for the dependence of import demand on the level of home income. One explanation is consumption driven: consumers buy more finished domestic and foreign goods, such as cameras and videocassette recorders, as home income rises. A second explanation is production driven: the imported goods are intermediate inputs, such as machinery and chemicals, required in producing the higher level of national output. Higher levels of income induce a greater volume of imports because more of such goods are needed immediately for home production and only indirectly for home consumption. In either case, the effect is the same: higher home output and income require a higher level of imports.

EQUILIBRIUM INCOME IN THE OPEN ECONOMY

We can now determine the equilibrium value of real national income in the open economy model just specified. If we substitute the relations in (11.3) into equation (11.2) we obtain

(11.4)
$$y = \bar{c} + \gamma y + \bar{i} + \bar{g} + \bar{x} - \bar{m} - \mu y$$

The autonomous components of domestic spending, $\bar{c}$, $\bar{i}$, and $\bar{g}$, can be summed and set equal to the term H, which represents all autonomous domestic demand for home produce. Therefore, (11.4) can be rewritten in simpler form as

(11.5)
$$y = \bar{H} + (\gamma - \mu)y + (\bar{x} - \bar{m})$$

Solving equation (11.5) for the value of y yields

(11.6)
$$y^\star = \frac{1}{1 - \gamma + \mu} [\bar{H} + (\bar{x} - \bar{m})]$$

This is an equilibrium value of y, because (11.6) represents the implicit condition that aggregate demand matches aggregate supply.

The expression under (11.6) is the equilibrium value for real national output or income in a simple open macroeconomy. Indeed, the closed economy can be treated as a special case of the expression under (11.6): in the closed economy, where foreign trade is entirely absent, the terms $\bar{x}$, $\bar{m}$, and μ will all be absent, so that (11.6) will compress to

(11.7)
$$y^\star = \frac{1}{1 - \gamma} \bar{H}$$

If we compare equations (11.6) and (11.7), it should be obvious that the magnitude of the multiplier will be *reduced* by the introduction of the parameter μ, the propensity to import. The import propensity, like the savings propensity out of home income, is a leakage from the stream of expenditure. It therefore reduces the expansionary effects of the autonomous demands for domestic goods. If, for example, the propensity to consume is 80 percent ($\gamma = 0.8$), the multiplier in the closed economy case $(1/[1 - \gamma])$ will be 5. With the same value for the propensity to consume and an import propensity of 10 percent ($\mu = 0.1$), the multiplier in the open economy case $(1/[1 - \gamma + \mu])$ will be smaller, approximately 3.3.

There is a further difference between closed and open economies. In the closed economy, the only autonomous expenditures are domestic, captured here by the term $\bar{H}$. But the open economy has an additional element of autonomous expenditures, the difference between exports (all of which are autonomous) and the autonomous component of imports. Total autonomous expenditures will increase if $\bar{x}$ exceeds $\bar{m}$, will stay unchanged if $\bar{x}$ equals $\bar{m}$, and will decrease if $\bar{x}$ is less than $\bar{m}$. The last case would have to be quite rare. For $\bar{x}$ to be less than $\bar{m}$, the autonomous component of imports would have to be sufficiently large that the current account would *always* be in deficit, regardless of the level of income or the magnitude of the propensity to import.

BALANCE OF TRADE

Assuming that $\bar{x} > \bar{m}$, Figure 11.1 depicts the relationship between national income and the balance of trade. The balance of payments on current account is represented along the vertical axis, and the level of real national income is represented along the horizontal axis.

The line segment from C to y^b in the upper area of the diagram shows the trade balance in surplus. The surplus diminishes as income increases, raising the total volume of imports relative to exports. When

FIGURE 11.1   National Income and the Balance of Trade

The balance of trade on current account falls as the level of national income rises.

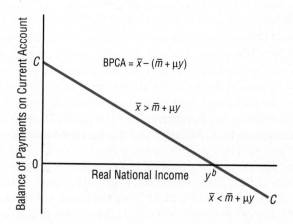

national income reaches the level y^b, the current account clears, or total exports and imports equalize. At higher levels of national income, the trade balance will be in deficit.

This model, so far, provides no way for external and internal balance to be achieved at the same time. Indeed, that such dual balance could be achieved is most unlikely. If trade is balanced, the internal sector will likely be out of balance; correspondingly, if income is at levels dictated by the conditions of internal balance, the foreign trade sector is likely to be either in surplus or in deficit.

To see this, consider the case where the trade balance has cleared (export and import volumes are exactly offsetting). Indeed, we may construct an argument that producers in the foreign sector will behave in such a way as to cause national income to adjust to the level, y^b, consistent with balanced trade. Such a scenario may be based upon rule-of-thumb adaptation by exporters to inventory changes. Suppose that, when the trade balance is in surplus, exporters find their inventories being run down at a faster than normal rate. This can prompt them to increase production, thereby pushing up output (and income) until import demand has risen to match export demand. When the current account is in a deficit position, exporters may find their inventories accumulating at a faster than normal rate and might take that as a signal to cut back on production. As their production declines, national output (and income) falls, thereby reducing import demand until it matches the volume of export demand.

This mechanism, slightly artificial though it is, will drive the foreign trade sector into equilibrium, such that $\bar{x} = m$. Since m has an autonomous component $\bar{m}$ and an endogenous component μy, this implies that $\bar{x} = \bar{m} + \mu y$, which gives a determinate value of national income at which trade is balanced. To be precise, when exports and imports equalize, the level of national income must be

(11.8) $$y^b = \frac{\bar{x} - \bar{m}}{\mu}$$

As (11.8) shows, the level of real national income compatible with balanced trade is the ratio of the gap between exports and the autonomous part of import demand to the propensity to import. (Indeed, the term $1/\mu$ can be described as the *balanced trade multiplier*.) y^b is the level of real national income that preserves *external* balance in an open economy.

So what is the condition for internal balance in this economy? If the foreign sector is in balance, the domestic economy will be qualitatively no different from a closed economy. Hence, the level of real national income that preserves *internal* balance (incomes earned equal to incomes spent) will be $y^\star$ in equation (11.7). But it would only be a matter of sheer coincidence if y^b and $y^\star$ took the same value, since each depends on entirely different parameters and there is no reason to believe that those parameters are connected in a way that will necessarily produce such a result. Hence, the conclusion: if income is the only variable that adjusts in an open economy, internal and external balance will not hold simultaneously.

If national income is at the level dictated by equation (11.7), $y^\star$, then external balance will not occur. If national income is at the level dictated by equation (11.8), y^b, then internal balance fails. From the standpoint of elementary algebra, we have two equations—(11.7) and (11.8)—to satisfy but only one unknown, y, to solve both of them.

EXCHANGE RATE

Economists traditionally have not been comfortable with arguments that lead to the conclusion that an economy can be beset by a fundamental and persistent disequilibrium. Even Keynes, who sought to present a theory of unemployment and underemployment crises, did so[2] from the standpoint of equilibrium rather than disequilibrium. So what can we do?

The dichotomy between balance in the external sector and imbalance in the internal sector, or vice versa, can be overcome if an additional unknown or variable is introduced into our system of equations. The variable customarily introduced is the *exchange rate*.

The exchange rate comes on the scene with the recognition that there are many different national currencies in the world—as many as there are countries. Each can be exchanged at some price for other nations' currencies. The price at which such bilateral currency transfers take place is known as the exchange rate.

Let us use the symbol e to represent the exchange rate, the foreign currency price measured in home currency, and treat the United States as the home country and Trinidad and Tobago as the foreign country. If \$1U.S. is equivalent in international markets to \$4TT, then the exchange rate, e, from the U.S. perspective is 1/4. This ratio is the amount of home currency that must be given up per unit of foreign currency.

The exchange rate affects the trade balance by converting domestic prices into foreign currency prices. Suppose, for instance, a U.S. importer is considering buying raw sugar grown in Jamaica or in Trinidad and Tobago. Suppose also that sugar is priced at \$180 per ton in Jamaican dollars and at \$120 per ton in Trinidad and Tobago dollars. If the exchange rates stand at 1/6 between U.S. dollars and Jamaican dollars and at 1/4 between U.S. dollars and Trinidad and Tobago dollars, then the importer would be faced with an identical \$30U.S. per ton price for

[2] In J. M. Keynes, *The General Theory of Employment, Interest and Money* (London: Macmillan, 1936).

sugar, regardless of the source. In the absence of any differences in quality or transport costs, the U.S. importer should be indifferent between either island's raw sugar.

Appreciations and Depreciations

If the Jamaican and the Trinidad and Tobago currency prices stay the same but (for whatever reason) the exchange rate between U.S. and Jamaican currency changes to 1/5, then the U.S. importer would have to pay $36U.S. per ton of Jamaican sugar and presumably would switch exclusively to Trinidad and Tobago sugar.

The rise in the U.S.-Jamaican exchange rate from 1/6 to 1/5 is an example of *depreciation* (or *devaluation*) in the home currency (in this case, U.S. dollars). If the exchange rate falls, an *appreciation* (or *revaluation*) in the home currency takes place. It will take more U.S. dollars ($1.20) to obtain six Jamaican dollars after the exchange rate has risen from 1/6 to 1/5. The U.S. dollar, therefore, has declined in value relative to the Jamaican dollar. But given unchanged Jamaican currency prices for their exports, prices for Jamaican-made goods will have gone up in U.S. currency, presumably leading to a decline in U.S. import demand for those goods.

Simultaneously, goods produced in the United States at unchanged U.S. dollar prices will be cheaper if purchased by holders of Jamaican currency. Jamaican import demand for U.S. exports should rise after the U.S. currency depreciates.

This example leads to the following generalization. When e, the exchange rate, increases—when the home currency depreciates—imports become more costly for home buyers, so import demand falls. Exports become less costly for foreign buyers, so export demand increases. Of course, if e, the exchange rate, falls—if the home currency appreciates—the opposite chain of events takes place. On this basis, we can alter our aggregate export and import demand functions to make both of them depend upon variations in the exchange rate:

$$x = x(e)$$
$$x'(e) > 0$$

and

$$m = m(y, e)$$
$$m'(y) > 0 \qquad m'(e) < 0$$

Export demand will rise with home currency depreciations, or increases in e. Import demand will fall with home currency depreciation, or increases in e, while continuing to rise and fall with rises and falls in national income.

Now, if we link movements in e to the relative demand and supply for home versus foreign currency, which we can do through the transactions requirements for trade, we are able to construct a model that can achieve both internal and external balance simultaneously. If export demand increases relative to import demand, foreigners will need more home country currency to buy home country goods. Their increased demand for home currency will lead to an improved relative value for home currency, putting downward pressure on e. This downward pressure corresponds to an appreciation of the home currency.

If import demand increases relative to export demand, domestic nationals will need more foreign currency to buy goods made abroad; they will seek to convert home currency into foreign currency to make their purchases. This should lead to a decline in the relative value of home currency, a depreciation, which is measured as an upward movement of the exchange rate.

We can conclude that when export demand is greater than import demand—when there is a surplus on current account—e will fall; an excess demand for home currency in the international currency market leads to an appreciation in its value. When export demand is less than import demand—when there is a deficit on current account—then e will rise; an excess demand for foreign currency in the international currency market leads to a depreciation in the value of home currency. Only when $x(e) = m(y,e)$ and there is a balance in foreign trade will the exchange rate stabilize, since there will be no excess demand for either currency.

EXCHANGE RATE AND INCOME EQUILIBRATION

We can now treat the exchange rate as the relative price that adjusts to bring about payments balance on current account. When outpayment of U.S. dollars (for example, to support import demand) is matched exactly by the inpayment of U.S. dollars to support foreigners' demand for U.S. exports, the exchange rate will have stabilized at an equilibrium value $e = e^\star$.

The following open economy model permits internal and external balance to occur simultaneously:

$$BPCA = x(e^\star) - m(y^\star, e^\star) = 0$$

$$y^\star = \left(\frac{1}{1-\gamma}\right)\bar{H}$$

Because trade balances, the domestic economy behaves like a closed economy. Internal balance now determines the equilibrium level of national income, $y^\star$. Given $y^\star$, the exchange rate adjusts to bring about external balance—to equate export and import demand.

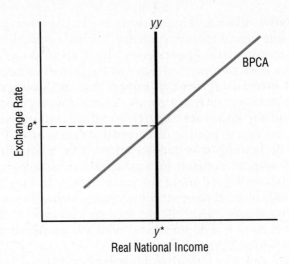

FIGURE 11.2   The Current Account and the Exchange Rate

As national income increases, a depreciation of the exchange rate (shown here as an increase in the value of *e*) is required in order to keep exports and imports in balance.

This model with two equations and two variables can easily be displayed, as in Figure 11.2. The curve *BPCA* is a set of all combinations of real national income and exchange rates consistent with balanced trade. Moving from left to right, as home income increases, import demand increases relative to export demand. To maintain equality between exports and imports, a higher exchange rate or a depreciation in the value of home currency is required. Therefore, the curve *BPCA* is positively sloped on a graph defined by *e* on the Y-axis and *y* on the X-axis.

The equilibrium level of real national income, $y^\star$, is determined directly from the ordinary consumption multiplier and the volume of autonomous domestic spending. That level appears as the vertical locus $yy^\star$ in Figure 11.2.

Plainly, once the exchange rate is introduced as a price that brings about completely balanced trade, the internal sector is insulated from the external sector. Domestic macropolicy measures, such as increased government spending, will have exactly the same effect in an open economy with balanced trade as in a closed economy. The key is faith in the power of exchange rate movements to foster alignment of export and import demand.

This faith will not, we fear, last very long. In the next section, the introduction of international capital markets into our model forces us to modify the idea that the exchange rate can always be relied on to balance exports and imports.

THE CAPITAL ACCOUNT

The focus so far has been on the balance of payments on current account. But the overall balance of payments also includes what is known as the *capital account*. Domestic nationals may buy foreign currency simply in order to buy foreign goods (as importers), but they may also seek foreign currency in order to purchase foreign assets. Such assets could range from foreign bank deposits to real estate to stocks and bonds; by purchasing them, domestic investors are able to seek out opportunities that may not be available at home and to diversify their portfolios as protection against various forms of investment risk. Similarly, foreign citizens may purchase home currency to buy domestic goods (which then become exports) or to buy assets in the home country.

When the level of asset acquisition in the home country by foreigners exceeds the level of asset acquisition abroad by domestic nationals, inpayments of home currency exceed outpayments. The home country experiences a payments surplus on capital account. Under reverse conditions, outpayments of home currency exceed inpayments. The home country then experiences a payments deficit on capital account.

Therefore, the status of the balance of payments on capital account depends on the direction of financial flows between the home country and abroad. The normal presumption is that capital inflows into the home economy will exceed capital outflows, leading to a capital account surplus, when the rate of return that is offered on domestic assets exceeds that offered in foreign countries, after adjusting for different levels of risk in different countries.

If r_d is the typical interest rate that can be earned by persons acquiring home assets, r_f is the typical interest rate earned by persons acquiring assets overseas, and $BPKA$ is the balance of payments on capital account, then $BPKA$ will exceed zero and be in surplus when r_d exceeds r_f. When r_d equals r_f, the balance of payments on capital account will equal zero. Finally, when r_d is less than r_f, the capital account balance will be negative or will be in deficit.

Allowing differentials between domestic and foreign interest rates to serve as the cornerstone of our model of capital flows, we can put together a simple specification of the payments balance on capital account:

$$BPKA = BPKA\left(\frac{r_d}{r_f}\right) \qquad BPKA'\left(\frac{r_d}{r_f}\right) > 0$$

This can be diagrammed, as in Figure 11.3. The simplest way to do this is to show the BPKA schedule as an increasing function of the home interest rate, treating the interest rate abroad as given. Thus, we reduce the BPKA to a function of domestic interest rates only: in effect, $BPKA = BPKA(r_d)$.

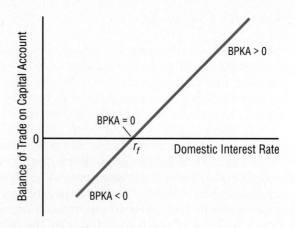

FIGURE 11.3 **The Balance on Capital Account**

The capital account will be balanced when the interest rate on domestic assets (r_d) just equals the interest rate on foreign assets (r_f).

While economists (as always!) are divided on the point, most people accept that it is generally better to have a current account surplus than to have a deficit. A surplus on current account amounts to a net addition to the stream of expenditures contributing to aggregate demand; a deficit amounts to a reduction. Furthermore, a deficit requires financing, typically by the acquisition of external debt. To meet such debt obligations, the country that runs the trade deficit eventually must either (*a*) tax its population more heavily, (*b*) run offsetting surpluses in the future, or (*c*) acquire additional debt from other sources to roll over the obligations to the initial set of creditors. Except in some very special circumstances, any of these options can lead to some obvious, and quite serious, problems.[3]

The relative desirability of surplus and deficit positions on capital account is not as transparent. A country running a surplus on capital account is one where inpayments by foreigners acquiring home assets exceed outpayments by domestic nationals acquiring assets overseas. The proceeds from these sales are not free of cost; they generally imply a commitment by domestic nationals to make interest and profit payments over time in the future. In a nutshell, a net capital inflow, or a capital

---

[3] An exception occurs when a country is able to issue debt denominated in its own currency. Then, a depreciation of the exchange rate can effectively reduce the value of those debts, placing the burden on the foreigners who do the lending. This is the situation of the United States, but it has the obvious limit that foreign creditors become increasingly unwilling to make new loans to countries that repeatedly burn them in this way.

account surplus, amounts to the buildup of external debt. This means, once again, the need (*a*) to raise future taxes, (*b*) to achieve future current account surpluses, or (*c*) to roll over the debt by borrowing from other sources, if the external debt is to be paid.

The Debt Crisis

Foreigners acquired domestic assets of developing countries in huge volume in the late 1970s and early 1980s. They did so mainly in the form of commercial bank loans by transnational banks. The total external debt of the developing countries therefore grew enormously; as of 1993 it stands in the vicinity of one trillion dollars, with about half owed to banks (and the rest to official creditors such as the International Monetary Fund and to governments).

This situation illustrates the pitfalls of too great a surplus on capital account. Prospects for full repayment of Third World debt have been dim for over a decade, and the effort to meet interest payments alone has led numerous developing countries—especially those in Latin America—to embrace austerity measures. These efforts to cut consumption levels and imports (see Figure 11.1) have had devastating effects on their populations. For many developing countries, the debt crisis that began in the 1980s is every bit as severe as the Great Depression of the 1930s was in the industrialized world.

Capital Account Deficits and Capital Exports

On the other side of the coin, *deficits on capital account* mean that outpayments exceed inpayments. In this case, domestic nationals are acquiring foreign assets of a greater value than domestic assets being acquired by foreigners. They are, in effect, exporting capital to other nations. Although the excess of outpayments over inpayments contributes directly to an overall payments imbalance in the near term, in principle it sets up a stream of interest payments in the future—assuming (of course) that foreigner debtors meet *their* obligations to domestic nationals! Today's capital account deficit lays the foundation for an inflow of income tomorrow as returns are realized on the foreign assets.

Capital Flight

In a special case known as *capital flight*, funds leave a country for reasons of politics or economic panic, mostly without being recorded and without expectation that they will return even if the short-term rate of return in the home country rises dramatically relative to that in the rest of the world. Capital flight is an especially important phenomenon in developing countries afflicted by the debt crisis, since funds have been removed from such countries to avoid appropriation by the authorities for use to meet payments due on the international debt.

The volume of capital flight is considerable. For the major Latin American debtor nations, estimates for the period 1976–1984 have run as high as $125 billion, more than one-quarter of the cumulative external debt of these developing countries.[4]

Despite the importance of capital flight, we do not deal with it in the rest of the chapter, nor do we consider movements of funds that leave the home country because of their origin in the illegal narcotics traffic or in the corrupt activities of public officials and rulers of some developing countries. Those funds are also unlikely to return to the home country in response to a rise in the interest rate offered at home relative to the interest rate that could be earned elsewhere in the world.

BALANCE OF PAYMENTS

The balance of payments is the sum of the balance on current account and the balance of capital account.[5] Therefore, we can express the balance of payments (BP) in symbols as

$$BP = BPCA + BPKA$$

$$BP = x(e) - m(y, e) + BPKA \left(\frac{r_d}{r_f} \right)$$

It is now possible to demonstrate how the IS-LM apparatus can be modified for the case of an open economy. The IS and LM schedules jointly identify the conditions of internal balance, and a new schedule, the BP schedule, identifies the conditions for external balance. (The open economy version of the IS-LM model is also known as the *Mundell-Fleming model*, after two economists whose studies were instrumental in its development.)

The complete open economy IS-LM model can be summarized with three equations in three unknowns:

(11.9) $y = c(y) + i(r_d) + \bar{g} + x(e) - m(y,e)$

(11.10) $\bar{M}^s = L(y,r_d)$

(11.11) $x(e) - m(y,e) + BPKA(r_d) = 0$

[4] Sunil Gulati, "Capital Flight: Causes, Consequences, and Cures," *Journal of International Affairs*, 42: No. 1 (Fall, 1988–1989), pp. 165–85.
[5] In what follows, the latter refers exclusively to capital flows, not capital flight.

Equation (11.9) is just a form of the IS schedule, which establishes the conditions for equality between investment and saving in the economy. It is altered from the closed economy case to incorporate net exports, $x - m$, but otherwise is the same: the equation tells us that equilibrium income varies inversely with the domestic rate of interest.

Equation (11.10) is the LM schedule, which establishes equality between the supply of money in the domestic economy, M^s, and the demand for money, L. It is exactly the same as in the closed economy case.

BP Schedule

Equation (11.11), finally, is something new. We call it the *BP schedule* because it establishes where and how the balance of payments comes into balance. In particular, the BP schedule tells us that any of three variables—exchange rate, income level, and domestic rate of interest—may adjust to ensure that the sum of the current and capital accounts is equal to zero.

Thus, there are three equations in this system and three unknowns: y, r_d, and e. Government expenditure and the money supply are treated as autonomous, policy-driven magnitudes. The foreign interest rate, r_f, is treated as given from the perspective of the home economy and can, therefore, be dropped from the capital account balance function. All variations in relative rates of return between home and foreign assets are dictated by changes in the domestic interest rate.

We start with the case of a fully adjusting economy characterized by completely flexible exchange rates. The exchange rate adjusts in response to the balance of payments position (and there is no intervention by the central bank in exchange markets). When there is a balance of payments surplus, the home currency appreciates in value, or e falls, leading to a decline in exports and a rise in imports until the surplus is eliminated. With a deficit, the home currency depreciates in value, or e rises, leading to a rise in exports and a fall in imports until, again, the deficit is extinguished. When the balance of payments is zero, the exchange rate has no tendency to change.

IS-LM-BP Model

The IS-LM-BP model appears in Figure 11.4 as a diagram with three schedules. We have drawn them to intersect at point A to display an economy exhibiting both internal and external balance simultaneously. Keep in mind that the IS curve provides all combinations of the home interest rate and level of real income that bring about equality of investment and saving at the prevailing exchange rate. The LM curve provides

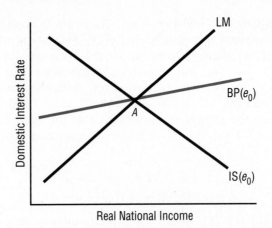

FIGURE 11.4   The Balance of Payments in an IS-LM Model

In an economy in both internal and external balance, the BP schedule shows the combination of domestic interest rate and national income consistent with payments balance at a given exchange rate. We have set e_0 so that the BP schedule intersects the IS and LM schedules at A. BP slopes upward, since a higher home interest rate attracts capital inflow and this offsets the decline in the current account as income rises.

all combinations of r_d and y that bring about equality of money supply and money demand; the domestic money market is treated here as independent of the influence of the market for foreign exchange.[6]

Finally, the BP curve provides all combinations of r_d and y that are also consistent with payments equilibrium at a given exchange rate. It is upward sloping because as r_d increases, net capital inflows increase, pushing the balance of payments toward a surplus position. At a given exchange rate, a higher level of income is then needed to restore a zero balance; it does so because the higher y reduces net exports and thus generates a current account deficit to offset the capital account surplus.

Changes in the exchange rate, e, may also occur. Since our axes are the domestic interest rate and the income level, shifts in e cause shifts in the position of the BP schedule, whereas changes in r_d and y lead to movements along a given BP schedule. At any given value of e, the BP

[6] The critical assumption that the domestic money supply is entirely independent of foreign currency flows is an unrealistic assumption, but it does make our analysis more manageable. To consider the domestic money supply autonomous is easier than to try to figure out the effects of foreign capital movements on domestic money. However, we would need to drop this assumption in order to analyze cases—and in the real world, there are many—where changes in the capital account lead directly to changes in domestic high-powered money. Similarly, we do not assume that any spending variations in either consumption or investment are linked directly to capital flows.

schedule thus divides the space into two regions: above or to the left of BP, the economy experiences payments surplus; below or to the right, the economy experiences deficit.

Monetary and Fiscal Policies with Floating Exchange Rates

Through exercises in which the policy variables are altered at the behest of the authorities, we can trace the repercussions on an open economy.

In an economy under a regime of *flexible exchange rates*, the authorities do not intervene to stabilize the value of e. Suppose such an economy had an LM curve steeper than the BP curve. In that case, what would be the consequences of a domestic monetary expansion?

The economy initially features full market clearing at point A. The first effect of a monetary expansion, as shown in Figure 11.5, is to cause the LM schedule to shift to the right to intersect the IS schedule at point B. At point B, the economy is in internal balance, but point B's lying to the right of the BP schedule indicates that the economy is now experiencing a payments deficit.

Note, too, the decline in the home interest rate relative to the rest of the world's. The home economy is therefore necessarily experiencing a net capital outflow (capital account deficit) at exchange rate e_0. The effect

FIGURE 11.5   Monetary Expansion in the Open Model

An expansionary monetary policy shifts the IS-LM equilibrium from A to B, causing a payments deficit. An exchange rate depreciation can then shift the IS and BP schedules, until a new equilibrium is reached at C.

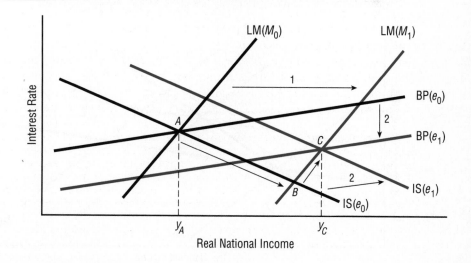

of the net capital outflow is reinforced by the rise in real national income, which will decrease net exports—both are reducing the balance of payments.

The payments deficit spurs the exchange rate to adjust: the exchange rate, e, rises; the home currency depreciates. As e increases, both the BP and IS schedules shift rightward. Exports are stimulated and imports are inhibited by the rising exchange rate, and this affects both schedules, as an examination of equations (11.9) and (11.11) shows. The process continues until the economy settles at a new general market-clearing position, point C in the diagram. The full effect of the monetary expansion is to raise the exchange rate from e_0 to e_1 and the level of real national income from y_A to y_C. The net effect on the home rate of interest, r_d, is ambiguous.

If, on the other hand, the BP schedule is steeper than LM, the exchange rate depreciation is more likely to lead to an increased domestic interest rate in the aftermath of a domestic monetary expansion. The successive positions the economy could take in that case are shown in Figure 11.6.

What about the effects of an increased volume of government spending in an IS-LM-BP world? We explore those effects in Figure 11.7, where LM is steeper than BP. If government spending is increased from G_0 to G_1, the IS curve will shift to the right, with the initial exchange rate at value e_2. The shift in IS produces conditions for internal

FIGURE 11.6   A Monetary Expansion Causing Higher Interest Rates

If the BP schedule is steeper than the LM schedule, indicating a low responsiveness of capital flows to changes in the interest rate, then the final market-clearing position of the economy may be at a higher interest rate after a monetary expansion than before.

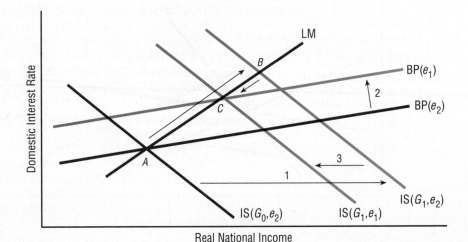

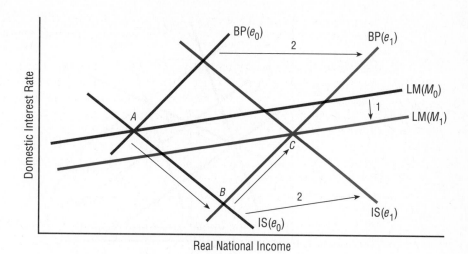

FIGURE 11.7   A Fiscal Expansion in an Open Economy

A fiscal expansion from (G_0, e_2) to (G_1, e_2) creates a capital inflow and balance of payments surplus. This is followed by exchange rate appreciation, which raises the BP schedule and dampens export demand, shifting the IS schedule back to the left. The gain in real national income is then reduced below what would occur in a closed economy.

balance at point B, but the foreign or payments sector will be in surplus at that point. In this situation, home currency should appreciate in value, or the exchange rate will decline from e_2 to e_1. Both BP and IS then will shift left, although not back to their original positions, since their movements must be compatible with the higher level of government expenditure. National income increases but by less than the amount that would have occurred in the closed economy.

When the BP schedule is steeper than the LM schedule, the effects of expansionary fiscal policy on real national income are magnified rather than dampened in comparison with the closed economy case. In this case, the increase in government spending pushes the economy into a payments deficit position instead of a surplus. This means, in turn, a rise in e from e_0 to e_1 as the exchange rate depreciates, leading to a further rightward shift in IS and a rightward shift in BP that produces real national income level y_C. This income level exceeds exceeds y_B, the level associated with the closed economy case (see Figure 11.8).

A Fixed Exchange Rate Regime

An alternative regime is one where the home currency's exchange rate is held fixed by the actions of the monetary authorities. The monetary authorities—the agents of the nation's central bank—"defend" the fixed

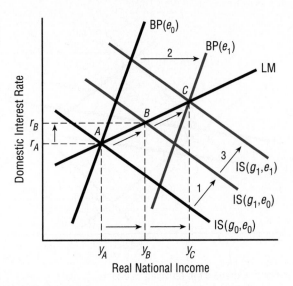

FIGURE 11.8   A Fiscal Expansion: Case II

If the BP schedule is steeper than the LM schedule, capital inflows from the rise in interest rates are small; there is a payments deficit, a depreciation of the exchange rate from e_0 to e_1, and a further rightward shift of IS, resulting in a further income increase from y_B to y_C.

exchange rate. They use their reserves of foreign currency to buy home currency in the foreign exchange markets to forestall a depreciation when their economy incurs a payments deficit. Similarly, they must buy foreign currency with home currency to prevent an appreciation when their economy incurs a payments surplus.

In the former case, the authorities seek to preserve an *overvalued* exchange rate for their nation's currency; in the latter case, they seek to preserve an *undervalued* exchange rate. The former typically is thought to be more difficult to accomplish than the latter, because a nation never has access to unlimited reserves of foreign currency. Overvaluation of an exchange rate cannot continue indefinitely. At a certain stage, dealers in foreign exchange markets may begin to speculate on the prospects of an eventual devaluation of the exchange rate. This opens another Pandora's box for policymakers. Nevertheless, fixed exchange rates have long held a certain appeal because of the stability they lend to decisions made by those who engage in transactions in international markets.[7]

[7] For those interested in this area, we highly recommend Charles Kindleberger's work on international financial instability *Manias, Panics and Crashes: A History of Financial Crises* (New York: Basic Books, 1978).

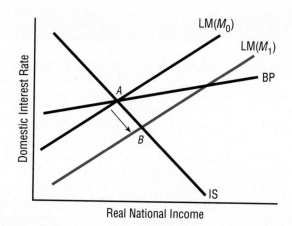

FIGURE 11.9   An Open Economy with Fixed Exchange Rates

Fixed exchange rates hold the BP schedule in place. Now, a monetary (or fiscal) expansion must cause a permanent deficit in the payments balance, draining the economy of foreign reserves.

Under fixed exchange rates, $e = \bar{e}$. We can explore the impact of expansionary monetary and fiscal policy from the standpoint of the Mundell–Fleming (open economy) model as well. Suppose the economy is in both external and internal balance at point A in Figure 11.9. An expansionary monetary policy will lead to a payments deficit at point B. The deficit must persist as long as the authorities continue to defend the exchange rate $\bar{e}$ by using foreign reserves to preserve the home currency's value in international markets.

There is an irreconcilable tension between domestic balance and balance in the foreign sector in this case. Without exchange rate flexibility, the consequence of an expansionary domestic monetary policy is simply to induce a payments deficit while raising real national income. The deficit occurs both because r_d falls (spurring a capital outflow) and because income rises (causing net exports to decline). There is no qualitative difference between a monetary expansion in this instance and the case where the BP curve has a steeper slope than LM.

If the authorities pursue an expansionary fiscal policy when LM is steeper than BP, the policy will raise national income and produce a surplus on current account. Here, market pressure for exchange rate appreciation is stymied by the authorities' purchases of foreign currency with home currency. The rise in r_d is so strong that higher capital inflows lead to a payments surplus, despite the adverse movement in the current account due to the income increase.

Taking a Closer Look

EXCHANGE RATES AND TRADE DEFICITS

The end of the Bretton Woods system of fixed but adjustable exchange rates is illustrated dramatically in Figures 11.B1 and 11.B2, which present the dollar/yen and dollar/pound exchange rates for the years 1960–1992.

The dollar/yen exchange rate was held at 360 yen to the dollar for the entire postwar period up until 1973. At this very low exchange rate, Japanese exports were highly competitive and grew very rapidly. With the end of fixed exchange rates, the dollar fell against the yen, as it has been doing episodically ever since. A significant exception is the period from 1981 to 1988, when the dollar rose quite sharply against the yen. This period coincided with a large expansion of Japanese exports to the United States.

The dollar/pound comparison tells a different story. The pound was overvalued compared to the dollar in the last years of Bretton Woods. You can see, in 1968, that the pound was *devalued*, from $2.80 to $2.40. Then, when floating rates were introduced, the pound fell again. During the high-dollar period of the 1980s, the dollar nearly reached one-for-one parity with the

FIGURE 11.B1   Exchange Rate: United States and Japan

Until the early 1970s, Japan maintained its exchange rate at 360 yen per dollar. This low rate enabled Japanese exports to grow very fast. When fixed exchange rates came to an end, the yen started to rise, and it has been rising, on and off, ever since. This reflects the increasing competitiveness and financial strength of the Japanese economy.

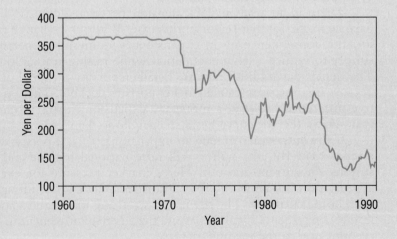

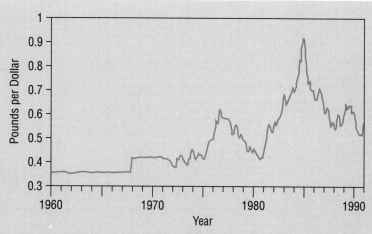

FIGURE 11.B2   **Exchange Rate: United States and Britain**

While the dollar has fallen against the Japanese yen, it has risen over the years against the British pound. Until the late 1960s, the pound was fixed at $2.80. It then was devalued to $2.40, where it remained until the system of fixed exchange rates dissolved in 1973. Since that time, the dollar/pound exchange rate has fluctuated a great deal.

FIGURE 11.B3   **U.S. Trade Deficit**

The years after 1970 saw a steady rise in the importance of trade to the U.S. economy. From 1980 to 1985, exports fell as a share of gross national product (GNP), while imports rose sharply. This was caused by a very great overvaluation of the dollar. The gap between imports and exports as a proportion of GNP measures the trade deficit or surplus. All are measured here in real terms.

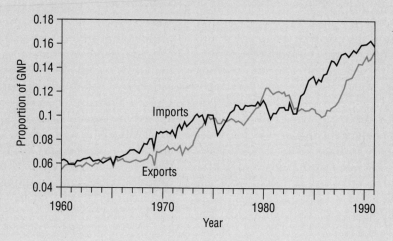

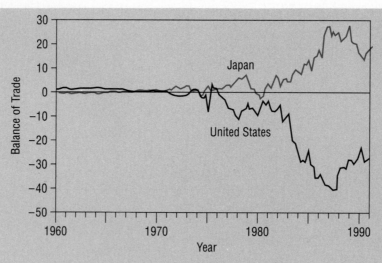

FIGURE 11.B4   Balance of Trade: United States and Japan

Both the United States and Japan had balanced trade until the mid-1970s. Since then, the United States has experienced large and increasing deficits, whereas Japan has enjoyed large surpluses. This was especially true in the 1980s. The scale on left shows the United States quarterly trade balance; the Japanese balance is not measured in a directly comparable unit.

pound, but it fell back again after 1987.

Some of the effects of changing exchange rates and other economic changes can be seen in Figures 11.B3 and 11.B4. The first shows the growth of exports and imports in the United States over thirty-two years. During periods when the dollar was comparatively low, such as the late 1970s and late 1980s, U.S. exports grew very rapidly. When the dollar was high, especially in the 1980s, exports stagnated while imports grew quickly, leading to large imbalances in trade.

Figure 11.B4 compares the U.S. balance of trade with that of Japan for the same thirty-two years. Both countries enjoyed nearly balanced trade until the mid-1970s; Japan's rapid export growth was balanced by rapid growth of imported products (especially food, oil, advanced machinery, and raw materials). Only in the late 1970s did chronic deficits appear in the United States and chronic surpluses appear in Japan. Both exploded in the 1980s. Much of the U.S. deficit and the Japanese surplus has been due to expanding exports of automobiles, electronic equipment, and machinery from Japan to the United States.

When BP is steeper than LM, a fiscal expansion will induce a payments deficit. As long as the exchange rate is fixed, such a deficit can be sustained again only through the depletion of foreign reserves. Once more, capacity to maintain such a regime is questionable, to say the least.

CLOSING REMARKS

Some final points need to be made to close the chapter. First, the relative slopes of BP and LM depend on the interest sensitivity of the capital flow function versus the interest sensitivity of the demand for money function. The more interest sensitive one or the other, correspondingly, the less steep the BP or the LM schedule.

Second, these relative slopes do not change the qualitative effects of *monetary* policy on real incomes and interest rates. They do matter quantitatively under both flexible and fixed exchange rate regimes, in the sense that policy effects are larger or smaller depending on which curve is steeper. But when we come to *fiscal* policy, the relative slopes of BP and LM matter both qualitatively and quantitatively. If LM is steeper, a policy of fiscal expansion produces a current account surplus; if BP is steeper, a deficit results.

Third, the attractiveness of fixed exchange rates depends in part on the degree to which exchange rates might have to fall to achieve trade balance. This depends upon the relative exchange rate elasticities of export and import demands. If those elasticities are small, then potentially huge and destabilizing adjustments would have to take place in the exchange rate to extinguish a payments deficit. The authorities may prefer to fix the exchange rate and let the income level adjust instead.

Fourth, ignoring capital flight, the potential effect of the foreign sector on the domestic money supply, and the potential direct effect of capital flows on domestic consumption and investment made exposition of models in this chapter easier—but at a price. The models presented were, in these respects, divorced from reality.

Certainly, if the home country has a high interest rate compared with the rest of the world, that should attract foreign buyers for domestic assets. The result should be a balance of payments surplus. With $e = \bar{e}$, both the IS and BP schedules are locked down. With IS and BP locked in place, only LM can shift to restore internal and external balance. That effect could come about when the accretion of reserves of foreign exchange due to the payments surplus increased domestic high-powered money and thereby the domestic money supply. Augmentation of the home supply of money would continue until the domestic interest rate fell and real income rose sufficiently to eliminate the surplus. The process is depicted in Figure 11.10 as a movement from point A to point B.

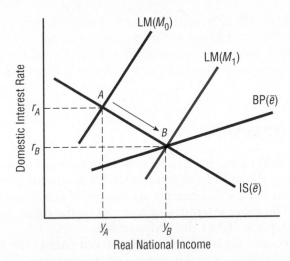

FIGURE 11.10   Monetary Adjustments to a Payments Surplus Under Fixed Exchange Rates

If the home interest rate is too high and the BP and IS schedules are fixed by the exchange rate, only a monetary expansion caused by capital inflow will eliminate a payments surplus.

Fifth, an endogenous domestic money supply—endogenously responsive to net capital flows—produces another avenue for adjustment even under a regime of fixed exchange rates. If, for some reason, the authorities do not want to see a monetary adjustment take place—perhaps they fear inflation—the central bank can seek to offset the rise in foreign reserves by selling bonds to reduce the stock of high-powered money back to its original level. If such a step succeeds, high-powered money, the foundation of the domestic money supply, will undergo a recomposition: more foreign assets and fewer domestic assets.[8] But the total volume of such money would not change.

The selling or buying of bonds by a central bank is an open market operation. An open market operation undertaken expressly to offset changes in foreign reserves due to payments imbalances is known as a *sterilization policy*. Sterilization cannot continue forever, either. Sterilization of a deficit involves offsetting losses of foreign assets by central bank acquisition of domestic bonds. Not only must the central bank buy, for example, U.S. savings bonds, but it must offset losses of reserves of foreign currency as well. Sensing that the central bank is in trouble,

[8] See Samuel Morley, *The Macroeconomics of Open Economies* (London: Edward Elgar, 1988), p. 99.

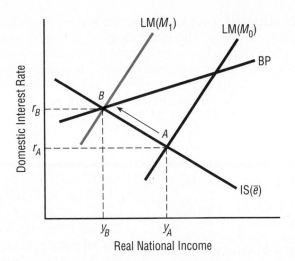

FIGURE 11.11   **Reserve Loss and Monetary Contraction Under Fixed Exchange Rates**

If the exchange rate is fixed and the home interest rate is too low, reserves will drain from the economy, forcing a monetary contraction that reduces national income, raises the home interest rate, and restores payments balance.

speculators will abound who anticipate an eventual currency devaluation. Moreover, by selling the home currency on the bet that a devaluation will occur, they can make it very difficult for the central bank to avoid one.

In the case of sterilization of a surplus, the speculators' actions in anticipation of a *revaluation* (appreciation) lead to pressure, in fact, to revalue the currency. In this case as well, the central bank will soon feel the pressure. And in both cases, we see the tenuousness of the authorities' capacity to genuinely control the money supply in an open economy.[9]

Sixth and finally, if the prevailing domestic interest rate is relatively low—so low that it produces a payments deficit—the loss of reserves can lead to a monetary contraction. This monetary contraction will bring about full market clearing as the economy moves from A to B in Figure 11.11. Defending the overvalued exchange rate at point A and sterilizing the deficit are particularly hard to do—but to accept adjustment via a monetary contraction is to accept a fall in home income.

In this chapter, we have little more than scratched the surface of the rich field of international macroeconomics; whole textbooks and courses

[9] Morley, *Macroeconomics,* pp. 99–101.

are devoted to this topic. We hoped here to provide an introduction, to show how some of the basic tools of macroeconomic analysis can be adapted to deal with international economic issues. Since the United States is now an open economy, with a comparatively high fraction of its GDP involved in international trade, this is an especially important point for U.S. students of the subject to recognize.

SPECIAL SECTION

An Introduction to North-South Analysis

In preceding chapters, we considered macroeconomic models from the perspective of a single country, whether the country's economy was closed or open to foreign trade. Here we extend our use of macroeconomic modeling to the interaction between two (or more) economies, each representing large blocs of nations in the world economy.

The customary way to partition the world economy is to distinguish between the more developed and less developed countries. The former we refer to as the North; the latter we refer to as the South. The North-South nomenclature suggests a geographic pattern that has the more affluent nations of the world typically situated in the Northern Hemisphere and the poorer nations of the world situated in the Southern Hemisphere. This nomenclature emerged in the 1970s in the context of calls by leaders of the poorer nations' for a "new world economic order."

For the purposes of global macroeconomic modeling, the North generally is treated as the industrialized, technically advanced, high-income region of the world. The North exports manufactured goods to the South. The South, treated as a region where agrarian activities predominate, technology is comparatively less advanced, and average incomes are low, exports primary products to the North.[1]

The accuracy of this pattern of specialization—the North as the manufactured-goods producer and the South as the primary-goods producer—has been called into question. Critics cite the rise of so-called postindustrial or "high"-technology activities in the affluent countries and of substantial industrialization in several Third World countries, most prominently Brazil, Mexico, the Republic of Korea, Singapore, Malaysia, Taiwan, and Hong Kong. Those who oppose the traditional North-South analysis argue that this pattern of specialiation applies to the world of the nineteenth century, not to the late twentieth century.

Nevertheless, large blocs of countries still fit the so-called "nineteenth-century" pattern of trade. Consequently, it seems legitimate to continue to utilize the traditional North-South approach for at least part of the analysis. Affluent nations such as the United States, Japan, Canada, and those of Western Europe remain far more industrialized than virtually all other nations of the world. And most nations of the Caribbean, Africa, and Southeast Asia remain, to this day, overwhelmingly producers and exporters of primary products.

Global macroeconomic modeling need not be wedded inflexibly to a two-region framework. If the existence of countries that specialized in producing high-technology goods (say microcomputing equipment) were important, then a third region of the world could be incorporated: a high-tech region. Similarly, the model could be extended to include a region representing the newly industrialized countries (NICs). Such extensions, while not easy, are feasible. In this special section, however, we will restrict our attention to the traditional two-region, North-South approach.

Two basic strategies can be used in setting up a world economy model. One is to treat the two regions as sharing the same fundamental structure—as operating from the same model—but differing in the values of certain parameters. A second is to treat the regions as possessing fundamentally distinct structures. In the first approach, the two economies are symmetrical; in the second approach, they are asymmetrical.

Symmetrical Approach

Using the first strategy, under which both regions are treated as having symmetrical economies, we will consider both the North and South to be simple, Keynesian open economies engaged in trade with one another. Each produces a commodity that the other can import for use, either as a consumption good or as an intermediate good. There is unemployment in both regions, so that output growth is possible. We further assume that the measures of output of each region are properly deflated so that output in both regions is measured in a common, inflation-adjusted unit.

Demand for the North's output can be expressed as

$$(11.S1) \quad y_n = c_n y_n + a_n + x_n - \mu_n y_n$$

In this equation, y_n is the North's output, c_n is the propensity to consume in the North, a_n is the North's real autonomous expenditure (investment, government spending, and autonomous consumption) on northern output, x_n is the real exports from the North to the South, and μ_n is the North's propensity to import. Thus northern demand is a positive function of northern income and of southern income but a negative function of the northern propensity to import from the South.

In parallel fashion, the demand for the South's output is

$$(11.S2) \quad y_s = c_s y_s + a_s + x_s - \mu_s y_s$$

Here y_s is the South's output, c_s is the propensity to consume in the South, a_s is the South's real autonomous expenditure on its own output, x_s are the real exports from the South to the North, and μ_s is the South's propensity to import.

The regions' interdependence arises precisely because the North's exports are the South's imports and the South's exports are the North's imports. Consequently, x_n and x_s can be rewritten as

$$(11.S3) \qquad x_n = \mu_s y_s$$

$$(11.S4) \qquad x_s = \mu_n y_n$$

Substitution of (11.S3) into (11.S1) reveals that the demand for the North's output depends not only on northern income but also (positively) on southern income; substitution of (11.S4) into (11.S2) demonstrates that the demand for the South's output depends on both regions' incomes as well:

$$(11.S5) \qquad \begin{aligned} y_n &= c_n y_n + a_n + \mu_s y_s \\ &\quad - \mu_n y_n \end{aligned}$$

$$(11.S6) \qquad \begin{aligned} y_s &= c_s y_s + a_s + \mu_n y_n \\ &\quad - \mu_s y_s \end{aligned}$$

Equations (11.S5) and (11.S6) provide a simple but instructive model of North-South interdependence that consists of two equations in two unknowns. The two unknowns are the output, or income, levels in each region. Solving the system for the equilibrium values of y_n and y_s, we obtain

$$(11.S7) \qquad y_n{}^\star =$$

$$\left(\frac{Q_n}{1 - Q_n Q_s \mu_s \mu_n} \right) (a_n + \mu_s Q_s a_s)$$

$$(11.S8) \qquad y_s{}^\star =$$

$$\left(\frac{Q_s}{1 - Q_n Q_s \mu_s \mu_n} \right) (a_s + \mu_n Q_n a_n)$$

where

$$Q_n = \frac{1}{1 - c_n - \mu_n}$$

$$Q_s = \frac{1}{1 - c_s - \mu_s}$$

The terms Q_n and Q_s are the open economy multipliers for each region in the absence of comprehensive interdependence of the type depicted here. They would be the multipliers if neither region's export activity depended on the other region's income level. In the actual situation, the first bracketed terms on the right side of equations (11.S7) and (11.S8) are the open-economy multipliers that apply when each region's income level influences the other's income level through trade. The interdependent multipliers are larger than the non-interdependent multipliers, scaled upward by the term in the denominator $(1 - Q_n Q_s \mu_s \mu_n)$, a number that is positive and smaller than one.

Notice that since the scale factor $(1 - Q_n Q_s \mu_s \mu_n)$ is the same for both regions, the region with the larger interdependent multiplier will be the one whose noninterdependent multiplier (Q_s, Q_n) is also larger. That is, the North's interdependent multiplier will be larger if $Q_n > Q_s$, and the South's multiplier will be larger if $Q_s > Q_n$.

Interdependence not only raises the multipliers for each region, it also leads to increases in the autonomous expenditures devoted to each region's output. To see this, examine the second bracketed terms on the right side of equations (11.S7) and (11.S8). In (11.S7), not only does the North's autonomous expenditure on the northern good determine its equilibrium level of output, but so does the South's autonomous expenditure on its own good. Indeed, the South's propensity to consume, μ_s, and its noninterdependent multiplier, Q_s, also appear in equation (11.S7). And an entirely parallel pattern of effects also exists for the determination of the South's level of output.

The critical question raised in North-South analysis is which region ultimately will have the higher level of income. The key factor is the propensity to import. The region that has the *lower* propensity to import will tend to have the *higher* income. For example, as the North's propensity to import, μ_n, gets smaller, the noninterdependent component of its multiplier, Q_n, becomes larger. This in turn reduces the positive effect of its domestic autonomous expenditures on the South's income level, while raising the positive effect on its own income level. In a sense, then, the region that is comparatively less import dependent will tend to have the superior income performance.[2]

In the real world, northern income levels are indeed higher. If we believed that both regions could be characterized as simple Keynesian economies of this type, we would be driven to conclude that the persistent income advantage held by the North is likely due to the North having a weaker propensity to import than the South: the income gap between North and South is sustained because the South is far more import dependent than the North. Although the two regions are structurally similar (both are simple Keynesian economies), the difference in the size of two important parameters in the model, their respective propensities to import, can determine the difference in their relative income levels.

We illustrate the case where the North's income level is above the South's in equilibrium in Figure 11.S1. Using equations (11.S5) and (11.S6), we can sketch the North's income as a function of both regions, and we can do the same for the South.

The North's income schedule appears as subscript N in the diagram, and the South's appears as subscript S. If the two schedules happened to intersect along the 45-degree line that bisects the diagram, both regions would have identical income levels. In that case, economic equality in a gross sense would exist between the two countries. But if the schedules intersect on either side of the 45-degree line, then one region is more affluent than the other.

We have drawn the schedules intersecting to the left of the 45-degree line, indicating that the

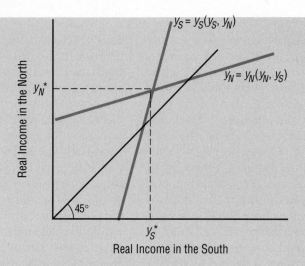

FIGURE 11.S1   Persistent Inequality in Real Incomes

When each country's income depends on the other's, then the economy with the smaller import propensity (North, in this case) will have the higher equilibrium national income.

equilibrium level of income is higher in the North. There is thus a gap in equilibrium incomes between North and South, hence persistent inequality.

Asymmetrical Model

The second strategy mentioned above is to treat North and South as structurally distinct regions. One such approach, popularized by Columbia University economist Ronald Findlay, is to view the North as a "Solow economy" (after MIT economist Robert Solow) and the South as a "Lewis economy" (after the late Princeton economist W. Arthur Lewis).[3]

The Solow economy in the North is a neoclassical growth economy, producing an investment good utilized in both regions. It experiences balanced growth, growing at a rate that maintains continuous full employment. In contrast, the Lewis economy in the South is an economy with an unlimited labor supply, due to the presence of a large subsistence agricultural sector from which wage labor can be drawn as needed. The South produces a primary product.

While the real wage is set in the North at whatever rate is consistent with full employment, the condition of surplus labor in the South means that the real wage is fixed institutionally, at a level not far above subsistence. Perhaps the real wage in the South is roughly equal to the average product of labor in the provision of foodstuffs in southern agriculture; thus, nonsubsistence workers in the South earn about as much as subsistence workers do.[4]

Findlay's investigation of a Solow North/Lewis South model proceeds on the terrain of growth theory. It should be clear at the outset that if the North starts out with a higher level of income and if the two regions end up growing at the same rate, there will be no change in the degree of international inequality over time. Nevertheless, there still will be a permanent disparity between the two regions in terms of average income levels. Indeed, Findlay presumes that the two regions will grow at the same rate, the rate that maintains full employment in the North.

We can refer to that rate as the *natural* growth rate in the North, n. In the North, both the available labor force and the available capital stock grow at the common rate n. The South does not have a natural rate of growth of its own, because it is the region with effectively unlimited supplies of labor. The constraint on growth in the South is its rate of capital accumulation, not the availability of labor.

The rate of capital accumulation in Findlay's Lewis South is dictated by savings activity in the South; savings is done exclusively by southern capitalists out of profits. Findlay identifies the southern profit rate with the marginal product of capital in the South, $f'(k_s)$, where k_s is the capital-labor ratio in the South. The institutionally fixed real wage, coupled with

profit maximization by southern entrepreneurs, leads to the equilibrium capital-labor ratio, $k_s = k_s^\star$.

If the southern capitalists' savings propensity is s, the absolute increase in the South's capital stock will be the following, measured in units of the North's good (the capital good):

$$(11.S9) \quad \Delta K_s = sPf'(k_s^\star)K_s$$

Here K_s is the South's capital stock. P is the terms of trade, the rate at which the North's capital good exchanges for each unit of the South's primary products (taking P_s and P_n as the price per unit of southern and northern goods, $P = P_s/P_n$). Dividing both sides of (11.S9) by K_s yields the proportional rate of increase in the South's capital stock, or the South's rate of capital accumulation:

$$(11.S10) \quad \frac{\Delta K_s}{K_s} = sPf'(k_s^\star)$$

Equation (11.S10) is the South's rate of growth. Since there is no constraint on southern growth set by labor availability, the South's growth rate must be fixed by the rate of increase in its available capital, which it must purchase from the North.

Now if the North and South come to grow at the same rate, the North's natural growth rate must coincide with the South's rate of capital accumulation. If that is the case, the following condition must hold:

$$(11.S11) \quad n = sPf'(k_s^\star)$$

Since n is given by the requirement that the North grow at a rate consistent with full employment, s is given by the habits and practices of southern capitalists, and $k_s^\star$ is determined by the existence of a fixed real wage in the South and the profit-maximizing behavior of southern capitalists, the only variable that can adjust to bring about equal growth rates is P, the terms of trade between South and North. The solution for P is the following:

$$(11.\text{S}12) \quad P^\star = \frac{P_s}{P_n} = \frac{n}{sf'(k_s^\star)}$$

This especially interesting result is, in effect, a long-run equilibrium value of the terms of trade. It is a long-run value in the sense that not only is there balanced growth in the North when this value obtains but there is also balanced growth in the world economy (i.e., between North and South).[5] The terms of trade for the South improve with a higher natural rate of growth in the North, deteriorate with an increase in the savings rate in the South (which amounts to increased demand for the northern good at each level of profits), and improve with an increase in the capital-labor ratio in the South, since diminishing returns lead to a fall in the marginal product of capital. The value of the long-run terms of trade is entirely independent of technical conditions of production and savings activity in the North.

Both regions will grow at the North's natural rate. However, it bears repeating that, although growth rates equalize between North and South, this still can be a recipe for persistent international inequality in incomes. As long as the North begins the dynamic process with an income lead, the proportionate differential in incomes will persist indefinitely, and the absolute differential will grow. In this case, however, there is no straightforward explanation for the origin of the gap. We could fill in the space with economic history. For example, we might look to the role of the Atlantic slave trade, or to colonialism and imperialism in separating rich and poor nations from the 1500s onward, as the ultimate origin of the distinction between economies that produce investment goods and those that do not.

By treating the North as a Solow economy, Findlay imputes full employment growth to the region. Of course, industrial economies are far from immune to unemployment, so this is not an entirely satisfactory way to depict their pattern of growth. When Solow first developed his model, he apparently conceived of full employment growth as a long-run tendency of the industrially advanced economies, certainly not as a continuous state of affairs among them. But thirty-six years after Solow first wrote, there is no persuasive evidence of a long-run tendency toward full employment in those economies either.

We could treat the North as an economy that does not grow at its natural rate but instead grows at Roy Harrod's *warranted* rate.[6] If we were to do this, we would replace the Solow North with a Harrod North while retaining the Lewis South. In a Harrod North, the growth rate will be determined by the rate of capital accumulation, which in turn is determined by the ratio of the North's saving rate (out of all categories of income, not just profits), z, to the capital-output ratio in the North, v. We can then substitute the term z/v for n on the left side of equation (11.S11). We leave the right side of the equation unchanged because the South still must buy its capital goods from the North:

$$\frac{z}{v} = sPf'(k_s{}^\star)$$

Now the long-run terms of trade will be

$$P^\star = \frac{z}{vsf'(k_s{}^\star)}$$

It is apparent from this equation that once the North is treated as a region with unemployment, the long-run terms of trade will no longer be independent of northern technology and savings activity. The parameter z, the northern saving rate, appears in the numerator, and the parameter v, the northern capital-output ratio, appears in the denominator. Thus, southern terms of trade will rise when northern savings rates rise and will rise again with improvements in northern technology that reduce the capital required for each unit of output.

Again, equality of growth rates brought about by adjustment in the terms of trade need not mean equality of incomes. If one region is wealthier at the outset, then interaction through a mechanism that leads both to grow uniformly only means that the richer region will stay richer by exactly the same proportion over time.

This brief, fairly bare-bones introduction to North-South models emphasizes the way in which they potentially can illuminate the nature of ongoing inequality between the more developed and less developed nations of the world. In many, many more ways, the models can be extended to explore a host of related issues. For example, in the Latin American structuralist analysis formalized primarily by Lance Taylor, monetary phenomena, exchange rate policy, the International Monetary Fund, and the international transmission of inflation via markup pricing play prominent roles. There is also a long, long-run examination, by André Burgstaller,[7] of industrialization and deindustrialization under shifting comparative advantage. But at the heart of the interest in global macromodeling in North-South fashion is the recognition of the vast disparity in income between rich and poor nations, and the development of systematic insights to explain the gap.

---

[1] For useful surveys of North-South models of trade and growth, see Ronald Findlay, "Growth and Development in Trade Models," in *Handbook of International Economics,* ed. R. W. Jones and P. B. Kenen, 1 (Amsterdam: Else-

vier Science Publishers, 1984), pp.185–236; Amitava K. Dutt, "Uneven Development in Alternative Models of North-South Trade," *Eastern Economic Journal*, 15 (April–June 1989), pp. 91–106.

[2] Does this suggest anything about the long-term comparative performance of the United States and Japan?

[3] See Ronald Findlay, "The Terms of Trade and Equilibrium in the World Economy," *American Economic Review*, 70 (June 1980), pp. 291–299. For the original papers by Solow and Lewis, see Robert M. Solow, "A Contribution to the Theory of Economic Growth," *Quarterly Journal of Economics*, 70 (February 1956), 65–94; W. Arthur Lewis, "Economic Development with Unlimited Supplies of Labour," *The Manchester School*, 28 (May 1954), pp. 139–191.

[4] Findlay also assumes the existence of neoclassical production functions in both regions and, hence, well-defined marginal products of labor and capital in both regions.

[5] Although the growth rates are uniform in Professor Findlay's long run, the rates of profit earned in each region may not be. This means that, even after installation, there will be an incentive to transfer capital between the regions, moving it away from the lower profit rate region toward the higher profit rate region. This leads to an alternative, long-period characterization of the terms of trade also consistent with persistent international inequality between North and South. See William Darity, Jr., "The Fundamental Determinants of the Terms of Trade Reconsidered: Long-Run and Long-Period Equilibrium," *American Economic Review* 80 (September 1990), pp. 816–828.

[6] Roy F. Harrod, "An Essay in Economic Dynamics," *Economic Journal*, 49: No. 1 (1939) pp. 14–33. The warranted growth rate is the rate that preserves balanced growth in the economy.

[7] See Lance Taylor, "South-North Trade and Southern Growth: Bleak Prospects from a Structuralist Point of View," *Journal of International Economics*, 11 (November 1981), pp. 589–601; Andre Burgstaller, "Industrialization, Deindustrialization, and North-South Trade," *American Economic Review*, 77 (December 1987), pp. 1017–18.

SUMMARY

The open economy can be analyzed by extending the simple Keynesian aggregate demand model. Consumption, exogenous government spending, and exogenous investment spending constitute the internal components of demand. Endogenous imports and exogenous exports determine the external balance. Import demand depends on the level of home income. Imports can be thought of as another form of consumption, or as intermediate goods. Once again, equilibrium is determined by the condition that aggregate demand equals aggregate supply. The multiplier is reduced when the propensity to import is included. Autonomous expenditures are changed by the difference between exports and the autonomous portion of imports. As income gets larger, the current account moves toward deficit.

Nothing in the aggregate demand model guarantees balanced trade at the equilibrium. One escape from an equilibrium with unbalanced trade is the possibility that exports adjust inventories to bring about balanced trade. In this model, a balanced trade multiplier determines national income. But then there is no reason why the balanced trade equilibrium necessarily would be the same as the equilibrium of the closed economy model. On the other hand, if income is the only variable that adjusts, internal and external balance will not necessarily hold at the same time.

To ensure that trade deficits (or surpluses) move toward balance, the exchange rate must be introduced. In a situation of trade deficit, the exchange rate will depreciate (while, in a situation of surplus, it will appreciate). This makes imports and exports also functions of the exchange rate. The effect is felt through the transactions demand for currency. When the currency needed for export demand exceeds the currency needed for import demand, the exchange rate will appreciate. In this more complex model, exchange rate movements ensure external balance, and the interest rate and income adjust to achieve internal balance.

An additional source of demand for foreign currency comes from the demand for foreign assets. The capital account is the difference between the acquisition of domestic assets by foreigners and domestic acquisition of foreign assets. Usually, differences in rates of return, adjusted for risk, determine whether a surplus or deficit exists on the capital account. The balance of payments on capital account is a function of the ratio of the domestic interest rate to the foreign interest rate. In general, current account deficits and capital account surpluses are viewed as economic problems because they imply a buildup of debts that must be paid in the future. Less-developed countries particularly have run into capital account surplus problems.

Together, the balance of payments on capital account and the balance of payments on current account determine the balance of payments. The balance of payments and the IS-LM apparatus taken together form the Mundell-Fleming model. In this model, the IS curve is the same as before, except that exports and imports are sensitive to exchange rate changes; the LM curve is exactly the same; the BP curve represents the balance of payments. The exchange rate, real income, and the interest rate adjust to equilibrate the balance of payments. At the intersection of the BP, IS, and LM curves, the economy is in equilibrium.

A monetary expansion under flexible exchange rates will cause a temporary balance of payments deficit. This deficit causes a currency depreciation. The currency depreciation shifts the IS and BP curves in such a way that all three curves intersect at a new, higher level of output. With an increase in government spending, national income is increased. If BP is insensitive to the interest rate, then the effect is magnified relative to the closed economy case. If BP is sensitive to the interest rate, then the effect is dampened.

In a system of fixed exchange rates, the government draws down or builds foreign reserves to counteract forces that would otherwise cause exchange rate movements. A monetary expansion in a fixed exchange rate regime causes income to rise and the interest rate to fall. But the balance of payments is out of equilibrium because the monetary authorities necessarily draw down foreign reserves. In the case of expansionary fiscal policy, income rises and, depending on the interest rate sensitivity of the balance of payments curve relative to the LM curve, the monetary authorities will have to draw down or build up reserves. In the long run, the accretion or depletion of reserves will cause the LM curve to shift to bring all three of the curves to a common point. Sterilization efforts cannot continue indefinitely, because speculators will force a revaluation or devaluation by selling or buying large amounts of home currency.

A recent trend in international economic theory is the development of North-South models. North-South models partition the world into two regions, the "developed" and the "less developed" countries. In general, the North exports manufactured goods, and the South exports primary goods. Two approaches to North-South modeling are a symmetrical and an asymmetrical approach.

In the symmetrical approach, the two regions have the same structure, but the values of parameters are different. When these models are solved, interdependence is shown by multipliers that depend on the parameters of the other regions. The interdependent multipliers are larger than the closed economy model multipliers. But the country with the larger domestic multiplier will have the larger overall multiplier regardless of the international effects. The country with the smaller propensity to import will have the highest income.

One example of an asymmetrical approach is Ronald Findlay's Lewis South and Solow North. The Lewis South has surplus labor, whereas the Solow North is growing at the neoclassical natural rate. Findlay assumes that both regions ultimately grow at the same rate. Thus, the proportional level of international disparity is maintained, and the absolute level of international disparity grows. The terms of trade are independent of any of the North's structural parameters. However, if we replace Solow's natural rate of growth with Harrod's warranted growth rate, then the North's parameters become important in the determination of the terms of trade.

Review Questions

1. Explain why a model that uses the exchange rate as the mechanism for equilibrating the current account is inadequate.

2. When the closed economy is opened to trade effects, the number of instruments available to policymakers is multiplied. Discuss the instruments added to the policymakers' arsenal in the open trade models. Be sure to discuss their pitfalls as well as their benefits.

3. Explain the problems confronting less developed countries who have encountered large surpluses on their capital accounts.

4. Why might an economist argue that a short-run surplus on the capital account is good?

5. With the help of the symmetrical North-South model, explain why a persistent trade deficit might be harmful.

6. The word *harmful* was used in the previous question. Why is this a possible misnomer for the situations described in North-South models? More generally, describe how, why, or when imbalances in the current account and the capital account are or are not *harmful*, in the strictest sense of the word.

Review Problems

1. Assume the following economy:

Consumption:	$C = 1,500 + .7y$
Investment:	$I = 2,000$
Government:	$G = 1,500$
Exports:	$X = 1,000$
Imports:	$M = 200 + .1y$

Calculate the equilibrium income in this economy. What is the trade balance? What is the open economy multiplier? If an autonomous increase of 800 in export demand occurred abroad, what would be the new equi-

librium? Construct a graph that shows what has occurred.

2. With the same economy, calculate a balanced trade equilibrium for both of the situations described above. What would export demand have to be for balanced trade at an income level of 14,500 and of 16,500? Draw a graph like that in Figure 11.1, indicating all of the cases discussed.

3. Using the more complete model that includes the exchange rate as an equilibrating mechanism for the current account, answer the following questions. Draw figures like 11.1, 11.2, and a simple Keynesian cross to indicate the effect of an increase of government spending. Assume the economy starts at equilibrium and in balance on the current account.

4. Using the Mundell-Fleming model and its associated graph, analyze the following situation. Starting from initial equilibrium, what is the effect of a fiscal contraction in a regime of floating exchange rates? What happens to the interest rate, income, and the exchange rate? If the answer depends on the relative elasticity of the balance of payments curve, analyze all cases.

5. Answer the same question as in question 4 for the case of a monetary contraction in a regime of flexible exchange rates.

6. Answer the same question as in question 4 for the case of a fiscal expansion in a regime of *fixed* exchange rates. Be sure to distinguish between short- and long-run effects and to discuss whether the balance of payments is in balance.

Suggested Readings

Charles Kindleberger, *Manias, Panics, and Crashes: A History of Financial Crises* (New York: Basic Books, 1978).

Samuel Morley, *The Macroeconomics of Open Economies* (London: Edward Elgar, 1988).

Graham Bird, *International Macroeconomics: Theory, Policy and Applications* (London: Macmillan).

William Scarth, *Macroeconomics: An Introduction to Advanced Methods* (Toronto: Harcourt Brace Jovanovich).

Richard T. Froyen, *Macroeconomics: Theories and Policies* (New York: Macmillan, 1983).

Rudiger Dornbusch, *Open Economy Macroeconomics* (New York: Basic Books, 1984).

R.W. Jones and P.B. Kenen, eds., *Handbook of International Economics,* Vol. 1 (Amsterdam: Elsevier Science Publishers, 1984).

Amitava K. Dutt, "Uneven Development in Alternative Models of North-South Trade," *Eastern Economic Journal,* Vol. 15:2, April-June 1989.

William Darity Jr., "The Fundamental Determinants of the Terms of Trade Reconsidered: Long-Run and Long-Period Equilibrium," *American Economic Review,* Vol. 80:4, September 1990.

Roy F. Harrod, "An Essay in Economic Dynamics," *Economic Journal,* 1939.

Chapter 12

THE POST-KEYNESIAN VISION

In this chapter, we turn to a third major line of macroeconomic argument, known as the post-Keynesian theory. Elements of this theory cover many topics already seen in other forms, including employment, prices, interest rates, and money. But post-Keynesians address these topics in ways that differ sharply from the new classical approach and that also have important differences from the new Keynesians. We summarize these differences by noting that post-Keynesians reject rational expectations and monetarism, the principles of new classical analysis that the New Keynesians tend to accept, while accepting (or at least being indifferent to) the notion of market clearing. Yet, post-Keynesians often arrive, by different methods, at policy conclusions that new Keynesians also support.

Post-Keynesians are a minority among macroeconomists. However, in our view, their work deserves notice and careful study, for it casts new and important light on some of the most basic problems modern economies face.

As you read this chapter, keep the following questions in mind:

- How can the money stock be endogenous, rather than policy-determined?
- What is the significance of a markup theory of prices?
- What influences are most important in determining the climate of profit expectations and therefore investment demand, in the post-Keynesian view?
- What is the post-Keynesian theory of interest rates and asset prices, and how do these variables affect investment demand?

• How do post-Keynesians attempt to assimilate technological change into their model of the economy's supply side?

Over the last eleven chapters, we have traced the development of the two main currents of macroeconomic theory, the Keynesian and the classical, ever since the great schism of the 1930s. We have seen how competing models emerged over time in reaction to each other and how they continue to compete to this day. We have shown how these models have tried to address the changing issues of their times, from the Great Depression and mass unemployment to the management of growth in the postwar years, to the stagflation of the 1970s, to the business cycle and trade problems that we face today.

Figure 12.1 illustrates the main developments of the past sixty years. As the figure indicates, John Maynard Keynes wrote *The General Theory of Employment, Interest and Money*[1] to challenge the classical idea that a free-market economy would tend automatically to full employment. Keynes presented a complex set of arguments, attacking classical concepts of the labor market and the capital market and introducing money and financial markets into the determination of real national product and employment for the first time. *Monetary production economics* would, he hoped, become the order of the day, displacing the *real-exchange economics* of the textbooks of his time.

A small but essential part of Keynes's argument, the fiscal multiplier, was captured in the earliest Keynesian model: the 45-degree diagram, or Keynesian cross. The Keynesian cross model provided a simple device for understanding mass unemployment, and a framework within which models of one particular aspect of Keynesianism—the theory of consumer behavior—could be explored. But because the cross ignored monetary policy and the money markets, it was not long regarded as a satisfactory synopsis of the whole Keynesian revolution. The Keynesian cross was soon superseded by the IS-LM model, which did incorporate some of the major Keynesian insights about money and interest, in particular the concepts of transactions demand and speculative demand for money.

IS-LM has proved a durable and flexible framework, and variations on the IS-LM theme remain in use in theoretical work today. But because IS-LM places Keynesian concepts in a general equilibrium framework and because many economists sought to integrate IS-LM with a supply-and-demand model of the labor market (through the Phillips curve), IS-LM is not uniquely and wholly Keynesian. Rather, IS-LM draws in part on classical as well as Keynesian sources of inspiration

[1] (London: Macmillan, 1936).

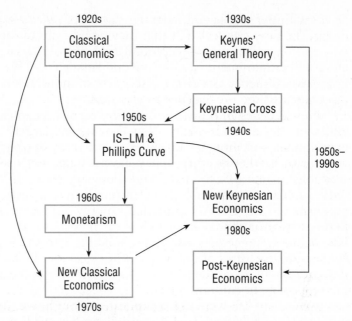

FIGURE 12.1   Macroeconomics Through Time

This figure shows the chain of developments in modern macroeconomics. Theories on the left are in the classical tradition; those on the right are Keynesian. Arrows show how each theory developed in reaction to what came before.

(indeed, IS-LM enjoyed an early designation as the "neoclassical synthesis" by some of its supporters). For this reason, it appears in the middle of our diagram—partly classical, partly Keynesian—and we consider the movement to IS-LM to have been a step away from Keynes's own economics and a step toward a restatement of the classical vision.

The monetarists, under Milton Friedman, mounted a rebellion against the synthesis represented by IS-LM and the Phillips curve. They sought to reestablish classical policy propositions about the neutrality of money and the political correctness of *laissez-faire*. But because the monetarists were working with the Keynesian tools (such as the consumption function), in an intellectual climate dominated by Keynesians and in which the old classical propositions had not regained credibility, theirs was a rebellion against Keynesianism even more than it was a restoration of the old classical system *per se*. In the diagram, the monetarists sit squarely in the classical tradition but arrows indicate that their ideas were developed out of the prevailing Keynesian ideas of the middle 1960s.

New classical economics was, as we have said, a palace revolt against monetarism. It aimed at replacing Friedman's *adaptive expec-*

tations with the supple and seductive notion of *rational expectations*. In so doing, the new classicals felt that they could fully restore, in a modern way and on a firm theoretical foundation, the old classical propositions about full employment equilibrium and laissez-faire. We thus depict the new classical theory as a direct descendent of monetarism and an indirect descendent of the pre-Keynesian classicals.

New Keynesian economics, finally, represents an effort to turn the tables on the new classicals. New Keynesians largely accept rational expectations and monetarism, as we have seen, but reject the essential concept of market clearing. They have sought, with some success, to reestablish some role for fiscal and monetary policy in a market economy. In this, they find it convenient to return to a version of IS-LM, in preference to the AS-AD (aggregate supply-aggregate demand) model that has become the favorite tool of the new classical camp. Nevertheless, the new Keynesians clearly are building with and in response to the conceptual structures of the new classicals; so we show the main line of descent running from the new classicals back over to the new Keynesians in the Keynesian column.

Now, as if life were not complicated enough, we turn to an enduring line of models that claim a more direct descent from Keynes's own work. These can be found on the right side of Figure 12.1 as *post-Keynesian economics*. Over the years, the post-Keynesians have remained somewhat aloof from the backs-and-forths of the mainstream Keynesians and the mainstream classicals. Indeed, many are equally critical of both traditions. Their attitude is reciprocated. As Robert Kuttner once put it, to the mainstream the post-Keynesians are "a tiny and despised sect that stubbornly refuses to disappear."[2]

Pay no attention, for the moment, to the bickering that goes on between theoretical traditions. Despite their small numbers, the post-Keynesians have continued to develop a body of macroeconomic theory that, we believe, has important insights for current policy issues. We devote the next two chapters to the post-Keynesian approach.

HOW DOES POST-KEYNESIAN ECONOMICS DIFFER?

Post-Keynesian economics is not just a minor variation on the New Keynesian themes. Instead, it represents an entire series of departures, challenging precisely those points on which the new Keynesians and the new classicals have come, after lengthy disputation, to agreement.

[2] Robert Kuttner, "The Poverty of Economics," *The Atlantic Monthly*, February 1985, pp. 74–84.

New classical economics rests, as we have seen, on three main ideas: market clearing, monetarism, and rational expectations. None can be taken as a literal description of the real world, but they do not need to be literal descriptions in order to be useful as theory. Workers and business-people in the real world need not be all-seeing and high-powered economic computers, constantly processing economic information in the optimal way, for the new classical ideas to be useful to economists (and students). The real issue is whether they are suitable as *abstraction*. Do these ideas lead to a vision of the economy that is broadly acceptable or to one that is profoundly misleading? Do they provide guidance for policy that is constructive, or guidance that is damaging? These are the important tests of a theory.

Post-Keynesians believe that the new classical abstractions really do not lead to useful generalizations about economic performance or policy. On this point, of course, the post-Keynesians and new Keynesians agree. But the two groups part company over reasons.

New Keynesians emphasize the potential failure of markets to clear and, in particular, the stickiness of real and nominal wages in the market for labor. But to post-Keynesians, the market clearing issue is somewhat beside the point: How can one discuss whether the aggregate labor market clears, when the real issue is whether, in any meaningful sense, an aggregate labor "market" actually exists?

Post-Keynesians acknowledge, of course, that many individual markets do exist—for commodities, for financial assets, and for differing types of labor. These particular and individual markets may or may not clear. But even if they do generally clear, that will not ensure that the economy *as a whole* will gravitate to full employment. What post-Keynesians doubt is the existence of a single overarching labor market, a market that ensures that full employment will prevail in the economy as a whole. They deny the usefulness, in other words, of the metaphor of supply and demand for labor as a whole, even while accepting that within actual markets on a smaller scale the forces of supply and demand do work, as a rule, to establish market-clearing quantities and prices.

With the market clearing question thus left in an ambiguous state, post-Keynesians focus their objections on the other two pillars of the new classical temple: monetarism and rational expectations. Since the new Keynesian model largely accepts both monetarism and rational expectations, the main post-Keynesian arguments against new classical economics also apply to the underpinnings of new Keynesianism. For this reason, post-Keynesianism needs to be treated as a distinct and separate theoretical tradition.

Discussion here will center on two points on which the post-Keynesians challenge monetarism and on one very sweeping objection that they make to rational expectations.

Endogenous Money

First, post-Keynesians do not believe that the money supply is controlled in any precise or regular way by the central bank. Rather, they argue, the central bank is generally *obliged* to supply the quantity of money that is demanded by economic agents. In particular, powerful borrowers such as large private corporations make decisions about how much they choose to borrow at any given time, and the monetary authorities cannot generally avoid providing the money and credit that would accommodate these demands. Thus, the active role of monetary policy is much more limited than monetarists, new classicals, and new Keynesians suppose, and the money supply itself cannot be treated as a policy variable but must be viewed as merely another (and not especially interesting) economic outcome.

A simple piece of institutional evidence exists for this viewpoint. The simplest textbook model of money creation, such as that discussed in Chapter 6, begins with a decision by the Federal Reserve to expand the monetary reserves of the banking system. This the Federal Reserve does by purchasing government securities on the open market. Bank reserves increase; interest rates fall; new investment borrowing is stimulated; and both the demand for new loans and the supply of reserves to meet that demand are enlarged.

As post-Keynesians observe, the real world works in quite a different way. In the real world, a very large part of bank credit is extended to businesses, especially large corporations. These actors negotiate lines of credit *in advance* with their commercial bankers. (For that matter, so do consumers who have prearranged limits on their credit cards.) These lines do not depend on whether the banking system has excess reserves with which to back a loan. Instead, when the corporation decides to borrow, it simply writes a check, and the bank automatically extends a new loan.

The bank, then, must seek reserves with which to back the loan. It could (in principle) get those reserves by calling in other loans, but that is extremely difficult to do in the real world and is not what banks actually do. Instead, banks borrow reserves from other banks. If the banking system as a whole is short of reserves, the federal funds rate (the rate on interbank lending of reserves) will rise. The central bank, seeing this, will react by adding reserves to the system. The money supply therefore rises and falls as much as borrowers, as a group, choose that it should.

On some occasions, of course, central bank policy becomes important. The central bank can control the short-term rate of interest. It may, from time to time, try to regulate the demand for credit by raising the rate of interest. The Federal Reserve in the United States did this, for example, in 1967, 1974, 1979, 1981, and 1989–1990. Alternatively, the central bank may try to stimulate demand for credit by lowering interest rates, as the Federal Reserve did for most of 1991 and 1992. This method of monetary control—manipulation of interest rates—is necessarily very imprecise. The effect of a reduction of interest rates on credit demand depends on the state of profit expectations (and future interest rate expectations) at any particular moment. If profit expectations are strong, a large rise in the interest rate may not be enough to quell loan demand. If profit expectations are weak, a large fall may not be enough to restore loan demand—a reality the Federal Reserve discovered in its efforts to stimulate recovery from the recession of 1991.

The key point, for post-Keynesians, is that a rise in interest rates works necessarily through a curtailment of private economic activity, through the mechanisms of recession and unemployment. For this reason, this type of policy is limited. The central bank has an overriding responsibility to act as *lender of last resort*, to prevent the kind of mass bankruptcies and bank failures that paralyzed the economic system during the 1930s. Therefore, even when active monetary policies are undertaken, post-Keynesians argue, they fall short of giving the central bank true discretionary command over the money supply.

Post-Keynesians believe, therefore, that it is not appropriate to represent the money supply curve as an exogenous policy instrument or as the vertical line characteristic of the monetarist model. The post-Keynesian money supply schedule is horizontal, as shown in Figure 12.2. In

FIGURE 12.2   Two Views of Money and Interest

Whereas monetarists believe that the central bank sets the money supply and lets the market determine the interest rate, post-Keynesians argue that the central bank sets the interest rate and lets money demand determine money supply.

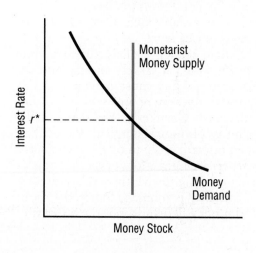
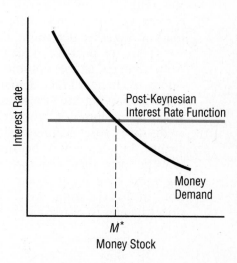

effect, the post-Keynesians replace the monetarist money supply policy function, $M^s = \bar{M}^s$, with an interest rate policy function:

$$(12.1) \hspace{5cm} r = \bar{r}$$

The money demand function, $M^d = M^d(r)$, thus determines M and not r. The central bank creates money as money is required by a shifting schedule of money demand. And since the money supply is not and cannot be closely controlled, the post-Keynesians reject the monetarist idea that the central bank is the master of the price level.

Markup Pricing

The post-Keynesians' second broad objection to monetarism concerns the theory of prices itself. Not only does the central bank not control the money supply, according to post-Keynesians, but the money supply does not drive the price level.

According to monetarism, the central bank first determines how much money to create, and the labor market sets the value of the real wage consistent with full employment. From these core facts, the general price level emerges: prices must settle to a level consistent with full employment real wages with the amount of money that the central bank has chosen to create.

Post-Keynesians have a very different view of the sequence of cause and effect. In the post-Keynesian view, money prices are very inertial; they are based, to a great extent, on the *money costs of production* prevailing at the immediately previous moment of time. To money costs, themselves the past prices of intermediate goods and the wages of labor, producers add a customary *markup*. The markup varies across products and industries, reflecting differing market conditions (or *degrees of monopoly power*), but it tends to be more or less stable over time. Costs and markup together determine the general price level.

Thus, to post-Keynesians, the main sequence of fluctuations runs from changes in the volume of production, at largely inertial money prices, to changes in the demand for credit, which must grow in order to finance growing inventories and capital investment and which will fall when the volume of production declines. Changes in the demand for credit then cause changes in the quantity of money supplied. Prices may change, but that will be because of an upward creep in costs, particularly in wage costs, that occurs when markets are tight and workers are enjoying some bargaining power with which to improve their relative position. In that situation, the chain of causality is running, indirectly, from price changes to changing credit and money demands, not the other way round.

To express this formally, we observe that the monetarist version of the equation of exchange, $MV = Py$, holds that V and y are constants, so that the chain of causality runs from M to P:

$$M\overset{\frown}{V} = \vec{P}\bar{y}$$

For the post-Keynesians, the equation of exchange still holds, but the price level at any given moment is the inertial variable, being a function of costs, C, in the preceding period and the markup, μ:

$$P_t = (1 + \mu)C_{t-1}$$

Therefore, with money supplied depending mainly on fluctuations in real output, the lines of causality for the most part run from y to M:

$$M\overset{\frown}{V} = \overset{\frown}{P}y$$

Occasionally, the central bank may (and does!) react to a creeping rise in costs (particularly wage costs) by raising the interest rate. But the first effect is inevitably on the volume of output and employment, not on the price level. Only by creating unemployment can the Federal Reserve contain wages and thereby slow the increase in the price level. Post-Keynesians insist that there is no market mechanism, working through expectations or otherwise, whereby reduction in money growth leads directly to a slowdown of inflation.

Markup pricing and real wage adjustment   The markup theory of pricing has another broad implication, one we have already encountered several times. If prices are set by a markup over wage costs, then adjusting nominal wages in the labor market cannot have the effect of reducing real wages and so creating the classical conditions for a fall of unemployment.

Under markup pricing, as we have just seen, the price level is determined within the productive system, essentially by a process of adding a profit margin to wages and other prime costs. The money supply then adjusts to meet the nominal transactions demands so created. Prices rise and fall with wages, while changes in the money supply are mainly a reflection, not a cause, of changes in real output and of cost-based inflationary pressures.

Because prices rise and fall with wages, changes in nominal wages generally will not bring about changes in real wages.[3] In the

---

[3] And because the money stock is endogenous, even a generalized fall of both wages and prices will not automatically lead to an increase in real demand, as often supposed, via the *real balance effect* (or increase in the purchasing power of an existing stock of money as prices fall).

post-Keynesian view, making *money* wages more flexible will not make *real* wages more flexible. There is no practical way to dissociate the determination of the aggregate price level (the denominator of the real wage) from the determination of money wages (in the numerator of the real wage). And since changes in money wages will not affect real wages, changes in money wages cannot reduce unemployment.

This is, of course, precisely the argument Keynes made at the start of *The General Theory*. Workers who resist cuts in money wages because they doubt that such cuts will lead to greater employment are, in the post-Keynesian view, entirely correct. Keynes's own words on this point are instructive: "It is fortunate that the workers, though unconsciously, are instinctively more reasonable economists than the classical school, inasmuch as they resist reductions of money-wages." According to Keynes and the post-Keynesians, workers implicitly recognize that the medicine so often prescribed for their unemployment is, in fact, a placebo because it fails to reduce the level of the real wage. The cure for unemployment, if there is one, must be made of more potent stuff.

Subjective Expectations

Even (perhaps especially) if a cut in the rate of increase of money wages will not lower real wages and raise employment, will workers not agree to such a cut simply in order to eliminate inflation? New classical economists would surely argue they would. In the new classical view, rational workers would adjust their nominal wage demands in response to the credible threat of tight money, because they would rationally expect the consequences of tight money to be unemployment, at least for themselves. Indeed, in this view, workers resisting money wage cuts will face unemployment, while their more compliant fellows get the jobs at the same real wage as before.

Post-Keynesians tend not to agree that the rational worker will necessarily behave in a cooperative way. They have a different view about how rational people evaluate the future, which raises the third major point of difference between post-Keynesians and new classicals: the treatment of expectations. We return to the case of the noncooperative workers below, but first a review of the underlying issues is useful.

For the new classical economics, rational expectations are the way in which the present is linked with the future. New classicists assume that economic actors form expectations about the future performance of the economy that (1) do not contain systematic errors and (2) cannot be improved by learning or otherwise changing the way those actors behave.

Again, criticizing the *descriptive realism* of this assumption is easy. Information is costly, so that for many economic actors it may not pay to be sufficiently well informed. Economic *rationality*—the ability to make logical decisions even when good information is available—is an assumption whose validity for a whole population may be doubted. Economic structures change; the absence of systematic errors in the past does not establish the validity of rational expectations in the future. And so on. There are many ways in which the rational expectations hypothesis does not accurately describe what goes on in the real world.

Yet, this objection does not really address the heart of the case for rational expectations. The real issue is not whether the hypothesis actually corresponds to the economic behavior of tens of millions of real people in the United States. It is whether the hypothesis forms a defensible basis for predicting that behavior. If so, then rational expectations provide a suitable basis for a working model of the economy. And this is all that careful advocates of rational expectations claim.

The post-Keynesian criticism aims at the heart of the specific claim that the rational expectations hypothesis makes. This is the claim that there exists, or can exist, an *objective* central tendency, average, or expected value, for the future values of major economic variables and that this average exists *independently of what it is expected to be*. If such a claim is valid, then the information-seeking actions of economic agents can indeed be conceived of in new classical terms, as an effort to discover the objective values. But if the claim is not valid, then the actual values may instead depend in crucial ways on whatever the subjective expectations of them happen to be. And in that case, the performance of the economy may become unstable in ways that are deeply incompatible with rational expectations.

We take up, very briefly, two aspects of this question. One is especially relevant to the post-Keynesian view of the determinants of the aggregate volume of investment (a subject covered in great detail below). It is known as the phenomenon of *animal spirits*, or purely subjective group behavior. The other goes back to those workers who won't cooperate with inflation-fighting nominal wage cuts; it can be described as a conflict between rational expectations and rational action. This sort of issue comes under the heading known to game theorists as the *prisoner's dilemma*.

Animal spirits The businessperson's decision to invest depends, as we learned long ago, on the interaction between the marginal efficiency of capital, or the expected profitability of a new investment, and the rate of interest that can be earned by doing nothing at all. Expected profitability depends, in part, on a set of outside conditions that are truly objective—for instance, on the degree of utilization of existing capacity and on current costs of production in relation to current prices at final sale.

But there is another element to expected profitability, one not so easy to pin down. Expected profitability also depends on the state of expectations of other entrepreneurs. These expectations, themselves among the objective conditions any individual entrepreneur must seek to discover, are important. If other entrepreneurs are planning investments at the same time, total demand conditions will be higher than otherwise, and final product prices and profitability may also be higher. But such expectations are unlike other objective conditions precisely in that they are not objective. They have no material basis, and if they change, then the character of rational behavior will change too.

Thus, let us suppose that confidence prevails. In that case, investment decisions will be strong, profits will be high—and confidence will be justified. But if confidence breaks down (which it may do independently of any external cause whatsoever), then entrepreneurs will cut their investment decisions, profits will fall, and again their failure of confidence will seem, after the fact, to have been justified.

Curiously, it is very difficult to distinguish this situation on the surface from something that might be predicted by the rational expectations model. The observer who postulates rational expectations will observe nothing in evident conflict with this postulate. Economic actors are not making systematic errors in their forecasts. Yet, there is still something wrong in what the postulate implies, because actors are not really seeking, or finding, an objective reality. They are *creating* reality, in the way that a herd of buffalo creates the reality of its own movement. Moreover, the reality can change, and since the causes are all in the mind, there is no good way to predict in which direction the herd will next move, or at what speed. With this metaphor in mind, economist Joan Robinson liked to say that the herd movements of investors and entrepreneurs could best be described as reflecting animal spirits.

In this tradition, post-Keynesian economists are skeptical of placing too much faith in the predictability of economic events. Economic uncertainty, they argue, is a prevailing feature of economic life. And dealing with uncertainty, as opposed to risk, involves dealing with a range of outcomes whose relative probabilities are unknown and cannot be calculated and for which it therefore makes no sense to calculate an expected value or central tendency, as expectations formation under rational expectations requires.

Prisoner's dilemmas   Given the existence of economic uncertainty, the other problem with rational expectations arises in the translation of expectations into action. A change in the expectations of individuals about the future does not necessarily mean a parallel change in their rational course of action.

Consider again the case of the workers who, in the new classical view, ought to keep their wage demands under control lest they provoke the wrath of the central bankers. Suppose that the central bankers are indeed fearsome, that their message is clear, and that the workers understand that the consequences of the central bankers carrying out their threats in the face of noncooperation is almost certainly a rise in unemployment.

Individual workers may well understand all this perfectly. But how can each be sure that all other workers also reason in the same way? Suppose some workers simply do not believe that the central bankers will act on their threats? Or some believe that the right course of action is to face the central bankers down? In that case, uncertainty about what other workers will do will drive even those workers who believe the central bankers are serious to a course of action opposite to what the rational expectations argument would call for.

Indeed, every worker's actions depend critically on what he or she expects other workers to do. Without absolute confidence that *all* workers will reduce their wage demands, it makes no sense for any one worker to risk cooperating with the central bank. (For example, maybe the central bank *will* back down and accommodate after all, leaving everyone employed and the cooperators with a reduction of real wage.) And since all workers reason the same way, all arrive at the same conclusion. Noncooperation pays, even though it may bring on a policy that will cause hardship and unemployment for some workers.

Some of the appropriate techniques for understanding and analyzing this phenomenon are to be found in *game theory*, which is a set of analytical techniques for dealing with fundamental uncertainty. The case of the workers described above is an elementary application of a situation in game theory known as the *prisoner's dilemma*.[4] Game theory in general provides one of the most exciting realms of current research in macroeconomics, among post-Keynesian economists and also among many orthodox economists as well.

These issues are also highly important in the real world. They have led many conservative economists to argue that the government must eliminate uncertainty, so far as possible, about its future policies. These economists are the main intellectual force behind efforts to enact money growth rules in the laws governing the Federal Reserve and to write amendments limiting federal government spending or balancing the budget into the Constitution of the United States. There has also been a large, if somewhat inconclusive, literature on the issue of *policy credibility*—whether policy is more effective if it is taken seriously by ordinary people.

---

[4] The prisoner's dilemma arises when two prisoners are interrogated separately about a crime. Each knows that if both refuse to confess, they cannot be convicted. But they also know that if they hold out while the other confesses, they will receive a stiff sentence while the confessor receives a light one. So both confess, both receive jail terms, and both are worse off than they would have been if each had been able to enforce cooperation on the other.

Game-theoretic concerns have also underpinned numerous recent real-world attempts in developing countries, including Argentina, Bolivia, Brazil, Israel, and Mexico, to coordinate expectations to stabilize their recent hyperinflations. These efforts, which represent a somewhat more direct approach to the management of economic uncertainty and its behavioral implications, are discussed in the special section following Chapter 13.

In sum, post-Keynesians believe that a world in which objective reality depends on subjective expectations cannot be modeled, as the new classical economics would have it, by assuming that expectations formation is merely a search for information. Rather, expectations must themselves be treated as an autonomous force. Moreover, the analysis of expectations about other people's expectations forces us away from the basic conclusions of the rational expectations model and into modes of analysis that address the issue of uncertainties that cannot themselves be quantified. Indeed, as we shall see in the special section at the end of the next chapter, post-Keynesians advocate a variety of policy interventions, known as *incomes policies*, that serve the purpose of influencing and coordinating the expectations of economic agents.

The nonexistence of the natural rate   A particular instance of conflict between the post-Keynesian perspective on expectations and that of the new classical economics shows its critical importance to a core proposition, namely whether there can or cannot exist a vertical Phillips curve and a natural rate of unemployment.

As you will recall, when the rational expectations hypothesis is embedded in the rest of the new classical framework, the result is a Phillips curve that is always vertical and the existence of a persistent natural rate of unemployment. The economy fluctuates around the natural rates of unemployment and output and actually resides there whenever expectations of inflation coincide with the inflation that actually occurs. Shifts in the natural rate may occur over time, but only as a result of structural changes in the economy. For example, an increase in the proportion of teenagers in the labor market may lead to a period of higher unemployment, because teenagers are less likely to remain in any one job for an extended time. Attempts to move away from the natural rate by altering the level of demand in the economy are bound to fail, to dissipate in inflation or deflation.

If expectations are an independent determining force behind investment and therefore employment, then the concept of a natural rate of unemployment loses its meaning. The actual rate of unemployment may be high or low, depending (in part) on whether the profit expectations of entrepreneurs are low or high. There is nothing irrational (even in the new classical sense) about either situation. In fact, whenever profit expectations are high, the unemployment rate will be low, and vice versa—

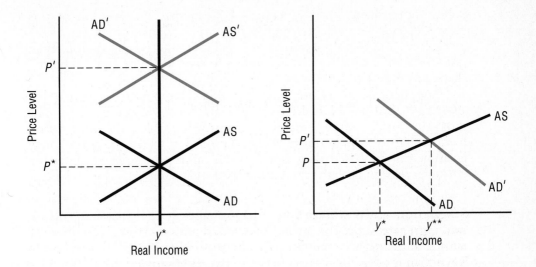

FIGURE 12.3   **Two Views of Aggregate Demand and Supply**

In the post-Keynesian view, shifts in aggregate demand alter the equilibrium level of
real income. There is no natural rate of output as in the new classical model.

just as expected. But there is no inherent tendency for the economy to
return to any given rate of unemployment once displaced from it (by a
shift of expectations). An *arbitrary* change in expectations can lead to a
change in *equilibrium* unemployment. It thus does not make sense to
speak of a *natural rate* of unemployment.

A simple way to see this disagreement is in terms of the two diagrams of Figure 12.3. Both show the interaction of aggregate supply and
aggregate demand, with each curve corresponding to a given expected
price level in the period in question. On the left, we have the new
classical view. It holds that the relationship between real aggregate supply and demand is mediated by the existence of a *natural rate of output*.
This is the output rate that corresponds to the natural rate of employment and unemployment, as determined in the labor market. Because of
rational expectations, a fully anticipated upward shift of aggregate demand will lead to a corresponding upward shift of aggregate supply: the
expected price level and the actual price level will both change, but real
output will not.

The diagram on the right approximates the post-Keynesian view.
Aggregate demand is downward sloping as before, indicating that, for a
given expected price level, a higher actual price level will yield a smaller
real quantity of output demanded (as prices rise relative to a fixed expectation, buyers demand fewer goods and services). But where new classical economics regards the value of aggregate demand as essentially

policy determined, post-Keynesians believe that the position of this curve depends on entrepreneurs' profit expectations (which determine investment and therefore purchasers' incomes) and is thus volatile in an essentially subjective way. It is fruitless to seek an "objective" expected change in the price level.

Suppliers are, therefore, unable to alter their expected supply in the short run to offset the real effects of a shift in aggregate demand. The short-run supply curve remains comparatively stable—the information from which to form a "rational expectation" on which the curve's new position can be based does not exist. If aggregate demand shifts for whatever reason, both the real output level and the price level will change.

Stagnation and exhilaration   Because aggregate demand is volatile and aggregate supply is stable, many different short-run equilibria of output and employment are equally plausible. Indeed, recent post-Keynesian models distinguish between two alternative states of the macroeconomy. In the *stagnationist* state, capitalists are gloomy, the rate of effective demand is low, and strongly expansionary fiscal and monetary policies are both sufficient and necessary to boost spirits, raise profits, and restore full employment. In the *exhilarationist* state, capitalists are eager, the rate of effective demand is high, and investment is restrained only by a high rate of interest—which may be due to government fiscal policies that are too expansionary for the prevailing conditions. In the exhilarationist world, post-Keynesians fall in line with new classicals, arguing for less-activist government policies. However, post-Keynesians do not think that the exhilarationist condition is everywhere and always the only one that applies.

INTEREST RATES, INVESTMENT, AND EMPLOYMENT

Isolating the major differences between post-Keynesians and the other modern schools ought to help define what post-Keynesians are against. But it is also necessary to describe what they are for and how they endeavor to model that. In this section, we present the first of several constructive elements of the post-Keynesian model.

To begin with a generalization, post-Keynesians believe that the problem of unemployment arises in the short run from fluctuations in the level of aggregate, or effective, demand.[5] *Effective demand* is the sum

[5] The terms *aggregate demand* and *effective demand* are practically interchangeable. We use effective demand when discussing the post-Keynesian model, simply because it is the more common usage in this context. However, the post-Keynesian usage is not identical with Keynes's usage in his *General Theory*.

of expenditure for consumption goods (by households and government), demand for investment goods (mainly by business), and the net demands of the foreign sector (exports minus imports).

What is special about this view? Once again, post-Keynesians do not believe any automatic mechanism exists that guarantees that the sum of these independently determined components will be sufficient to buy back the entire national product at full employment. In particular, post-Keynesians follow Keynes in rejecting the idea (shared by new classicals and new Keynesians) that the forces of supply and demand in the labor market will play this role. Therefore, it is necessary to analyze each component separately. And if any one major component is unstable, post-Keynesians would conclude, that part can be described as the cause of instability in employment.

As we learned from our early treatment of the consumption function, consumption expenditure is a comparatively stable stream over time. It is also, for the most part, predictable once current money incomes are known. Government expenditure is also highly stable and predictable. Export demand is not so predictable, because it depends on foreign incomes that lie beyond the reach of a national model. But short of modeling the whole world economy, nothing much can be done about that. That leaves *investment demand* as the most volatile and yet most potentially predictable element in the effective demand equation. Post-Keynesians therefore tend to insist that an understanding of fluctuations in investment is the key to an understanding of unemployment.

The first critical need in a theory of investment is for a theory of the rate of interest. Post-Keynesians have built their theory around the core idea that the rate of interest is an *exogenous* force, both short-term and long-term. This exogeneity has a profound consequence, which is the non-neutrality of policies (both monetary and fiscal) affecting aggregate demand. This quite complex issue is fundamentally not treated in the mainstream of contemporary macroeconomics; therefore, we devote sufficient space and care to clarify it.

Classical Interest Rate Theory Once Again

New Keynesians and new classicals appear to get their theory of the determination of interest rates from the same place: the microeconomic theory of marginal product pricing. You have already seen how this theory underlies the conventional conception of the labor market. According to it, real wage rates offered (along the demand curve for labor) are determined by the *marginal productivity of labor*. Businesses will hire workers just up to the point where the output of the last worker hired compensates for the wage he or she must be paid. Meanwhile, the supply curve of labor is upward sloping, which reflects the *marginal disutility of work* to the worker and the fact that wages must rise to induce workers to give up valuable leisure time. Thus, equilibrium of real wages and employment is jointly determined by the interaction of labor supply and labor demand.

In parallel fashion, the marginal productivity theory holds that real interest rates offered (along the demand curve for capital) will vary with the marginal productivity of the capital stock. As more capital is employed, this marginal productivity falls; thus, the demand curve for capital is downward sloping. And the equilibrium (of real interest rates and new investment) is determined in the market for capital (sometimes called the market for loanable funds) by the interaction between this downward-sloping demand curve for capital and an upward-sloping supply curve of saving. The latter reflects the increasing reward (real interest rate) that is required to induce savers to forgo consumption today in favor of investment that may yield higher consumption tomorrow.

In this new classical/new Keynesian view of the world, the long-term interest rate has nothing to do with the volume of employment. The interest rate determines, rather, the proportion of income that will be saved and, in conjunction with the physical productivities of the capital stock, the choice of techniques and capital intensities of production. If the interest rate falls, a more capital-intensive technique will be used; if it rises, a less capital-intensive technique may be employed. These decisions may influence *the rate* at which an economy grows and the composition of output as between investment and consumption goods, but they are irrelevant to the volume of employment and output that will pertain at any given moment. (It is quite possible to have, for instance, full employment and no net investment, so long as everyone is productively employed in making consumption goods with the existing capital stock. This will occur at a very high rate of interest.) Thus, new classicals and new Keynesians alike downplay the role of the interest rate when they discuss the problem of unemployment.

Post-Keynesian Problems with the Classical View

A key problem with this theory, post-Keynesians believe, is that the concept of a capital stock is not meaningful outside of highly simplified models.[6] Where there are diverse types of capital goods (as in the real

[6] Specifically, models that treat capital and output as though they consisted of a single homogeneous substance. Such models are known in economics as "corn models" because, in the case of corn, the output (corn to eat) and the principal element of capital (seed corn) are the same thing. More-fanciful terms for the kind of capital involved include *putty* and (Joan Robinson's suggestion) *leets* (steel, spelled backwards).

world, where capital includes everything from rakes and shovels to machine tools and aircraft), the measurement of the physical volume of the capital stock, in terms of some consistent physical unit (tons, yards, hours of rental time), literally makes no sense. There is no such thing as a physical unit of capital in the real world.[7] Hence, it is impossible to establish a downward-sloping (marginal productivity) relationship between the demand for capital and the real interest rate, as the loanable funds theory of the interest rate requires.

Indeed, it can be shown that, in general, there is no reason why lower real interest rates will be associated with a more intensive use of capital, nor higher interest rates with a less intensive use. Thus, in the post-Keynesian view, the idea of an equilibrium, or natural, rate of interest as the central tendency of a capital market turns out to be logically impossible to defend.[8] Post-Keynesians therefore reject the capital market view of interest rate determination and take up an alternative perspective in which the interest rate becomes a critical determinant of the volume of employment.

The Post-Keynesian Alternative

For the most part, post-Keynesians return to the theory of the interest rate set forth in Keynes's *General Theory*. That alternative viewpoint requires that we distinguish between interest rates on assets created for only a short period of time (say, ninety days or six months) and interest rates on assets created for long periods (say, three years or more).

Short-term assets are highly *liquid*, which means that they are easy to buy and sell at their face value. The reason for this is straightforward: anyone who buys a ninety-day bill has to wait only that length of time, at a maximum, before the original issuer is obliged to redeem the bill at face value.

For long-term assets, such as corporate and government bonds and household mortgages, the situation is very different. They need not be redeemed until the very distant future. In the meantime, they may trade freely among investors but at a variable price. In particular, if the long-term interest rate rises, then a long-term bond issued earlier at a lower interest rate will fall in value, while if the long-term interest rate falls, long-term bond prices will rise. For this reason, long-term bond in-

---

[7] This makes capital quite different from, at least, unskilled labor, which can be measured in physical units (hours of labor time). The measurement of the capital stock in terms of money values, though often employed in statistical work, does not resolve this problem, since a key issue at stake is the means whereby the prices of capital goods are themselves determined.

[8] For a detailed treatment of these issues, we recommend Geoffrey Harcourt, *Some Cambridge Controversies in the Theory of Capital* (Cambridge: Cambridge University Press, 1972).

vestments are considered to be speculative, or risky, even though there may be little chance that the issuer will actually fail to pay the interest and principal when they fall due. So, long-term interest rates tend to be higher than short-term rates and also to be governed by a number of market forces—such as changes in expectations about economic conditions in the future—that do not affect the short-term rate of interest.

Post-Keynesians regard the short-term interest rate as set for practical purposes by the central bank, as illustrated by equation (12.1) and Figure 12.2. Moreover, the market in which the central bank operates is a market for money, not for capital. Short-term interest is the reward, not for accumulating capital but for buying the government debts that the central bank wishes to issue and, correspondingly, for forgoing the liquidity advantages of keeping cash in the wallet.

Thus, the determination of the short-term rate is entirely straightforward. What is interesting, in the post-Keynesian view, is what happens when the short-term rate changes. For while new classicals and new Keynesians alike see the investment decision as consisting largely of a comparison between the interest rate and a *given* investment demand schedule (set by the real rate of return on capital investment), post-Keynesians insist that the operation of asset markets fundamentally ties the expected profitability of new investment itself to fluctuations in the rate of interest. And so, when the short-term interest rate changes, it has a fundamental effect on the incentives to hold money as opposed to other assets and, through that effect, on the prices of all capital assets and on the rate of investment. We turn now to a more detailed examination of this process.

Expectations, asset prices, and investment   As all economists agree, effective demand for investment goods depends on the difference between the expected profitability of investment projects, on the one hand, and the rate of interest, on the other. The rate of interest is the *opportunity cost* of embarking on physical investment—the amount that one could earn by doing nothing, or the amount that one counts as the base cost if one chooses to borrow in order to invest.

At this point, for a theory of expected profits, economic thought runs in two directions. The mainstream theory returns, once again, to the capital market: the expected return on new investment must be a function of the marginal physical productivity of the capital stock, which in turn depends on whether an economy is endowed with a lot of capital relative to its labor force, or only a little.

The post-Keynesians have rejected the idea that the profitability of new investment depends in any coherent way on the raw size of the previously existing capital stock. So they must look for some other basis on which entrepreneurs can make this calculation. They find it in a theory that helps us understand how capital assets are priced. In parti-

Taking a Closer Look

INTEREST RATES: REAL AND NOMINAL, SHORT AND LONG

The charts that accompany this box illustrate the course of interest rates over the past three decades in several major industrial countries.

Note first that there is no such thing as "the" interest rate. Many different interest rates exist, each corresponding to an asset of a particular type, maturity, and risk. In Figure 12.B1, we show three or four similar rates for four countries: a discount rate, a call rate, a bank (or prime) rate, and a bond rate.

The *discount rate* is an administered rate, set by the decision of the central bank. It is also, typically in all charted countries, the lowest interest rate most of the time. It is the rate at which banks can borrow from the central bank in order to maintain their liquidity (and meet their reserve requirements). Since the discount rate is the lowest rate, central banks generally limit the amount of discount lending any individual bank can do. Banks are also reluctant to press for discount loans; an excessive eagerness to make up required reserves at the discount window may be taken as a sign of imprudent banking practices, inviting unwelcome scrutiny from regulators. We show discount rates for the United States, France, and Japan. Of these countries, the United States makes the most use of changes in the discount rate,

whereas France makes little use of this instrument of policy.

The *call rate*, an overnight rate on loans (*call money*) between banks, is the market rate that tends to be most closely aligned with the discount rate. (In the United States, the interest rate most similar to a call rate is known as the *federal funds rate*.) The rates are similar to discount rates for an obvious reason: banks use call loans to meet their reserve requirements, which is exactly the same reason they may go to the discount window. Thus, the two rates will tend to move together if the discount rate is permitted to move at all. However, there will be occasions when the central bank restricts access to discount loans while refusing to raise the discount rate; at such times, if loan demand is very great, the call rate will rise far above the official discount rate. As you can see in Figure 12.B1, this happened in Japan in 1975 and 1981 and in France throughout the first half of the 1980s.

Rates that banks charge each other (on overnight loans) and rates they charge their customers (on loans that may range up to three to five years) diverge widely. In Figure 12.B1, the U.S. prime rate and the British bank rate illustrate the best rates that commercial borrowers can generally obtain from

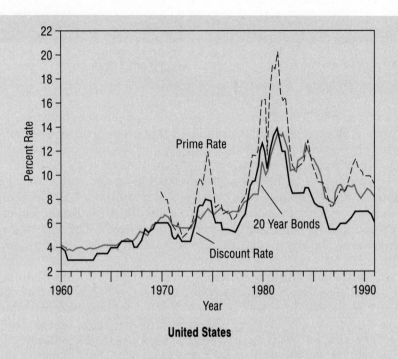

United States

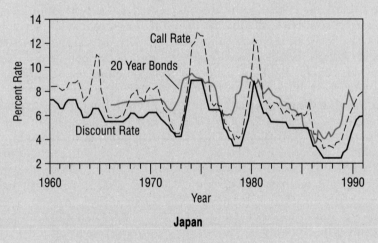

Japan

FIGURE 12.B1   Interest Rate Comparisons

banks. In the U.S. case, the prime rate has risen especially far above short-term money market rates during period of tight money, as in 1974–1975, 1980, and 1981–1982. These times were good for bank profits, not so much fun for bank borrowers. However, the normal

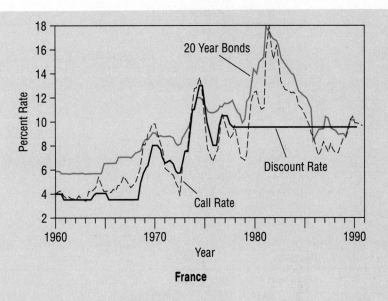

France

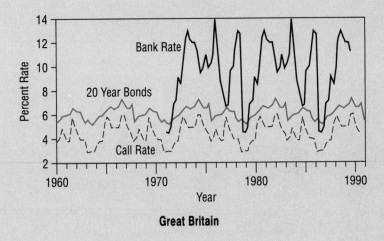

Great Britain

difference between bank rates and the marginal cost of funds is evidently much less in the United States than in Britain; this may reflect a greater competitiveness of the U.S. banking system.

A long-term rate is illustrated by the twenty-year bond rate. In all the countries, long-term interest rates tend to be higher than the short rate, and by a fairly consistent amount. This reflects the greater

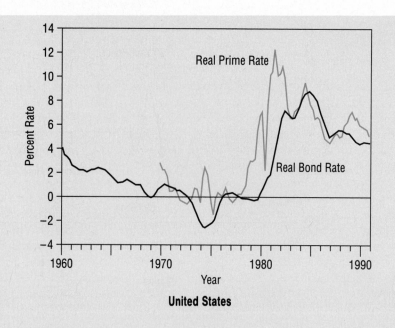

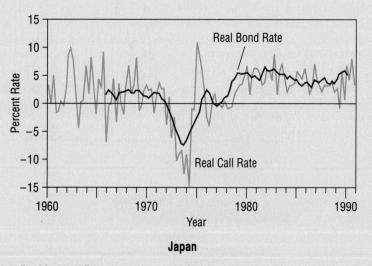

FIGURE 12.B2   Real Interest Rates

risk in long-term lending and
(closely related) the reduced liquidity of long-term assets. (Even safe
ones, such as government bonds,
are subject to price fluctuations.)

The relationship between interest rates on loans of different
maturities is known as the *yield
curve*. Since long rates tend to lie
above short, except in moments of

extremely tight policy, the yield curve is normally upward sloping. This is certainly true in the U.S. case. But note how much steeper the yield curve has become in the 1980s than it was before, as measured by the bond rate over the discount rate. Also, even very good bank rates, such as the prime rate, often lie above the lowest-risk long bond rate. This reflects the higher risk involved in loans to private companies than in loans to the government.

Real interest rates are calculated by subtracting a measure of actual or anticipated inflation from nominal, or money, interest rates. For short-term interest rates, this is relatively straightforward: simply subtract current inflation from the interest rate. But for long-term credit instruments, the calculation of a real interest rate is necessarily imprecise because the relevant measure of inflation is *expected future inflation* over the length of the particular loan. No measure of this expected rate of inflation exists, as it is a purely subjective notion.

Figure 12.B2 shows real short-term interest rates and an estimated long-term real interest rate for the United States and Japan. Interestingly, these charts illustrate how much measures of the real rate of interest can vary over time. You may ask whether this is consistent with a model that attributes such rates to an equilibrating process between the supply of savings and the demand for investment. Also, note how much higher the real interest rate became in the United States after 1980. New classical economists would tend to attribute this to an inward shift in the supply curve of savings (due to declining personal savings and budget deficits) or to an outward shift in the demand curve for investment. Keynesians, especially post-Keynesians, would focus on a shift to a much more restrictive monetary policy. For them, the rise in nominal interest rates brought on the fall in inflation rates, and the high real rate is merely an artifact of this policy change.

cular, the post-Keynesian theory focuses on the difference in price between the cost of production of capital assets and the expected price at which a new capital asset can be sold.

For this reason, a theory of *asset prices* must and does underlie the determination of the relative levels of effective demand and cost of supply. This theory determines prices for commodities that can be stored once they are produced, that can be sold, and resold, and the new production of which constitutes that most volatile element of effective demand, the manufacture of investment goods. We need a theory of asset prices, based on rational behavior (profit seeking by firms and utility seeking by individuals) but under the climate of uncertainty that post-Keynesians believe to be the essential feature of investment decision making in the real world.

Prices facing the entrepreneur   Our theory properly begins at the level of the individual economic agent, in particular the businessperson or entrepreneur. This person—the central figure in the story—has access to capital and must decide on its disposition. We therefore develop our picture of the entrepreneur with care.

At any time, the entrepreneur must choose between one of three possible courses of action: (1) purchase a capital asset (say, a house or a plot of land or a piece of equipment) now, paying the present *spot price* (*SP*) for that asset; (2) place an order for such a capital asset to be delivered at some time in the future, thereby contracting to pay the *forward price* (*FP*) (the price that must be paid now for delivery at some future date) for that asset; (3) place no order at all, in which case the funds may lie idle, earning the going rate of interest. In the latter case, if the entrepreneur chooses to remove funds from the bank at a later date to buy the commodity, he or she will pay the spot price prevailing at that time.

Calculations concerning the profitability of each course of action depend on a third concept, namely today's *expected price* (*EP*) of the commodity at that future date. While the spot and forward prices are observable at any given time, the expected future price of a commodity is purely subjective. *EP* exists solely in the mind of the entrepreneur and will differ from one entrepreneur to another. If *EP* is high, options 1 or 2 will be taken, depending on the relationship between the spot and the forward price. If *EP* is low, then the money may sit in the bank.

The investment choice   Now consider the entrepreneur's choice. When is it best to purchase an asset? Clearly, when one can expect a profit from doing so, relative to keeping funds on deposit at the bank. It is easy to see this process at work in, for example, the case of a fine old painting. Why would a speculator (who is not interested in art for its own sake) buy an old work of art? Because, and only because, it may become more valuable at some time in the future than it is today. In particular, if the expected future price of the painting is so much higher than the present price that it apparently will pay to take money from the bank (forgoing the interest that would be earned there) and invest it in the painting instead, then the speculator will be moved to make the transaction. The ratio of the expected future to the current spot price, EP_{t+1}/SP_t is the expected appreciation, or *expected yield*, $1 + q$, of this commodity.

Of course, our speculator must also make provision to protect the painting and to guard it against both damage and thieves. For this purpose, he may hire a guard, and he may take out an insurance policy. The cost of doing so, over the year he expects to hold the painting, is the *carrying cost, c*. And, in making the choice of the painting as against some other purchase, he will also take into account how readily the painting might be sold for cash if that suddenly became necessary. This implicit valuation (which might be fairly low in the case of a painting) is the *liquidity premium, l*.

Combining the three factors, *q, c,* and *l*, yields the *own-rate of interest* on the purchase of the painting (a concept suggested to Keynes by his friend, the Italian economist Piero Sraffa):

$$i = q - c + l$$

We can go further than this, to say quite definitely *how much* money our entrepreneur will shift from bank account to art collection. He will move just enough so that, in a subjective estimation, the own-rate of interest on additional paintings acquired falls to equal the rate of interest on bank deposits. For, as each new painting is added to the art collection, we may presume that the spot price rises relative to the price that our entrepreneur expects the paintings will fetch in, say, a year's time.[9] Thus, the expected return on the speculation declines. Eventually, the spot price becomes so high, relative to the expected price, that our speculator calculates that he would be better off leaving the money in the bank. At that point, the speculation stops. The own-rate of interest of paintings has adjusted to be equal to the market rate of interest on money.

This gives us a first basic proposition:

The own-rate of interest on assets (when measured in terms of money) tends to adjust to equal, at the margin, the rate of interest on money.

Of course, putting aside the temptations of counterfeiting, old paintings cannot be newly produced. For this reason, while an auction market will exist, it is unlikely that there will also exist a *forward market* in such items. Forward markets are most useful, and best organized, around commodities produced and released on a regular schedule (e.g., wheat, corn, and soybeans).

Where assets are traded in forward markets, it normally (except in cases of glut) will cost more to order an asset for delivery immediately

---

[9] Either the speculator must bid a higher and higher spot price in order to bring additional paintings to market, or he must purchase paintings with lower and lower prospects for future appreciation. In either case, the own rate of interest must fall as additional paintings are bought.

than to order the same asset to be delivered, say, one year hence.[10] The ratio of these two prices, *SP/FP,* is defined as the *spot premium* of the asset in question. EP_{t+1}/FP measures is the return that can be earned by buying forward now rather than for spot delivery a year hence.[11] This is a reward for providing, to the supplier, the assurance that a sale can be made a year hence at a definite price.[12]

The same general process is at work in the forward markets for all producible commodities, or in any contract market at all—such as the market for housing, where the consumer chooses between old houses currently on the spot market and equivalent new construction, contracted now for later delivery (a private forward market). In such markets, the spot price cannot rise indefinitely relative to the forward price. For, as the spot price rises, raising the liquidity premium and lowering the own-rate of interest on the asset, there is an increasing incentive to buy the commodity on the forward market (to order a new house rather than buy an old one). This incentive provides a safety valve for rising demand with the result that forward prices will rise and fall alongside those in the spot markets.

Thus we arrive at a second basic proposition:

Spot prices and forward prices of producible assets must move together.

With producible commodities, yet a fourth price must be considered. This is the *supply*, or *cost*, *price* (*CP*) that will bring forth additions, at some date in the future, to whatever presently expected supplies may be.[13] The cost price, plus a markup, yields the expected price at which a newly produced commodity may (at some time in the future) be sold. If the forward price at which that commodity can be sold today for deliv-

---

[10] It is necessary to compensate those parties who store commodities to make them available on the spot market; a direct order to the factory avoids such costs of storage. In the case of a glut, much forward market activity of any kind is unlikely, except for commodities that cannot be stored.

[11] Consider the situation in which the spot price does not change over a year's time. The person who buys spot at the beginning and sells at the end has no profit to show on the year. The person who buys forward at the beginning for delivery at the end and then closes out the position by selling spot at the end earns the spot premium on the commodity in question.

[12] Alternatively, the premium that must be paid for spot delivery can be thought of as a type of *liquidity premium*, an extra sum that must be paid if the person wishes to have the commodity immediately rather than at some future date.

[13] Meanwhile, the expected future spot price, so critical to the case of the nonreproducible painting, fades somewhat in importance. In the case of housing, expected increases in the prices of the existing stock (for example, due to expected increases in population density or wealth in a metropolitan region) are mainly important insofar as they affect the current prices of the housing stock. There is little that will affect the expected future price that will not also affect the current price.

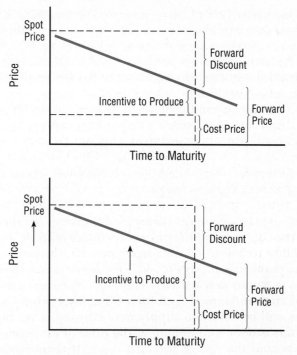

FIGURE 12.4   Present and Future Prices

Spot prices are related to forward prices by a stable premium, or discount (see upper diagram). When interest rates fall, spot prices rise, pulling up forward prices and increasing the expected profitability of production (lower diagram).

ery in the future rises above the cost price, a powerful incentive comes into play. It becomes profitable to sell, on the forward market, commodities that do not yet exist and to contract for their production in the intervening time;[14] the prospective yield for the *producible* asset is thus $1 + q' = FP/CP$. Figure 12.4 summarizes these relationships.

Importance of sticky costs   Production itself, therefore, depends critically on a certain stickiness in the relationship of these four prices. That is, the pressure of equilibration between current (let us say, high) spot prices and current forward prices *must* work to slow the fall of the forward price toward the cost price. The ability of a contractor to make a forward sale at a price higher than the cost of producing a commodity is

[14] The same incentive comes into play in the absence of well-organized forward markets, if the expected price rises sufficiently above the cost price. However, this is a much riskier activity. In housing, it is known as building "on spec," and it has been the ruin of many a builder.

the essential nature of entrepreneurial profit. Without this margin, entrepreneurship would not exist, and new production would not occur beyond the barest requirements of subsistence.

Moreover it *must* be the case that the current contractual supply price does not rise instantly to the forward price. So long as there is stickiness—specifically, a stickiness of wages, since labor costs are the principal cost of production—there is the possibility of profit in production. And into this breach will pour the entrepreneurs.

This brings our third proposition:

> *Production of reproducible assets occurs when forward prices exceed the cost price by a sufficient margin.*

Consider again the example of housing. In a boom, existing stocks become "tight," and the price of available housing starts to rise. If houses available today are becoming expensive, house buyers will realize at some point that it pays to wait for new houses to be built. Thus, they will enter into construction contracts (forward market purchase). Forward market demand, and forward market prices, will rise also. Developers will be happy to supply new housing at the higher forward price. But this is only true so long as the price of new construction (cost price) lags behind the rise of forward price. If there were no such lag, there would be no increased profit in organizing the production of new houses, and the demand for new housing would not be met.

Why do construction workers (and contractors and suppliers) allow for stickiness in their costs? Post-Keynesians are happy to accept some of the new Keynesian reasons for rational stickiness in this context. Most fundamentally, construction workers want to work, and they rationally recognize that someone must be willing to hire them. If they did not hold their own prices at least somewhat steady in the face of rising demand, then the incentive to engage in new construction activity would simply cease to exist.

Summary: Why is there investment?   We have presented three basic propositions:

1. The own-rate of interest on assets (when measured in terms of money) tends to adjust to equal, at the margin, the rate of interest on money.
2. Spot prices and forward prices of producible assets must move together.
3. Production of reproducible assets occurs when forward prices exceed the cost price by a sufficient margin.

The first proposition implies that when the interest rate on money falls, the spot price of all storable and tradable assets must rise to bring down their own-rates of interest to the money rate. The second proposition tells us that the forward price for producible assets will then rise to keep the forward price in line with the spot price. And according to the third proposition, so long as costs of production lag behind the rise in the forward price, a rise in the forward price will lead to a greater expected profitability of new investment.

The theory we have sketched here[15] thus links the current and forward prices of a commodity, the conditions of its production, and the expectations that may prevail about the trend of demand. All are connected with the prevailing rate of interest on financial assets. With these elements, post-Keynesians propose an explanation of why an incentive may exist for expanding or contracting the current volume of production. Three features of the theory bear repeating.

First, it rests largely, but not entirely, on subjective expectations about future prices. Entrepreneurs do not know whether demand will be high or low a year hence or whether supply prices will have risen or fallen. But they must form judgments about these matters, and they do. Moreover, we can predict the direction of influence of some current events on future events, not because we can read people's minds but because current assets and future products are substitutes for each other. And markets exist in which rights to one can and do trade for rights to the other.

Second, changes in the money rate of interest play a pervasive role. Any cut in interest must force a rise of every spot price to restore the equality of the own-rate of interest to the money rate of interest. Since the expected price in the future is partly dependent on supply conditions and is therefore sluggish, if not sticky, the main price adjustment must occur in the spot market. Spot prices must rise, triggering a parallel rise in forward prices (to preserve the spot premium), and there is, automatically and inevitably, an increased incentive to produce.

Third, our economic system fortunately has arranged itself so that while capital asset markets (e.g., housing, machinery, bulk commodities) clear rapidly by means of price adjustments, labor markets do not. For it is precisely the stability of labor markets that opens up the prospect for profits in production of investment goods. If labor markets were more flexible, if workers *did* offer their employment at varying rates and with full information about expected future profit conditions, then all of the excess return to any endeavor would get transferred by contract to the workers in every case. Entrepreneurship, which depends on the hope for not ordinary but high returns, could never emerge in such a world. The opportunities for new forms of productive activity would never be exploited. The new Keynesians *do* have a point when they offer plausible reasons for wages being sticky. But it is not merely the effectiveness of

[15] Which is an exposition of the argument made in Keynes, *The General Theory*, Chap. 17.

government policy that depends on wage stickiness; the very existence of net investment itself depends on it.

The Long-Term Interest Rate and the Fisher Effect

We have told our story, so far, in terms of the short-term, or money, rate of interest. This is the rate that affects spot asset prices and, therefore, the expected profitability of investment.

What is the importance of the long-term rate? The long-term rate of interest is important to the *financing* of business investment. Businesses rarely prefer to finance long-term investment projects in short-term debt markets; to do so exposes them to an additional element of financial market risk. If short-term interest rates rise during the life of the project, they have to bear the dual burden of rising costs and declining profitability. If, however, they have financed their investment with a fixed-interest bond or bank loan, then at least the cost side of the ledger remains under control.

How is the long-term rate of interest determined? In the post-Keynesian view, it measures two fundamental social forces. One, mentioned earlier, is the required compensation to lenders for the speculative risk, specifically the price risk, associated with long-term bonds. This accounts for the fact that long-term rates tend to rise with the term to maturity of the asset.

The other factor has to do with the expected future stream of short-term rates of interest. This expected future stream is important for a simple reason: lenders have the choice of buying a long bond today or of lending for short periods of time and enjoying a variable stream of interest returns as short-term rates fluctuate over time. If they expect short-term rates to rise in the future, they may refuse to lend at long term, unless and until long-term rates rise to cover this expectation.

Normally, of course, there may be no reason for the future to differ from the present, and so no reason to think that short-term interest rates (e.g., the overnight or the thirty-day rate) will be either higher or lower a year from now than they are today. In that case, the expected stream of future short-term rates will have no effect on the current long-term rate, and movements of the short-term rate will tend to foreshadow movements in long-term rates. But if lenders have a strong reason to think that short-term rates are either high or low for some temporary reason, then the long-term rate may not follow the movements in the short rates. For example, in the winter of 1991–1992, short-term rates were pushed very low by the Federal Reserve, but long-term rates remained extremely high. One possible explanation is that lenders generally did not expect that low short-term interest rates would last.

Thus, the nominal long-term interest rate, which is critical for the financing of business investment, is very largely a matter of *social convention*. It is no more nor less than what is expected by the balance of opinion between lenders and borrowers, based on their expectations of the future stream of short-term interest rates (a purely subjective expectation) and their attitudes toward risk. The long-term interest rate can be influenced (to some extent) by policymakers, who may throw their weight in the financial markets behind raising it or lowering it.[16] But in the main, Keynes and the post-Keynesians believe the long-term interest rate is sociologically determined without necessary reference to physical, technological, or productive forces. For this reason, it is likely to be extremely slow to react to changes in circumstances affecting those forces. This is why we may say that the post-Keynesian long-term interest rate is (for practical purposes) exogenous.

Exogenous does not mean unimportant. Indeed, we can now trace an argument showing how the long-term interest rate affects employment. As you will recall, the actual burden of any debt depends not only on the nominal interest rate but also on the amount of inflation that occurs while the debt is outstanding, and therefore on the real value of the principal that eventually is repaid. To take this into account, we define the *real interest rate* as equal to the current nominal, or money, interest rate minus the *expected future rate of inflation* over the lifetime of the particular debt.

The expected future rate of inflation is an extremely nebulous concept, since we have no concrete information about what will happen in the future. But as a behavioral matter, expected inflation is likely to vary, in part, with changes in the present state of effective demand. When the economy is running near full employment and workers are restive, inflation fears tend to rise; when the economy is in recession, both actual inflation and expected future inflation tend to fall.

According to investment theories that go as far back as the basic Keynesian models, the real long-term rate of interest, in conjunction with the expected profitability of projects, determines the volume of investment. But because the nominal long-term rate of interest is extremely slow moving, we may have a situation in which the real long-term rate varies inversely with movements in effective demand.

When the rate of growth of effective demand falls, for example because of a fall in the (actual and expected) rate of inflation, a given

[16] In particular, policymakers may seek to drive down the long-term rate by promising that the sequence of short-term rates that will hold over a long period into the future will be kept low. But this is extremely difficult to do, since current policymakers cannot bind the actions of future policymakers. In fall 1991, Chairman Alan Greenspan discovered this problem: the Federal Reserve drove down the short-term rate of interest, but the long-term rates stubbornly refused to follow.

nominal long-term rate of interest automatically corresponds to a higher real rate of interest. Investment will then fall (because fewer projects seem worth financing), and unemployment will rise. Correspondingly, if the rate of growth of effective demand rises, expected inflation will rise, the real rate of interest on long-term investment will automatically fall, and investment, profits, employment, and output will rise even more. (This is known as the *Fisher effect*, after the U.S. economist Irving Fisher.)

Two important points about this process must be noted. First, it is independent of what may happen in the labor market—it does not depend in any way on real or money wages being "too high." Second, in times of slump the Fisher effect cannot be offset by reducing money wages! For, if money wages fall, prices will fall too (see the preceding arguments about markup pricing), and real interest rates will rise even more. Thus, the Fisher effect works to exacerbate the business cycle, not to relieve it. And, in the post-Keynesian view of the world, the classical adjustment mechanisms not only do not work, they often work in precisely the wrong direction.

A THEORY OF THE CAPITAL STOCK

Another main point that differentiates post-Keynesian economics from its competitors concerns the treatment of the existing capital stock. As already noted on several occasions in this chapter, new classicals and new Keynesians accept a very simple vision of supply and demand in the market for capital, governed by falling marginal physical productivity of capital and its derivative, a downward-sloping investment demand function. Post-Keynesians reject this conceptualization.

What post-Keynesians propose in its place is also quite simple: a model of the existing stock of capital based on the fact that factories and equipment installed at different times are likely to operate at different physical productivities and different unit costs. In particular, old capital equipment is generally less efficient than new capital equipment. To show the implications of this very simple point, we draw a two-sector picture of the manufacturing economy, in which there is a qualitative distinction between the processes that produce capital (or investment) goods and the processes that use these goods to produce products for mass consumption.

Capital and Consumer Goods

The big difference between capital and consumer goods industries lies in the fact that the design of capital goods conveys changes in technology into the production process. Through the incorporation of new techniques in new capital equipment, users of capital goods can gradually change the stream of consumer goods reaching the public. This fact conditions the way capital goods can be, and are, made. Capital goods are produced by highly skilled and well-paid talent using precise but flexible equipment; they are adapted to the particular requirements of each production process into which they flow; their social function is to incorporate advances in science and technique and thereby renew the process of production.

Conversely, consumer goods are produced through the cooperation of labor and previously installed capital goods. As a broad (and by no means watertight) generalization, capital goods are *custom* goods; consumer goods are *mass-produced* goods. Because consumer goods are mass-produced, their production requires the cooperation of capital goods installed over long periods of time. That is, new consumer goods are not just produced on new equipment; they may be produced on equipment that is itself quite old and whose technology was largely fixed into place at the time it was installed.

New Technology

For the above reason, changes in technique spread comparatively rapidly through the capital goods sector. In computers or aircraft or structural engineering, virtually the whole industry moves forward with the cutting edge of technical change. Old computers and old airplanes and old bridges continue in use, but older designs for new versions of these products drop out of service as soon as new and superior designs emerge. Since learning is rapid, the marginal cost of production of new capital goods tends to be flat, or even declining, within the broad limits of available capacity. Moreover, there is no margin of second-best technique (incorporating the older, outmoded designs) that is acceptable to purchasers in tight markets. Boeing cannot put the 727 back into production just because 757s are scarce, nor will the eight-bit Osborne I (the original personal computer) be resurrected if a shortage of Sun Workstations suddenly develops.

The fast-changing nature of capital goods production helps determine how profits—or more precisely, economic rents—are earned in this sector. That is, the capital goods producer with the new technique to sell is, for a limited time only, a monopolist who has the entire demand curve for the (newly created) industry all to itself. The monopolist picks off early consumers at the high prices they are willing to pay; these are known as *reservation prices*. Then, as production proceeds and cumulative volume grows larger, prices fall and the firm moves down the demand curve. We call this process *transient dynamic price discrimination*. Success depends on maintaining a monopoly position at least long enough to

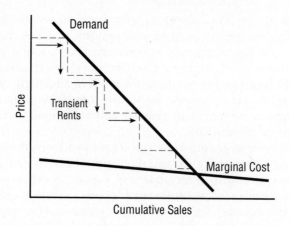

FIGURE 12.5   **Transient Price Discrimination in Capital Goods Production**

New capital goods are introduced at high prices, permitting recovery of research costs and extracting "rents" from the buyers most eager to get the product. Then prices fall toward marginal costs of production as the market expands.

recover fixed costs; once imitators move in, price collapses to marginal costs.

Figure 12.5 illustrates the movement of prices for a newly introduced capital good; the area under the demand curve and above the marginal cost curve reflects the *rental income* of a successful technological innovator.

In practice, therefore, the capital goods industry is very much like a lottery. The first producer to market clears the big prizes that come with having access to those early customers willing to pay the highest prices for new products. For this reason, in capital goods production, there is an enormous advantage to having the best designers, the best scientists, the best engineers, and the best start-up production team. To obtain such talent, firms must bid for it; so the highly credentialed skills that can compete for first-rank status are in the position of those who pass through initial drawings of a lottery and emerge as the finalists for the grand prize.

Ultimately, a large share of the transient technological rents that may be earned by companies that score a technological coup must be shared with the workers who were responsible for achieving it; otherwise, they will simply leave for a better employer. It is no accident that, while there is little evidence of unusually large profits in the capital goods sector (there are many losers alongside each winner), workers of all kinds in this sector are the highest paid in industry. They are receiving the *industry-specific labor rents* that reflect their strong position as sellers of labor services in their industry.

Economist Joseph A. Schumpeter spoke of "gales of creative destruction" in the technological process. By this phrase, he meant to emphasize both the permanence and irreversibility of technological change and the disruption and disorder that goes with it. The competition of capital goods producers is a winner-take-all, devil-take-the-hindmost affair that changes the nature of the world. It "so displaces its equilibrium point," Schumpeter wrote, "that the new one cannot be reached from the old one by infinitesimal steps. Add as many mail coaches as you please, you will never get a railway thereby."[17]

Moreover, it is a competition not between the infinitude of perfect competitors of classical theory but between monopolists and would-be monopolists: "The introduction of new methods of production and new commodities is hardly conceivable with perfect—and perfectly prompt—competition from the start. And this means that the bulk of what we call economic progress is incompatible with it."[18] In another place, Schumpeter summed up:

> But in capitalist reality it is not that kind of competition which counts but the competition from the new commodity, the new technology, the new source of supply, the new type of organization . . .—competition which commands a decisive cost or quality advantage and which strikes not at the margins of the profits and the outputs of the existing firms but at their foundations and their very lives. This kind of competition is as much more effective than the other as a bombardment is in comparison with forcing a door, and so much more important that it becomes a matter of comparative indifference whether competition in the ordinary sense functions more or less promptly; the powerful lever that in the long run expands output and brings down prices is in any case made of other stuff.[19]

We now investigate the application of Schumpeter's vision to the other sector of the economy, namely the mass production of consumer goods.

Best Practice and the Margin of Obsolescence

Consumer goods must, virtually by definition, be produced in bulk. As a functional necessity, then, there must usually be multiple factories for

[17] *Theory of Economic Development* (Cambridge, Mass.: Harvard University Press, 1955), p. 64.
[18] Joseph A. Schumpeter, *Capitalism Socialism and Democracy* (London: George Allen & Unwin, 1976), p. 105.
[19] Ibid., pp. 84–85.

any particular class of goods. This means, in turn, that factories produced at different times and according to different designs must coexist. It is not possible to scrap all previous factories every time a new factory is built. Instead, new and best-practice factories are added to a stream of preexisting factories, all producing common (or similar) products but by differing processes. The final consumer is unaware of and generally indifferent to the vintage of the equipment on which the product was produced.

At any given time, there is a "book of blueprints" from which alternative factory designs and production techniques may be chosen. *Best-practice* technique is simply the least-cost way available for producing at a predetermined scale, at the moment at which a blueprint is chosen. After that moment, the design of the factory is (comparatively speaking) fixed. Small modifications can be made, new equipment can be installed, and production techniques can be upgraded as workers and managers learn better and more efficient ways to work with the equipment they have. But in the main, the die is cast: the basic technology has been chosen, and the factory cannot convert to an entirely new technology should one come along.

Once a factory has been built, unit costs will decline over time (at least at first) as bugs are worked out of the system. But, in general, no amount of retrofitting and innovative adaptation of techniques in an existing plant can keep unit costs falling as rapidly as for new plants, as the nature of best-practice technique—of the initial factory design—evolves. Generally then, the cost advantages enjoyed by new plants decay as they get older. Over time, any given factory is headed inexorably toward the *margin of obsolescence*. Once it reaches that margin, it is a candidate for the scrapheap.

Price-Cost Profile

Over an industry as a whole, there must exist at any time a profile of capital assets involved in the production of any particular good—a profile that ranges from the most to the least efficient, from best practice to the margin of obsolescence. Figure 12.6 illustrates such a price-cost profile. We can easily superimpose a demand function and so derive the quantity that will be produced and the price that will be charged. Moreover, the area between the profile and the price gives us the economic rents, or profits, associated with each possible level of production.

Consumers do not know in which factory, whether best-practice or nearly obsolescent, a particular television set or automobile was made. Therefore, the price of the product cannot depend on this. Instead, the price must be set just high enough so that the highest-cost (and, presum-

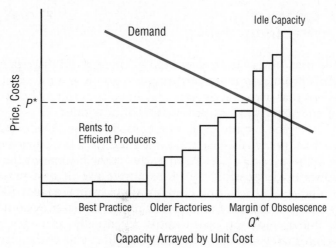

FIGURE 12.6   **Costs and Prices in Mass Production**

In a mass-production industry, rents accrue to producers who are closest to the best-practice technique. The position of the demand curve determines how many factories can operate, the price at which output will be sold, and the profits to the most efficient producers.

ably, oldest) factory can cover its costs and remain in production. The *differential* between highest cost (ergo the price) and the prevailing unit in any particular factory determines the profit earned on a unit produced in that factory. At the given price, the more efficient producers are earning *efficiency rents*, which reflect their low unit costs of production compared with the marginal producers. Meanwhile, the total gap between prices and costs determines total profits, and the distribution of plants of varying vintages and cost profiles across firms determines the distribution of profits across firms.

Is this profile merely a classical supply curve? In the very short run, it may seem so; if demand were to shift upward, then idle capacity would be brought into service, and prices would rise to cover the higher unit costs of that capacity. But this concept of a supply curve does not hold up over any substantial period of time, as we shall see. Why? Time and technology move in but one direction. Old plants and equipment are scrapped when they become obsolete and so disappear off of the right end of the price-cost profile. And new plants and equipment arrive at the lower left of the diagram, embodying the lowest available unit costs of production. Thus, unlike the classical supply curve, movement along the price-cost profile is not reversible, and the profile itself changes shape as technologies evolve.

The Corporation and
Technological Immortality

One final observation may help us understand the relationship between plants producing mass-consumption goods and the companies or corporations that own and operate existing plants and make decisions concerning the acquisition or production of new ones.

Imagine the life cycle of a company (e.g., DeLorean Motors, Kaypro Computer) that enters a mass industry with just one product produced in just one place. At first, this company enjoys the benefits of high profits made possible by its exclusive use of best-practice production techniques. But, as time goes on, this advantage fades. When the company's plant is superseded by a new plant built later by someone else, it will no longer enjoy top-profit status. Eventually, as it ages, profits will fade and ultimately vanish. The end of the life cycle of the plant is also the end of the life cycle of the company itself.

Needless to say, this is a fate most manufacturing enterprises would greatly like to avoid. In fact, large manufacturing enterprises do not often go out of existence simply because their plants age and technologies change. To the contrary, corporate survival is much longer than the survival of individual plants. Indeed, stable or only slowly changing market shares among big firms are a feature of many industries over long

FIGURE 12.7   Stability of Corporate Market Shares

Corporations A, B, and C may each operate a range of factories of differing age, scales, and efficiencies. So long as all corporations introduce new factories at about the same time and scrap old ones at about the same time, they will maintain their relative positions in the industry.

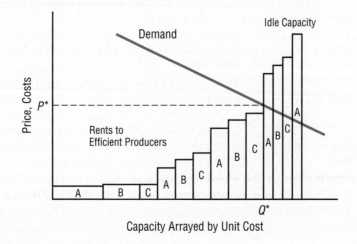

Capacity Arrayed by Unit Cost

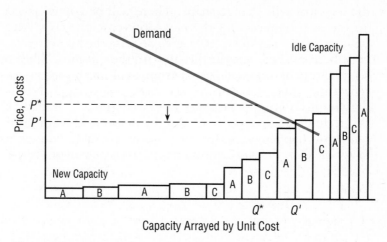

FIGURE 12.8   Effects of New Investment

New investment takes the form of new factories, operating at larger scales with lower unit costs. Total production increases, and prices fall; inefficient plants are forced to close. Total profits may rise or fall, and they are redistributed across producers. Note how company C is losing market share and profitability in this example.

periods of time and across major technological transitions. The biggest corporations are, for practical purposes, immortal. Shakeouts, bankruptcies, and liquidations do occur, but they are not everyday events.

How is this remarkable stability achieved? The answer can only be that major firms arrange to maintain similar production structures and technical profiles. We show this in Figure 12.7 by dividing our hypothetical cost-price profile into plants owned by different corporations (labeled A, B, and C in the diagram). Each major enterprise must maintain facilities of several vintages, approximately spanning the vintages of the industry as a whole. The profitability of each enterprise will vary with changes in industry demand as a whole, so firms will achieve a measure of stability with respect to each other. The smallest viable firm size for the long run is then determined not by the smallest efficient plant size but by the minimum size required to maintain such a facsimile of the whole industry's technical profile.

How do similar cost-price profiles emerge in different firms without explicit collusion between them? It must be that the largest consumer goods manufacturers make investment decisions in similar ways and at similar times, so that the pattern of new investments comes to reflect the distribution of the existing capital stock.

Figure 12.8 illustrates what happens when a significant technological breakthrough occurs, such as might permit a large increase in the minimum efficient scale of a plant. In such a case, the technical profile of the industry will change shape. There will be a new, larger flat portion on the left, representing the new, low-cost capacity. Also, the profile will not rise so rapidly to the right, because the highest-cost capacity will have been pushed even further toward the margins. Since price must be set to clear the markets, competition will mean that prices must fall to reflect the lower costs of the new high-cost margin. Note that we have drawn only two new factories in our diagram. Company C has missed this technological opportunity, and you can read from the diagram what will now happen to its profits and its market share as its remaining factories face the stiff competition from the new, low-cost facilities opened up by A and B.

CONCLUSION

So much for the basics. In this chapter, we have covered the whole range of post-Keynesian departures from the new classical/new Keynesian mainstream. These include new theories of money and interest, of the general price level, of expectations, of asset prices and investment, and finally of the evolution of technology, changes in the capital stock, and the role of the corporation. Quite a range!

We turn in the next and final chapter to the presentation of a model based on all of these elements, one that will provide a clear expression of the macroeconomic and policy implications of the post-Keynesian vision.

SPECIAL SECTION

Industrial and Technology Policies[1]

Industrial and related commercial technology policies are the new kids on the economic policy block. Unlike, say, the budget deficit, their conceptualization is recent, and they remain vaguely defined in the eyes of the public, the press, and even of Congress and the ad-

ministration. Indeed, there remains considerable skepticism, particularly among economists, as to whether such policies are needed at all.

Advocates of industrial and commercial technology policies— among them Laura Tyson, chair of President Clinton's Council of Economic Advisers—argue that major U.S. manufacturing industries have suffered a serious loss of competitive stature in world markets. They believe that this decline is not being offset in time by market forces and that macroeconomic policy—particularly changes in the exchange rate—cannot do the job alone. They point to the apparent successes of explicit industrial strategies, especially in Japan.

All of these views remain controversial. Opponents counter that the convergence of foreign industries on U.S. performance levels is a natural and perhaps inevitable process. They believe that existing problems *can* be remedied by changing macroeconomic policies and that government intervention—in particular, technological choices—is likely to do more harm than good. And they argue that the Japanese experience may not be applicable to conditions in the United States.

Post-Keynesian economists tend to be more sympathetic than most others to the need for explicit policies to foster rapid development of industrial and commercial technologies. You can get an idea of why this is so from our discussion in this chapter of the cost-price profile facing industries. If foreign enterprises in the model we describe come to dominate the low-cost, highly efficient portions of an industry's capital structure, then domestic firms, relegated to the position of high-cost producers, obviously will suffer a profit squeeze and loss of market share. Unless they manage to reestablish themselves as low-cost producers, they will continue to lose ground over time and will eventually be forced

out of business. Government help may be needed to reverse such a pattern of decline or to allow an emerging industry to get a technological jump on its competitors from overseas.

From a policy standpoint, these and similar arguments carry weight. And President Clinton has, in effect, overridden the objections and started down the path of developing industrial and technology policies. What should these policies be? This section briefly highlights the nature of the current industrial competitiveness problem, as seen by advocates of industrial and technology policies, and outlines plausible strategies for the longer run.

The Industrial Performance Problem

Research suggests that U.S. manufacturing industries and their problems fall into three broad and substantially distinct classes: advanced technology industries, heavy or capital-intensive industries, and light or labor-intensive industries. Within these categories, not all industries are suffering competitiveness problems, and not all of those that are suffer to an equal degree. But broadly speaking, each category is characterized by a different set of economic and technological problems, and each needs an individualized policy treatment.

Advanced Technology Industries
Advanced technology industries are a diverse and surprisingly large

group, comprising about a quarter of U.S. manufacturing employment in our classification—as many as five million workers. They include aerospace, communications, and electronic equipment, advanced electrical machinery, photographic equipment, pharmaceuticals, and many parts of the chemical industry. In addition, the competitive performance and wage behavior of such energy- and resource-intensive industries as paper and food processing, though not commonly thought of as "advanced," have closely tracked that of others in this group. Thus, a qualitatively cohesive set of industries can be thought of as including both traditional areas of comparative advantage (known as "Ricardo goods" to trade economists) and the advanced industries whose comparative advantage is created by increasing returns, innovative design, and technological leadership.

Advanced industries as a group still enjoy the best trade performance in U.S. manufacturing. Collectively, they usually run a trade surplus, and they maintained nearly balanced trade even in the worst years of the U.S. trade deficit. A few sectors within the group now run chronic deficits, but these tend to be offset by surpluses in other sectors. These industries are also the most strongly rooted in the high skills of U.S. workers and in the good infrastructure and plentiful land and resources of the United States. They are the least likely of U.S. industries to pack up and move. Their overall employment has held constant over the years, as growing markets, product innovation, and product differentiation have offset the labor-saving effects of rapid productivity gains.

The United States' advanced industries have nonetheless suffered a loss of world market share and technical leadership, especially in the past ten years. Their problems stem, we believe, from four main sources. First, the massive overvaluation of the dollar from 1981 through 1986/87 gave foreign competitors a matchless opportunity to challenge U.S. leadership in many sectors. Second, this price disadvantage was compounded by distortions in the pattern of world growth in the 1980s. The United States grew more strongly than did Europe or the Third World but was, by the same token, unable to maintain the growth of external markets that our advanced industries require. Third, foreign challengers benefited from government assistance (the European Airbus) and protected domestic markets (Japan's advanced electronics sector), while comparable assistance was not widely available to U.S. advanced industries. Finally, where the U.S. government did and does support advanced research, the "technology push" structure of those efforts has made it difficult to convert their products (in defense, space, energy, medicine) into viable new commercial technologies.

Heavy (Capital-Intensive) Industries   Heavy industries in the United States include, most importantly, automobiles and steel but also the producers of engines and turbines, construction equipment, glass and glassware, and the output of sawmills and planing mills. They are characterized by complex manufacturing and assembly processes, intensive use of capital equipment, and production mainly for mass markets. Altogether, nearly two million workers are now employed in such industries— following sharp losses in employment in the mid-1980s. Though less skilled on average than workers in advanced technology, they remain more highly paid and are among the best-paid and most highly unionized workers in manufacturing.

Until the early 1980s, certain U.S. heavy industries (particularly producers of construction equipment, engines, and nonelectrical machinery) enjoyed rapidly growing external markets. Indeed, the growth in these markets had actually offset the increase of imports in steel and automobiles over the 1970s, giving this group of industries as a whole a stable trade position. But in the development bust of the early 1980s, these external markets collapsed, and with the long overvaluation of the dollar that followed, many never recovered. Meanwhile, those heavy industries oriented mainly to the domestic market, especially autos and bulk carbon steel, confronted intense import competition and a sharp erosion of their competitive position in the domestic market. All in all, about half a million jobs were lost in heavy industries in the 1980s, and the relative wage position of workers in these industries slipped. As a group, heavy industries are now inward looking and import competing, and they are powerfully oriented toward a political strategy of trade protection.

The problems of U.S. heavy industry result from four main, interrelated causes. First has been inadequate innovation and capital investment and, in consequence, the comparative obsolescence of plant and equipment. Second, these industries face intensive competition not only from Europe and Japan but also from Korea, Mexico, Brazil, and other emergent industrial powers, many of whom put heavy industry at the center of a development strategy. Third and fourth are, again, the decline of external markets and overvaluation of the dollar. We attach much less significance to an often-mentioned fifth cause, namely the high level of U.S. wages. Wage costs are a comparatively small part of total costs in heavy manufacturing, and nonwage-cost differentials drive international competition in these industries.

Light (Labor-Intensive) Industries
Labor-intensive industries include especially the manufacture of garments and shoes and the assembly of many consumer goods, from

sporting goods and toys to jewelry. These face a high degree of threat from foreign competition originating in the Third World. And in these industries, wage differentials matter. International wage gaps in these sectors can reach ten to one after adjustment for productivity differentials, and this is in industries where labor accounts for the major part of total cost. While U.S. labor-intensive manufacturing will not disappear, there is essentially no way that U.S. workers can maintain their position against competition of this sort, and they have not done so. Wages are falling in these industries, and jobs are migrating overseas.

Principles for Industrial Policy

The task of launching industrial policies that are anything other than the *ad hoc* result of defense policy and the politics of special interests is daunting. Existing federal efforts in the industrial and technological domains traditionally have not, with the exception of agriculture, been designed to promote industrial-commercial competitiveness. Moreover, while one may glibly say that such policies should correct the damage of the 1980s and put the United States on a sure footing for the twenty-first century, the degree of policy design, consensus, and coordination required for successful action is not small. Not only is *systematic* and *explicit* industrial technology policy a new venture for this country, but it must be exe-

cuted in a federal structure fragmented, decentralized, and governed by parochial interests.

Clearly, many factors affecting industrial performance have little to do with the development, adoption, and diffusion of technologies. Some of the most important of these factors are macroeconomic. During the 1980s, the high U.S. dollar and stagnation in overseas markets imposed huge cumulative damage on U.S. industries. The loss of export sales and intense import competition systematically forestalled the kind of investments and strategies required for businesses to continue to compete effectively in the long run. Siege mentalities and extraordinary competitive stress spawned temporary coping mechanisms that, among other things, left investment underfunded and created companies with inappropriately narrow product lines. These basic problems cannot be cured by industrial policy alone.

Industrial policies must be rooted in a number of broader preconditions, including changes in macroeconomic policy. Particularly indispensable are a competitive dollar and a strategy to promote and sustain global economic growth. These are the two key elements in a macroeconomic policy that maintains a favorable climate for the adjustment of U.S. industry to global competitive conditions. Without growing foreign markets for U.S. exports, specific policies to help particular industries or to foster particular lines of technological progress will not stand much chance.

The basic objective of industrial policy should be to cultivate the technological basis of industrial comparative advantage. While only one of several factors that affect the day-to-day world of economic competition, technology is ultimately the main source of dynamic competitive strength. Technological dynamism underlies new product and materials innovations, the ability to differentiate products in the marketplace, and improved levels of efficiency and productivity. In addressing these issues, industrial technology policies have rather clear tasks: to help correct the damage U.S. competitive stature suffered during the 1980s and to ensure that the U.S. industrial technology base is properly positioned for future global competition.

The broad sketch of U.S. industrial problems provided above indicates that different policy principles must apply for prospective actions in each main industry class. This is largely because their problems lie in different realms of technological activity. And even though technological success is typically thought to result from research and development efforts, the available industrial technology policy tool kit extends far beyond simple support for R&D. It includes tax credits, procurement practices, regulations, and government-to-industry technology transfer. With a judicious selection from among these tools, industrial technology policies can affect the commercial adoption of technology and the market for new innovations, as well as the development of new technologies themselves.

Advanced Technology Advanced industries benefit from a comparative advantage, long enjoyed by the United States, in scientific research and industrial innovation. This comparative advantage does not result from fixed factor endowments but is created by knowledge and labor skills that cumulate over time. Moreover, there is compelling historical evidence from around the world that advanced technology sectors benefit from and thrive on government assistance.

Spillovers exist. The economic returns from high technologies are not fully appropriated by the firm, but they are (to some degree at least) internal to the country. Economies of concentration exist in sectors that innovate extremely quickly, and skilled workers migrate far more easily within national boundaries than across them. National policies that promote advanced technologies are therefore likely to generate national gains. And even though some new technologies diffuse so quickly that national appropriability appears to be weakening, accelerated growth in advanced technology markets clearly seems to be a positive-sum exercise for the world economy as a whole. For all of these reasons, advanced technologies remain the most promising areas for industrial promotion.

The United States has, over history, pursued aggressive technology policies—though generally not mainly for commercial and civilian reasons. It still promotes science and technology research more than any other country. Unless one is prepared to argue that these efforts have been uniformly unsuccessful, the philosophical argument that government is inherently unable to make good technology decisions is difficult to accept. To the contrary, government may be the only body, apart from government-granted monopolies such as the old AT&T (which ran the largest private research institute in the world, Bell Labs), that can support R&D on the scale that major technological change requires. This is an area where uncertainties of all kinds cloud research and market decisions and where the exact applications of fundamentally new technologies are frequently unforeseen. Technological choice, then, often becomes a shot in the dark. Governments can take such shots; private corporations often cannot or will not assume the risk of doing so on a comparable scale.

In light of this record, the question of whether government should or should not play such a role seems misstated. The real questions are what kind of a role it should play and at what stage in the process?

A good case can be made that U.S. technology policy in recent times has been too heavily weighted toward the esoteric and expensive and insufficiently oriented toward the commercial and practical. This is partly due to the influence of the laissez-faire ideological tradition. It is also partly the result of the military orientation of much government R&D and of the role the scientific community has played in U.S. science and technology policy.

New policies aimed at advanced industry will probably try to remedy deficiencies of past technology policy. They are likely to foster the development of new (and emerging) *civilian* technologies, their adoption by the advanced sectors, and the rapid growth of markets for their products, here and abroad. A good example is the Clinton Administration's proposal for a network of fiber-optic "data superhighways," an idea with substantial potential to generate new developments in the information industries. Other policy approaches may include negotiated access to product markets in other advanced countries, the imposition of domestic regulatory standards aimed at speeding the uptake of cleaner and safer technologies, and judicious use of government procurement power.

Heavy Industry   The task facing U.S. heavy industries is not so much to develop fundamentally new technologies as it is to seize opportunities where they already exist. Virtually all heavy industries confront the challenge of transforming their capital base to match the manufacturing, quality, and cost positions of major foreign competitors. Hard policy choices exist here since, in a world of scarce public resources, a key issue facing policymakers must be whether to play a hard game of catch up in all, some, or none of the heavy industries.

Heavy industries are those for which installed capacity is very large and for whom a basic pattern of technology is built in at the beginning—many plants and mills, once built, are essentially frozen in their technological time. Return to the industrial forefront therefore implies massive scrapping of old plants and construction of new plants, along technological lines pioneered by more recent entrants across the globe. To some extent, this process is continually under way; it is part of the market mechanism. The question, however, is whether the process moves quickly enough and whether government should intervene to speed it along, to foster the replacement of outmoded processes and techniques with new ones.

Of the heavy industries, the most threatened are steel and autos. They have already seen major transformations, through retooling and redesign by U.S. auto companies, in Japanese transplant operations in autos, and with the development of minimills in steel. But clearly, much remains to be done. Both autos and steel still face unrelenting challenges from foreign producers in an environment of worldwide overcapacity, and many other heavy industries are also under threat.

The question is how to respond. Assume for the moment that the United States made an across-the-board investment in heavy industry. Even if that process succeeded, it is not clear what would have been achieved. In all likelihood, the result would be industries as good as, or perhaps only marginally better than, those that already exist in other countries. Meanwhile, global overcapacity would be worse, and the U.S. heavy industry work force would still expect higher wages than its competition would, in spite of adverse market conditions and an absence of decisive productivity advantages that would justify such differentials. It may be a losing game.

Policies aimed at heavy industry should, therefore, be cautious and selective. Support for individual industries should be based on multiple criteria, especially the following: current competitive standing; the degree of effort required to restore productivity and cost advantages; upstream and downstream linkages (e.g., the supplier network feeding into automobile manufacturing and the insurance and services that result from auto employment and sales); barriers to new market entry (which may be prohibitive once all factors are considered); and long-term needs of the manufacturing sector as a whole.

Where strategic interventions are required, attention should focus on the larger public purposes that may be served. For example, renewal of the machinery industry should take into account the needs of a large-scale reconstruction of civilian public infrastructure; initiatives affecting autos should weigh the future of the transportation system. Given the existing patterns of global capacity and the comparative distribution of labor skills, a shrinking in the overall role for heavy industry in the U.S. economy is probably appropriate. The goal of industrial policy should be limited to supporting industrial clusters that serve important public purposes and that, once revitalized, will not require indefinite public support.

Light Industry   Policies aimed at labor-intensive manufactures generally have little by way of a technological component. They should, instead, foster fair competition on the one hand and graceful adjustment for workers on the other. Fair competition means pressing the more successful Third World competitors to raise their wages and living standards and to otherwise reduce the wage gap (after adjustment for productivity differences) between themselves and the United States. Graceful adjustment means retraining the young and retiring the old as jobs in these areas continue to shrink. The fail-

ure to provide adequately for the welfare of workers who are displaced as labor-intensive industries constrict has long been a serious omission in U.S. public policy.

Long-Term Strategies

Over the longer term, industrial policy design should strive to leave durable institutions and procedures for fostering the development and rapid uptake of new commercial technologies and the renewal of technology-enhancing infrastructure. In particular, the government needs a greater independent capability to judge new technological possibilities, opportunities, and risks.

Federal Research Facilities and Research Funding   Federal laboratories (e.g., the nuclear weapons research facilities at Livermore, California, and Los Alamos, New Mexico) are strongly oriented toward either nonpatentable basic research or mission-specific technology development. They probably have little potential for systematic commercial spin-offs. The apparent need, in our view, is less to convert the national laboratory system to a competitiveness mission than to create and place such a mission within the federal R&D establishment more broadly conceived. This may involve the dedication of new labs to industrial missions or the creation of new programs within individual laboratories. Similarly, federal funding of industrial technology needs to be institutionalized in a way to benefit broad classes of industry and to avoid the tendency for a few large projects to absorb all available resources.

Regulatory   Policies   Present federal Office of Management and Budget (OMB) review of federal regulatory policies, through the Office of Information and Regulatory Analysis, has been largely designed to slow the implementation of new standards that are opposed by businesses and other affected interest groups. In our view, regulations affecting industry should instead be reviewed at the design stage to ensure that opportunities to maximize the competitive benefits of regulatory compliance are acted upon. Where choices exist in implementing a regulation that will help with the uptake of new and cost-reducing technologies, policy should work to ensure that those choices are taken.

Infrastructure Development
New technologies often enter the civilian economy in the wake of the provision of new public infrastructure goods: airports, road networks, communications lines, and so on. Presently, discussions focus on fiber-optic communications highways and high-speed passenger rail proposals. In addition, consideration should be given to energy-conserving technologies (including prominently the new information

technologies) and on those that might reduce the dependence of the country on road transport (e.g., carless railroad freight technology) may be appropriate. Decision making on new infrastructure should be capable of an ongoing review of needs; projects should be designed in such a way that partial benefits can be realized before final completion. Probably the best way to meet these objectives is to establish a national infrastructure bank with good technical and project review capabilities—a kind of internal version of the World Bank, aimed at promoting domestic rather than foreign economic development.

External   Market   Development
Finally, the United States needs comprehensive measures to promote its technologies in foreign markets. Further debt reduction in Latin America and Eastern Europe and new credits by the former Soviet Union would be useful first steps. Beyond this, the reconstruction of East—Central Europe and former Soviet Bloc countries via technical assistance for infrastructure and energy development, environmental cleanup, and communications networks would help to create enduring markets for U.S. equipment and to aid new democratic governments. Given the financial enormity of this task, it is of course appropriate to make the modernization of the "Eastern" economies a joint effort of the industrially advanced countries.

Conclusion

In our view, the task of developing industrial technology policy is a legitimate government function. It should, however, be pursued systematically, and new aspects of these policies should be introduced only as time and developing expertise bring confidence that this can be done with success. The early emphasis must be on development of new technologies; later efforts need to shift emphasis toward commercialization. The broad objective should be to create a flexible, ac-countable, and expert federal technology establishment that in effect defies all of the stereotypes. The challenge for those who favor active competitiveness policies is not to dismiss the skeptics but to show by action and experience that smart and effective policy design is possible.

---

[1] This section is adapted from James Galbraith and Maria Papadakis, "New Directions in Industrial and Technology Policies," *Stanford Law and Policy Review,* forthcoming.

SUMMARY

Post-Keynesians claim to be the most direct descendants in the Keynesian tradition. They attack two pillars of the new classical temple: rational expectations and monetarism. The third pillar, market clearing, is considered a moot point. Unlike both the new Keynesian and the new classical schools, post-Keynesians do not believe in a single unified labor market.

Some post-Keynesians believe that the money supply is endogenous and that monetary authorities are obliged to supply whatever quantity of money is demanded. Because large lines of credit exist, loans are made automatically as borrowers increase their demand for money. In general, the monetary authorities accommodate the swings in money demand. A more or less effective policy consistent with this viewpoint is to control interest rates on lines of credit.

The post-Keynesian theory of prices is an inertial one based on markup pricing. Post-Keynesians insist that trying to control prices by controlling the money supply is not effective, because controlling the money supply actually causes credit to tighten. With markup pricing, the wage level in large measure controls the price level. Lowering the nominal wage does not lower the real wage; therefore, a fall in the nominal wage does not imply a fall in unemployment.

Post-Keynesians do not believe that rational expectations form a defensible basis for predicting behavior. In particular, they do not believe an objective central tendency for values of economic variables exists independent of its own expectation. Investors' expectations are in a sense self-fulfilling. If investors believe good business conditions will exist in the future and therefore they invest, then good demand conditions will exist. The subjective nature of these expectations is called "animal spirits." The unpredictable nature of investment is the basis for true uncertainty as opposed to calculable risk.

Furthermore, post-Keynesians argue, rational predictions do not always lead to rational action. This is illustrated by way of a "prisoner's dilemma," where all parties know they would better off cooperating but still do not.

Nor do the post-Keynesians accept the existence of a natural rate of unemployment. Instead, they believe the state of expectations determines the level of equilibrium employment. In contrast to the new classicals, post-Keynesians believe that the short-run aggregate supply curve is fixed, at least as it applies to private business enterprises. The aggregate demand curve can shift up or down as investor expectations change. Two general conditions exist: a stagnationist environment, where wage increases stimulate demand, and an exhilarationist environment, where profit increases stimulate demand.

Post-Keynesians believe that mass unemployment in the short run is usually due to insufficient effective demand. Instability in any component of effective demand will be sufficient to render employment unstable. But investment is the most markedly unstable element in aggregate demand.

Post-Keynesians also assert that long-term investments are risky by their very nature and therefore have a higher interest rate than short-term investments; short-term interest rates are set by the central bank. As do virtually all economists, post-Keynesians believe that investment depends on the difference between the profit rate and the interest rate.

Profitability, in the post-Keynesian view, depends on the difference between the cost of production of capital assets and the expected price at which they can actually be sold. To be more exact, profitability is determined by the own-rate of interest, which depends on the expected yield, the carrying cost, and the liquidity premium of the asset. Investments are made until the own-rate of interest falls to meet the bank loan rate of interest, called the own-rate of interest on money. Post-Keynesians also discuss forward prices. These prices move together with spot prices in the case of producible assets to achieve uniformity of all assets' rates of interest measured in money terms.

When forward prices exceed the cost price sufficiently, production of reproducible assets will occur. A certain stickiness must exist to maintain the difference between these two prices. Many post-Keynesians accept the new Keynesians' views on this issue but argue that cost stickiness, rather than being a defect, is an essential element of a successful economic system.

Long-term investment projects are formed in long-term debt markets. The long-term interest rate depends on the compensation necessary for speculative risk and on the expected stream of short-term interest rates. Future short-term rates of interest are very uncertain. The long-term rate of interest is therefore largely a matter of social convention and can be viewed as exogenous. It is slow to move; therefore, perking up the rate of investment by manipulating the long-term rate of interest is difficult.

Post-Keynesians differentiate between the production of capital goods and of consumption goods. New techniques are incorporated into the production process through the design of capital goods. By the nature of the production process, capital goods are generally custom goods. Consumption goods are generally mass-produced and can use physical capital that may be quite old. Capital good production is dynamic. In the capital sector, innovators are able to capture monopoly rents called transient technical rents. The capital sector in general has low profits, but with the need for creativity, wages are high.

In the consumer goods industry, the best-practice technique is used to build a plant. Over time, unit costs will decline as fixed costs are recovered. But at the same time, the plant is headed toward obsolescence. The price of a consumer good is set just above the price needed to cover costs in the least efficient plant. The more efficient plants all earn efficiency rents. This is not, however, a classical supply curve, because it is not reversible. As plants reach obsolescence, they are scrapped. To keep from becoming defunct, corporations maintain many plants that span the various possible vintages of capital.

Review Questions

1. Chapters 10–12 used rational expectations, monetarism, and market clearing as starting points for discussion. Discuss the various stances taken on these issues by the monetarists, the new classicals, the new Keynesians, and the post-Keynesians.

2. Discuss the concept of endogenous money as used by post-Keynesians. In particular, how do expectations fit into this discussion?

3. In the questions to Chapter 10, it was casually observed that prices seem to be sticky downward more than they are sticky upward. Have the post-Keynesians offered any further insights into this phenomenon? Explain.

4. Using the various prices and costs introduced in this chapter, explain how the investment decision is made.

5. Using the analysis of vintages of capital stocks made in this chapter, explain the demise of some actual company or group of companies.

6. Compare post-Keynesian macroeconomic theory's ability to explain and predict growth and development with the abilities of the other theories to do the same.

Review Problems

1. Draw a diagram with interest rates and money on the axes. Reconstruct the demand and supply schedules for money, using post-Keynesian reasoning about the endogenicity of the money stock. Then derive the LM schedule and draw both the IS and LM schedules on a diagram with interest rates and real income on the axes. What is the shape of the LM schedule? Is money neutral under these conditions? (Hint: Think carefully about the consequences of a change, either an increase or a decrease, in the quantity of money.)

2. Assume that prices are governed in general by a markup over costs. Now suppose there is a sharp jump in oil prices of the kind that occurred in 1974 and 1979. What will happen to prices in general? Suppose that consumers respond to the rise in prices by reducing their demand for goods. In a post-Keynesian world, what will happen to prices, output, and employment?

3. Businesses frequently borrow from commercial banks to meet payrolls, cover inventory costs and supplies, and otherwise finance their next round of production. Loans require businesses to meet interest obligations. Suppose businesses now include interest payments as part of costs in their markup pricing decision. What will happen to prices, investment, output, and employment in the event that the Federal Reserve decides to pursue a tight money policy?

4. Explain the paradox of fiscal and monetary policies under stagnationist and exhilarationist conditions.

5. Keynes and the post-Keynesians attribute three main properties to any economic asset: carrying cost, yield, and liquidity premium. Which is the most important in determining the own-rate of return on each of the following: (a) wheat, (b) real estate, (c) steel, (d) money.

6. If we know that the own-rate of return is -1 percent per year on wheat, 1 percent on real estate, 3 percent on steel, and 2 percent on money, what is the expected annual appreciation or depreciation for wheat, real estate, and steel?

7. As we have learned, post-Keynesian investment theory rests on the view that production of reproducible assets is prompted by forward prices exceeding cost prices by an adequate margin. Explain, then, the post-Keynesian rejection of rational expectations in favor of a purely subjective view of expectations.

8. In what sense is it valid to say that, under the terms of post-Keynesian theory, the money rate of interest "rules the roost"?

9. Should we expect to find a systematic relationship between long-term and short-term rates of interest? If so, why, and what is that relationship? If not, why not?

10. Given the post-Keynesian view on the role of new technologies, what policies could be pursued by a national government to accelerate the pace of technological change?

Suggested Readings

Geoffrey Harcourt, *Some Cambridge Controversies in the Theory of Capital* (Cambridge: Cambridge University Press, 1972).

Joseph A. Schumpeter, *Capitalism, Socialism and Democracy* (London: George Allen & Unwin, 1976).

Chapter 13

THE Z-D MODEL AND THE BUSINESS CYCLE

Looking Forward

In this chapter, we assemble the main elements of Chapter 12 into a post-Keynesian model of the determination of output and prices. We then use that model to illustrate how post-Keynesians view the problems of recession, inflation, depression, and boom. The chapter concludes with a survey of incomes policies—past, present, and potential.

   As you read this final chapter, make sure you can answer these questions:

- What determines the level of effective demand in this model?
- How does effective demand interact with the cost of supply to determine the equilibrium volume of output and employment?
- Why is this equilibrium unstable?
- What are the consequences of periodic recessions for the supply side of the economy? For the interaction of large corporations?
- How can interest rate policy influence the business cycle? How about policies that directly influence the setting of wages and prices?

Chapter 12 presented the major elements of the post-Keynesian vision, including endogenous money, markup pricing, subjective expectations, and complete theories of asset pricing and of technological change. Now we show how to organize these elements into the traditional broad categories of supply and demand, but in this case, supply and demand for output as a whole. In this way, we can create a third complete model of the determination of national income and output, alongside the IS-LM and AS-AD models of previous chapters. We call this final alternative the *Z-D model*, following the terminology of its originator, Sidney Weintraub of the University of Pennsylvania, whose work in the late 1950s formed the foundation of the American post-Keynesian effort.[1]

Why another model? Primarily because the AS-AD and IS-LM alternatives do not accurately represent the post-Keynesian vision. They are not built out of the elements presented in the last chapter, and they include other elements (such as rational expectations in the case of the AS-AD model) that post-Keynesians reject. For this reason, neither model can come to grips with the central macroeconomic problem of concern to post-Keynesians: the possibility that a free economy may suffer a systemic, sustained failure to achieve and maintain full employment.

The AS-AD model represents the new classical vision and incorporates the elements of the new classical theory. Aggregate demand (the quantity of real goods that will be purchased at differing prices of output) and aggregate supply (the quantities that will be offered at differing prices) interact to determine a unique price level and volume of transactions. The AS-AD model is concerned with showing that the conditions under which the actual and the expected price levels coincide correspond to achievement of a "natural" rate of output and a "natural" rate of employment.

Under AS-AD, indeed, all sustained states can be thought of as natural—if something persists, it must be an equilibrium (for if it were not, it could not be sustained). By the same token, departures from sustained states are merely fluctuations—if something does not persist (a temporary bout of unemployment, for example), there is no point in worrying about it. Therefore, there is no place in the AS-AD picture for the Great Depression (or for any persistent deviation from full employment).[2] A sustained period of unemployment that is neither natural nor self-correcting cannot be accounted for by the theory. It is easy to see how this vision is inconsistent with post-Keynesian belief.

---

[1] Sidney Weintraub, *An Approach to the Theory of Income Distribution* (Philadelphia: Chilton Co., 1958) and *Classical Keynesianism, Monetary Theory and the Price Level* (Philadelphia: Chilton Co., 1961).

[2] Pushing this argument to its logical end, some new classical economists have questioned whether the Great Depression really occurred. They argue that what people thought at the time was a depression was actually a period of rapid technological change and industrial displacement. Moreover, they argue that the situation was made to seem worse than it actually was by flaws in the economic data available at that time. Correspondingly, some new classical economists also argue that the modern business cycle is actually driven by exogenous forces of technological change. The new classical theory of the *real business cycle* is a continuing development in current literature.

The IS-LM model is, of course, free of rational expectations and natural rates of output, and it does incorporate such authentically Keynesian ideas as a shiftable marginal efficiency of capital schedule and a demand for money function that includes interest-dependent speculative demands. Moreover, if monetary and fiscal policies are set wrong, IS-LM can generate an unemployment equilibrium. IS-LM has, therefore, been the framework of choice for Keynesian models for decades, and the new Keynesians still employ it for certain purposes today.

But post-Keynesians are not comfortable with IS-LM either. One reason, which we have already discussed in detail, has to do with the treatment of price inflation under IS-LM, in particular with the ad hoc marriage of the IS-LM model to the purely empirical Phillips curve. Post-Keynesians never liked the Phillips curve, even when it was riding high in the 1960s. Partly, this was because the Phillips curve lacked a theoretical foundation, whereas post-Keynesians felt that a truly Keynesian theory had to be built on the theory of asset and commodity prices that is actually found in Keynes's *General Theory*.[3] Thus, post-Keynesians were not particularly surprised when the Phillips curve collapsed. (On the other hand, they tend to dispute the suggestion that the curve's collapse should be taken as the proof of the failure of Keynesian economics.)

The post-Keynesians wanted a model that could capture Keynes's own central characterization of the Great Depression, as a period of *equilibrium unemployment*. They also wanted a Marshallian model, with a steady-state equilibrium and with clear internal dynamics that would drive economic actors toward or away from the equilibrium outcomes, as circumstances might dictate. In this way, they hoped to build a conceptual framework that did not bias its user toward the judgment that full employment was the normal condition of society and unemployment was abnormal. Rather, they hoped for a model under which both conditions might occur (as post-Keynesians believe they do in the real world) and that would illuminate the conditions and the policies under which full employment might be obtained.

As it turns out, the elements of the post-Keynesian vision are well suited to constructing a model with these properties. The key is to model not the operation of markets but the behavior, specifically the hiring and production decisions, of business firms. In this context, the notions of demand and supply take on meanings somewhat different from what we are used to in economics but closer to ordinary business usage. In the post-Keynesian model, we isolate the features that are mainly *subjective,* having to do with expected market conditions in the future, on the demand side; we reserve the features that are mainly *objective,* having to

[3] J. M. Keynes, *The General Theory of Employment, Interest and Money* (London: Macmillan, 1936).

do with known costs of production, availability of credit, and so on, to the supply side. Then we can show how a given state of expectation will drive individual firms, and all firms collectively, toward an equilibrium value of current production and employment.

EFFECTIVE DEMAND

How does a business firm decide how many people it should hire in the period immediately ahead? The post-Keynesian answer to this question begins with an estimate of the size of the market. Are business conditions improving or declining? Is demand for the firm's product rising or falling? Are prices going up or down? How much can be sold, and at what prices? In other words, what is the *expected state of effective demand?*

Our conventional theory of the labor market frames this question in terms of a technical relationship between the *marginal revenue product* of a worker (how much revenue an additional worker will add) and the wage. In this view, prices and wages are fixed by the market and known to the firm, and firms can sell all they choose at the going price. Therefore, market conditions are essentially a given, and the key to the firm's decision to hire or fire is simply the extent of diminishing returns to labor in the firm's own processes of production. Firms are said to hire up to the point at which an additional worker's increment to output, sold at the market price, is just offset by the wage paid. Presumably, hiring decisions are continually being made by managers and refined by engineers, whose job is to seek ever more efficient ways to extract additional output from any given number of workers.

Post-Keynesians argue that the principal strategic question facing the firm is external, not internal. The most important elements of the marginal revenue product do not have to do with the technical question of how much additional output an additional worker can or will produce. Indeed, this is a fairly trivial calculation in most cases, as firms have a long experience with their production facilities and are well aware of how many workers they would require to produce at different levels of output.

Rather, the major uncertainty facing business firms is the uncertainty of their markets. The planning departments of such firms are concerned with assessments of shifting price, demand, and market conditions. Their staff comprises economists (who predict overall market conditions), product designers (who adjust the firm's output to new technological opportunities and shifts in consumer tastes), and advertisers (who try to persuade consumers that the product offered is in fact the product desired). It is no accident, in this view, that the top professionals in corporate life are concerned with such issues (along with finance), whereas production specialists often take a secondary position.

One way to capture the state of expectation of the firm is in terms of the *expected price of output*. The better the economic conditions are expected to be, the higher the price the firm expects to receive on its products. And the higher the price that products are expected to bring, the more of them (other things equal) the firm will pay to produce. Expected price of output is thus an index of confidence in the future profitability of doing business, a convenient way of expressing the state of optimism or pessimism that may prevail at any given time.

We can relate each possible expected price of output for the firm to an optimal level of employment for that firm. Such a schedule appears in Figure 13.1 on the left. The curve is steep at lower price levels and tapers off as prices get higher. This suggests that low expected prices are associated with a general pessimism, which only a significant boost to prices and profitability can dislodge. Higher prices, on the other hand, are associated with increasing optimism, causing firms to add workers relatively more quickly as conditions improve. Moreover, as prices get higher, additional firms may enter the market. We show a schedule for a second entrant with a dotted line.

To find out the relationship between expected prices and employment in the economy as a whole, simply sum the employment intentions of each firm at each expected price level for output. This amounts to adding individual firm demand-expectation schedules horizontally to arrive at the aggregate schedule shown in Figure 13.1 on the right. This is the schedule of effective demand, or (as we shall call it in this chapter)

FIGURE 13.1   Effective Demand and Employment

Each company decides how many workers to hire, based on its own assessment of future market conditions. The total number of jobs offered is the sum of these individual subjective decisions.

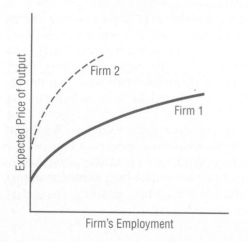
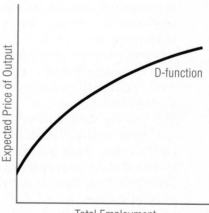

the *D-function*. Since different firms enter at different expected price levels, this function flattens even more markedly as expected prices rise than do the schedules for individual firms.

The *D*-function shows employment for each expected level of prices (or, if you like, for each *state of confidence* about economic conditions immediately ahead). Read the other way, the function also gives a kind of composite value for the expectation of the price of output that would coincide with each level of employment that may occur. The slope of this curve is positive: as employment rises, so will both the aggregate demand for goods and the prices that can be charged for them. But the same forces that cause firms to react optimistically, to add workers at higher expected price levels, also bring about, or reflect, a diminishing increase of expenditure and therefore of price increases as employment grows. For example, at higher levels of employment, there may be higher levels of personal saving or higher levels of imports, which hold down output prices and the rise of expected profitability.

COST OF SUPPLY AND COMPETITIVE PRICE

Of course, a rise in employment will not continue indefinitely, even as expected prices continue to rise. Eventually, as they expand employment, firms will find that their per unit costs of production start rising. Perhaps a certain factor of production becomes relatively scarce, forcing up its price, or less-skilled and therefore less-efficient labor must be hired, causing a fall in per worker productivity and a rise in per unit costs. So long as marginal unit costs rise less rapidly than marginal unit revenues, employment can continue to grow and profits to rise. But at some point, marginal costs rise above marginal revenues; actual profits are maximized, and employment growth will stop.

The schedule of firm-level marginal unit costs for different levels of employment appears in Figure 13.2 on the left. It curves upward as employment increases, because (in the short run) firms use their lowest-cost equipment and their highest-value workers before they bring less-efficient processes and people into service. This curve is nothing more than a smoothed version of the price-cost schedule shown in Chapter 12, modified here to measure employment rather than units of capacity on the horizontal axis.

Adding these cost schedules for different firms together, we again sum horizontally. The result, called the *Z-function*, appears in Figure 13.2 on the right. Since profit-maximizing firms hire up to the point where marginal costs just equal price, this function shows the *profit-maximizing level of total employment* for all firms taken together, at any given actual price of output.

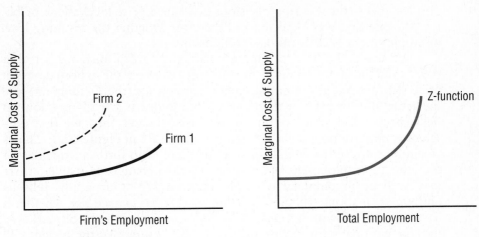

FIGURE 13.2   Cost of Supply

The Z-function shows the level of marginal cost incurred by firms at each level of employment. Since profits are maximized when price is set to equal marginal cost, the Z-function also shows the profit-maximizing level of employment for each expected price of output.

In calculating the Z-function, we assume that the path of money wage rates and other costs are comparatively predictable for the short run. Firms thus ask themselves what would be the best number of employees to hire for each possible price of output. The sum total that would be hired under profit maximization gives the position of the Z-function for that price of output.

DETERMINATION OF EMPLOYMENT AND PRICES

Why can't firms simply move to the profit-maximizing point on the Z-function and stop there? The answer to this question, and the nub of the post-Keynesian model, lies in the fact that the future is unknown. At each moment of time, firms cannot say with certainty what the actual price level in the next period will be. Therefore, they cannot simply choose the profit-maximizing employment level on the Z-function.

What firms can do—indeed, the best they can do—is make a guess and then hire accordingly. The sum of these separate guesses is reflected in the D-function. The D-function, not the Z-function, thus governs the actual hiring decisions of firms. What the Z-function tells us is whether—given markup pricing based on costs at the margin of obsolescence—those hiring decisions generate a price level above or below the one that was expected and therefore whether the resulting level of employment is or is not an equilibrium.

For any given level of employment, the vertical distance between the D- and the Z-functions is the difference between the expected output price that generated the employment decision (on the D-function) and the actual output price at that level of employment (the Z-function). If the expected and actual output prices just coincide, then we find ourselves at employment level $N^\star$ and price level $P^\star$ in Figure 13.3. This is an equilibrium in the Marshallian sense: there is no further tendency for the level of employment or the price level to change. However, there may well be involuntary unemployment at $N^\star$. Our model tells us nothing at all about whether the labor market has cleared nor whether it has cleared at full employment. Why? Because there is no labor market in the conventional sense in this model. We only know that the system will not raise or lower employment above or below $N^\star$ unless it is disturbed.

To repeat, there is nothing to say that $N^\star$ corresponds in any conceptual way to *full employment*. It is the profit-maximizing level of employment for firms. There may well be workers who would like to work

FIGURE 13.3   Effective Demand and Supply Price

In the Z-D model, the equilibrium level of employment occurs when the expected price level that determines employment coincides with the actual price level that results. But this equilibrium is unstable: a small shock to employment will reduce actual and then expected prices, in a downward spiral.

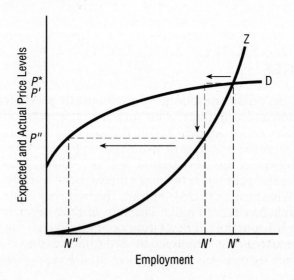

at the prevailing wage or even lower but who cannot find work because employers expect that costs would outrun the further gain in output prices at higher levels of employment. Thus, this model equilibrium is perfectly consistent with the notion of *involuntary unemployment* in Keynes's own sense of that term.

DYNAMICS OF THE Z-D SYSTEM

If expected and actual output prices differ, then the level of employment cannot be an equilibrium. Since the causality runs from the expected output price to the level of employment to the actual output price and back to the expected output price, we can now trace out some dynamics that will show what happens if we are displaced from an equilibrium position and whether or not our model will push us toward an equilibrium if we start away from one.

Figure 13.3 illustrates what may happen. At the equilibrium level of employment $N^\star$, the Z- and D-functions intersect, and actual and expected price levels coincide. Suppose that a small shock occurs, reducing total employment from $N^\star$ to N'. Since high-cost capacity is the first to be retired, the actual effect of this reduction on prices is much greater. Actual prices fall from $P^\star$ to P'. Now, suddenly, the model is far away from its original equilibrium position.

What happens then? It must depend on what happens to the state of profit and price expectations. If expected prices fall to the level of actual prices, the result will be a large reduction in employment, all the way back to N''. If, on the other hand, entrepreneurs believe that the reduction in actual prices is merely a temporary phenomenon, a blip on the economic radar screens, then price expectations will stick at $P^\star$, and the employment level will soon recover. All depends, therefore, on what happens to price expectations in the face of the shock.

Well, what will happen to price expectations? An adaptive expectations model would predict that price expectations will follow the actual price. A rational expectations model might predict the reverse: since the shock itself is a random phenomenon, it should not affect price expectations for the period ahead. What would the post-Keynesian model predict?

If we follow our general model of the capital stock presented in Chapter 12, entrepreneurs will assume that the initial reduction of employment from $N^\star$ to N' was accompanied by a permanent reduction in the capital stock, along the margins of obsolescence of each firm. Therefore, they will know that the initial employment level cannot be recovered and therefore the competitive price level has in fact declined. Rationally, they will adjust their price expectations downward; they then

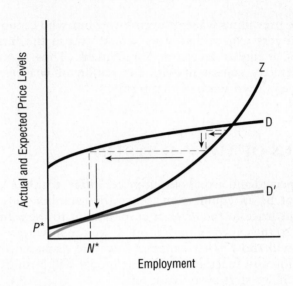

FIGURE 13.4   A Depression Equilibrium

In the aftermath of a small shock to employment, actual and then expected prices fall, depressing employment. Eventually, the D-function itself shifts downward as a depression psychology takes hold, and a low-level or depression equilibrium may be established.

will cut their hiring and raise their firing—and the economy will tumble into a slump. We have reached an important conclusion about the dynamics of the Z-D model: *an equilibrium employment level is unstable.*

If the economy is left to its own devices, the enveloping gloom may eventually lead firms to cut the number of workers that they would hire at any and each level of prices. This would lead to a downward shift in the D-function itself, so that the *equilibrium* value of prices and employment falls, along the Z-function. We may end up at a new equilibrium, characterized by endemic gloom and mass unemployment, at $N\star$ and $P\star$ in Figure 13.4.

Is there any "natural" way out of such a situation? Indeed there is. A low-employment equilibrium raises the possibility that a small shock to expected prices in the upward direction can lead to an improvement in conditions. Suppose something happens that displaces employment just a little upward from $N\star$ in Figure 13.5 on the right. The actual price level will now suddenly jump above the value that was expected. If firms see this as a harbinger of recovery, they will adjust their expectations, and their hiring, along the D-function (D'). Of course, there are plenty of unemployed who are happy to take the jobs that are now offered. Suddenly, more people are at work, and prices are recovering further. There is, as well, pressure to start investing again to bring down costs

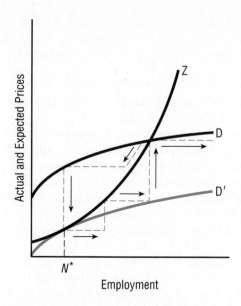
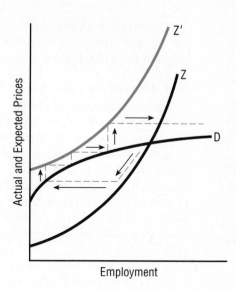

FIGURE 13.5   A Slump and Recovery

The "natural" way out of the slump is to wait until expected prices fall so low that a small shock causes actual prices to exceed them, thus starting an upward cycle. Keynes's solution was to raise government spending and cut taxes or interest rates so that actual prices received would rise again, starting the recovery without waiting for expectations to fall further.

and hold the Z-function in line. Investment activity, of course, raises employment still further. The economy is off on a disequilibrium expansion. Eventually, the D-function will shift upward, and investment will restore the Z-function so that equilibrium may be attained at high employment.

This method of recovery is perfectly viable. The problem is that it may take many years of depression before the D-function shifts downward by enough to end the downward phase of the cycle. And until that happens, the groundwork for an autonomous expansion cannot be laid. In the Great Depression, Keynes felt that the time was too long, that it might run to decades if government did not intervene. In many subsequent recessions, U.S. presidents and members of Congress have felt the same way.

Can government do anything? If so, what? The answer is at least twofold. At the simplest level, government may try to raise the price expectations of firms. Following the strategy of Herbert Hoover in 1928, politicians will constantly assure the public that "prosperity is just around the corner." Or, following the strategy of the National Recovery

Administration in the early New Deal, government may actively intervene to promote higher prices. If it succeeds, the entrepreneurs' expected
value of the price level will rise, and employment decisions (along the D-
function) will recover. Unfortunately, this strategy is unlikely to succeed, precisely because firms know that the structure of costs has shifted.
Therefore, they are likely to resist the blandishments of politicians that
contradict the mandates of common sense.

That leaves the government with the alternative, a Keynesian solution to the business slump: raise the position of the Z-function, thereby
raising the actual profitability of any given level of private employment.
How can this be done? Easily: by government-provided jobs, public
investments in infrastructure and housing, military spending, or any
other available means. As Joan Robinson wrote (see Chapter 2): "If you
can't pay men to do something sensible, pay them to do something
silly."

Now, when firms arrive at a collective level of employment, they
discover that actual prices received and profitability are higher than they
had anticipated they would be. Moving out along the D-function, they
raise their optimal employment. But this only raises prices and profitability still further! With the addition of fiscal or monetary stimulus, the
government has succeeded in curtailing the recession and setting off a
cycle of recovery and expansion. Figure 13.5B illustrates the process of
recovery set in motion by Keynesian demand policy. In due course,
private investment in new technologies will shift the Z-function back
downward and to the right, reestablishing a high-level employment
equilibrium (see Figure 13.5).

DYNAMICS OF INFLATION

Suppose an expansion is under way, whether set off initially by Keynesian macropolicy or by the private forces of entrepreneurial optimism.
Suppose now that the expansion is proceeding, that the D-function has
shifted upward, and that the economy is approaching a high employment equilibrium once again. What guarantees that it will stop there?
The answer is that there is no guarantee at all. Indeed, there is every
reason to fear that the economy will grow past the point of equilibrium
employment and then simply continue to grow.

As it does, the Z-function will once again curve toward the vertical;
costs per unit of employment will rise. At the same time, there may be a
feedback effect on the D-function. The expected rise in workers' nominal incomes caused by accelerating inflation of costs may shift upward
the expected price level associated with each level of employment. In that
case, the D-function becomes unhinged, and a constant level of employ-

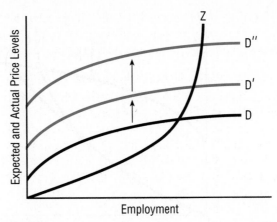

FIGURE 13.6   An Inflationary Spiral

In an inflationary spiral, expected increases in incomes generate a continuing upward shift in effective demand; costs rise in step with expected income, raising prices with little or no effect on employment.

ment is associated with an ever increasing dollar flow of incomes and costs. We have a runaway spiral of inflation (see Figure 13.6).

Can such a process be stopped? One obvious way is to reverse the Keynesian policies of Figure 13.5 (on the right): downshift the Z-function, cutting spending, raising taxes and interest rates, and lowering realized prices at each level of employment. But post-Keynesians also argue that direct intervention in setting wages and other costs, or *incomes policies*, can play a useful role.

If successful, such policies serve two purposes. First, they straighten out and flatten the Z-function. Optimal employment levels rise as expected prices rise, since wages and other costs per hour of work are kept constant (Figure 13.7). Incomes policies thus automatically move the equilibrium level of employment to the right, toward full employment. No other active change in policy, neither fiscal nor monetary, is required.[4]

Second, effective incomes policies dampen the rise in inflationary expectations. They thus stop the upward shift of the D-function that tends to occur when inflation gets out of control. By stabilizing the D-function and flattening the Z-function, incomes policies help hold the line against a potential runaway spiral of inflation expectations and inflation.

[4] Of course, wage controls may not work for very long. They reduce real wages; and while this might be good for employment, workers whose real wages are restrained don't like it. If opposition is strong enough, then wage controls will tend to break down over time.

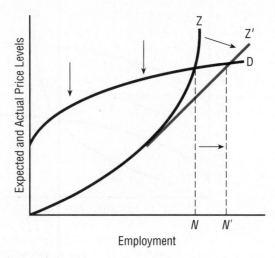

FIGURE 13.7   Effect of Incomes Policy

Wage controls reduce supply price at high levels of employment while holding back
the rise in expected prices. They therefore can raise the equilibrium level of employment, at least temporarily.

ARE RECESSIONS USEFUL?

We now have to confront an extremely unpleasant and controversial
possibility: that recessions, with all of the unemployment, dislocation,
and human misery they cause, may actually play an integral role in the
development of the kind of economy we have.

The first argument along these lines arises from the possibility,
examined above, of a destabilizing, inflationary boom. Suppose that, for
reasons of ideology or doubts about the effectiveness of the effort, the
government decides it will not impose any form of wage or cost controls. Then its options are quite grim. If it does not actually cause a
recession, the inflationary boom may continue and turn into hyperinflation. A do-nothing policy is likely to be considered untenable in such a
situation, and the government may begin to pray for recession in the
way that a drought-stricken farmer may pray for rain.

Corporations and other business enterprises may also regard a recession as a necessary evil under certain circumstances. We saw in the last
chapter that, in a recession, all firms with some of the very oldest capacity will be tempted to scrap that capacity rather than attempt to maintain
it through a period of slack demand. The workers in the doomed facilities lose their jobs. And the total available capacity in the industry declines—not just for the duration of the slump itself but for as long as it
takes for new capacity to be built when the D-function shifts back out.

In the ensuing boom, on the other hand, firms reap the benefits of the previous scrapping. All firms will then confront a shortage of capacity, a shortage large enough to accommodate new investment by all of the firms presently in the market. All of them will benefit by building anew. And so long as no firm tries to disrupt the established division of market shares in its investment planning—however that division may originally have come about—the industry as a whole will avoid a destructive period of overcapacity once the new factories come into production.[5]

So, there may be a social function to occasional downturns in business activity, painful though they are, in the modern capitalist economy. That is, recessions provide a signal for major consumer goods companies to scrap older facilities at the same time. As they do so, they clear away older, high-cost capacity and make room for the addition of new, low-cost capacity and the introduction of new technologies in the upturn that will follow. Without a prior round of scrapping, such new investment is highly risky: if too much new capacity is created, there could be an oversupply, a price war, and a precipitous decline of profits. Periodic recessions therefore help to ensure that each major company can make investment plans without fear of destabilizing the industry as a whole.

Once large-scale scrapping has occurred, the social function—so to speak—of the recession has been served. Price levels have fallen, and unemployment is high both among consumer goods workers and among the producers of new capital goods, who have been idled while the process of net disinvestment worked itself out. But now there are opportunities galore. Outward shift in the D-function re-creates the potential for profits in the production of consumer goods, and the projected shortage of capacity that now emerges signals the need for plant and equipment to be built. No sooner is the slump over than an investment boom is on. Figure 13.8 illustrates the shift in both functions that occurs as new investment kicks in.

THE NEW POLITICAL BUSINESS CYCLE

Let us now use the Z-D framework to consider the politics of the business cycle.

[5] In practice, many industries are characterized by a core of large firms and a fringe of small producers (each of whom operates only one or two plants). The latter may be producers of specialized products catering to a niche market within the industry, or they may be high-cost producers who have not yet been squeezed out of existence. Sometimes, new fringe producers are created by the sale of older, high-cost production facilities to their own workers, which is an alternative to scrapping.

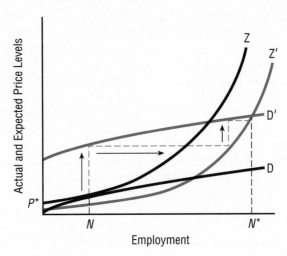

FIGURE 13.8   An Investment-Led Boom

In the recovery, rising profit expectations raise employment, and new investments push down unit costs. The result is to create a new high-employment equilibrium.

A recession, as we have seen, may be kicked off by nothing more than a temporary downward movement of the expected price level. But if expectations of growth are robust, that may not be enough. Particularly, if we are on the right side of the Z-D equilibrium and facing the inflationary pressures that evidently result, there may be no natural force that will get those pressures under control within a short period of time.

But a government intent on recession and controlling policy levers has a powerful alternative. It can cut its own spending and raise taxes, thereby depriving the economy of purchasing power. Even more potently, it can raise interest rates, which as we saw in the last chapter will have a depressing effect on all commodity and asset prices.

The consequence of such policies is to downshift the Z-function, as shown in Figure 13.9. This results in decreased sales, decreased cash flow, and decreased profit expectations at each level of employment for all plants and firms. Just as a boom psychology can be artificially implanted, so too can the psychology of recession.

An interesting policy dilemma emerges. Recessions, which nobody likes, nevertheless may be deemed necessary to eliminate an inflationary boom. They also serve the social function of permitting investment plans to be made in ways that permit the preservation of market stability between firms. They thus occur, in part, because policy decisions make them happen and through the use of the instruments of policy—mainly, in the real world, tight monetary policy and high interest rates—to depress the Z-function.

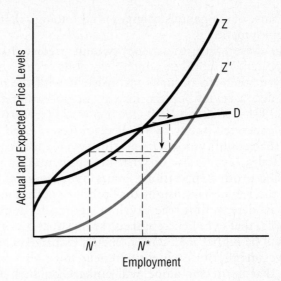

FIGURE 13.9   A Government-Induced Recession

If the government wants a recession, it can cut prices received at each level of employment by raising interest rates or through a tighter fiscal policy. These measures can turn an incipient boom into a slump.

Yet, recessions must happen not too frequently. If the next recession is expected too soon, the rise in expected profitability (recovery of effective demand) that is necessary to bring about the postrecession rise in investment will not occur. For the government, then, the trick is to bring about a "recession to end recessions": a downturn that is expected to be followed by stable growth without inflation. Needless to say, this is a little like bringing about a "war to end wars"; it is easier said than accomplished. And governments that promise such things are often rightly distrusted by the voters.

The contrast between this new political view of the business cycle and those of the new classical and new Keynesian schools is instructive.

New Political versus
New Classical Cycles

New classical economics has not yet succeeded in promulgating a general theory of why business cycles occur. So far, the most prevalent view in that camp holds that business cycles emerge because of random errors in the profit expectations of entrepreneurs, or because of unexpected shocks to demand administered by government policy or outside events, or because of exogenous changes in technology that generate fluctuations in employment.

In these cases, the theory would predict that recessions must be unexpected. A world in which recessions occur when government policies want them to occur is inconsistent with the new classical perspective. Yet, a review of the history of postwar recessions (1970, 1974, 1980, 1981–1982, and 1990–1991) shows that *every case* involved a deliberate, concerted policy by the Federal Reserve and the administration to slow the economy down. And this was no secret at the time to anyone with a clear-eyed view of what the policymakers were up to.

The profit expectations errors hypothesis is, of course, borrowed from the Keynesian insight that profit expectations are an autonomous force in determining the level of aggregate demand. It may be, for example, that every entrepreneur knows that his or her profits individually will be higher if all entrepreneurs embark on an ambitious program of investment. But each entrepreneur must also contemplate the possibility that he or she alone will embark on such a program—and face financial ruin when the high overall level of demand on which individual profitability depends fails to materialize. In this case, it is individually rational for each entrepreneur not to invest. And since all reason alike, their failure to invest confirms each of them in their initial pessimism. Rather than risk hanging separately, all are hanged together.[6]

Most everyone will concede that coordination failures are a potent source, potentially at least, of recessions and depressions. But are they what actually happens in practice? We think not, for two reasons. First, one doesn't need the coordinations failure explanation to account for recessions that were willed by policymakers in the first place. Second, the coordination failure explanation tends to point toward purely governmental remedies for recession. For example, it would seem that truly massive investments in public works projects, tax cuts, and the like, would be required to plug the gap left by a coordination failure and that only such massive action might have the effect of breaking entrepreneurs away from their collective despondency. Yet, we find in practice that very small measures do quite well—the average increase in fiscal stimulus between the recession and the recovery in the United States is only eight-tenths of 1 percent of gross domestic product (GDP). Yet, early into the recovery, a radical shift of investor confidence and behavior often occurs. This does not seem consistent with the dark and powerful forces of the prisoner's dilemma.

---

[6] As noted in an earlier chapter, a failure of *expectations coordination* can be modeled as problem of *game theory*; coordination failures of this type are known as *prisoner's dilemmas*.

New Political versus
New Keynesian Cycles

New Keynesians hold diverse views about why recessions happen. Some stress the importance of external shocks to the economy, such as the increase in oil prices in 1973 and 1979. These cause a reduction of aggregate supply, by making the existing volume of output more costly to produce and putting a squeeze on profits at current prices. In principle, such a squeeze can start a process of plant closings and rising unemployment. Unfortunately for this explanation, the econometric evidence fails to support the idea that shocks alone can account for the magnitude of the business cycle that the U.S. economy has experienced in recent decades.

Others in the new Keynesian camp agree with us that the actions of domestic policymakers are more important. They argue that these actions occur in response to popular and political revulsion against rising rates of inflation. Recessions are caused in order to "break the cycle of inflationary expectations" and to permit a resumption of growth later on at lower inflation rates. Pursuing this line, still others have developed models of the *electoral business cycle*,[7] which lead to predictions that governments will bring on recessions immediately after their election so they can enjoy a boom in the period before the next election.

There is something to the now conventional wisdom about recessions and elections. It seems clear to us, for example, that the recession of 1970 was engineered with a view to controlling inflation before the 1972 election and that the recession of 1981 was engineered with an eye to having a strong, noninflationary recovery under way by 1984. The electorate, for whatever reasons, does not like inflation and is prepared to tolerate high unemployment for a short time in order to get rid of it. Moreover, the electorate does respond favorably to periods of high growth with low inflation, which have tended to occur with some frequency in presidential election years. As Edward Tufte expressed the matter: "It is apparent that the way to defeat the tradeoff between inflation and unemployment in the short run is to hold a presidential election."[8]

But the electoral connection cannot be the whole story. If it were, the election-year recession under Jimmy Carter in 1980 and the failure of the Bush administration to precipitate a recession in 1989 would become equally inexplicable. In the former case, the administration acted against

[7] William Nordhaus of Yale University figures prominently here. See his essay, "The Political Business Cycle," *Review of Economic Studies,* 42 (April 1975), pp. 169–190. See also Edward Tufte, *Political Control of the Economy* (Princeton, N.J.: Princeton University Press, 1978).

[8] Edward F. Tufte, *Political Control of the Economy* (Princeton, N.J.: Princeton University Press, 1978), p. 22.

its own clear political self-interest and paid for it at the polls. In the latter, the administration gambled against the most electorally favorable course of action. Why would rational politicians do such risky and/or foolish things? One possibility is that even elected governments sometimes act in the interests of constituencies whose interests conflict with those of the politicians themselves.

NEW POLITICAL CYCLES AND PARADOXES OF ECONOMICS

In view of the evidence, our new political view holds up pretty well. It accounts for the observed fact that recessions are often initiated in broad daylight by overt acts of government policy. It accounts for the fact that restrictive policies enjoy, at first and for a short time, the overwhelming support of business, even though their immediate and most dramatic effects are on business profits. It incorporates and explains the dramatic effects of recessions on inflation, but as a by-product rather than as the underlying cause of the recessionary policy. And it explains why policy can turn around quickly once the recessionary point has been made and why a strongly expansionary policy does not immediately bring inflation back after only a few months of high unemployment and massive disinvestment.

Pro-cyclical Investment Spending

The new political view of the business cycle also explains why the pattern of investment spending is strongly procyclical. In the downturn, there is no demand for investment goods, and the sectors devoted to construction of plant and the manufacture of equipment suffer the deepest unemployment. But as soon as the economy starts back to work, the capital goods sector moves very quickly, almost overnight, toward full employment. Indeed, most of the new investment of the business cycle upturn gets under way early on, while the overall unemployment rate remains high.

This is quite inconsistent with the new Keynesian theory, which would predict that investment would be slow at first and as long as large amounts of unutilized capacity remained in existence. New Keynesians would argue that only when existing plant reached full employment should one expect to see a recovery of new investment. But in fact, recessions signal the demise of old equipment, which is not available to be revived in the recovery; as a result, the recovery of capital goods spending comes early, rather than late, in the business cycle.

Pro-cyclical Productivity Growth

The same phenomenon may lie behind the observation that productivity growth, the rate of increase of output per unit of measured input, is higher in the early stages of an expansion than later on. This observation, known as the *Verdoorn Law*, seems paradoxical to traditional theory. If the high-cost producers are idled in the slump, average productivity should rise; and when these same high-cost producers are called back in the recovery, average productivity should fall. Productivity gains from new investment, moreover should occur late in the cycle, when new investments are at last being made, rather than early on, which is when we actually observe them.

Under the view we think more reasonable, average productivity will grow most slowly toward the end of a business cycle expansion, when investment slows down in (rational) expectation of a coming recession. Firms will add extra shifts to their existing plants rather than risk making large new capital expenditures and being rendered illiquid in a credit crunch. Average productivity growth will be most rapid in the early stages of the expansion, because the new capacity that comes online (after a period in which the investment itself takes place) will be lower-cost and higher-productivity than the average for installed plant and equipment.

Pro-cyclical Real Wages

A final virtue of the new political model of the business cycle, when coupled to our two-sector model of the economy, lies in its ability to explain the oftentimes procyclical movement of real wages, which is another apparent puzzle to both the new Keynesian and the new classical schools.

New classicals tend to regard increases in employment as movements along a demand-for-labor function. This function is derived from a production function characterized by diminishing marginal productivity; therefore, it must be downward sloping. If a fall of unemployment results from an autonomous shift outward of an upward-sloping labor supply curve, then the resulting equilibrium will again be characterized by lower real wage. In this model, it is not easy to explain an apparent fact: that real wages rise most sharply when employment is growing most quickly.

Nor does a focus on the market for labor help resolve the paradox. To the contrary, when unemployment is high, the competition for work is most intense. One would not expect rising real wages until labor markets become tight. Reasoning in this way led Keynesians to the Phillips curve, which postulated that inflationary pressures result from the attempt by workers to exploit their relative scarcity and raise wages when unemployment is low. Again, this seems quite inconsistent with what we find in the real world, where real wages rise most rapidly in the early phases of an expansion, despite continuing high unemployment, and where the increase of real wages slows down dramatically later in the expansion, despite the fact that unemployment is low.

In the framework we have presented, these results are easily explained. When the recovery begins, there is a large increase in employment in the capital goods sector, as firms scramble to place their orders for the expansion of low-cost, best-practice capacity. Capital goods workers are highly paid. Thus, raising the employment of workers in capital goods industries should raise the real wage of manufacturing workers overall. And as the expansion proceeds and additional consumer goods workers are hired, at lower wages, to staff the factories that are newly created, average real wages should fall. Finally, in the next slump, it is capital goods workers who lose their jobs. This imparts a sharp downward kick to average real wages, again in the same direction of movement as the business cycle.

This pattern of movement's consequences for the functional distribution of income, between wages and profits, is also interesting. The increase in gross investment results in an increase in gross profits to firms. But who actually receives those gross profits? They accrue in substantial part to the workers in the capital goods firms, who receive them as surplus returns. They are recorded in the national income accounts as wages (there is no entry for "windfall profits on human capital"), but from an economic standpoint, they are profit (or rental) rather than wage income. Thus, when the business cycle upturn begins after a recession, it is measured wage income (and in the capital goods sector, at that) that rises most quickly in response to rising investment. Only later on, when new factories come on-line and the consumer goods sector returns to full production, do measured profits (which are actually rents earned by all factories whose costs are lower than price) catch up, and these accrue to the large consumer goods–producing firms.[9]

In sum, we find that a theory of profits and wages that is based on a conceptual division of the economy into capital and consumer goods–producing sectors and that incorporates in a reasonable way the generation and the diffusion of new technologies into the manufacturing process has a lot to tell us about the mechanisms of the business cycle. Further, this theory seems richer and more plausible in significant respects than either of its principal competitors. It is also based more

---

[9] Evidence can be adduced from the wage equations in James Galbraith and Paulo Du Pin Calmon, "Relative Wages and International Competitiveness in U.S. Manufacturing Industry," LBJ School of Public Affairs Working Paper No. 56 (1990).

completely, in our judgment, on the traditions of three of the deepest thinkers on macroeconomics that economics has produced: Keynes (the theory of effective demand, supply price, and the rate of interest), Kalecki (the framework of income distribution), and Schumpeter (the theory of technological change).

CAN THE BUSINESS CYCLE BE MANAGED?

As a broad rule, new classical economics views business cycles as resulting from random errors made by economic agents. New Keynesian economics sees them as the result of outside shocks to the economy, whose own source and explanation are not really part of the problem that economists set out to explain. Neither theory leads to a strong belief that business cycles can or should be managed by government intervention.

In the post-Keynesian view, business cycles occur mainly because of political pressures to make them occur. These pressures, in turn, reflect the interests of certain groups in the economy, in particular the interest of large producers in controlling costs of production. The purpose is served in two distinct ways: the slump disciplines labor, and it clears away the older, high-cost capital equipment in a way that makes possible the subsequent renewal and transformation of the capital stock without disturbing the relative position of the business groups themselves. Thus, recessions and booms are part and parcel of the way an economy such as that of the United States organizes itself.

Needless to say, we do not think that this is attractive. Moreover, this system may self-destruct as the United States economy becomes more and more open to international trade. Each recession leads to scrapping of the most backward capacity, which is the oldest capacity and which is American capacity. But when the expansion comes, the new plants are increasingly built overseas, in Third World nations—not to take advantage of superior technologies but to take advantage of grossly inferior wages. The human costs of this process to U.S. workers, who find their careers abruptly terminated with little prospect of new jobs that match their current living standards, are very large.

The function of the business cycle—to clear the way for full and efficient employment of the capital goods–producing sector in the renewal of the capital stock—is indispensable to a technologically progressive economy.[10] The question is, Can this function be served in a more efficient and less harmful way? The answer would appear to be yes. The

---

[10] Indeed, one can argue that the failure of the full employment economies of the socialist world lies in their failure to find a way to get rid of old factories and designs. The East German car known as the Trabant, for example, was not too obsolete when it was introduced in 1964. But by 1989 . . . !

world provides examples of successful capitalist economies that manage to maintain their technological and competitive positions without resort to periodic mass unemployment.

This is achieved by two main means. In Japan, as in France and many developing nations, the coordination of investment decisions traditionally has not been left to the business cycle. Rather, it occurs through a planning mechanism, accompanied by a high degree of direct state control over the distribution of credits to finance investment. The result is a more stable distribution of investment over time, a more efficient use of the resources of the capital goods sector, and a higher average rate of growth than the United States has enjoyed. The price on the other side is the necessary existence of a state bureaucracy endowed with far more power over industrial decision making than exists here. These state bureaucracies are themselves far from infallible, and the Japanese and French experiences are both littered with examples of misallocated investments. The question is only whether one imperfect system might be preferable to another.

The second means of adjustment without crisis is epitomized by Sweden. There, investment decisions remain in private hands. But the state plays a far larger role than in the United States or in France or Japan in ensuring that workers make a successful transition from old industrial pursuits to new ones. A national policy of *wage solidarity* puts firms under pressure to maintain their technological advantages in order to be able to continue to pay high wages. And extensive programs exist to aid the retraining and, where necessary, relocation of industrial workers. The result is a kind of forced-draft process of investment, which again results in a more efficient use of the resources of the capital goods industry and a higher and more stable rate of growth. (Sweden also maintains a pool of funds for low-interest investment lending that is blocked in periods of strong demand and released for use when unemployment threatens; this helps stabilize the D-function without dictating specifically which investment projects are to be built.)

Thus, there appear to be three main possibilities for economies that wish to maintain technological competitiveness and high living standards. They can intervene directly in investment decisions. They can conduct an active policy of macroeconomic stabilization, while reducing political pressures for recessions by actively promoting the industrial transitions that recessions achieve. Or they can allow the business cycle to do this work, as the United States does. The trouble with the latter approach is, while it economizes on the direct application of resources to government, it allows a far larger volume of resources, in the capital goods sector that is periodically forced to lie idle, to run to waste. For this reason, it is comparatively inefficient. In this comparative inefficiency, we believe, lies much of the explanation of the relative decline of the U.S. economy since 1970.

SPECIAL SECTION

Incomes Policies—Old Attempts and New Ideas

Mandatory wage and price controls have not been used in the United States since 1973. The last vestige of a voluntary *incomes policy*, a system of wage and price guidelines administered by the Council on Wage and Price Stability under the Carter administration, was abolished when Carter left office in 1981. But even today, when inflation threatens, politicians, old-fashioned liberals, and even ordinary people sometimes think that a return to such measures might be needed. Incomes policies are still widely used outside the United States, in countries as diverse as Israel, Poland, Argentina, and Brazil and in ways that reflect some of the most up-to-date macroeconomic thinking. This section provides some of the theory and history of this policy tool.

Simple models of supply and demand send a clear message about price controls. Consider Figure 13.S1, where $P^\star$ represents the market-clearing price of a certain good. If the government tries to control the price and sets a ceiling price at P_c, below the market-clearing price, more will be demanded than will be supplied, and shortages will quickly emerge. On the other

FIGURE 13.S1   Price Control in a Competitive Market

Imposing price ceilings that are below equilibrium values in competitive markets will only cause shortages, equal in this case to $Q' - Q_c$.

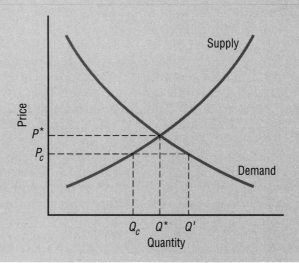

hand, if the controlled price is set at a ceiling price that is above $P\star$, the controls will have no effect; the market price and not the control price will apply. Only if the government happens to set the controlled price exactly at $P\star$ will all be well: the quantity demanded and the quantity supplied will balance exactly. But in that case, why bother with the controls?

If this logic somehow seems too simple, your instincts are driving you in the right direction. The arguments that surround the actual application of wage and price controls do not occur in the textbook context of free, efficient, and perfectly competitive markets. Rather, they occur in the real world of monopoly power, imperfect information, unstable inflation, and—usually if not always—war.

Wage and price controls have been used on and off in North America since colonial times. The earliest uses were always *selective*, or aimed at particular goods and services, and usually in response to the pressures of wartime. For example, the Commonwealth of Virginia controlled the export price of tobacco in 1619, and the Commonwealth of Massachusetts imposed controls on wage rates in 1630. None of these or other measures lasted in fixed form for very long.[1]

The Revolutionary War posed the problem of controls in the face of exceptionally powerful demand pressures. State-by-state price fixing was sought at a New Haven convention in 1779, but weak cooperation by some of the new states led to comprehensive failure. The Southern states were never involved in the price-fixing plans, and in the face of a national crisis, only a national solution could have worked. The Revolutionary War was therefore financed largely by inflationary money issue, the famous Continentals.

The nineteenth century was a long interlude of laissez-faire, during which government stayed out of the business of fixing prices. Even in the Civil War—which saw the introduction of an income tax, mandatory military conscription, and paper money (greenbacks) unbacked by gold (among many other modern, and short-lived, measures)—the government let the markets set the prices of goods and services. As a result, the Civil War was also a highly inflationary time.

World War I

World War I ushered in the modern age of wartime price management. It was the first truly industrial war, and success depended on mobilizing U.S. productive capacity for war purposes in a very short period of time. The government's main problem was to acquire, from private industry, a very large share of the total production of such basic industrial supplies as steel, coal, rubber, and cotton. Moreover, it had to do so without generating either rampant inflation or exorbitant profits for the supplying firms, both of which would have been (and had been, during the Civil

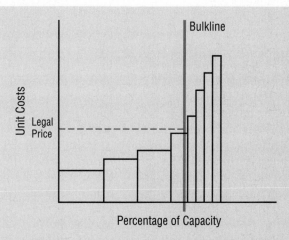

FIGURE 13.S2   Bulkline Pricing

Under the bulkline system, the government set a price adequate to provide a "fair" profit to the more efficient producers, and requisitioned that bulk at the controlled price. Producers unable to make a profit at that price had to fend for themselves.

Source: Adapted from Hugh Rockoff, *Drastic Measures: A History of Wage and Price Controls in America* (New York: Cambridge University Press, 1984).

War) the natural consequence of relying solely on free market forces.

The solution was known as *bulkline pricing*. Under this system, the government would set a single price for each major product, calculated to be sufficient to bring forth the "bulk" of the output of an industry, taking into account the fact that different firms within a single industry have different production costs. Thus, as shown in Figure 13.S2, the bulkline for steel might be set at 80 percent of steel output, and a price would be set that would yield fair profits to firms producing about 80 percent of the nation's steel. This price would not be high enough to meet the costs of the

marginal, high-cost producers, which would have to accept losses or else not do business with the government. Meanwhile, the government would issue orders of curtailment to the main steel-demanding industries, such as automobiles, to bring total demand into balance with available civilian supply.

Bulkline pricing worked tolerably well for a short period, and World War I, for the United States, was mercifully short. But a sharp inflation of uncontrolled prices took place nevertheless, and the complexities of selective price controls led the most influential analysts to believe that even more-comprehensive measures would be needed the next time around.

World War II

That next time came in 1941, with the Japanese attack on Pearl Harbor and the entry of the United States into World War II. Within a few days, the Pacific fell to the Japanese, and natural rubber and other strategic commodities abruptly became scarce. As the nation mobilized for war on a scale never before attempted, wartime planners confronted an equally unprecedented task of holding down inflation under conditions of prolonged and total war.

John Kenneth Galbraith was the young economist to whom the task of organizing wartime price controls was first entrusted. At first, Galbraith believed that the main problems would arise with those larger industrial enterprises who would gain monopoly power in wartime situations. The war would create captive government markets on the one hand and reduce alternative sources of supply on the other.[2] The remedy, it was thought, was to fix major industrial prices at levels corresponding to (prewar) competitive output (and marginal costs) and so to prevent the exercise of monopoly power.

Unfortunately, the initial program of selective controls did not address the problem of wartime excess demand. The war generated an immense flow of new incomes without a corresponding increase in goods that civilians could purchase and consume. This started driving up prices in the markets that were competitive, even while the mar-

kets that were monopolistic maintained comparative price stability. Price inflation accelerated, and it looked for a while as if the Office of Price Administration (OPA) had been heading off in the wrong direction.

On April 28, 1942, just four months after Pearl Harbor, the OPA issued the general maximum price regulation, which became known as the "General Max." This regulation froze all prices, from a ton of steel to a cup of coffee, at the highest levels achieved in March 1942. The effect was to create a temporary climate of overall price stability, arresting inflation and making it possible for the price controllers to address the deeper problems of controls. Then, working at a furious pace while the freeze lasted, OPA developed substitute specific price schedules for individual commodities and so created the basic framework for price controls over the next year.

According to Hugh Rockoff, three problems faced the controllers at this point. First, the General Max froze temporary relative price anomalies into place, creating difficult situations for retailers whose prices had been temporarily out of line with their costs when the freeze hit. Second, since the maximum prices were set for each retailer at the March 1942 level, the introduction of new products to the stores after that date became a loophole in the controls. Third, the General Max was extremely difficult to enforce, because different prices for the same commodity in different stores were entirely legal, depending on what the situation had been in March 1942.

In April 1943, President Roosevelt issued a hold-the-line order. The order instituted a comprehensive freeze of wages and prices that lasted for the rest of the war. Compared to selective controls and even to the General Max, the hold-the-line policy had several advantages. It was enforceable, simple, and comprehensive. OPA was able to enlist, across the country, volunteer boards of civilian price control monitors, who joined in the task of ensuring that controls remained in effect. These boards also administered rationing of scarce commodities (such as butter and sugar). Controls remained largely effective through 1946, and World War II was thus the first major war in U.S. history that was not accompanied by a runaway inflation.

Writing after the war about the experience of controls, Galbraith emphasized not their implications for monopoly but their macroeconomic effects.[3] What "hold-the-line" really meant was control not only over the *actual* rate of inflation but also over the *expected* rate of inflation. By issuing the order, Roosevelt helped inspire confidence that inflation would not be allowed during the war. This meant that idle money balances and money invested in war bonds at interest rates of only 2 percent would be safe from the ravages of inflation and available to spend on civilian goods after the war. With confi-

dence that prices would not rise, people were willing to set aside most of their excess incomes, and savings rates rose to 25 percent of gross national product (GNP)—the kind of figure that nowadays we associate with South Korea or Japan. Meanwhile GNP doubled, so that by 1944 Americans were saving the value of one-half of what GNP had been in 1940. World War II thus saw the emergence of controls as part of a strategy of macroeconomic stabilization—which is how they have been used ever since.[4]

The Kennedy-Johnson Guideposts

President John F. Kennedy's administration saw the first modern application of wage-price policy in peacetime. Kennedy did not impose controls, nor did his Democratic successor, Lyndon Johnson. Instead, they articulated what became known as an *incomes policy*, consisting of *guideposts* for the setting of wages and prices. The guideposts did not have the force of law, but they were far from being strictly voluntary in practice—as President Kennedy showed in a famous confrontation with United States Steel in 1962. U.S. Steel was forced by White House pressure to roll back an announced price increase.

The theory behind guideposts, explicitly post-Keynesian, originated with Sidney Weintraub of the University of Pennsylvania in the late 1950s. Weintraub was concerned with the rates of wage change that would be compatible with stable prices and full employment in a growing economy. He observed that if the average rate of wage change could be limited to the average rate of growth of labor productivity, then, on average, prices would be stable. In general, if W and P are the wage rate and the price level, if γ/N is the output/labor ratio or rate of labor productivity, and if there is a markup α that determines the relation of wages to prices, then

$$P = (1 + \alpha) \, W \left(\frac{N}{\gamma}\right)$$

and, converting to rates of growth,

(13.S1) $\dot{P} = \dot{\alpha} + \dot{W} + (\dot{N} - \dot{\gamma})$

Equation (13.S1) tells us that the rate of inflation will be the sum of changes in the markup and changes in the wage rate, minus any improvement in labor productivity. Thus, if markups are stable and productivity improves at 3 percent per year, then an average wage gain of 3 percent will lead to stable prices.

The guidepost policy consisted of urging that all workers receive annual pay increases equal to the rate of productivity growth plus an allowance for the previous year's inflation. Wages and profits in that case would provide no additional spur to inflation, which would continue at the low rates of the early 1960s. Full employment could be approached through fiscal and monetary stimulus, such as the income tax cuts of 1964, without setting off what was called a *wage-price spiral.*

Nixon's Controls

President Richard Nixon took office in 1969 as an avowed opponent of both controls and guidelines and proceeded within his first days in power to scrap the wage-price guidepost strategy.[5] By that time, inflation was accelerating anyway as a consequence of the Vietnam War, and it appeared to be moving in line with influential estimates of the Phillips curve. Nixon's response, at first, was the traditional one. Tight money and high interest rates were thrown into the battle, and in 1970 the nation entered its first recession since the late 1950s. Unfortunately, the recession did not cure inflation, which by the summer of 1971 had hardly fallen despite an increase of over one million unemployed. The vaunted Phillips curve, so accurate in its predictions of accelerating inflation as unemployment fell, did not run in reverse.

Nixon's response, on August 15, 1971, was to introduce the nation's first extended peacetime period of mandatory wage and price controls. His controls strategy moved in phases. First, beginning on August 15, 1971, there was a complete ninety-day freeze on all wages and prices (phase one). Then, as soon as administrative bodies (the Pay Board and Cost of Living Council) could be brought into existence, the comprehensive freeze was replaced with an OPA-like structure of administered price and wage schedules (phase two). These restrictions lasted for about a year, were relaxed at the beginning of 1973, then reimposed (phase three), and abandoned in 1974.

The purposes, effects, and long-range consequences of this program have been among the most hotly disputed topics in the modern history of economic policy. We know, of course, the raw facts. Immediately following the imposition of the wage-price freeze in August 1971, the economy went into a spectacular and sustained surge of growth. Real GNP rose by 5 percent in the following year alone, after having grown only 2.8 percent in 1971. Inflation, which the recession of 1970–1971 had not reduced below the then-frightening rate of 5.9 percent, fell to 3.3 percent in 1972. President Nixon was safely reelected in a 49-state landslide.

Then the economy went off the rails. Through 1973, worldwide commodity prices had been on a sharp upswing, fueled in part by the strong growth of U.S. demand. This culminated in October 1973 with the Yom Kippur War in the Middle East and the decision by the Organization of Petroleum Exporting Countries (OPEC) to quadruple the price of oil. Suddenly, by mid-1974, U.S. inflation was running away (6.2 percent in 1973, 11.0 percent in 1974), while real economic growth simultaneously slowed to a dead halt.

In the face of this history, the 1971–1973 experience of price con-trols finds few defenders. The conservative view of Nixon's controls, given the presuppositions of monetarist and new classical theory, is that they contributed nothing to output growth and nothing even to the control of inflation except perhaps in the very short run. Monetarists have argued that the 1973–1974 period does not disturb the observed historical relationship between money growth and inflation rates. Thus, they claim, had the Federal Reserve not run up the money supply in 1972, the inflation of 1973–1974 would not have occurred. Controls, in this view, at best displaced inflation from before until after the 1972 election.

We credit the controls with helping to produce the strong burst of growth in 1972. How did controls contribute? By stabilizing, for a time, inflation expectations and so ensuring that the expansionary monetary policies implemented from late 1971 onward by the Federal Reserve under Chairman Arthur Burns would indeed boost real output rather than prices in the short run.[6] Thus, we believe that the controls worked and that the inflation that followed in 1973 and after was only in part due to the expansionary policies of 1972. Other, partly independent factors included the external shocks to commodity and oil prices and the fact that controls were removed while the boom was still on. But Nixon and the Federal Reserve are still subject to criticism for applying controls for short-run political effect, for removing them at the worst possible moment, and for destroying the credibility of controls as a policy instrument in future administrations.[7]

Carter to Reagan to Bush

President Jimmy Carter's experiments with wage and price policy were never so bold as President Nixon's. Carter did maintain a Council on Wage and Price Stability, which set voluntary standards and tried valiantly to ward off the rising inflation rates of the late 1970s. And in 1979, Labor Secretary Ray Marshall negotiated a "social compact" with the leadership of U.S. labor unions. The compact seems to have had a distinct effect in holding down nominal wage settlements in that year and in 1980. However, prices went on up anyway, real wages fell, and the voters rewarded Carter by throwing him out of office.[8]

Just as President Nixon had begun his term by dismantling the Kennedy-Johnson guidelines, so President Reagan opened his administration by abolishing the Council on Wage and Price Stability. Then, with the recession brought on by supertight monetary policies in 1981–1982, the actual rate of inflation fell—as it typically does in deep recessions. So President Reagan was able to pursue economic expansion after 1982 with a relatively low rate of inflation.

Reagan's recovery was blessed, as the early stages of economic recoveries always have been, by a relatively high rate of produc-

tivity growth and an absence of new inflationary pressures. What is more remarkable, and unprecedented, is that in the economic expansion that lasted from 1983 through 1989, inflation rose very little, despite the complete absence of a formal incomes policy of any kind.

We believe the reason for this can be summed up in one word: imports. Reagan's recovery and expansion was the first in modern U.S. history to be accompanied by a flood of imports of manufactured goods, many of them from low-wage developing countries. The effects on U.S. wage levels were dramatic: relative wages fell through the 1980s in those industrial areas where low-wage competition was strongest. And even the traditional wage-setting industries of the United States, especially the automotive sector, felt for the first time the strong competitive pressure of lower foreign wage levels. Thus, wage settlements remained moderate through the expansion, and the inflation rate did not rise. The price of high employment was not rising inflation, as in the old days of the Phillips curve, but instead a large and seemingly incorrigible deficit in the balance of trade.

President George Bush remained as resistant as Reagan to active intervention on wages and prices. Therefore, in 1989 and 1990, when inflation rates began to push back up past 5 percent a year, the Federal Reserve reacted once again with a policy of high interest rates, tight money, and slow economic growth. The resulting recession of 1990–1992 brought both the inflation rate and the trade deficit under control, but at a heavy price in unemployment and lost industrial production. Apparently, the key to a steady, noninflationary expansion with balanced trade and without incomes policies has not yet been found.

Ideas for the Future

What is the future of wage-price policies? If we ever see them again in the United States, it will probably be in a new crisis, and economists will have very little influence on how controls are put into effect. Nevertheless, there are still economists who believe that the issues surrounding the design of incomes policy are important and that they merit some consideration even when the prospect of seeing controls in practice is remote. Moreover, there is a growing body of new experience around the world with both the theory and practice of incomes policies, and this bears examination as Americans increasingly realize that not all of the solutions to our economic problems will necessarily be found at home.

Incentive Strategies: TIP, MAP and Share   One all-American approach to the design of incomes policy has been to emphasize the role of individual incentives. Mainstream economists, including William Nordhaus of Yale (a member of Carter's Council of Economic Advisers), Larry Seidman of the

University of Delaware, David Colander of Middlebury College, and the late Abba Lerner have proposed various schemes to generate economic rewards for moderate wage-setting behavior. The proposals of Nordhaus, Seidman, and others are known as a *tax-based incomes policy*, or *TIP*. TIPs would consist of imposing a surtax on wage settlements over and above an annual guideline, on the theory that such a tax would discourage high wage settlements and, therefore, wage-driven inflation. The Lerner-Colander variation, known as the *market anti-inflation program,* or *MAP*, would establish a system of transferable coupons whereby rights to raise wages would be rationed in the economy. Under MAP, the government would limit wage increases by limiting the total issue of coupon rights, and individual firms could bid for those rights according to their need for higher-paid labor.

TIP and MAP proposals were, for a time, a minor growth industry among academic economists, who argued that they would be self-enforcing and thus avoid the administrative difficulties that plague the administration of wage and price guidelines over any prolonged period in peacetime. Unfortunately, political leaders and economists with administrative experience in government were never convinced that the administrative problems truly could be avoided or that the TIP/MAP proposals were sufficiently promising to make an experiment worthwhile. To date, there have been no experiments with either idea anywhere in the world.

A final, and much more revolutionary, suggestion along similar lines is owed to Martin Weitzman of Massachusetts Institute of Technology. It is known as the *share economy*.[9] Weitzman calls for eliminating altogether the system of hourly wage compensation for labor. In its place, he proposes a system whereby a firm would pay all of its workers a fixed proportion of its gross receipts. Thus, total labor compensation would depend on total sales and would be a variable rather than a fixed element of firm costs.

Under this system, if a large firm chose to add an additional worker to its payroll, that would have the effect of reducing the pay owed to all other workers in that firm. Thus (to bring in some language from microeconomics), the marginal cost of adding a worker would lie below the earnings of that worker and also presumably below that worker's marginal revenue product. Large firms would therefore have an incentive to hire as many workers as possible. According to Weitzman, this would virtually guarantee full employment while preventing the surge of labor costs with which full employment is often associated in the wage system.

What of this idea? We believe Weitzman's suggestion has both merits and problems. The unemployed would be big gainers. On the other hand, high-wage workers would be losers, since they would in effect be paying the wages of the newly hired. And whether the scheme would successfully stabilize the macroeconomy has been a matter of vigorous debate. A full discussion lies well beyond our purpose here, but we are confident that the share economy itself lies far beyond the scope of practical politics, at least in our lifetimes.

Heterodox Shock Policies   A second broad line of argument in favor of incomes policies has taken root since the mid-1980s and represents, we believe, the future of the genre. This line emphasizes, as did John Kenneth Galbraith in the late 1940s, the macroeconomic aspects of incomes policy rather than its effects on individual incentives. In particular, the new emphasis falls on the problem of coordinating a reduction in inflation expectations so as to reduce the cost of moving from high to low inflation. Often, nowadays, the tools of game theory are used to frame these issues (although, we will not be concerned with the technicalities of game theory here.)

The game-theoretic argument is quite straightforward. One of the reasons inflation persists is simply that the great mass of economic actors in the economy, both firms and workers, believe that it will persist. So they make allowances for future inflation in their current contracts and in other economic behavior. For example, if inflation is expected to be 50 percent over the next year, everyone insists (and everyone else agrees) on at least a 50 percent inflation allowance in all yearlong economic agreements. The need to validate all those agreements, when the time comes, effectively forces the government to print enough money to ensure that 50 percent inflation does in fact occur.[10]

The key to breaking this *inertial inflation* is to find a way to change everybody's expectations at once. Having done that, one must then validate the change of expectations with changes in substantive policies, such as reductions in the budget deficit and in the issue of printing-press money. In this way, the combination of "inflation stabilization with incomes policy support" can, in principle, ensure that an instant shift from high- to low-inflation equilibrium does in fact occur.[11] Thus the game-theoretic approach leads to "shock therapy" for inflation—in contrast to the gradualism of the TIP and MAP proposals.

Since the middle 1980s, Argentina, Bolivia, Brazil, Israel, Mexico, and Poland have all experimented with *heterodox shock* cures for rampaging inflation. Typically, these programs have involved (1) a price freeze; (2) a fiscal squeeze, implemented by cutting public subsidy programs and/or by raising taxes; and (3) a monetary reform, usually involving a change in the name of the currency (from pesos to australes in Argentina and from cruzeiros to cruzados and then new cruzados and finally back to cruzeiros in Brazil). The purpose of monetary reform is to convert all economic contracts, which were written under the assumption of continued high inflation in the old currency, to new terms reflecting an assumption of low or zero inflation in the new currency. In this way, the whole economy could, in principle, shift from one set of assumptions about inflation to another set of assumptions overnight.

The results of heterodox shock therapy have been mixed. There was one unqualified success, in Israel, whose fiscal situation was much helped by a large loan from the United States. In Mexico, which was also able to negotiate a substantial debt reduction (and later, a free trade agreement with the United States) as its program went into effect, the results are strongly positive so far but their sustainability remains in doubt. In Poland, we have seen mixed reports. Advocates of the shock therapy point to the rapid marketization of the Polish economy that has occurred, whereas skeptics point to a collapse of heavy industry and rising unemployment. In Bolivia, the picture is similarly cloudy. Bolivia managed to stabilize a rampant hyperinflation, in part by stopping all payments on its external debt, but the economic misery of one of the world's most impoverished countries remains an intractable long-term issue.

In Argentina and Brazil, the initial programs succeeded in stopping inflation, at least at first. But they also produced a surge of real demand, an economic boom, that led to their undoing after a year or so. This pattern of temporary success against inflation, followed by a year or so of prosperity and then disaster, provides perhaps the most interesting illustration of the strengths and weakness of heterodox shocks.

For many reasons, economic growth tended to go out of control in the wake of the heterodox shocks. In part, the Brazilian and Argentine governments miscalculated the postinflation status of fiscal policy: they did not realize how much real tax burdens would be reduced by an end to inflation. In part, a renewed climate of financial stability fostered the resurgence of huge new markets for consumer credit, and consumers went on a credit-driven buying spree that could not have been foreseen. In part, politicians (particularly in Brazil) decided to milk the boom for electoral advantage. As a result, inflation returned in both countries within little more than a year, and both learned that the same rabbit cannot be pulled from a hat twice.

All in all, the high inflations that plague developing countries with weak tax structures and heavy foreign debts seem destined to remain among the most intractable economic problems. Yet, where heterodox adjustment strategies have failed, they have nevertheless failed in interesting ways. And where they have succeeded, in full or in part, they have opened new vistas for eventual policy innovations in the more advanced industrial countries. Thus, they have contributed significantly to a better understanding both of the inflation process and of the means whereby more resourceful, disciplined, and powerful governments—such as the United States—might deal in the future with a problem of rising inflation.

---

[1] For history, we rely heavily on Hugh Rockoff's excellent study, *Drastic Measures: A History of Wage and Price Controls in America* (New York: Cambridge University Press, 1984).

[2] This view reflected both the antibusiness perspective of the New Deal and the most exciting theoretical developments of the economics of that time, which had to do with the theory of monopoly and imperfect competition.

[3] John Kenneth Galbraith, *A Theory of Price Control* (Boston: Houghton-Mifflin, 1952).

[4] In the Korean War, the same essential strategies were employed as in World War II (though without rationing), again with reasonable success.

[5] One of Nixon's first jobs as a young Washington lawyer had been at the Office of Price Administration during World War II. It was an assignment he did not advertise in his later political career.

[6] If controls did affect the expected rate of inflation (as we believe), then they raised the real value of expected future demand over the period 1971–1973 and thus expected profitability. In this way, they could have contributed materially to the boom.

[7] Econometric work on the effects that the 1971–1973 controls had on inflation from 1971 through 1975 has yielded mixed results. For example, Princeton economist Alan Blinder (a New Keynesian and member of the Council of Economic Advisors under President Clinton) has found that the controls did

have some downward effect on inflation overall through this period; New Classical (and Bush administration official) Michael Darby found that controls actually raised the postcontrol rate of inflation. Econometric work by James Galbraith suggests another interesting possibility: that Nixon's controls raised real wages (by about 2 percentage points over and above what can be accounted for by other known effects on wages) because they held down prices more than they held down nominal wage rates. This may have been a reason why the administration that imposed wage and price controls earned such an evidently rich reward for it at the polls. Blinder, Darby, and other studies are summarized in Rockoff, *Drastic Measures*, p. 218. Galbraith's work with Paulo Du Pin Calmon is in Lyndon B. Johnson School of Public Affairs Working Paper #56, 1990.

[8] The falling real wages of the late Carter years are also an econometric finding of Galbraith's, still present after controlling for the effect of falling GNP growth in 1980.

[9] Martin Weitzman, *The Share Economy* (Cambridge, Mass.: Harvard University Press, 1984). Weitzman's main purpose in advancing this plan was to help eliminate chronic unemployment, rather than to cure inflation. Nevertheless, because the two issues are closely connected, discussing his ideas at this point in the text is useful.

[10] If it does not do so, the consequence will be sky-high real interest rates, a wave of bankruptcies, and economic depression—costs that democratically elected governments usually find much too difficult to pay.

[11] The phrase in quotation marks is the title of an important paper (New York: Group of 30, 1986) by Rudiger Dornbusch and Mario Henrique Simonsen, a former finance minister of Brazil.

SUMMARY

A model can be constructed that rejects the central features of the new classical model. It also moves away from the Keynesian interpretation represented by the merger of the IS-LM diagram and the Phillips curve.

The first step in this process is to model the production and hiring behavior of firms rather than the behavior of markets. In this analysis, effective demand is based on subjective expectations, and the supply analysis concentrates on objective costs. The decisions expected of firms are based on the price expected to prevail in the market at the time when they bring their product to market. Higher expected prices reflect better market conditions, causing firms to anticipate that they can sell more goods profitably. Employment and aggregate demand are therefore a positive function of price. This analysis is the basis of the D-function.

The second part of the analysis is the Z-function, which is based on the objective conditions of production. As output and employment increase, the costs per unit of output increase, producing a positively sloped Z-function. The Z-function determines the actual price prevailing in the market by way of a markup pricing mechanism. The intersection of the Z and D-functions constitutes an equilibrium. At this point, the expectation of prices equals the price level that would cover costs and yield maximum profits at that level of employment, and there is no reason for movement from this point. But, consistent with Keynes's observation, there is the possibility of involuntary unemployment. This equilibrium exists with no reference whatsoever to the labor market.

The equilibrium described by the Z and D-function analysis is not stable. If, for some reason, expectations of prices are temporarily pushed down from the equilibrium price, there are forces that will cause the level of employment to continue to fall. Once production has fallen, obsolescent plants will be put out of service. This will cause overall efficiency to increase lowering the expectations of price in the next period. The lower price expectations will lead to even lower employment and output. In fact, with a generally worse business climate, the D-function is expected to shift down. The flip side to this is that an upward cycle occurs if price expectations are temporarily increased.

The policy solution to depressions in the Z-D analysis is similar to that derived from the IS-LM analysis, namely to have the government increase its spending. The increase in government spending shifts up the Z-function and starts an upward spiral in the economy. Once an economy has embarked on this upward spiral, the possibility for inflation exists, as the Z-function can turn very steep and the D-function shifts up with the expectations of inflation. The post-Keynesians recommend an incomes policy to control inflation. This policy acts by flattening the Z-function and stabilizing the D-function.

Interestingly, in the post-Keynesian analysis, recessions can serve a useful purpose. They allow the renovation of the manufacturing base through the replacement of outdated plants. In fact, the post-Keynesians emphasize that the government may endeavor to induce recessions for these very reasons. The problem is that eventually the public will incorporate these recessions into their expectations and the expected rebounds will not occur.

The post-Keynesian theory of the business cycle is based on evidence that the government induces recessions. This theory of the business cycle, in conjunction with their separation of the economy into capital goods and consumer goods sectors, can explain the procyclical nature of several economic aggregates. The procyclicity of investment and the capital goods sector is explained by the fact that in the beginning of the recovery, scrapped capacity must be replaced with new plants. Since wages are highest in the capital goods sector, wages are likely to be procyclical. The procyclicity of productivity is also due to the new productive capacity. However, in the later stages of the boom, since the bust is expected, additions to production are made by adding shifts rather than plants.

Lately, in the United States, this process of renewing the economy appears to have been short-circuited. Rather than scrapped plants being replaced, productive capacity is increased by building new plants in low-wage countries. The answer to this problem is to promote better planning either through direct government intervention in investment decisions or by promoting industrial transitions.

Review Questions

1. Compare and contrast the post-Keynesian view of business firm behavior with the views of other schools of thought explored in this book.

2. Post-Keynesians claim to have better captured the actual behavior of firms across the business cycle. What, if any, elements of firm behavior have they not adequately described? Can these elements be incorporated into their theory?

3. Why are recessions necessary when there is full employment and high inflation? Why can't the economy continue in this state?

4. In post-Keynesian theory, how would increases in population be handled? Would there be shifts in the Z or D curves? Explain.

5. Explain exactly how the aggregate demand curve of the post-Keynesians managed to reverse completely the slope found for every other aggregate demand curve we have looked at.

6. Richard Nixon instituted wage and price controls to manage inflation. Assess the effectiveness of his policy. Was his policy consistent with the post-Keynesian policy prescription for inflation? Explain.

Review Problems

1. Prepare graphs of relevant economic statistics to answer the following question: How well has the election cycle theory of the business cycle performed?

2. Use the Z-D analysis to assess the effects of a tax cut for firms that invest in new plant capacity. Compare your analysis with the results predicted by the IS-LM analysis and the new classical analysis.

3. With the end of the Cold War, many commentators have spoken of a newly available peace dividend. Analyze its effects with Z-D analysis.

4. Suppose the Z-function is drawn so that it intersects the D-function twice. Analyze the first intersection of the curves in terms of stability. Can you think of any economic phenomena explained by this intersection?

5. On the same sheet of paper, draw an investment-led boom and the results of Keynesian policy with the Z-D analysis. How do they differ? Describe why one outcome is preferable to the other. Can you think of a better policy than the so-called Keynesian policy?

6. Employment is on the abscissa of the *Z-D* graph. What sleight of hand caused the switch from output to employment on this axis? Add a single graph to the analysis to make the link from employment to output obvious. Show an investment-led boom with this amended analysis. Is anything added to the analysis? Comment.

Suggested Readings

Edward F. Tufte, *Political Control of the Economy* (Princeton: Princeton University Press, 1977).

Hugh Rockoff, *Drastic Measures: A History of Wage and Price Controls in America* (New York: Cambridge University Press, 1984).

John Kenneth Galbraith, *A Theory of Price Control* (Boston: Houghton-Mifflin, 1952).

Martin Weitzman, *The Share Economy* (Cambridge: Harvard University Press, 1984).

Index